THE FIRST URBAN CHURCHES 3
EPHESUS

WRITINGS FROM THE GRECO-ROMAN WORLD SUPPLEMENT SERIES

Clare K. Rothschild, General Editor

Number 9

THE FIRST URBAN CHURCHES 3
EPHESUS

Edited by
James R. Harrison and L. L. Welborn

S\B\L PRESS

Atlanta

Copyright © 2018 by SBL Press

All rights reserved. No part of this work may be reproduced or transmitted in any form or by any means, electronic or mechanical, including photocopying and recording, or by means of any information storage or retrieval system, except as may be expressly permitted by the 1976 Copyright Act or in writing from the publisher. Requests for permission should be addressed in writing to the Rights and Permissions Office, SBL Press, 825 Houston Mill Road, Atlanta, GA 30329 USA.

Library of Congress Cataloging-in-Publication Data

First urban churches / edited by James R. Harrison and L. L. Welborn.
      volumes cm. — (Society of Biblical Literature. Writings from the Greco-Roman world Supplement series ; Number 7)
  Includes bibliographical references.
  Contents: 1. Methodological foundations.
  ISBN 978-1-62837-102-4 (v. 1 : pbk. : alk. paper) — ISBN 978-1-62837-104-8 (v. 1 : ebook) — ISBN 978-1-62837-103-1 (v. 1 : hardcover : alk. paper)
  ISBN 978-0-88414-111-2 (v. 2 : pbk. : alk. paper) — ISBN 978-0-88414-112-9 (v. 2 : ebook) — ISBN 978-0-88414-113-6 (v. 2 : hardcover : alk. paper)
  ISBN 978-0-88414-234-8 (v. 3 : pbk. : alk. paper) — ISBN 978-0-88414-235-5 (v. 3 : ebook) — ISBN 978-0-88414-236-2 (v. 3 : hardcover : alk. paper)

  1. City churches. 2. Church history—Primitive and early church, ca. 30–600. 3. Cities and towns—Religious aspects—Christianity. I. Harrison, James R., 1952– editor.
  BV637.F57 2015
  270.109173'2—dc23   2015021858

Printed on acid-free paper.

Contents

Abbreviations vii

An Epigraphic Portrait of Ephesus and Its Villages
    James R. Harrison 1

An Ephesian Tale: Mystery Cults, Reverse Theological
Engineering, and the Triumph of Christianity in Ephesus
    Guy MacLean Rogers 69

The Jewish Community in Ephesus and Its Interaction with
Christ-Believers in the First Century CE and Beyond
    Paul Trebilco 93

Acclaiming Artemis in Ephesus: Political Theologies in Acts 19
    Bradley J. Bitner 127

The Gladiator Graveyard of Ephesus as Evidence for the Study
of Martyrdom
    Mikael Haxby 171

Ἐκκλησία in Ephesians as Godlike in the Heavens, in Temple,
in γάμος, and in Armor: Ideology and Iconography in Ephesus
and Its Environs
    Fredrick J. Long 193

From Zeus or by Endoios? Acts 19:35 as a Peculiar Assessment
of the Ephesian Artemis
    Stephan Witetschek 235

Ephesian Cultic Officials, Their Benefactors, and the Quest
for Civic Virtue: Paul's Alternative Quest for Status in the
Epistle to the Ephesians
 James R. Harrison 253

Ephesus and the Numismatic Background to νεωκόρος
 Michael P. Theophilos 299

Contributors 333
Primary Sources Index 337
Modern Authors Index 355

Abbreviations

Primary Sources

1 Apol.	Justin, *Apologia 1*
1 Macc	1 Maccabees
1QM	War Scroll
1QpHab	Pesher Habakkuk
2 Bar.	2 Baruch
Ad Aen.	Servius, *Ad Aeneid*
Agalm.	Porphyry, *Peri agalmatōn*
Ag. Ap.	Josephus, *Against Apion*
Ann.	Tacitus, *Annales*
Ant.	Josephus, *Jewish Antiquities*
Anth. Gr.	*Anthologia Graeca*
Ant. rom	Dionysius of Halicarnassus, *Antiquitates romanae*
Apoc. Sedr.	Apocalypse of Sedrach
Apol.	Lucian, *Apologia*
Ars	Horace, *Ars poetica*
Astr.	Manilius, *Astronomica*
Aug.	Seneca, *Divus augusta*; Suetonius, *Divus Augustus*
Bel	Bel and the Dragon
Ben.	Seneca, *De beneficiis*
Car.	Historia Augusta, *Caracalla*
Carm.	Catullus, *Carmina*
Clem.	Seneca, *De clementia*
Comp.	Galen, *De comparanda medicina*
Conc. Apam.	Dio Chrysostom, *De Concordia cum Apamensibus* (*Or.* 40)
Dei cogn.	Dio Chrysostom, *De dei cognition* (*Or.* 12)
Deipn.	Athenaeus, *Deipnosophistai*
Descr.	Pausanias, *Graeciae descriptio*

Diatr.	Musonius Rufus, *Diatribai*
Diogn.	Diognetus
Ep.	Martial, *Epigrams*; Seneca, *Epistulae morales*
Eph.	Ignatius, *Letter to the Ephesians*
Epict. diss.	Arrian, *Epicteti dissertationes*
Fug.	Philo, *De fuga et inventione*
Geog.	Dionysius Periegetes, *Geographical Description of the Inhabited World*; Strabo, *Geographica*
Geor.	Vergil, *Georgica*
Hist.	Livy, *Historia Romae*
Hist. Alex.	Q. Curtius Rufus, *Historiae Alexandri Magni Macedonensis*
Hist. Aug.	Historia Augusta
Hist. eccl.	Eusebius, *Historia ecclesiastica*
Hist. rom.	Cassius Dio, *Historia Romana*; Velleius, *Historia Romana*
Hom. Act.	John Chrysostom, *Homiliae in Acta apostolorum*
Inst.	Quintilian, *Institutio oratoria*
Iph. taur.	Euripides, *Iphigenia taurica*
J.W.	Josephus, *Jewish War*
Leg.	Athenagoras, *Legatio pro Christianis*; Cicero, *De legibus*
Legat.	Philo, *Legatio ad Gaium*
Leuc. Clit.	Achilles Tatius, *Leucippe et Clitophon*
Ling.	Varro, *De lingua latina*
LXX	Septuagint
Magn.	Ignatius, *Letter to the Magnesians*
Mart.	Tertullian, *Ad martyras*
Mart. Pol.	Martyrdom of Polycarp
Metam.	Apuleius, *Metamorphoses*; Ovid, *Metamorphoses*
Mos.	Philo, *De vita Mosis*
MT	Masoretic Text
Nat.	Pliny, *Naturalis historia*
Nat. d.	Cicero, *De natura deorum*
Onom.	Julius Pollux, *Onomasticon*
Or.	Dio Chrysostom, *Orationes*
Peregr.	Lucian, *De morte peregrini*
Pers.	Aeschylus, *Persae*
Phld.	Ignatius, *Letter to the Philadelphians*

Praem	Philo, *De praemiis et poenis*
Praep. ev.	*Praeparatio evangelica*
Ps. Sol	Psalms of Solomon
QG	*Questions and Answers on Genesis*
Rep.	Cicero, *De republica*
Rhod.	Dio Chrysostom, *Rhodiaca* (*Or.* 31)
Sat.	Horace, *Satirae*; Persius, *Satirae*
Satyr.	Petronius, *Satyricon*
Sib. Or.	Sibylline Oracles
Spec.	Philo, *De specialibus legibus*
Spect.	Tertullian, *De spectaculis*
Stoic. rep.	Plutarch, *De Stoicorum repugnantiis*
Strat.	Polyaenus, *Stratagemata*
T. Benj.	Testament of Benjamin
T. Job	Testament of Job
Theb.	Statius, *Thebaid*
Tib.	Suetonius, *Tiberius*
Tob	Tobit
Tranq.	Seneca, *De tranquillitate animi*
Troph. dyn.	Galen, *Peri trophon dynameos*
Tu. san.	Plutarch, *De tuenda sanitate praecepta*
Vesp.	Aristophanes, *Vespae*
Vit. beat.	Seneca, *De vita beata*
Wis	Wisdom of Solomon

Secondary Sources

AAMS	Advances in Archaeological and Museum Science
AB	Anchor Bible
ABD	Freedman, David Noel, ed. *Anchor Bible Dictionary.* 6 vols. New York: Doubleday, 1992.
AC	*L'antiquité classique*
ACS	American Classical Studies
ADRA	Association pour la diffusion de la recherche sur l'Antiquité
AGJU	Arbeiten zur Geschichte des antiken Judentums und des Urchristentums
AGROS	Accessible Greek Resources and Online Studies
AIIN	*Annali dell'Istituto Italiano di Numismatica*

AJA	*American Journal of Archaeology*
AJEC	Ancient Judaism and Early Christianity
AK	*Archiv für Kulturgeschichte*
ANF	Roberts, Alexander, and James Donaldson. *The Ante-Nicene Fathers: Translations of the Writings of the Fathers down to A.D. 325.* 10 vols. Buffalo: Christian Literature, 1885–1887.
ANRW	*Aufstieg und Niedergang der römischen Welt: Geschichte und Kultur Roms im Spiegel der neueren Forschung.* Part 2, *Principat.* Edited by Hildegard Temporini and Wolfgang Haase. Berlin: de Gruyter, 1972–.
ANSMN	*American Numismatic Society Museum Notes*
Antichthon	*Antichthon: Journal of the Australian Society for Classical Studies*
AÖAWPH	Anzeiger der Österreichischen Akademie der Wissenschaften—philosophisch-historischen Klasse
APSP	*American Philosophical Society Proceedings*
AR	*Archiv für Religionswissenschaft*
Arch	*Archaeology*
ASV	American Standard Version
AZGKJ	Aschkenas: Zeitschrift für Geschichte und Kultur der Juden
BA	*Biblical Archaeologist*
BAGD	Bauer, Walter, William F. Arndt, F. Wilbur Gingrich, and Frederick W. Danker. *Greek-English Lexicon of the New Testament and Other Early Christian Literature.* 3rd ed. Chicago: University of Chicago Press, 2000.
BAR	*Biblical Archaeology Review*
BASOR	*Bulletin of the American School of Oriental Research*
BBR	*Bulletin for Biblical Research*
BCH	*Bulletin de correspondance hellénique*
BDAG	Danker, Frederick W., Walter Bauer, William F. Arndt, and F. Wilbur Gingrich. *Greek-English Lexicon of the New Testament and Other Early Christian Literature.* 3rd ed. Chicago: University of Chicago Press, 2000.
BDF	Blass, Friedrich, Albert Debrunner, and Robert

	W. Funk. *A Greek Grammar of the New Testament and Other Early Christian Literature*. Chicago: University of Chicago Press, 1961.
BECNT	Baker Exegetical Commentary on the New Testament
BEFAR	Bibliothèque des écoles françaises d'Athènes et de Rome
BEHEH	Bibliothèque de l'École des hautes études, ive section: Sciences historiques et philologiques
BerMatÖAI	Berichte und Materialen herausgegeben vom Österreichischen Archäologischen Institut
BETL	Bibliotheca Ephemeridum Theologicarum Lovaniensium
BHGNT	Baylor Handbook on the Greek New Testament
BHL	Blackwell Handbooks in Linguistics
Bib	*Biblica*
BIS	Biblical Interpretation Series
BJS	Brown Judaic Studies
BKG	Bilkent Kültür Girişimi
BMC	*Coins of the Roman Empire in the British Museum*. Edited by Harold Mattingly and R. A. G. Robert Andrew Glindinning Carson. 6 vols. London: Trustees of the British Museum, 1923–1962.
BNTC	Blackwell's New Testament Commentaries
BP	The Bible and Postcolonialism
BS	Mazar, Benjamin, Moshe Schwabe, Baruch Lifshitz, and Nahman Avigad, eds. *Beth Sheʿarim*. English ed. 3 vols. New Brunswick, NJ: Rutgers University Press, 1973–1976.
BSGRE	Brill Studies in Greek and Roman Epigraphy
BSL	Biblical Studies Library
BTB	*Biblical Theology Bulletin*
BTS	Biblical Tools and Studies
BTTK	*Belleten Türk Tarih Kurumu*
BZ	*Biblische Zeitschrift*
BZNW	Beihefte zur Zeitschrift für die neutestamentliche Wissenschaft
CAH	Cambridge Ancient History
CBET	Contributions to Biblical Exegesis and Theology

CBQ	*Catholic Biblical Quarterly*
CCCHBulg	Coin Collections and Coin Hoards from Bulgaria
CCR	Cambridge Companions to Religion
CCS	Cincinnati Classical Studies
CCSA	Corpus Christianorum: Series Apocryphorum
CGCI	Head, Barclay V. *Catalogue of the Greek Coins of Ionia*. Edited by Reginald Stuart Poole. A Catalogue of the Greek Coins in the British Museum 14. London: Trustees of the British Museum, 1892. Coins referenced are in the Ephesus section.
CH	*Church History*
CIG	Boeckh, August, ed. *Corpus inscriptionum graecarum*. 4 vols. Berlin: Akademie der Wissenschaften. 1828-1877.
CIL	Mommsen, Theodor, et al., eds. *Corpus Inscriptionum Latinarum*. Berlin: Reimerus, 1862–.
CIRC	Cambridge Introduction to Roman Civilization
CJ	*Classical Journal*
CL	Collection Latomus
CNT	Commentaire du Nouveau Testament
Colloq	*Colloquium*
COMES	Civitatum Orbis Mediterranei Studia
ConBNT	Coniectanea Biblica: New Testament Series
CPJ	Tcherikover, Victor A, Alexander Fuks, and Menachem Stern, eds., with an epigraphical contribution by David M. Lewis. *Corpus Papyrorum Iudaicarum*. 3 vols. Jerusalem: Hebrew University; Cambridge: Harvard University Press, 1957–1964.
CQ	*Catholic Quarterly*
CSJud	Studies in Christianity and Judaism/Études sur le christianisme et le judaïsme
DEAR	Ruggiero, Ettore de, ed. *Dizionario epigráfico di antichità romane*. 4 vols. Rome: Pasqualucci, 1895–1919.
DNP	Cancik, Hubert, and Helmuth Schneider. *Der neue Pauly: Enzyklopädie der Antike*. 16 vols. Stuttgart: Metzler, 1996–2003.

DocsAug	Ehrenberg, Victor, and A. H. M. Jones, eds. *Documents Illustrating the Reigns of Augustus and Tiberius*. Oxford: Clarendon, 1949.
DRB	Douay-Rheims Bible
EBib	Etudes bibliques
EC	*Early Christianity*
ECAM	Early Christianity in Asia Minor
EHS.G	Europäische Hochschulschriften, Reihe 3, Geschichte und ihre Hilfswissenschaften.
EIL	Wilmanns, Gustavus. *Exempla inscriptionum Latinarum in usum praecipue academicum*. 2 vols. Berlin: Weidmannos, 1873.
EJÖAI	Ergänzungshefte zu den Jahresheften des Österreichischen Archäologischen Institutes
EKKNT	Evangelisch-Katholischer Kommentar zum Neuen Testament
EP	Evangelical Perspectives
ESV	English Standard Version
ETSP	E. Togo Salmon Papers
FBBS	Facet Books, Biblical Series
FES	Oberlietner, Wolfgang, ed. *Funde aus Ephesos und Samothrake*. Vol. 2 of *Katalog der Antikensammlung*. Vienna: Kunsthistorisches Museum, 1978.
FiE	Forschungen in Ephesos
FSI	*Forensic Science International*
GCRW	Greek Culture in the Roman World
GRBS	*Greek, Roman, and Byzantine Studies*
GSCLA	Gorgias Studies in Classical and Late Antiquity
GW	God's Word Translation
HAG	Homer Archaeological Guides
HCSB	Holman Christian Standard Bible
Historia	*Historia: Zeitschrift für alte Geschichte*
HMCH	Hidryma Meletōn Chersonēsou tou Haimou
HS	Hellenic Studies
HSCP	*Harvard Studies in Classical Philology*
HTR	*Harvard Theological Review*
HTS	Harvard Theological Studies
HUT	Hermeneutische Untersuchungen zur Theologie

HvTSt	*Hervormde Teologiese Studies* (*HTS Teologiese Studies/HTS Theological Studies*)
Hypomnemata	Hypomnemata: Untersuchungen zur Antike und zu ihrer Nachleben
IAG	Moretti, Luigi. *Iscrizioni agonistiche greche.* Rome: Signorelli, 1953.
IBM	*The Collection of Ancient Greek Inscriptions in the British Museum.* 4 vols. Oxford: Clarendon, 1874–1916.
ICC	International Critical Commentary
IEph	Wankel, Hermann, et al., eds. *Die Inschriften von Ephesos.* 8 vols. in 11. IK 11–17. Bonn: Habelt, 1979–1984.
IErythrai	Engelmann, Helmut, and Reinhold Merkelbach. *Die Inschriften von Erythrai und Klazomenai.* IK 1. Bonn: Habelt, 1972.
IF	Istanbuler Forschungen
IFS	In the Footsteps of the Saints
IG	*Inscriptiones Graecae.* Editio Minor. Berlin: de Gruyter, 1924–.
IJHS	*International Journal of the History of Sport*
IJO	Noy, David, et al., eds. *Inscriptiones Judaicae Orientis.* 3 vols. TSAJ 99, 101, 102. Tübingen: Mohr Siebeck, 2004.
IK	Inschriften griechischer Städte aus Kleinasien
IKyme	Engelmann, Helmut, ed. *Die Inschriften von Kyme.* IK 5. Bonn: Habelt, 1976
IMagnMai	Kern, Otto. *Die Inschriften von Magnesia am Meander.* Berlin: Spemann, 1900.
IPergamon	Fränkel, Max, and Christian Habicht, eds. *Die Inschriften von Pergamon.* 2 vols. Altertümer von Pergamon 8. Berlin: Spemann, 1890–1895.
IPriene	Blümel, Wolfgang, and Reinhold Merkelbach, eds., in collaboration with Frank Rumscheid. *Inschriften von Priene.* IK 69. Berlin: Habelt, 1906.
ISmyrna	Petzl, Georg, ed. *Die Inschriften von Smyrna.* 2 vols. in 3 parts. IK 23–24. Bonn: Habelt, 1982–1990.

IStratonikeia	Şahin, Mehmet Çetin, ed. *Die Inschriften von Stratonikeia*. 2 vols. in 3 parts. IK 21–22. Bonn: Habelt, 1981–1990.
ITS	International Theological Studies
JAC	*Jahrbuch für Antike und Christentum*
JASP	Jutland Archaeological Society Publications
JBL	*Journal of Biblical Literature*
JDAI	*Jahrbuch des Deutschen Archäologischen Instituts*
JETS	*Journal of the Evangelical Theological Society*
JGRChJ	*Journal of Greco-Roman Christianity and Judaism*
JHS	*Journal of Hellenic Studies*
JL	Jerome Lectures
JNAA	*Journal of the Numismatic Association of Australia*
JNG	*Jahrbuch für Nümismatik und Geldgeschichte*
JÖAI	*Jahreshefte des Österreichischen archäologischen Instituts*
JRA	*Journal of Roman Archaeology*
JRASup	Journal of Roman Archaeology Supplement
JRS	*Journal of Roman Studies*
JRSM	Journal of Roman Studies Monographs
JSH	*Journal of Sport History*
JSJSup	Supplements to the Journal for the Study of Judaism
JSNT	*Journal for the Study of the New Testament*
JSNTSup	Journal for the Study of the New Testament Supplement Series
JSOT	Journal for the Study of the Old Testament
JTS	*Journal of Theological Studies*
KEK	Kritisch-exegetischer Kommentar über das Neue Testament
KernosSup	Kernos Supplément
KJV	King James Version
KTAH	Key Themes in Ancient History
LBS	Linguistic Biblical Studies
LCL	Loeb Classical Library
LNTS	The Library of New Testament Studies
LP	Thomasson, Bengt E. *Laterculi praesidum*. 3 vols. Götteborg: Radius, 1984–1990.

LSJ	Liddell, Henry George, Robert Scott, Henry Stuart Jones. *A Greek-English Lexicon*. 9th ed. with revised supplement. Oxford: Clarendon, 1996.
MAII	Missione archeologica Italiana di Iasos
MAMA	Calder, W. M., Alan Cameron, J. Cullen, and Barbara Levick, eds. *Monumenta Asiae Minoris antiqua*. London: Manchester University Press; Longmans, Green, 1928–.
MedAnt	*Mediterraneo Antico*
MEFR	*Mélanges de l'École française de Rome*
MnemSup	Mnemosyne bibliotheca classica Batava supplementum
MONG	*Mitteilungen der Österreichischen Numismatischen Gesellschaft*
NA^{28}	*Novum Testamentum Graece*, Nestle-Aland, 28th ed.
NASB	New American Standard Bible
NC	*The Numismatic Chronicle*
NEA	*Near Eastern Archaeology*
NedTT	*Nederlandsch theologisch tijdschrift*
NET	New English Translation
NewDocs	Horsley, Greg H. R., and Stephen Llewelyn, eds. *New Documents Illustrating Early Christianity*. North Ryde, NSW: The Ancient History Documentary Research Centre, Macquarie University, 1981–.
NHMS	Nag Hammadi and Manichaean Studies
NICNT	New International Commentary on the New Testament
NIDNTTE	Silva, Moisés, ed. *New International Dictionary of New Testament Theology and Exegesis*. 2nd ed. 5 vols. Grand Rapids: Zondervan, 2014.
NIV	New International Version
NLT	New Living Translation
NovT	*Novum Testamentum*
NovTSup	Supplements to Novum Testamentum
NR	Numismatique romaine
NTL	New Testament Library
NTOA	Novum Testamentum et Orbis Antiquus
NTS	*New Testament Studies*
NTSR	New Testament for Spiritual Reading

NZ	*Numismatische Zeitschrift*
ÖAI	Österreichisches Archäologisches Institut
ÖAW	Österreichischen Akademie der Wissenschaften
OCM	Oxford Classical Monographs
ÖFN	Österreichische Forschungsgesellschaft für Numismatik
OGIS	Dittenberger, Wilhelm. *Orientis graeci inscriptiones selectae*. 2 vols. Leipzig: Hirzel, 1903–1905.
OLD	Glare, P. G. W., ed. *Oxford Latin Dictionary*. Oxford: Clarendon, 1982.
Paradosis	Paradosis: Contributions to the History of Early Christian Literature and Theology
PBSR	*Papers of the British School at Rome*
Paideia	Paideia: Commentaries on the New Testament
PG	Migne, Jacques-Paul, ed. Patrologia Graeca [= Patrologiae Cursus Completus: Series Graeca]. 162 vols. Paris: Migne, 1857–1886.
PIR	*Prosopographia Imperii Romani Saeculorum I. II. III*. 3 vols. 2nd ed. Berlin: de Gruyter, 1933.
P.Lond.	Kenyon, Frederic George, H. I. Bell, and Walter Ewing Crum, eds. *Greek Papyri in the British Museum*. 7 vols. London: British Museum, 1893–1917.
P.Magd.	Lesquier, Jean, ed. *Papyrus de Magdola: Réédités d'après les originaux*. Paris: Leroux, 1912.
P.Oxy.	Grenfell, Bernard P., et al., eds. *The Oxyrhynchus Papyri*. London: Egypt Exploration Fund, 1898–.
PW	*Paulys Realencyclopädie der classischen Altertumswissenschaft*. New edition by Georg Wissowa and Wilhelm Kroll. 50 vols. in 84 parts. Stuttgart: Metzler & Druckenmüller, 1894–1980.
QT	*Quaderni Ticinese*
RAC	Klausner, Theodor, et al., eds. *Reallexikon für Antike und Christentum*. Stuttgart: Hiersemann, 1950–.
RBS	Resources for Biblical Study
REG	*Revue des ètudes grecques*
RevPhil	*Revue de philology*
RGRW	Religions in the Graeco-Roman World

RIC	Mattingly, Harold, ed. *The Roman Imperial Coinage*. 10 vols. London: Spink, 1923–1994. Citations of volume 2.1 are to the 2nd edition.
RivB	*Rivista biblica italiana*
RPC	Burnett, Andrew, Michel Amandry, and Pere Pau Ripollès, eds. *Roman Provincial Coinage*. London: British Museum Press; Paris: Bibliothèque nationale, 1992–.
RRA	Rhetoric of Religious Antiquity
R&T	*Religion and Theology*
RSAH	Routledge Studies in Ancient History
RVV	Religionsgeschichtliche Versuche und Vorarbeiten
SAAA	Studies on the Apocryphal Acts of the Apostles
SAPERE	Scripta Antiquitatis Posterioris ad Ethicam Religionemque Pertinentia
SBG	Studies in Biblical Greek
SBLDS	Society of Biblical Literature Dissertation Series
SBLSP	Society of Biblical Literature Seminar Papers
SBS	Stuttgarter Bibelstudien
SCJud	Studies in Christianity and Judaism
SCO	*Studi classici e orientali*
SEG	*Supplementum epigraphicum graecum*. Amsterdam: Gieben, 1923–.
SFCB.SP	Spätantike—Frühes Christentum—Byzanz, Reihe B: Studien und Perspektiven
SIDA	Scripta Instituti Donneriani Aboensis
SIG	Dittenberger, Wilhelm. *Sylloge inscriptionum graecarum*. 3rd ed. 4 vols. Leipzig: Hirzel, 1915–1924.
SNGCop	*Sylloge nummorum Graecorum. The Royal Collection of Coins and Medals, Danish National Museum*. 12 vols. Copenhagen: Munksgaard, 1942–1979.
SNGLewis	Carradice, Ian, ed. *Lewis Collection in Corpus Christi College, Cambridge*. Vol. 6 of *Sylloge nummorum Graecorum*. 2 parts. London: Oxford University Press, 1972–1992.
SNGMün	Klose, Dietrich O. A., ed. *Ionien*. Vol. 20 of *Sylloge nummorum Graecorum Deutschland: Staatliche Munzsammlung München*. Munich: Hirmer, 1995.

SNGParis	*Sylloge nummorum Graecorum France: Bibliothèque nationale; Cabinet des médailles*. Paris: Bibliothèque Nationale, 1983–.
SNGRighetti	Kapossy, Balázs, ed. *Katalog der Sammlung Jean-Pierre Righetti im Bernischen Historischen Museum*. Vol. 2 of *Sylloge nummorum Graecorum Schweiz*. Bern: Haupt, 1993.
SNGvA	Aulock, Hans von, and Gerhard Kleiner, eds. *Sammlung von Aulock*. Vol. 1 of *Sylloge nummorum Graecorum Deutschland*. 18 parts. Berlin: Mann, 1957–1968.
SNTSMS	Society for New Testament Studies Monograph.
SNTW	Studies of the New Testament and Its World
SP	Sacra Pagina
SR	*Studies in Religion*
SSR	Studies in Rhetoric and Religion
SSRH	Sociological Studies in Roman History
TAM	Kalinka, Ernst, et al., eds. *Tituli Asiae Minoris*. Vienna: Hoelder, 1901–.
TANZ	Texte und Arbeiten zum neutestamentlichen Zeitalter
TAPA	*Transactions of the American Philological Association*
TDGR	Translated Documents of Greece and Rome
TDNT	Kittel, Gerhard, and Gerhard Friedrich, eds. *Theological Dictionary of the New Testament*. Translated by Geoffrey W. Bromiley. 10 vols. Grand Rapids: Eerdmans, 1964–1976.
TENTS	Texts and Editions for New Testament Study
TNTC	Tyndale New Testament Commentaries
TOOSup	Topoi Orient-Occident Supplément
TSAJ	Texte und Studien zum antiken Judentum
TU	Texte und Untersuchungen
TynBul	*Tyndale Bulletin*
UH	Urban History
USQR	*Union Seminary Quarterly Review*
VING	Veröffentlichungen des Institutes für Numismatik und Geldgeschichte

VNK	Veröffentlichungen der Numismatischen Kommission
WBC	Word Biblical Commentary
WGRWSup	Writings from the Greco-Roman World Supplement Series
WMANT	Wissenschaftliche Monographien zum Alten und Neuen Testament
WSt	*Wiener Studien*
WUNT	Wissenschaftliche Untersuchungen zum Neuen Testament
YCS	Yale Classical Studies
YLT	Young's Literal Translation
YPA	*Yearbook of Physical Anthropology*
ZNW	*Zeitschrift für die Neutestamentliche Wissenschaft und die Kunde der älteren Kirche*
ZPE	*Zeitschrift für Papyrologie und Epigraphik*

An Epigraphic Portrait of Ephesus and Its Villages

James R. Harrison

In a book neglected by modern scholars, *Ephesos im Spiegel seiner Inschriften*,[1] Dieter Knibbe and Bülent İplikçioğlu discussed the history of Ephesus and its culture. What makes their exposition so valuable is that it is an epigraphic portrait of the city, containing fifty-seven translated inscriptions, each with a brief commentary attached. This chapter will also look at the social life of Ephesus through the "mirror" of its inscriptions. These bilingual texts (Greek and Latin) now comprise a corpus of well over 3,750 inscriptions.[2] The limitations of inscriptions as sources of evidence for any ancient city have to be acknowledged. As texts, they are elitist, providing little insight, for example, into the life of the poor at the base of the social pyramid.[3] They can be highly fragmentary or damaged, are often removed from their original archaeological context, and are random in their survival. Furthermore, as Knibbe and İplikçioğlu concede, "Their disadvantage is that they are merely flashes in the large framework of events, and that even their sum total does not provide a coherent his-

---

1. Dieter Knibbe and Bülent İplikçioğlu with Friedrich Schindler, *Ephesos im Spiegel seiner Inschriften* (Vienna: Schildler, 1984). At the outset, it should be stated that references to the deutero-Pauline epistles (Ephesians, Colossians, 2 Thessalonians, and the Pastorals) by their traditional attribution (i.e., Paul), both in this essay and in other essays in this volume, do not imply acceptance of Pauline authorship on the part of the editors, who recognize that the vast majority of historical-critical New Testament scholarship accepts the pseudonymous origins of the deutero-Pauline epistles.

2. This is the estimate of Greg H. R. Horsley ("The Inscriptions of Ephesos and the New Testament," *NovT* 34 [1992]: 121). By contrast, Knibbe and İplikçioğlu postulates that there may well be over five thousand Ephesian inscriptions (*Ephesos*, 10).

3. The only use of πτωχός ("poor man") in the Ephesian inscriptions is Christian (IEph 7.2.4301, citing Ps 131:15–16 LXX).

torical picture."[4] Nevertheless, their contemporaneity with the events and issues reported gives them a valuable edge over our mostly later literary evidence, riddled as it is with aristocratic bias.

In this essay I will explore the ideology of the Ephesian inscriptions for insight into the religious culture, social relations, and civic life of Ephesus and its countryside. My approach will necessarily be selective, bypassing the history, literature, archaeology, iconography, and numismatics of Ephesus,[5] focusing instead on aspects of the urban and village context of the early Ephesian believers as revealed in the inscriptions and proceeding in many instances by case studies. Topics to be covered include the messages conveyed by the buildings of Ephesus; the neighboring villages; indigenous and imperial cults; elites and associations; the Jews of Ephesus; slavery in the city; spectacles, games, and processions; and, finally, the social world of graffiti. Throughout the footnotes I will highlight the contribution of the other essays in this volume to this picture of Ephesus.

1. Ephesus, Mythology, and Its Buildings: Disseminating Symbolic Messages

It is beyond the scope of this chapter to discuss the many inscriptional dedications to benefactors for erecting structures within Ephesus.[6] Suffice it to say, a vast range of individuals and organizations built at Ephesus, including the Roman ruler, the governor of Asia Minor, consuls, Asian asiarchs and *archiereis*, local magistrates, priests and priestesses, unknown officials, military personnel, local associations, the city of Ephesus itself, those with access to revenues from sacred institutions, and, finally, a child

---

4. Knibbe and İplikçioğlu, *Ephesos*, 10.

5. See Gilbert Wiplinger and Gudrun Wlach, *Ephesus: One Hundred Years of Austrian Research* (Vienna: ÖAI, 1996); Dieter Knibbe, *EPHESUS—ΕΦΕΣΟΣ: Geschichte einer bedeutenden antiken Stadt und Portrait einer modernen Grossgrabung im 102. Jahr der Wiederkehr des Beginnes österreichischer Forschungen (1895–1997)* (Frankfurt am Main: Lang, 1998); Peter Scherrer, *Ephesus: The New Guide*, trans. Lionel Bier and George M. Luxon, rev. ed. (Istanbul: Ege Yayınlan, 2000); Jerome Murphy-O'Connor, *St. Paul's Ephesus: Texts and Archaeology* (Collegeville, MN: Liturgical Press, 2008). See also Michael P. Theophilos's essay in this volume.

6. For a summary of construction in Ephesus, see L. Michael White, "Urban Development and Social Change in Imperial Ephesos," in *Ephesos, Metropolis of Asia: An Interdisciplinary Approach to Its Archaeology, Religion, and Culture*, ed. Helmut Koester, HTS 41 (Valley Forge, PA: Trinity Press International, 1995), 52–54.

who donated a building (IEph 3.690).[7] In any case, most building projects were sponsored by locals. What we need at the outset is some type of understanding about how the buildings of Ephesus connected with Artemis, the Roman ruler, and the mythology of the Ephesian past and what messages were being conveyed to contemporaries. This not only raises questions about the identity of Ephesus in the imperial period but also about the ideological intentions of its benefactors. An exploration of the founder myth of Androclus and its expression in the edifices and processions of Ephesus provides a revealing case study.

1.1. Ephesus and the Foundation Myth of Androclus: A Study of the Processional Way of Artemis

The incorporation of Artemis worship into the foundation mythology of the city is a fascinating and important study. A significant change in the processional route of Ephesian Artemis, the Via Sacra, had occurred by the imperial era. The old archaic and classical route, which had incorporated beautiful seaside vistas, was replaced by a new landlocked, territorial alternative, necessitated by the resiting of the city in the Hellenistic age (281 BCE) due to the silting of the Ephesian harbor. As we will later see, the later second-century procession of the statues through Ephesus, funded by a bequest of C. Vibius Salutaris, reinforced for Ephesian citizens the realities of Roman control and power in provincial Asia Minor. Nevertheless, this new route was intimately connected to the traditional Ephesian foundation myths. Along the processional way of Artemis were sites associated in various ways from the second century BCE to the second century CE with the founder (κτίστης) of Ephesus, Androclus. The foundation story is well known from the literary sources.[8] Androclus, the son of the legendary King Codrus of Athens, had been told in a Delphic oracle that he would found a new city through the signs given by a wild boar and fish, which, according the foundation myth, led him inexorably

---

7. Angela V. Kalinowski, "Patterns of Patronage: The Politics and Ideology of Public Building in the Eastern Roman Empire (31 BCE–600 CE)" (PhD diss., University of Toronto, 1996), 43–67.

8. Athenaeus, *Deipn.* 8.361d–e; Strabo, *Geog.* 14.12.21; Pausanias, *Descr.* 7.2.8–9. For discussion, see Elisabeth Rathmayr, "Die Präsenz des Ktistes Androklos in Ephesos," *AÖAWPH* 145 (2010): 19–60. The English translations of the Androclus inscriptions below are indebted to the German translations of Rathmayr.

to establish a settlement at the site of Ephesus, expelling the local populations of the Lydians and Leleges upon arrival. But what importance did Androclus still retain for imperial Ephesus and how was the myth incorporated into the processional worship of Artemis?

The Ephesian inscriptions underscore the continuing importance of Androclus to Ephesus in Roman times and the religious vitality of the myth. The prytanis Tullia is honored by having her beneficence brought to the attention of Artemis and Hestia, who both continuously help her with her civic role in the famous city of Androclus (IEph 4.1064 [first/second century CE]):

> O you goddess of the very best and wise city founded by Androclus, always virgin Hestia, and you, the greatest person among the gods, Artemis, are always and everywhere helpers of Tullia: (the noteworthy fact is that) she has been a prytanis willingly and richly with you (in your city), by using her wealth abundantly for every good cause.

Elsewhere Androclus is named the founder of the city (IEph 2.501 [second/third century CE]), whereas the Ephesians themselves are called the Ἀνδροκλίδαι, the descendants of Androclus (IEph 5.1548; 7.1.3079). There is reference to the "day of Androclus," on which oil was distributed to all the gymnasia (IEph 3.644). The benefactor, Vedius Papianus Antoninus, is also eulogized with ancestral "founder" ideology: "the most distinguished senator and the benefactor since the times of the ancestors and *ktistēs* of our fatherland" (IEph 7.1.3079 [Antonine period]). Remarkably, another inscription depicts Androclus as still protecting and guarding the city through the agency of his pro-Roman benefactors:

> Androclus, the city's *ktistēs*, has restored the guards under the guidance of Aur. Nikostratos, who is also called Eupalis, son of Eupalios, loyal to the emperor. (IEph 2.501)

Finally, an inscription in honor of the new Asian proconsul Messalinus flatters him in highly adulatory terms for his restoration of the Ephesian theater, portraying him as being greater than the founder of the city:

> Behold the mighty arch, the robust foundation walls of the theater, and admire the worthy (new) founder of well-known Ephesus, who is still more prominent than Androclus, Messalinus, the great ruler of the great (province) Asia. (IEph 6.2044 [fourth/fifth century CE])

The continuing vitality of the Androclus myth and its interconnection with Artemis and imperial cult is also seen in the way that the new processional route, devised with the help of Salutaris's bequest (104 CE), incorporated sites honoring Androclus. First, on Curetes Street (the ancient *embolos*) past the Magnesian Gate is the heroon of Androclus himself, built in the second century BCE and staking out symbolically the Athenian heritage of Ephesus in the early Hellenistic age. A fragmentary relief, among many others in the heroon, shows Androclus on horseback with a flying cape, chasing with a spear an unknown object that, on the basis of parallels from an Ephesian coin and a relief in the Temple of Hadrian,[9] can only be a boar, an obvious allusion to the foundation myth.[10] The message of Androclus's heroon, as Diana Y. Ng suggests,[11] has "intercity and international audiences in mind."

Second, the Nymphaeum of Trajan, located in the southwest of Curetes Street, exhibited a colossal, partly nude statue of the Roman ruler, a statue of his adoptive father Nerva, and a statue of a youthful hunter, identified with Androclus, with a statue of Apollo standing opposite—another clear allusion to the Delphic origins of the foundation myth.[12] Nor must we forget the substantial deflected glory that accrued to the benefactor Claudius Aristion, who was an asiarch (IEph 2.427), high priest of the city, and temple warden of the imperial cult (IEph 2.234, 235, 237, 239, 241, 424a, 425a, 461, 508; 3.638; 7.2.4105, 5113). He was one of two benefactors who funded the Nymphaeum (IEph 2.424 [102/114 CE]) and various other projects (IEph 2.425; 7.1.3217a–b). In sum we are seeing here the intersection of imperial and elite Ephesian benefactors, who draw upon the foundational myths of Ephesus and the rerouted processional way of Artemis in order to enhance the social and political impact of their patronage.[13] Finally, the traditional Ionic warrior image of Androclus

---

9. For the coin, see Rathmayr, "Die Präsenz des Ktistes Androklos," 152, figs. 1–2. For the Hadrian relief, see pp. 57–59, figs. 17–19.

10. For full discussion, see Hilke Thür, "Der ephesische Ktistes Androklos und (s)ein Heroon am Embolos," *JÖAI* 64 (1995): 70, 82–83; Thür, "The Processional Way in Ephesos as a Place of Cult and Burial," in Koester, *Ephesos*, 160; Diana Y. Ng, "Manipulation of Memory: Public Buildings and Decorative Programs in Roman Cities of Asia Minor" (PhD diss., University of Michigan, 2007), 192–99.

11. Ng, "Manipulation of Memory," 209.

12. See ibid. For the statue, see Rathmayr, "Die Präsenz des Ktistes Androklos," 152, fig. 11.

13. See the discussion in Ng, "Manipulation of Memory," 209.

(cf. Pausanias, *Descr.* 7.2.6–9) is redefined for a new understanding that fits the providential and peaceful ordering of history by Artemis and the Roman ruler.[14]

Third, in the northeast of the city, in the aediculated hall of the baths of Vedius, was found another sculpture of a youthful figure, identified as Androclus by "the nearby find of a dog's paw resting on tufts of boar bristles—another obvious reference to the mythical boar hunt."[15] The Baths of Vedius, belonging to the larger gymnasium complex, would have been one of the sites where oil was dispensed to the athletes on the day of Androclus, as noted before.[16] As we have already seen, the benefactor of the gymnasium, Vedius Papianus Antoninus, who will be discussed later, was also acclaimed like Androclus as the founder of the city. Thus the Ephesian elites acquired substantial personal honor by their benefaction of projects associated with the legendary founder of the city.

Fourth, among the many statues carried in processional way was most likely a silver image of Androclus (IEph 1a.27, l. 183 [CE 104]: "and a silver image [of Androclus?]"). Even though the restoration is uncertain and has been challenged,[17] it is virtually assured by the fact that since three sites honoring Androclus have been carefully incorporated into the processional itinerary of C. Vibius Salutaris, it is impossible to conceive that the statue of Androclus was somehow omitted from the procession, even if the procession was dominated by images of Artemis.

Thus, as Ng concludes regarding Ephesian building activities,[18] "the elite priority of self-promotion in the cases of Aristion, Vedius, and Salutaris all borrow from the prestige and authority of Ephesus's mythical foundation and legendary founder." What is especially surprising is that both Artemis and the Roman ruler "muscle in" on the prestige of Androclus. We are witnessing here in the early Second Sophistic era the honoring of the mythic past and ancestral figures in Asia Minor (e.g., the civil basilica

---

14. Ng writes: "By choosing another identity for Androklos, one that emphasized his participation in a divinely preordained hunt, the program at the Nymphaeum of Trajan turned away from a foundation legacy of conflict and towards one of peaceful fulfillment of prophecy, implying that Roman rule and the cooperation of elites was similarly preordained" (ibid., 208).

15. Ibid., 214.

16. Ibid., 215–16.

17. See ibid., 220, n. 74 for a strong rebuttal of such skepticism.

18. Ibid., 227.

at Aphrodisias, the theater reliefs at Hierapolis), as part of the articulation of local civic identity in the face of increasing Romanization. The pro-Roman Asian elites, however, comfortably incorporate the local honoring of the founder figures and the mythological past within the wider Roman honorific system and their local urban building activities.

It is not without significance, therefore, that in the "processional" hymn of Paul (or the pseudonymous author) in Eph 1:3–14, in which he proceeds across the ages from our pretemporal election to our future inheritance, he continually reverts to our incorporation in our founder figure, Christ (Eph 1:3b, 4a, 6b, 7a, 9b, 10b, 10c, 11a, 12b, 13a, 13b). In light of the evidence above, this interminably long sentence in Greek expresses its processional and theological impact as it moves relentlessly across the papyrus, emphasizing repeatedly our grace, blessing, and security in Christ—our soteriological founder—and in his predestinating Father.

2. The Relationship of City to Countryside: The Villages of the Kaystros Valley

An important area of study of the ancient world, which remains relatively neglected in classical and New Testament studies, is the relationship of the city to the surrounding countryside and its villages.[19] The composers of the Ephesian inscriptions were well aware that the polis included its hinterland as well. Several examples will suffice. IEph 1a.7.2 (98/97 or 94/93 BCE) speaks of "the Ephesians who live in Ephesus or in the countryside" (l. 11; cf. l. 15). Similarly, IEph 1a.8 (86/85 BCE) celebrates "the

---

19. See John Rich and Andrew Wallace-Hadrill, eds., *City and Country in the Ancient World* (London: Routledge, 1991); Andrew P. Gregory, "Village Society in Hellenistic and Roman Asia Minor" (PhD diss., Columbia University, 1997); Peter Lampe, "The Phrygian Hinterland South of Temenothyrai (Uşak)," *EC* 7 (2016): 381–94. For the importance of village and hinterland studies in New Testament scholarship on the polis and the social constituency of the early Christians, see Thomas A. Robinson, *Who Were the First Christians? Dismantling the Urban Thesis* (Oxford: Oxford University Press, 2017). On the hinterland of Ephesus, see Recep Meriç, *Das Hinterland von Ephesos: Archäologisch-topographische Forschungen im Kaystros-Tal*, EJÖAI 12 (Vienna: ÖAI, 2009), not seen by me. On the difference between city and village, see James R. Harrison, "The First Urban Churches: Introduction," in *Methodological Foundations*, vol. 1 of *The First Urban Churches*, ed. James R. Harrison and L. L. Welborn, WGRWSup 7 (Atlanta: SBL Press, 2015), 3–7.

protection, safety, and salvation both of the temple of Artemis and of the city and its countryside" (ll. 16–17). An undated dedication (IEph 5.1786) refers to an Ephesian erecting a monument "on behalf of himself and the villages." Finally, in an inscription honoring an Ephesian advocate (IEph 3.802, ll. 21–22), the various posts of his career are listed, including being "sole police magistrate of the countryside."

While the references above underline the importance of the surrounding countryside in Ephesian identity, there is substantial epigraphic reference to villages belonging to the hinterland territory of Ephesus. François Kirbihler has demonstrated from the Ephesian inscriptions that there were twelve Ephesian villages in the Kaystros valley,[20] either designated a κώμη ("village") or a κατοικία ("settlement"). He argues that Ephesus would have been able to increase its territorial share of the villages in the valley unhindered until the end of the second century BCE, assuming that Lysimachus's resiting and refounding of the city in 281 BCE did not extend much beyond Larisa. If the 86/85 BCE grant of Ephesian citizenship (IEph 1a.8, ll. 42–47) to the *paroikoi* ("sojourners") was only extended to the recently established communities like Larisa and Tire, then, Kirbihler concludes, much of the Kaystros valley must have belonged to Ephesus by the first century BCE, stretching from beyond the borders of Larisa and Tire to Hypaipa and Dios Hieron.[21]

Thus the civic life of the villages in the Kaystros valley represents an important dimension of our understanding of Ephesus as a city. The name of the Ephesian village of the Boukolianoi, for example, derives from its main occupation, the tending of cattle, throwing indirect light on the provisioning of Ephesus with food and sacrifices from its nearby villages.[22] Again, like many other Phrygian villages, there is frequent mention in the village inscriptions of the imposition of fines for the violation of tombs and ritual procedures, issues of cultic sensitivity that brought additional

---

20. Frannçois Kirbihler, "Territoire civique et population d'Éphèse (Ve siècle av. J.-C.-IIIe siècle apr. J.-C.)," in *L'Asie Mineure dans l'Antiquité: Échanges, populations et territories; Regards actuels sur une peninsula; Actes du Colloque International de Tours, 21–22 Octobre 2005*, ed. Hadrien Bru, François Kirbihler, and Stéphane Lebreton (Rennes: Presses Universitaires de Rennes, 2009), 316.

21. Kirbihler, "Territoire civique et population d'Éphèse," 315. For a map of the Ephesian hinterland territory, see p. 333.

22. Gregory, "Village Society," 375. Note IEph 7.1.3276: "[He will give to the village of the B]oukolianoi [denarii - - -]."

income to the village coffers and reflected wider Hellenistic practices.[23] But we will concentrate on the villages of Larisa (IEph 7.1.3271–75), Boneita (IEph 7.3251), and Almoura (IEph 7.1.2350, 7.1.2352–3264). These illuminate aspects of daily life of the villages (e.g., funeral customs, occupations, magistrates, economic relations), their buildings and benefactors, their indigenous deities and relations with the city of Artemis, and the worship of the Roman ruler.

First, in the village of Larisa, a dedication is made to Zeus Olympios Soter and the Roman ruler Hadrian by an "emperor-loving" benefactor, who erects a "statue" of the Roman ruler and builds "the slaughterhouse near it [τὸ [περὶ αὐτον] μάκελλον] from the revenue of the village" (IEph 7.1.3271). Diodorus erects two deer to Ephesian Artemis (IEph 7.1.3272), whereas Dionysios Diadumenos dedicates an Artemis statue (7.1.3273). What overall picture emerges from these vignettes of village life in Larisa in the Ephesian hinterland?

We note the deep penetration of the imperial cult into the local village life of Ionia, though the traditional Greek deities are still conspicuously rendered honor ahead of the Roman ruler. Nevertheless, wealthy local benefactors honor the Caesars with statuary in civic places and contribute in unspecified ways to village-funded building projects such as the macellum. This particular building undoubtedly functioned as a meat market, but an analogy with the macellum at Pompeii is perhaps apposite here.[24] Was the μάκελλον at Larisa, like Pompeii, a place where sacrifices to the Roman ruler were offered in the building's facilities, such as in an imperial cult room adjacent to the nearby imperial statue? Although this scenario is entirely speculative, the close proximity of Larisa's meat market to the ruler's statue is intriguing and may suggest some type of cultic connection.[25]

---

23. For fines in Ephesian villages, see IEph 7.1.3453 (Chrondrianon village), 3292 (Thyairenon village); 7.2.3701 (village of the Kilbianoi), 3703 (unnamed village). I am grateful to Gregory for these references ("Village Society," 607) and discussion (pp. 215–16, 297–99, 495).

24. Scholars are divided on the presence of an imperial cult room said to be at the *macellum* ("market") of Pompeii. For the evidence, see Alastair Small, "The Shrine of the Imperial Family in the Macellum at Pompeii," in *Subject and Ruler: The Cult of the Ruling Power in Classical Antiquity*, ed. Alastair Small, JRASup 17 (Ann Arbor, MI: Journal of Roman Archaeology, 1996). However, note the highly dismissive remarks of Mary Beard, *Pompeii: The Life of a Roman Town* (London: Profile, 2008), 301.

25. Beard rightly notes that there is uncertainty about the regularity of animal slaughter in the imperial cult: "But exactly how often the distinctive, full-blown animal

Notwithstanding the centrality of the indigenous and imperial cults, the goddess Artemis, the protector of Ephesus and its countryside, makes her presence felt by means of her honorific statues throughout the village. Most important of all, Larisa is styled a "sacred settlement" ([ἡ Λαρει] σηνῶν ἱερὰ κατοικία [IEph 7.1.3274, l. 8]), demonstrating that the village "clearly formed part of the scattered estates of the Artemision in the Kaystros valley," as Andrew P. Gregory notes. He concludes, "The self-identity of the inhabitants of these sacred communities was very much bound up with the cult of the *local* deity, just as their social and economic ties bound them to the priestly economy."[26]

Gratifyingly, we know more about the relationship of Almoura to Ephesus than Larisa. Strabo indicates the proximity of Almoura to Ephesus and how it came to be under Ephesian control:

> The third Larisa is a village in the territory of Ephesus in the Caÿster Plain; it is said to have been a city in earlier times, containing a temple of Larisaean Apollo and being situated closer to Mt. Tmolus than to Ephesus. It is one hundred and eighty stadia distant from Ephesus, and might therefore be placed under the Maeonians. But the Ephesians, having grown in power, later cut off for themselves much of the territory of the Maeonians, whom we now call Lydians. (*Geog.* 13.3.2)[27]

Most of the epigraphic texts of Almoura are conventional enough. IEph 7.1.3250 is a dedication of a fountain to an unknown god of the Almouroi and to the Roman ruler Gaius Caligula. If the editor is correct in suggesting that the damaged section of the dedication is probably a reference to an indigenous deity of Almoura, then the indigenous deities are again given primacy over the Roman ruler in honorific rituals, a feature of the Ephesian civic inscriptions also. Various local dignitaries are also commended for living καλῶς ("well") and κοσμίως ("decently" [IEph 7.1.3253–54]). In the case of the goddess Artemis, Aurelius Salluvius Timotheus is eulogized as a "pious and voluntary *neopoios* of our lady Artemis" (IEph 7.1.3263). Thus the epigraphic portrait of Almoura coheres with what we already know from Larisa.

---

slaughter took place—rather than the cheaper 'shorthand' of wine, incense and grain, thrown onto the flames of an altar—we can only guess" (*Pompeii*, 293).

26. Gregory, "Village Society," 36 (my emphasis).

27. Translation from Horace Leonard Jones, trans., *Strabo: Geography; Books 13–14*, LCL 223 (Cambridge: Harvard University Press, 1929).

But the foundation of P. Aelius Menecrates for Demeter and Men (IEph 7.1.3252) affords us unique insight into the indigenous religious life of Almoura and its benefaction culture.[28] The benefactor Menecrates is said to have brought back a basket set in silver and dedicated it to the priesthood of Demeter (IEph 7.1.3252, ll. 1–7). Seemingly, the basket had somehow managed to get lost amidst the equipment of the mysteries of Demeter,[29] but the circumstances of its disappearance and rediscovery are not specified. The sacred basket (κάλαθος) would have contained the sacred objects (ἱερά) that were carried around in the procession.[30] Menecrates also dedicates to Men, the protecting deity of the village, a silver standard that was to be conducted in the procession preceding the celebration of the mysteries (IEph 7.1.3252, ll. 7–11). The remainder of the inscription explains how Menecrates dedicated "workshops" (or "stores" [ἐργαστήρια]) at the front of his house (IEph 7.1.3252, ll. 14–15), the revenues of which provided for the costs of the incense burnt for Demeter in her mysteries. On the day of the procession of the κάλαθος, those male villagers who had been chosen by lot (IEph 7.1.3252, ll. 17–18) to participate in the cortège were entertained at a lavish banquet, along with the village archons (ll. 17–21), which was to be held at Menecrates's house each year until he died (ll. 21–22). This inscription reveals that some of the Ephesian elites also possessed houses in the villages of the hinterland. These wealthy luminaries ensured not only the provision for and superintendence of the indigenous cults, thereby demonstrating their *eusebeia* ("piety") toward the gods, but also, in the pursuit of *philotimia* ("love of honor"), enabling them to cultivate the goodwill of the local dignitaries and magistrates by means of their hospitality.

Second, concerning the village of Boneita, we learn from IEph 7.1.3251 that there is an agora at the site (ἐν τῇ ἀγορᾷ [l. 9]), providing clear evidence for commercial activity in the form of periodic markets. There is also an official designated the *argyrotamias* (ἀργυροταμίου [l. 15]) and the village

---

28. See the excellent discussion of Harry W. Pleket, "Nine Greek Inscriptions from the," *Talanta* 2 (1970): 61–74, to which my account is indebted.

29. Ibid., 62.

30. Ibid., 63. For examples of processions at Ephesus, note the circular procession of the statues commencing from and ending at the Temple of Artemis funded by C. Vibius Salutaris (IEph 1a.27) and the ancestral processions and nights festivals of the gods in the city (IEph 1a.10).

also possesses the status of a sacred *katoikia*.³¹ The reference to the *argyrotamias* cannot be dismissed as more likely belonging to Almoura, as the editor of IEph 7.1 urges, simply because of the presence of the same official in that village (ἀργυροτ[αμίου] [IEph 7.1.3250, l. 6]). This conclusion, as Gregory rightly notes,³² is "remarkably shortsighted" in its dismissal of the administrative and commercial complexity of the hinterland villages, especially those designated *katoikia*, as both Boneita (IEph 7.1.3251, l. 12) and Almoura were (IEph 7.1.3250, ll. 6–7; cf. 3250, l. 3; 3256; 3262, ll. 14–15; 3263, ll. 12–13). Sophistication in civic administration and economic relations, therefore, was not just confined to the larger villages of the Kaystros valley and Ephesus but also characterized some of the smaller villages as well.

In sum, a very rich understanding of the indigenous gods, the protective role of Artemis, and the importance of imperial worship in the surrounding villages of Ephesus in the Kaystros valley has emerged. We now turn to a brief discussion of Ephesus and its gods, which has admittedly been an area of intense research, in hopes of grasping elements of distinctiveness as opposed to what is entirely typical.

3. Ephesian Artemis, the Imperial Rulers, and the Indigenous Gods

Scholars have intensively investigated the relationship of Ephesus to Artemis and its cult. Areas of research have included the mysteries of Artemis, the procession of statues funded by the foundation of C. Vibius Salutaris, the collision of the early Christians with Artemis worship, the power of Artemis over rival magicians and the spirit world, Ephesus as a *neōkoros* of Artemis, the role of the Artemision in the daily life of Ephesus and its relationship to the imperial cult, the holy days of Artemis, the relation of Artemis to the other local indigenous gods of Ephesus, the priestesses and *neopoioi* of Artemis, and Artemis and the legend of the Seven Sleepers, among many other areas of investigation.³³ Readers are encouraged to

---

31. Note, too, the *katoikia* of the Siklianoi (IEph 7.1.3287A), Kalbianoi (IEph 7.2.3701), and Palkeanon (IEph 7.2.3850).

32. Gregory, "Village Society," 89, n. 234.

33. For the mysteries of Artemis, see Rosalinde A. Kearsley, "The Mysteries of Artemis at Ephesus," *NewDocs* 6:196–202; Guy MacLean Rogers, *The Mysteries of Artemis of Ephesos: Cult, Polis, and Change in the Graeco-Roman World*, Synkrisis

consult this continually increasing corpus of scholarship. I will not reiterate here what is said in my accompanying essay in this volume regarding the elites.[34] It discusses the imperial cult during the Julio-Claudian era;

(New Haven: Yale University Press, 2012); Ruth M. Léger, "Artemis and Her Cult" (PhD diss., University of Birmingham, 2015). See also Guy MacLean Rogers's essay in this volume, "An Ephesian Tale: Mystery Cults, Reverse Theological Engineering, and the Triumph of Christianity in Ephesus." For the procession of statues funded by the foundation of C. Vibius Salutaris, see Rogers, *The Sacred Identity of Ephesos: Foundation Myths of a Roman City* (London: Routledge, 1991); Dieter Knibbe, "Via Sacra Ephesiaca: New Aspects of the Cult of Artemis," in Koester, *Ephesos*, 141–54. For the collision of the early Christians with Artemis worship, see Rick Strelan, *Paul, Artemis, and the Jews in Ephesus*, BZNW 80 (Berlin: de Gruyter, 1995); see also Werner Theissen, *Christen in Ephesos: Die historiche und theologische Situation in vorpaulinischer und paulinischer Zeit und zur Zeit der Apostelgeschichte und der Pastoralbriefe* (Tübingen: Franke, 1990); Paul Trebilco, *The Early Christians in Ephesus from Paul to Ignatius*, WUNT 166 (Tübingen: Mohr Siebeck, 2004; repr., Grand Rapids: Eerdmans, 2007). For the power of Artemis over rival magicians and the spirit world, see Clinton E. Arnold, *Ephesians, Power and Magic: The Concept of Power in Ephesians in Light of Its Historical Setting*, SNTSMS 63 (Cambridge: Cambridge University Press, 1989; repr. Grand Rapids: Baker, 1992); James R. Harrison, "Artemis Triumphs over a Sorcerer's Evil Art," *NewDocs* 10:37–47. For Ephesus as a *neōkoros* of Artemis, see Rosalinde A. Kearsley, "Ephesus: Neokoros of Artemis," *NewDocs* 6:203–5; Steven J. Friesen, *Twice Neokoros: Ephesus, Asia and the Cult of the Flavian Imperial Family*, RGRW 116 (Leiden: Brill, 1993). See also Stephan Witetschek, "From Zeus or by Endoios? Acts 19:35 as a Peculiar Assessment of the Ephesian Artemis," in this volume. For the role of the Artemision in the daily life of Ephesus and its relationship to the imperial cult, see François Kirbihler and Lilli Zabrana, *Archäologische, epigraphische und numismatische Zeugnisse für den Kaiserkult im Artemision von Ephesos: Der Kult der Dea Roma und des Divus Iulius unter dem Triumvirat*, EJÖAI 83 (Vienna: Österreichisches Archäologisches Institut, 2014), 101–31; Ulrike Muss, "The Artemision in Early Christian Times," *EC* 7 (2016): 293–312. For the holy days of Artemis, see Richard E. Oster, "Holy Days in Honour of Artemis," *NewDocs* 4:74–82. For the relation of Artemis to the other local indigenous gods of Ephesus, see Richard E. Oster, "Ephesus as a Religious Center under the Principate, I: Paganism before Constantine," *ANRW* 18.3:1661–728. For the priestesses and *neopoioi* of Artemis, see James R. Harrison, "Family Honour of a Priestess of Artemis," *NewDocs* 10:30–36; Harrison, "A 'Worthy' *neopoios* Thanks Artemis," *NewDocs* 10:48–54. For Artemis and the legend of the Seven Sleepers, see Jacques Bonnet, *Artémis d'Éphèse et la légende des sept dormants* (Paris: Librairie Orientaliste Paul Geuthner, 1977).

34. See James R. Harrison, "Ephesian Cultic Officials, Their Benefactors, and the Quest for Civic Virtue: Paul's Alternative Quest for Status in the Epistle to the Ephesians," in this volume.

the corruption involving the priests of Artemis at the time of Claudius; the civic virtue of the priests, priestesses, and benefactors of Artemis; and a numismatic evaluation of how Ephesus speaks about its relation to Artemis and the Roman rulers. What follows is a brief overview of select epigraphic evidence relating to Artemis, the indigenous deities, and the integration of the imperial cult with Ephesian religious life.

An early inscription from Ephesus (IEph 1a.2 [second half of the fourth century BCE]) recounts a diplomatic disaster involving the worship of Artemis. Ephesian priests and ambassadors had been sent to the Ephesian-founded Temple of Artemis in Sardis, with the result that local miscreants, who had "violated the holy (ceremonies) and insulted the envoys," now faced the death penalty. The inscription not only underscores the inviolable sanctity of the Artemis ceremonies, but it also reveals the reason for the diplomatic mission: "(to present) robes to Artemis in accordance with ancestral custom." This reveals how the worship of Artemis had spread to the cities of the Greek world and shows that the cultic imprimatur of Ephesian Artemis was seen to be critical in certain instances,[35] though, in this case, with disastrous results. The cultic relationship between Sardis and Ephesian Artemis was again reaffirmed several centuries later when Sardis sent to Ephesus to acquire images of Artemis in order to expel the results of the plague, believed to be the "evil art of a sorcerer," which was decimating Sardis at the time (165 CE).[36]

The international reputation of Ephesian Artemis is heavily emphasized in a decree proposing the honoring of the goddess throughout the entirety of her own month and during the festival of the Artemisia.[37] As IEph 1a.24 (162–164 CE) explains:

> Since the goddess Artemis, leader of our city, is honored not only in her own homeland, which she has made the most illustrious of cities through her own divine nature, but also among the Greeks and also the barbarians, the result is that everywhere her shrines and sanctuaries have sprung up, and temples have been founded for her and altars dedicated

---

35. IEph 4.1408 also mentions the sending of "temple administrators" from Ephesus "for the sacrifices that are in Phygela." See Gregory Stevenson, *Power and Place: Temple and Identity in the Book of Revelation*, BZNW 107 (Berlin: de Gruyter, 2001), 62, n. 169.

36. See Harrison, "Artemis Triumphs"; Rogers, *Mysteries of Artemis*, 225–26.

37. Note the Ephesian boy comedian who won "the contest at the great festival of the Artemisia" (IEph 5.1606).

to her because of the visible manifestations [ἐπιφανείας] effected by her. And this is the greatest proof of the reverence surrounding her, that a month is named after her, Artemision among us, and Artemisius among the Macedonians and among the other Greek nations and among the cities within their borders. During this month, festivals and sacrifices are performed, particularly in our city, the nurturer of its own Ephesian goddess.[38] (ll. 8–22)

What is intriguing is the implication in the decree that the worship of Artemis overcomes ethnic, linguistic, and cultural barriers between Greeks and barbarians by virtue of its unifying influence. Artemis also imposes the blessings of her own calendar upon historically fractious city-states—the Macedonians, Greek cities, and the cities within their borders—with the result that the reverence of her cult is promoted throughout the Greek world. A common identity in Artemis, therefore, is established among the Greek city-states for the entire month of Artemision/Artemisius, pacifying whatever tensions there might be across the Greek world. This alternative message of the "good news" of Artemis was a rival to the apostolic gospel (cf. Acts 19:23–41).[39] The early Christian dismantling of the dividing wall of hostility between Jew and gentile in Christ's cross also addresses ethnic and cultural divisions (Eph 2:14b), as does Paul's indebtedness to Greek and barbarian (Rom 1:14). However, as Guy MacLean Rogers rightly comments,[40] the increased devotion to Artemis not only honors the goddess abroad but also enhances the financial well-being of Ephesus through the increased goods and services required for all the new extra holy days and festival celebrations. Ephesus nurtures her own goddess and profits financially in so doing.

But, in the worldview of our inscription, this is effected by the "visible manifestations" (ἐπιφανείας) of divine Artemis. By contrast, the appearance of the language of "epiphany" in the New Testament is reserved for the epiphany (ἐπιφάνεια) of God and Christ (2 Thess 2:8; 1 Tim 6:14; 2 Tim 1:10; 4:1, 8; Titus 2:13). Moreover, the gift of Ephesian citizenship to new recipients was inscribed in the Temple of Artemis in the city (IEph 5.1448–55). It is not surprising, therefore, that the new citizenship

---

38. See Rogers, *Mysteries of Artemis*, 222–24. Translated by S. R. Llewelyn.
39. IEph 5.1448: "[And that they make a thank offering] for the good tidings to Artemis [[εὐ]αγγέλια τῆι Ἀρτέμιδι]." See Bradley J. Bitner, "Acclaiming Artemis in Ephesus: Political Theologies in Acts 19," in this volume.
40. Rogers, *Mysteries of Artemis*, 224.

of gentile believers, who are no longer strangers and aliens (Eph 2:12, 19), is presented in the Epistle to the Ephesians as a case of Jew and gentile growing together into a holy temple in the Lord, a dwelling place for God (2:21–22). In light of this theological and social counterpointing, the ideological collision between Artemis and early Christianity was present from the very beginning of the expansion of the apostolic gospel into the eastern Mediterranean basin.[41] Consequently, the cult of Artemis came to be considered demonic by the Christians, as the following, much later (fifth century CE) inscription illustrates:

> Having destroyed a deceitful image of demonic Artemis, Demeas set up this sign of truth, honoring the driver-away of idols, God and the cross that victorious immortal symbol of Christ. (IEph 4.1351)[42]

The significance of Artemis in the Roman world, as opposed to the Greek world, is demonstrated by the Julio-Claudian and Flavian gifts and honorific dedications to the goddess. For example, Augustus erected "the sacred boundary pillars of the roads and watercourses" to the honor of the goddess (IEph 5.1523–1524). The council and people of Ephesus also praise Trajan as the city's

> own founder and savior because of his unsurpassed gifts to Artemis, granting to the goddess the right to inherited and ownerless property and her own laws, and providing supplies of grain from Egypt and who ma[d]e the harbor navigable, both diverting and … the river Kaystros which dam[aged the] harbor because of the … (IEph 2.274, ll. 8–16)

This does not mean, however, that the Ephesians somehow diminish the status of the Caesars in thanking the ruler and his family for beneficence.[43] The Ephesians, in response to T. Aelius Antoninus's gift of imperial spectacles and sacrifices to the city on his birthday, adopt the traditional language of reciprocity for the veneration and requital of the gods in expressing their gratitude and indebtedness to the Roman ruler: "As far

---

41. See Richard E. Oster, "The Ephesian Artemis as an Opponent of Early Christianity," *JAC* 19 (1976): 24–44.

42. This and the following quote translated by S. R. Llewelyn.

43. See also Fredrick J. Long, "Ἐκκλησία in Ephesians as Godlike in the Heavens, in Temple, in γάμος, and in Armor: Ideology and Iconography in Ephesus and Its Environs," in this volume.

as is humanly possible, to repay the benefactions of the gods, we continue repaying eagerly" (IEph 1a.21, ll. 39–41). Note, too, the provincial assembly of hymn singers in Asia who sang "hymns to the Augustan household" and accomplished "sacrifices to the Augustan gods, leading festivals and banquets" (IEph 7.2.3801, ll. II,18–19 [41–54 CE]; cf. 1a.18d, ll. 4–24, esp. ll. 12–13 [44 CE]).[44]

However, in this process of the lyrical veneration of Artemis and the adulation of the imperial benefactors, the other indigenous Greek gods are definitely not overlooked. There is mention, for example, of the Temple of the Samothracian gods and their altars (1Eph 1a.20, l. 71), the sacrificial and liturgical responsibilities of the prytanis in the worship of Demeter and the gods (IEph 1a.10 [third century CE]), and the thanksgiving of the priestess Favonia Flacilla to multiple deities (IEph 4.1060). Nor is the chief god of the Greek pantheon forgotten, but rather he is worshiped in his local expression (Zeus Ktesios) as the god of the storeroom: "Having vowed, I, Cornelianus, set up for you, Lord Zeus Ktesios, this altar" (IEph 4.1240). Even in the imperial cult, the Roman ruler Hadrian was still hailed as resembling "Zeus Olympios" in his beneficence (IEph 2.267–71a) and the sons of Drusus Caesar were hailed as the sons of Zeus, the "new Dioscoroi" (IEph 7.2.4337). In sum, the world of Ephesus was full of gods, both in the heavens and on the earth (cf. 1 Cor 8:5–6), and the Ephesians were scrupulous in showing their allegiance to them.

We turn now to the quest for honor among the Ephesian elites and how that intersected with the local trades and mercantile associations of Ephesus.

4. The Ephesian Elites and the Associations: Rivalry and the Quest for Honor

The civic elites of Ephesus have been widely discussed, whether they are asiarchs (cf. Acts 19:31), powerful Ephesian families such as the Vedii, benefactors like C. Vibius Salutaris, priestesses of Artemis, male and female benefactors of the city, sponsors of paideia (including the library

---

44. Translation from Richard S. Ascough, Philip A. Harland, and John S. Kloppenborg, eds., *Associations in the Greco-Roman World: A Sourcebook* (Waco, TX: Baylor University Press, 2012), §160. See also Harland, "Honours and Worship: Emperors, Imperial Cults and Associations at Ephesus (First to Third Centuries CE)," *SR* 25 (1996): 319–34.

of Celsus), *agōnothetai* of the games, or members of Ephesian gerousia.[45] This section focuses on how the quest for honor among the Ephesian elites and the local associations could easily unravel into the destructive force of *invidia* ("jealousy") with its alienating consequences for social relations.

An example of the operation of *invidia* is found in a letter from Antoninus Pius, which commends the generosity of the Ephesian benefactor Vedius Antoninus (IEph 5.1491 [145 CE]). The letter, set out below, reveals the dark underside of the benefaction system where the Ephesian elites competed for social precedence:

> Imperator Caesar Titus Aelius Hadrianus Antoninus Augustus, son of the deified Hadrianus, grandson of the deified Traianus Parthicus, great grandson of the deified Nerva, *pontifex maximus*, holding tribunician power for the eighth time, twice hailed *imperator*, four times consul, father of his country, to the chief magistrates, council and people of Ephesus greeting. The generosity which Vedius Antoninus lavishes on you I have learned not so much from your letters as from his. Wishing to obtain assistance from me for the embellishment of public works that he had offered you, he informed me how many and how big buildings he is contributing to the city. But you do not appreciate him properly. Now I have granted him all that he asked, appreciating that he prefers

---

45. See Francçois Kirbihler, "Les notables d'Ephèse: Essai d'histoire sociale (133 av. J.-C.–262 ap. J.-C.)" (PhD diss., University of Tours, 2003). For civic elites as asiarchs, see Rosalinde A. Kearsley, "Some Asiarchs in Ephesos," *NewDocs* 4:46–55. For civic elites as powerful Ephesian families, see Guy MacLean Rogers, "The Constructions of Women at Ephesos," *ZPE* 90 (1992): 215–23; Angela V. Kalinowski, "The Vedii Antonini: Aspects of Patronage and Benefaction in Second Century Ephesos," *Phoenix* 56 (2003): 109–49; François Kirbihler, "Le rôle public des femmes à Éphèse à l'époque impériale: Les femmes magistrats et liturges (Ier s.–IIIe s. apr. J.-C.)," in *Femmes, cultures et sociétés dans les civilisations méditerranéennes et proche-orientales de l'Antiquité*, ed. Francçoise Briquel-Chatonnet et al., TOOSup 10 (Paris: de Bocard, 2009), 67–92. For civic elites as benefactors like C. Vibius Salutaris, see Rogers, *Sacred Identity of Ephesos*. For civic elites as priestesses of Artemis, see Harrison, "Family Honour." For civic elites as male and female benefactors of the city, see Kalinowski, "Patterns of Patronage." For civic elites as sponsors of paideia, see James R. Harrison, "Sponsors of Paideia: Ephesian Benefactors, Civic Virtue and the New Testament," *EC* 7 (2016): 346–67. For civic elites as *agōnothetai* of the games, see James R. Harrison, "Paul and the *Agōnothetai* at Corinth: Engaging the Civic Values of Antiquity," in *Roman Corinth*, vol. 2 of *The First Urban Churches*, ed. James R. Harrison and L. L. Welborn, WGRWSup 8 (Atlanta: SBL Press, 2016), 286–91. For civic elites as members of Ephesian gerousia, see Colin Bailey, "The Gerousia of Ephesus" (PhD diss., University of British Columbia, 2006).

to make the city more majestic not in the customary manner of public figures who for the sake of immediate popularity expend their generosity on spectacles and distributions and the prizes of games, but in a manner that looks to the future. This letter was transmitted by his Excellency, the proconsul Claudius Julianus. Farewell.[46]

Apparently, after consulting with the boule regarding the building of a new structure at Ephesus, Vedius Papianus Antoninus had written to Antoninus Pius regarding the embellishment of the public work, but the Ephesians had clearly not written to the Roman ruler regarding the fact that the project was underway and that they were supportive of the project and its mooted decoration. Antoninus Pius takes this as a case of the Ephesians not properly appreciating their benefactor—a damning assessment of the Ephesian elites from the perspective of Greco-Roman reciprocity system. Several questions emerge. What building did Vedius intend to embellish and why? Why did he approach Antoninus Pius regarding the issue? Why had the Ephesians been so churlish about his plans? What was the result of this exchange for Vedius Antoninus? What differentiates Vedius from other Ephesian benefactors?

First, the inscription gives us no indication which building at Ephesus is in mind, but most likely it is the Vedius bath-gymnasium complex in the north of the city (IEph 2.431), which was dedicated in 146–148 CE after the correspondence with Antoninus Pius.[47] Angela V. Kalinowski argues that Vedius was probably targeting as clients "the powerful mercantile and manufacturing classes in Ephesus that operated in the stoa of Servilius and probably lived near the gymnasium and the Koressos gate."[48] The evidence for this is the general proximity of the Vedius bath-gymnasium complex to the trade booths of the various associations (including the bath attendants [IEph 6.2078]). Additionally, there were reserved seats in the latrines of the gymnasium complex for a whole variety of trade associations (IEph 2.454a–f).[49] Even more important are the honors accorded Vedius by the

---

46. For the translation and full exposition of the letter, see Kalinowski, "Patterns of Patronage," 102–27.

47. For full discussion, see Kalinowski, "Patterns of Patronage," 110–16. On the Vedius bath-gymnasium complex, see Martin Steskal and Martino La Torre, *Das Vediusgymnasium in Ephesos: Archäologie und Baubefund*, FiE 14.1 (Vienna: ÖAW, 2008).

48. Kalinowski, "Patterns of Patronage," 116. For full argument, see pp. 114–16

49. For translation, see Ascough, Harland, and Kloppenborg, *Associations in the Greco-Roman World*, §172.

Ephesian associations.[50] The strong reciprocal bond between Vedius and the trade associations is evident in the association inscription of the woolworkers who honor him as "founder of the city of the Ephesians" (IEph 3.727). A statue was set up for Vedius by the association of the wine tasters in the Scholastika baths by the Ephesian council and the people, detailing the full *cursus honorum* of his magistracies and benefactions on behalf of the city (IEph 3.728 [162–163 CE]).[51] The temple builders also call him their founder and benefactor (IEph 7.1.3075) and the teachers near the Mouseion honor him (IEph 6.2065). The support base of the mercantile and manufacturing groups of city not only provided Vedius with alternative pathways of honor via the local associations, but it also boosted his civic profile among influential sections of the city, enabling him to broker local trades and financial contacts, including the bankers (IEph 2.454a), that could prove useful for his future building projects, as well as the current bath-gymnasium complex.

Second, the reason for approaching Antoninus Pius was, as Kalinowski argues, to provide the Roman ruler with the opportunity to decorate the gymnasium with a hall devoted to the imperial cult, including the erection of statues of the Roman ruler, his family, and, perhaps, Vedius himself.[52] This likelihood is reinforced by the fact that Antoninus Pius "granted him all that he asked." The deflected glory to Vedius in such a project would have been inestimable.

Third, there is little doubt that the *invidia* of Vedius's rivals explains their recalcitrance in writing to the Roman ruler about the progress of the bath-gymnasium complex. Several pieces of evidence confirm this. In the

---

50. I am indebted to the discussion in Kalinowski, "Patterns of Patronage," 117–19.

51. For translation, see Ascough, Harland, and Kloppenborg, *Associations in the Greco-Roman World*, §170. On the issue of whether the Ephesian inscriptions had a "proper" *cursus honorum*, see François Kirbihler, "Un cursus honorum à Éphèse? Quelques réflexions sur la succession des magistratures de la cité à la époque romaine," in *Folia Graeca in honorem Edouard Will: Historica*, ed. P. Goukowsky and C. Feyel, Études anciennes 51 (Nancy: ADRA, 2012), 67–107.

52. Kalinowski, "Patterns of Patronage," 120–22. Wiplinger and Wlach write of the Vedius gymnasium: "In the middle of the west side, a particularly magnificent furnished room, with rich two-storey tabernacle architecture, opens onto the palaestra. A shallow niche in the middle of the west side contains a base, upon which a statue of the Emperor could well have been placed, and the foundation of an altar—the room is therefore called the Emperor Hall" (*Ephesus*, 46; cf. 47, fig. 57).

highly effusive imperial letter of Constantius II honoring the benefactor Flavius Philippus, we read of the potential danger of excessive civic fame provoking the jealousy of others:

> Even when we too are silent, his extraordinary deeds shine forth. In their light he stood out brilliantly as so great and gifted man that with the grace of affection he rose above envy [*invidiam*]. For it could not happen that he provoked arrows of jealousy against himself who made it his purpose to be more pleasing to his emperor. (IEph 1a.41, ll. 17–20 [CE 344])[53]

Moreover, in the case of the Ephesian benefactor, Claudius Aristion, the destructive effects of the *invidia* of his fellow citizens were personally felt when he was arraigned before Trajan's court for treason. As Pliny elaborates,

> Claudius Aristion pleaded his case. He was the leading citizen of the Ephesians, generous, and one who sought popularity in a harmless way; for this reason he had aroused the envy [*invidia*] of people of a vastly different character who had suborned an informer against him. He accordingly was cleared of the charge and acquitted. (*Ep.* 6.31)

Finally, to cite another Ephesian example, the unknown Philip appropriated for his own honor much later one of Celsus's four personifications of virtue at Celsus's library—"The Good Sense (or 'Intention') of Philip" ("Ἔννοια Φιλίππου [IEph 7.2.5110])—by removing the honorific inscription of Celsus and replacing it with a new one of his own.[54]

Clearly, in each case above, the high status and prominent profile of Ephesian benefactors had rankled some of their contemporaries. This either elicited *invidia* or provoked accusations of treason on their part. Others who were aggrieved either appropriated or erased the virtue of the luminary where possible.[55] As we have seen, a similar fate had befallen Vedius at Ephesus, but he was eventually vindicated, with the Ephesians being forced to acknowledge before the Antoninus Pius that they had

---

53. Translated by L. J. Swift and J. H. Oliver, "Constantius II on Flavius Philippus," *AJP* 83 (1962): 248–50.

54. For details, see Harrison, "Sponsors of Paideia," 353.

55. See James R. Harrison, "The Erasure of Honour: Paul and the Politics of Dishonour," *TynBul* 66 (2016): 161–84.

received benefactions from him: "You make known to me who already knows of it the generosity which Vedius Antoninus has vouchsafed you, he who has contributed also the gifts which he received from me toward the decoration of the city" (IEph 5.1492 [CE 150]).[56]

It is worthwhile pondering what precisely differentiated Vedius from his powerful Ephesian rivals. As we have seen, Antoninus Pius perceptively commented that, in contrast to his contemporaries, who, for the "sake of immediate popularity expend their generosity on spectacles and distributions and the prizes of games," Vedius did so "in a manner that looks to the future." Those contemporaries who, like Vedius, had also undoubtedly contributed to public works in Ephesus, would have thought that they were investing in "the future" as well. But, in the case of the bath-gymnasium complex, Vedius courted imperial favor, and even more remarkably, turned strategically to the trades and mercantile associations for the endorsement and strategic placement of his building project.[57] Very few Ephesian citizens were able to enlist such wide-ranging sponsorship across the social echelons for a transformative building program in Ephesus. The contemporaries of Vedius seethed internally with *invidia* at how he had so comprehensively bested them at their own game.

5. The Jews of Ephesus: Julius the ἀρχιατρός and the Association of Physicians

In this section, we will focus upon a specific people group living within ancient Ephesus: namely, the diaspora Jews.[58] Our literary evidence regarding the Ephesian Jews from the mid-first century BCE onwards is reasonably extensive. The Jewish historian Josephus charts with great

---

56. Kalinowski, "Patterns of Patronage," 124.

57. I am not suggesting that all Ephesians associations forged connections with the provincial imperial cult (e.g., IEph 1a.18d, ll. 4–24; 7.2.3801), acted as benefactors (e.g., IEph 1a.20), possessed worldwide connections (e.g., the Dionysiac artists in IEph 1a.22), or could exercise significant local sway (e.g., the silversmith riot in Acts 19:23–41; IEph 2.425, 547, 585, 586; 3.636; 6.2212, 2441; or the bakers' strike at Ephesus in IEph 2:215). The small guilds of the nut sellers (IEph 6.2709) and the bed builders (IEph 6.2213) would have been insignificant, among many others. See Harland, "Honours and Worship."

58. For the other ethnic groups in provincial Asia, see the Ephesian inscription, found in the agora, that lists the provincial people groups of Asia by their dioceses (IEph 1a.13 [70/79 CE]).

clarity the privileges that the Ephesian Jews had strategically managed to extract from the Romans by the early imperial period: an exemption from military service; the right to maintain the law, Sabbath, and ancestral customs; and the continuance of tithing to the Jerusalem temple (*Ant.* 14.228-230, 234, 238-240, 262-264; 16.160-165, 167-168, 172-173; cf. Philo, *Legat.* 315-316).[59] It is important, however, to realize that the exemption from military service only applied to the *smaller* group of Jews possessing the Roman citizenship (*Ant.* 14.234, 240), an exemption also possibly covering all other Jews with Roman citizenship in Asia Minor (*Ant.* 14.231-232).[60] Paul Trebilco has argued that from 49 BCE there were increasing tensions in Ephesus between the Jews and indigenous residents over the distinctive lifestyle of the Jewish community, which, in the view of their opponents, was indelibly defined by their boundary markers (Sabbath and other feasts, Law, tithe-giving, etc.).[61] John M. G. Barclay rightly notes that there must have been a number of socially and economically prominent Jews at Ephesus to provoke such opposition from their enemies.[62] But the tensions seem to disappear under the reign of Augustus by 2-3 CE, with the Jews melding into Ephesian society as a well-known, city-wide, prosperous, and socially quietist group, even if this inference is initially drawn from the silence regarding further conflicts in our sources.[63] Finally, in terms of the New Testament evidence, the book of Acts mentions the presence of Jewish exorcists (Acts 19:13-16), the high priest Sceva (19:14), and a synagogue in the city at the time of Paul's visit (18:19, 26a; 19:8-9a). The existence of a synagogue is also implied in Josephus (*Ant.* 14.227) and Philo (*Legat.* 31). According to Trebilco, there may have

---

59. For an excellent discussion of the Jews in provincial Asia, see John M. G. Barclay, *Jews in the Mediterranean Diaspora: From Alexander to Trajan (323-117 CE)* (Edinburgh: T&T Clark, 1996), 259-81. For an epigraphic and archaeological discussion of the Jews at Ephesus, see Horsley, "Inscriptions of Ephesos," 121-27.

60. For discussion, see Paul Trebilco, *Jewish Communities in Asia Minor*, SNTSMS 69 (Cambridge: Cambridge University Press, 1991), 172-73. See also Trebilco, "The Jewish Community in Ephesus and Its Interaction with Christ-Believers in the First Century CE and Beyond," in this volume.

61. Trebilco, *Early Christians*, 40-41.

62. Barclay, *Jews in the Mediterranean Diaspora*, 271.

63. Trebilco, *Early Christians*, 41, including n. 190. More widely in Asia, see Trebilco, *Jewish Communities in Asia Minor*, 183-84.

been more than one synagogue in the city, as was the case with Jewish communities elsewhere in Asia Minor.⁶⁴

The archaeological evidence, however, for a Jewish presence in Ephesus is almost nonexistent in comparison to, for example, the Jewish synagogue, inscriptions, and shops at Sardis. A menorah, often overlooked in modern discussions, has been carved into the steps leading up to the entrance of the Celsus library, incised by an unknown Jewish resident of the city sometime after the construction of the library.⁶⁵ A fragment of a marble block, possibly from the synagogue, has been found in the narthex of the domed church at Ephesus with the word τό θυσιαστήριον ("altar"), accompanied by an incised menorah to its right (IEph 7.2.4130 = IJO 2.31:153 [fourth century CE or later]). There is also (1) a glass flask (painted with a menorah, ethrog, lulav, and shofar); (2) four lamps with menorahs; (3) a Jewish magical amulet with a menorah, but found in the area between Ephesus and Smyrna; and (4) another Jewish amulet, a carnelian gemstone, written in Greek on the obverse and in Hebrew on the reverse.⁶⁶ Lines 6–8 of the Greek text on the gemstone renders a Jewish invocation that is clearly reminiscent of Exod 3:14 LXX (ἐγώ εἰμι ὁ ῏Ων: "I am who I am"). The text of the amulet says: "(You) whom myriads of angels tend, O ever-living Adonaie, for You are the one who is (<ἀ>ίζων, Ἀδωναίε ὢν γὰρ εἶ)."⁶⁷

---

64. Trebilco, *Early Christians*, 44.

65. This important piece of evidence is often overlooked in discussions of Celsus's library; see, e.g., Scherrer, *Ephesus*, 130–32; Volker Michael Strocka, "The Celsus Library in Ephesus," in *Ancient Libraries in Anatolia: Libraries of Hattusha, Pergamon, Ephesus, Nysa* (Ankara: Middle East Technical University Library, 2003), 33–43. For details of the menorah, see *IJO* 2:151; Dieter Knibbe, *Ephesus: Geschichte einer bedeutenden antiken Stadt und Portrait einer modernen Grossgrabung* (Frankfurt am Main: Lang, 1998), 123, n. 296.

66. For full details, see A. Thomas Kraabel, "Judaism in Western Asia Minor under the Roman Empire, with a Preliminary Study of the Jewish Community at Sardis, Lydia" (PhD diss., Harvard University, 1968), 56–57 (reproducing the Greek text of the amulet); Horsley, "Inscriptions of Ephesos," 125; Trebilco, *Early Christians*, 48, n. 224.

67. Translation from Kraabel, "Judaism in Western Asia Minor," 57. The original text was published in Josef Keil, "Ein rätselhaftes Amulett," *JÖAI* 32 (1940): 79–84, unavailable to me. Horsley rightly points to the problem of provenance of the gem: "The item was purchased at Smyrna in 1912, and was claimed to be from Ephesos. Not included in *I.Eph*" ("Inscriptions of Ephesos," 125).

But the most helpful material evidence we have regarding the presence of the Jews in Ephesus comes from the public inscriptions, even though the documents are later than the New Testament period. Several Jewish inscriptions, in addition to the altar stone noted above, have been found.[68] There is mention of

1. the (possibly) Jewish-named M. Aurelius Sambathius (*IJO* 2.34 [third century CE]) at a grave site, a name given, some have argued, to Jews born on the Sabbath;[69]
2. a funerary monument to the "official doctor" or "chief doctor" (ἀρχιατρός) Julius (IEph 5.1677 = *IJO* 2.32 [Antonine period]);
3. the acclamation for the "ruler of the synagogue" (ἀρχισυνάγωγος) and the elders (IEph 4.1251 = *IJO* 2.32 [fifth century CE]); and
4. a gravestone for a priest (ἰαιρέος) named Marcus Mussius (IEph 5.1676 = *IJO* 2.33 [200 CE]).[70]

What do we learn about Jewish enculturation in Ephesian society from the epigraphic evidence? Our case study of Julius the ἀρχιατρός is instructive in this regard. Not only does the career of Julius illustrate the issues associated with enculturation, but it also opens up a further opportunity to study another member of the Ephesian civic elite, as well as the association of physicians with whom he would have had contact. As noted above, in a funerary monument from Ephesus, there is reference to the "official"

---

68. For discussion, see Steven M. Baugh, "Paul and Ephesus: The Apostle among His Contemporaries" (PhD diss., University of California, 1990), 81–86; G. H. R. Horsley, "Jews at Ephesos," *NewDocs* 4.116:231–32; Trebilco, *Early Christians*, 43–48; *IJO* 2:152–62. The text is cited in full by Buagh, "Paul and Ephesus."

69. Baugh raises the possibility that Sambathios may have been "a Jewish convert to Christianity" on the basis of the appearance of a (Sa)mbathios—note, however, that the name is restored—in an Ephesian tomb with the Christian symbols of the cross and Alpha-Omega sign (IEph 6.2306k) ("Paul and Ephesus," 85). For other Christian instances of the name, see Horsley, "Jews at Ephesos." However, see Horsley's critique of this position, noting that (1) in some papyri, σάμβαθον refers to a container and not to the Sabbath, and (2) the cross and other Christian symbols could have been added subsequently to a Jewish inscription ("Inscriptions of Ephesos," 126–27). For full discussion, see Trebilco, *Early Christians*, 47, n. 220.

70. See also the letter of bishop Hypatios mentioning the Jews at Ephesus (*IJO* 2.35).

or "chief" doctor Julius (ἀρχιατροῦ), his wife Julia, and their children. The inscription is set out below:

> (This monument is that) of Ju(lius ?) … the Chief Doctor (and of) his wife, Julia … and of their children. May they live! [[ζῶ]σιν] [This] tomb is cared for by the Jews ['Ιουδέοι] [in Ephe]sus." (IEph 5.1677 = IJO 2.32)[71]

If Julius is a Jew, as is highly likely,[72] we gain here keen insight into how well the Ephesian Jews had integrated as a people group into Ephesian civic life. Steven M. Baugh has observed that the sentiment ζῶσιν was a commonplace on non-Jewish Ephesian tombs,[73] demonstrating how the Jews "had assimilated many of the practices of their neighbors despite their existence as a distinct social group." By contrast, Baugh opines that the *Hasidim* of Palestine would have refused such a convention.[74] But this imposes a Palestinian matrix upon the cultural context of diaspora Jews and, in the process, misunderstands the reason for Ephesian Jews choosing such a widespread funerary motif. So what is the religious ethos of our Ephesian inscription?

In the case of the Ephesian Jews such as Julius and Mussius (IEph 5.1676 = IJO 2.33), the more open-ended ζῶσιν or ζῇ was probably adopted because it could embrace the varied postmortem expectations within the Ephesian Jewish community (e.g., Sheol [Hades], immortality of the soul, bodily resurrection?).[75] The funerary expression would certainly not

---

71. For discussion, see Baugh, "Paul and Ephesus," 84–85; Trebilco, *Jewish Communities in Asia Minor*, 173–74; *IJO* 2:155–57. Baugh correctly comments that, like other ancient association (e.g., "the guild of the silversmiths" [IEph 6.2212]), "the Jewish community appears to take on the function of a guild and burial society for its members" ("Paul and Ephesus," 85).

72. The singular form ζῇ ("May he live!") is also used in the Ephesian inscription of the Jewish priest Marcus Mussius (IEph 5.1676 = *IJO* 2.33). The care of Julius's tomb, along with the grave of Mussius, by the Jewish community would be highly unlikely if he were an unbelieving gentile.

73. On the hereafter in the Jewish funerary inscriptions, see Joseph S. Park, *Conceptions of Afterlife in Jewish Inscriptions with Special Reference to Pauline Literature*, WUNT 2/121 (Tübingen: Mohr Siebeck, 2000).

74. Baugh, "Paul and Ephesus," 84.

75. On Sheol/Hades, see *BS* 2.127, *CIJ* 2.1530; Pieter Willem van der Horst, *Ancient Jewish Epitaphs: An Introductory Survey of a Millennium of Jewish Funerary Epigraphy (300 BCE–700 CE)* (Kampen: Kok Pharos, 1991), 151–52, 156–57. On the soul, see *CIJ* 2.1530; van der Horst, *Ancient Jewish Epitaphs*, 156–57. On the resur-

alienate their gentile neighbors, and it allowed flexibility regarding the public expression of the diverse beliefs of the Ephesian Jewish community about the afterlife. Moreover, ζῶσιν may have acquired additional force as a sentiment because of its perceived resonances with the redemptive activity of the Old Testament "living God" (Deut 5:6; Josh 3:10; Jer 10:10) over against the lifelessness of the gentile idols and their inability to save (Ps 115:3–7; Isa 41:21–24; 43:10–13; 44:6–23; 45:20; Jer 10:1–16). What ultimately mattered was that the Ephesian Jews would "live" with their "living" God, entrusting their final postmortem journey to him in a prayer wish (ζῶσιν). We must remember that because diaspora Jews were summoned to seek the welfare of the city (Jer 29:7), it was appropriate for some of them to be honored with the conventional Greco-Roman inscriptional moral accolades and coronal honors as a sign of their devotion to the well-being of the city.[76] So, in this case, the Ephesian Jews adopted a routine and inoffensive funerary sentiment to express implicitly their communal postmortem faith beliefs.

There is little doubt that Julius was a high-status Ephesian citizen, given that the city's inscriptions mention several other prominent individuals holding the office of ἀρχιατρός (IEph 3.622; 4.1161–67; 7.1.3239).[77] The status was underscored by the edict of a triumvir who freed doctors from liability to taxes and liturgies (IEph 7.2.4101 [first century BCE]), freedom from liturgies being an honor traditionally accorded prominent benefactors.[78] Ephesian doctors could gain further kudos by competing in the city's two-day Asclepian games, which involved "theoretical," "surgery,"

---

rection, see *BS* 2.194 ("Good luck with your resurrection!"); van der Horst, *Ancient Jewish Epitaphs*, 118.

76. Baruch Lifshitz, *Donateurs et fondateurs dans les synagogues juives: Répertoire des dédicaces grecques relatives à la construction et à la réflection des synagogues* (Paris: Gabalda, 1967), §§13, 33.

77. On the status of Julius as "official doctor," note Trebilco, *Jewish Communities in Asia Minor*, 173–74: "Such officially recognized public physicians were paid by the city and their principal task was to give medical attention to citizens." There is little doubt, therefore, that Julius treated the general Ephesian community and not just his fellow Jews.

78. On ἀλειτούργητος ("free from the public burdens"), see James R. Harrison, *Paul's Language of Grace in Its Graeco-Roman Context*, WUNT 2/172 (Tübingen: Mohr Siebeck, 2003; repr., Eugene, OR: Wipf & Stock, 2017). For Ephesian epigraphic examples of ἀλειτούργητος, see IEph 2.219; 3.946, 956a; 7.2.4337.

"problem-solving," and "surgical instruments" contests (IEph 4.1162).[79] Certainly, as this particular inscription shows, the "chief physicians" of Ephesus were not only the directors of the contests but also competitors in and winners of the games.

But to what extent did Julius maintain boundary markers between himself and the other Ephesian physicians? The latter sacrificed to "ancestor Asclepius and to the Sebastoi" (IEph 3.719) and, as noted, staged competitions in honor of Asclepius (IEph 4.1162)?[80] As the ἀρχιατρός, Julius must have belonged to the "association [τὸ συνέδριον] of [physicians] from the Mouseion in [Eph]esus" (IEph 6.2304), presumably being on familiar terms with the "instructors in the Mouseion" (IEph 6.2065; 7.1.3068). Undoubtedly, he would have been exposed to the association's banqueting and cultic activities, having to negotiate not only issues of food purity but also the dedication of food to idols at its private celebrations.[81] Moreover, how one skirted the idolatrous statues—ubiquitous in any Greco-Roman city, including the Ephesian Mouseion with (presumably) its statue of Asclepius—was an issue that consumed rabbinic debate in antiquity.[82] Did Julius absent himself from banquets and professional occasions involving idolatry, as occasion demanded, while going to other events that were less compromising? Or did he simply treat the idols as nonexistent powers with no ability to act punitively or to save and thus attend important occasions in freedom of conscience regarding idolatry? We simply do not know. But while there may have been differing views among the Ephesian Jews regarding the limits of their integration into

---

79. For a translation of this inscription, see Philip A. Harland, "Victors in Competitions of Physicians—Rufinus (138–161 CE)," Associations in the Greco-Roman World: An Expanding Collection of Inscriptions, Papyri, and Other Sources in Translation, https://tinyurl.com/SBL4209b.

80. See Philip A. Harland, *North Coast of the Black Sea, Asia Minor*, vol. 2 of *Greco-Roman Associations: Texts, Translations and Commentary*, BZNW 204 (Berlin: de Gruyter, 2014), §129.

81. On rabbinic thought on idolatry and laws concerning gentile food, see Peter J. Tomson, *Paul and the Jewish Law: Halakha in the Letters of the Apostle to the Gentiles* (Assen: Van Gorcum, 1990), 151–76.

82. See Yaron Z. Eliav, "Roman Statues, Rabbis, and Greco-Roman Culture," in *Jewish Literatures and Cultures: Context and Intertext*, ed. Anita Norich and Yaron Z. Eliav, BJS 349 (Providence, RI: Brown Judaic Studies, 2008), 99–116. For an Ephesian statue of Asclepius at the Selçuk Museum, see Cengiz Topai, *Ephesus Museum Selçuk*, trans. P. Rhode (Istanbul: BKG, 2010), 43.

Ephesian society, it would seem that Julius, as an ἀρχιατρός, was able to differentiate between the legitimate civic demands of his professional life, maintaining the Jewish boundary markers as required and maintaining the corporate expression of his faith in the synagogal community of Ephesus. Certainly his fellow Jews who looked after his grave saw no problem with his faith commitment.

6. The Slaves of Ephesus

The role and status of slaves has been intensively investigated in classical and New Testament studies,[83] but little work has been done in exploring slavery in the Ephesian inscriptions. After the initial exploratory work of Steven M. Baugh and Sjef van Tilborg, a breakthrough has come with the innovative and incisively argued thesis of Katherine Ann Shaner on slavery in the Ephesian epigraphic and iconographic evidence.[84] In terms of studies on Ephesian freedmen, Colin Bailey's excellent discussion of G. Stertinius Orpex has also filled in an important gap.[85] This section will

---

83. On slavery in the ancient world, see William Linn Westermann, *The Slave Systems of Greek and Roman Antiquity* (Philadelphia: American Philosophical Society, 1955); Thomas Wiedemann, *Greek and Roman Slavery* (London: Croom Helm, 1981); Keith R. Bradley, *Slaves and Masters in the Roman Empire: A Study in Social Control* (New York: Oxford University Press, 1987); Bradley, *Slavery and Society at Rome* (Cambridge: Cambridge University Press, 1994); Moses I. Finley, *Ancient Slavery and Modern Ideology*, ed. Brent D. Shaw, exp. ed. (Princeton: Wiener, 1998); Sandra R. Joshel, *Slavery in the Roman World*, CIRC (Cambridge: Cambridge University Press, 2010). On slavery and the New Testament, see Dale B. Martin, *Slavery as Salvation: The Metaphor of Slavery in Pauline Christianity* (New Haven: Yale University Press, 1990); Allen Dwight Callahan, Richard A. Horsley, and Abraham Smith, eds., *Slavery in Text and Interpretation*, Semeia 83/84 (1998): passim; Jennifer A. Glancy, *Slavery in Early Christianity* (Oxford: Oxford University Press, 2002); J. Albert Harrill, *The Manumission of Slaves in Early Christianity*, HUT 32 (Tübingen: Mohr Siebeck, 1995); Harrill, *Slaves in the New Testament: Literary, Social and Moral Dimensions* (Minneapolis: Fortress, 2006).

84. Baugh, "Paul and Ephesus," 62–66; Sjef van Tilborg, *Reading John in Ephesus*, NovTSup 83 (Leiden: Brill, 1996), 86–90; Katherine Ann Shaner, "The Religious Practices of the Enslaved: A Case Study of Roman Ephesos" (ThD diss., Harvard Divinity School, 2012). The references cited herein are from Shaner's thesis, but her book will be published this year as *Enslaved Leadership in Early Christianity* (Oxford: Oxford University Press, 2017).

85. Bailey, "Gerousia of Ephesus," 91–95.

explore the presence of high status freedmen at Ephesus, the curious case of slaves acting as cobenefactors with their masters at the Harbor House, the slave market of the agora, and, finally, the revealing Persicus decree and the pictorial evidence regarding slaves in Terrace House 2. What light does this evidence throw on early Christian attitudes towards slavery?

6.1. High Status Ephesian Freedmen of the First Century CE

6.1.1. G. Stertinius Orpex

G. Stertinius Orpex—freedmen of G. Stertinius Maximus, the *consul suffectus* of 23 CE—is accorded honors by the council and the people in IEph 3.720,[86] along with his daughter Marina. The most detailed account of the benefactions of Orpex is found in a funerary inscription (IEph 7.2.4123; cf. IEph 6.2113), discovered in the Scholastika baths of Ephesus, which outlines a foundation that he sets up for the boule and gerousia of Ephesus. There are also other inscriptions that throw light on his beneficent activities. Orpex is honored in IEph 3.720 for continuing to show piety towards the god (εὐσε[βῶς] διακείμεν[ον πρὸς τὴν θεόν] - - -), presumably by paying for the sacrifices or for the statue of the god, but since the inscription is fragmentary and restored, we cannot be certain. Again, Orpex and his family dedicate a wall and other parts of the stadium to Artemis Ephesia and Nero (IEph 2.411). But what do we know about Orpex himself and his rise to prominence?

From the Latin text of IEph 7.2.4123, we learn that Orpex was a "bookkeeping clerk" (*scriba librarius*). This compound term, *scriba* added to *librarius* ("copyist"), denotes a superior type of *librarius*. The word was often applied to the quaestorian clerks at Rome (Cicero, *Nat. d.* 3.3; CIL 1.1297, 1298; 2.1809), who administered the treasury (*ex aerario* [CIL 6.1816]) and kept the public books. It could be viably proposed that Orpex, possibly a public slave in Rome, administratively helped the consul G. Stertinius Maximus, but, more likely, he dealt with the praetors and other lower level officials of the city. Governors in the provinces also had two of these treasury clerks as account keepers (Livy, *Hist.* 38.55.5), but whether this avenue of service was later open to Orpex in the senatorial provinces

---

86. Van Tilborg speculates that Orpex was a member of the council (*Reading John in Ephesus*, 86).

(Asia, possibly?) is unknown. Bailey has suggested that Orpex, after settling at Ephesus, became "a trade agent for his former master or engaged in business of his own."[87] The former alternative would be more feasible, in my opinion, especially now that Orpex was a freedman (*libertus*) of G. Stertinius Maximus.[88] Needless to say, these tentative suggestions about the career of Orpex as a public slave at Rome and, subsequently, as an upwardly mobile freedman and agent at Ephesus, are entirely speculative. Nevertheless, it shows us what the social possibilities for a person like Orpex were, the elite circles that he may have moved in, and how he had accrued substantial wealth in the process. But what did Oprex and his daughter intend in establishing such a generous foundation at Ephesus?

The benefactions flowing from his foundation are set out below in the Greek text:

(Latin text)
Gaius Stemtinius Orpex, freedman [*libertus*] of the consular Gaius Stertinius Maximus, who was once a bookkeeping clerk, lies here, as does Stertinia Quieta, a freedwoman [*liberta*] of Gaius; and Gaius Stertinius Marinus, the son of Gaius, who lived eight years; and Gaius Stertinius Asiaticus, the son of Gaius, who lived three years; and Stertinia Prisca, the daughter of Gaius, who lived eight years.

(Greek text)
This one with his daughter Marina ... dedicated in the gymnasium a statue of Asclepius with Health and Sleep with all their adornments, and they also donated to the *boule* of the Ephesians and to the priests five thousand denarii, so that beside their statues which are in the Tetragonus agora ... those who are present might receive a distribution of an equal number of drachmae; and they donated to the *gerousia* two thousand five hundred denarii, so that they might receive an annual distribution at a rate of two denarii each; in the same way, they donated to the same *gerousia* another one thousand five hundred denarii, so that from the interest of this money each year men who have been selected by lot might receive three denarii each at the places for a feast and so that from the remaining thirty denarii they might receive twenty for ... and ten for a tragic performance; and in the same way to each ... and three pounds

---

87. Bailey, "Gerousia of Ephesus," 91.
88. Van Tilborg proposes that the *liberta* (freedwoman) Stertinia Quieta is the wife of Orpex (*Reading John in Ephesus*, 86).

... on the Kalends of May ... and in the same way five hundred for the *geronteion*. (IEph 7.2.4123; cf. IEph 6.2113)[89]

From IEph 7.2.4123 we know that a foundation was established by Orpex and Marina, stipulating that:

1. a donation of 5,000 denarii was be provided so that cash distributions might be made to the members of the boule and priests in equal allocations;
2. a donation of 2,500 denarii was to be provided so that cash distributions might be made to the members of the gerousia at two denarii each;
3. a further 1,500 denarii lottery was to be established for select members of the gerousia, chosen by lot, who would receive another three denarii from the interest.

In addition to the foundation, which constitutes the central part of the inscription, there is mention of the dedication of a statue of Asclepius with Health and Sleep and mention of other donations to be used for various purposes at different occasions. Was Orpex both a member of the boule and gerousia? Does this explain his very generous donations to each body? We do not know. But, if so, he was reciprocating the personal honor that each body had conferred upon him in the past. Or was he—as an ex-slave who had risen to elevated status and wealth in Ephesus—simply rendering his gratitude to the city and its civic gods for the opportunities provided? The fact that the foundation is made in conjunction with his wealthy and socially prominent daughter also enhances his family prestige. At the very least, therefore, gratitude and *philotimia* are the fundamental motivations behind the foundation of Orpex.

6.1.2. Mazaeus and Mithridates

The Mazaeus-Mithridates Gate, a three-bayed arch, was the south gate of the Tetragonus (Commercial) Agora. It stands at right angles to the Celsus Library, which was built much later.[90] The visual dimension of Ephesian benefaction culture is well represented by this grandiose monument, with

---

89. Translation from Bailey, "Gerousia of Ephesus," §72.
90. For the restored gate, see Wiplinger and Wlach, *Ephesus*, 126–27, figs. 170–71.

its large honorific inscription rendered in Greek and Latin, and prominently displayed, so that passers-by could not miss it as they drew closer.[91] As Kalinowski notes, "The viewer's eye would then be drawn up the columns of the facade to rest on the entablature, where the text was carved in large letters, usually over 7 cm. in height."[92] The letters of the Mazaeus-Mithridates gate were probably bronze (but possibly gilded) in antiquity.[93] The dominant position of the Latin text on the entablature—both in terms of the inscription's length and, by contrast, the recessed placement of the vastly abbreviated Greek text in the attic of the monument—also demonstrates how Latin could be used as the language of political control in the provinces.[94] The appearance of Latin here is made all the more remarkable by the fact that Greek is almost universally used at Ephesus with honorific dedications and statues to the Roman ruler, changing only in the third century CE to Latin.[95] The bilingual inscription, dedicated by the freedmen of Augustus (*liberti Augusti*) Mazaeus and Mithridates, is set out below (IEph 7.1.3006 [4/3 BCE]). It is highly significant that the dedicators of the inscription address their Roman patrons in their own language:[96]

(Latin text)
For Imperator Caesar Augustus, son of the god, pontifex maximus, consul for the twelfth time, with tribunician power for the twentieth time, and for Livia, (wife) of Caesar Augustus. For Marcus Agrippa, son

---

91. Statues would have also accompanied the inscriptions. Emily Victoria Olson writes: "The statues themselves do not survive, but cuttings atop the attic cornice of the gate confirm that statues of the imperial family once stood there" ("Contextualizing Roman Honorific Monuments: Statue Groups of the Imperial Family from Olympia, Ephesus and Lepta Magna" [PhD diss., University of North Carolina, 2013], 119). The formula of the inscription perhaps indicates that the statues of Augustus and Livia were on the left bay, whereas those of Marcus and Agrippa were placed on the right (Charles Brian Rose, *Dynastic Commemoration and Imperial Portraiture in the Julio-Claudian Period* [Cambridge: Cambridge University Press, 1997], 172–74, no. 112).

92. Kalinowski, "Patterns of Patronage," 72.

93. Ibid. 72, n. 15.

94. Ibid. 61.

95. Werner Eck, "The Presence, Role and Significance of Latin in the Epigraphy and Culture of the Roman Near East," in *From Hellenism to Islam: Cultural and Linguistic Change in the Roman Near East*, ed. Hannah M. Cotton et al. (Cambridge: Cambridge University, 2009), 25–26.

96. Ibid., 25.

of Lucius, consul for the third time, imperator, with tribunician power for the sixth time and for Julia, daughter of Caesar Augustus. Mazaeus and Mithridates for their patrons [*patronis*].

(Greek text)
Mazaeus and Mithridates for their patrons [[τοῖς] πά[τ]ρωσι] and for the demos.[97]

Significantly, the inscription honors not only the Roman ruler but also the female members of the Julian family, Augustus's wife Livia and daughter Julia, along with Augustus's adopted political heir and son-in-law, Marcus Agrippa. The plural form of "patron" (*patronis*; πάτρωσι) underscores the familial scope of the freedmen's indebtedness. The triple-bayed arch was probably erected as a response to the death of Agrippa in 12 BCE, or possibly even conceived during the trip of Agrippa and Julia in the East (16–13 BCE), because Julia is clearly presented as the husband of Agrippa.[98] A statue of Lucius Caesar was subsequently added to the arch in 2 CE, along with its inscription, accompanying the other (now lost) statues of Augustus, Livia, Agrippa, and Julia (IEph 7.1.3007). Charles Brian Rose feasibly suggests that Lucius's statue was erected after his death and was placed to the right of Augustus and Livia since Lucius was named as the son of the ruler.[99] Thus, as Kalinowski states, "This monumental entranceway was a demonstration of the wealth that these imperial freedmen had accumulated in the service of their patrons, a testament to their loyalty, and a reminder of the power of Rome."[100] Nearby was found the grave inscription of Mithridates himself (IEph 3.851), an appropriate funereal

---

97. Translation from Rosalinde A. Kearsley, ed., *Greeks and Romans on Imperial Asia: Mixed Language Inscriptions and Linguistic Evidence for Cultural Interaction until the End of III AD*, IK 59 (Bonn: Habelt, 2001), §151. In view of our later section on graffiti, it should be noted that in the apsidal niche of the eastern passage of the gate is the graffito "Whoever urinates here will be tried in court" (Selahattin Erdemgil, *Ephesus* [Istanbul: Net Turistik Yayinlar, 1986], 87).

98. Rose, *Dynastic Commemoration*, 172–74. Olson, "Contextualizing Roman Honorific Monuments," 119, n. 47. Olson adds, "The left bay was dedicated by Mazaeus to Augustus and Livia, the right by Mithridates to Agrippa and Julia." This division of dedication would make sense in view of the fact that Mithridates is a *libertus* of Agrippa (Mithradates Agrippae l(ibertus) [IEph 3.851]).

99. Rose, *Dynastic Commemoration*, 172–74.

100. Kalinowski, "Patterns of Patronage," 61.

placement given that, in the Augustan period, Curetes Street was lined with ancient graves, though it is entirely possible that "the donors themselves may have been buried in annexes of the gate."[101] Last, the monument has been strategically positioned, marking "a major intersection known as the Triodos, which was the mythical birthplace of Artemis and Apollo."[102] The Apolline connection is especially significant in this context because Augustus claimed special affiliation with the god.[103] In sum, the two Augustan freedmen not only donated a spectacular provincial monument in honor of the Julian ruler and his family but also incorporated an important strand of the religious underpinning of Augustus's rule by means of its careful placement in the city. The reflected glory in erecting a monument like this would have been enormous.

6.2. Slave "Benefactors" at the Customs House of the Harbor of Ephesus

Varro tells us that slaves regularly passed through the harbor of Ephesus (*Ling.* 25.8.21),[104] so we would perhaps expect some epigraphic confirmation of the presence of slaves in the region of the harbor. We know from the *Lex portorii Asiae* (75 BCE–72 CE) that for the tax farmers of the Asian cities, including those at Ephesus, the customs rates for slaves was five denarii per slave, reduced to two and a half denarii from 17 BCE onwards (ll. 10–12, 20, 98 [Cottier]).[105] Fortunately for us, confirmation comes in the dedication of a new fishing customs house, erected by the trade association of the fishermen and fishmongers at Ephesus and made

---

101. Olson, "Contextualizing Roman Honorific Monuments," 119, n. 49.

102. Ibid., 119, n. 47.

103. See John F. Miller, *Apollo, Augustus, and the Poets* (Cambridge: Cambridge University Press, 2009).

104. On the harbor of Ephesus, see Heinrich Zabehlicky, "Preliminary Views of the Ephesian Harbor," in Koester, *Ephesos*, 201–15. The reworking of the harbor quay and seawall, due to silting, was noted in the Ephesian inscriptions (IEph 1a. 24 [CE 146/47]; cf. Strabo, *Geog.* 14.1.24b [641c]; Tacitus, *Ann.* 16.23). For the remains of the harbor wall, see Wiplinger and Wlach, *Ephesus*, 145, pl. 192. On the other harbor repairs predating 147 CE (IEph 6.2061 [102–114 CE]; 7.1.3006 [105 CE]; 2.274 [129 CE]), see Zabehlicky, "Preliminary Views," 205.

105. Michel Cottier et al., *The Customs Law of Asia* (Oxford: Oxford University Press, 2008). For discussion, see Julien Ogereau, "Customs Law of the Roman Province of Asia (*Lex portorii Asiae*)," *NewDocs* 10:95–109.

out to Nero, Julia Agrippina, Octavia, and the demos of the Romans and of the Ephesians (IEph 1a.24 [CE 54–59]; cf. IEph 5.1503).

The onomastic data provided by the inscription, itself nearly two meters high and found in the harbor area of Ephesus, provides important insights into the social milieu of early Christianity.[106] But among the list of donations for the construction of the customs house, along with the names of the associating members contributing to it, we come across the following intriguing reference to slave "benefactors" contributing toward the building expenses (IEph 1a.20a–b, ll. 66–71):

> L. Fabricus Vitalis was works superintendent and deviser of the construction of the work. He also dedicated at his own expense, with his wife and their *threptoi* [τῶν ἰδίων φρεπτῶν], two columns, the ones beside the temple of the Samothracian gods, with the adjacent altars.

Among the names of contributors, there are also names of slaves (e.g., Onesimus, Epaphroditus [IEph 1a.20a, l. 37; 20b, ll. 44, 46]), each of whom donate an unknown amount of denarii to the building funds. Additional slave names occur among the security guards (Phorbus, Secundus [IEph 1a.20b, ll. 32, 34), each of whom contribute one thousand bricks to the building.[107] So the presence of slaves in the harbor region of the city is confirmed. But what do we make of the slave "benefactors" mentioned?

There is no indication from our text that Onesimus, Epaphroditus, Phorbus, and Secundus were upwardly mobile freedmen who might have had access to more substantial financial reserves. Where Onesimus and Epaphroditus got their money is unknown, but it may have been a very modest total of denarii: we are simply unable to say since our text is fragmentary. The sizeable boon of one thousand bricks from the "watchmen" Phorbus and Secundus remains an unsolved puzzle, but the benefaction may have simply been a case of their providing the labor in making the bricks, with a wealthy benefactor, either their own master or someone else in the association, providing the raw materials. Alternatively, it could be,

---

106. For translation and discussion of the decree, see Greg H. R. Horsley, "Inscriptions of Ephesos," 127–35; Horsley, "A Fishing Cartel in First-Century Ephesos," *NewDocs* 5:95–114.

107. Shaner, "Religious Practices of the Enslaved," 60. Horsley also mentions Paulinus, Dionysios, Xanthos, and Zosimos as additional slave candidates ("Fishing Cartel," 109).

as Greg H. R. Horsley suggests, that the donation has come from their own *peculium*.[108] But Shaner is correct, I believe, in suggesting that L. Fabricus Vitalis is the *sole* benefactor who provided the two columns. His slaves were only mentioned in order to enhance his own status as a slave-owning patron over against the other, lower-status donors.[109]

6.3. The Slave Market in the Ephesian Agora

Shaner has discussed the existence of the slave market (σταταρίον) at Ephesus, though such a structure has not yet been identified from the archaeological remains of the city. However, we have evidence of its existence, in addition to the Persicus Decree discussed below, in the form of two statue bases, each of which, Shaner argues, was originally positioned in the Tetragonus Agora.[110] First, C. Sallustius Crispus Passienus, proconsul of Asia in 42/43 CE, is described as an "advocate" or "defender" (*pat[rono]*) of "those who carry out business in the slave market" ([*qui i]n statario ne[g]otiantor* [IEph 7.1.3025]). We know of the existence of slave markets, slave brokers, and slave dealers from inscriptional texts in other cities,[111] but we learn little else in terms of detail. Clearly the Romans are interested in the smooth running of the provincial slave markets at Ephesus (IEph 7.1.3025), no doubt because of the lingering memories of destabilizing slave revolts in the republican past. Further, the wealthy elite builders of slave markets (*MAMA* 5.1.260), including the prosperous slave dealers who are also able to sponsor the festival days of the Caesars (*OGIS* 2.524), are firmly entrenched in the higher echelons of the honor system. Social hierarchy is maintained at the expense of enslaved human bodies.

Second, Ti. Claudius Secundus, a former slave on the basis of his name "Secundus" (IEph 3.646),[112] is now honored as a freedman by "those who carry out business in the slave market" (*qui in statario negotiantor*).

---

108. Horsley, "Fishing Cartel," 110.
109. Shaner, "Religious Practices of the Enslaved," 61.
110. Ibid., 64.
111. E.g., *MAMA* 6.260, Phrygia: "he built the slave market and the altar from his own (funds)"; *OGIS* 2.524, Thyatiris: "The workers of the slave market and the slave brokers honored Alexanderer a slave dealer, (the son of) Alexander, and erected (this monument)."
112. Shaner, "Religious Practices of the Enslaved," 64. For examples of "Secundus" as a slave name, see *CIL* 5.600; 6.7861; 9.5125; 10.202; 11.4382; 14.4506; etc.

A patron of the state of the Ephesians (*favisori civitatis Ephesiorum* [IEph 3.646]) and known from other Ephesian epigraphic honors (IEph 3.857, l. 3; 5.1544, l. 5), this upwardly mobile freedman was accorded an especially large statue, judging by the size of its base.[113] Shaner observes from this honorific transaction that "Secundus's status as a freedperson complicates the social hierarchies among enslaved/free—those who broker slaves honor a former slave with a statue."[114] There is considerable truth in the paradoxical social reversal highlighted by Shaner. However, the status of being an imperial freedman in the provinces was certainly worth highlighting publicly, as the Ephesian inscriptions testify.[115] In the case of the opportunities of advancement offered by the imperial *cursus honorum* for freedmen of the Roman ruler, the status of one's master, the ruler of the empire, would outshine one's servile origins, even though the indelible stain of slavery still remained.[116] The inscriptions of G. Stertinius Orpex and Mazaeus and Mithridates, discussed above, clearly demonstrate this.

6.4. The Persicus Decree and the Hierarchy of Slavery at Ephesus

Found in the theater of Ephesus, the decree of P. Fabius Persicus (IEph 1a.17–19 [44 CE]) deals with a variety of issues, ranging from the sale of priesthoods, the financial administration of the city, and matters relating to the Artemisium. The critical section of this large decree relating to slaves occurs in IEph 1a.18b:

---

113. Shaner, "Religious Practices of the Enslaved," 64.

114. Ibid., 64.

115. Freedmen of the Caesars appear regularly in the Ephesian inscriptions: e.g., freedmen of Augustus (IEph 3.859, 859a; 5.1564), Nero (7.2.4123), Domitian (3.853), and Trajan (3.858). However, inscriptions of lower status slaves also appear. Note the inscription in Latin on ivory tesserae certifying inspection by Calyx, slave of Autronicus (IEph 2.562).

116. Henrik Mouritsen, *The Freedmen in the Roman World* (Cambridge: Cambridge University Press, 2011), 11–33. See also Susan Treggiari, *Roman Freedmen during the Late Republic* (Oxford: Clarendon, 1969). Greg H. R. Horsley discusses P.Oxy. 46.3312, which mentions the paradox of the upwardly mobile Hermaios, who, although possibly a private citizen, journeyed to Rome "and became a freedman of Caesar in order to take appointments" ("Joining the Household of Caesar," *NewDocs* 3:1.7–9; cf. Arrian, *Epict. diss.* 1.19.32; Lucian, *Apol.* 1).

Likewise as many as provide the service of public slaves [δούλων δημοσίων], though they be free [ἐλεύθεροι], and burden the public purse with excessive expenditure ought to be released with public slaves [δούλων δημοσίων] substituted in place of their service. Likewise, it is my pleasure that public slaves [δημοσίους δούλους], who are said to purchase infants at whatever price and to dedicate them to Artemis that their slaves [οἱ δοῦλοι αὐτῶν] might be raised from her revenue, provide for their own slaves [τοῖς ἰδίοις δούλοις]. (ll. 14–18)[117]

Baugh discerns four lower-status groups that are identified by Persicus in the extract above, namely,

1. free men (ἐλεύθεροι) who engage in employment at cost to the public purse, work in Persicus's view more appropriately assigned to the public slaves;
2. public slaves (δοῦλοι δημόσιοι) who, in Persicus's view, should ideally replace the free day laborers currently employed in various public services;
3. an entrepreneurial group of public slaves (δημόσιοι δοῦλοι) who had purchased young children (*threptoi*) at the slave market, with a view to training them as temple slaves at the expense of Artemis; and
4. slaves who own their own slaves (οἱ ἴδιοι δοῦλοι).[118]

It is beyond the scope of our discussion to investigate the complexities of this decree more fully. Suffice it to say, the presence of young children to be purchased at the slave market is clearly indicated, but whether they were adopted foundlings (θρεπτοί) or the babies of slaves is difficult to say.[119]

---

117. For discussion, see Baugh, "Paul and Ephesus," 70–73; Shaner, "Religious Practices of the Enslaved," 82–97, esp. 89–97. Translated by S. R. Llewelyn.

118. In the view of Baugh, "these people would presumably hold the lowliest social position at Ephesus. Even if they were freed, they would still be the freedmen of slaves, and thus derive little social advancement" ("Paul and Ephesus," 73).

119. Baugh, "Paul and Ephesus," 73, n. 142. On *threptoi*, see Archibald Cameron, "ΘΡΕΠΤΟΣ and Related Terms in the Inscriptions of Asia Minor," in *Anatolian Studies Presented to W. H. Buckler*, ed. William Mitchell Calder and Josef Keil (Manchester: Manchester University Press, 1939), 27–62; Teresa Giulia Nani, "ΘΡΕΠΤΟΙ," *Epigraphica* 5/6 (1943/1944): 45–84; Marijana Ricl, "Legal and Social Status of *Threptoi* and Related Categories in Narrative and Documentary Sources," in Cotton, *From Hellenism to Islam*, 93–114.

Persicus also forbids the δημοσίοι δοῦλοι from buying the slaves of slaves for the Temple of Artemis. Shaner argues that the real problem is that "confusion in social position results when babies, owned by public slaves, are dedicated to Artemis, the city-goddess, whose patronage of the city ensures the sustainability of the public slaves."[120] In other words, concerns over social stratification issues, as well as the draining away of income from the Temple of Artemis, is at the heart of Persicus's concerns. But the social hierarchy at all levels is consistently reaffirmed in Persicus's decree, and where ambiguities emerged, the status quo is strongly endorsed.[121]

6.5. Slaves and the Wealthy Ephesian Households: The Evidence of Terrace House 2

The final strand of evidence regarding Ephesian slavery is a series of wall paintings of slaves in Taberna 45 in Terrace House 2. On the south, east, and west walls are depictions of clothed female slaves each with a drink, drinking vessel, flowers, garlands, and perfume containers.[122] Another servant, whose sex is not clearly identified, is shown with two glass bowls.[123] The two servants in the "Theater Room" wall painting, one clearly a female, offer wine from a jug and fish on a platter.[124] The paintings are cleverly poised because the servants seem to turn toward the visitors in the room to offer their various expressions of hospitality.[125] However, a more voyeuristic and sexual form of hospitality is offered the guests in Residential Unit 1 in the wall paintings of naked servants, female and male, one adorned with a necklace, others offering a garland or a fish on a platter or gesticulating welcome.[126]

---

120. Shaner, "Religious Practices of the Enslaved," 90–91.

121. Shaner writes, "Persicus's concern in the decree is for kyriarchal ordering of the cult, and the subordination of public slaves to their appropriate roles, at least in Persicus's opinion, ensures proper order" (ibid., 91).

122. See Norbert Zimmermann and Sabine Ladstätter, eds., *Wall Painting in Ephesos from the Hellenistic to the Byzantine Period* (Istanbul: Ege Yayınları, 2011), 129, figs. 232, 234–238.

123. See ibid., 129, fig. 233.

124. See ibid., 89, figs. 138.5–6.

125. Ibid., 130.

126. Ibid., 116, figs. 200–3.

Here we see a visual representation of the somatic rhetoric of slavery in antiquity, explored expertly by Jennifer A. Glancy.[127] Glancy argues that the characterization of slaves as "bodies" meant that slaves were routinely exposed to abuse and penetration. They served as surrogate bodies (absorbing violence directed against their masters) or as female bodies (sources for children and lactation) and sexual surrogates. While these paintings provide modern historians with evidence of the abusive corporeal dimension of slavery in the ancient household, in actuality the paintings provided a titillating perspective of slave "hospitality" for elite male viewers in the room. The cultured rendering of the subject matter in Terrace House 2 should not deceive us regarding the unsavory reality of what were the proprietorial attitudes to slave bodies by the elites.

6.6. The New Testament and Slavery from an Ephesian Perspective

Several brief comments on the consequences of the Ephesian epigraphic and iconographic portrait of slavery for the New Testament are apposite. First, Shaner is correct in pointing to the paradoxical social reversals that could take place in master, freedmen, and slave relations. The Stoic Seneca, a contemporary of Paul, highlights the common humanity that unites slave and master (*Ep.* 31.11; 44.1; 47.10; cf. *Ben.* 3.28.1; *Vit. beat.* 24.3). He emphasizes the friendship that slaves could offer members of a household, reminding masters of their own "moral" slavery and exhorting them to mete out restrained and fair punishments (*Ep.* 47.16–20). With the conversion of Onesimus, however, the status of Onesimus was elevated from household slave to the familial status of brother-in-Christ (Phlm 15–16) and coworker with Philemon (11, 16b). The humorous reversal of client-patron relationships is also potent. Paul sends Onesimus back to Philemon, the provider of hospitality in his house church (Phlm 2), but, ironically, Philemon must now accept his former slave as a guest in his own house (17) as the Lord's freedman (cf. 1 Cor 7:22) and as Paul's emissary and coworker (Phlm 11–13, 16b, 17b). We are witnessing here a radical change in servile status that exceeds anything envisaged by the humane Seneca, though Glancy views Seneca more as a self-interested and practical manager of his household than as a humanitarian.[128] The

---

127. Glancy, *Slavery in Early Christianity*, 9–38.
128. Ibid., 137–38.

paradox of Philemon recedes when the epistle is contrasted with the social attitudes of Paul's Roman contemporaries.

Glancy rightly challenges traditional exegetical approaches to 1 Thess 4:3–8, 1 Cor 5:1–13, and 1 Cor 6:12–20. She argues that in separating *porneia* from the body of Christ, Paul does not satisfactorily address the issue of the abuse of enslaved prostitutes by their masters, either inside or outside the house church. Female slaves in particular—unless manumitted (cf. 1 Cor 7:21)—were left vulnerable to sexual exploitation. This seriously questions the extent that social leveling was experienced in Paul's house churches, despite Paul's famous "Magna Carta" of humanity (Gal 3:28; cf. Col 3:11). The gravamen of Glancy's argument has genuine bite. The adjustments Paul (or the pseudonymous author) makes to hierarchical master-slave relationships in the household codes seem minimal by contrast (Eph 6:5–9; Col 3:21–4:1; cf. 1 Tim 6:1–2). The potential of sexual abuse of slaves by Christian masters is not directly addressed by the apostle, other than Paul's general warnings against lust and fornication in Eph 4:22 and 5:3–5, which, admittedly, preface his later household codes (Eph 5:20–6:9; cf. 1 Thess 4:4–6a). For Paul, seemingly, our transformation in Christ explicitly challenged ancient proprietary attitudes to other people's bodies in the household and in the *ekklēsia*. With that articulated, he did not feel that he had to address explicitly sexual relations between slave and master in the household codes. To what extent this change hardened hierarchical and proprietary attitudes towards slaves within and outside of the churches is another issue.

7. Spectacles, Games, Contests, and Processions at Ephesus

Spectacles, games, contests, and processions at Ephesus have attracted the interest of scholars over the years.[129] Again, as with our section on

---

129. See Louis Robert, "Sur des inscriptions d'Éphèse: Fêtes, athletes, empereurs, épigrammes," *RevPhil* 41 (1967): 7–84; Irene Ringwood Arnold, "Festivals of Ephesos," *AJA* 76 (1972): 17–22; Lilian Portefaix, "Ancient Ephesus: Processions as Media of Religious and Secular Propaganda," in *The Problem of Ritual: Based on Papers Read at the Symposium on Religious Rites Held at Åbo, Finland, on the Thirteenth–Sixteenth of August 1991*, ed. Tore Ahlbäck, SIDA 15 (Åbo: Donner Institute, 1993), 195–210; Rogers, *Sacred Identity of Ephesos*; Stephen Andrew Brunet, "Greek Athletes in the Roman World: The Evidence from Ephesus" (PhD diss., University of Texas, 1998); Brunet, "Olympic Hopefuls from Ephesos," *JSH* 30 (2003): 219–35; Michael J. D. Carter, "The Presentation of Gladiatorial Spectacles in the Greek East: Roman Culture

the Ephesian elites above, our primary focus will be upon the competitive nature of ancient Ephesus as revealed in its spectacular, agonistic, and processional culture.

Ephesus was no exception to the Romanization of the Greek East in its adoption of Roman spectacles of gladiatorial combat and wild animal fights. The significant archaeological find of a mass burial pit at Ephesus with the bones of slain gladiators—part of a cemetery with tombstones depicting gladiatorial combat—underscores this, as does the iconography of Ephesian gladiator lamps.[130] The Ephesian theater, where the spectacles were held, had assigned seating for offices and groups that was indicated by seating inscriptions. However, at Ephesus, these were not inscribed on the seats themselves but rather on the back of statue bases throughout the theater, which had been donated by C. Vibius Salutaris (IEph 1a.27). These bases were surmounted by the statue with the dedication of Salutaris on the front of the base, while on the reverse were the particular civic groups (council, tribe, and various other organizations), for which each enclosure (*cuneus*) of the theater was reserved. As Tamara Jones explains, "these seating arrangements were not newly instituted and the bases were merely making manifest what was already in practice."[131] We have only two inscriptions (*SEG* 34.1168a–d [ca. 128 CE]; IEph 6.2083–87) that show some of the categories of enclosure in the seating sections. The seating reflects the hierarchical nature of Ephesian society at spectacles with the places of the "most illustrious council," "council of elders," and "strategos," as well as individuals from Ceramus, being among the extant Ephesian inscriptions.[132]

---

and Greek Identity" (PhD diss., McMaster University, 1999); Karl Grossschmidt and Fabian Kanz, *Gladiatoren in Ephesos: Tod am Nachmittag; Eine Ausstellung im Ephesos Museum Seluk, seit 20. April 2002* (Wein: ÖAI, 2002); Stefan Feuser, "A Stroll along the Sea: The Processional Way in Ephesus and the Littoral," *CHS Research Bulletin* 3.1 (2014): https://tinyurl.com/SBL4209c.

130. See Michael Haxby, "The Gladiator Graveyard of Ephesus as Evidence for the Study of Martyrdom," in this volume. For all the gladiatorial lamps at the Selçuk Museum, see P. Büyükkolanci, "Kleinfunde mit Gladiatorendarstellungen im Ephesos Museum," in Grossschmidt, *Gladiatoren in Ephesos*, 93–95; S. Ladstätteweverer, "Lampen mit Gladiatorendarstellungen aus den Hanghaüsern in Ephesos," in Grossschmidt, *Gladiatoren in Ephesos*, 97–102.

131. See Tamara Jones, "Seating and Spectacle in the Graeco-Roman World" (PhD diss., McMaster University, 2008), 121.

132. Ibid., 337.

However, Ephesian epigraphy is replete with references to gladiators, and there is a graffito of gladiators in Residential Unit 4 of Terrace House 2.[133] In particular, the splendid iconography of the tombstones of the gladiators—which, with few exceptions, are housed now at the Selçuk Museum—displays their battles against each other, their fights with wild animals, and their glorious victory poses.[134] The inscriptions of Ephesus do not preserve any details about the victories of the gladiators, unlike many gladiator inscriptions elsewhere (e.g., Thasos [*IG* 12.8.549]).[135] However, a particularly interesting Ephesian inscription, recorded on a slab of white marble (IEph 4.1182 [early second century CE]), is a family of gladiators who were owned by an asiarch:

(column 1): Family of gladiators of
(column 2): T. Claudius Tatianus Julianus, Asiarch.[136]

This phenomenon is widespread among the urban elite, who own not only the family of gladiators but also their support staff and the *damnati* (καταδίκοι, i.e., the prisoners of war, barbarians, and the criminals who were condemned to be executed at the midday games; cf. 1 Cor 4:9). The *lanistae* (managers of teams of gladiators) and priests of the imperial cult were the particular groups who acquired these families.[137] However, the reference in our inscription to the asiarch Julianus owning the family is explained by the fact that asiarchs carried out high priestly roles, with the two titles "asiarch" and "*archiereus*" being virtually synonymous by

---

133. See Zimmermann and Ladstätter, *Wall Painting in Ephesos*, 92, fig. 144. These were first charted systematically by Louis Robert, *Les gladiateurs dans l'orient grec* (Amsterdam: Hakkert, 1971), 195–202, §§199–222. Note the wall painting of a boy gladiator in Residential Unit 2 Terrace House 2 (Zimmermann and Ladstätter, *Wall Painting in Ephesos*, 89, fig. 138.7 [Room 14b]).

134. For all the gladiatorial reliefs at the Selçuk Museum, see A. Zülkadiroglu and C. Içten, "Gladiatorenreliefs in der Ausstellung," in Grossschmidt, *Gladiatoren in Ephesos*, 75–82; Mustafa Büyükkolanci, "Neue in Venatoren- und Gladiatorenreliefs im Ephesos Museum," in Grossschmidt, *Gladiatoren in Ephesos*, 83–88. For detailed descriptions of the iconography accompanying the relevant gladiatorial inscriptions, see Carter, "Presentation of Gladiatorial Spectacles," 351–54, §§263, 266–269, 271–273, 275–277, 279, 281, 283–285.

135. See Carter, "Presentation of Gladiatorial Spectacles," 252.

136. Translated, Ascough, Harland, and Kloppenborg, *Associations in the Greco-Roman World*, §167.

137. Carter, "Presentation of Gladiatorial Spectacles," 266.

the third century CE.[138] The size and prestige of the Ephesian spectacles offered by the high priests is seen from the third century inscription of Marcus Aurelius Daphnus (IEph 7.1.3070): "Asiarch of the three temples in Ephesus, who held a *munus* in his homeland with thirty-nine pairs (of gladiators) fighting *apotomos* for thirteen days, and who killed Libyan beasts."[139] The cost of mounting this particular gladiatorial spectacle would have been prohibitive for any other than the elites, given the extended period and numbers of combatants. It is also difficult to estimate the finances required for acquiring the beasts, but it must also have been equally taxing, given other Ephesian epigraphic references to the killing of large numbers of lions in spectacles.[140] Thus the asiarchs and *archiereis* sponsor this most Roman form of popular entertainment in honor of the ruler at Ephesus,[141] surpassing their contemporaries in the quest for *philotimia* by virtue of their prestigious role in the imperial cult and by their generosity in mounting glorious spectacles, the status significance of which would been obvious to all members of the social pyramid.

As far as the games at Ephesus, the Ephesian *agōnothetai* ("presidents of the games") coordinated and dispensed beneficence by administering the festivals and sacrifices to Artemis and by maintaining the sanctity of the month of Artemision and its accompanying games. A good example is the honorific decree eulogizing T. Aelius Marcianus Priscus, the president of the games. The decree highlights his contribution to the Artemisia in this manner: "He was first [πρῶτον] to conduct the festival in its entiret[y] and obtained festal holidays for the entire month named after the goddess and established the Artemisiac contest and increased the prizes for the

---

138. Ibid., 205–6. In terms of high priests, IEph 6.2061 (103–116 CE) says that Titus Flavius Monrtanus, *archiereus* of Asia, "completed the theatre, dedicated it during his high priesthood, and gave both gladiators and wild beast hunts" (ll. 8–10). Another unnamed Ephesian elite benefactor offers "four days of gladiators fighting with arms sharpened" (Eph 3.810, l. 1 [180–220 CE]).

139. Regarding the technical term *apotomos*, Michael J. D. Carter writes, "Combats qualified as *apotomos* were especially bloody and so probably reflect more dangerous or fatal (and so expensive) shows" ("Archiereis and Asiarchs: A Gladiatorial Perspective," *GRBS* 44 [2004]: 46).

140. Robert, *Les gladiateurs dans l'orient grec*, 195–96, §§198–200; §198 mentions the slaughter of twenty-five lions over a five-day period. See Chris P. Eplett, "Animal Spectacula of the Roman Empire" (PhD diss., University of British Columbia, 2001).

141. However, note that the scribe of the boule, Lucius Cerrinus Paetus, is said "to conduct spectacles for the five days" from the public funds (IEph 1a.21 [138 CE]).

contestants and erected statues for the ones who won" (IEph 1a.24c, ll. 6–14).[142]

In terms of the contests and their winners, we have already mentioned the competitions for physicians and the victory of a boy comedian at Ephesus. Several major inscriptions from different cities outline the competitions that the pantomime Ti. Julius Apolaustus had won across the Hellenic world, including the very old Greek competition of the Ephesia at Ephesus (IEph 6.2070–71).[143] This shows us how the *koinon Asias* "could diverge from the regular festivals not only by including official disciplines more suited to Roman tastes," such as the gladiatorial competitions, but also by introducing mimes and pantomimes as further contests.[144] In terms of Ephesus itself, on the basis of an inscription (*IAG* 84), Brunet argues that the games of Ephesus were ranked third in the ancient world by the athletes competing.[145] Indeed, there are 106 inscriptions honoring all types of athletes at Ephesus, with the prospect of still more being discovered.[146] The investigation required to come to grips with such an enormous database is beyond the scope of this chapter. Thus we will confine ourselves to two interesting examples and draw some conclusions from them.

First, the victory inscription of the boxer Photion, whose home city was Laodicea on the Lycus, details with precision his victories by age division, region, and order of occurrence (IEph 5.1605 [after CE 174]). The victories of Photium in the age division of "young men" in Asia Minor are recounted in this manner: (1) two victories in Ephesus (Koina of Asia in Ephesus; Epinikia in Ephesus); (2) two in his home town (Koina of Asia in Laodicea, Ecumenical Deia Sebasta in Laodicea); (3) one in Miletus (Didymeia in Miletus). These provincial fights

---

142. A sister and brother make contributions by equipping the race course ([ἐν τῷ στ]αδίῳ), presiding at the festival of the Artemisia, and conducting the games at the great Pythia and for the Chrysophoroi (IEph 5.1618). In another fragmentary inscription honoring the victory of an Ephesian charioteer (IEph 4.1086A) is also mention of the race course at Ephesus (στ[α]δίῳ). For a brief commentary on this rare charioteer monument in western Asia Minor, only one among three others (see IPergamon 1.10–12; IMagnMai 127; IKyme 46), see Brunet, "Greek Athletes in the Roman World," 316, §11.

143. William J. Slater, "The Pantomine Iulius Apolaustus," *GRBS* 36 (1995): 263–92.

144. Ibid., 281–82.

145. Brunet, "Greek Athletes in the Roman World," 15–16.

146. For the epigraphic catalogue of Ephesian athletes, see ibid., 293–477.

are followed by his fights in the age division of "men." Photion expands his range of competitions internationally by moving from further victories in Asia Minor (Traianeia Deiphileia in Pergamon, Ecumenical Deia Sebasta in Laodicea, Ephesea) to fights in Italy and the Peloponnese (Eusebeia in Puteoli, Sebasta in Naples, Aspis in Argos), and then, as an internationally famous boxer, returning again to further bouts in Asia Minor (Artemisia in Ephesus).[147]

We know the result of Photion's boxing career after the sequence of fights outlined above. He went on to win at Olympia, as a papyrus (P.Lond. 3.1178, l. 84 [CE 194]) indicates by according the boxer the honorific "Olympionikes" (Φωτίων Καρπίνος Λαδίκευς καὶ Ἐφέσιος, πύκτης Ὀλυμπιονείκης). Photion organized his boxing career strategically, gaining experience in the lower age division by competing in familiar local and regional bouts before, upon moving to the higher age competition, testing himself on the international stage and gaining the ultimate prize at Olympia. This inscription gives us keen insight into the peripatetic world of the ancient athlete, who sought personal glory contest by contest, region by region, and continent by continent, with a view to enhancing the honor of his family and his city. The athletic elites, like their modern counterparts, were always travelling to the next contest. Ephesus, like other ancient cities, deeply imbibed this culture of the beautiful, strong, and victorious.[148]

Second, another important Ephesian inscription (IEph 5.1613 [after CE 132]; cf. IEph 4.1133) honors a runner who has won the original athletic *periodos* ("circuit") of ancient Greece (i.e., Olympia in Prusa, Pythia in Delphi, Nemea, and Isthmia).[149] Several other important claims are made about this athlete. He was "unbeaten" ([ἄλ]ειπτος), and very unusually, he had won victories in the *stadion* (180 m) and *diaulos* (ca. 400 m) races, as

---

147. For commentary on this inscription, see Brunet, "Greek Athletes in the Roman World," 343–45, §28.

148. On male beauty contests in antiquity, see Nigel B. Crowther, "Male Beauty Contests in Greece: The Euandria and Euexia," *AC* (1985): 285–91; James R. Harrison, "Paul and the Ancient Athletic Ideal," in *Paul's World*, ed. Stanley E. Porter, Pauline Studies 4 (Leiden: Brill, 2008), 102–3.

149. For discussion, with a differently restored text to IEph 5.1613 at various junctures, see Brunet, "Greek Athletes in the Roman World," 332–34, §28. The IEph editor's claim that the athlete is possibly Demaratos is to be rejected since he was active in the Augustan age, whereas our athlete competed in the reign of Hadrian (Brunet, "Greek Athletes in the Roman World," 334).

well as the pentathlon,[150] in the same session at Isthmia "once for all" (ἅπαξ). Most striking of all, in an unnamed race, he had arrived "alone and first (μό[νο]ς καὶ πρπῶτ[ος]) coming into the registration (of competitors) having stopped all (his) rivals" well before the race had begun. His towering reputation had scared all the other competitors away! Other victories occurred at the Panathenaia in Athens, the Panhellenic games, and the Hadrianeia. What we are witnessing here is not only the stratospheric boasting of ancient athletes and their cities but also how increasingly difficult it was becoming by the second century CE to establish new claims of athletic primacy that had not already been accomplished before.[151] Ancient cities were assiduous record keepers of their various athletic competition results, as were the athletes themselves.[152] Remarkably, our Ephesian competitor had established new grounds for boasting in an already jam-packed arena of fame.

Last, we have already referred to the procession of Demeter and Men at Ephesus and the village of Almoura, as well as C. Vibius Salutaris's procession of the statues out from and back to the Temple of Artemis throughout the entire city. As noted at the outset of the chapter, the route of the processional way of Ephesian Artemis in the archaic and classical period—which was intimately related to the sea and its shoreline—had to change due to the silting of the harbor at Old Ephesus. But with the relocation of the city in the Hellenistic age (including the relocation of the waterfront 150 meters to the west) and the heavy rebuilding of the city in the Roman period, the spectacular vistas of the old procession were lost, having been replaced, by the time of Salutaris, with a "terrestrial, landlocked festival."[153] Where the cleansing of the cult image of Artemis took place in Roman times is unknown, but it could have taken place at the seashore in Classical times.[154] Irrespective of the site (village or city) or the route (landlocked or seaside), it is clear that processions in Ephesus and its surrounding territories were an expression of the vital religious core of the city and its inhabitants, urban and rural, and its continued prosperity at

---

150. Brunet restores [ὁπλίταν] (a footrace in hoplite armor) instead of [πένταθλον] in the IEph edition ("Greek Athletes in the Roman World," 332, §28).

151. For discussion, see ibid., 21–41, 82–84.

152. The *agōnothetēs* determined the wording of the inscription, in conjunction with the athletes (ibid., 93–94), with cities and synods being assiduous record keepers (pp. 41–58).

153. Feuser, "Stroll along the Sea," 5, §3.

154. Ibid., 4, §5; 6, §3.

the hands of beneficent gods. By the time of Salutaris, however, there was a visible shift in power realities in Ephesian processional culture. As Lilian Portefaix astutely observes,

> The presence of statues, representing Roman instruments of power, in the temple of Artemis Ephesia elevated Roman rule into the domain of the gods, and the placing of these statues in the theatre made the presence of Roman power tangibly conscious to the members of the Popular Assembly, reminding them of their position as citizens of a city subordinate to Rome. The tension between Roman rule and Greek spiritual culture became clear in the Salutaris bequest.[155]

8. The Social World of the Ephesian Graffiti

The study of the social world revealed by the graffiti of Greco-Roman antiquity is still a relatively new discipline, with major studies of the phenomenon in Roman Asia Minor being so far confined to Aphrodisias, Smyrna, and Iasos.[156] However, apart from several recent studies of the graffiti in Terrace House 2 in Ephesus and the "inscribed images" of the Ephesian theater,[157] the other graffiti of the city, as far as I am aware, have

---

155. Portefaix, "Ancient Ephesus," 207.

156. See Peter Kegan, *Graffiti in Antiquity* (London: Routledge, 2014). Additionally, note Jean-Charles Moretti, "Graffites de la Palestre du lac à Délos," *BCH* 122 (1998): 201–12; Rex E. Wallace, *An Introduction to Wall Inscriptions from Pompeii and Herculaneum* (Wauconda: Bolchazy-Carducci, 2005); Jennifer A. Baird and Claire Taylor, eds., *Ancient Graffiti in Context*, RSAH 2 (New York: Routledge, 2011); Kristina Milnor, *Graffiti and the Literary Landscape in Roman Pompeii* (Oxford: Oxford University Press, 2014). For Aphrodisias, see Angelos Chaniotis, "Graffiti in Aphrodisias: Images—Texts—Contexts," in Baird and Taylor, *Ancient Graffiti in Context*, 191–207. For Smyrna, see Roger S. Bagnall, *Everyday Writing in the Graeco-Roman East* (Berkeley: University of California Press, 2011), 7–26; Bagnall et al., eds., *Graffiti from the Basilica in the Agora of Smyrna* (New York: New York University Press, 2016). Since the basilica find of graffiti at Smyrna, discussed by Bagnall above, another important collection of Greek graffiti has been found in the agora of Smyrna in 2013, belonging to the second and further centuries CE. For details, see https://tinyurl.com/SBL4209d. For Iasos, see Cristina Servadei, "Graffiti con schemi di gioco nell'agorà di Iasos: Esempi dalla stoà orientale," in *Il tempio distilo d'età ecatomnide e l'architettura ionica*, vol. 1 of *Iasos: L'area a sud dell'agorà*, ed. Nicoló Masturzo, Archaeologica 176, MAII 6 (Rome: Bretschneider, 2016), 16–22.

157. See Hans Taeuber, "Graffiti," in *Das Hanghaus 2 in Ephesos: Die Wohneinheit 6; Baubefund, Ausstattung, Funde*, ed. Hilke Thür and Friedrich Krinzinger, FiE

not been seriously discussed. They provide keen insight into the religious and philosophical beliefs, shame culture, scatological humor, political and social viewpoints, games, and astronomy of the Ephesians.

Perhaps the most celebrated graffito on the modern "tourist trail" at Ephesus displays a left foot with a cross placed above it, accompanied by, to the right, a bust of a woman wearing a wall crown and, to the left, a heart with a triangular symbol at its top (IEph 2.580).[158] This graffito can be seen carved on Marble Street, dated by Werner Jobst to the fifth century CE.[159] According to the modern tourist guides, the graffito advised visiting sailors and Ephesian males to proceed along the Arcadian Way from the harbor to the crossroads of Marble and Curetes Streets, whereupon, struck by the alluring image of the enigmatic woman, the men knew that they would have their sexual desires satisfied by heading towards the brothel on the left side of the street opposite the Celsus Library.[160] However, this lurid construction falls apart upon closer examination.[161] First, the woman more

---

8.9 (Vienna: ÖAW, 2010), 122–25 and 472–78; Sabine Ladstätter, with Barbara Beck-Brandt, Martin Steskal, and Norbert Zimmermann, *Terrace House 2 in Ephesos: An Archaeological Guide*, trans. Nicole M. High, HAG 12 (Istanbul: Altan Basim, 2013), 184–88; Elisabeth Rathmayr, "The Significance of Sculptures with Associated Inscriptions in Private Houses in Ephesos, Pergamon, and Beyond," in *Inscriptions in the Private Sphere in the Greco-Roman World*, ed. Rebecca Benefiel and Peter Keegan, BSGRE 7 (Leiden: Brill, 2015), 146–78; Charlotte Roueché, "Images of Performance: New Evidence from Ephesus," in *Greek and Roman Actors: Aspects of an Ancient Profession*, ed. Pat Easterling and Edith Hall (Cambridge: Cambridge University Press, 2002), 254–81.

158. Scherrer argues that the heart is pierced with an arrow (the triangular symbol) (*Ephesus*, 156). However, as Edwin M. Yamauchi observes, "some have interpreted the triangular symbol as the female pudenda" (*New Testament Cities in Asia Minor: Light from Archaeology on Cities of Paul and the Seven Churches* [Grand Rapids: Baker, 1980; repr., Eugene, OR: Wipf & Stock, 2003], 102). The subjectivity in assessing the meaning of the individual components of the graffito is apparent.

159. Werner Jobst, "Das 'öffentliche Freudenhaus' in Ephesos," *JÖAI* 51 (1976/1977): 67.

160. Other additions to the tourist guide lore include reference to the hole in the marble above the heart: the cost of entry into the brothel, it is proposed, is the amount of coins required to fill the hole. Alternatively, the "heart" is said to represent in actuality a wallet filled with coins. My own Turkish tourist guide at Ephesus pointed to the five card-like projections above the woman's head and humorously quipped that this represented the credit card facility for the brothel! Such proposals tell us more about the imagination of modern tourist guides than sober archaeological analysis.

161. Scherrer dismisses as incorrect the proposal that the graffito was "a signboard for the so-called 'House of Pleasure'" (*Ephesus*, 156).

likely represents the mural crowned goddess Tyche (Fortune),[162] famous among other mural crowned civic goddesses (e.g., Hestia, Cybele). Second, rather than being a "unified message," the image "may be a case of multiple graffiti on the same cobblestone, created by different writers who wished to communicate distinct messages."[163] Third, the identification of the nearby two-storied residential building as a brothel is questionable. In a latrine adjacent to the Varius Bath complex, a fragmentary dedication, inscribed on an architrave and datable to the period after Domitian's rule, mentions, so it is argued, a brothel (παιδισκήοις [IEph 2.455]). But the location of the brothel is unknown. As Thomas McGinn states, "The structure located behind the latrine, which was once thought to be a brothel, is almost certainly a Roman peristyle house and not the purpose-built brothel that the inscription seems to imply."[164] Fourth, under the entry for παιδισκεῖος in the revised supplement of LSJ, the authors note that παιδισκήοις in IEph 2.455, our graffito, has "uncertain significance."[165] Further, it seems highly unlikely that the denotation of "prostitute" makes any sense in what is (in a full reconstruction) an honorific dedication to Artemis and Trajan or (in a minimalist reconstruction of the inscription) a dedication to an unknown Caesar. Thus the translation traditionally proposed for the key word in our architrave, "brothel," is at best unproven or, more likely, misconceived. Fifth, even if the traditional translation is correct, Thomas McGinn and Werner Jobst suggest that "the inscription may have been taken from another, unknown location for reuse in its findspot."[166] With so many uncertainties emerging, the popular tourist guide patter about the graffito ought to be abandoned in scholarly circles.

---

162. Margherita Guarducci (*Epigrafi di carattere private*, vol. 3 of *Epigrafia Greca* [Rome: Istituto Poligrafico dello Stato, 1974], 73–74), cited in IEph 2.580 (p. 243), says that the graffito consists of "images of feet (or soles) … and surmounted by the bust of the deity" (Italian original translated here). For the Tyche identification, see Otto Friedrich August Meinardus, "The Alleged Advertisement for the Ephesian Lupanar," *WSt* 7 (1973): 244–49, cited in Yamauchi, *New Testament Cities in Asia Minor*, 102.

163. Anise K. Strong, *Prostitutes and Matrons in the Roman World* (Cambridge: Cambridge University Press, 2016), 262.

164. Thomas McGinn, *The Economy of Prostitution in the Roman World: A Study of Social History and the Brothel* (Ann Arbor: University of Michigan Press, 2004), 225.

165. LSJ revised supplement, s.v. "παιδισκεῖος." For the dating, see Jobst, "Das 'öffentliche Freudenhaus,'" 65, 69.

166. McGinn, *Economy of Prostitution*, 225; Jobst, "Das 'öffentliche Freudenhaus,'" 65, 69.

An equally interesting example is the graffito found in the latrine of the gymnasium at Ephesus. Presented in hexameters, the text runs as follows:

> Moving with your foot and long raising with the fist of your hand
> and coughing from your heart, and shaking your whole body
> from the fingers' ends, (until) relieving (yourself) you cheered of joy,
> may your belly never give you pain after you've come to my home. (IEph 3.456.1)

We see here the potential social disaster for the host and the embarrassment for the guest that could be occasioned by food poisoning during hospitality in the host's home.[167] The shame culture is implied in this instance, rather than explicitly stated, because the bowel evacuation relieves the sufferer of the potential effects of any food poisoning. Mutual relief on the part of the guest and host is humorously underscored.[168]

Another graffito in iambics was also found in the latrine of the Ephesian gymnasium (IEph 2.456.2). It advocates a Stoic approach to life, characterized by strict personal discipline. The wise person, having abandoned the seductions of a life of unrestrained hedonism, should not become disgruntled over the personal success of the morally unworthy. Such fruitless mutual comparison not only provokes internal distress for the morally worthy but it also diverts them from the path of true virtue:

> If we do not choose a fugitive life
> drinking or luxuriating or free (from any constraint),
> (then) we always cause ourselves distress
> (by) seeing unworthy people more successful (than ourselves).[169]

---

167. I am indebted to Dr. Julien Ogereau for this insight and the translation.

168. The importance of carefully planned hospitality, in which the needs of guests are scrupulously catered for, is underscored by the appreciative graffito note recorded on the garden painting in the courtyard of residential unit of Terrace House 2 in Ephesus: "Attalianos, the boy, commemorated the beautiful hospitality" (Ladstätter, *Terrace House 2*, 167).

169. The Ephesian inscriptions and wall paintings show considerable interest in the Greek philosophers, highlighting Socrates the Athenian (IEph 2.560.1, 3) and Chilon the Spartan (IEph 2.560.2), one of the famous Seven Sages (see James R. Harrison, "The Seven Sages, The Delphic Canon and Ethical Education in Antiquity," in *Ancient Education and Early Christianity*, ed. Matthew Ryan Hauge and Andrew W. Pitts, LNTS 533 [London: Bloomsbury T&T Clark, 2016], 71–86). In terms of wall paintings in Terrace House 2, Socrates is again isolated as an important Greek figure

Another Ephesian latrine graffito evinces interest in popular philosophy by caricaturing one of its better-known motifs, though it draws upon a familiar trope of banquet poetry. But the topos is profaned by reducing its more serious sentiments to toilet humor. At face value, IEph 2.561.1 reads thus: "(Choose) the right time [ὥραν] or death [θάνατον]." What is the meaning of this puzzling graffito? Volker Michael Strocka argues that it refers to the defecatory process. The importance of timely digestion and defecation in everyday life is critical; otherwise, metaphorically speaking, the bodily results of delay or excess, both for those in the act of defecating and for those waiting to defecate, can be "deadly" in their effects.[170]

---

for Ephesians (Ladstätter, *Terrace House 2*, 82, fig. 47). In IEph 7.2.4340 and 3.789, there is mention, respectively, of a "Platonic" and "eclectic" philosopher. More generally, φιλόσοφοι are frequently honored in the inscriptions at Ephesus (IEph 3.616, 789; 5.1958; 6.2066; 7.2.3901, 4340). The sophist Soterus, for example, is eulogized in IEph 5.1548 in this manner: "Twice did the Androclidae summon from Athens me Soterus, a sophist, first by decrees of the Council; and on me first as a reward for virtue in life and wisdom of speech they resolved by way of honor to bestow numberless gifts." There is also a highly fragmentary inscription that is possibly a philosophical diatribe (SEG 33.960 [second century CE]). We read, too, in a dossier from 42 BCE, that immunity is granted for professors, sophists, and doctors (*SEG* 56.1219, a revision of *SEG* 31.952). Finally, a delightful caricature of philosophers and their pseudo-wisdom is found in the latrine of residential unit 2 in Terrace House 2 (Ladstätter, *Terrace House 2*, 185; Zimmermann and Ladstätter, *Wall Painting in Ephesos*, 87–88, figs. 136–37). As Ladstätter explains, "the scrawny men are not discussing high truths, but instead the right time, and are thus reminding the users of the latrine to hurry" (*Terrace House 2*, 185). On the physiognomy of identifying philosophers as a group in the wall paintings, see Zimmermann and Ladstätter, *Wall Painting in Ephesos*, 88. It is worth remembering that in Terrace House 2, the cultured Socrates is presented sympathetically elsewhere in a wall painting. As Zimmerman and Ladstätter write (88 n. 293), "The latrine paintings are therefore an example of self-conscious and selected irony, with which one wanted one wanted to distance oneself from the traditional keenness to display education and culture displayed elsewhere." For similar satirical pictures and graffiti on wall paintings from a tavern at Roman Ostia (100 CE), see https://tinyurl.com/SBL4209e. On Paul and ancient toilet humor, see James R. Harrison, "'Laughter is the Best Medicine': St. Paul, Well-Being, and Roman Humour," in *Well-Being, Personal Wholeness and the Social Fabric*, ed. Doru Costache, Darren Cronshaw, and James R. Harrison (Newcastle upon Tyne: Cambridge Scholars Press, 2017), 209–40.

170. See Volker Michael Strocka, *Die Wandmalerei der Hanghäuser in Ephesos*, FiE 8.1 (Vienna: ÖAW, 1977), 88–89, cited in IEph 2.561.1 (p. 230). On the "right time" motif in the graffito of philosophers from Ephesian Terrace House 2, see the footnote directly above. See also Zimmermann and Ladstätter, *Wall Painting in Ephe-*

But, as Felix Preisshofen has observed, the text is ambiguous, since ὥρα also means "the spring" or "prime of life," effectively the equivalent of the phrase ἥβη ἄνθος ("[the] bloom of youth").[171] The connection between ὥρα, θάνατος, and banquet poetry becomes apparent in the poetic epigrams of Nicarchus (late first century CE).[172] Nicarchus spells out the desirability of maintaining attendance at banquets notwithstanding the ravages of age and death's inevitable approach while also affirming the desirable extension of the "bloom of youth."[173] Although toilet humor touches the base of the social pyramid as much as its apex, the clever ambiguity of this graffito points to a composer and audience familiar with the tropes of banquet poetry.

Curses against people who urinate in inappropriate spots are also standard fare in the Ephesian graffiti. We have already noted the presence of a urination curse scrawled on the Mazaeus-Mithridates Gate. Artemis and Hekate are angered by people urinating, respectively, in Domitian Street and in the agora (IEph 2.569, 567). There is even a prohibition against urinating in a *kamara* (chamber) in a dream (IEph 2.568a.1–2). How seriously

---

sos, 88, fig. 137 on the graffiti "Three out of none" in the latrine of Residential Unit 2 as another encouragement to the toilet user to hurry up.

171. For the Preisshofen citation, see Strocka, *Die Wandmalerei der Hanghäuser*, 88–89, referenced in IEph 2.561.1 (p. 230).

172. On poets at banquets, see the contemporary of Nero, Lucillius: "You know the rule of my little banquets. To-day, Aulus, I invite you under new convivial laws. No lyric poet shall sit there and recite, and you yourself shall neither trouble us nor be troubled with literary discussions" (*Anth. Gr.* 11.10). All translations of *Anthologia Graeca* are from W. R. Paton, ed. and trans., *The Greek Anthology*, 5 vols., LCL 67–68, 84–86 (Cambridge: Harvard University Press, 1916–1918). For examples of banquet poems, see Statius, *Theb.* 1.5; Martial, *Ep.* 6.42. On Roman feasts, see Katherine M. D. Dunbabin, *The Roman Banquet: Images of Conviviality* (Cambridge: Cambridge University Press, 2003).

173. "Must I not die? What care I if I go to Hades with gouty legs or in training for a race? I shall have many to carry me; so let me become lame, if I wish. As far as that goes, as you see, I am quite easy, and never miss a banquet" (*Anth. Gr.* 5.38). "Nicarete, who formerly was in the service of Athene's shuttle, and stretched out many a warp on the loom, made in honour of Cypris a bonfire in front of her house of her work-basket and bobbins and her other gear, crying, 'Away with you, starving work of wretched women, that have power to waste away the bloom of youth [νέον τήχειν ἄνθος].' Instead the girl chose garlands and the lyre, and a gay life spent in revel and festivity. 'Cypris,' she said, 'I will pay you tithe of all my gains. Give me work and take from it your due'" (*Anth. Gr.* 6.285).

these urinating curses, not studied in the scholarly literature,[174] should be taken is a moot point. The particular Ephesian sites where the graffiti were found are not "sacred" in the same way that ancient grave sites are, where, universally in the Greco-Roman world, vicious imprecations are brought against anyone who would interfere with the remains or the site itself.[175] It may be that these particular Ephesian curses are just a form of scatological humor, but, equally, perhaps because the site is associated with particular cultic activities or honoring significant dignitaries, the curse is serious.[176] Both options have to be left open.

Some of the Ephesian graffiti have a clear political and social intent. A graffito from Terrace House 2, apartment 2, for example, underscores the ubiquity and eternity of the Roman Empire: "Rome, queen over all, your power will never end" (IEph 2.599).[177] Among scribblings on a column of

---

174. Note, however, the very helpful web article of Michael Gilleland, "Commit No Nuisance," *Laudator temporis acti*, https://tinyurl.com/SBL4209f. Gilleland points to a range of evidence, including a splendid first-century CE temple bas-relief of Zeus throwing thunderbolts at a kneeling, defecating man (John R. Clarke, *Looking at Laughter: Humor, Power, and Transgression in Roman Visual Culture* [Berkeley: University of California Press, 2007], 60–62). Several Latin inscriptions regarding the gods' wrath towards defecating and urinating offenders are also cited in English translation (*CIL* 3.1966; 4.7716; 6.13740). Additionally, for literary references, see Plutarch, *Stoic. rep.* 22.2; Persius, *Sat.* 1.112–114; Suetonius, *Nero* 56; Aristophanes, *Vesp.* 393–94; Horace, *Ars* 470–72; Horace, *Sat.* 1.8.37–39; Petronius, *Satyr.* 71.8; Hist. Aug., *Car.* 5.7.

175. See Johan Strubbe, ed., *ΑΡΑΙ ΕΠΙΤΥΜΒΙΟΙ: Imprecation against Desecrators of the Grave in the Greek Epitaphs of Asia Minor; A Catalogue*, IK 52 (Bonn: Habelt, 1997). In regard to the sanctity of statues, Eliav argues that both Greco-Roman world and the rabbis classified the cultural and physical *context* of statues, dividing them into "worshiped" or "nonworshiped" ("Roman Statues, Rabbis, and Greco-Roman Culture"). Thus the rabbis could dismiss the nonworshiped statues as nonidolatrous and Greco-Romans could befoul the same statues with feces and urine with no religious threats precisely because of the public perception of the sculpture as noncultic.

176. For sophisticated scatological humor, see Catullus's criticism of his unfaithful lover Lesbia and her paramours: "And here all her good and blessed lovers come, and truly, rather unsuitably, all her insignificant and back alley adulterers; and first among all these longhaired pansies, son of rabbity Iberia, is you Egnatius, whose good is marked by a bushy beard and teeth cleaned with Spanish urine" (Catullus, *Carm.* 37). Translation from Casey C. Moore, "Invective Drag: Talking Dirty in Catullus, Cicero, Horace and Ovid" (PhD diss., University of South Carolina, 2015), 47.

177. Also in Terrace House 2, apartment 2 is a painted wall picture of a fish, identified by its graffito as the "*kephalos* fish" species (IEph 2.561c).

the east hall of the agora is a graffito criticizing the pompous: "A pompous man [σεμνός]: I do not suffer (him)" (IEph 2.577.4).[178] While the character trait of pomposity could well be the general target here, more likely the Ephesian aristocratic elites are in view, given their inherited wealth, social precedence, and the endless roll call of their civic magistracies and public honors (inscriptions, statuary) throughout the city.

Two final examples demonstrate the usefulness of graffiti in civic contexts. An inscription on a stone board—which was used as a play board in the east vestibule of Marble Street, a little to the north of the corner of Marble and Curetes Streets—has this warning about the perils of gaming: "The dice table, having much (luck?), will give pleasure through (the) loss of gold" (IEph 2.556). The Greek letters, along with their message, are spread across the thirty-six-space field of the *ludus latrunculorum*, a strategy board game for two players popular across the Roman Empire.[179] Finally, though technically not popular graffiti, markings for the equinoxes and the solstices, summer and winter, are found on a sundial now housed in the Selçuk Museum (IEph 2.433).[180]

9. Conclusion

While the epigraphic evidence has its limitations, its contemporaneity ushers one into the daily life and preoccupations of ancient Ephesians in a way that the literary evidence does not. One is held hostage to the class bias, jaundiced perceptions, and selectivity of the author in the ancient literature. By contrast, the inscriptions provide the reader with the discourse of the inhabitants, Roman officialdom, local power brokers and institutions of Ephesus, caught up as they were in its vast array of activities and debate across the urban spaces and the nearby villages. The inscriptions and graffiti were read by the literate; explained by bystanders to the illiterate; heard when the honorific inscriptions, association bylaws, and imperial decrees were publicly proclaimed aloud; or were interpreted for the viewer by the accompanying statue, iconography, and the local build-

---

178. Note the positive use of σεμνός in IEph 2.577.3: "Worthy of respect [σεμνός], worthy of respect [σεμνός] (is) a young child."

179. For Latin inscriptional examples of the *ludus latrunculorum*, see Reinhold Merkelbach, "Ephesische Parerga (12): Eine tabula lusoria für den ludus latrunculorum," *ZPE* 28 (1978): 49.

180. For the sundial, see Topai, *Ephesus Museum Selçuk*, 64.

ing in which the inscription was erected. Through the inscriptions, the ancient Ephesians still speak to us across the centuries, inviting us to enter into their illustrious and thrice-*neōkoros* city.

Bibliography

Arnold, Clinton E. *Ephesians, Power and Magic: The Concept of Power in Ephesians in Light of Its Historical Setting.* SNTSMS 63. Cambridge: Cambridge University Press, 1989. Repr. Grand Rapids: Baker, 1992.
Arnold, Irene Ringwood. "Festivals of Ephesos." *AJA* 76 (1972): 17–22.
Ascough, Richard S., Philip A. Harland, and John S. Kloppenborg, eds. *Associations in the Greco-Roman World: A Sourcebook.* Waco, TX: Baylor University Press, 2012.
Bagnall, Roger S. *Everyday Writing in the Graeco-Roman East.* Berkeley: University of California Press, 2011.
Bagnall, Roger S., Roberta Casagrande-Kim, Akin Ersoy, and Cumhur Tanriver, eds. *Graffiti from the Basilica in the Agora of Smyrna.* New York: New York University Press, 2016.
Bailey, Colin. "The *Gerousia* of Ephesus." PhD diss., University of British Columbia, 2006.
Baird, Jennifer A., and Claire Taylor, eds. *Ancient Graffiti in Context.* Routledge Studies in Ancient History 2. New York: Routledge, 2011.
Barclay, John M. G. *Jews in the Mediterranean Diaspora: From Alexander to Trajan (323 BCE–117 CE).* Edinburgh: T&T Clark, 1996.
Baugh, Steven M. "Paul and Ephesus: The Apostle among His Contemporaries." PhD diss., University of California, 1990.
Beard, Mary. *Pompeii: The Life of a Roman Town.* London: Profile, 2008.
Bonnet, Jacques. *Artémis d'Éphèse et la légende des sept dormants.* Paris: Librairie Orientaliste Paul Geuthner, 1977.
Bradley, Keith R. *Slavery and Society at Rome.* Cambridge: Cambridge University Press, 1994.
―――. *Slaves and Masters in the Roman Empire: A Study in Social Control.* New York: Oxford University Press, 1987.
Brunet, Stephen. "Greek Athletes in the Roman World: The Evidence from Ephesus." PhD diss., University of Texas, 1998.
―――. "Olympic Hopefuls from Ephesos." *JSH* 30 (2003): 219–35.
Büyükkolanci, Mustafa. "Neue in Venatoren- und Gladiatorenreliefs im Ephesos Museum." Pages 83–88 in *Gladiatoren in Ephesos: Tod am Nachmittag; Eine Ausstellung im Ephesos Museum Seluk, seit 20. April*

2002. Edited by Karl Grossschmidt and Fabian Kanz. Wein: ÖAI, 2002.

Büyükkolanci, P. "Kleinfunde mit Gladiatorendarstellungen im Ephesos Museum." Pages 93–95 in *Gladiatoren in Ephesos: Tod am Nachmittag; Eine Ausstellung im Ephesos Museum Seluk, seit 20. April 2002*. Edited by Karl Grossschmidt and Fabian Kanz. Wein: ÖAI, 2002.

Callahan, Allen Dwight, Richard A. Horsley, and Abraham Smith, eds. *Slavery in Text and Interpretation. Semeia* 83/84 (1998).

Cameron, Archibald. "ΘΡΕΠΤΟΣ and Related Terms in the Inscriptions of Asia Minor." Pages 27–62 in *Anatolian Studies Presented to W. H. Buckler*. Edited by William Mitchell Calder and Josef Keil. Manchester: Manchester University Press, 1939.

Carter, Michael J. D. "Archiereis and Asiarchs: A Gladiatorial Perspective." *GRBS* 44 (2004): 41–68.

———. "The Presentation of Gladiatorial Spectacles in the Greek East: Roman Culture and Greek Identity." PhD diss., McMaster University, 1999.

Chaniotis, Angelos. "Graffiti in Aphrodisias: Images—Texts—Contexts." Pages 191–207 in *Ancient Graffiti in Context*. Edited by Jennifer A. Baird and Claire Taylor. Routledge Studies in Ancient History 2. New York: Routledge, 2011

Clarke, John R. *Looking at Laughter: Humor, Power, and Transgression in Roman Visual Culture*. Berkeley: University of California Press, 2007.

Cottier, Michel, Michael H. Crawford, C. V. Crowther, Jean-Louis Ferrary, Barbara Levick, Olli Salomies, and Michael Wörrle, eds. *The Customs Law of Asia*. Oxford: Oxford University Press, 2008.

Crowther, Nigel B. "Male Beauty Contests in Greece: The Euandria and Euexia." *AC* (1985): 285–91.

Dunbabin, Katherine M. D. *The Roman Banquet: Images of Conviviality*. Cambridge: Cambridge University Press, 2003.

Eck, Werner. "The Presence, Role and Significance of Latin in the Epigraphy and Culture of the Roman Near East." Pages 15–42 in *From Hellenism to Islam: Cultural and Linguistic Change in the Roman Near East*. Edited by Hannah M. Cotton, Robert G. Hoyland, Jonathan J. Price, and David J. Wasserstein. Cambridge: Cambridge University, 2009.

Eliav, Yaron Z. "Roman Statues, Rabbis, and Greco-Roman Culture." Pages 99–116 in *Jewish Literatures and Cultures: Context and Intertext*. Edited by Anita Norich and Yaron Z. Eliav. BJS 349. Providence, RI: Brown Judaic Studies, 2008.

Eplett, Chris P. "Animal Spectacula of the Roman Empire." PhD diss., University of British Columbia, 2001.
Erdemgil, Selahattin. *Ephesus*. Istanbul: Net Turistik Yayinlar, 1986.
Feuser, Stefan. "A Stroll along the Sea: The Processional Way in Ephesus and the Littoral." *CHS Research Bulletin* 3.1 (2014): https://tinyurl.com/SBL4209c.
Finley, Moses I. *Ancient Slavery and Modern Ideology*. Edited by Brent D. Shaw. Exp. ed. Princeton: Wiener, 1998.
Friesen, Steven J. *Twice Neokoros: Ephesus, Asia and the Cult of the Flavian Imperial Family*. RGRW 116. Leiden: Brill, 1993.
Gilleland, Michael. "Commit No Nuisance." *Laudator Temporis Acti*. https://tinyurl.com/SBL4209f.
Glancy, Jennifer A. *Slavery in Early Christianity*. Oxford: Oxford University Press, 2002.
Gregory, Andrew P. "Village Society in Hellenistic and Roman Asia Minor." PhD diss., Columbia University, 1997.
Grossschmidt, Karl, and Fabian Kanz. *Gladiatoren in Ephesos: Tod am Nachmittag; Eine Ausstellung im Ephesos Museum Seluk, seit 20. April 2002*. Wein: ÖAI, 2002.
Guarducci, Margherita. *Epigrafi di carattere private*. Vol. 3 of *Epigrafia Greca*. Roma: Istituto Poligrafico dello Stato, 1974.
Harland, Philip A. "Honours and Worship: Emperors, Imperial Cults and Associations at Ephesus (First to Third Centuries CE)." *SR* 25 (1996): 319–34.
―――. *North Coast of the Black Sea, Asia Minor*. Vol. 2 of *Greco-Roman Associations: Texts, Translations and Commentary*. BZNW 204. Berlin: de Gruyter, 2014.
―――. "Victors in Competitions of Physicians—Rufinus (138–161 CE)." Associations in the Greco-Roman World: An Expanding Collection of Inscriptions, Papyri, and Other Sources in Translation. https://tinyurl.com/SBL4209b.
Harrill, J. Albert. *The Manumission of Slaves in Early Christianity*. HUT 32. Tübingen: Mohr Siebeck, 1995.
―――. *Slaves in the New Testament: Literary, Social and Moral Dimensions*. Minneapolis: Fortress, 2006.
Harrison, James R. "Artemis Triumphs over a Sorcerer's Evil Art." *NewDocs* 10:37–47.
―――. "The Erasure of Honour: Paul and the Politics of Dishonour." *TynBul* 66 (2016): 161–84.

———. "Family Honour of a Priestess of Artemis." *NewDocs* 10:30–36.

———. "The First Urban Churches: Introduction." Pages 1–40 in *Methodological Foundations*. Vol. 1 of *The First Urban Churches*. Edited by James R. Harrison and L. L. Welborn. WGRWSup 7. Atlanta: SBL Press, 2015.

———. " 'Laughter Is the Best Medicine': St. Paul, Well-Being, and Roman Humour." Pages 209–40 in *Well-Being, Personal Wholeness and the Social Fabric*. Edited by Doru Costache, Darren Cronshaw, and James R. Harrison. Newcastle upon Tyne: Cambridge Scholars Press, 2017.

———. "Paul and the *Agōnothetai* at Corinth: Engaging the Civic Values of Antiquity." Pages 271–326 in *Roman Corinth*. Vol. 2 of *The First Urban Churches*. Edited by James R. Harrison and L. L. Welborn. WGRWSup 8. Atlanta: SBL Press, 2016.

———. "Paul and the Ancient Athletic Ideal." Pages 81–110 in *Paul's World*. Edited by Stanley E. Porter. Pauline Studies 4. Leiden: Brill, 2008.

———. *Paul's Language of Grace in Its Graeco-Roman Context*. WUNT 2/172. Tübingen: Mohr Siebeck, 2003. Repr., Eugene, OR: Wipf & Stock, 2017.

———. "The Seven Sages, The Delphic Canon and Ethical Education in Antiquity." Pages 71–86 in *Ancient Education and Early Christianity*. Edited by Matthew Ryan Hauge and Andrew W. Pitts. LNTS 533. London: Bloomsbury T&T Clark, 2016.

———. "Sponsors of Paideia: Ephesian Benefactors, Civic Virtue and the New Testament." *EC* 7 (2016): 346–67.

———. "A 'Worthy' *neopoios* Thanks Artemis." *NewDocs* 10:48–54.

Horsley, Greg H. R. "A Fishing Cartel in First-Century Ephesos." *NewDocs* 5:95–114.

———. "The Inscriptions of Ephesos and the New Testament." *NovT* 34 (1992): 105–68.

———. "Joining the Household of Caesar." *NewDocs* 3:7–9.

Horst, Pieter Willem van der. *Ancient Jewish Epitaphs: An Introductory Survey of a Millennium of Jewish Funerary Epigraphy (300 BCE–700 CE)*. Kampen: Kok Pharos, 1991.

Jobst, Werner. "Das 'öffentliche Freudenhaus' in Ephesos." *JÖAI* 51 (1976/1977): 61–84.

Jones, Horace Leonard, trans. *Strabo: Geography; Books 13–14*. LCL 223. Cambridge: Harvard University Press, 1929.

Jones, Tamara. "Seating and Spectacle in the Graeco-Roman World." PhD diss., McMaster University, 2008.

Joshel, Sandra R. *Slavery in the Roman World*. Cambridge Introduction to Roman Civilization. Cambridge: Cambridge University Press, 2010.

Kalinowski, Angela V. "Patterns of Patronage: The Politics and Ideology of Public Building in the Eastern Roman Empire (31 BCE–600 CE)." PhD diss., University of Toronto, 1996.

———. "The Vedii Antonini: Aspects of Patronage and Benefaction in Second-Century Ephesos." *Phoenix* 56 (2003): 109–49.

Kearsley, Rosalinde A. "Ephesus: Neokoros of Artemis." *NewDocs* 6:203–5.

———, ed. *Greeks and Romans on Imperial Asia: Mixed Language Inscriptions and Linguistic Evidence for Cultural Interaction until the End of III AD*. IK 59. Bonn: Habelt, 2001.

———. "The Mysteries of Artemis at Ephesus." *NewDocs* 6:196–202.

Kegan, Peter. *Graffiti in Antiquity*. London: Routledge, 2014.

Keil, Josef. "Ein rätselhaftes Amulett." *JÖAI* 32 (1940): 79–84.

Kirbihler, François. "Le rôle public des femmes à Éphèse à l'époque impériale: Les femmes magistrats et liturges (Ier s.–IIIe s. apr. J.-C.)." Pages 67–92 in *Femmes, cultures et sociétés dans les civilisations méditerranéennes et proche-orientales de l'Antiquité*. Edited by Francçoise Briquel-Chatonnet et al. TOOSup 10. Paris: de Bocard, 2009.

———. "Les notables d'Éphèse: Essai d'histoire sociale (133 av. J.-C.–262 ap. J.-C.)." PhD diss., University of Tours, 2003.

———. "Some Asiarchs in Ephesos." *NewDocs* 4:46–55.

———. "Territoire civique et population d'Éphèse (Ve siècle av. J.-C.–IIIe siècle apr. J.-C.)." Pages 301–33 in *L'Asie Mineure dans l'Antiquité: Échanges, populations et territoires; Regards actuels sur une peninsula; Actes du Colloque International de Tours, 21–22 Octobre 2005*. Edited by Hadrien Bru, François Kirbihler, and Stéphane Lebreton. Rennes: Presses Universitaires de Rennes, 2009.

———. "Un cursus honorum à Éphèse? Quelques réflections sur la succession des magistratures de la cité à la époque romaine." Pages 67–107 in *Folia Graeca in honorem Edouard Will: Historica*. Edited by P. Goukowsky and C. Feyel. Études anciennes 51. Nancy: ADRA, 2012.

Kirbihler, François, and Lilli Zabrana. *Archäologische, epigraphische und numismatische Zeugnisse für den Kaiserkult im Artemision von Ephesos: Der Kult der Dea Roma und des Divus Iulius unter dem Triumvirat*. EJÖAI 83. Vienna: Österreichisches Archäologisches Institut, 2014.

Knibbe, Dieter. *EPHESUS—ΕΦΕΣΟΣ: Geschichte einer bedeutenden antiken Stadt und Portrait einer modernen Grossgrabung im 102. Jahr der*

Wiederkehr des Beginnes österreichischer Forschungen (1895–1997). Frankfurt am Main: Lang, 1998.

———. *Ephesus: Geschichte einer bedeutenden antiken Stadt und Portrait einer modernen Grossgrabung*. Frankfurt am Main: Lang, 1998.

———. "Via Sacra Ephesiaca: New Aspects of the Cult of Artemis Ephesia." Pages 141–54 in *Ephesos, Metropolis of Asia: An Interdisciplinary Approach to Its Archaeology, Religion, and Culture*. Edited by Helmut Koester. HTS 41. Valley Forge, PA: Trinity Press International, 1995.

Knibbe, Dieter, and Bülent İplikçioğlu with Friedrich Schindler. *Ephesos im Spiegel seiner Inschriften*. Vienna: Schildler, 1984.

Koester, Helmut. *Ephesos, Metropolis of Asia: An Interdisciplinary Approach to Its Archaeology, Religion, and Culture*. HTS 41. Valley Forge, PA: Trinity Press International, 1995.

Kraabel, A. Thomas. "Judaism in Western Asia Minor under the Roman Empire, with a Preliminary Study of the Jewish Community at Sardis, Lydia." PhD diss., Harvard University, 1968.

Ladstätter, Sabine, with Barbara Beck-Brandt, Martin Steskal, and Norbert Zimmermann. *Terrace House 2 in Ephesos: An Archaeological Guide*. Translated by Nicole M. High. HAG 12. Istanbul: Homer Kitabevi, 2013.

Ladstättoweverer, S. "Lampen mit Gladiatorendarstellungen aus den Hanghaüsern in Ephesos." Pages 93–95 in *Gladiatoren in Ephesos: Tod am Nachmittag; Eine Ausstellung im Ephesos Museum Seluk, seit 20. April 2002*. Edited by Karl Grossschmidt and Fabian Kanz. Wein: ÖAI, 2002.

Lampe, Peter. "The Phrygian Hinterland South of Temenothyrai (Uşak)." *EC* 7 (2016): 381–94.

Léger, Ruth M. "Artemis and Her Cult." PhD diss., University of Birmingham, 2015.

Lifshitz, Baruch. *Donateurs et fondateurs dans les synagogues juives: Répertoire des dédicaces grecques relatives à la construction et à la réflection des synagogues*. Paris: Gabalda, 1967.

Martin, Dale B. *Slavery as Salvation: The Metaphor of Slavery in Pauline Christianity*. New Haven: Yale University Press, 1990.

McGinn, Thomas. *The Economy of Prostitution in the Roman World: A Study of Social History and the Brothel*. Ann Arbor: University of Michigan Press, 2004.

Meinardus, Otto Friedrich August. "The Alleged Advertisement for the Ephesian Lupanar." *WSt* 7 (1973): 244–49.

Meriç, Recep. *Das Hinterland von Ephesos: Archäologisch-topographische Forschungen im Kaystros-Tal.* EJÖAI 12. Vienna: Österreichisches Archäologisches Institut, 2009.
Merkelbach, Reinhold. "Ephesische Parerga (12): Eine tabula lusoria für den ludus latrunculorum." *ZPE* 28 (1978): 48–50.
Miller, John F. *Apollo, Augustus, and the Poets.* Cambridge: Cambridge University Press, 2009.
Milnor, Kristina. *Graffiti and the Literary Landscape in Roman Pompeii.* Oxford: Oxford University Press, 2014.
Moore, Casey C. "Invective Drag: Talking Dirty in Catullus, Cicero, Horace and Ovid." PhD diss., University of South Carolina, 2015.
Moretti, Jean-Charles. "Graffites de la Palestre du lac à Délos." *BCH* 122 (1998): 201–12.
Mouritsen, Henrik. *The Freedmen in the Roman World.* Cambridge: Cambridge University Press, 2011.
Murphy-O'Connor, Jerome. *St. Paul's Ephesus: Texts and Archaeology.* Collegeville, MN: Liturgical Press, 2008.
Muss, Ulrike. "The Artemision in Early Christian Times." *EC* 7 (2016): 293–312.
Nani, Teresa Giulia. "ΘΡΕΠΤΟΙ." *Epigraphica* 5/6 (1943/1944): 45–84.
Ng, Diana Y. "Manipulation of Memory: Public Buildings and Decorative Programs in Roman Cities of Asia Minor." PhD diss., University of Michigan, 2007.
Ogereau, Julien. "Customs Law of the Roman Province of Asia (*Lex portorii Asiae*)." *NewDocs* 10:95–109.
Olson, Emily Victoria. "Contextualizing Roman Honorific Monuments: Statue Groups of the Imperial Family from Olympia, Ephesus and Lepta Magna." PhD diss., University of North Carolina, 2013.
Oster, Richard E. "The Ephesian Artemis as an Opponent of Early Christianity." *JAC* 19 (1976): 24–44.
———. "Ephesus as a Religious Center under the Principate, I: Paganism before Constantine." *ANRW* 18.3:1661–728.
———. "Holy Days in Honour of Artemis." *NewDocs* 4:74–82.
Park, Joseph S. *Conceptions of Afterlife in Jewish Inscriptions with Special Reference to Pauline Literature.* WUNT 2/121. Tübingen: Mohr Siebeck, 2000.
Paton, W. R., ed. and trans. *The Greek Anthology.* 5 vols. LCL 67–68, 84–86. Cambridge: Harvard University Press, 1916–1918.

Pleket, Harry W. "Nine Greek Inscriptions from the Cayster-Valley in Lydia: A Republication." *Talanta* 2 (1970): 55–88.

Portefaix, Lilian. "Ancient Ephesus: Processions as Media of Religious and Secular Propaganda." Pages 195–210 in *The Problem of Ritual: Based on Papers Read at the Symposium on Religious Rites Held at Åbo, Finland, on the Thirteenth–Sixteenth of August 1991*. Edited by Tore Ahlbäck. SIDA 15. Åbo: Donner Institute, 1993.

Rathmayr, Elisabeth. "Die Präsenz des Ktistes Androklos in Ephesos." *AÖAWPH* 145 (2010): 19–60.

———. "The Significance of Sculptures with Associated Inscriptions in Private Houses in Ephesos, Pergamon, and Beyond." Pages 146–78 in *Inscriptions in the Private Sphere in the Greco-Roman World*. Edited by Rebecca Benefiel and Peter Keegan. BSGRE 7. Leiden: Brill, 2015.

Rich, John, and Andrew Wallace-Hadrill, eds. *City and Country in the Ancient World*. London: Routledge, 1991.

Ricl, Marijana. "Legal and Social Status of *Threptoi* and Related Categories in Narrative and Documentary Sources." Pages 93–114 in *From Hellenism to Islam: Cultural and Linguistic Change in the Roman Near East*. Edited by Hannah M. Cotton, Robert G. Hoyland, Jonathan J. Price, and David J. Wasserstein. Cambridge: Cambridge University Press, 2009.

Robert, Louis. *Les gladiateurs dans l'orient grec*. Amsterdam: Hakkert, 1971.

———. "Sur des inscriptions d'Éphèse: Fêtes, athlètes, empereurs, épigrammes." *RevPhil* 41 (1967): 7–84.

Robinson, Thomas A. *Who Were the First Christians? Dismantling the Urban Thesis*. Oxford: Oxford University Press, 2017.

Rogers, Guy MacLean. "The Constructions of Women at Ephesos." *ZPE* 90 (1992): 215–23.

———. *The Mysteries of Artemis of Ephesos: Cult, Polis, and Change in the Graeco-Roman World*. Synkrisis. New Haven: Yale University Press, 2012.

———. *The Sacred Identity of Ephesos: Foundation Myths of a Roman City*. London: Routledge, 1991.

Rose, Charles Brian. *Dynastic Commemoration and Imperial Portraiture in the Julio-Claudian Period*. Cambridge: Cambridge University Press, 1997.

Roueché, Charlotte. "Images of Performance: New Evidence from Ephesus." Pages 254–81 in *Greek and Roman Actors: Aspects of an Ancient*

Profession. Edited by Pat Easterling and Edith Hall. Cambridge: Cambridge University Press, 2002.
Scherrer, Peter. *Ephesus: The New Guide*. Translated by Lionel Bier and George M. Luxon. Rev. ed. Istanbul: Ege Yayinlan, 2000.
Servadei, Cristina. "Graffiti con schemi di gioco nell'agorà di Iasos: Esempi dalla stoà orientale." Pages 16–22 in *Il tempio distilo d'età ecatomnide e l'architettura ionica*. Vol. 1 of *Iasos: L'area a sud dell'agorà*. Edited by Nicoló Masturzo. Archaeologica 176. MAII 6. Rome: Bretschneider, 2016.
Shaner, Katherine Ann. *Enslaved Leadership in Early Christianity*. Oxford: Oxford University Press, 2017.
———. "The Religious Practices of the Enslaved: A Case Study of Roman Ephesos." ThD diss., Harvard Divinity School, 2012.
Slater, William J. "The Pantomine Iulius Apolaustus." *GRBS* 36 (1995): 263–92.
Small, Alastair. "The Shrine of the Imperial Family in the Macellum at Pompeii." Pages 115–41 in *Subject and Ruler: The Cult of the Ruling Power in Classical Antiquity*. Edited by Alastair Small. JRASup 17. Ann Arbor, MI: Journal of Roman Archaeology, 1996.
Steskal, Martin, and Martino La Torre. *Das Vediusgymnasium in Ephesos: Archäologie und Baubefund*. FiE 14.1. Vienna: ÖAW, 2008.
Stevenson, Gregory. *Power and Place: Temple and Identity in the Book of Revelation*. BZNW 107. Berlin: de Gruyter, 2001.
Strelan, Rick. *Paul, Artemis, and the Jews in Ephesus*. BZNW 80. Berlin: de Gruyter, 1995.
Strocka, Volker Michael. "The Celsus Library in Ephesus." Pages 33–43 in *Ancient Libraries in Anatolia: Libraries of Hattusha, Pergamon, Ephesus, Nysa*. Ankara: Middle East Technical University Library, 2003.
———. *Die Wandermalerei der Hanghäuser in Ephesos*. FiE 8.1. Vienna: ÖAW, 1977.
Strubbe, Johan, ed. *ΑΡΑΙ ΕΠΙΤΥΜΒΙΟΙ: Imprecation against Desecrators of the Grave in the Greek Epitaphs of Asia Minor; A Catalogue*. IK 52. Bonn: Habelt, 1997.
Swift, L. J., and J. H. Oliver. "Constantius II on Flavius Philippus." *AJP* 83 (1962): 247–64.
Taeuber, Hans. "Graffiti." Pages 122–25, 472–78 in *Das Hanghaus 2 in Ephesos: Die Wohneinheit 6; Baubefund, Ausstattung, Funde*. Edited by Hilke Thür and Friedrich Krinzinger. FiE 8.9. Vienna: ÖAW, 2010.
Theissen, Werner. *Christen in Ephesos: Die historiche und theologische Situ-*

ation in vorpaulinischer und paulinischer Zeit und zur Zeit der Apostelgeschichte und der Pastoralbriefe. Tübingen: Franke, 1990.

Thür, Hilke. "Der ephesische Ktistes Androklos und (s)ein Heroon am Embolos." *JÖAI* 64 (1995): 63–104.

———. "The Processional Way in Ephesos as a Place of Cult and Burial." Pages 157–200 in *Ephesos, Metropolis of Asia: An Interdisciplinary Approach to Its Archaeology, Religion, and Culture*. Edited by Helmut Koester. HTS 41. Valley Forge, PA: Trinity Press International, 1995.

Tilborg, Sjef van. *Reading John in Ephesus*. NovTSup 83. Leiden: Bill, 1996.

Tomson, Peter J. *Paul and the Jewish Law: Halakha in the Letters of the Apostle to the Gentiles*. Assen: Van Gorcum, 1990.

Topai, Cengiz. *Ephesus Museum Selçuk*. Translated by P. Rhode. Istanbul: BKG, 2010.

Trebilco, Paul. *The Early Christians in Ephesus from Paul to Ignatius*. WUNT 166. Tübingen: Mohr Siebeck, 2004. Repr., Grand Rapids: Eerdmans, 2007.

———. *Jewish Communities in Asia Minor*. SNTSMS 69. Cambridge: Cambridge University Press, 1991.

Treggiari, Susan. *Roman Freedmen during the Late Republic*. Oxford: Clarendon, 1969.

Wallace, Rex E. *An Introduction to Wall Inscriptions from Pompeii and Herculaneum*. Wauconda: Bolchazy-Carducci, 2005.

Westermann, William Linn. *The Slave Systems of Greek and Roman Antiquity*. Philadelphia: American Philosophical Society, 1955.

White, L. Michael. "Urban Development in Social Change and Imperial Ephesos." Pages 27–79 in *Ephesos, Metropolis of Asia: An Interdisciplinary Approach to Its Archaeology, Religion, and Culture*. Edited by Helmut Koester. HTS 41. Valley Forge, PA: Trinity Press International, 1995.

Wiedemann, Thomas. *Greek and Roman Slavery*. London: Croom Helm, 1981.

Wiplinger, Gilbert, and Gudrun Wlach. *Ephesus: One Hundred Years of Austrian Research*. Vienna: ÖAI, 1996.

Yamauchi, Edwin M. *New Testament Cities in Asia Minor: Light from Archaeology on Cities of Paul and the Seven Churches*. Grand Rapids: Baker, 1980. Repr., Eugene, OR: Wipf & Stock, 2003.

Zabehlicky, Heinrich. "Preliminary Views of the Ephesian Harbor." Pages 201–15 in *Ephesos, Metropolis of Asia: An Interdisciplinary Approach to*

Its Archaeology, Religion, and Culture. Edited by Helmut Koester. HTS 41. Valley Forge, PA: Trinity Press International, 1995.

Zimmermann, Norbert, and Sabine Ladstätter, eds. *Wall Painting in Ephesos from the Hellenistic to the Byzantine Period*. Istanbul: Ege Yayinlari, 2011.

Zülkadiroglu, A., and C. Içten. "Gladiatorenreliefs in der Ausstellung." Pages 75–82 in *Gladiatoren in Ephesos: Tod am Nachmittag; Eine Ausstellung im Ephesos Museum Seluk, seit 20. April 2002*. Edited by Karl Grossschmidt and Fabian Kanz. Wein: ÖAI, 2002.

An Ephesian Tale:
Mystery Cults, Reverse Theological Engineering, and the Triumph of Christianity in Ephesus

Guy MacLean Rogers

Over the last one hundred years or so, many scholars and theologians have argued that the rise and development of Christianity out of Judaism was linked somehow to the popularity of Greco-Roman mystery cults during the Hellenistic and early Roman imperial periods.[1] At least some historians connected these contemporaneous religious phenomena because they argued that ancient Greco-Roman mystery cults were *Erlösungsreligionen*, or religions of salvation, in the same way that Christianity (allegedly) was.[2] Both mystery cults and early Christianity offered adherents the possibility of avoiding death or of having some kind life after death.

More recently, however, Walter Burkert argued against the idea that mystery cults promised to help against the reality of death for humans or gave them any hope of some kind of rebirth or resurrection.[3] There is no conclusive "pagan" evidence that the vast majority of initiates into Greco-Roman mystery cults believed that their initiations would help against the certainty of death or lead to some kind of rebirth.[4] Although initiations into the mysteries of some gods and goddesses did involve the

---

I would like to dedicate this article to the memory of my late friend Dieter Knibbe.

1. E.g., Odo Casel, *The Mystery of the Christian Worship*, ed. Burkhard Neunheuser (London: Darton, Longman & Todd, 1962; repr., New York: Crossroad, 1999).

2. Richard Reitzenstein, *Die hellenistischen Mysterienreligionen nach ihren Grundgedanken und Wirkungen* (Stuttgart: Teubner, 1910).

3. Walter Burkert, *Ancient Mystery Cults* (Cambridge: Harvard University Press 1987), 23, 29.

4. The Eleusinian mysteries may be a partial exception; see Burkert, *Ancient Mystery Cults*, 90–92, 100–101.

promise of *sōtēria* (safety, salvation), the kind of *sōtēria* sought in these cults by initiates was a here-and-now kind of salvation.[5] What most initiates were seeking from their initiations into the mysteries was help or aid while they were still among the living.

Why does the question of the relationship between early Christianity and ancient mystery cults matter to anyone, apart from a few academic specialists in the histories of ancient polytheism and early Christianity? The proposed link between ancient mystery cults and early Christianity might matter, not only to scholars but also to the broader public, because, if such a link could be proved, it could help to explain the still largely puzzling historical development whereby large numbers of polytheists eventually became monotheists of the Abrahamic tradition(s).

Mystery cults in Ephesus and elsewhere in the Greco-Roman World should be studied first of all for their own sake(s), if for no other reason than the fact that the evidence for such cults dates from the archaic period, hundreds of years before the (r)evolution of Christianity out of Judaism during the first century CE. Mystery cults are integral to the study of Greco-Roman civilization itself. But their collective story may nevertheless be part of a hugely important one for world history, too—in fact, the largest and most significant narrative about the relationship between the ancient and modern worlds, namely, how it came to pass that the majority of people living on the face of the earth today are monotheists of one of the Abrahamic traditions, as every survey of the religious affiliations of the more than seven billion people alive today indicates.[6]

So what do we know about the existence of mystery cults in Ephesus, one of the most important cities (*poleis*) of the Greco-Roman World? Can the evidence for those cults there be used to establish either ritual or theological links to or with nascent Christianity in Ephesus? Can the history of mystery cults in Ephesus help us to understand how and why a Roman Empire largely of polytheists eventually became one of monotheists?

The vast majority of the surviving evidence for mystery cults in Ephesus relates to the celebration of the mysteries of Artemis. I will discuss some of that evidence below. But first I would like to explore briefly some of the other mystery cults in the city, in part because so little scholarly attention has been paid to them in the past.

---

5. On the benefits of initiation into the mysteries of Isis and Sarapis, see Burkert, *Ancient Mystery Cults*, 16.
6. See https://www.census.gov/popclock/.

Mystery cults may have existed in Ephesus before the fifth century BCE, but there is no conclusive evidence for their existence before that time. In fact, it is not until we reach the fourth century BCE that we begin to find irrefutable indications of the existence of such cults, and the preponderance of evidence for these cults dates to the early Roman Empire. Of course, these conclusions may be a function of the random survival of evidence. But the absence of unequivocal epigraphical, numismatic, archaeological, or literary evidence for mystery cults in Ephesus before the fifth century BCE suggests that such cults did not exist in the city during the archaic and early classical periods. How and why these cults appeared in the city after the fifth century BCE remain questions that I hope to address elsewhere. Whenever and however mystery cults (other than those of Artemis) arose, the best attested of the mystery cults in Ephesus are those of Demeter and Kore (and the Sebastoi or Roman emperors), Dionysos, Aphrodite Daitis, and possibly Samothrace.

In inscriptions dated to the reign of Tiberius, references to "Demetriastai" or "before the city Demetriastai," may suggest that the Demetriastai before the polis were members of an association of initiates, because later we find "Demetriastai before the polis" and *mystai* of Dionysus Phleus mentioned together in an inscription found in the then-village of "Ayasoluk" (Selçuk) (IEph 5.1595, ll. 3–6; 7.2.4337, ll. 10, 27). In the inscription from the reign of Tiberius, the worshipers of Demeter arranged for images or statues of their benefactors to be set up in a publicly visible place (IEph 7.2.4337).[7] As Jeanne and Louis Roberts argued many years ago, Demetriastai "before the city" does not mean initiates who were somehow physically based or located in front of the city but initiates who represented themselves collectively as defenders of the polis.[8]

A priestess of Sebaste Demeter Karpophoros named Servilia Secunda is also mentioned in the inscription from the reign of Tiberius, in which the Demetriastai in the polis honored benefactors who were also priests and priestesses (IEph 7.2.4337, l. 17). Given her name, Servilia Secunda was probably a Roman citizen herself, or the priestess at least came from a family of Roman citizens.

---

7. Philip A Harland, *Associations, Synagogues, and Congregations: Claiming a Place in Ancient Mediterranean Society* (Minneapolis: Fortress, 2003), 117.

8. See Jeanne Robert and Louis Robert, *Exploration, histoire, monnaies et inscriptions Paris*, vol. 1 of *Fouilles d'Amyzon en Carie* (Paris: de Boccard, 1983), 172–76; Robert and Louis, "Bulletin épigraphique," *REG* 96 (1983): 387.

From a letter to the Roman proconsul Lucius Mestrius Florus from Lucius Pompeius Apollonius, dated from after 88 or 89 CE, we know that *mystēria* and sacrifices were performed in Ephesus by *mystai* or initiates (along with the priestesses) to Demeter Karpophoros (Fruitbearer), Demeter Thesmophoros (Lawbearer), and the god emperors each year with great purity and lawful customs (IEph 2.213, ll. 3–8). In the letter, Apollonius went on to assert that the practices were protected by kings and emperors as well as the proconsul of the period, as contained in their enclosed letters (IEph 2.213, ll. 8–11).

The letter thus indicates that mysteries and sacrifices to Demeter Karpophoros and Thesmophoros and to the Roman emperors were being made by initiates by the late first century CE. Moreover, the mysteries and sacrifices, at least those to Demeter Karpophoros and Thesmophoros, must date to the period when Ephesus was under the power of kings, although we do not know how far back into the time before the formation of the Roman province of Asia and Ephesus's incorporation into that province the practices date. Also, there was some kind of written record or dossier of letters acknowledging the rights of the initiates available to be cited by Apollonius on behalf of the initiates. An altar dedicated to the god emperors and to the *mystai* by Serapion, the secretary of the boule and his children, probably to be dated to the reign of Antoninus Pius, demonstrates that the imperial mysteries were celebrated at least into the mid-second century CE (IEph 5.1506, ll. 1–9).

An inscription from the late first century or early second century CE then mentions a priest for life of Dionysus Phleus (T. Varius Nikostratos) and a priest for life of the Eleusinian goddesses (C. Licinnius Maximus [IEph 4.1270]). These goddesses surely must be Demeter and Kore, and the inscription suggests mysteries in some sense related to those performed at Eleusis outside of Athens (although details are not specified). Another inscription, dated to 120 CE, refers to Rutilius Bassus, a priest of Demeter Karpophoros (IEph 4.1210).[9] The inscription from 120 CE refers to the dedication of a *naos* of Demeter and the things in front of it by Rutilius Bassus (IEph 4.1210, ll. 1–12). An altar of Pluto, Demeter Karpophoros, and Kore was found on the southeast slope of Panayirdag (IEph 4.1228, ll. 1–3).

---

9. Cf. IEph 4.1233; 5.1486, possibly 1538; 6.2038; 7.1.3217b, l. 20.

There are then references to "Demetriastai before the polis," to *mystai* of Dionysus Phleus (IEph 5.1595, ll. 3–6), and to mysteries of Demeter in the endowment inscription of the priest of Demeter P. Aelius Menekrates for Demeter and the god Men dated to ca. 140 CE (IEph 7.1.3252, ll. 6–7). In the inscription Menekrates is honored for having dedicated income from shops he owned to buy a basket set in silver for use during the procession that took place during the celebration of Demeter's mysteries (ll. 11–12).[10] He also dedicated a silver sign to be carried in processions preceding the mysteries and sacred banquet for the god Men (ll. 7–11).[11]

During the reign of Commodus, from a list of priests who belonged to some kind of cult association, we know of the existence of a priest of Demeter and also of Kore (IEph 5.1600, l. 63; cf. l. 47). Another imperial era inscription refers to *Koure Plouteos* (IEph 6.2104, l. 3). This should mean the Kore is envisioned as giving wealth. Finally, there is a reference to Demeter Karpotokos (Giving birth to fruit), in a late antique dedicatory inscription of Flavius Anthemius Isidorus (IEph 4.1305, l. 5).

All of the explicit evidence for the celebrations of mysteries of Dionysus begins after the battle of Actium. Around 25 or 24 BCE Presbon, the son of Antaios was priest of Dionysus Phleus Poimantrios (Shepherding the Flock) (IEph 1a.9b, l. 17; 3.902, ll. 6, 15–16).[12] At the end of the first century CE, or at the beginning of the second century, there was a priest for life of Dionysus Phleus, T. Ouarios Neikostratos, (a cult associated with that of the Eleusinian gods) (IEph 4.1270, ll. 3–6). During the reign of Trajan a Dionysian association dedicated a monument of some kind to Dionysus and to Trajan; some scholars have speculated that this inscription perhaps implies that Trajan himself was a member of the association of worshippers (IEph 7.1.3329, ll. 1–3).[13] The appearance of a *palaios gerōn*

---

10. For discussion, see Harry W. Pleket, "Nine Greek Inscriptions from the Cayster-Valley in Lydia," *Talanta* 2 (1970): 61–75, no. 4; Marc Kleijwegt, "Textile Manufacturing for a Religious Market: Artemis and Diana as Tycoons of Industry," in *After the Past: Essays in Ancient History in Honour of H. W. Pleket*, ed. Willem Jongman and Marc Kleijwegt, MnemSup 233 (Leiden: Brill, 2002), 115.

11. For worship of the Phrygian god Men in Asia Minor, see Eugene N. Lane, "Men: A Neglected Cult of Roman Asia Minor," *ANRW* 18.3:2161–74.

12. Presbon was prytanis of the polis in 26 or 25 BCE. For Dionysus Phleus, see Reinhold Merkelbach, *Die Hirten des Dionysos: Die Dionysos-Mysterien der römischen Kaiserzeit und der bukolische Roman des Longus* (Stuttgart: Teubner, 1988), 19–20 nn. 16 and 17.

13. Harland, *Associations, Synagogues, and Congregations*, 156.

(some kind of cultic position) in the inscription may signify that the association was one involved in the celebration of the mysteries of Dionysus, although this is not certain (IEph 7.1.3329, ll. 4–5).[14]

During the reign of Hadrian, Dionysius Periegetes refers to Dionysian choruses of dancing women in Ephesus (*Geog.* 826–842).[15] An inscription from the agora attests to the celebration of a winter festival in honor of Dionysus between 140 and 150 CE, and another, undated inscription from the agora refers to a Baccheion, where the devotees of the cult perhaps assembled (IEph 3.661, l. 20; 2.434, ll. 1–2). Because of inscriptions that were perhaps originally incised somewhere in or around the banqueting hall on Panayirdag or on the wall revetments of the single room building directly south of it, Keil argued that there was at least one meeting place of devotees of Dionysus on the Panayirdag.[16] Strabo tells us that the association of the *technitai* (artists) of Dionysus was based in Ephesus after fleeing from Teos, and we know from an inscription dated to the reign of Pius that the *technitai* about Dionysus were present in the city at the time (Strabo, *Geog.* 14.1.29; IEph 1a.22, ll. 35–36). C. Flavius Furius Aptus was perhaps a priest in the cult of Dionysus Oreios Bacchios during the reign of Marcus or Commodus.[17]

There were mysteries of Dionysus celebrated during the reign of Hadrian, and there was an association of initiates called "the initiates before the polis" (IEph 2.275, ll. 7–8). The association included a priest of Dionysus (IEph 2.275, l. 8), a hierophant (IEph 2.275, ll. 9–10), an *epimelētēs* (a manager [IEph 2.275, ll. 10–11]), a *mystagōgos* (a leader of initiates [IEph 2.275, ll. 8, 13]), and a *hymnōdos* (a choral singer [IEph 2.275, ll. 14]). An undated inscription refers to a dedication of wands to Dionysus by the hierophant Mundicius and his son the agonothete Mundicius (IEph 4.1211, ll. 1–8).

In addition, many fragments of lists of the *mystai* of Dionysus before the polis during the reign of Hadrian have been found in the theatre of

---

14. See also the editors' note in IEph.

15. See Richard E. Oster, "Ephesus as a Religious Center under the Principate, I," *ANRW* 18.3:1674.

16. For the initiates, see IEph 5.1601, 1602.

17. IEph 2.502, ll. 6–8; 2.502a, ll. 4–6; 3.675, ll. 4–5; 3.834, l. 9?; 4.1099.1, ll. 1–3; 4.1099.2, ll. 1–2; 4.1267, ll. 1–2; 5.1932a, ll. 1–2; 7.1.3064, ll. 1–3. The epithet *Oreios* (of the mountain) is probably a reference to Dionysus's role as leader of bacchants on mountains.

Ephesus (IEph 5.1601, 1602). In these lists there are references to a priest (IEph 5.1601a, l. 4), an official who was *enthronios* ("enthroned" [5.1601a, l. 7]), a *hydraulos* (a musician of some kind [5.1601a, l. 8]), a *hieroslogos* (a declaimer of a sacred story [5.1601a, l. 9]), a *thyrsophoros* (a wand bearer [5.1601e, l. 4]),[18] and many other individuals who sacrificed (5.1601a, l. 2). An undated inscription refers to *boukoloi* (cowherds) of Dionysus in the form of a bull (IEph 4.1268, ll. 1 and 4).[19] In the bouleuterion of the upper city, the figure of a silenus (one of Dionysus's usual companions) supports the construction of the *skēnē* building; on the head of the silenus, there is a basket (*kistē* or *liknon*) in which there is a phallus and crescent.[20] The most striking image in artistic representations of the celebrations of Dionysian mysteries generally is the erect phallus in a winnowing basket.[21] A reference to Achilles Tatius's hero Leucippe (wearing the clothing of Melite during an all-night festival), who is called a bacchant by Sosthenes, may imply that at least part of the Dionysian mysteries were celebrated at night after the mid-second century CE (*Leuc. Clit* 6.4–5).

During the reign of Commodus, the *sakephoroi*[22] *mustai*,[23] emperor-lovers, of the *propatoros* (founder) god Dionysos Koreseitos honored the new Dionysos (Commodus) with a statue (IEph 2.293, ll. 4–8). The reference to Koreseitos may indicate that there was a sanctuary for Dionysus connected with this cult in the section of Ephesus known as Koressos.[24]

A list of priests, probably of members of an association for the worship of Dionysus, from the reign of Commodus names G. Ioulios Epagathos as a priest of the founder god Dionysus (as well as Dios Panhellenios and Hephaistos [IEph 5.1600, ll. 2–4]).[25] This inscription perhaps means that

---

18. For another wand bearer, see IEph 4.1268, l. 2; 5.1982, l. 6.

19. For the *boukoloi* elsewhere in Asia Minor, see Harland, *Associations, Synagogues, and Congregations*, 49.

20. Maria Aurenhammer, "Sculptures of Gods and Heroes from Ephesos," in *Ephesos, Metropolis of Asia: An Interdisciplinary Approach to Its Archaeology, Religion, and Culture*, ed. Helmut Koester, HTS 41 (Valley Forge, PA: Trinity Press International, 1995), 269.

21. Walter Burkert, *Greek Religion* (Cambridge: Harvard University Press, 1985), 95.

22. Wearing the coarse, goat-hair cloth of the sect.

23. The same title of the association appears in IEph 4.1250, l. 1.

24. See Aurenhammer, "Sculptures of Gods and Heroes," 267.

25. Epagathos was also a prytanis, secretary of the demos, and *hymnōdos*, *boularchos*, and *architektōn* of the goddess, as stated in IEph 5.1600, ll. 4–7; cf. 4.1061, ll. 2–8,

we should understand there to have been mysteries of Dionysus, Zeus Panhellenios,[26] and Hephaistos at the time. In the list also appears (probably) the office of the hagnearch (IEph 5.1600, ll. 8, 52, 54), an *epimelētēs* of the mysteries (ll. 10–11), and a hierophant (l. 33).

The priest of Dionysus Phleus T. Ouarios Neikostratos was a Roman citizen and secretary of the demos of Ephesus (IEph 4.1270, ll. 3–5; 2.476, l. 1). The priest of the cult of Dionysus during the reign of Hadrian, Claudius Romulus, was a Roman citizen and also a prytanis sometime between 100 and 103 CE (IEph 2.275, l. 9; 4.1020, ll. 1–3).[27] The hierophant Claudius Eubios was also a Roman citizen (IEph 2.275, ll. 9–10), and the Roman citizen and *epimelētēs* of the mysteries M. Antonius Drosus (IEph 2.275, ll. 10–11) had dedicated a statue of an athlete (IEph 4.1129, ll. 2–6) and also appears repeatedly in a list of *mystai* of Dionysus for the polis (IEph 5.1601a, l. 3 and passim). The leader of the initiates Theodotos Proklion was a peregrine, as was his choral singer son, Proklos (IEph 2.275, ll. 12–14). M. Aurelius Menemachus, the priest in the cult of Dionysus from the reign of Commodus, was also a high priest (asiarch) and prytanis (IEph 1a.47, l. 26; 2.293, ll. 8–10; 4.1075 ll. 6–9). C. Flavius Furius Aptus, perhaps a priest in the cult of Dionysus Oreios Bacchios, was alytarch of the Ephesian Olympics as well as the owner of luxury apartment 6 in Terrace House 2, which featured two statues of Aphrodite that flanked the staircase that led from the atrium of the apartment to a private basilica

---

in which Epagathos appears as prytanis, gymnasiarch, *philosebastos hymnōdos*, secretary of the demos, *boularchos, eirēnarchos, agoranomos*, and *architekton* of the goddess in the prytaneion. The god Pan is also mentioned in line 48 of the inscription, leading some scholars to conclude that worship of Pan, who by tradition had nourished Dionysus, was incorporated into the celebration of Dionysus's mysteries; see Aurenhammer, "Sculptures of Gods and Heroes," 269. In the Kunsthistorisches Museum in Vienna, there is a statue group of Pan with the infant Dionysus from Ephesus, confirming the linkage during the Roman imperial period to which the group belongs.

26. Zeus Patroios had been worshipped in Ephesus since the fifth century BCE; there seems to have been some kind of sanctuary for Zeus on Panayirdag, as we can tell from a series of inscriptions found (or emanating from) there, including a fifth century BCE stele for Zeus Patroios and Apollo Patroios (IEph 2.101), an inscription from ca. 300 BCE under a relief (which shows Meter and Apollo) that mentions Zeus Patroios and Apollo (2.102), and two fifth-century BCE inscription that both mention a *hieron* of Zeus Patroios (2.103, 104).

27. Another priest of Dionysus Phleus for life, T. Ouarios Neikostratos, who was also a secretary (IEph 2.476), is mentioned in IEph 4.1270, ll. 3–5, an inscription from the late first or early second century CE.

(IEph 2.502, ll. 6–8; 2.502a, ll. 4–6; 4.1099.1, ll. 1–3; 4.1099.2, ll. 1–2).[28] In fact, Dionysian imagery is found all over Terrace House 2, whose inhabitants belonged to the socioeconomic elite of imperial Ephesus, and an approximately 2-meter tall statue of Dionysus was set up in a prominent location at a fountain house on the north side of the *embolos*.[29]

An inscription from the reign of Commodus indicates that by the late second century CE, the *mystai* of Dionysus Phleus[30] were associated with the Demetriastai before the polis (IEph 5.1595, ll. 2–6). At the time, the association included a priest (for life), the Roman citizen T. Aurelius Plutarchos (IEph 5.1595, ll. 2–7), the hierophant and Roman citizen P. Claudius Aristophanes (IEph 5.1595, ll. 7–9), and the *epimelētēs* Saturneilos (IEph 5.1595, ll. 9–12).

In the list of priests from Commodus's reign, Epagathos was also a prytanis, secretary of the demos, and *hymnōdos*, *boularchos*, and *architektōn* of the goddess (IEph 5.1600, ll. 4–7). The hierophant Patroklos was a peregrine (IEph 5.1600, l. 33). In the lists of *mystai* of Dionysus before the polis, the Roman citizen M. Aurelius Drosos was an *epimelētēs* of the mysteries (IEph 2.275, ll. 10–11) and dedicated a statue of an athlete (4.1129, ll. 2–6). M. Antonius Artemidorus was *ergepistatēs pythionikēs hiereus* (some kind of superintendent of cultic works [IEph 2.276, ll. 16–18]). Unfortunately, the lists are too fragmentary for us to establish how many of the *mystai* were Roman citizens and what public offices they held.

Images of Greek-styled Aphrodite were the most popular of all ideal sculpture(s) types in the city during the Hellenistic and Roman periods.[31] We also know that there was a temenos of the goddess and a temple of Aphrodite Hetaira.[32] But we know nothing about the details of Aphrodite's mysteries. Our only tangible piece of evidence is that during the third century CE, there were brother and sister initiates of Aphrodite Daitis who had set up an altar for the goddess (IEph 4.1202, ll. 1–7).[33] Aphrodite

---

28. Aurenhammer, "Sculptures of Gods and Heroes," 261.

29. The statue is now displayed in the Ephesus Museum in Selçuk, inv. no. 769.

30. Dionysus Phleus also appears in IEph 3.902, ll. 6–7, in a list of priests dated to the last quarter of the first century BCE.

31. Aurenhammer, "Sculptures of Gods and Heroes," 260.

32. Polyaenus, *Strat.* 5.18; Athenaeus, *Deipn.* 13.573a. Near the southern edge of the Roman imperial-era harbor, there also seems to have been a shrine of Aphrodite related to an association of merchants from Rhodes. But we have no idea whether this shrine was connected to the celebration of mysteries.

33. For the cult, see Josef Keil, "Aphrodite Daitis," *JÖAI* 17 (1914): 145–47; Kurt

Daitis has been identified with Aphrodite Automata or Epidaetida mentioned by Servius, but this is not certain.³⁴

Finally, in the "Customs Law" for the province of Asia, which has been dated between 54 and 59 CE, there is mention of a Samothrakion (IEph 1a.20.70–71). This shrine has not been discovered, but its existence should indicate the celebration of rites, perhaps, *mystēria* in honor of the well-known Samothracian gods in Ephesus, by the mid-first century CE.

Thus there were mysteries of Demeter and Kore, the Roman emperors, Dionysus, Aphrodite, and (probably) the Samothracian gods celebrated at one time or another in Ephesus. Most of the evidence for the existence of these cults and the activities of their supporters comes from the Roman imperial period. Whether that is a result of (changing?) epigraphic habits or the histories of the cults themselves is unknown. Detailed analysis of the cults, however, reveals organizational differences among them and different rituals, which should probably be connected to the very different sacred stories (*hieroi logoi*) about the individual gods and goddesses that formed part of the theological background to the cults. Most importantly for the topic of this paper (that is, opening up for discussion the question of the relationship between mystery cults in Ephesus and early Christianity), however, the evidence may seem dissatisfying. If some or any kind of salvation was offered to initiates into the cults of Demeter and Kore, the Roman emperors, Dionysus, Aphrodite, and the Samothracian gods, that is not revealed in the mainly epigraphical, imperial-era evidence that we have for them.

On the other hand, some of the inscriptions do show that there were people who advertised (epigraphically) group identities related to these cults that they carried with them after they took part in whatever rites comprised the celebrations of the various mysteries. The initiates into the cults of Demeter and Dionysus, who later, at least, allowed themselves to be represented epigraphically as "for the city," made a series of collective claims to roles as defenders of the polis. It is therefore not the case, as we have so often read or been told, that initiates into these cults only formed individual ritual or theological identities, such as *mystēs* or *mystai* (the title of initiates across many mystery cults), that only applied to the time periods of the initiations. Group identities related to specific activities and

---

Latte, "Aphrodite in Ephesos," *AR* 17 (1914): 678–79; Dieter Knibbe and Bülent İplikçioğlu, "Neue Inschriften aus Ephesos VIII," *JÖAI* 53 (1981/1982): 147, no. 164.

34. Oster, "Ephesus as a Religious Center," 1667–68.

values, such as the Demetriastai *pro poleōs* were formed (and later represented epigraphically), and thus the sizes, activities, and values of these groups can be compared to those of early Christian groups in Ephesus and elsewhere. Interestingly, it has recently become clear as a result of a massive study of early Christianity in Ephesus that we should be speaking not about early Christianity but perhaps about multiple Christianities at the very same time, since we know that there were Pauline and Johannine (and other) Christian groups operating within the city during the second half of the first century CE (and before).[35]

Still yet another pattern emerges. Behind the organizational, ritual, and theological differences among the mystery cults for which we have evidence, a consistent sociopolitical profile of those who were involved in the cults comes into focus, based upon comparative prosopographical research. Almost all of the men and women who subsidized and took part in these cults at the level of performing rituals were well-off Roman citizens of Ephesus. The significance of this is related to another important question about mystery cults that may have implications for evaluating whether the people who were involved in subsidizing and performing in such cults were possible candidates for experimentation with other cults or systems of religious belief such as early Christianity or Christianities. Based upon the evidence we have thus far, the men and women who participated in the celebration of the mysteries of Demeter and Kore, the Roman emperors, Dionysus, Aphrodite, and the Samothracian gods were thoroughly integrated into the societal structures of euergetism and political status seeking of the Greco-Roman polis.

Of course, we cannot rule out the possibility that some members of Ephesus's socioeconomic elite might have had an interest in Judaism and/or nascent Christianity, as we know was the case elsewhere. But the epigraphical evidence at any rate suggests that the citizens such as P. Aelius Menekrates, who subsidized the basket for use during the procession during the celebration of Demeter's mysteries, wanted to have advertised publicly their support of these cults and their own integration into the status structures and hierarchies of the polis, the province, and the Roman Empire.

---

35. Paul Trebilco, *The Early Christians in Ephesus from Paul to Ignatius*, WUNT 166 (Tübingen: Mohr Siebeck, 2004; repr., Grand Rapids: Eerdmans, 2007), 101–3, 152–54, 196, 235–36, 292, 347–50, 402–3, 443–45, 503–6, 586–88, 626–27, 681–83, 711, 712–17.

A third conclusion follows from our brief chronological review of the evidence for these other mystery cults in the city. At present there is no evidence for the continued existence of these cults after the mid- to late third century CE. Why all of these cults seem to disappear together at the same time during the mid- to late third century CE is a question to which I will return below.

But what about the celebrations of the mysteries of Artemis of Ephesus? Could those celebrations or the experiences of the initiates into Artemis's mysteries in Ephesus be seen as somehow providing a ritual or theological bridge to the rise of Christianity in the city?

Mysteries of Artemis may have been celebrated in Ephesus during the archaic or early classical periods. But no literary, epigraphic, or archaeological evidence substantiates the existence of such celebrations during these time periods. Rather our first piece of tangible evidence for the existence of mysteries of Artemis dates to the reign of Commodus, an inscription that refers back, however, to the foundation of the polis of Arsinoe on what would become the physical site of Hellenistic and Roman Ephesus (IEph 1a.26, ll. 2–3). The inscription makes reference to mysteries and sacrifices and the erection of a temple and a cult statue of the savior, probably Artemis (IEph 1a.26, ll. 3–4). The inscription also refers to an order by Lysimachus (Alexander the Great's former bodyguard) that the members of the gerousia should receive (money) to feast and to sacrifice to the goddess (IEph 1a.26, ll. 5–6). Elsewhere, I have argued that Lysimachus quite possibly created the mysteries and sacrifices centered upon Artemis as a savior goddess essentially as a grateful response for her aid in his military and political struggles against Demetrios Poliorketes (for control of the polis) and in order to help integrate the citizens of his new polis of Arsinoe into its intertwined religious and political structures.[36] From a broader perspective, my point was that what mystery cults (such as those of Artemis of Ephesus) were cannot be abstracted from events and developments in high politics and from the history of the polis itself.

The vast majority of our evidence for the mysteries of Artemis, however, comes from the period after the battle of Actium, fought on September 2, 31 BCE. In many ways, both in form and substance, the evidence

---

36. Guy MacLean Rogers, *The Mysteries of Artemis of Ephesos: Cult, Polis, and Change in the Graeco-Roman World*, Synkrisis (New Haven: Yale University Press, 2012), 75–83.

arose out of that decisive turning point in the history of Roman imperium and the Mediterranean world as a whole.

Two years after the battle of Actium, the geographer Strabo provided his readers with the single most important piece of information about the general festival held in Ortygia (about five miles south of the city center of Ephesus) and the mystic sacrifices of the Curetes. After describing the grove of Ortygia and the story of Leto giving birth to Artemis and Apollo there with the help of the Curetes, Strabo says,

> A general festival is held there annually; and by a certain custom the youths vie for honor, particularly in the splendor of their banquets there. At that time, also, an association [*archeion*] of Curetes holds symposiums and performs certain mystic sacrifices. (*Geog.* 14.1.20)[37]

We do not know exactly what constituted the mystic sacrifices Strabo mentions. But clearly mystic sacrifices are related at least semantically to a cluster of terms used elsewhere to describe the act of initiating people into the mysteries (*myein*), to describe the process itself (*myēsis*), and to describe those who undergo an initiation (*mystēs* or *mystai* in the plural).[38]

By the reign of Tiberius (14–37 CE) at the latest, yearly lists of Curetes were inscribed on the various architectural elements of the Doric façade of the stoa that led into the prytaneion of the Upper Agora of Ephesus. In these lists, the names of the six yearly Curetes follow the names of the prytanis of the year. Following the names of the Curetes on most of the surviving lists are the names of individuals eventually designated as *hierourgoi* (cult attendants). The lists of prytanes, Curetes, and cult attendants were put up at least into the middle of the third century CE. Among his other lasting contributions to our understanding of Ephesian epigraphy and history, Dieter Knibbe was the first to put these sometimes very fragmentary inscriptions into a plausible chronological order.[39]

---

37. Translation slightly modified from Strabo, *Geography: Books 13–14*, trans. Horace Leonard Jones, LCL 233 (Cambridge: Harvard University Press, 1929). Jones renders *archeion* as "a special college."

38. For the semantic cluster, see Burkert, *Ancient Mystery Cults*, 7–10.

39. Dieter Knibbe, *Der Staatsmarkt: Die Inschriften des Prytaneions; Die Kureteninschriften und sonstige religiöse Texte*, FiE 9.1.1 (Vienna: ÖAI, 1981). Subsequent efforts to redate and reorder some of the lists have not been convincing. Those who have pointed out some of the difficulties with Knibbe's ordering have failed to provide comprehensive accounts of their own.

From the office titles of the cult attendants, such as *hierophantēs* (hierophant), an office title that is usually restricted to those who revealed the mysteries in Ephesus and elsewhere, we can reconstruct at least some of the rituals and rites that took place during the celebration of the mysteries of Artemis over a two-hundred-year period at the height of the Roman empire. We can chart how the celebrations were expanded during the late first and early second century CE, including the addition of the procession subsidized by C. Vibius Salutaris that was timed to coincide with the celebrations that took place on Thargelion 6 each year, at a time when the polis itself was undergoing an urban expansion and elaboration. We also can trace the creation of a vocabulary of piety, set out in these very visible public texts, in which the prytanes' and the Curetes piety, not only with respect to Artemis, but also the Roman emperors was articulated.

From the names and office titles of the prytanes and Curetes, we also can reconstruct a kind of changing sociological profile of the men and women who were responsible for paying for and enacting the mysteries over more than two centuries. It comes as no great shock to learn that the vast majority of those men and women were Roman citizens (or belonged to families of Roman citizens) of bouleutic status, though not necessarily members of the boule's top tier, the so-called *dekaprōtoi*. Celebrating the mysteries of Artemis was, in effect, a kind of (Greco-Roman) family business in Ephesus during the first and second centuries CE. That profile is consistent with the sociological portrait of the men and women who celebrated the mysteries of the other gods and goddesses in the city during the same period, even if our information for the latter is supported by far less evidence. The contrast with the sociological profile of at least some of the Christians who belonged to the Pauline group in Ephesus is striking; according to one reading of Rom 16:6–15 as an embedded letter of Paul to Ephesus, none of the twenty-six names of Christians listed from the letter show the individuals named to have been Roman citizens.[40]

As far as the question of the purpose of celebrating Artemis's mysteries is concerned, unfortunately, we have only one explicit text, dated to the year 211 or 212 CE, which apparently was part of the inscribed and displayed record of a question put to an oracle, from which we learn that the prytanis of the city had celebrated the mysteries and sacrifices for the sake

---

40. Helmut Koester, "Ephesos in Early Christian Literature," in Koester, *Ephesos*, 123–24.

"of our common salvation" (IEph 4.1077). It is probably for the sake of the common salvation of the polis that the prytanis served that the mysteries were celebrated.

Moreover, just as in the cases of the other mystery cults in the city, our evidence for the celebration of Artemis's mysteries ceases in the middle of the third century CE. In my book about the mysteries of Artemis and the polis of Ephesus, I advanced a theory about why these cults died out in the mid-third century CE. The theory was based upon an interpretation of the "secret" behind the celebration of Artemis's mysteries. My hypothesis was that the Ephesians stopped celebrating the mysteries of Artemis because of a breakdown in the reciprocal logic of the relationship between the Ephesians and Artemis that the celebrations both exemplified and reinforced.[41] Moreover, the story of the decline of the mysteries cannot be separated from the story of the demise of Ephesus's bouleutic order during the third century CE. That theory is grounded in the ancient epigraphical and archaeological evidence for the bouleutic order of the city.[42] But I also try to show how the whole story of the cult might fit into anthropological, evolutionary, and neurobiological theories of adaptation and change.[43]

For the purposes of this brief investigation, what I would like to do here is to suggest that even if the sociopolitical profiles of those who celebrated Artemis's mysteries (and the other mysteries in the city) and the early Christians in Ephesus were very different, there is room in my account for a related story. That is a story about the ways in which Christian writers such as Paul, the author of the Pauline Letter to the Ephesians, and Ignatius of Antioch appropriated the language of initiating people into the mysteries and turned that language towards their own ends when they wrote letters while they (arguably) were in Ephesus or to Ephesus. They did so precisely because they must have been aware of the existence and popularity of the cults described above (and other well-known mystery cults in the contemporary empire), to which the Curetes' inscriptions and many other pieces of evidence still bear witness. While many of the references that these writers made to mysteries were fairly general and/or related to ideas and theological concepts drawn from the rich Jewish scriptural traditions, at least a few of the references indicate

---

41. Rogers, *Mysteries of Artemis*, 251–55, 279–85.
42. Ibid., 243–55.
43. Ibid., 285–88.

more than a passing familiarity with at least some aspects of the polytheist mystery cults.[44]

As is well known, the apostle Paul spent slightly less than three years in Ephesus (fall of 52 to spring of 55 CE).[45] During his extended stay in the city at that time, unless he never walked along the Basilica stoa of the Upper Agora, he must have seen the lists of *Kouretēs* inscribed on the architectural elements of the prytaneion, the earliest surviving texts of which were displayed during the reign of Tiberius (IEph 4.1001).[46] From these texts we know that the mysteries of Artemis were being celebrated in the city while Paul was in Ephesus.[47] It was perhaps no accident that writings of his dated to this period contain repeated references to a mystery or mysteries.

In 1 Corinthians, written in Ephesus during spring of 54 CE (16:8–9),[48] for instance, Paul wrote of God's mystery and the wisdom not of this world or of the rulers of this world but the wisdom of God, hidden in a mystery, that God predetermined for our glory before time began (1 Cor 2:6–7). Commentators have seen these passages as referring to the meaning that God had revealed in the message of the cross and have traced out the Semitic language background to Paul's use of the term *mystērion*.[49] Later on in the same letter Paul spoke of himself and his fellows as stewards (*oikonomous*) of the mysteries of God (1 Cor 4:1). In imperial Ephesus the *oikonomoi* served as treasurers in charge of sacred monies of the gods (see IEph 2.541; 7.2.3513a, l. 7; 7.2.3513b, l. 5). Near the very end of the letter Paul revealed a mystery (*mystērion*) to his readers: they would not all sleep, but would be changed, in a moment, in the twinkling of an eye, at the last trumpet (1 Cor 15:51). This extract has

---

44. For Paul's citations of the scriptures of Israel, see J. Ross Wagner, "Paul and Scripture," in *The Blackwell Companion to Paul*, ed. Stephen Westerholm (Malden, MA: Wiley-Blackwell, 2011), 154–71, esp. 155–57 for a very useful table of citations.

45. For the chronology, see Acts 20:31; Rainer Riesner, "Pauline Chronology," in Westerholm, *Blackwell Companion to Paul*, 19.

46. Rogers, *Mysteries of Artemis*, 123, 128.

47. Kouretes's lists put up possibly while Paul was in the city at this time might include IEph 4.1005–8.

48. Riesner, "Pauline Chronology," 16, 19.

49. Joseph A. Fitzmyer, *First Corinthians: A New Translation with Introduction and Commentary*, AB 32 (New Haven: Yale University Press, 2008), 171; Raymond E. Brown, *The Semitic Background of the Term "Mystery" in the New Testament*, FBBS 21 (Philadelphia: Fortress, 1968), 40–50.

been interpreted as the passing on of a divine truth that had been hidden, and the multifarious resonances with passages from the Hebrew Bible have been persuasively detailed.[50]

Most strikingly, however, also near the end of the missive, Paul claimed that even if he had the gift of prophecy and understood all the mysteries (*ta mystēria panta*) and all the knowledge, and if he had all the faith to move mountains but did not have love, he was nothing (1 Cor 13:2). The phrase "all the mysteries" (13:2) may be an allusion to Paul's discussion of wisdom and its relation to the hidden counsels of God, the so-called heavenly secrets of 1 Cor 2:1.[51]

But a similar phrase appears in the fragmentary decree of the *synedrion* of the Ephesian gerousia, dated to the reign of Commodus, but referring back to the foundation of the polis of Arsinoe (later Ephesus) by Lysimachus during the early third century BCE.[52] In lines 3–4 of that inscription, Lysimachus is credited with having made an arrangement for "*ta men alla] panta peri te mystēriōn kai thysiōn*"—"all the things concerning the mysteries and sacrifices" (IEph 1a.26, ll. 3–4). The phrase in the inscription might refer not just to the mysteries of one divinity but to all the mysteries carried out at the time, possibly of all the divinities for whom such cults were organized. But a later, imperial era inscription of a priestess of Artemis uses another, similar formulation to describe her celebration of *panta ta mystēria tēs theou*, all the mysteries or rites of the goddess alone (IEph 7.1.3059, ll. 3–4). A comparable formulation is also used in the early third century CE "thanks" inscription of the prytanis Favonia Flaccilla, who had celebrated all the mysteries (*ta mystēria panta*) for a year (IEph 4.1060, l. 7). Paul's use of the phrase *ta mystēria panta* in a letter written in Ephesus, therefore, may be an allusion to what was a kind of local shorthand for the celebration of Artemis's mysteries, just as the mysteries of Demeter and Kore at Eleusis were commonly called *ta mystēria* or "the Mysteries *tout court*."[53]

In Philippians, perhaps composed during the period when Paul was imprisoned in Ephesus (during the winter of 54/55 CE [Phil 1:18–27;

---

50. Fitzmyer, *First Corinthians*, 603–5.
51. Ibid., 493.
52. For extended discussion of the inscription, see Rogers, *Mysteries of Artemis*, 71–88.
53. Burkert, *Ancient Mystery Cults*, 4.

2:24]),[54] Paul told the Philippians, with reverence and trembling, to "continue working out what your own salvation means" (*tēn heautōn sōtērian katergazesthe* [Phil 2:12]). The salvation envisioned here might refer to the well-being of the Christian community at Philippi or their relationship to god.[55] Salvation could also be communal for polytheists however, as we have seen from the inscription put up by a prytanis who had celebrated the mysteries and sacrifices probably for the sake of "our common salvation" in 211 or 212 CE (IEph 4.1077, ll. 5–7). Salvation in mystery cults was not only for the sake of individual safety.

The late first-century CE Letter to the Ephesians probably was not written by Paul and probably was not addressed only to the Ephesians but rather to the saints and faithful in Christ (Eph 1:1). This means that it was intended to be sent to all the churches.[56] We cannot exclude the possibility, however, that all of the churches included Ephesus. If this letter was also sent to Ephesus at the time, it is interesting that at the exact time when the Ephesians were expanding the scale of the celebration of the mysteries of Artemis,[57] there are multiple references to mysteries and salvation in the letter, including a famous passage in which the author writes about the mystery or secret (*to mystērion*) that was made known to him by revelation (*kata apokalupsin* [Eph 3:3]). According to one interpretation of this phrase, the core of the revealed secret was Christ and the incorporation of the gentiles into God's people.[58] Arguably, a similar revelation was made known to initiates into the mysteries at Eleusis during the celebration of the mysteries when the Athenians in silence revealed to the *epoptai* the most perfect epoptic secret, a reaped ear of grain.[59]

From the early second century CE, there is also the Trajanic-era letter of Ignatius of Antioch to the Ephesians (the longest of Ignatius's letters), with

---

54. Trebilco, *Early Christians in Ephesus*, 83–87; Riesner, "Pauline Chronology," 15, 19.

55. John Henry Paul Reumann, *Philippians: A New Translation with Introduction and Commentary*, AB 33B (New Haven: Yale University Press, 2008), 387.

56. Koester, "Ephesos in Early Christian Literature," 124.

57. Rogers, *Mysteries of Artemis*, 172, 184–85.

58. Markus Barth, *Ephesians 1–3: A New Translation with Introduction and Commentary*, AB 34 (New York: Doubleday, 1974), 329–30. For interpretation of the theme, see also John Paul Heil, "Paul and the Believers of Western Asia," in Westerholm, *Blackwell Companion to Paul*, 88–89.

59. On the disclosure of the Eleusinian secret by Diagoras and Hippolytus, see Burkert, *Ancient Mystery Cults*, 90–92.

its repeated references to the mysteries. These include a passage in which Ignatius wrote that "You are all fellow travelers [*synodoi*], god-bearers [*theophoroi*], temple-bearers [*naophoroi*], Christ-bearers [*Christophoroi*], holiness-bearers [*hagiophoroi*], and in every way are adorned [*kekosmemenoi*] by the commandments of Jesus Christ" (Ign., *Eph.* 9).[60] Such a description of a procession of men bearing sacred objects has been compared to the description of the *theophoroi* in the well-known festival inscription of Demosthenes of Oinoanda.[61] The passage in Ignatius, however, might also be compared to the account of the procession of statues subsidized by C. Vibius Salutaris in Ephesus in 104 CE. In that procession, thirty-one gold and silver type-statues and images (altogether) of the emperor Trajan, his wife Plotina, Artemis (9), the Roman people, the gerousia, the equestrian order, the *ephēbeia*, Augustus, the demos, all of the tribes of Ephesus, Androclus, Lysimachus, Euonumos, Pion, Athena Pammousos, and Sebaste Homonoia Chrysophoros were stipulated to be carried from the pronaos of the Temple of Artemis through the city along a circular route on a number of occasions every year, including during the *sōtēria*, by the guards of the Artemision, two *neopoioi*, the beadle, the *chrysophoroi*, and a sacred slave of Artemis (IEph 1a.27, ll. 148–213, 464–66, 470–73).[62] While *theophoroi* are not mentioned as carrying the sacred images of Artemis in the Salutaris bequest, there is no doubt that the specified individuals in the procession in Ephesus carried images of divinities. Moreover, we know that there was a special priestess in Ephesus whose job it was to adorn the stature of the great goddess Artemis, the *kosmēteira*.[63] Ignatius also makes reference to fellow initiates of Paul, in effect making the great Apostle himself into one of the *mystai* (*Eph.* 12.2).[64]

In citing these texts, with their clear allusions to the celebrations of mysteries, I am not trying to revivify the theory that early Christianity itself was

---

60. For this passage and its relationship to mystery associations generally, see Allen Brent, *Ignatius of Antioch: A Martyr Bishop and the Origin of Episcopacy* (London: T&T Clark, 2007), 80–83.

61. Ibid., 82.

62. Guy MacLean Rogers, *The Sacred Identity of Ephesos: Foundation Myths of a Roman City* (London: Routledge, 1991), 80–126.

63. IEph 3.742, l. 2; 3.792, ll. 3–4; 3.875, l. 6; 3.892, ll. 7–8; 3.980, ll. 7–8; 3.983, ll. 3–4; 3.984, ll. 2–3; 3.989, ll. 7–8; 3.993, l. 6; 3.994, ll. 2–3; 5.1655, l. 4; 5.1872a, l. 2; 6.2902, ll. 1–2; 7.1.3072, l. 15; 7.2.4337.

64. For a reading of passage in light of the Pauline influence in Ephesus, see Trebilco, *Early Christians in Ephesus*, 686–87.

a kind of mystery religion or that what the Curetes did on Thargelion 6 in Ortygia resembled or was homologous with what Jews or later Christians did when they assembled in Ephesus (for which we have nowhere near as much information as we do about the rituals that took place during the celebrations of the mysteries of Artemis during the early Roman Empire). On the contrary, one of the conclusions to be drawn from my study of mystery cults in Ephesus is that the cults themselves show considerable variation with respect to offices and rituals and that there are no exact analogies between the celebrations of the Greco-Roman mysteries in the city and what we know the various Christian groups in the city were doing from close study of the relevant passages in Acts.[65] The extravagant banquets held by youths in Ephesus during the celebrations of Artemis's mysteries, for instance, were nothing like the simple, communal meals shared by Christians. Nor am I denying the relevance of the Jewish literary traditions for understanding the language of secrets and mysteries revealed in Paul's letters and in the other texts I have cited. Systematic study of Paul's letters does indeed show that Paul took great pains to situate his good news "in relation to a broad and dynamic Jewish tradition."[66] Paul's thought in general is "deeply rooted in the Jewish Scriptures, from which he draws not only citations and vocabulary, but large patterns of thought."[67]

What I am suggesting, however, is that, in the absence of a large number of texts providing us with detailed information about exactly who the Jews or Christians in the city actually were (in the same kind of detail that the Curetes's inscriptions provide), the letters of Paul, the pseudo-Pauline author, and Ignatius might at least tell us something about who these authors imagined they were speaking to and why they also evoked the celebrations of polytheist mysteries. Paul, the pseudo-Pauline author, and Ignatius used the language of the Greco-Roman mystery cults because of the well-documented popularity of these cults at the time. The language of the mysteries formed part of the broader cultural "encyclopedia" within which these authors composed their missives and were part of the thought world(s) of at least some of their intended audiences.[68] Those audiences perhaps understood the depth and breadth of the scriptural traditions of

---

65. Koester, "Ephesos in Early Christian Literature," 126–31.
66. Wagner, "Paul and Scripture," 157.
67. John M. G. Barclay, "Paul, Judaism, and the Jewish People," in Westerholm, *Blackwell Companion to Paul*, 194.
68. For the cultural "encyclopedia" of Paul, see Wagner, "Paul and Scripture," 161.

Judaism well enough to get all of the allusions to Israel's sacred texts that the letters alluded to. But by the second century CE, it was also no secret either to polytheists or Christians how popular the mysteries of Artemis and the other gods and goddesses of Ephesus were.

BIBLIOGRAPHY

Aurenhammer, Maria. "Sculptures of Gods and Heroes from Ephesos." Pages 251–74 in *Ephesos, Metropolis of Asia: An Interdisciplinary Approach to Its Archaeology, Religion, and Culture*. Edited by Helmut Koester. HTS 41. Valley Forge, PA: Trinity Press International, 1995.

Barclay, John M. G. "Paul, Judaism, and the Jewish People." Pages 188–20 in *The Blackwell Companion to Paul*. Edited by Stephen Westerholm. Malden, MA: Wiley-Blackwell, 2011.

Barth, Markus. *Ephesians 1–3: A New Translation with Introduction and Commentary*. AB 34. New York: Doubleday, 1974.

Brent, Allen. *Ignatius of Antioch: A Martyr Bishop and the Origin of Episcopacy*. London: T&T Clark, 2007.

Brown, Raymond E. *The Semitic Background of the Term "Mystery" in the New Testament*. FBBS 21. Philadelphia: Fortress, 1968.

Burkert, Walter. *Ancient Mystery Cults*. Cambridge: Harvard University Press, 1987.

———. *Greek Religion*. Cambridge: Harvard University Press, 1985.

Casel, Odo. *The Mystery of the Christian Worship*. Edited by Burkhard Neunheuser. London: Darton, Longman & Todd, 1962. Repr., New York: Crossroad, 1999.

Fitzmyer, Joseph A. *First Corinthians: A New Translation with Introduction and Commentary*. AB 32. New Haven: Yale University Press, 2008.

Furnish, Victor Paul. *Second Corinthians: Translated with Introduction, Notes, and Commentary*. AB 32A. New York: Doubleday, 1984.

Gathercole, Simon J. "Paul's Christology." Pages 172–87 in *The Blackwell Companion to Paul*. Edited by Stephen Westerholm. Malden, MA: Wiley-Blackwell, 2011.

Harland, Philip A. *Associations, Synagogues, and Congregations: Claiming a Place in Ancient Mediterranean Society*. Minneapolis: Fortress, 2003.

Heil, John Paul. "Paul and the Believers of Western Asia." Pages 79–92 in *The Blackwell Companion to Paul*. Edited by Stephen Westerholm. Malden, MA: Wiley-Blackwell, 2011.

Keil, Josef. "Aphrodite Daitis." *JÖAI* 17 (1914): 145–47.

Kleijwegt, Marc. "Textile Manufacturing for a Religious Market: Artemis and Diana as Tycoons of Industry." Pages 81–134 in *After the Past: Essays in Ancient History in Honour of H.W. Pleket*. Edited by Willem Jongman and Marc Kleijwegt. MnemSup 233. Leiden: Brill, 2002.

Knibbe, Dieter, *Der Staatsmarkt: Die Inschriften des Prytaneions; Die Kureteninschriften und sonstige religiöse Texte*. FiE 9.1.1. Vienna: ÖAI, 1981.

Knibbe, Dieter, and Bülent İplikçioğlu. "Neue Inschriften aus Ephesos VIII." *JÖAI* 53 (1981/1982): 87–150.

Koester, Helmut. "Ephesos in Early Christian Literature." Pages 119–140 in *Ephesos, Metropolis of Asia: An Interdisciplinary Approach to Its Archaeology, Religion, and Culture*. Edited by Helmut Koester. HTS 41. Valley Forge, PA: Trinity Press International, 1995.

Lane, Eugene N. "Men: A Neglected Cult of Roman Asia Minor." *ANRW* 18.3:2161–74.

Latte, Kurt. "Aphrodite in Ephesos." *AR* 17 (1914): 678–79.

Merkelbach, Reinhold. *Die Hirten des Dionysos: Die Dionysos-Mysterien der römischen Kaiserzeit und der bukolische Roman des Longus*. Stuttgart: Teubner, 1988.

Oster, Richard E. "Ephesus as a Religious Center under the Principate, I: Paganism before Constantine." *ANRW* 18.3:1661–728.

Pleket, Harry W. "Nine Greek Inscriptions from the Cayster-Valley in Lydia." *Talanta* 2 (1970): 55–88.

Reitzenstein, Richard. *Die hellenistischen Mysterienreligionen nach ihren Grundgedanken und Wirkungen*. Stuttgart: Teubner, 1910.

Reumann, John Henry Paul. *Philippians: A New Translation with Introduction and Commentary*. AB 33B. New Haven: Yale University Press, 2008.

Riesner, Rainer. "Pauline Chronology." Pages 9–29 in *The Blackwell Companion to Paul*. Edited by Stephen Westerholm. Malden, MA: Wiley-Blackwell, 2011.

Robert, Jeanne, and Louis Robert. "Bulletin épigraphique." *REG* 96 (1983): 76–191.

———. *Exploration, histoire, monnaies et inscriptions Paris*. Vol. 1 of *Fouilles d'Amyzon en Carie*. Paris: de Boccard, 1983.

Rogers, Guy MacLean. *The Mysteries of Artemis of Ephesos: Cult, Polis, and Change in the Graeco-Roman World*. Syncrisis. New Haven: Yale University Press, 2012.

———. *The Sacred Identity of Ephesos: Foundation Myths of a Roman City*. London: Routledge, 1991.

Strabo. *Geography: Books 13–14*. Translated by Horace Leonard Jones. LCL 233. Cambridge: Harvard University Press, 1929.

Trebilco, Paul. *The Early Christians in Ephesus from Paul to Ignatius*. WUNT 166. Tübingen: Mohr Siebeck, 2004. Repr., Grand Rapids: Eerdmans, 2007.

Wagner, J. Ross. "Paul and Scripture." Pages 154–71 in *The Blackwell Companion to Paul*. Edited by Stephen Westerholm. Malden, MA: Wiley-Blackwell, 2011.

The Jewish Community in Ephesus and Its Interaction with Christ-Believers in the First Century CE and Beyond

Paul Trebilco

For the earliest Christian *ekklēsia*, the local Jewish community was generally an important dimension of the polis. This was certainly the case in Ephesus. Accordingly, the relationship between the Christian *ekklēsia* and the Jewish community in the city of Ephesus will be considered here. The evidence from Josephus, Philo, and some inscriptions suggests that in the first century CE, the Jewish community in Ephesus was significant and could also act as a unified body. After presenting some of this evidence, I will discuss the extent to which the Jewish community and the Christ-believing communities in the city interacted with each other. I will then draw a number of conclusions from this evidence.

1. The Jewish Community in Ephesus

1.1. The Foundation of the Community

The origins of the Jewish community in Ephesus are unknown. Josephus has two passages in which he gives dubious claims regarding Jewish citizenship in Ephesus and Ionia, one in 312–281 BCE (*Ag. Ap.* 2.39) and the other in 262–246 BCE (*Ant.* 12.125–126).[1] But the implication that

---

1. See Paul Trebilco, *Jewish Communities in Asia Minor*, SNTSMS 69 (Cambridge: Cambridge University Press, 1991), 167–69; John M. G. Barclay, *Jews in the Mediterranean Diaspora: From Alexander to Trajan (323 BCE–117 CE)* (Edinburgh: T&T Clark, 1996), 260–61; Barclay, *Against Apion*, vol. 10 of *Flavius Josephus: Translation and Commentary* (Leiden: Brill, 2007), 190. In *Ag. Ap.* 2.39, Josephus writes that the Jews at Ephesus "bear the same name as the indigenous citizens, a right which they received

Jews were living in Ephesus in the third century BCE seems likely.[2] It is significant then that by the time of Paul's mission in Ephesus around 52 CE,[3] the Jewish community may have lived in Ephesus for over three hundred years.

1.2. The Level of Organization of the Jewish Community

A range of documents relating to Jews in Ephesus or more generally in Asia, dated from 49 BCE to 2/3 CE, are given by Josephus and Philo.[4] We see the community actively approaching ruling bodies to gain the right of assembly so they could meet together regularly (see *Ant.* 14.227) or for permission to build a synagogue[5] and the right to administer their own

---

from Alexander's successors," that is, Seleucus Nicator (all translations of Josephus are from the LCL). See also *Ant.* 12.119-21. In *Ant.* 12.125-126, Josephus claims that the Jews of Ionia were granted citizenship by Antiochus II Theos (262-246 BCE).

2. See Tessa Rajak, *The Jewish Dialogue with Greece and Rome: Studies in Cultural and Social Interaction*, AGJU 48 (Leiden: Brill, 2001), 304.

3. See Paul Trebilco, *The Early Christians in Ephesus from Paul to Ignatius*, WUNT 166 (Tübingen: Mohr Siebeck, 2004), 53.

4. See *Ant.* 12.125-128; 14.223-227, 228-230, 234, 240, 262-264; 16.27-30, 59-60, 162-165 (which concerns Asia in general), 167-168, 172-173; *Ag. Ap.* 2.38-9; Philo, *Legat.* 315. Although some aspects of these documents may be questionable, they contain material that is probably reliable. The authenticity of these decrees has been defended by Miriam Pucci Ben Zeev, *Jewish Rights in the Roman World: The Greek and Roman Documents Quoted by Josephus Flavius*, TSAJ 74 (Tübingen: Mohr Siebeck, 1998), 139-290, 357-68; see also Barclay, *Jews in the Mediterranean Diaspora*, 262-64; Erich S. Gruen, *Diaspora: Jews amidst Greeks and Romans* (Cambridge: Harvard University Press, 2002), 85-86. Jews in Ephesus or Ionia are not mentioned in 1 Macc 15:16-25.

5. No synagogue has yet been found in Ephesus. However, the existence of a synagogue in Ephesus seems to be implied in the decree cited in *Ant.* 14.227, dated to 43 BCE, where the Jews are given permission "to come together for sacred and holy rites in accordance with their law." See Donald D. Binder, *Into the Temple Courts: The Place of the Synagogues in the Second Temple Period*, SBLDS 169 (Atlanta: Scholars Press, 1999), 280-81. Philo, *Legat.* 315, addressed to Ephesus, may perhaps also imply the existence of a synagogue. Furthermore, Acts provides evidence for a Jewish synagogue in the mid-first century (18:19, 26; 19:8-9). An inscription of the Imperial period mentions *archisynagogoi* and presbyters. It reads: "τῶν ἀρχισυναγωγῶν καὶ τῶν πρεσβ(υτέρων) πολλὰ τὰ {τα} ἔτη" (IEph 4.1251); see Greg H. R. Horsley, "An *Archisynagogos* of Corinth?," *NewDocs* 4.113:215, no. 23; date in Horsley, "The Inscriptions of Ephesos and the New Testament," *NovT* 34 (1992): 122. Another undated inscription

finances (see, e.g., *Ant.* 14.262–264; 16.27–30, 167–168, 172–173). They also took active measures to ensure that they could send the temple tax to Jerusalem, which shows the community in Ephesus retained strong links with Jerusalem and with the temple. We see the retention of facets of Jewish identity then.

These documents also provide evidence for the communal life of the Jews of Ephesus and show that on some occasions they acted as a united body. In *Ant.* 14.262–264, Josephus preserves a decree, probably to be dated in 42 BCE, which reads:

> Decree of the people of Ephesus. "In the presidency of Menophilus, on the first of the month Artemision, the following decree was passed by the people on the motion of the magistrates, and was announced by Nicanor. Whereas the Jews in the city [τῶν ἐν τῇ πόλει Ἰουδαίων] have petitioned the proconsul Marcus Junius Brutus, son of Pontius, that they might observe their Sabbaths and do all those things which are in accordance with their native customs without interference from anyone, and the governor has granted this request, it has therefore been decreed by the council and people that as the matter is of concern to the Romans, no one shall be prevented from keeping the Sabbath days nor be fined for so doing, but they shall be permitted to do all those things which are in accordance with their own laws."

---

reads "]τὸ θυσιαστήριον" (altar or sanctuary), followed by a menorah (IEph 4.4130). It seems very likely that this was from a synagogue. See Josef Keil, cited in IEph 7, p. 433; Clive Foss, *Ephesus after Antiquity: A Late Antique, Byzantine, and Turkish City* (Cambridge: Cambridge University Press, 1979), 45; Horsley, "Jews at Ephesos," *NewDocs* 4.116:231. The stone was found in the Cathedral of St. Mary, and Foss suggests the synagogue was in this area of the city. However, we may wonder if there were actually multiple synagogues in the city. We know that other large cities such as Rome had more than one synagogue, and the wording in Acts 19:8–10 could allude to the particular synagogue where Christians normally met, until tensions developed with the Jewish community and Paul departed from that particular synagogue with his supporters; see Irina Levinskaya, "The Traces of Jewish Life in Asia Minor," in *Neues Testament und hellenistisch-jüdische Alltagskultur: Wechselseitige Wahrnehmungen; III. Internationales Symposium zum Corpus Judaeo-Hellenisticum Novi Testamenti 21.–24. Mai 2009, Leipzig*, ed. Roland Deines, Jens Herzer, and Karl-Wilhelm Niebuhr, WUNT 274 (Tübingen: Mohr Siebeck, 2011), 350. Cf. Stephan Witetschek, *Ephesische Enthüllungen 1: Frühe Christen in einer antiken Großstadt; Zugleich ein Beitrag zur Frage nach den Kontexten der Johannesapokalypse*, BTS 6 (Leuven: Peeters, 2008), 162–63.

Here "the Jews in the city" of Ephesus have argued their case with the proconsul, who has responded favorably; subsequently the council and people of Ephesus have granted the proconsul's request that the Jews should be allowed to observe the Sabbath and follow their own customs. This action by "the Jews in the city" indicates their ability to act as a united body.

Furthermore, in *Ant.* 16.172–173, Josephus records a letter, probably to be dated between 9 and 2 BCE, in which the proconsul Julius Antonius stated that "the Jews dwelling in Asia" had approached him when he was in Ephesus and asked that he might confirm their right to observe their own customs.[6] Although here the Jews of Asia seem to be acting together, that the proconsul's letter was written to people in Ephesus suggests that the Jews in the city were a very significant group within the wider group of Jews in Asia; this is unsurprising, given that Ephesus was the leading city in the area. Both these documents from the first century BCE show that the Jews of Ephesus were able to act as a united community.[7]

We have very few inscriptions from Jews in Ephesus, but we do have two inscriptions from the second century CE that show that the Jewish community could be conceived of as a united community by Jews themselves at this time.[8] One epitaph reads:

[τὸ μνημεῖόν (?) ἐστιν] Ἰο[υλίου ?]
[   ] ἀρχιιατροῦ [καὶ]
[τῆς γυναικ]ὸς αὐτοῦ Ἰουλίας
[   ]ης καὶ τέκνων αὐτῶν.
[ζῶ]σιν.
[ταύτης τῆ]ς σοροῦ κήδον-
[ται οἱ ἐν Ἐφέ]σῳ Ἰουδέοι.

---

6. See also *Ant.* 16.167–168 and, concerning the Jews in Asia, *Ant.* 16.160–165.

7. In the decree cited in *Ant.* 16.168, dated to around 14 BCE and addressed to the magistrates, council, and people of Ephesus, Agrippa states that anyone who steals sacred monies of the Jews and takes refuge in a place of asylum will not be handed over to the local magistrates but rather will be "turned over to the Jews under the same law by which temple-robbers are dragged away from asylum." This suggests the Jews of Ephesus were recognized as acting together and as being able to exercise some judicial powers; see Binder, *Into the Temple Courts*, 282. Again, it suggests some form of united organization.

8. For other Jewish finds from Ephesus (four menorah and three oil lamps), see Renate Pillinger, "Jüdische Alltagskultur in Ephesos und Umbegung im Spiegel der Denkmäler," in Deines, Herzer, and Niebuhr, *Neues Testament und hellenistisch-jüdische Alltagskultur*, 86–94.

This is the tomb of Julius … *archiatros*, and of his wife Julia, … and of their children, while living. The Jews in Ephesus are charged with care of this tomb. (IEph 5.1677, ll. 1–7 = *IJO* 2.32)⁹

Here a Jew, whose name was probably Ἰουλίος, entrusts the care of his tomb to the local Jewish community, which he probably calls οἱ ἐν Ἐφέ]σῳ Ἰουδέοι. This implies that the community was seen as one group. A second inscription from the late second century reads:

Τὸ μνημεῖόν ἐστι Μαρ. Μουσσίου ἱαιρέος. ζῆ. κήδονται οἱ Ἰουδαῖοι.

This tomb is that of Marcus Moussios, priest. He made this while living. The Jews are charged with its care. (IEph 5.1676 = *IJO* 2.33)

Here the Jews as a group are charged with caring for this tomb. The maintenance of tombs was an important matter in antiquity. That in these two cases the task of looking after a tomb was assigned to the Jews suggests that there was some mechanism by which this would happen. These two inscriptions therefore imply that the Jews of Ephesus had some formal organizational structure and that the Jews of the city identified themselves as a coherent community.¹⁰

It is quite common for associations in Ephesus to be mentioned in inscriptions in conjunction with the care of tombs. One undated example reads:

τοῦτο τὸ [μνη]|μεῖόν ἐστιν [—]|λείνου Ἀττάλ[ου] | καὶ Ἀττάλου Ἀ[λε]||ξάνδρου. τού[του] | τοῦ μνημείου [καν]|ναβαρίων ἡ συ[νερ]|γασία κήδεται.

---

9. Translations are my own unless otherwise stated. Date from Guy MacLean Rogers, "Demetrios of Ephesos: Silversmith and Neopoios?," *BTTK* 50 (1986): 881, n. 16. David Noy dates it as "second or third century" (*Italy [excluding the City of Rome], Spain and Gaul*, vol. 1 of *Jewish Inscriptions of Western Europe* [Cambridge: Cambridge University Press, 1993], 102). That Ioulios was an *archiatros* suggests that at the time it was written at least some Jews had some standing in the city.

10. One could object that a person would always want to *claim* that a community was united in a context like an epitaph, even if it was not. But my point here is that the epitaph *could* have spoken of a particular group within the wider Jewish community, which would not indicate that the whole Jewish community could be conceived of as a unified whole but rather that it was made up of a number of potentially disparate entities.

This memorial belongs to ... *Name* son of Attalus and Attalus son of Alexander. The guild of hemp workers takes care of this memorial. (*SEG* 43.812)[11]

Here the same verb that is found in our two Jewish inscriptions—κήδω—is used in the middle voice for the activity of caring for the tomb by the guild of hemp workers. Associations have some form of organization and are united groups. Clearly the same can be said of the Jewish community.

The evidence from Josephus and these two Jewish inscriptions shows that the Jews in Ephesus could be spoken of as a body, suggesting they had a level of organization and had adopted a united, city-wide organizational structure. This is a significant finding, particularly given my interest here in how the Jewish community might respond to the mission of Christ-believers in their midst.

Why did the Jewish community adopt a united organizational form, particularly given that it is not the only possible structure they could have adopted?[12] Firstly, the documents preserved by Josephus suggest that political expediency may have encouraged the Jews to adopt this structure or reinforced this structure if it had already developed. Faced with challenges to their rights,[13] the Jews of Ephesus needed to adopt a united front

---

11. Dieter Knibbe, Helmut Engelmann, and Bülent Iplikçioglu, "Neue Inschriften aus Ephesos XII," *JÖAI* 62 (1993): 138, no. 43. Translation from Philip A. Harland's website, https://tinyurl.com/SBL4209h, ID# 10458. For other inscriptions that mention association in conjunction with the care of tombs or the enforcement of fines, see Richard S. Ascough, Philip A. Harland, and John S. Kloppenborg, eds., *Associations in the Greco-Roman World: A Sourcebook* (Waco, TX: Baylor University Press, 2012), 161 (IEph 6.2212, 2103, 2200a, 2446; 7.1.3216), 175 (IEph 6.2213, 2226 [= SEG 49.2427], 2304, 2402; 7.2.4117); Çengiz Içten and Helmut Engelmann, "Inschriften aus Ephesos und Kolophon," *ZPE* 120 (1998): 86–88, no. 7 (= SEG 48.1363).

12. See further Paul Trebilco, "Jews, Christians and the Associations in Ephesos: A Comparative Study of Group Structures," in *100 Jahre Österreichische Forschungen in Ephesos: Akten des Symposions Wien 1995*, ed. Herwig Friesinger and Fritz Krinzinger (Vienna: ÖAW, 1999), 325–34.

13. As noted above, the Jews had experienced mistreatment and hostility over issues such as keeping the Sabbath and sending temple tax to Jerusalem and over Jewish rights in general; see *Ant.* 14.230, 262–264; 16.27–8, 57–60, 167–168, 172–173; Philo, *Legat.* 315; see further Barclay, *Jews in the Mediterranean Diaspora*, 264–78; Trebilco, *Early Christians in Ephesus*, 40–41; Bradley Ritter, *Judeans in the Greek Cities of the Roman Empire: Rights, Citizenship and Civil Discord*, JSJSup 170 (Leiden: Brill, 2015), 207–29.

in arguing with the city authorities and the Roman administration. This is clear, for example, in *Ant.* 12.125–128, where the Ionians agitated against the Jews of Ionia, which increased the need for Jewish unity so that they could defend the retention of their customs (see also *Ant.* 16.27–60).

A second, related reason was that of the Jewish temple tax. It is clear from the decrees preserved by Josephus that at times the cities of Asia sought to prevent the Jews from sending the temple tax to Jerusalem (e.g., *Ant.* 16.28, 45). A key reason for this seems to have been the difficult economic situation of the province of Asia for most of the first century BCE. Some cities seem to have resented a significant amount of gold being sent each year to Jerusalem and the consequent harm this caused to the local economy. These cities therefore sought to prevent the export of the temple tax by the Jewish community.[14] Faced with this sort of threat, the Jews of Ephesus needed to present a united front to argue their case.

Thirdly, these inscriptions may indicate that care of tombs was also one of the reasons that the Jews in Ephesus became a united group. Clearly care of graves was very important, and so this too may have led to the Jewish community becoming united and functioning like a city-wide association in this way.

There may well have been additional reasons that led to this city-wide sense of unity. We can suggest these included a sense of belonging together due to the common ties of their ethnicity, marriage within the community, observing the same customs, and the life of the synagogue community or communities.

That they were a united community is significant for our discussion. The Jewish community had a structure that meant that they could oppose the activity of someone like Paul or the growth of the Christ-believing community. It places them even more in the foreground for the growth of the Christ-believing groups.

1.3. The Jewish Community's Standing in the City

The decrees given by Josephus and Philo also indicate that by the mid-first century BCE, there was a sizeable and significant Jewish community in Ephesus. It seems to have been sufficiently noteworthy in the eyes of the city of Ephesus that Jews in the city were sending what must have been

---

14. Barclay, *Jews in the Mediterranean Diaspora*, 264–78.

significant amounts of money to Jerusalem for action to be taken to stop this from occurring (*Ant.* 16.27–30, 163, 167–168, 172–173). Furthermore, some Jews seem to have been sufficiently prominent in the city that it was annoying when they kept the Sabbath or refused to appear in court on that day. The result was that they were fined for observing the Sabbath (*Ant.* 14.262–264) or were perhaps required to give a bond so that they would appear in court on the appropriate day (*Ant.* 16.164–165).[15] These seem to be the actions of the city against a significant community in their midst rather than against a tiny and insignificant group that could be ignored or easily coerced.[16] They were also able to lobby successfully to restore their privileges after an infringement. Hence, as John M. G. Barclay notes, "these are Jews sufficiently articulate and well-connected (and with sufficient funds) to be able to take their protests to the highest authorities, with at least occasional success."[17] The documents also show that some Jews in Ephesus possessed Roman citizenship (see *Ant.* 14.228, 234, 240).[18] All of this suggests the community had some prominence within the life of the city.

1.4. The Size of the Jewish Community in Ephesus

Brian McGing has shown how very little hard data we have available to us with regard to the size of Jewish communities.[19] The only real indication that we have with regard to the Jewish community in Ephesus comes from the decrees preserved by Josephus, which suggest the Jewish com-

---

15. Note that *Ant.* 16.162–165 concerns the Jews in Asia in general.

16. See Barclay, *Jews in the Mediterranean Diaspora*, 271–72. He notes with regard to Jewish communities in Asia that "in general one can only explain gentile hostility on the grounds that the Jewish community was of influence and importance—perhaps growing importance—within the life of the city" (276).

17. Ibid., 271.

18. See also Trebilco, *Jewish Communities*, 172–73; Barclay, *Jews in the Mediterranean Diaspora*, 271; Binder, *Into the Temple Courts,* 280; Gruen, *Diaspora,* 87.

19. Brian McGing, "Population and Proselytism: How Many Jews Were There in the Ancient World?," in *Jews in the Hellenistic and Roman Cities,* ed. John R. Bartlett (London: Routledge, 2002), 88–106. See also Abraham Wasserstein, "The Number and Provenance of Jews in Graeco-Roman Antiquity: A Note on Population Statistics," in *Classical Studies in Honour David Sohlberg,* ed. Ranon Katzoff, Yaakov Petroff, and David M. Schaps (Ramat Gan: Bar-Ilan University Press, 1996), 307–17.

munity of the city was reasonably sizeable.[20] Perhaps it numbered in the many hundreds by the first century CE? Comparative data from Sardis and Aphrodisias from a much later period, at least, suggests that some Jewish communities in Asia Minor could be of this size.[21]

Some scholars have estimated that the Jewish diaspora made up around 10 percent of the population of the Mediterranean, while Walter Ameling has suggested the Jews in Asia Minor made up less than 5 percent of the total population.[22] Either figure would give a far larger number of Jews in Ephesus than my suggestion of many hundreds, but as McGing has shown, all our estimates are really guesses.[23] Given that the population of Ephesus was perhaps 200,000, 5–10 percent would be a population of

---

20. See, for example, *Ant.* 16.27: "It was also at this time, when they [Agrippa and Herod] were in Ionia, that a great multitude of Jews, who lived in its cities ..." (see also 16.166). Philo writes of Asia and Syria that "the Jews are very numerous in every city" (*Legat.* 245). But clearly these texts do not give definite numerical data.

21. The Sardis synagogue may have been able to seat one thousand people (it is only an estimate by the archaeologist), and the Aphrodisias inscription lists sixty-nine Jews and fifty-two "Godfearers"; see Trebilco, *Jewish Communities*, 41, 152–53. There has been ongoing debate about the dating of both the Sardis synagogue and the Aphrodisias inscription. Botermann has suggested that the Sardis building might have become a synagogue only in the mid-fourth century; see Helga Botermann, "Die Synagoge von Sardes: Eine Synagoge aus dem 4. Jahrhundert?," *ZNW* 81 (1990): 103–21. Jodi Magness dates the building to the sixth century ("The Date of the Sardis Synagogue in Light of the Numismatic Evidence," *AJA* 109 [2005]: 443–75). Marcus Rautman argues for the late fourth and fifth centuries ("Daniel at Sardis," *BASOR* 358 [2010]: 53). Pieter Willem van der Horst dates the Aphrodisias inscription to "the late fourth or fifth, perhaps even sixth century CE" (*Saxa judaica loquuntur: Lessons from Early Jewish Inscriptions*, BIS 134 [Leiden: Brill, 2015], 39).

22. See Wayne A. Meeks, *The First Urban Christians* (New Haven: Yale University Press, 1983), 34; Walter Ameling, "Die jüdischen Gemeinden im antiken Kleinasien," in *Jüdische Gemeinden und Organisationsformen von der Antike bis zur Gegenwart*, ed. Robert Jütte and Abraham Peter Kustermann, AZGKJ 3 (Vienna: Böhlau, 1996), 30.

23. Accordingly, Rick Strelan estimates there were up to 25,000 Jews in the city (*Paul, Artemis, and the Jews in Ephesus*, BZNW 80 [Berlin: de Gruyter, 1996], 181). Thomas A. Robinson thinks 75,000 is the upper limit (*The Bauer Thesis Examined: The Geography of Heresy in the Early Christian Church* [Lewiston, NY: Mellen, 1988], 114). Binder thinks "the other literary sources [apart from Acts] imply a sizable Jewish population in the city" (*Into the Temple Courts*, 282). Pieter W. van der Horst thinks there were around one million Jews in Asia Minor ("Jews and Christians in Aphrodisias in the Light of Their Relations in Other Cities of Asia Minor," *NedTT* 43 [1989]: 106–7).

10,000–20,000 Jews. Even the low figure of 2 percent would give a population of around 4,000.

Whatever was the case, I suggest that the Jewish community was a sizable and united community with some standing in the city. It was a significant part of the polis.

2. The Jewish Community and the Early Christians in Ephesus

What interaction might there have been between this Jewish community and the Christ-believing communities in the city? How might the presence of such a Jewish community have impacted the growth and development of the Christ-believing communities in Ephesus? What might the realities have been on the ground? Before discussing this, we can note some difficulties we encounter in this discussion.

First, all the evidence we have for interaction between Jewish and Christ-believing communities in Ephesus comes from Christian sources. This is unsurprising, given the paucity of evidence we have for Jewish communities in the city, particularly in the Common Era, but it does mean that we are generally seeing these interactions from one perspective alone—the Christian one. It also means that in my discussion below, I will go through successive Christian sources.

Second, we need to remind ourselves that many of the early Christ-believers were, of course, ethnically Jewish. When we consider what might be thought of as Jewish ideas among Christ-believers, we need to ask if they come from Jews *or* from Jewish Christians *or* from gentile Christians who have adopted Jewish attitudes. Perhaps such ideas and practices came from Jewish Christians who, of course, continued to see themselves as Jews, rather than from non-Christian Jews. In addition, Jewish influence could be from Jewish tradition or Jewish writing and so could be a textual influence, mediated solely by Christ-believers.

Third, many have argued that Jewish communities in Asia Minor and elsewhere in the diaspora were very diverse, with local factors such as the time and circumstances of the foundation of the community and relationships with the wider community and with city officials considerably impacting the development and nature of the Jewish community.[24] Simi-

---

24. See further Trebilco, *Jewish Communities*, 188; Strelan, *Paul, Artemis, and the Jews*, 173.

larly, early Christian communities were clearly very diverse. Accordingly, while we can suggest what might be happening in Ephesus on the basis of evidence for either Jewish or Christian communities *elsewhere*, such suggestions can only ever be very tentative.

2.1. Paul and Acts[25]

According to Acts, Apollos was active in the synagogue in Ephesus, and there he met Priscilla and Aquila, who "explained the Way of God to him more accurately" (Acts 18:26).[26] Sometime afterwards, Christ-followers were to be found within the synagogue,[27] for in Acts 18:27 we read: "And when he [Apollos] wished to cross over to Achaia, the brothers and sisters [οἱ ἀδελφοί] [in Ephesus] encouraged him and wrote to the disciples to welcome him." These ἀδελφοί were Jewish believers in Jesus within the synagogue in Ephesus. We are not told how they came to faith, but the most likely supposition from within Luke's narrative is that they had been converted through the ministry of Priscilla and Aquila.

In Acts 19:1 we are told that Paul returns to Ephesus and then in Acts 19:8-10 we read:

> He [Paul] entered the synagogue and for three months spoke out boldly, and argued persuasively about the kingdom of God. When some stubbornly refused to believe and spoke evil of the Way before the congregation, he left them, taking the disciples with him, and argued daily in the lecture hall of Tyrannus. This continued for two years, so that all the residents of Asia, both Jews and Greeks, heard the word of the Lord.[28]

---

25. Paul gives no clear evidence for opposition from Jews in Ephesus in his letters. In 1 Cor 15:32, he writes of fighting wild animals in Ephesus, which is almost certainly a reference to non-Christians opponents, and in 1 Cor 16:8-9, he says there are "many adversaries" in Ephesus. In both cases, some of these opponents could be Jews, but in neither case is this certain.

26. All biblical quotations are from the NRSV. On Acts 18:19-21, see Trebilco, *Early Christians in Ephesus*, 110-11. For arguments that the Acts material relating to Ephesus can be regarded as basically authentic, see pp. 104-7 and the sources cited there.

27. Acts 18:26 might be taken to suggest there was only one synagogue in Ephesus, which may be unlikely if the Jewish community in the city was large. But as noted above with regard to Acts 19:8-10, Acts 18:26 need only be a reference to the particular synagogue in Ephesus in which the Christians were active.

28. Note also Acts 19:17.

According to this text, Paul preached for three months in the synagogue in Ephesus and then encountered opposition from some Jews. Three months is a particularly long time for Paul to stay in the synagogue[29] and shows that some Jews were receptive. This is confirmed by the note in 19:9 that when Paul finally left the synagogue, he took with him a number of believers, who were clearly Jewish Christians and perhaps some Godfearers.

This picture of Paul—who calls himself "the apostle to the gentiles"[30]—at work in the synagogue has often been questioned, particularly since Paul never mentions preaching in synagogues in his letters. However, it is clear from 2 Cor 11:24 ("Five times I have received from the Jews the forty lashes minus one"),[31] written shortly after Paul left Ephesus, that he did keep going to the synagogue. Such a punishment was administered by the synagogue for a wide range of serious offences; that Paul endured this punishment five times shows that he was often rejected by synagogue communities but also that did not lightly give up his commitment to preach to his compatriots and continued to attend synagogues and submit to their discipline.[32] This suggests that in many of the cities Paul visited, he would go to the synagogue, even if he had been punished recently elsewhere (see Gal 4:29; 1 Thess 2:15–16). In light of this, Paul's own anguish over the lack of response to the gospel by his fellow Jews in Rom 9–11 can be seen as his reflection on his own experience of the rejection of the gospel (Rom 9:30–3; 10:16–19, 21; 11:7, 11–15, 20, 25, 28).[33] It is also historically plausible

---

29. Compare Pisidian Antioch (Acts 13:13–14, 42, 44–52) and Thessalonica (Acts 17:2, 5–9).

30. See Rom 1:5, 13–14; 11:13–14; 15:15–21; Gal 1:16; 2:7–9; cf. Rom 15:16.

31. See also 1 Cor 9:20; Barclay, *Jews in the Mediterranean Diaspora*, 393–95. Paul also speaks of the gospel as addressed "to the Jew first and also to the Greeks" (Rom 1:16); see also Rom 2:9–10; 3:9; 9:1–5; 10:1, 12; 1 Cor 1:24; 7:18; Gal 3:28. The punishment is based on Deut 25:1–3. We have no record of where any of these floggings occurred, but Acts portrays several occasions prior to the writing of 2 Corinthians when Paul could have received the thirty-nine lashes; see Acts 13:45, 50; 14:5; 18:12. In 2 Cor 11:26, Paul also speaks of being in danger from his own people. Thus the consistent pattern in Acts of Paul being in conflict with the synagogue (see, e.g., 13:44–52; 17:1–5, 13–14; 18:5–7) is quite plausible.

32. See Stanley K. Stowers, "Social Status, Public Speaking and Private Teaching: The Circumstances of Paul's Preaching Activity," *NovT* 26 (1984): 64. That Paul continued to consider himself a Jew, with the right to present his brand of Judaism, is clear from Rom 9:1–5; 11:1; 1 Cor 9:19–23.

33. See also 2 Cor 3:14. In light of these passages, we can suggest that his description of the gospel as "to the Jew first and also to the Greek" is also autobiographical.

that the Christ-followers in Ephesus left the synagogue with Paul because of disagreement with other Jews (see Acts 19:9). This refusal to believe is exactly what Paul writes of in Rom 9.

But, of course, this does not mean there was no further contact between Christ-followers and the Jewish community in Ephesus. Clearly some Jews could have heard Paul in the Hall of Tyrannus; this is Luke's implication when he states that Paul argued there daily and then summarizes: "This continued for two years, so that all the residents of Asia, both Jews and Greeks, heard the word of the Lord" (Acts 19:10). This suggests some Jews were present in the Hall of Tyrannus along with Greeks, and there is no reason to doubt this since it is entirely credible that some Jews would have continued to be interested in Paul's preaching, even after he had left the synagogue. Of course, some Jews could well have gone to the Hall of Tyrannus to refute Paul and to convince other listeners (including other Jews) that he was wrong.[34] So we can suggest that there would be ongoing contact with Jews, after the departure from the synagogue of 19:9; it was simply the preaching of Christ within the walls of the synagogue that ceased.

This ties in with one element of the account of the Ephesian riot of Acts 19:23-41. In 19:33-34 we read:

> Some of the crowd gave instructions to Alexander, whom the Jews had pushed forward. And Alexander motioned for silence and tried to make a defense before the people. But when they recognized that he was a Jew, for about two hours all of them shouted in unison, "Great is Artemis of the Ephesians!"

The most likely interpretation of this event is that the Jew Alexander was put forward in order to distance the Jewish community from the Christ-believers and so to prevent harm coming to the Jews.[35] Alexander wished to make it clear to the other Ephesians present that the troublemaker Paul should *not* be associated with the Jewish community of the city. Rather, Paul represented a renegade faction. However, this backfired, since the

---

34. Note that Luke says in Acts 19:10 that "Jews ... heard the word of the Lord," which does not imply they necessarily agreed.

35. See Ernst Haenchen, *The Acts of the Apostles: A Commentary* (Oxford: Blackwell, 1971), 574, n. 7; 575; on the unevenness in the story see Trebilco, *Early Christians in Ephesus*, 160; for arguments for its historicity, see 160-61.

crowd did not distinguish between Jews and Jewish Christ-believers, and the crowd also knew that Jews did not worship Artemis; in their highly pro-Artemis mood, they reacted to Alexander's presence. But Alexander's actions and underlying concern make perfect sense: the Jewish community was concerned that its hard-fought yet somewhat vulnerable position in the city should not be jeopardized. That the Jewish community would want to act in defense of its rights is in keeping with the evidence from Josephus that shows the Jewish community in Ephesus, and communities elsewhere, sought to defend these rights, as we have seen.[36] This suggests that their position in the city could easily be disrupted. It also suggests that although Paul had left the synagogue many months before, the Jewish community continued to be concerned about his preaching and that they themselves distinguished between their community and the Pauline Christ-believers and sought to assert and preserve their distinctive identity compared with these Christ-believers. It also seems likely that the on-going relationship between (some members of) the Jewish community and the Christ-believers could have been difficult.[37]

2.2. The Pastoral Epistles[38]

Many have argued that 1 and 2 Timothy were written to Christ-followers in Ephesus, probably between 80 and 100 CE (see 1 Tim 4:1; 2 Tim 2:26; 3:13).[39] As he writes, the Pastor faces opponents who have already had a considerable impact among the readers and whom he regards as posing

---

36. See Trebilco, *Jewish Communities*, 8–19; Trebilco, *Early Christians in Ephesus*, 38–43; Justin Taylor, *Commentaire Historique (Act. 18,23–28,31)*, vol. 5 of *Les Actes des deux Apôtres*, EBib 30 (Paris: Librairie Lecoffre, 1996), 51–52.

37. See Robert F. Stoops, "Riot and Assembly: The Social Context of Acts 19:23–41," *JBL* 108 (1989): 73–91.

38. With regard to Ephesians, there is the issue of textual uncertainty in Eph 1:1, which means we cannot be sure that it was written to Ephesus. Even if it was written to the city, the difficulty of extrapolating from the text (e.g., Eph 2:11–22) to actual ongoing relations between Christians and contemporary Jews in Ephesus is such that it cannot be included here. See also my "Reading Ephesians in Ephesus: A Letter to Pauline *and* Johannine Christ-Followers?," in *Ephesus as a Religious Center under the Principate*, ed. Trevor W. Thompson, James Walters, and Allen Black (Tübingen: Mohr Siebeck, forthcoming).

39. See also Trebilco, *Early Christians in Ephesus*, 197–209 and the references cited there.

a dangerous threat.[40] The opponents are clearly within the community[41] rather than outsiders who have travelled to Ephesus to influence this community. Accordingly they are to be seen as Christ-believers rather than Jews.

Most scholars would agree that there was a Jewish dimension to the teaching of the Pastor's opponents.[42] The opponents are first introduced in 1 Tim 1:3-4 where Timothy is instructed to order certain persons "not to occupy themselves with myths and endless genealogies that promote speculations" (μηδὲ προσέχειν μύθοις καὶ γενεαλογίαις ἀπεράντοις, αἵτινες ἐκζητήσεις παρέχουσιν). While some commentators think the reference is to the myths used by gnostics, there is little to support this view, and in Titus 1:14 the Pastor criticizes the opponents for "paying attention to *Jewish* myths" (προσέχοντες Ἰουδαϊκοῖς μύθοις; see also Tit 1:10; 3:9.).[43] Although the term *myth* need not mean the same thing every time the Pastor uses it, it seems likely that Jewish myths are also meant in 1 Tim 1:3-4, since the Pastor goes on in 1 Tim 1:6-11 to speak of "some people" who desire to be "teachers of the law" (νομοδιδάσκαλοι), which in this context is clearly the Jewish law.[44] Hence the Pastor connects the myths with Judaism and the law, which suggests that both myths and genealogies are to be understood against a Jewish background.

---

40. See I. Howard Marshall in collaboration with Philip H. Towner, *A Critical and Exegetical Commentary on the Pastoral Epistles*, ICC (Edinburgh: T&T Clark, 1999), 42.

41. Hence they are spoken of as having shipwrecked the faith in 1 Tim 1:19-20, and Timothy is told to command "certain people" not to teach any different doctrine (1 Tim 1:3; 4:11), which indicates that they are within the community. See also 1 Tim 1:5-6; 2 Tim 2:18; 3:8; Trebilco, *Early Christians in Ephesus*, 211-12.

42. See for example Strelan, *Paul, Artemis, and the Jews*, 155.

43. See Philip H. Towner, *The Goal of Our Instruction: The Structure of Theology and Ethics in the Pastoral Epistles*, JSNTSup 34 (Sheffield: JSOT Press, 1989), 28; William D. Mounce, *Pastoral Epistles*, WBC 46 (Nashville: Nelson, 2000), lxx. For the connection with gnostic views, see, for example, Walter Schmithals, "The Corpus Paulinum and Gnosis," in *The New Testament and Gnosis: Essays in Honour of Robert McL. Wilson*, ed. Alastair H. B. Logan and Alexander J. M. Wedderburn (Edinburgh: T&T Clark, 1983), 117.

44. Philip H. Towner, *The Letters to Timothy and Titus*, NICNT (Grand Rapids: Eerdmans, 2006), 120-31. This is also shown by the contact between the list in 1 Tim 1:9-10 and the Decalogue.

In the Pastor's opinion, the opponents did not use the law "lawfully" (νομίμως) because they said the law applied to all,[45] whereas for the Pastor, "the law is laid down not for the innocent but for the lawless and disobedient," whom he goes on to list (1 Tim 1:9–10). This suggests that the opponents thought the Jewish law continued to be valid for Christ-believers to some extent, certainly in ways the Pastor thought were now wrong. The Pastor probably objected to the way the opponents used the law as a source for their speculations (1 Tim 1:3–4) and in order to argue for their ascetic views relating to food, a view that may have reflected Jewish food laws (1 Tim 4:1–3).[46] The opponents seem to have argued that both of these elements of their teaching were relevant to all Christ-believers. By contrast, the Pastor regards it as illegitimate to use the law to regulate the Christian life; the law is not for the righteous (1 Tim 1:9).

In 1 Timothy, the reference to the Jewish character of the opponents is found when the teaching is first introduced in 1 Tim 1:4, 7–11; as Marshall notes "it is presumably intended to colour our reading of what follows."[47] It seems likely then that the opponents included Jewish Christ-believers and/or gentile Christ-believers influenced by such Jewish believers, who maintained the validity of at least some significant parts of the law for believers.

But did the opponents develop what can be seen as Jewish dimensions of their teaching *at least in part* because of the influence of, or in interaction with, the local Jewish community in Ephesus? Certainly, the totality of the content of the opponents' teaching cannot be explained *solely* from Jewish influence or as based on Jewish teaching. For example, the opponents' belief that the resurrection has already passed (2 Tim 2:18)[48] cannot be seen as developed *solely* under the impact of the Jewish community and must come from somewhere else. Indeed, it can be argued that strong dimensions of their teaching were developments from *within* the Pauline tradition itself,

---

45. As well as arguing for the validity of the food laws (see 1 Tim 4:1–3), they seem to have been developing esoteric myths and genealogies from the law (see 1 Tim 1:4). The Pastor asserts in 1 Tim 1:8–11 that the proper function and role of the Old Testament law is not to serve as a source of such myths and genealogies but rather to expose sin.

46. See Mounce, *Pastoral Epistles*, lxx.

47. Ibid., 44; see also 195, n. 115.

48. On this see Trebilco, *Early Christians in Ephesus*, 218–22. The freedom currently given to women (as is suggested by 1 Tim 2:8–15, for example, and what is said about widows in 1 Tim 5) can also not readily be explained from a Jewish background alone.

and so may be independent of *any* influence outside of the Christian community. Further, as we have seen, the evidence from Acts suggests that at the end of the Pauline mission, the Pauline community in Ephesus had a significant Jewish element. Perhaps some of these Jewish Christians from Paul's time (or gentiles influenced by them) were part of "the opponents" and over time developed some of the Jewish dimensions of the opponents' teaching, quite independently of interaction with non-Christian Jews in the city.[49]

But while Jewish influence from the Ephesian Jewish community cannot explain all the views presented as held by the opponents, it may still be a factor. In coming to their views—including those that do have Jewish roots—were the opponents influenced, to some extent at least, by the prominent and sizable Jewish community in the city? Was this one factor behind the opponents promoting the Jewish law, for example? Perhaps the significant and sizeable Jewish community in Ephesus may have exerted an influence on the opponents as they developed their views, *as well as* their teaching reflecting the fact that they themselves were probably Jewish Christians within the Christian community.[50] Were both these factors significant with regard to the development of the prominent Jewish dimensions of the opponents' teaching? Unfortunately we can only raise, rather than answer, these questions.

2.3. John's Gospel

In my view strong arguments can be mounted that John's Gospel was written in Ephesus, although, of course, this issue is much debated.[51]

Stephen Wilson, like many others, thinks John's Gospel can be read as evidence for both the history and the present situation of the Johannine community. On this view, "the depiction of Jews and Judaism in John expresses the troubled history of the relationship between his community

---

49. See also Werner Thiessen, *Christen in Ephesus: Die historische und theologische Situation in vorpaulinischer und paulinischer Zeit und zur Zeit der Apostelgeschichte und der Pastoralbriefe*, TANZ 12 (Tübingen: Francke, 1995), 86 and n. 311.

50. It seems unlikely that Jewish Christ-believers from somewhere else were influential in the development of the opponents' teaching, since the Pastor says nothing about such visitors; if he had, then such travelers could be teaching these facets of Jewish practice. There is no evidence in 1 and 2 Timothy that circumcision was an issue. If the Jewish community was exerting an influence on the Christians in Ephesus, then such influence did not include circumcision.

51. See Trebilco, *Early Christians in Ephesus*, 241–63.

and the synagogue."⁵² On such a view, all that is said about "the Jews" in John's Gospel does indeed "fit" with what we know of the actual Jewish community in Ephesus, in the sense that "the Jews" in the Gospel are presented as a strong community, opposed to the Christian group, and able to act forcibly against them.⁵³ Such an argument is compatible with our evidence for the actual Jewish community in the city.

However, I do not think that we can include John's Gospel here as evidence for interaction between Jews and Christians *in Ephesus*, since, following Richard Bauckham and a number of other scholars, I take the view that the gospels were written for all Christians and so I do not think John's Gospel can be used to reconstruct the history of a particular community.⁵⁴ But I note that many would want to follow the view that Wilson propounds.

2.4. The Johannine Letters

I would argue that the Johannine Letters give evidence for a Johannine community in and around Ephesus and that shortly prior to 1 John being written, a group we can call the secessionists had left that community.⁵⁵ Some have argued that the secessionists were Jews who denied that Jesus was the Messiah.⁵⁶ This would be in view in 1 John 2:22: "Who is the liar but the one who denies that Jesus is the Christ?" If this was the case, perhaps such Jews came to their view under the influence, at least in part, of the Jewish community in Ephesus.

However, it is very unlikely that the secessionists were Jews who rejected Jesus as the Messiah. Firstly, 1 John 2:19 makes it clear that the secessionists had once been within the community, which shows that they were not non-Christian Jews. Secondly, if the secessionists were Jews who rejected Jesus as the Messiah, we would expect the author to deal with the

---

52. Stephen G. Wilson regards this as "a universally recognized fact" (*Related Strangers: Jews and Christians, 70–170 C.E.* [Minneapolis: Fortress, 1995], 73).

53. They can cast them out of the synagogue (John 9:22; 12:42; 16:2) and may even be able to put some Christians to death (John 16:2; cf. 10:28; 15:18).

54. See Trebilco, *Early Christians in Ephesus*, 237–41; see Richard Bauckham, ed., *The Gospels for All Christians: Rethinking the Gospel Audiences* (Grand Rapids: Eerdmans, 1998).

55. See 1 John 2:18–26; 4:1–6; 2 John 7–9. For their location in Ephesus, see Trebilco, *Early Christians in Ephesus*, 241–71.

56. See Daniel R. Streett, *They Went Out from Us: The Identity of the Opponents in First John*, BZNW 177 (Berlin: de Gruyter, 2011).

Scriptures at some length, but in fact there are no Old Testament quotations, and very few allusions, in 1 and 2 John.[57] It seems clear then that the secessionists are Christians with a different Christology. Thirdly, that the secessionists did have a different Christology is in keeping with the emphasis of 1 John on Jesus as the Son of the Father (e.g., 1 John 1:4; 2:22-24) rather than on Jesus as Messiah.[58]

There are no dimensions of the Johannine Letters in which we can detect interaction with the local Jewish community.[59] As has often been noted, the Johannine community seems to be an insulated group, as evidenced by its in-group language and its attitude to "the world."[60] While the letters show some interaction with Old Testament tradition and language (although this is surprisingly small),[61] there are no signs of interaction with contemporary Jews in the city at the time of writing. We may suggest that it is because of the evident insularity of the community, resulting perhaps from schism, that we do not see more obvious signs of contact between the community addressed in the letters and the Jewish community.[62]

2.5. Revelation

We do not have any direct evidence for contact or conflict between the Ephesian Christian community addressed in Rev 2:1-7 and the Jewish community in Ephesus.[63]

---

57. See n. 61 below.

58. See further Judith M. Lieu, *I, II and III John: A Commentary*, NTL (Louisville: Westminster John Knox, 2008), 105-6.

59. Interestingly, Ἰουδαῖος, found seventy times in John's Gospel, does not occur in 1-3 John.

60. See Trebilco, *Early Christians in Ephesus*, 385-92. For negative references to "the world," see 1 John 2:15-17; 3:1, 13; 4:1, 3, 5; 5:4-5, 19; 2 John 7. Positive references are found in 1 John 2:2; 4:9, 14.

61. See "the antichrist" (1 John 2:18, 22; 4:3; 2 John 7) and Cain (1 John 3:12), for example. See also Donald A. Carson, "1-3 John," in *Commentary on the New Testament Use of the Old Testament*, ed. Gregory K. Beale and Donald A. Carson (Grand Rapids: Baker Academic, 2007), 1063-67.

62. Wilson, writing of the Johannine community, notes: "As internal divisions became more prominent, the problem of Judaism faded into the background, so that while it retains its place in the final redaction of the Gospel it goes unmentioned in the letters" (*Related Strangers*, 73).

63. Of course, John the Seer himself was undoubtedly a Jewish Christian and was

However, in Rev 2:9 and 3:9 John writes of "the synagogue of Satan" in Smyrna and Philadelphia. Note Rev 2:9: "I know your affliction and your poverty, even though you are rich. I know the slander on the part of those who say that they are Jews and are not, but are a synagogue of Satan."

In my view, the most likely interpretation of these verses, though it is hotly disputed,[64] is that they concern people who are non-Christian Jews but whom John considers to have now forfeited the right to call themselves Jews because they reject Christ and attack his followers. Because they actively oppose and slander Christians (βλασφημία [2:9]),[65] John regards them as aligning themselves with Satan, the Great Accuser (Rev 12:10). Hence for John, they are a synagogue not of God (as the Jews themselves would have claimed) but of Satan.[66] In John's eyes, it is the members of the church who are the true Jews.[67] This suggests that the Christian communities in Smyrna and Philadelphia were in conflict with their local Jewish communities.

However, John does not mention Jews in his letter to the Christians in Ephesus in Rev 2:1–7. Perhaps John is silent about conflict between Christians and Jews in Ephesus because conflict was not an issue for the addressees there, in contrast to Christians in Smyrna and Philadelphia. Or perhaps we should note that John's letters, to some extent at least,

---

deeply embedded in the Old Testament and perhaps had significant links with Ephesus, but my concern here is with the Christian community in Ephesus.

64. The other view is that they are gentile Christians; see Wilson, *Related Strangers*, 163; David Frankfurter, "Jews or Not? Reconstructing 'the Other' in Rev 2:9 and 3:9," HTR 94 (2001): 403–25. Michele Murray, *Playing a Jewish Game: Gentile Christian Judaizing in the First and Second Centuries CE*, SCJud13 (Waterloo, ON: Wilfrid Laurier University Press, 2004), 73–81. Murray writes that Rev 2:9 and 3:9 refer to Christians who "are accused of falsely identifying themselves as Jews" (p. 99).

65. βλασφημία is strong language, elsewhere used of the activity of the beast and the whore; see Rev 13:1, 5, 6; 17:3. Jan Lambrecht argues that here it refers to slander against Christians rather than blasphemy against God and Christ ("Jewish Slander: A Note on Rev 2,9–10," in *Collected Studies on Pauline Literature and on the Book of Revelation* [Rome: Pontificio Istituto Biblico, 2001], 329–39).

66. See Elisabeth Schüssler Fiorenza, *The Book of Revelation: Justice and Judgment* (Philadelphia: Fortress, 1985), 116.

67. See Leonard L. Thompson, *The Book of Revelation: Apocalypse and Empire* (Oxford: Oxford University Press, 1990), 90; see also Jan Lambrecht, "Synagogues of Satan (cf. Rev 2,9 and 3,9): Anti-Judaism in the Apocalypse," in *Collected Studies on Pauline Literature*, 341–56.

have an exemplary character.[68] This would mean that what is said to one church has a representative or paradigmatic function for the other six churches in Asia (and elsewhere in the province, and further afield, too). What is said of one church, in this case about conflict with the Jews, may well apply to others, though probably to a lesser degree. This is hinted at by John at the end of each proclamation when he writes, "Let anyone who has an ear listen to what the Spirit is saying to the *churches*" (e.g., Rev 2:7). Certainly, just because nothing is said on a topic to one particular church, does not mean that that church was totally uninvolved in that regard. Clearly what is said to one church applies to that church, but what is said to a particular church has at least some relevance to another, as the refrain in Rev 2:7 (and 2:11, 17, 29; 3:6, 13, 22; 13:9) suggests. In particular, we cannot say that there was no conflict between Christians in Ephesus and the Jewish community in the city at the time of Revelation *solely* on the basis of John's silence.

However, it remains significant that we *do not have direct evidence* for that conflict; it is simply likely to have been the case because it occurred in nearby Smyrna and Philadelphia.

2.6. Ignatius

Ignatius wrote to Ephesian Christians between 105 and 110 CE,[69] and he says nothing to that community about contemporary Jews. However, in writing to the Christians at Magnesia, Ignatius warns them against living "according to Judaism" and keeping the Sabbath (*Magn.* 8–10).[70] In *Magn.* 10.3 he writes: "It is outlandish to proclaim Jesus Christ and practice Judaism," which suggests that some Christians were involved in Jewish practices, of which the Sabbath is clearly one. However, it is not clear that they did so under the direct influence of Jews.[71]

In *Phld.* 6.1 we read: "But if anyone should interpret Judaism to you, do not hear him. For it is better to hear Christianity from a man who is circumcised than Judaism from one who is uncircumcised." In the second

---

68. See Peter Hirschberg, *Das eschatologische Israel: Untersuchungen zum Gottesvolkverständnis der Johannesoffenbarung*, WMANT 84 (Neukirchen-Vluyn: Neukirchener Verlag, 1999), 117–18.
69. See Trebilco, *Early Christians in Ephesus*, 629–31.
70. See Murray, *Playing a Jewish Game*, 84–86
71. See ibid., 86–87.

sentence quoted here, Ignatius refers first of all to a Jewish Christian who is promoting Christian faith and then to a gentile who is promoting Judaism. What he goes on to say in the letter suggests these are gentile *Christians*;[72] that is, there are gentile Christians who, according to Ignatius, were preaching or promoting Jewish practices. We do not know *why* these gentile Christians were doing this. As Michele Murray comments: "Gentile Christians in Asia Minor may have continued with prior practices of Jewish rites adopted when they were God fearers on the periphery of the synagogue: they simply did not change their lifestyle when they became Christians.... Or, perhaps in the setting of a vibrant diaspora Judaism, gentile Christians became exposed to Judaism through social interaction with Jews."[73] But Ignatius is silent about this in relation to Ephesus.

2.7. The Acts of John

The Acts of John are probably to be dated to around 150–160 CE,[74] and many of the activities of John recounted in the Acts of John occur in Ephesus. Although the provenance of this work is debated, Pieter J. Lalleman and others have argued that it was written in Asia Minor, and this is the most likely possibility.[75] Accordingly, the text may well have some knowledge of the contemporary situation in Ephesus and wider Asia Minor at the time it was written.

The only place in the text where Jews are mentioned is in Acts of John 94, where we read: "Now, before he [Jesus] was arrested by the lawless Jews, who received their law from a lawless serpent, he gathered us all together and said, 'Before I am delivered up to them, let us sing a hymn to the Father, and go forth to what lies before us.'"[76] This reflects the gospels,

---

72. See Wilson, *Related Strangers*, 164; Murray, *Playing a Jewish Game*, 88–91.

73. Murray, *Playing a Jewish Game*, 91.

74. See Pieter J. Lalleman, *The Acts of John: A Two-Stage Initiation into Johannine Gnosticism*, SAAA 4 (Leuven: Peeters, 1998), 268–70; Harold W. Attridge, "The Acts of John and the Fourth Gospel," in *From Judaism to Christianity: Tradition and Transition; A Festschrift for Thomas H. Tobin, S. J., on the Occasion of His Sixty-Fifth Birthday*, ed. Patricia Walters, NovTSup 136 (Leiden: Brill 2010), 256.

75. See Lalleman, *Acts of John*, 256–68; Helmut Engelmann, "Ephesos und die Johannesakten," *ZPE* 103 (1994): 297–302.

76. Note Richard I. Pervo, "Johannine Trajectories in the Acts of John," *Apocrypha* 3 (1992): 48, where he writes that the Acts of John "display scarcely a trace of affinity with or derivation from Judaism."

where Jesus is arrested by other Jews (see Matt 26:47–56; Mark 14:43–47; Luke 22:47–53; John 18:2–12). However, Acts of John 94 clearly demonstrates an anti-Jewish sentiment, since it describes them as "lawless Jews," and adds that the Jewish law was delivered by "a lawless serpent," which is clearly a reference to Satan.[77] Perhaps in this, the Acts of John is influenced by but goes beyond the Gospel of John, which the author of the Acts of John clearly knows.[78]

Thus, there may simply be a textual explanation for what is said in Acts of John 94, and it is hard to know if this antipathy is in any way influenced by interactions between the Christian author of the Acts of John and contemporary Jews. There is no further evidence in the Acts of John for any such interaction, and it is noteworthy that the author of the Acts of John makes no other comments about Jews in the text. Hence, the Acts of John give no clear evidence for any contemporary interactions between himself and the Jewish community.[79]

2.8. Justin Martyr

Justin's *Dialogue with Trypho*, written around 155–160 CE[80] in Rome, was set in Ephesus according to Eusebius (*Hist. eccl.* 4.18.6), perhaps on the basis of a well-established tradition. It purports to be a historical dialogue. Judith Lieu argues that it is entirely reasonable to think that Justin did have discussions with a Trypho in Ephesus in the way suggested in the *Dialogue*. His readers would also regard this as reasonable.[81]

Although we cannot regard Justin's work as a reliable record of an actual debate, both Justin and his readers could well have seen Ephesus as

---

77. See Pervo, "Johannine Trajectories," 48, n. 6.
78. See John 8:44: "You are from your father the devil, and you choose to do your father's desires." See also Lalleman, *Acts of John*, 110–23; Attridge, "Acts of John," 258–65. Eric Junod and Jean-Daniel Kaestli relate this reference to the serpent to John 8:44 (*Textus alii Commentarius*, vol. 2 of *Acta Iohannis*, CCSA 2 [Turnhout: Brepols, 1983], 643–44).
79. Lalleman thinks that the community behind the Acts of John "has gained a considerable distance from the Jewish context in which its Gospel [of John] originated" (*Acts of John*, 121).
80. See Judith Lieu, *Image and Reality: The Jews in the World of the Christians in the Second Century* (Edinburgh: T&T Clark, 1996), 103.
81. See ibid., 103–4; see also Timothy J. Horner, *Listening to Trypho: Justin Martyr's Dialogue Reconsidered*, CBET 28 (Leuven: Peeters, 2001), 179–89.

a suitable and realistic venue for a debate between a learned Christian and a learned Jew concerning matters such as Jesus and the law.[82] This suggests that it is reasonable to think that there were these sorts of discussions in Ephesus around 160 CE.

What does this suggest about the interaction between Jews and Christians in Ephesus? It at the least suggests that each community was reasonably knowledgeable about the other and that there may have been in-depth debates and disputes "conducted in a civilized tone"[83] about a range of matters.

2.9. Polycrates

According to Eusebius, around 190 CE, Polycrates, bishop of Ephesus, described 14 Nisan as the day "when the people [ὁ λαός] remove the leaven."[84] Bauckham notes that this cannot simply be derived from Exod 12:15, but rather reflects contemporary Jewish practice and the language that was used for that practice.[85] We note also the use of ὁ λαός for the Jewish people; this term is found in Jewish inscriptions in Asia Minor (*IJO* 2.26.4 [Nysa], 44.3 [Smyrna], 181.2 [Appia], 206.5 [Hierapolis])[86] and so probably reflects contemporary Jewish language. Accordingly, Bauckham notes that Polycrates "can speak of things Jewish in an accurately Jewish way."[87] This may in part be due to Polycrates living in close proximity to the large Jewish community of the city and perhaps being part of a church with a strongly Jewish-Christian background. In this small way then we see the interaction of Jews in Ephesus with some Christians towards the end of the second century.

---

82. See Thompson, *Book of Revelation*, 143.

83. Wilson, *Related Strangers*, 283; see also Horner, *Listening to Trypho*, 187–88.

84. See Polycrates, quoted in Eusebius, *Hist. eccl.* 5.24.2–7.

85. Richard Bauckham, "Papias and Polycrates on the Origin of the Fourth Gospel," *JTS* 44 (1993): 31–33.

86. See also Emil Schürer, *The History of the Jewish People in the Age of Jesus Christ*, rev. and ed. Geza Vermes, Fergus Millar, and Martin Goodman, vol. 3.1 (Edinburgh: T&T Clark, 1986), 89–90.

87. Bauckham, "Papias and Polycrates," 37.

2.10. The Synod of Laodicea

The Synod of Laodicea (ca. 363 CE), which related to Christians in Asia and so is relevant to those in Ephesus, prohibited Christians from practicing their religion with Jews, in particular, "celebrating festivals with them," "keeping the Sabbath," and "eating unleavened bread" during the Passover. The Synod decreed that Christians should work on the Sabbath and read the gospels as well as the Jewish Scriptures on Saturday (Canons 16, 29, 37, 38).[88] This is highly revealing and indicates significant Jewish influence on the life of Christian communities in the mid-fourth century.[89]

3. Conclusion

We have seen that there is good—though limited—evidence for a sizable, significant, and (at least to some extent) united Jewish community in Ephesus in the first and second centuries CE. We can suggest then that this Jewish community was a significant group in the city and also in the foreground for the Christians in Ephesus. Furthermore, given that the first Christ-believers were Jews who would have been involved in both the Jewish synagogue and the Christ-believing assembly, and given that so much was shared between the two groups, it seems likely that actual interaction between Jews and Christians might well have been ongoing or at least might have occurred at a range of points.

We see this interaction in Acts, where we learn that Paul and others preached in a synagogue in Ephesus and had some success, but they also provoked a negative response and left the synagogue as a group. According to Acts 19, during the riot in the theater there was an attempt to distance the Jewish community from the growing Christ-believing group.

However, apart from Acts, New Testament texts provide very limited *explicit* evidence for the interaction between the Jewish community and the Christ-believers in Ephesus. There is no clear evidence from the Johannine Letters or from Revelation. In the Pastorals there is evidence for a Jewish dimension to the opponents' teaching, but this teaching could well have been developed by Jewish Christians themselves (or gentiles influenced by Jewish Christians), rather than being a development that resulted

---

88. Ulrich Huttner, *Early Christianity in the Lycus Valley*, AJEC 85, ECAM 1 (Leiden: Brill 2013), 291–314.

89. See further van der Horst, "Jews and Christians," 118.

directly from interaction with the Jewish community in the city. Ignatius and the Acts of John also provide no evidence for contemporary interaction between the two communities relating to Ephesus.

But then the evidence of both Justin Martyr and Polycrates—limited as it is—suggests some real interaction between Jews and Christians in Ephesus. Also, the much later Synod of Laodicea—admittedly not Ephesus but of relevance to Ephesus—shows some real convergences of practice between the two communities.

Accordingly, we have a variegated picture of interaction. Overall, the *lack* of visibility of the Jewish community in most of the texts from Ephesus that we have discussed is surprising. This is particularly the case because we have suggested that the Jewish community was sizeable and prominent in the city, as well as being well organized and united. It would be in the foreground for the growing community of Christ-believers, and we would expect there to be ongoing interaction between Jews and Christians. A well-organized and united Jewish community would also be well placed to object to the growth of the Christian community in the city and to oppose the Christian community in an organized and coherent fashion through synagogue discipline and other means. The Jews might also have been able to go to the authorities to at least raise issues of concern, which is what we consistently see in the documents preserved by Josephus.[90]

So clearly we would expect the Jewish community to feature more in the Christian literature from Ephesus. Can we explain the apparent lack of interaction between the two groups in our texts then? We have a number of options to consider.

Firstly, perhaps this supposed lack of interaction is simply related to the nature of our evidence. With regard to Christian evidence, of course, most of the New Testament consists of occasional documents that are responding to particular and often in-house issues. We only know about the practice of the Lord's Supper in Pauline churches because this had been a highly contentious issue in Corinth and so Paul wrote about it. Without this, we would have no evidence about the practice of the Lord's Supper. Perhaps, then, the relationship with the Jewish community was not contentious, or at least it was not addressed in our occasional documents. This in itself would be a significant insight. But certainly the evidence in Paul's

---

90. In these documents, when Jewish privileges were infringed or other significant issues challenged the community, they acted to address the problem.

letters and in Acts suggests that in the early period such relations were contentious. So this argument seems less than likely as an explanation for later silence on the matter.

Secondly, perhaps this supposed lack of interaction is simply related to the accident of preservation. I have already noted the scarcity of Jewish evidence from the first century CE onwards. Further, if we had an early Christian figure from Ephesus who wrote explicitly about matters relating to Judaism, then we would know much more about relations between the Jewish community and Christ-believers, at least from the perspective of that author. So perhaps a key reason is simply what has been preserved and what has been lost.

Thirdly, perhaps the Christian communities of Ephesus were introverted and insular. Did the Christians somehow live in isolation from the Jews? Did this insularity or isolation perhaps mean that they did not relate to the Jewish community as a community?[91] This is possible but seems less likely, given the amount of interaction we know of elsewhere.

Fourthly, we might think that size is a factor here. If the Jewish community in Ephesus numbered in the many thousands, as seems possible, then perhaps a number of small Christ-believing groups totaling a few hundred at the most[92] could isolate themselves from a very large Jewish community and thus pass "under the radar." This might particularly be the case with Christ-believers meeting predominantly in house churches.[93] But Acts 19:8–10 suggests that even a small Christian community might be of concern to the Jewish community. That Paul endured the synagogue punishment of thirty-nine lashes five times (2 Cor 11:24) also shows that diaspora synagogues were concerned about just one person (admittedly an

---

91. Or perhaps the Jewish community was not at all related in *actual practice* to the Christians? See Andrew S. Jacobs, "The Lion and the Lamb: Reconsidering Jewish-Christian Relations in Antiquity," in *The Ways That Never Parted: Jews and Christians in Late Antiquity and the Early Middle Ages*, ed. Adam H. Becker and Annette Yoshiko Reed, TSAJ 95 (Tübingen: Mohr Siebeck, 2003; repr., Minneapolis: Fortress, 2007), 102 and n. 25.

92. For discussion about the size of the Christian community in Ephesus, see Robinson, *Bauer Thesis*, 120; see also Mikael Tellbe, *Christ-Believers in Ephesus. A Textual Analysis of Early Christian Identity Formation in a Local Perspective*, WUNT 242 (Tübingen: Mohr Siebeck, 2009), 47 and n. 213.

93. However, on this, see Edward Adams, *The Earliest Christian Meeting Places: Almost Exclusively Houses?*, LNTS 450 (London: Bloomsbury T&T Clark, 2013).

influential person) disrupting their community through Christian preaching.

Fifthly, did a "parting of the ways" at an early point lead to very limited interaction between the Jewish community and the Christ-believing communities? This seems highly *unlikely*. Here I think of Adam H. Becker and Annette Yoshiko Reed's book, *The Ways That Never Parted*. They write that in choosing this title:

> We wish to call attention to the ample evidence that speaks against the notion of a single and simple "Parting of the Ways" in the first or second century CE and, most importantly, against the assumption that no meaningful convergence ever occurred thereafter.... we suggest that Jews and Christians (or at least the elites among them) may have been engaged in the task of "parting" throughout Late Antiquity and the early Middle Ages, precisely because the two never really "parted" during that period with the degree of decisiveness or finality needed to render either tradition irrelevant to the self-definition of the other, or even to make participation in both an unattractive or inconceivable option.[94]

Certainly, the (admittedly very limited) evidence from Justin Martyr, Polycrates of Ephesus, and the later Synod of Laodicea shows ongoing interaction did occur between Jews and Christians in Ephesus, which suggests it may well have happened earlier too.

But sixthly, a key factor here is the diversity of both Judaism and early Christianity. This diversity in both cases is well known across Asia Minor[95]—but what about diversity *within* Ephesus? Such diversity is fairly clear in Ephesus as far as the early Christians are concerned—where virtually all those who have considered the evidence recently would suggest that there were a number of different Christ-believing communities in the city.[96] Such diversity is less well documented for the Jews in Ephesus.

---

94. See Annette Yoshiko Reed and Adam H. Becker, "Introduction: Traditional Models and New Directions," in Becker and Reed, *Ways That Never Parted*, 22–23.

95. For Jewish communities, see Trebilco, *Jewish Communities*. For early Christianity, see for example Richard E. Oster, "Christianity in Asia Minor," *ABD* 1:938–54.

96. See for example, Tellbe, *Christ-Believers in Ephesus*, 39–47. He thinks "there were various types or groups of Christ-believers in Ephesus towards the end of the first and the beginning of the second century.... However, when it comes to the possibility of reconstructing clearly distinguishable communities or groups of Christ-believers in Ephesus, I remain more pessimistic" (47).

Indeed, I have suggested that they could act as a united body—but there could still have been different synagogue communities that displayed significant diversity on a range of issues.[97] We need think only of the range of synagogue communities in Rome and the evidence for diversity there within the Jewish community.[98]

This would mean that different groups within the early Christian communities in Ephesus and within what we might call the Jewish *communities* in Ephesus could sustain different levels of interaction and different relationships with the other grouping. Some Christians might have had virtually no interaction with Jews (perhaps the group represented in the Johannine Letters), while other Christian groups may have had significant and ongoing interaction with Jewish groups (as shown by Justin and Polycrates). Such diversity and difference may have been evident among the different synagogues in Ephesus, too.

On this view, our evidence relating to Ephesus would predominantly come from those Christ-believing groups that had little interaction with local Jewish communities, at least at the time represented by our evidence. But there might well have been other groups of both Jews and Christians who would have told a quite different story.

Finally, in *The Ways That Never Parted*, Becker and Reed write of "the inadequacy of any monolithic model that seeks to theorize the relationships between 'Judaism' and 'Christianity' *without considering the socio-cultural and discursive specificities that shaped interactions between Jews and Christians in different cultural contexts, geographical locales, and social strata.*"[99] I hope this study has shown the importance of specific context and of geographical locale and has again underlined the point that it is risky to generalize from one polis to another.

---

97. Thus the different synagogue communities could act together when this was important (and when they were facing external pressure, for example) but could also be quite different in many other areas of their communal life, including their interactions with others such as Christians.

98. See Margaret H. Williams, who argues that "everything we know about the Roman Jewish community in particular and synagogal structures in general tells us that a considerable degree of diversity is to be expected, not total uniformity" (*Jews in a Graeco-Roman Environment*, WUNT 312 [Tübingen: Mohr Siebeck, 2013], 133).

99. Adam H. Becker and Annette Y. Reed, preface to Becker and Reed, *Ways That Never Parted*, x; emphasis added.

Bibliography

Adams, Edward. *The Earliest Christian Meeting Places: Almost Exclusively Houses?* LNTS 450. London: Bloomsbury T&T Clark, 2013.

Ameling, Walter. "Die jüdischen Gemeinden im antiken Kleinasien." Pages 29–55 in *Jüdische Gemeinden und Organisationsformen von der Antike bis zur Gegenwart.* Edited by Robert Jütte and Abraham Peter Kustermann. AZGKJ 3. Vienna: Böhlau, 1996.

Ascough, Richard S., Philip A. Harland, and John S. Kloppenborg, eds. *Associations in the Greco-Roman World: A Sourcebook.* Waco, TX: Baylor University Press, 2012.

Attridge, Harold W. "The Acts of John and the Fourth Gospel." Pages 255–65 in *From Judaism to Christianity: Tradition and Transition; A Festschrift for Thomas H. Tobin, S. J., on the Occasion of His Sixty-Fifth Birthday.* Edited by Patricia Walters. NovTSup 136. Leiden: Brill 2010.

Barclay, John M. G. *Against Apion.* Vol. 10 of *Flavius Josephus: Translation and Commentary.* Leiden: Brill, 2007.

———. *Jews in the Mediterranean Diaspora: From Alexander to Trajan (323 BCE–117 CE).* Edinburgh: T&T Clark, 1996.

Bauckham, Richard, ed. *The Gospels for All Christians: Rethinking the Gospel Audiences.* Grand Rapids: Eerdmans, 1998.

———. "Papias and Polycrates on the Origin of the Fourth Gospel." *JTS* 44 (1993): 24–69.

Becker, Adam H., and Annette Yoshiko Reed. Preface to *The Ways That Never Parted: Jews and Christians in Late Antiquity and the Early Middle Ages.* Edited by Becker, Adam H., and Annette Yoshiko Reed. TSAJ 95. Tübingen: Mohr Siebeck, 2003. Repr., Minneapolis: Fortress, 2007.

Binder, Donald D. *Into the Temple Courts: The Place of the Synagogues in the Second Temple Period.* SBLDS 169. Atlanta: Scholars Press, 1999.

Botermann, Helga. "Die Synagoge von Sardes: Eine Synagoge aus dem 4. Jahrhundert?" *ZNW* 81 (1990): 103–21.

Carson, Donald A. "1–3 John." Pages 1063–67 in *Commentary on the New Testament Use of the Old Testament.* Edited by Gregory K. Beale and Donald A. Carson. Grand Rapids: Baker Academic, 2007.

Engelmann, Helmut. "Ephesos und die Johannesakten." *ZPE* 103 (1994): 297–302.

Foss, Clive. *Ephesus after Antiquity: A Late Antique, Byzantine, and Turkish City.* Cambridge: Cambridge University Press, 1979.

Frankfurter, David. "Jews or Not? Reconstructing 'the Other' in Rev 2:9 and 3:9." *HTR* 94 (2001): 403–25.
Gruen, Erich. S. *Diaspora: Jews amidst Greeks and Romans.* Cambridge: Harvard University Press, 2002.
Haenchen, Ernst. *The Acts of the Apostles: A Commentary.* Oxford: Blackwell, 1971.
Hirschberg, Peter. *Das eschatologische Israel: Untersuchungen zum Gottesvolkverständnis der Johannesoffenbarung.* WMANT 84. Neukirchen-Vluyn: Neukirchener Verlag, 1999.
Horner, Timothy J. *Listening to Trypho: Justin Martyr's Dialogue Reconsidered.* CBET 28. Leuven: Peeters, 2001.
Horsley, Greg H. R. "An *Archisynagogos* of Corinth?" *NewDocs* 4.113:213–20.
———. "The Inscriptions of Ephesos and the New Testament." *NovT* 34 (1992): 105–68.
———. "Jews at Ephesos." *NewDocs* 4.116:231–32.
Horst, Pieter Willem van der. "Jews and Christians in Aphrodisias in the Light of Their Relations in Other Cities of Asia Minor." *NedTT* 43 (1989): 106–21.
———. *Saxa judaica loquuntur: Lessons from Early Jewish Inscriptions.* BIS 134. Leiden: Brill, 2015.
Huttner, Ulrich. *Early Christianity in the Lycus Valley.* AJEC 85. ECAM 1. Leiden: Brill, 2013.
Içten, Çengiz, and Helmut Engelmann. "Inschriften aus Ephesos und Kolophon." *ZPE* 120 (1998): 83–91.
Jacobs, Andrew S. "The Lion and the Lamb: Reconsidering Jewish-Christian Relations in Antiquity." Pages 95–118 in *The Ways That Never Parted: Jews and Christians in Late Antiquity and the Early Middle Ages.* Edited by Adam H. Becker and Annette Yoshiko Reed. TSAJ 95. Tübingen: Mohr Siebeck, 2003.
Junod, Eric, and Jean-Daniel Kaestli. *Textus alii Commentarius.* Vol. 2 of *Acta Iohannis.* CCSA 2. Turnhout: Brepols, 1983.
Knibbe, Dieter, Helmut Engelmann, and Bülent İplikçioğlu. "Neue Inschriften aus Ephesos XII." *JÖAI* 62 (1993): 113–50.
Lalleman, Pieter J. *The Acts of John: A Two-Stage Initiation into Johannine Gnosticism.* SAAA 4. Leuven: Peeters, 1998.
Lambrecht, Jan. "Jewish Slander: A Note on Rev 2,9–10." Pages 329–39 in *Collected Studies on Pauline Literature and on the Book of Revelation.* Rome: Pontificio Istituto Biblico, 2001.

———. "Synagogues of Satan (cf. Rev 2,9 and 3,9): Anti-Judaism in the Apocalypse." Pages 341–56 in *Collected Studies on Pauline Literature and on the Book of Revelation*. Rome: Pontificio Istituto Biblico, 2001.
Levinskaya, Irina. "The Traces of Jewish Life in Asia Minor." Pages 347–57 in *Neues Testament und hellenistisch-jüdische Alltagskultur: Wechselseitige Wahrnehmungen; III. Internationales Symposium zum Corpus Judaeo-Hellenisticum Novi Testamenti 21.–24. Mai 2009, Leipzig*. Edited by Roland Deines, Jens Herzer, and Karl-Wilhelm Niebuhr. WUNT 274. Tübingen: Mohr Siebeck, 2011.
Lieu, Judith M. *I, II and III John: A Commentary*. NTL. Louisville: Westminster John Knox Press, 2008.
———. *Image and Reality: The Jews in the World of the Christians in the Second Century*. Edinburgh: T&T Clark, 1996.
Magness, Jodi. "The Date of the Sardis Synagogue in Light of the Numismatic Evidence." *AJA* 109 (2005): 443–75.
Marshall, I. Howard, in collaboration with Philip H. Towner. *A Critical and Exegetical Commentary on the Pastoral Epistles*. ICC. Edinburgh: T&T Clark, 1999.
McGing, Brian. "Population and Proselytism: How Many Jews Were There in the Ancient World?" Pages 88–106 in *Jews in the Hellenistic and Roman Cities*. Edited by John R. Bartlett. London: Routledge, 2002.
Meeks, Wayne A. *The First Urban Christians: The Social World of the Apostle Paul*. New Haven: Yale University Press, 1983.
Mounce, William D. *Pastoral Epistles*. WBC 46. Nashville: Nelson, 2000.
Murray, Michele. *Playing a Jewish Game: Gentile Christian Judaizing in the First and Second Centuries CE*. SCJud 13. Waterloo, ON: Wilfrid Laurier University Press, 2004.
Noy, David. *Italy (excluding the City of Rome), Spain and Gaul*. Vol. 1 of *Jewish Inscriptions of Western Europe*. Cambridge: Cambridge University Press, 1993.
Oster, Richard E. "Christianity in Asia Minor." *ABD* 1:938–54.
Pervo, Richard I. "Johannine Trajectories in the Acts of John." *Apocrypha* 3 (1992): 47–68.
Pillinger, Renate. "Jüdische Alltagskultur in Ephesos und Umgebung im Spiegel der Denkmäler." Pages 85–98 in *Neues Testament und hellenistisch-jüdische Alltagskultur: Wechselseitige Wahrnehmungen; III. Internationales Symposium zum Corpus Judaeo-Hellenisticum Novi Testamenti 21.–24. Mai 2009, Leipzig*. Edited by Roland Deines, Jens

Herzer, and Karl-Wilhelm Niebuhr. WUNT 274. Tübingen: Mohr Siebeck, 2011.
Pucci Ben Zeev, Miriam. *Jewish Rights in the Roman World: The Greek and Roman Documents Quoted by Josephus Flavius.* TSAJ 74. Tübingen: Mohr Siebeck, 1998.
Rautman, Marcus. "Daniel at Sardis." *BASOR* 358 (2010): 47–60.
Rajak, Tessa. *The Jewish Dialogue with Greece and Rome: Studies in Cultural and Social Interaction.* AGJU 48. Leiden: Brill, 2001.
Reed, Annette Yoshiko, and Adam H. Becker. "Introduction: Traditional Models and New Directions." Pages 1–34 in *The Ways That Never Parted: Jews and Christians in Late Antiquity and the Early Middle Ages.* Edited by Adam H. Becker and Annette Yoshiko Reed. TSAJ 95. Tübingen: Mohr Siebeck, 2003.
Ritter, Bradley. *Judeans in the Greek Cities of the Roman Empire: Rights, Citizenship and Civil Discord.* JSJSup 170. Leiden: Brill, 2015.
Robinson, Thomas A. *The Bauer Thesis Examined: The Geography of Heresy in the Early Christian Church.* Lewiston, NY: Mellen, 1988.
Rogers, Guy MacLean. "Demetrios of Ephesos: Silversmith and Neopoios?" *BTTK* 50 (1986): 877–83.
Schmithals, Walter. "The Corpus Paulinum and Gnosis." Pages 107–24 in *The New Testament and Gnosis: Essays in Honour of Robert McL. Wilson.* Edited by Alastair H. B. Logan and Alexander J. M. Wedderburn. Edinburgh: T&T Clark, 1983.
Schürer, Emil. *The History of the Jewish People in the Age of Jesus Christ.* Revised and edited by Geza Vermes, Fergus Millar, and Martin Goodman. Volume 3.1. Edinburgh: T&T Clark, 1986.
Schüssler Fiorenza, Elisabeth. *The Book of Revelation: Justice and Judgment.* Philadelphia: Fortress, 1985.
Stoops, Robert F. "Riot and Assembly: The Social Context of Acts 19:23–41." *JBL* 108 (1989): 73–91.
Stowers, Stanley Kent. "Social Status, Public Speaking and Private Teaching: The Circumstances of Paul's Preaching Activity." *NovT* 26 (1984): 59–82.
Streett, Daniel R. *They Went Out from Us: The Identity of the Opponents in First John.* BZNW 177. Berlin: de Gruyter, 2011.
Strelan, Rick. *Paul, Artemis, and the Jews in Ephesus.* BZNW 80. Berlin: de Gruyter, 1996.
Taylor, Justin. *Commentaire Historique (Act. 18,23–28,31).* Vol. 5 of *Les Actes des deux Apôtres.* EBib 30. Paris: Librairie Lecoffre, 1996.

Tellbe, Mikael. *Christ-Believers in Ephesus: A Textual Analysis of Early Christian Identity Formation in a Local Perspective.* WUNT 242. Tübingen: Mohr Siebeck, 2009.

Thiessen, Werner. *Christen in Ephesus: Die historische und theologische Situation in vorpaulinischer und paulinischer Zeit und zur Zeit der Apostelgeschichte und der Pastoralbriefe.* TANZ 12. Tübingen: Francke, 1995.

Thompson, Leonard L. *The Book of Revelation: Apocalypse and Empire.* Oxford: Oxford University Press, 1990.

Towner, Philip H. *The Goal of Our Instruction: The Structure of Theology and Ethics in the Pastoral Epistles.* JSNTSup 34. Sheffield: JSOT Press, 1989.

———. *The Letters to Timothy and Titus.* NICNT. Grand Rapids: Eerdmans, 2006.

Trebilco, Paul. *The Early Christians in Ephesus from Paul to Ignatius.* WUNT 166. Tübingen: Mohr Siebeck, 2004.

———. *Jewish Communities in Asia Minor.* SNTSMS 69. Cambridge: Cambridge University Press, 1991.

———. "Jews, Christians and the Associations in Ephesos: A Comparative Study of Group Structures." Pages 325–34 in *100 Jahre Österreichische Forschungen in Ephesos: Akten des Symposions Wien 1995.* Edited by Herwig Friesinger and Fritz Krinzinger. Vienna: ÖAW, 1999.

———. "Reading Ephesians in Ephesus: A Letter to Pauline *and* Johannine Christ-Followers?" In *Ephesus as a Religious Center under the Principate.* Edited by Trevor W. Thompson, James Walters, and A. Black. WUNT. Tübingen: Mohr Siebeck, forthcoming.

Wasserstein, Abraham. "The Number and Provenance of Jews in Graeco-Roman Antiquity: A Note on Population Statistics." Pages 307–17 in *Classical Studies in Honour David Sohlberg.* Edited by Ranon Katzoff, Yaakov Petroff, and David M. Schaps. Ramat Gan: Bar-Ilan University Press, 1996.

Williams, Margaret H. *Jews in a Graeco-Roman Environment.* WUNT 312. Tübingen: Mohr Siebeck, 2013.

Wilson, Stephen G. *Related Strangers: Jews and Christians, 70–170 C.E.* Minneapolis: Fortress, 1995.

Witetschek, Stephan. *Ephesische Enthüllungen 1: Frühe Christen in einer antiken Großstadt; Zugleich ein Beitrag zur Frage nach den Kontexten der Johannesapokalypse.* BTS 6. Leuven: Peeters, 2008.

Acclaiming Artemis in Ephesus: Political Theologies in Acts 19

Bradley J. Bitner

1. Great Is Artemis of the Ephesians!

Twice in the narrative of Acts 19:23–40, the auditor is confronted with a collective shout:

καὶ γενόμενοι πλήρεις θυμοῦ ἔκραζον λέγοντες· μεγάλη ἡ Ἄρτεμις Ἐφεσίων.
And becoming full of wrath they began to shout, saying, "Great is Artemis of the Ephesians!" (19:28; all biblical translations are mine)

φωνὴ ἐγένετο μία ἐκ πάντων ὡς ἐπὶ ὥρας δύο κραζόντων· μεγάλη ἡ Ἄρτεμις Ἐφεσίων.
There came one voice from them all for about two hours shouting, "Great is Artemis of the Ephesians!" (19:34)

First, the silversmiths in 19:28, stirred by their fellow craftsman Demetrius, erupt in a cry of "Great is Artemis of the Ephesians!" Then, once the artisans and their shout spill into the streets of Ephesus, the resulting uproar reaches a crescendo in the theater in 19:34. There, for two hours, the assembled crowd cries out in rhythmic unison, "Great is Artemis of the Ephesians!"[1] Within the soundscape of 19:23–40, these dual

---

1. In Acts 19:28, D05 (Bezae) adds δραμόντες εἰς τὸ ἄμφοδον ("running into the street") before ἔκραζον and omits the article (ἡ) before Ἄρτεμις. In 19:34, D05 again omits the article (ἡ) before Ἄρτεμις, while B03 (Vaticanus) doubles the acclamation (twice: μεγάλη ἡ Ἄρτεμις Ἐφεσίων, μεγάλη ἡ Ἄρτεμις Ἐφεσίων). On these shifts in detail and emphasis, see Josep Rius-Camps and Jenny Read-Heimerdinger, *A Comparison with the Alexandrian Tradition, Acts 18.24–28.31: Rome via Ephesus and Jerusalem*, vol. 4 of *The Message of Acts in Codex Bezae* (London: T&T Clark, 2009), 59–78.

acclamations resonate powerfully, animating the confusion and shaping the action within the narrative.[2]

Yet these identical cries as such have not been a focus in most New Testament scholarship on Acts 19. Rather, the attention of readers is normally directed to two attending features of the text. On the one hand, it is Artemis Ephesia herself, the great goddess of the polis, who has received extensive consideration.[3] As the object of the double acclamation—and therefore its sonic center—this is understandable. But an almost exclusive concentration on the one acclaimed may have muted our apprehension of the form and function of the acclamations themselves. On the other hand, the turmoil or *stasis* surrounding the acclamations has rightly occasioned much reflection.[4] Nevertheless, the nexus between the dual acclamations

---

2. The narrative spaces resound with rumblings: τάραχος (19:23), σύγχυσις (19:29), κράζω (19:28, 32, 34), συστροφή (19:40), στάσις (19:40), θόρυβος (20:1). See Charles H. Talbert, *Reading Acts: A Literary and Theological Commentary on the Acts of the Apostles*, Reading the New Testament (New York: Crossroad, 1997), 179: "The paragraph is held together by the refrain, 'Great is Artemis of the Ephesians' (vv. 28 and 34)."

3. Important literature on Artemis Ephesia in relation to Acts 19 includes Richard E. Oster, "The Ephesian Artemis as an Opponent of Early Christianity," *JAC* 19 (1976): 27–44; Oster, "Holy Days in Honour of Artemis," *NewDocs* 4:74–82; Paul Trebilco, "Asia," in *Graeco-Roman Setting*, vol. 2 of *The Book of Acts in Its First Century Setting*, ed. David W. J. Gill and Conrad Gempf (Grand Rapids: Eerdmans, 1994), 316–57; Christine M. Thomas, "At Home in the City of Artemis: Religion in Ephesos in the Literary Imagination of the Roman Period," in *Ephesos, Metropolis of Asia: An Interdisciplinary Approach to Its Archaeology, Religion, and Culture*, ed. Helmut Koester, HTS 41 (Valley Forge, PA: Trinity Press International, 1995), 81–117; Rick Strelan, *Paul, Artemis, and the Jews in Ephesus*, BZNW 80 (Berlin: de Gruyter, 1996); Rainer Schwindt, *Das Weltbild des Epheserbriefes: Eine religionsgeschichtlich-exegestiche Studie*, WUNT 148 (Tübingen: Mohr Siebeck, 2002), 63–134; C. L. Brinks, "'Great is Artemis of the Ephesians': Acts 19:23–41 in Light of Goddess Worship in Ephesus," *CBQ* 71 (2009): 776–94; Guy MacLean Rogers, *The Mysteries of Artemis of Ephesos: Cult, Polis, and Change in the Graeco-Roman World*, Synkrisis (New Haven: Yale University Press, 2012). See also James R. Harrison, "Family Honour of a Priestess of Artemis," *NewDocs* 10:30–36; Harrison, "Artemis Triumphs over a Sorcerer's Evil Art," *NewDocs* 10:37–47; Harrison, "A 'Worthy' *neopoios* Thanks Artemis," *NewDocs* 10:48–54.

4. Notably: Robert F. Stoops, "Riot and Assembly: The Social Context of Acts 19.23–41," *JBL* 108 (1989): 73–91; Jeffrey M. Tripp, "A Tale of Two Riots: The Synkrisis of the Temples of Ephesus and Jerusalem in Acts 19–23," *JSNT* 37 (2014): 86–111. For additional literature, see Richard I. Pervo, *Acts: A Commentary*, Hermeneia (Minneapolis: Fortress, 2009), 484–502; Craig S. Keener, *15:1–23:35*, vol. 3 of *Acts: An Exegetical Commentary* (Grand Rapids: Baker Academic, 2014), 2898–924.

and this political narrative of riot and assembly has not been adequately explored. Surprisingly, some speak of these acclamations only as "cries of worship" or "prayer chants." To fail to see these cries as *acclamations*, however, is to miss much of their sociopolitical import.[5] Others indeed note just how well the Artemis acclamations match the form of extant ancient acclamations. But they fail to dwell on their political-theological functions in civic, provincial, and imperial settings or to emphasize how a greater understanding of the Artemis acclamations might sharpen our reading of Act 19 generally.[6]

There are suggestive observations among commentators who have paused to consider the role of the acclamations in Luke's literary presentation, but there is no consensus beyond the fact that they bring extra "local color" to Acts 19. Alfred Loisy recognized, as have many since, that the cries of 19:28 and 19:34 preserve the acclamatory language of the inscriptions, but he suspected they were part of the work of a redactor in 19:23-40; in any case, they were not particularly significant for what narrative theology there is in the final form of Acts 19.[7] Ernst Haenchen, noting the work of Erik Peterson on the *Heis Theos* acclamations, agreed as to the traditional form and reckoned that the "two hour pandemonium of the crowd [19:34] illustrates the—actually powerless—fanaticism of the heathens."[8] But, considering the passage to be a Lukan literary fiction (with the acclamations as a novelistic touch), Haenchen remained slightly puzzled as to the larger

---

5. E.g., Stoops, "Riot and Assembly," 84; Brinks, "Great is Artemis," 785, 788-90. Pervo prefers the language of "ritual shout" (19:28) and "ritual cultic chant" (19:34) (*Acts*, 486 [cf. 494]).

6. C. K. Barrett comments only on details of grammatical form (*Introduction and Commentary on Acts XV-XXVII*, vol. 2 of *A Critical and Exegetical Commentary on the Acts of the Apostles*, ICC [London: T&T Clark, 1998], 928, 934). Talbert, having noted that the acclamations are integral to the narrative, fails to comment on just how this is the case (*Reading Acts*, 179-81).

7. Alfred Loisy, *Les acts des apôtres* (Paris: Nourry, 1920), 744-56.

8. Ernst Haenchen, *The Acts of the Apostles: A Commentary* (Oxford: Blackwell, 1971), 573-75. See Erik Peterson, *Heis Theos: Epigraphische, formgeschichtliche und religionsgeschichtliche Untersuchungen zur antiken "Ein-Gott"-Akklamation; Nachdruck der Ausgabe von Erik Peterson 1926 mit Ergänzungen und Kommentaren von Christoph Markschies, Henrik Hildebrandt, Barbara Nichtsweiss, Ausgewählte Schriften 8 (Würzberg: Echter, 2012). This includes Peterson's initial work on the Εἷς Θεός acclamations (published in 1926) and four previously unpublished essays by Peterson, as well as commentary, *addenda et corrigenda* by the editors.

narrative purpose of the outcry, especially as it relates to the "Jewish intermezzo" of 19:33–40.[9] Gerd Lüdemann views the acclamations as adding to the dramatic intensity of the narrative. But he, too, thinks Luke is testing his narrative inventiveness and has difficulty seeing their significance in relation to any narrative-theological whole.[10]

In contrast to these older, source-critical assessments, Peter Lampe argued in 1992: "Not a single thought need be wasted on [considering Luke's] literary dependence. Rather, Acts 19 is written by someone who is intimately familiar with the Ephesian scene."[11] Among recent interpreters, Paul Trebilco and Richard I. Pervo agree with the estimation that the acclamations are among several details that provide such intimate local knowledge, but they differ as to what this implies for Luke's historical sources and the dating of the composition of Acts.[12] Pervo argues that "function is more important than diction" and implies that the acclamation of 19:28 lends the silversmiths a certain, limited political power in civic terms.[13] With others, Pervo thinks that the two hour acclamation of 19:34 provides a literary parallel with the two years of Paul's public teaching in 19:10.[14] Rowe sees the acclamation of 19:28 as "narratively intelligible" in relation to the prospect of the disintegration of Artemis-related economics in Ephesus; for him, the acclamation of 19:34 works as a kind of narrative dilation that allows the *grammateus* enough time to arrive in the theatre and quell the uproar. Thus, the acclamations are primarily effective and realistic literary devices.[15] Craig S. Keener, in his detailed treatment of Acts 19, notes briefly the political resonances that acclamations might have, observing only that the repeated chants in these

---

9. Haenchen, *Acts of the Apostles*, 577–78.

10. Gerd Lüdemann, *Early Christianity according to the Traditions in Acts: A Commentary*, trans. John Bowden (London: SCM, 1989), 216–17.

11. Peter Lampe, "Acta 19 im Spiegel der ephesischen Inschriften," *BZ* 36 (1992): 66.

12. Trebilco seems content to see Lukan sources and historicity converging in the narrative ("Asia," 316–57). Pervo will cede to Luke no historical-narrative "kudos" (*Acts*, 485–502). On some of the larger methodological issues involved, see Stephan Witetschek, "Artemis and Asiarchs: Some Remarks on Ephesian Local Colour in Acts 19," *Bib* 90 (2009): 334–55.

13. Pervo, *Acts*, 494.

14. Ibid., 497. See also Rius-Camps and Read-Heimerdinger, *Comparison with the Alexandrian Tradition*, 77.

15. C. Kavin Rowe, *World Upside Down: Reading Acts in the Graeco-Roman Age* (Oxford: Oxford University Press, 2009), 44–46.

verses fit "rather precisely the local evidence" and were deployed as acts "of religious fervor."[16]

Only when we step outside the mainstream of New Testament scholarship do we perceive a somewhat different estimation of the Artemis acclamations in Acts 19 by epigraphists and ancient historians. Three such scholars in particular merit close attention. First, Peterson, an epigraphist and early church historian, observed in his magisterial study of 1926, *Heis Theos*, that one encounters no more vivid example of an ancient acclamation than that found in Acts 19:28, 34.[17] But in a subsequent shorter essay, posthumously published only in 2012 by Christoph Markschies, Peterson argued that the Artemis acclamations in Luke's narrative (especially that in 19:34) were merely the literary tip of an historical-ritual iceberg. Auditors of this account of the two hour acclamation in the theater would, by Peterson's reckoning, have understood it to be merely the initial element in a chain of acclamations.[18] Although Peterson does not develop this insight, it implies new possibilities for our reading of the Acts 19 narrative in acclamatory context, possibilities we will develop below. Second, in 1997, the ancient legal historian Reinhard Selinger discussed the role of the Artemis acclamations in the narrative of the *Demetriosunruhen* (Demetrius riots).[19] Not only, contends Selinger, do certain narrative details come across as eminently plausible from the point of view of Roman civic and legal history, but the whole is also coherent: events unfold in a consistent and almost automatic fashion, with the acclamations contributing materially to the narrative.[20] Like Peterson, Selinger's familiarity with the sociology of ancient acclamations allows him to perceive those narrated by Luke as political and ritual speech acts.[21] But Selinger, too, fails to explore further what precise effect(s) these Artemis acclamations have in the narrative theology of Acts 19. Finally, a recent essay by Angelos Chaniotis on the ritual functions of acclamatory epithets in ancient political

---

16. Keener, *15:1–23:35*, 2899, 2923.
17. Peterson, *Heis Theos*, 141.
18. Ibid., 590. He suggests there would have followed positive acclamations for the emperor, the provincial governor, and the Ephesian magistrates, as well as denunciatory acclamations against Paul and the Christians.
19. Reinhard Selinger, "Die Demetriosunruhen (Apg. 19,23–40): Eine Fallstudie aus rechtshistorischer Perspektive," *ZNW* 88 (1997): 242–59.
20. Selinger, "Die Demetriosunruhen," 259.
21. Ibid., 254. He notes: "The wording of the acclamation itself was of secondary importance. The main point was its effect."

and agonistic settings emphasizes their competitive nature.[22] Chaniotis connects the Ephesian Artemis acclamations to a rich seam of epigraphical evidence and suggests a reading of Acts 19 that takes careful note of competing political theologies.[23]

What then do we make of these select observations from the history of interpretation?[24] Initially, we see a basic consensus that the Artemis acclamations lend a vivid, Ephesian tenor to the narrative. The author of Acts knows both Ephesus and acclamations well and constructs his narrative in a thoroughly coherent manner and with locally resonant terminology. Additionally, and related to the first point, we notice that among mainstream New Testament scholars, few see the dual acclamations as thematically significant for an overall interpretation of Acts 19.[25] Instead, and most importantly for the purposes of this essay, we see that what these treatments lack is a precise definition of acclamations as political-theological speech acts and, as a result, a full appreciation of their narrative-theological function in Acts 19. Furthermore, we observe that among those who bring an epigraphical and ancient historical perspective to the narrative of Acts 19, and specifically to the acclamations, Peterson, Selinger, and Chaniotis are representative voices urging us to attend more closely to the resonances that might echo in an ancient auditor's ear.

In view of this, our aim is to listen afresh to the roiling crowds in Ephesus as they acclaim their civic goddess in order that we might grasp the significance of these acclamations in their sociopolitical and narrative-theological contexts. To do so we will first detail the character and function of ancient acclamations, dwelling on a kind of "script" that emerges from examples that overlap terminologically and conceptually

---

22. Angelos Chaniotis, "Megatheism: The Search for the Almighty God and the Competition of Cults," in *One God: Pagan Monotheism in the Roman Empire*, ed. Stephen Mitchell and Peter Van Nuffelen (Cambridge: Cambridge University Press, 2010), 112–40.

23. Chaniotis, "Megatheism," 126, n. 56. See also Nicole Belayche, "*Deus deum … summorum maximus* (Apuleius): Ritual Expressions of Distinction in the Divine World in the Imperial Period," in Mitchell and Van Nuffelen, *One God*, 141–66.

24. For a substantial review of the history of scholarship on Acts 19, see Scott Shauf, *Theology as History, History as Theology: Paul in Ephesus in Acts 19*, BZNW 133 (Berlin: de Gruyter, 2005).

25. This is generally the case regardless of whether the interpreter views the passage as historically plausible or not, rooted in first-century eyewitness report or a later, redacted (or invented) "Lukan" invention.

with Acts 19. Then, we will begin to draw out the interpretive significance of these observations for the collision of political theologies in the Ephesus narrative.

2. Acclamations and Acclamatory Scripts in Antiquity

To this point, we have insisted on considering the shouts of Acts 19:28, 34 as *acclamations*.[26] We now offer a definition of our key term: an acclamation is a "rhythmically-formulated, sing-song-like or recited cry, with which a crowd expresses approval, praise and congratulations, or disapproval, imprecation and demand."[27] Acclamations were thus powerful speech acts. They represent a communicative mode across many ancient cultures whereby groups of people gave vocal expression to a consensus that was variously affective and volitional as well as religious and political.[28] Even when acclamations erupted spontaneously, they were shaped

---

26. For the application of ancient acclamations to the text of 1 Cor 3:5–4:5, drawing on some of the following evidence, see Bradley J. Bitner, *Paul's Political Strategy in 1 Corinthians 1–4: Constitution and Covenant*, SNTSMS 163 (Cambridge: Cambridge University Press, 2015), 275–85.

27. Theodore Klauser, "Akklamation," *RAC*, col. 216. See also J. Schmidt, "Acclamatio," *PW*, cols. 147–50; Ettore De Ruggiero "Acclamatio," *DEAR*, cols. 72–76; *OLD*, s.v. "*acclamatio*."

28. In addition to the works of Peterson and Chaniotis already cited, important studies of acclamations include Jean Colin, *Les villes libres dans l'Orient gréco-romain et l'envoi au supplice par acclamations populaires*, CL 82 (Brussels: Latomus, 1965); Louis Robert, "Une épigramme satirique d'Automédon et Athènes au début de l'Empire (Anth. Pal. XI-319)," *REG* 94 (1981): 360–61; B. Baldwin, "Acclamations in the Historia Augusta," *Athenaeum* 59 (1981): 138–49; Charlotte Roueché, "Acclamations in the Later Roman Empire: New Evidence from Aphrodisias," *JRS* 74 (1984): 181–99; Roueché, "Floreat Perge," in *Images of Authority: Papers Presented to Joyce Reynolds on the Occasion of Her Seventieth Birthday*, ed. Mary Margaret Mackenzie and Charlotte Roueché (Cambridge: Cambridge Philological Society, 1989), 206–28; Gregory S. Aldrete, *Gestures and Acclamations in Ancient Rome* (Baltimore: Johns Hopkins University Press, 1999); Clifford Ando, *Imperial Ideology and Provincial Loyalty in the Roman Empire* (Berkeley: University of California Press, 2000), esp. 200–5; Gregory Rowe, *Princes and Political Cultures: The New Tiberian Senatorial Decrees* (Ann Arbor: University of Michigan Press, 2002); Hans-Ulrich Wiemer, "Akklamationen im spätromischen Reich: Zur Typologie und Funktion eines Kommunikationsrituals," *AK* 86 (2004): 55–73; Thomas Kruse, "The Magistrate and the Ocean: Acclamations and Ritualised Communication in Town Gatherings in Roman Egypt," in *Ritual and Communication in the Graeco-Roman World*, ed. E. Stavrianopoulou, KernosSup 16

by and performed with reference to highly scripted and ritualized communicative dynamics in the first-century Mediterranean world.[29] Established rhythms, set titles and phrases,[30] and patterns of repetition and variation provided a framework or script within which to improvize.[31] In narrative, key verbs and cognates[32] signal the presence of an acclamation. Often, as in Acts 19, acclamatory *formulae* appear as direct discourse.[33] But such

---

(Liège: Centre international d'étude de la religion grecque antique, 2006), 297–315; Angelos Chaniotis, "Acclamations as a Form of Religious Communication," in *Die Religion des Imperium Romanum: Koine and Konfrontationen*, ed. Hubert Cancik and Jörg Rüpke with Franca Fabricius (Tübingen: Mohr Siebeck, 2008), 199–218; Kathleen Coleman, "Public Entertainments," in *The Oxford Handbook of Social Relations in the Roman World*, ed. Michael Peachin (Oxford: Oxford University Press, 2011), 345–50.

29. E.g., Tertullian, *Spect.* 16: "a united shout of common madness" (*unius dementiae una vox est*). Acclamations, in Greek and Latin, were common throughout the first century and across the Roman Empire. But verbatim acclamations are attested directly in the early period primarily in literary evidence and graffiti. Most other epigraphical and papyrological evidence for acclamations appears later because of trends in recording practices and the development of protocols, but we can be confident that the later evidence preserves patterns relevant in the first century. See Bitner, *Paul's Political Strategy*, 275–85.

30. E.g., Μέγας/Μεγάλη; Αὔξι/Αὔξε; Νικᾷ/Νεικᾷ/Νικᾷς; Εἷς/Εἷς Θεός. For further acclamatory *formulae*, see Peterson, *Heis Theos*; Roueché, "Acclamations"; Chaniotis, "Megatheism."

31. Aldrete, *Gestures and Acclamations*, 140–47; Rowe, *Princes and Political Cultures*, 82–83.

32. Those in Greek include ἐπιφωνέω, προσφωνέω, εὐφήμι, ἐπευφήμι, ἐκβοάω, κραυγάζω, κράζω, ἐπιφώνημα (-ησις), προσφώνημα (-ησις), φωνή, βοή, ἐκβόησις, ἔπαινος, εὐφημία. Third-person plural verbs of speaking and answering, especially when accompanied by ὁμοθυμαδόν ("with one accord") also often signal acclamation. Further examples and Latin equivalents in Klauser, "Akklamation," col. 216. See also Peterson, *Heis Theos*; Colin, *Les villes libres*.

33. E.g., *TAM* 5.1:75 (Sattai in Lydia): "Εἷς Θεὸς ἐν οὐρανοῖς. Μέγας Μὴν Οὐράνιος. Μεγάλη δύναμις τοῦ ἀθανάτου θεοῦ" (One god in heaven! Great is Heavenly Mes! Great is the power of the immortal god!); see Chaniotis, "Megatheism," 135. We also know of acclamations scratched or painted informally, sometimes as graffiti or *dipinti*: Peter Keegan, *Graffiti in Antiquity* (London: Routledge, 2014). See also Angelos Chaniotis, "Graffiti in Aphrodisias: Images—Texts—Contexts," in *Ancient Graffiti in Context*, ed. Jennifer A. Baird and Claire Taylor, RSAH 2 (New York: Routledge, 2011), 191–207. Acclamations (e.g., Εἷς Θεός) are also found, sometimes with iconography, on gems, amulets, and medallions; see, e.g., Catherine Hezser, *Jewish Literacy in Roman Palestine*, TSAJ 81 (Tübingen: Mohr Siebeck, 2001), 437; Jeffrey Spier, *Late Antique and Early Christian Gems*, SFCB.SP 20 (Wiesbaden: Reichert, 2007).

formulas were not empty or merely expressive; the form of acclamation was always connected with its function. That is to say, acclamations were deployed to *accomplish* something within religious and political life. For philosopher Giorgio Agamben, to whose theory of acclamation we will return below, acclamations of the kind we have in focus "constitute a threshold of indifference between politics and theology;" indeed, rather than being simply "ornament[s] of political power," acclamations in some sense "found and justify" the glory of powers profane and divine.[34] Therefore, it is important to keep in view that in a variety of ethnic and social settings—Jewish, Greek, and Roman—acclamations *communicated* effectively; they gave voice to groups of people who may or may not have had official status or representation in civic and political contexts, and their messages were recognized by all who heard. Acclamations expressed the power—and the political theology—of the people. Let us illustrate some of these communicative dynamics by examining several ancient texts that preserve elements of acclamatory scripts relevant to what we overhear in Acts 19.

To begin with, Jews from many eras were familiar with and participated in acclamations in political and religious settings. We see this in various biblical and intertestamental texts.[35] By the first century, both in Palestine and in the diaspora, Jews knew well how to leverage acclamations within a Roman provincial context. There were the raucous acclamations of the crowds in the passion narratives of the gospels (Matt 27:21–26; Mark 15:13–14; Luke 23:18–25; John 19:6, 12, 15–16).[36] Acts itself testifies to another classic instance of acclamation in 12:20–23 where Herod Agrippa

---

34. Giorgio Agamben, *The Kingdom and the Glory: For a Theological Genealogy of Economy and Government*, trans. Lorenzo Chiesa with Matteo Mandarini (Stanford: Stanford University Press, 2011), 229–30.

35. E.g., acclamations of covenant loyalty in Exod 19:8 (after the display of divine power in thunder, lightning, and thick darkness on Sinai); 24:3 (in a collective shout of covenant ratification); Ezra 3:12–13 (shouts of grief from some and joy from others at the construction of the "Second Temple"). Of obvious relevance are the oft-cited acclamations from Bel 18 (Μέγας ἐστὶν ὁ Βηλ) and 41 (Μέγας ἐστὶ κύριος ὁ θεός), the context being a crafted anti-idol polemic and dramatic theological reversal as the king sees Daniel preserved by Israel's Lord.

36. For "aretological acclamations" and the compositional structure of (especially) Mark's Gospel, see Gerd Theissen, *The Miracle Stories of the Early Christian Tradition*, ed. John Kenneth Riches, trans. Francis McDonagh, SNTW (Edinburgh: T&T Clark, 1983), 71–72, 212–15.

is acclaimed: "And the demos [people] was crying aloud, 'The voice of a god and not of a man!'" (ὁ δὲ δῆμος ἐπεφώνει, Θεοῦ φωνὴ καὶ οὐκ ἀνθρώπου [Acts 12:22]).[37] In literature outside the New Testament, Josephus also attests the Jewish experience of acclamation. We read of the inhabitants of Jerusalem, clad in festal garments, receiving M. Agrippa with acclamations in 16 BCE (Josephus, *Ant.* 16.2).[38] Josephus also recounts his own acclaim, as a representative of Roman power, by a crowd of Galileans in a fraught political context. Faced with hostile opposition by one named Jonathan, Josephus is protected by a series of vigorous acclamations while Jonathan and his companions are acclaimed *against* by the crowd (Josephus, *Vita* 48). What these examples demonstrate is that first-century Jews, including those present in the Ephesian streets and theater in Acts 19, were well versed in the use of acclamations. Acclamatory functions such as the exaltation of a deity and engagement in political competition involving a range of local and provincial magistrates comprised familiar elements of the Jewish and biblical experience.

Further examples only fill out for us the available acclamatory scripts. It becomes evident more widely in ancient Mediterranean culture that some acclamations were more welcome than others and, furthermore, that acclamatory spaces and occasions mattered. In one of his orations, the wealthy orator Dio Chrysostom comments

> [A] resolution of commendation voted by you from your seats in the assembly is a splendid distinction; but other peoples, even if they burst their lungs with cheering, seem not to show honor enough. (*Rhod.* 109)[39]

Here it is clear that the most welcome effect of an acclamation, at least in terms of the civic elite of the Greek East, was the transferral of honor and glory to a worthy recipient. A regular, lawful assembly populated by respectable and authorized citizens was the ideal setting for this, preferable even to loud cheering from the masses in less formal civic spaces. In part, this was because popular acclamations in open public spaces could be less predictable, more difficult to control, and could even become menacing. In

---

37. Cf. Josephus, *Ant.* 8.2, which preserves a longer account of the same episode.
38. For a similar example almost certainly involving diaspora Jews in Alexandria, see the acclamation of Germanicus (CE 19) in P.Oxy. 25.2435 r.
39. Translation from J. W. Cohoon and H. Lamar Crosby, trans., *Dio Chrysostom: Discourses 31–36*, LCL 358 (Cambridge: Harvard University Press, 1940).

his *De morte peregrini*, Lucian describes his aging protagonist attempting to play on the emotions of the crowd by threatening (rhetorically) to take his own life. The crowd's reaction was mixed and had immediate effect:

> The more witless among the people began to shed tears and call out: "Preserve your life for the Greeks!" But the bolder part shouted out, "Carry out your purpose!" by which the old man was immoderately upset.... That "Carry out your purpose!" assailing him quite unexpectedly caused him to turn still paler ... and even to tremble slightly, so that he brought his speech to an end. (*Peregr.* 33 [trans. Harmon, slightly adapted])

The power and scripted nature of popular acclamations, and their conjunction with sociopolitical dynamics, authorized civic spaces, and magistrates, appears lucidly in a papyrus text from Egypt. The acclamatory details of this text warrant a treatment *in extenso*:

> as the ... festival gathering took place [the people exclaimed, "..., to the Romans] for all eternity the rule of the Romans! The lords Augusti! Long live the prefect, long live the Katholikos! Long live the prytanis, bravo, glory of the city, Hurrah, Dioscorus, you foremost of citizens! Everything that is good will be increased under your administration, you initiator of good things! The Nile loves you as the blessed (Hesies) and rises! Long live he, who loves his fellow citizens, long live he, who loves moderation, initiator of good things, founder of the city! ... Bravo.... A conferment (of honor) should be passed for the prytanis for the city! Long live the prefect, long live the Katholikos! Beneficent prefect, beneficent Katholikos! We beseech you, Katholikos, concerning the prytanis: a conferment (of honor) should be ratified for the prytanis, the conferment should be ratified today, this is the first and foremost duty, the most important duty!" (P.Oxy. 1.41, lines 1–16 [ca. 300 CE])[40]

---

40. All P.Oxy 1.41 translations are from Kruse, "The Magistrate and the Ocean." This text from Oxyrhynchus attests the record of a public gathering and demonstrates how even in relatively small provincial cities, these acclamatory scripts were known and used effectively. Although this is much later than the New Testament period, it presents a richly detailed view of the various aspects of acclamations that are present but only glimpsed more or less piecemeal in first-century texts. For full commentary, see Kruse, "Magistrate and the Ocean," 297–315. Chaniotis points to similar dynamics in the city of Akraiphia in Boiotia (Central Greece) in the mid-first century, where a wealthy benefactor by the name of Epameinondas was competitively acclaimed (see *IG* 7.2711, 2712; "Megatheism," 128).

In this text we hear a crowd (the demos) roaring wave on wave of acclamation for a local magistrate.[41] In a festival setting, with other provincial magistrates present, the demos leverages its acclamatory intensity in a spontaneous, yet scripted, manner. The string of rhythmic acclamations ascribes honorific titles and glory to a local figure who has evidently been a generous benefactor.[42] But the acclamations are not merely expressive or affective; they enunciate a pointed request that places pressure upon the local government to honor Dioscorus the prytanis (president of the civic council). This communicative effect is not lost on those listening, as we see next. What follows—in the back and forth between the magistrates and the people—is illustrative of further communicative dimensions in this scenario of acclamation:

> The prytanis said: "I welcome your honors and am most gratified by them. I urge you that these tokens (of your honor) be postponed to a legitimate meeting [εἰς καιρὸν ἔννομον], at which you may make them with authoritative force and I can accept them with assurance." (P.Oxy. 1.41, lines 16–19)

Hearing the crowd's acclaim and its attendant demand, the prytanis Dioscorus responds graciously but with caution. He urges the crowd to bring their honorific acclaim to a lawful assembly so that their requests can be officially heard and granted. But the people will not be put off so easily. They persist in their enthusiastic demands and continue to embed their acclaim for the Prytanis within further acclamations for figures imperial, provincial, and local. As Thomas Kruse notes, there are three types of acclamation present in this text: utterances of praise, rehearsals of meritorious deeds, and concrete demands.[43]

> The demos cried: "You are worthy of many conferments...! The lord Augusti, all victorious! For the Romans the power of the Romans forever! Long live the prefect, savior of the less well off! O Katholikos, we urge you, Katholikos: the prytanis for the city, the lover of justice for the city, the founder of the city! We beseech you, Katholikos, preserve the

---

41. See Kruse, "Magistrate and the Ocean," 308–10.

42. The exact nature of Dioskoros's benefactions is not made explicit. See Kruse, "Magistrate and the Ocean," 302–4.

43. Ibid., 314.

city for the emperors! Beneficent Katholikos! The ... for the city, he who loves his fellow citizens for the city."

Aristion, the *syndikos*, said, "We shall present [your requests] to the faithful council."

The demos: "We ask, Katholikos, for the guardian of the city, the founder for the city! Faithful strategos, peace of the city! Hurrah, Dioskourides, foremost of citizens! Hurrah Seuthes, foremost of citizens, Isarchon, Isopolit! True, faithful *syndikos*! Long life to all who love the city! May the lords Augusti live forever! (P.Oxy. 1.41, lines 19–30)

In reflecting on this text, Kruse remarks that what is exceptional about its acclamations "is that they are not examples of brief spontaneous applause ... expressed in formulaic phrases as a reaction to individual utterances, but rather *a dramatic production of the ritualised speech of the crowd, which develops in a crescendo like manner.*"[44] The crowd is active, urgent, and presses its demands with superlative, competitive titles ("glory of the city," "foremost of citizens," "initiator of good things," "founder of the city"), improvising on a communicative script in an opportune moment.[45] Although the papyrus does not record the eventual outcome from the lawful assembly that surely followed, we are left with little doubt that Dioscorus received the honors that the demos demanded for him.

Altogether the examples cited thus far begin to fill out for us a kind of flexible acclamatory script; the focus of honor in each case has been a local worthy or magistrate. What we have not yet seen, however, is the way in which deities are scripted in among local, provincial, and imperial recipients of acclamation. This emerges clearly in a *tableau* involving acclamations at the sailing festival of Isis depicted by Apuleius in his *Metamorphoses*.[46] Lucius, having been recently restored by the goddess Isis to human form from that of an ass, narrates the scene:

---

44. Ibid., 310, emphasis added.

45. Some wonder if "claqueurs," such as those brought by Nero from Alexandria to Rome in the first century (Suetonius, *Nero*, 20, 3), may not have organized the phrases ahead of time and deployed themselves strategically among the crowd in order that they might instigate and sustain the acclamations. See Kruse, "Magistrate and the Ocean," 311–12.

46. On the ritual aspects in this text, see Jörg Rüpke, *The Religion of the Romans*, trans. Richard Gordon (Cambridge: Polity, 2007), 92–93.

When we arrived at the temple itself, the chief priest and those who carried the divine images and those who had already been initiated into the awesome inner sanctuary were admitted into the goddess's private chamber, where they arranged the breathing effigies in their prescribed places. Then one of this group, whom everyone called the scribe [*grammatea dicebant*], stationed himself before the door and summoned the company of the *pastophori* [shrine-bearers]–the name of a consecrated college–as if calling them to an assembly [*in contionem vocato*]. Then from a lofty platform he read aloud from a book verbatim, first pronouncing prayers for the prosperity of the great Emperor, the Senate, the knights, and the entire Roman people, for the sailors and ships under the rule of our world-wide empire. Then he proclaimed, in the Greek language and with Greek ritual, the opening of the navigation season. The crowd's acclamation which followed confirmed that his words had been auspicious to all [*Quam vocem feliciter cunctis evenire signavit populi clamor insecutus*]. Then, steeped in joy, the people brought forward boughs and branches and garlands and kissed the feet of the goddess, who stood on the steps, fashioned of silver. (*Metam.* 11.17)[47]

This scene reveals much of interest and relevance. Divine images of the goddess are carried by attendants who emerge from the temple and assemble before the people. Out of a liturgical book, a scribe reads prayers for a variety of Roman authorities and for sailors in the coming navigation season. The crowd then responds with acclamations and joyous celebration, bringing offerings and even kissing the feet of the silver Isis. In the larger context of Lucius's miraculous transformation, this is a fitting novelistic celebration of the power and presence of the goddess.

Yet the fictive narrative works because Apuleius involves recognizable aspects of Isis worship, including an acclamatory script, within a larger, familiar local and imperial framework. As Peterson observes, the prayers proclaimed by the scribe find an echo in the acclamations of the people. Both are scripted such that participants know what to say and how to say it, doing so in such a way that it comes across as appropriately spontaneous.[48] The prayers to Isis demonstrate a kind of gradation—moving through levels of Roman imperial and provincial authority and on to the

---

47. Translation from J. Arthur Hanson, ed. and trans., *Apuleus: Metamorphoses Books 7–11*, LCL 453 (Cambridge: Harvard University Press, 1989).

48. See also Peterson, *Heis Theos*, 603–5 ("Vota, Akklamationen, Gebete"). Peterson considers this book of prayers as a precursor to the protocolled acclamations of the imperial senate and ecclesial synods in subsequent centuries.

local sailors about to embark. The result is that imperial politics, local politics and economics, and divine worship are so many political-theological strands woven tightly together according to an acclamatory-ritual pattern. There is a mutual reinforcement whereby the political theology of a very localized site (Cenchreae in Apuleius's narrative) is both supported by and supportive of Roman imperial ideology in a comprehensive and powerful manner. Acclamatory script here is no empty ritual. Isis and her silver image(s) are at the center of a larger formulary that articulates an approved and living public identity for all those involved.

In summary, our introduction to acclamations as speech acts and political-theological scripts lends sharper definition to our expectations as auditors of Acts 19. First, we saw that among Jews, Greeks, and Romans, acclamations were familiar speech acts that picked up and amplified—sometimes spontaneously—known titles and phrases. In addition, they could be deployed with reference to persons human and divine. Furthermore, this deployment was a public and powerful expression of common will—most often transferring honor and glory, frequently also making demands, sometimes heaping up scorn or disapprobation, and usually expressing a combination of these elements. Finally, we began to see how acclamations were a central aspect of public rituals that defined and reinforced a local and an imperial ideology, a potent combination of politics and theology. Especially with respect to certain local deities whose celebrity was often widespread in the Roman Empire, these acclamatory scripts were integral to the competitive, political-theological rituals involved in what has been called "megatheism."

3. Early Imperial Ephesian Megatheism

What is *megatheism*? Chaniotis, who coined the term, uses it "as a designation of piety which was based on a personal experience in the presence of god, represented one particular god as somehow superior to others, and was expressed through oral performances (praise, acclamations, hymns) accompanying, but not replacing, ritual actions."[49] Already we see how the acclamatory scripts we explored above are an important element in the larger phenomenon Chaniotis describes. Furthermore, Chaniotis draws attention to the localized nature of acclamatory megatheism in the early

---

49. Chaniotis, "Megatheism," 113.

imperial period. That is, certain deities were volubly championed in certain locales. A network emerges involving piety, religious experience, local and competitive acclamation of a particular deity, and a focus on certain divine attributes, all articulated in conjunction with other public rituals. What this network highlights for us is that to understand fully the significance of the Artemis acclamations we must set them first in megatheistic, and ultimately in Ephesian, context. Studies by Chaniotis and Guy Rogers now enable us to do both to a greater degree than ever before.

Chaniotis portrays megatheism as competitive political theology at a personal and local level. Put crudely, it was in many ways a contest of "Our god(dess) is greater than yours!" Chaniotis presents a portrait sketched largely from the epigraphic evidence. This is because it is inscribed media that give the most detailed access to the affective formularies and civic settings of the piety and politics involved. An examination of the inscriptions leads Chaniotis to conclude that geographically diverse communities in the early empire employed a "shared vocabulary" (in which the *Heis* and *Megas/Megalē* acclamations figure prominently) to engage in a competitive "dialogue."[50] Acclamations and "acclamatory epithets" such as *Megas* were basic strategies utilized in this dialogue. Chaniotis notes, "As acclamations were experienced not only by those who performed them, but also by the audiences which attended festivals and processions, *a koine of 'acclamatory epithets' could easily be developed* and an epiklesis transferred from one divinity to another."[51]

Turning to the inscribed acclamations studied by Peterson, Chaniotis concurs that, rather than being strictly monotheistic, the *Heis Theos* formula was often deployed competitively to designate one deity "as unique within a polytheistic system."[52] Moreover, in a detailed treatment of inscriptions (and graffiti), Chaniotis demonstrates that acclamations of deities tended to do at least four things: (1) they linked the piety of the one acclaiming to a personal experience of the deity's power and presence; (2) they focused on specific attributes of that deity; (3) they elevated one deity (with local significance) over others; and (4) they attempted to assert and even leverage a special relationship to that deity. He provides striking examples illustrating these acclamatory pragmatics.

---

50. Ibid., 119.
51. Ibid., 130 (italics mine).
52. Ibid., 119.

Acclaiming Artemis in Ephesus

One such example is an inscription exhibiting all of these features and dating to 57 CE. It comes from rural Roman Lydia in Asia Minor, some 175 kilometers inland from Ephesus.

```
1   Μεγάλη Μήτηρ Μηνὸς Ἀξιοττη-
    νοῦ · Μηνὶ Οὐρανίῳ Μηνὶ Ἀρτεμι-
    δώρου Ἀξιοττα κατέχοντι Γλύ-
    κων Ἀπολλωνίου καὶ Μύρτιον Γλύ-
5   κωνος εὐλογίαν περὶ τῆς ἑαυτῶν
    σωτηρίας καὶ τῶν ἰδίων τέκνων ·
    σὺ γάρ με, κύριε, αἰξμαλωπιζόμε-
    νον ἠλέησες · Μέγα σοι τὸ ὅσιον,
    μέγα σοι τὸ δίκαιον, μεγάλη νείκη,
10  μεγάλαι σαὶ νεμέσεις, μέγα σοι
    τὸ δωδεκάθεον τὸ παρὰ σοὶ κα-
    τεκτισμένον ἠχμαλωτίσθην
    ὑπὸ ἀδελφοῦ τέκνου τοῦ Δημαι-
    νέτου, ὅτι τὰ ἐμὰ προέλειψα καὶ
15  σοι βοίθεαν ἔδωκα ὡς τέκνῳ ·
    σὺ δὲ ἐξέκλεισές με καὶ ἠχμα-
    λώτισάς με οὐχ ὡς πάτρως, ἀλλὰ
    ὡς κακοῦργον · μέγας οὖν ἐστι
    Μεὶς Ἀξιοττα κατέχων · τὸ εἰκα-
20  νόν μοι ἐποίησας · εὐλογῶ ὑμεῖν ·
    ἔτους ρμβ', μη(νὸς) Πανήμου β'
```

1   Great is the Mother of Mes Axiottenos!
    To Heavenly Men, Men Artemidorou ruling
    over Axiotta, Glykon, son of Apollonius, and
    Myrtion the wife of Glykon (set up this) praise
5   because of the safety of themselves
    and of their children.
    For you showed mercy upon me, O Lord,
    when I was imprisoned. Great is your
    holiness! Great is your justice! Great (your)
10 victory! Great your acts of revenge! Great is
    the Dodekatheon which is located next to you!
    I was imprisoned
    by my brother's son Demainetos,
    because I abandoned my property and gave
15 you my support as if to a child.
    But you locked me out and imprisoned me as

> if I were not (your) uncle, but
> as if I were a criminal. Great therefore is
> Meis ruling over Axiotta! The sufficiency
> 20 you accomplished for me! I praise you!
> In the year 142, on the 2nd day of the month
> Panemos. (*SEG* 53.1344)[53]

These *Megas/Megalē* acclamations are set within a larger text best described as a "thanksgiving offering." As Chaniotis notes, "Its dedication involved some form of ritual action (e.g., a libation or a sacrifice) as well as an exaltation in the presence of an audience.... The phrase 'for you O Lord showed mercy when I was a captive' reflects what Glykon said aloud when he came to the sanctuary of Mes to set up his inscription.... It was in the presence of images or symbols of the gods [the Dodekatheon] that Glykon performed his acclamations."[54] Thus, first of all, Glykon piously acclaims Mes on the basis of a personal experience of the god's intervention on his behalf (ll. 7–8, 19–20).[55] Secondly, in doing so, Glykon focuses on distinct attributes of Mes—his dwelling in heaven; that he is *kyrios*; his holiness, justice, vengeful acts, and sufficiency (ll. 1–2, 8–10, 19–20).[56] Thirdly, there are suggestions that Mes is set in superior position to other deities (ll. 10–11).[57] Fourthly, by the use of the title "Axiottenos" (l. 1), a term related to "ruling" (l. 3), Mes is linked politically to Glykon's locale of Axiotta.[58] Not to be missed is the implication in Glykon's acclamation

---

53. Ibid., 122–26. The *editio princeps*, with an English translation (slightly adapted here), is Hasan Malay, "A Praise on Men Artemidorou Axiottenos," *Epigraphica Anatolica* 36 (2003): 13–18. See also Angelos Chaniotis, "Ritual Performances of Divine Justice," in *From Hellenism to Islam: Cultural and Linguistic Change in the Roman Near East*, ed. Hannah Cotton et al. (Cambridge: Cambridge University Press, 2009), 115–53.

54. Chaniotis, "Megatheism," 124.

55. Chaniotis gathers several other inscriptions that demonstrate this element of personal or corporate encounter with a deity's power, for example, the acclamation in response to the so-called Panamara rain miracle of Zeus in 42 BCE; see IStratonikeia 10, l. 13: ἔτι δὲ ἀναβοών[των] μεγάλῃ τῇ φωνῇ Μέγαν εἶναι Δία Πανάμαρον ("and now crying out with a loud voice, 'Great is Zeus Panamaros!'").

56. SEG 53.1344 notes the possibility that these may also represent "divine personifications." See Malay, "Praise on Men," 16.

57. Chaniotis, "Megatheism," 125.

58. Mes was a regional deity, linked elsewhere by epithets to other locales (e.g., Mes Motylleites). See ibid., 114.

that Mes has punished his nephew who mistreated him (ll. 11–20). We are thus reminded that—as complex, scripted speech acts—acclamations may ascribe honor to a deity such as Mes while simultaneously heaping dishonor on another agent. Indeed, the double effect of this acclamatory reality in Glykon's thanksgiving attests his experience of the deity's power and presence. In short then, Chaniotis's overall impression of this megatheistic network is striking: "Glykon's text reflects a coherent theology, which was in part influenced by and in part opposed to competing religious conceptions of the divine."[59]

This example of a less well-known Anatolian deity serves to illustrate in one brief text important constituent features of megatheism.[60] If Mes is acclaimed thus, how much more might we expect to see such megatheism enacted in relation to more popular deities?[61] In fact, these features do recur with regularity across the Mediterranean in the early imperial period, in large urban centers as well as rural villages, and for deities with an even wider geographic appeal than Mes. As it happens, in emphasizing the competitive context of the political claims and cultic practices related to megatheism, Chaniotis highlights one particular goddess as a paradigm: Ephesian Artemis.[62]

With these insights from Chaniotis in mind, we turn to the work of Guy MacLean Rogers in order to set Artemis Ephesia in local acclamatory and megatheistic context. Doing so will bring us nearly to the point of returning, with greater sensitivity, to the double acclamation and the whole narrative of Acts 19. Megatheism in Ephesus was thoroughly Artemis centered, all the more so as the early Roman imperial period progressed. Rogers, in his recent synthetic treatment, has demonstrated how Artemis worship was perhaps *the* central element of Roman Ephesian political theology. Particularly in the Julio-Claudian period, this fundamental part

---

59. Ibid., 125.

60. For a collection of inscriptions relating to Mes (Men) and his connection with Pisidian Antioch and Acts 13, see Greg H. R. Horsley, "The Great Power of God," *NewDocs* 3:31–32. See also Horsley, "Expiation and the Cult of Men," *NewDocs* 3:20–31, esp. pp. 30–31, where Horsley proposes, "It is not too speculative to suggest that the sort of argument which could have been brought against Paul and Barnabas to have them expelled was that their message was a threat to the city's main god and his cult, and would draw adherents away from the worship of Men.... Acts is quite silent about the god, but this attempt to read between the lines may be worth further reflection."

61. Mes/Men does appear at Ephesus, e.g., alongside Demeter in IEph 7.1.3252.

62. Chaniotis, "Megatheism," 114–15.

of public life in Ephesus underwent a dynamic restructuring.[63] Indeed, Rogers effectively places Artemis in megatheistic perspective, noting that her mysteries, processions, festivals, and related acclamations formed "the oral and possibly written script that the Ephesians used to negotiate their legal, political, and religious relations with their city rivals in Asia, with the Roman Senate, and with the Roman emperor himself."[64] In order to see how this came to be, we briefly summarize several observations of Rogers that are especially relevant to our investigation.

First, from the time of Octavian/Augustus, there was an explicit Roman sanctioning and reshaping of Artemis worship in Ephesus. This involved a careful reconfiguration of associated civic rights, privileges, and even spaces such that local cult became increasingly intertwined with provincial and imperial politics.[65] By 6/5 BCE, an Augusteum (Temple of Augustus) was constructed in connection with the Artemision. Around the same time, as part of the Roman-Ephesian revolution Rogers narrates, the Curetes (key players in the Artemis cult) were transferred from the Artemision to a prytaneion much more centrally located in the so-called upper (Tetragonus) agora of Ephesus.[66] Thus, by early in the first century, Augustus, the goddess Roma, and Artemis had been closely interlinked by Ephesian politics, architecture, processional routes, and sightlines.[67] The Artemis cult, which had always figured prominently in Ephesian civic identity, maintained its pivotal role, but now with distinct Roman entailments.

Specifically, by the time of Tiberius, the narrative of Artemis's birth had become the defining feature of Ephesian political-theological identity. This was the case within the polis, in ambassadorial negotiation with Rome, and in competition with other cities such as Delos, Smyrna, Pergamon, Eleusis, and Athens who claimed privileged links with Artemis or similar deities who had their own mystery cults (Tacitus, *Ann.* 3.60–63).[68]

---

63. Rogers, *Mysteries of Artemis of Ephesos*.
64. Ibid., 143.
65. Ibid., 115–18.
66. For the full version of how this relocation not only placed the Curetes in the center of Ephesian civic space but also gave authority to civic (and not temple) officials—namely, the prytanis, the boule, and the demos—who carefully managed the Artemis birth narrative and the celebration of the mysteries in relation to Ephesian political interests in the first century, see ibid., 119–21.
67. Ibid., 93–103.
68. See ibid., 122–23, 140–44, 156–58.

Political prestige and privileges, a sense of local identity, and economic benefits were wrapped up in this intercivic struggle.[69] For Ephesus, it was Artemis who supplied all of the megatheistic clout for the ongoing competition.

Further striking evidence for the conjunction of loyalty to the emperor with Artemis piety comes in the titles adopted and advertised by the Curetes and other cult attendants in the mid- to late first century and beyond. Prior to circa 54 CE, the Curetes were honored primarily as *eusebeis* (reverent/pious) with regard to their service to the goddess.[70] But from the time of Nero through to the Flavian era the epithets *philosebastos* (devoted to the emperor) and *philartēmidos* (devoted to Artemis) were added to *eusebeis*. The balanced parallelism in the terms is evocative of a carefully calculated double piety. Rogers adjudges the combination of these titles for the keepers of the Artemis cult to be the "local manifestation of a common [Roman imperial] religious language"; it was a "public strategy" with the goal of leveraging devotion to Artemis in a manner that represented fidelity to Rome and thereby secured the peace and prosperity of Ephesus.[71]

In this same vein, in 80/81 CE the Ephesian *grammateus* L. Herennius Peregrinus described himself as *hagnou kai philartēmidos* (pure and devoted to Artemis) as he set up a statue and inscribed its base in honor of the Roman proconsul C. Laecanius Bassus Caecina Paetus (IEph 3.695).[72] In doing so, the *grammateus* was clearly linking his civic piety to Artemis with Roman loyalty within the provincial network of power. This conjunction continued well into the second century and is exemplified in

---

69. Ibid., 158: "When we read between the lines of the first-century lists of Curetes, what we see, then, is the professionalization and the beginning of the commercialization of the celebrations of the mysteries of Artemis, as directed by the polis of Ephesus through the prytaneis. The Ephesians modernized the mysteries in part to construct and reinforce a distinct, local identity but also to make the experience of initiation available to the population of a city that Seneca observed was the second largest in the eastern Roman empire by the mid-first century."

70. Ibid., 158: "The epithet no doubt was a clear indication of their belief in her divinity and power. But the linguistic choice also was intended to establish a shared sense of appropriate piety with other members of the demos and readers of the texts [inscribed Curetes lists]."

71. Ibid., 162.

72. Lines 15–19: Λουκίου Ἐρεννίου | Περεγρείνου ἁγνοῦ | καὶ φιλαρτέμιδος, | τοῦ γραμματέως | τοῦ δήμου τὸ β'. See Rogers, *Mysteries of Artemis of Ephesos*, 159–60.

the Salutaris foundation inscription dedicating money, statues, and typestatues to Artemis and her civic keepers in Ephesus for use in festivals, processions, and public distributions of cash. In two inscriptions from 104 CE, C. Vibius Salutaris is repeatedly honored, in both Greek and Latin, as *philartēmis kai philokaisar* (IEph 1.27, 33).[73] For his lavish expense, it was decreed that Salutaris was to be publicly proclaimed and crowned in the Ephesian assembly as one who worked earnestly on behalf of the city and who was "devoted to Artemis" (*philartēmin* [IEph 1.27, ll. 84–90]).[74] To be devoted to Artemis was to be loyal to Rome. By implication, to be a devoted provincial subject meant—at least in Ephesus—that Artemis was the goddess whom one must not ignore, much less challenge, in her megatheistic hegemony. To do so would be both un-Roman and un-Ephesian, certainly by the mid-first century, if not earlier.

If such was indeed the case, what were the personal and corporate experiences of Artemis to which local piety was linked? Which divine attributes of Artemis were celebrated in Ephesian political-theological settings?[75] Undoubtedly, the mysteries were an ongoing setting for encounters with Artemis. But even beyond the circle of elite and subelite initiates, her attributes were known and celebrated. Persistently over time, Artemis was known as Savior (*Sōteira*) and Helper (*Boēthēs*), the One Who Hears Prayers (*Epēkoos*).[76] She was a goddess of epiphany (*Epiphaneia*) and One Who Does Not Lie (*Ou Pseudētai*). On the basis of her attributes, Artemis was offered thanks (in the form of dedicatory thanksgiving prayers, *eucharisteiai*) and her name was invoked (*horkizō*) by her

---

73. IEph 1.27, ll. 451–52: Γάϊος Οὐείβιος, Γ. υἱ(ός), Οὐωφεστεῖνα, Σαλουτάριος, φιλάρ|τεμις καὶ φιλόκαισαρ διάταξιν. IEph 1.33, ll. 4–5 (Lat.), 15–16 (Gk.): C. Vibius, C. f., Vofent., Salutaris, philartemis et | philocaesar ... Γάϊος Οὐείβιος, Γ. υἱός, Οὐωφεστεῖνα, Σαλουτάριος, | φιλάρτεμις καὶ φιλόκαισαρ. See also IEph 1.36a, ll. 4–6; 36b, ll. 4–6; 36c, ll. 4–6; 36d, ll. 4–6. On the Salutaris foundation, see Guy MacLean Rogers, *The Sacred Identity of Ephesos: Foundation Myths of a Roman City* (London: Routledge, 1991).

74. [ὡς σπουδά]ζοντα καὶ φιλάρ|τεμιν (ll. 89–90).

75. For general attributes of Artemis considered diachronically, with evidence, see Strelan, *Paul, Artemis, and the Jews*, 48–52. What follows summarizes and augments some of the data collected there.

76. For Artemis as Savior, see, e.g., an undated imperial inscription to C. Atticus Iulius, priest of Artemis Soteira: Γ(άϊος) Ἰούλιος | Ἄττικος ἱερεὺς Ἀρ|τέμιδος Σωτεί|ρας Σεβαστοῦ γένους (IEph 4.1265). See also IEph 3.606, ll. 4–5. For Artemis as One Who Hears Prayers, see, e.g., IEph 2.504, l. 1; 505.1, l. 1; 505.2, l. 1: Ἀρτέμιδι ἐπηκόῳ (all 114/115 CE).

devotees.[77] By the turn of the second century, in the Salutaris foundation inscription (IEph 1.27) alone, Artemis is described as

- "the greatest goddess Artemis [τὴν μεγίστην θεὸν Ἄρτεμιν], from whom the most beautiful things come to all" (ll. 12–13)[78]
- "the foundress [of the city]" (τὴν ἀρχηγέτιν [l. 20])
- "golden Artemis [with her] two stags" (Ἄρτεμις χρυσέα ... καὶ αἱ ... ἔλαφοι δύο [ll. 157–58])[79]
- "Artemis the torch bearer" (Ἄρτεμις λαμπαδηφόρος [l. 168])[80]
- "the most manifest and greatest goddess Artemis" (τῆς τε ἐπιφανεστάτης καὶ μεγίστης θεᾶς Ἀρτέμιδος [ll. 344–45])
- "the lady Artemis" (τῆς κυρίας Ἀρτέμιδος [l. 363])

What these epithets of Artemis demonstrate is how the goddess was experienced and remembered, in her power and presence, by those who were devoted to her. As even this cursory list makes evident, she was particularly acclaimed, thanked, and celebrated for offering salvation/safety, for her powerful manifestations, for being the founder of the city, and for her overall greatness. Lady (*kyria*) Artemis of the Ephesians was far and away the biggest goddess in town and her appeal was multilayered and multidirectional.[81] Artemis lorded it over Ephesus, and Ephesus lauded their connection to the great Lady over that of all other cities.

---

77. See also Greg H. R. Horsley, "Giving Thanks to Artemis," *NewDocs* 4:127–29. The same term is used of the Jewish exorcists in Acts 19:13.

78. For a variant spelling within the same inscription, see ll. 224–25: τῆς μεγίστης θεᾶς Αρ[τέμιδος].

79. See also Rogers, *Sacred Identity of Ephesos*, 112–13: "The golden type-statue of Artemis with her stags evoked her immortality. Artemis with her burning torch, however, was the thread which ran through the entire procession, and no doubt was intended to evoke the mysteries of Ortygia and Solmissos, the annual re-enactment of Artemis' birth. Ephesian civic identity began with this event, an event which predated the existence of the Greek city. The birth of Artemis at Ephesos remained central to the Ephesians' sense of their place in the world of AD 104."

80. See also Rogers, *Sacred Identity of Ephesos*, 111, 115: "Artemis with her torch lit the way to the Ephesians' ultimate sense of identity—and stole both the first and the last scenes of the procession" (p. 115).

81. In fact, Artemis was so appealing that she was worshiped and (ac)claimed elsewhere, as the Ephesians delighted to point out. She appears, for example, as Artemis Laphria at Patrai and Artemis Orthia in the Pelopponese and with many other localized epithets in locations across the Mediterranean. See Tobias Fischer-Hansen

Within early imperial Roman Ephesus, therefore, there were many groups closely associated with Artemis who had vested interests in her greatness. Not only the Curetes, the boule and demos, and local and provincial elites praised her; they were joined by local craftsmen who acclaimed Artemis and who honored those who honored her. In describing the civic processional route laid out in the Salutaris inscription, Rogers remarks,

> Merchants and craftsmen from all the different guilds of Ephesus bought and sold goods brought into the harbour which gave Ephesus its wealth; the silversmith's riot which the Apostle Paul started probably originated in one of the stalls of the [Tetragonos] agora.[82] No doubt Salutaris' procession would have aroused at least some interest among the shopkeepers and shoppers from Ephesus and the surrounding cities as they haggled over their wares.[83]

Artemis economics and civic religion fused acutely in the guild of the silversmiths; their handiwork was almost certainly plied in the Tetragonus Agora. Their presence has also left traces along nearby Arkadiane Street, which led from the theater area down toward the harbor (IEph 2.547.1, 547.2).[84] Sometime after the 50s CE, M. Antonius Hermeias, himself a silversmith and a *neopoios* (cult official), was laid with his wife in a tomb looked after by the association of silversmiths (IEph 6.2212).[85] At the end of the first century, the silversmiths set up a statue base for Tiberius Claudius Ariston, who was three times high priest of Asia, prytanis and *neōkoros*, on account of his construction projects that beautified the city

---

and Birte Poulsen, eds., *From Artemis to Diana: The Goddess of Man and Beast* (Copenhagen: University of Copenhagen, 2009). Furthermore, when Artemis is acclaimed together with other deities elsewhere, for example, alongside Pythian Apollo and Hecate in Delphi, she takes a back seat to the most prominent god or goddess according to the local megatheistic script. See Chaniotis, "Megatheism," 126–27. Finally, recall that Ephesus ensured their megatheistic claim on Artemis as their founder and chief civic goddess over against Delos in the Tiberian embassy of 26 CE (Tacitus, *Ann.* 3.61.1–2). See Rogers, *Mysteries of Artemis of Ephesos*, 140–43.

82. Only completed in the reign of Nero; see Rogers, *Sacred Identity of Ephesos*, 100–101, maps of processional route at 196–97.

83. Ibid., 101.

84. These are two identical topos inscriptions on columns: ἀργυροκόπων. Did these mark a gathering space? Guild offices? Commercial shop fronts?

85. See also Greg H. R. Horsley, "The Silversmiths at Ephesos," *New Docs* 4:7–10.

(IEph 2.425.10).[86] These social interrelations sit comfortably within the civic framework of a megatheism focused on Artemis. Silversmiths, elite civic and provincial figures, the Artemis temple economy and cult, and Rome are interwoven in a commercial and honorific web. Even when she is not explicitly mentioned in texts such as these, the epiphanic aura of Artemis shines at the center of the Ephesian political theology and economy in connection with the titles of officials (*neopoios, prytanis, neōkoros*) who were linked to her public cult. We know from Acts 19 that the silversmiths were accustomed to generating acclamations for Artemis. Evidence also demonstrates that the guild itself was capable of basking in reflected acclaim. An undated inscription reads:

May the guild (or company) of the living(?) silversmiths increase!
Ἄυξει τὸ πλῆθος τῶν ἀργυροχόων τῶν ζώντων (IEph 1.585)[87]

In a gloriously refracted reciprocity, the manifest magnificence of Artemis cast its light back upon those who honored her with their labor, their voices, and the works of their hands. Those in Ephesus who acclaimed her great (*Megas/Megalē!*) experienced a certain flourishing (*Auxei!*), as did their city, which was later called "the nurturer of its own Ephesian goddess" (ἐν [τῇ] | ἡμέτερᾳ πόλει τῇ τροφῷ τῆς ἰδίας θεοῦ τῆς Ἐφ[εσί]|ας [IEph 1.24b, ll. 22–23]).

Thus was megatheism in first-century Ephesus focused on Artemis in her greatness and glory. It was a glory articulated for the "leader of [the] city" (ἐπειδὴ ἡ προεστῶσα τῆς πόλεως [IEph 1.24b, l. 8]) on account of her "divine nature" (διὰ τῆς ἰδίας θειότητος [l. 10]) and "visible manifestations" (διὰ | τὰς ὑπ' αὐτῆς γεινομένας ἐναργεῖς ἐπιφανείας [ll. 11–13]), a glory generated by civic reverence, and a glory focused—especially in the act of acclamation—on her "divine name" (τοῦ θείου | ὀνόματος [ll. 24–25]). As a result, the Ephesians might conceivably countenance a modicum of inter-

---

86. See also the later IEph 2.276, 586; 3.636; SEG 34.1094. The same kind of web focused on other deities in different locales: for a working group (συνεργασία) of silversmiths and goldsmiths, a local benefactor, and the cult of Athena at Smyrna, see ISmyrna 721 (*CIG* 3154).

87. See also Horsley, "Silversmiths at Ephesos"; Philip A. Harland, ed., *North Coast of the Black Sea, Asia Minor*, vol. 2 of *Greco-Roman Associations: Texts, Translations, and Commentary*, BZNW 204 (Berlin: de Gruyter, 2014), 247. Cf. IEph 7.1.3090: "May it increase forever, the great city of the Ephesians!" ([εἰς τοὺς αἰῶνας] αὔξι, ἡ μεγάλη Ἐφε[σίων πόλις]).

(or even intra-) civic competition in the polytheistic spirit of Greco-Roman megatheism. But woe betide any who suggested that a competing deity might seriously challenge Artemis—especially in Ephesus itself—and who dared to critique the civic hegemony of the goddess who owed so much to the handiwork and verbal acclaim of her people.[88] Just how far would Artemis, not to mention her Ephesian minders and their Roman masters, allow her glory to be eclipsed by another?[89]

4. Glory, the Efficacy of Acclamation

Our application of the framework of megatheism to Artemis and Ephesus suggests a glory focused on the name of the goddess, for in her name were latent all her celebrated attributes. Acclamation was the culturally scripted verbal explosion of this glory—an outburst in honor of Artemis that might simultaneously praise the city and its elites, acknowledge the sanctioning authority of Rome, and be directed against other divine competitors and their cities or devotees. Acclamations wielded glory as both tribute and weapon. These facts are consonant with the observations of Agamben alluded to earlier that acclamations, in the "political archaeology of glory," may be seen to "found and justify" political power.[90] In this vein, Agamben argues that the all-important efficacy of acclamation is in fact *glory*.

Agamben's reflections are important for us as we pivot from our examination of ancient acclamatory scripts as a critical component of Greco-Roman megatheism back to the text of Acts 19 and the urgent acclamations for Artemis that prompted our investigation. Building on Peterson's work with the *Heis Theos* acclamations and connecting it even to our contemporary "society of spectacle,"[91] Agamben remarks:

> As is the case of every acclamation, its effect and function are more important than the comprehension of its meaning. The audience who, today, in a French or American concert hall cry out "bravo," might not know its

---

88. This is the point made by Martin Ebner, *Die Stadt als Lebensraum der ersten Christen* (Göttingen: Vandenhoeck & Ruprecht, 2012), 25–26.

89. IEph 1.24b, ll. 32–34: "For in this way, with the improvement of the honoring of the goddess, our city will remain more glorious [ἐνδοξοτέρα] and more blessed for all time."

90. Agamben, *Kingdom and the Glory*, 168.

91. See Guy Debord, *The Society of the Spectacle*, trans. D. Nicholson-Smith (New York: Zone, 1994).

precise meaning or the grammar of the Italian term (not varying it even if it is said of a woman or to more than one person), but they know perfectly well the effect that the acclamation must produce. It rewards the actor or virtuoso and obliges him to return to the stage. Those who know about show business go so far as to claim that actors need applause in the same way one needs nourishment. This means that, in the sphere of doxologies and acclamations, the semantic aspect of language is deactivated and appears for a moment as an empty rotation; and, yet, it is precisely this empty turning that supplies it with its peculiar, almost magical, efficacy: that of producing glory.[92]

We may well take issue with Agamben's assumptions concerning the "empty rotation" of acclamatory language (and the empty divine throne he mentions elsewhere), but it is difficult to deny his conclusions regarding the quasi-magical efficacy of acclamations as they produce and wield glory. Acclamations are indeed powerfully doxological.[93] In line with Peterson's study of antique acclamations, Agamben affirms that they are at the same time consensual, democratic, and therefore political. A people who acclaim in unison are united; they are to a significant degree identified and defined corporately by their acclamation. In their very utterance, acclamations generate, sustain, and set the parameters for a polity just as much as they articulate a theology.[94]

In returning with these insights to the guildhall and theater spaces of Ephesus, we now grasp more fully the meaning—or rather, the efficacy—of the repeated, sustained acclamations for Artemis on that day during Paul's long sojourn in the city. The silversmiths took up a cry that exalted their chief civic goddess, their profession, and their benefactors. But it was also an acclamation of indignation against Paul and—as we shall see presently—against his fellow Jews, his gospel, and his Jesus. As the acclaimers spilled into the streets and swelled their numbers in the theater,

---

92. Agamben, *Kingdom and the Glory*, 232. Agamben ultimately links acclamations to the consensual basis of public law and political theology, arguing that "consensual democracy, which Debord called 'the society of the spectacle' and which is so dear to the theorists of communicative action, is a glorious democracy, in which the *oikonomia* is fully resolved into glory and the doxological function, freeing itself of liturgy and ceremonials, absolutizes itself to an unheard of extent and penetrates every area of social life" (259).

93. See especially ibid., 197–259 ("The Archaeology of Glory").

94. Ibid., 167–96, 253–59.

the volume grew along with the consensus. In the acclaim for Artemis there was not only commercial and cultic rage; there was also a growing political-theological expression of identity. For the gathered populace, this "Great is Artemis of the Ephesians!" and the linked acclamations for local benefactors and for the house of the Caesars, which surely accompanied it according to script, expressed what it meant to be gloriously Ephesian. This articulation—over against any other ethnic identity or *politeia*—was what it meant to be Ephesian under Rome. For two hours on at least one occasion, Luke tells us, the glory of Ephesus rumbled and swelled before the *grammateus* finally stilled and dismissed the irregular assembly.[95]

5. Acclamation and Opposing Political Theologies in Acts 19

We are now ready to return to the text of Acts 19 with an understanding of acclamatory scripts, Artemis megatheism in Ephesus, and the focal glory of acclamations that generates, sustains, and defends a political theology. How, we must ask, might this delineation of the efficacy of acclamation help us better understand not simply the dual acclamations of 19:28, 34 but the progression and selectivity of the whole cloth of Luke's Ephesian narrative?

Thus far we have spoken of Acts 19 as a unit, within which 19:23–40 and the acclamations for Artemis sit. But is this the proper narrative unit for interpretation? Views are divided on this point, precisely because it is linked with how the overall structure of Acts is understood. Giuseppe Betori and Ben Witherington III are representative of those who see 19:20(–22) as a major "seam" connecting 19:23–40 more nearly to what follows than to what precedes.[96] Those who see 19:21 as the beginning of a distinct "travel narrative" also tend to interpret 19:23–40 less (at least in

---

95. For the structure, attendees, and seating blocs of regular Ephesian assemblies in the Salutaris inscription, see Guy MacLean Rogers, "The Assembly of Imperial Ephesos," *ZPE* 94 (1992): 224–28.

96. Giuseppe Betori, "La strutturazione del libro degli Atti: Un proposta," *RivB* 42 (1994): 3–34. Betori proposes the following: (introduction) 1:1–11; (1) 1:12–8:4; (2) 8:16–14:28; (3) 14:27–16:5; (4) 15:35–19:22; (5) 19:20–28:31; (conclusion) 28:14b–31. He sees pivotal, overlapping "seams" at 1:12–14; 8:1b–4; 14:27–28; 15:35–16:5; 19:20–22; 28:14b–16. Ben Witherington III focuses on the widely acknowledged "word of the Lord increased" hinges at 6:7; 9:31; 12:24; 16:5; and 19:20, proposing six "panel-sections": 1:1–6:7; 6:8–9:31; 9:32–12:24; 12:25–16:5; 16:6–19:20; 19:21–28:31 (*The Acts of the Apostles: A Socio-rhetorical Commentary* [Grand Rapids: Eerdmans, 1998]). Both, therefore, see 19:20–22 as a key interpretive moment, but one that inserts a kind of

narratival-thematic terms) in light of 19:1–20.[97] But others see strong reasons for taking 19:1–40 as a tightly coherent unit. Charles H. Talbert places it within the larger section 13:1–28:31, seeing especially the geographical focus on Ephesus in 18:2–20:1 as important.[98] Scott Shauf locates Acts 19 as the climax of a "panel" that stretches from 15:36–19:40(20:1) and offers a detailed defense for interpreting 19:23–40 very tightly within 19:1–40. His reasons, basically three, are "both structural and thematic": (1) Paul's time in Ephesus forms the "high point" of his overall ministry and mission; (2) the *egeneto de* of 19:1 sets it off from the preceding unit and 20:1 (*meta de*) clearly begins a new section; and (3) the Ephesian "episodes" of chapter 19 form a coherent, thematic thread, explicable by Luke's desire to highlight the success of Paul, his proclamation, and his Jesus.[99] Shauf's argument will be confirmed by our observations concerning the narrative-theological function of the acclamations for Artemis as they relate to the whole of chapter 19.[100]

Both acclamations are voiced in the so-called riot narrative at the climax of Acts 19:1–40. The whole is a highly crafted narrative, Shauf argues, that divides into six subunits, given here with distinctive thematic elements identified in each:

1. 19:1–7[101] baptism into the name of Jesus
   Paul's hands and the Holy Spirit

---

caesura, marking off 19:23–40 from what precedes and seeing it (esp. Witherington, *Acts of the Apostles*, 583) primarily as preparatory for Acts 21 and following.

97. Keener, *15:1–23:35*, 2860: "The brief notice in 19:21–22 shifts the narrative's focus toward Rome, preparing for Paul's custody in Acts 21–28, just as Luke 9:51–52 shifts the gospel's focus toward Jerusalem, preparing for Jesus's passion." But see Shauf, *Theology as History*, 235–37. Pervo remarks, "The variety of plans presented for Acts ... indicates not only the use of different models (thematic, geographical, literary) but also Luke's propensity toward a fluid, overlapping technique" (*Acts*, 20–21).

98. Talbert, *Reading Acts*, 165–72.

99. Shauf, *Theology as History*, 143–44. Cf. John Chrysostom, who suggests a coherence to 19:1–40: "Again danger; again uproar. Do you see the renown? There came twofold miracles. They contradicted it. Such is the way the threads alternate through the whole texture [οὔπω διὰ πάντων ὑφαίνεται τὰ πράγματα]" (*Hom. Act.* 45.3 [PG 60.317]).

100. With Shauf, *Theology as History*, 144, it is important to note that approaching 19:1–40 in this manner as the primary unit of coherence does not imply its isolation from the whole flow of Acts.

101. Ibid., 144–61.

2. 19:8–12[102]   Paul's proclamation
                 God's power through Paul
3. 19:13–17[103] Sceva's seven sons
                 power in relation to the names of Paul and Jesus
                 magnifying the name of Jesus
4. 19:18–20[104] confession of practices
                 burning of books[105]
                 word of the Lord increases and prevails
                 "strength of response called forth by the power of God's work in the city"[106]
5. 19:21–22[107] Paul's plans as God's plan for him to leave Ephesus
                 Paul is *not* driven out of Ephesus
6. 19:23–40[108] "the conflict of the spreading Christian mission with pagan religion"[109]
                 riot focused on "the status of Artemis and her relationship to the city"[110]

In considering Luke's historiographical and theological selectivity in composing this arrangement, Shauf concurs with many who see the summary statements of 19:17 ("and the name of the Lord Jesus was being magnified") and 19:20 ("in this way mightily did the word of the Lord increase and prevail") as critical for understanding the entire Ephesian

---

102. Ibid., 161–77.
103. Ibid., 177–226.
104. See ibid., 226–34, where he forwards several strong objections to the traditional interpretation of the *praxeis* and *perierga* of 19:18–19 as specifically "magical," in line with the spells found in Egyptian magical papyri. What Shauf does not consider is whether the deeds and scrolls in question might relate to the mystery cults of Artemis and other figures ritually celebrated in Ephesus, especially from the Roman imperial period. See Rogers, *Mysteries of Artemis of Ephesos*, 293–302, 311–12; cf. Walter Burkert, *Ancient Mystery Cults* (Cambridge: Harvard University Press, 1987), 58, 70–72. If this link were made definitively, it would set up a new resonance and narrative progression between 19:18–20 and what follows in 19:23–40. But see Pervo, *Acts*, 479–81.
105. Shauf, *Theology as History*, 144–61.
106. Ibid., 234.
107. Ibid., 234–40.
108. Ibid., 240–63.
109. Ibid., 241.
110. Ibid., 248.

episode.[111] What is striking, but rarely noted, is that both these statements have clear resonance with the acclamations for Artemis which follow. Indeed, both employ verbal cognates—*megalunō* in 19:17 and *auxanō* in 19:20—of two of the most common acclamations we have witnessed in the evidence canvassed above (*Megas/Megalē, Auxi/Auxei*).[112] Furthermore, the magnification of the name of the Lord Jesus in 19:17 begins, in the context of our argument, to suggest strongly that Artemis is not the only deity receiving acclamations in Acts 19. It is quite possible we are meant to hear, not merely a generalizing summary in 19:17, but specific echoes of verbal acclaim for the name of Jesus.[113]

What Shauf further proposes, however, is of special interest for our investigation of the political-theological efficacy of the acclamations that follow in 19:23-40. He argues that Luke has structured the narrative such that 19:23-40 shares significant compositional and thematic features with both 19:1-7 and 19:13-17. First, when seen in the flow of the chapter, 19:1-7 and 19:23-40 are similar in that they are the extended subunits narrating specific events in detail. But whereas the emphasis of the particularity of 19:1-7 is on the name of Jesus, that in 19:23-40 is clearly on the name of Artemis. Second, 19:13-17, with its emphatic summary focused on the magnification of the name of Jesus in 19:17,[114] highlights Paul's extraordinary success in Ephesus; similarly, 19:23-40 highlights the same

---

111. Ibid., 272-78. See Pervo, *Acts*, 479-82; Keener, *15:1-23:35*, 2852. Note the variant word order, emphasizing *the Lord*, in the "growth" statement in 19:20 in the text of NA[28]: Ὁυτως κατὰ κράτος τοῦ κυρίου ὁ λόγος ηὔξανεν καὶ ἴσχυεν (cf. 6:7 καὶ ὁ λόγος τοῦ θεοῦ [D = κυρίου] ηὔξανεν καὶ ἐπληθύνετο ὁ ἀριθμός τῶν μαθητῶν; 12:24 ὁ δὲ λόγος τοῦ θεοῦ ηὔξανεν καὶ ἐπληθύνετο). There is, however, considerable variation in the mss at 19:20. See also Jerome Kodell, "'The Word of God Grew': The Ecclesial Tendency of Λόγος in Acts 1,7; 12,24; 19,20," *Bib* 55 (1974): 505-19.

112. Luke appears to know the most popular acclamatory language, also using αὐξάνω in his "growth statement" at 12:24 (ὁ δὲ λόγος τοῦ θεοῦ ηὔξανεν καὶ ἐπληθύνετο), there in contrast to the acclamations for Herod in 12:22. See IEph 7.1.3090: [εἰς τοὺς αἰῶνας] αὔξι, ἡ μεγάλη Ἐφε[σίων πόλις] ("May it increase forever, the great city of the Ephesians!").

113. Shauf, *Theology as History*, 274, notes that the imperfect ἐμεγαλύνετο indicates the "extended character of this magnification." See also, at pp. 293-97, his extended comments on this in relation to Acts 19 and wider Lukan usage of μεγαλύνω.

114. See John A. Ziesler, "The Name of Jesus in the Acts of the Apostles," *JSNT* 4 (1979): 35-37.

success of Paul's mission, but by a "negative" focus on the magnification of the name of Artemis.

Although Shauf does not explicitly argue on this basis, it becomes evident that the respective focus on the opposing divine names in 19:1–17 and 19:23–40 balances and integrates the narrative theology of the unit. Tracing the distribution and uses of the divine names of Jesus and Artemis in the chapter makes this case visually:

19:1–17
- in order that they might believe in the one coming after him, that is in Jesus (19:4)
- they were baptized into the name of the Lord Jesus (19:5)
- Then some ... undertook ... to invoke the name of the Lord Jesus (19:13)
- I adjure you by the Jesus whom Paul proclaims (19:13)
- Jesus I know and Paul I recognize, but who are you? (19:15)
- and they magnified the name of the Lord Jesus (19:17)

19:23–40
- silver shrines of Artemis (19:24)
- the temple of the great goddess Artemis (19:27)
- and that she may even be deposed from her magnificence, she whom all Asia and the world revere (19:27)
- Great is Artemis of the Ephesians! (19:28)
- Great is Artemis of the Ephesians! (19:34)
- the city of the Ephesians is the temple keeper of the great Artemis (19:35)

The effect of this careful balance of divine names is to construct a contest of gods *kata kratos*.[115] In effect, what we see in Acts 19 is competing political theologies set in a building narrative. It is a megatheistic antago-

---

115. Shauf, *Theology as History*, 248; see also Joachim Molthagen, "Die ersten Konflikte der Christen in der griechisch-römischen Welt," *Historia* 40 (1991): 42–76. See also the reasons adduced by Rius-Camps and Read-Heimerdinger for seeing the narrative of Acts 19 as setting up a "direct and sustained rivalry" between Paul's proclamation and Artemis-worship. Many of these reasons apply even if one does not adopt the readings of the so-called Western text (*Comparison with the Alexandrian Tradition*, 64–77).

nism not between two cities as such, but within Ephesus itself, between Jesus and his growing number of believers and Artemis with her devoted, assembled civic throng. According to Duffy, at the semiotic level of the narrative there is a "shadow program" in 19:23–40 whereby, among other oppositions, we see two in particular: (1) Demetrius played off against Paul and (2) the Artemis shrines countered by Paul's anti-idolatry polemic.[116]

In this regard, Duffy notes the careful "maxi-structure" of 19:23–40.[117]

Introduction (23–24)
A Demetrius *gathers* the silversmiths (25a)
  B Demetrius's speech (25b–27)
    C Silversmiths *stir up* the crowd (28a)
      D Acclamation (28b)
        E Riot narrative (29–34a)
      D' Acclamation (34b)
    C' Clerk *calms* the crowd (35a)
  B' Clerk's speech (35–40a)
A' Clerk *dismisses* the assembly (40b)
Summary and transition (19:41–20:1)

Although she is not alone in pointing to the important placement of the acclamations in 19:28, 34, Duffy's structural outline helpfully brings to the fore their centrality in the subunit 19:23–40. Without the acclamations, the "riot narrative" would cohere less tightly, lacking its doxological center(s); likewise, the magnification of Jesus's name (19:17) and the increase of the word of the Lord (19:20)—both resulting from divine action through Paul's ministry—lose significant force if Artemis is not acclaimed and the crowd is dismissed in the final Ephesian subunit. If this argument concerning the flow and structure of the narrative of Acts 19 and its thematic focal points indeed emerges from the text, then we may make several further observations on the basis of our consideration above of acclamations, their causes, and their effects.

Why do the acclamatory outbursts occur just here in 19:28 and 19:34? To begin with, in 19:28, the initial acclamation is in response to Demetri-

---

116. Maureen E. Duffy, "The Riot of the Silversmiths at Ephesus (Acts 19:23–40): A Synchronic Study Using Rhetorical and Semiotic Methods of Analysis" (PhD diss., University of St. Paul, Ottawa, 1994), 126–28.
117. Ibid., 71.

us's speech, most often seen as highlighting the economic threat posed by Paul's gospel. But the cause of the disturbance was not merely economic.[118] Rather, the wrath incited by his speech was the result of a megatheistic economics and was stirred up by Paul's proclamation on Demetrius's own lips.[119] Since there is no explicit object following the *akousantes* in 19:28, we must infer that the acclamatory anger is caused by Paul's persuasive idol polemic (*ho Paulos houtos peisas* [19:26]) enumerated in 19:25b–27. In those verses, Demetrius outlines a triple threat: (1) the silversmiths' share of Artemis-related business may become dangerously exposed (*eis apelegmon elthein* [19:27]);[120] (2) the temple (economy?) of Artemis may become devalued (*eis outhen logisthēnai* [19:27]);[121] and (3) Artemis herself might be overthrown from her megatheistic hegemony (*kathaireisthai tēs megaleiotētos autēs* [19:27]). Within the context of acclamatory megatheism, this outburst in 19:28 makes even more sense: for their part, the craftsmen sense that the political theology of Roman Ephesus is under threat.

Then, in 19:34 the second, more prolonged acclamation is sparked by Alexander's non-speech (19:33). For those in the crowded theater, it was the recognition of Alexander's Jewish demeanor (*epignontes de Ioudaios estin* [19:34]) that led to two hours of acclamation. The implied causes of this "Jewish intermezzo" become clearer in megatheistic focus. First, the Jews were also linked to a sustained idol polemic that frequently rendered them at best suspicious and at worst dangerous in the eyes of non-Jews.

---

118. Rightly seen by Rowe, who claims the collision of the gospel with Artemis worship "rests ultimately on the theological affirmation of the break between God and the cosmos" in Paul's anti-idol polemic (*World Upside Down*, 50–51). Shauf, *Theology as History*, 248: economic concerns "recede thematically."

119. As Shauf notes, Demetrius's speech "adds information about Paul's ministry in Ephesus that has not previously been narrated" (*Theology as History*, 281). See also Duffy, "Riot of the Silversmiths," 127. John Chrysostom also hears the glory of the gospel and its efficacy through Paul in the speech of Demetrius (*Hom. Act.* 45.4 [PG 60.320]).

120. Usually translated "disrepute," ἀπελεγμός is a rare term related to ἀπελέγχω that can signify divine prosecution in the confession inscriptions of Asia Minor (e.g., *TAM* 5.1:499). See Angelos Chaniotis, "Under the Watchful Eyes of the Gods: Divine Justice in Hellenistic and Roman Asia Minor," in *The Greco-Roman East: Politics, Culture, Society*, ed. Stephen Colvin, YCS 31 (Cambridge: Cambridge University Press, 2004), 1–43.

121. See also the perceptive reading of Tripp, "Tale of Two Riots."

Second, the Jews were a recognized *politeuma* within Roman Ephesus and the province of Asia.[122] As a result, it was natural for such a megatheistic acclamation to be directed against the Jews just as it might be against another city.[123] This political-theological hypothesis is only confirmed if we grant the overwhelming likelihood of Peterson's initial reading of Acts 19:34 as an abbreviated form of a string of surging acclamations. On this interpretation, and in light of the pattern of acclamatory scripts explored above, rather than understanding Luke to be reporting a single line shouted monotonously in praise of Artemis for the entire two-hour period in 19:34, we ought instead to apprehend an acclamatory sequence on the order of:

> Great is Artemis of the Ephesians! Great is Imperator Caesar! Long may he live! The power of the Romans forever! Great is the proconsul, justice for the city! Bravo the *grammateus*, you preserve the city for the emperors! Long live the prytanis, lover of Artemis, initiator of good things! Great is Artemis, founder of the city! May she triumph over her enemies! May she increase! May the city of the Ephesians increase![124]

If we grant that Luke leads us toward some such scenario in Acts 19:34, then we perceive more lucidly the efficacy and multiple directions in which the megatheistic acclamation would have run—in praise of Artemis, of Rome, of magistrates and honorands at various levels, in support of the glory of Roman Ephesus, and, importantly, against those groups who broke with this consensus, whether Jews or Jesus-acclaimers.

Finally, in 19:35–39 we hear the speech of the *grammateus* in response to the crowd. It is important to note that he addressed neither Artemis

---

122. See Mikael Tellbe, *Christ-Believers in Ephesus: A Textual Analysis of Early Christian Identity Formation in a Local Perspective*, WUNT 242 (Tübingen: Mohr Siebeck, 2009), 57–75.

123. Or, indeed, enemies within the city, e.g., ὅλη ἡ πόλις τοῦτο λέγι· τοὺς ἐχθρούς | σου τῷ ποταμῷ. | ὁ μέγας θεὸς τοῦτο παράσχῃ ("This entire city says, 'Your enemies to the river! May this great god grant this!'"). Inscription from Charlotte Roueché, *Aphrodisias in Late Antiquity: The Late Roman and Byzantine Inscriptions Including Texts from the Excavations at Aphrodisias Conducted by Kenan T. Erim*, JRSM 5 (London: Society for the Promotion of Roman Studies, 1989), no. 83.xi.

124. This is a fictional composite based on known acclamatory scripts. See Roueché, "Acclamations," 189: "Those to be acclaimed are honoured in descending order of importance." Cf. acclamations for Dioskoros above (P.Oxy. 1.41) and the comments of Peterson (*Heis Theos*, 590).

nor Demetrius and his fellows first, but rather the *city* and its relation to the goddess and her temple (*tēn Ephesiōn polin neōkoron* [19:35]).[125] In many respects, he responded to the triple threat outlined by Demetrius, but in nearly reverse order. Ultimately, he urged calm on five grounds: (1) the universal acclaim received by Artemis (19:35–36); (2) the ritual blamelessness of "these men" (19:37); (3) the open courts where economic charges might be lawfully brought (19:38), (4) the regular civic assembly as the proper setting for further complaints (19:39); and (5) the danger of *stasis* and concomitant Roman displeasure (19:40). If not before, certainly here we witness the political-theological strands of Artemis, Ephesus, and Rome woven tightly together. Yet the clerk's response is to some degree ambiguous within Luke's narrative. Are Paul and his Jesus a threat or not to Ephesus? to Rome? The clerk seems to think not. Yet if 19:17 and 19:20, with the magnification of the name of Jesus and the spectacular increase of the word of the Lord, serve as linchpins of the textual unit, then the reader is given to know differently.

6. Each City's Own Proper Gods

In his recapitulation of the Artemis incident of Acts 19, Chrysostom remarks

> For each city had its own proper gods [κατὰ πόλιν γὰρ αὐτοῖς ἦσαν θεοί]. They thought to make their voice a barrier against the divine Spirit. Children indeed, these Greeks! And their feeling was as if by their voice they could recover her reverential awe, and undo what had taken place…. See, a disorderly multitude! (*Hom. Act.* 42.3 [PG 60.299])

What Chrysostom hints at but does not press is the nascent clash of political theologies in Roman Ephesus in Luke's narrative. Whether we prefer the megatheism of Chaniotis or the "competitive cartels of memes" proposed by Rogers,[126] a focus on the religious and political context, scripts, and efficacies of the acclamations in Acts 19:28, 34 highlights this clash as one of Luke's primary communicative purposes in composing the

---

125. Cf. John Chrysostom, *Hom. Act.* 45.4 (PG 60.320); Shauf, *Theology as History*, 248, 262.

126. Rogers proposes a sociobiological paradigm for understanding the culturally situated behaviors in the conflicts among Judaism, Christianity, and Artemis worship in Roman Ephesus (*Mysteries of Artemis of Ephesos*, 287–88).

chapter. It was a conflict irrupting around the proclamation of the name of the Lord Jesus in first-century Ephesus. But it would take several centuries, during which time the competition continued, until at last the glory of Artemis was truly overthrown.[127] Even so, well before a Christian called Demeas tore down an image of Artemis in 354 CE, raising in its place a cross (IEph 4.1351), the megatheistic triumph of the Christ was imaginatively narrated. Although it was in the Acts of John, and not in connection with Paul, its language resonates with the acclamatory political theologies of Acts 19:

> And while John was saying this, of a sudden the altar of Artemis split into many pieces, and all the offerings laid up in the temple suddenly fell to the floor and its glory was shattered.... Then the assembled Ephesians cried out, "There is but one God, the God of John! There is but one God who has mercy upon us, for you alone are God!"... But John stretched out his hands and with uplifted heart said to the Lord, "Glory to you, my Jesus, the only God of truth, for you gain your servants by elaborate means." And having said this he said to the people, "Rise up from the ground, men of Ephesus, and pray to my God, and acknowledge his invisible power that is openly seen, and the wonderful works that were done before your eyes. Artemis should have helped herself.[128] (Acts of John 42–43)

In the estimation of Rogers, Artemis was eventually unable to help herself because she and her mysteries, although acclaimed well into the third century, engendered no *ekklēsia*, no *politeia* such as that "propagated by the Apostle Paul."[129] The site marked by Luke in the roar of the gathered crowd in Acts 19:34 was one in which the contest he recorded already signaled the insufficiency of a merely consensual glory to sustain the goddess and her city. Rather, the reader of Acts 19 who can imaginatively hear at a distance those acclamations is counseled to consider the need for divine agency (19:11), the proclamation and presence of a truly great name (19:17), a gospel engendering visible growth (19:20), and (for the

---

127. Ibid., 251–56, 279–85.
128. See Knut Schaferdiek, "The Acts of John," in *Writings Relating to the Apostles; Apocalypses and Related Subjects*, vol. 2 of *New Testament Apocrypha*, ed. Wilhelm Schneemelcher, rev. ed. (Louisville: Westminster John Knox, 1992), 187–89. Cf. Sib. Or. 5.293–299, cited in Shauf, *Theology as History*, 240.
129. Rogers, *Mysteries of Artemis of Ephesos*, 290–91.

time being) a ruling power whose structures are at the least well ordered and permissive (19:38–40). For those directly in the wake of Paul's sojourn in the city who had experienced the extraordinary power of his God, it was enough that Ephesus acclaimed its Artemis while they clung by faith to the Lord Jesus Christ (20:21) and his kingdom that Paul proclaimed (19:8; 20:25).

Bibliography

Agamben, Giorgio. *The Kingdom and the Glory: For a Theological Genealogy of Economy and Government*. Translated by Lorenzo Chiesa with Matteo Mandarini. Meridian. Stanford: Stanford University Press, 2011.

Aldrete, Gregory S. *Gestures and Acclamations in Ancient Rome*. Baltimore: Johns Hopkins University Press, 1999.

Ando, Clifford. *Imperial Ideology and Provincial Loyalty in the Roman Empire*. Berkeley: University of California Press, 2000.

Baldwin, B. "Acclamations in the Historia Augusta." *Athenaeum* 59 (1981): 138–49.

Barrett, Charles Kingsley. *Introduction and Commentary on Acts XV–XXVII*. Vol. 2 of *A Critical and Exegetical Commentary on the Acts of the Apostles*. ICC. London: T&T Clark, 1998.

Belayche, Nicole. "*Deus deum ... summorum maximus* (Apuleius): Ritual Expressions of Distinction in the Divine World in the Imperial Period." Pages 141–66 in *One God: Pagan Monotheism in the Roman Empire*. Edited by Stephen Mitchell and Peter Van Nuffelen. Cambridge: Cambridge University Press, 2010.

Betori, Giuseppe. "La strutturazione del libro degli Atti: Un proposta." *RivB* 42 (1994): 3–34.

Bitner, Bradley J. *Paul's Political Strategy in 1 Corinthians 1–4: Constitution and Covenant*. SNTSMS 163. Cambridge: Cambridge University Press, 2015.

Brinks, C. L. "'Great Is Artemis of the Ephesians': Acts 19:23–41 in Light of Goddess Worship in Ephesus." *CBQ* 71 (2009): 776–94.

Burkert, Walter. *Ancient Mystery Cults*. Cambridge: Harvard University Press, 1987.

Chaniotis, Angelos. "Acclamations as a Form of Religious Communication." Pages 199–218 in *Die Religion des Imperium Romanum: Koine and Konfrontationen*. Edited by Hubert Cancik and Jörg Rüpke with Franca Fabricius. Tübingen: Mohr Siebeck, 2008.

———. "Graffiti in Aphrodisias: Images—Texts—Contexts." Pages 191–207 in *Ancient Graffiti in Context*. Edited by Jennifer A. Baird and Claire Taylor. RSAH 2. New York: Routledge, 2011.

———. "Megatheism: The Search for the Almighty God and the Competition of Cults." Pages 112–40 in *One God: Pagan Monotheism in the Roman Empire*. Edited by Stephen Mitchell and Peter Van Nuffelen. Cambridge: Cambridge University Press, 2010.

———. "Ritual Performances of Divine Justice." Pages 115–53 in *From Hellenism to Islam: Cultural and Linguistic Change in the Roman Near East*. Edited by Hannah Cotton, Robert G. Hoyland, Jonathan J. Price, and David J. Wasserstein. Cambridge: Cambridge University Press, 2009.

———. "Under the Watchful Eyes of the Gods: Divine Justice in Hellenistic and Roman Asia Minor." Pages 1–43 in *The Greco-Roman East: Politics, Culture, Society*. Edited by Stephen Colvin. YCS 31. Cambridge: Cambridge University Press, 2004.

Cohoon, J. W., and H. Lamar Crosby, trans. *Dio Chrysostom: Discourses 31–36*. LCL 358. Cambridge: Harvard University Press, 1940.

Coleman, Kathleen. "Public Entertainments." Pages 345–50 in *The Oxford Handbook of Social Relations in the Roman World*. Edited by Michael Peachin. Oxford: Oxford University Press, 2011.

Colin, Jean. *Les villes libres dans l'Orient gréco-romain et l'envoi au supplice par acclamations populaires*. CL 82. Brussels: Latomus, 1965.

Debord, Guy. *The Society of the Spectacle*. Translated by D. Nicholson-Smith. New York: Zone, 1994.

De Ruggiero, Ettore. "Acclamatio." *DEAR*, cols. 72–76.

Duffy, Maureen E. "The Riot of the Silversmiths at Ephesus (Acts 19:23–40): A Synchronic Study Using Rhetorical and Semiotic Methods of Analysis." PhD diss., University of St. Paul, Ottawa, 1994.

Ebner, Martin. *Die Stadt als Lebensraum der ersten Christen*. Göttingen: Vandenhoeck & Ruprecht, 2012.

Fischer-Hansen, Tobias, and Birte Poulsen, eds. *From Artemis to Diana: The Goddess of Man and Beast*. Copenhagen: University of Copenhagen, 2009.

Haenchen, Ernst. *The Acts of the Apostles: A Commentary*. Oxford: Blackwell, 1971.

Hanson, J. Arthur, ed. and trans. *Apuleus: Metamorphoses Books 7–11*. LCL 453. Cambridge: Harvard University Press, 1989.
Harland, Philip A. *North Coast of the Black Sea, Asia Minor*. Vol. 2 of *Greco-Roman Associations: Texts, Translations, and Commentary*. BZNW 204. Berlin: de Gruyter, 2014.
Harrison, James R. "Artemis Triumphs over a Sorcerer's Evil Art." *NewDocs* 10:37–47.
———. "Family Honour of a Priestess of Artemis." *NewDocs* 10:30–36.
———. "A 'Worthy' *neopoios* Thanks Artemis." *NewDocs* 10:48–54.
Hezser, Catherine. *Jewish Literacy in Roman Palestine*. TSAJ 81. Tübingen: Mohr Siebeck, 2001.
Horsley, Greg H. R. "Expiation and the Cult of Men." *NewDocs* 3:20–31.
———. "Giving Thanks to Artemis." *NewDocs* 4:127–29.
———. "The Great Power of God." *NewDocs* 3:31–32.
———. "The Silversmiths at Ephesos." *New Docs* 4:7–10.
Keegan, Peter. *Graffiti in Antiquity*. London: Routledge, 2014.
Keener, Craig S. *15:1–23:35*. Vol. 3 of *Acts: An Exegetical Commentary*. Grand Rapids: Baker Academic, 2014.
Klauser, Theodore. "Akklamation." *RAC*, cols. 216–33.
Kodell, Jerome. "'The Word of God Grew': The Ecclesial Tendency of Λόγος in Acts 1,7; 12,24; 19,20." *Bib* 55 (1974): 505–19.
Kruse, Thomas. "The Magistrate and the Ocean: Acclamations and Ritualised Communication in Town Gatherings in Roman Egypt." Pages 297–315 in *Ritual and Communication in the Graeco-Roman World*. Edited by E. Stavrianopoulou. KernosSup 16. Liège: Centre international d'étude de la religion grecque antique, 2006.
Lampe, Peter. "Acta 19 im Spiegel der ephesischen Inschriften." *BZ* 36 (1992): 59–76.
Loisy, Alfred. *Les Acts des Apôtres*. Paris: Nourry, 1920.
Lüdemann, Gerd. *Early Christianity according to the Traditions in Acts: A Commentary*. Translated by John Bowden. London: SCM, 1989.
Malay, Hasan. "A Praise on Men Artemidorou Axiottenos." *Epigraphica Anatolica* 36 (2003): 13–18.
Molthagen, Joachim. "Die ersten Konflikte der Christen in der griechisch-römischen Welt." *Historia* 40 (1991): 42–76.
Oster, Richard E. "The Ephesian Artemis as an Opponent of Early Christianity." *JAC* 19 (1976): 27–44.
———. "Holy Days in Honour of Artemis." *NewDocs* 4:74–82.

Pervo, Richard I. *Acts: A Commentary*. Hermeneia. Minneapolis: Fortress, 2009.

Peterson, Erik. *Heis Theos: Epigraphische, formgeschichtliche und religionsgeschichtliche Untersuchungen zur antiken "Ein-Gott"-Akklamation; Nachdruck der Ausgabe von Erik Peterson 1926 mit Ergänzungen und Kommentaren von Christoph Markschies, Henrik Hildebrandt, Barbara Nichtsweiss*. Ausgewählte Schriften 8. Würzberg: Echter, 2012.

Rius-Camps, Josep, and Jenny Read-Heimerdinger. *A Comparison with the Alexandrian Tradition, Acts 18.24–28.31: Rome via Ephesus and Jerusalem*. Vol. 4 of *The Message of Acts in Codex Bezae*. London: T&T Clark, 2009.

Robert, Louis. "Une épigramme satirique d'Automédon et Athènes au début de l'Empire (Anth. Pal. XI–319)." *REG* 94 (1981): 360–61.

Rogers, Guy MacLean. "The Assembly of Imperial Ephesos." *ZPE* 94 (1992): 224–28.

———. *The Mysteries of Artemis of Ephesos: Cult, Polis, and Change in the Graeco-Roman World*. Synkrisis. New Haven: Yale University Press, 2012.

———. *The Sacred Identity of Ephesos: Foundation Myths of a Roman City*. London: Routledge, 1991.

Roueché, Charlotte. "Acclamations in the Later Roman Empire: New Evidence from Aphrodisias." *JRS* 74 (1984): 181–99.

———. *Aphrodisias in Late Antiquity: The Late Roman and Byzantine Inscriptions Including Texts from the Excavations at Aphrodisias Conducted by Kenan T. Erim*. JRSM 5 London: Society for the Promotion of Roman Studies, 1989.

———. "Floreat Perge." Pages 206–28 in *Images of Authority: Papers Presented to Joyce Reynolds on the Occasion of Her 70th Birthday*. Edited by Mary Margaret Mackenzie and Charlotte Roueché. Cambridge: Cambridge Philological Society, 1989.

Rowe, C. Kavin. *World Upside Down: Reading Acts in the Graeco-Roman Age*. Oxford: Oxford University Press, 2009.

Rowe, Gregory. *Princes and Political Cultures: The New Tiberian Senatorial Decrees*. Ann Arbor: University of Michigan Press, 2002.

Rüpke, Jörg. *The Religion of the Romans*. Translated by Richard Gordon. Cambridge: Polity, 2007.

Schaferdiek, Knut. "The Acts of John." Pages 152–71 in *Writings Relating to the Apostles; Apocalypses and Related Subjects*. Vol. 2 of *New Testament*

Apocrypha. Edited by Wilhelm Schneemelcher. Rev. ed. Louisville: Westminster John Knox, 1992.

Schmidt, J. "Acclamatio." *PW*, cols. 147–50.

Schwindt, Rainer. *Das Weltbild des Epheserbriefes: Eine religionsgeschichtlich-exegestiche Studie*. WUNT 148. Tübingen: Mohr Siebeck, 2002.

Selinger, Reinhard. "Die Demetriosunruhen (Apg. 19,23–40): Eine Fallstudie aus rechtshistorischer Perspektive." *ZNW* 88 (1997): 242–59.

Shauf, Scott. *Theology as History, History as Theology: Paul in Ephesus in Acts 19*. BZNW 133. Berlin: de Gruyter, 2005.

Spier, Jeffrey. *Late Antique and Early Christian Gems*. SFCB.SP 20. Wiesbaden: Reichert, 2007.

Stoops, Robert F. "Riot and Assembly: The Social Context of Acts 19.23–41." *JBL* 108 (1989): 73–91.

Strelan, Rick. *Paul, Artemis, and the Jews in Ephesus*. BZNW 80. Berlin: de Gruyter, 1996.

Talbert, Charles H. *Reading Acts: A Literary and Theological Commentary on the Acts of the Apostles*. Reading the New Testament. New York: Crossroad, 1997.

Tellbe, Mikael. *Christ-believers in Ephesus: A Textual Analysis of Early Christian Identity Formation in a Local Perspective*. WUNT 242. Tübingen: Mohr Siebeck, 2009.

Theissen, Gerd. *The Miracle Stories of the Early Christian Tradition*. Edited by John Kenneth Riches. Translated by Francis McDonagh. SNTW. Edinburgh: T&T Clark, 1983.

Thomas, Christine M. "At Home in the City of Artemis: Religion in Ephesos in the Literary Imagination of the Roman Period." Pages in 81–117 in *Ephesos, Metropolis of Asia: An Interdisciplinary Approach to Its Archaeology, Religion, and Culture*. Edited by Helmut Koester. HTS 41. Valley Forge, PA: Trinity Press International, 1995.

Trebilco, Paul. "Asia." Pages 316–57 in *Graeco-Roman Setting*. Vol. 2 of *The Book of Acts in Its First Century Setting*. Edited by David W. J. Gill and Conrad Gempf. Grand Rapids: Eerdmans, 1994.

Tripp, Jeffrey M. "A Tale of Two Riots: The Synkrisis of the Temples of Ephesus and Jerusalem in Acts 19–23." *JSNT* 37 (2014): 86–111.

Wiemer, Hans-Ulrich. "Akklamationen im spätromischen Reich: Zur Typologie und Funktion eines Kommunikationsrituals." *AK* 86 (2004): 55–73.

Witetschek, Stephan. "Artemis and Asiarchs: Some Remarks on Ephesian Local Colour in Acts 19." *Bib* 90 (2009): 334–55.

Witherington, Ben, III. *The Acts of the Apostles: A Socio-rhetorical Commentary*. Grand Rapids: Eerdmans, 1998.
Ziesler, John A. "The Name of Jesus in the Acts of the Apostles." *JSNT* 4 (1979): 28–41.

The Gladiator Graveyard of Ephesus as Evidence for the Study of Martyrdom

Mikael Haxby

In 1993, excavators near the site of the Hellenistic city Ephesus in present-day Turkey were looking for a key branching point in the city's ancient Via Sacra, a wide road leading from the city to the Temple of Artemis a mile or so away. Their calculations as to the location of the intersection were slightly off, due to an unexpected turn in the road, and instead they uncovered a section of the Via Sacra flanked on both sides by an ancient necropolis.[1] Within this necropolis, they found a gladiator graveyard.[2]

---

1. Dieter Knibbe and Wolfgang Pietsch, "Via Sacra—Damianosstoa," *JÖAI* 63 (1994): 17–18. Excavators were searching for the Stoa of Damianus, a massive arched covering for the Via Sacra, and they were specifically looking to discover how the stoa was constructed at a key branching point in the Via Sacra. The Stoa of Damianus was constructed in the early third century under the auspices of T. Flavius Damianus, the city's leading benefactor and intellectual at the time. Knibbe, "Via Sacra Ephesiaca: New Aspects of the Cult of Artemis Ephesia," in *Ephesos, Metropolis of Asia: An Interdisciplinary Approach to Its Archaeology, Religion, and Culture*, ed. Helmut Koester, HTS 41 (Valley Forge, PA: Trinity International, 1995), 148–50.

2. Beside the road stood the buildings of the necropolis, several small grave houses and many grave walls, freestanding single blocks of crude brick and cement erected at various angles. Both of the grave houses were built along the Stoa of Damianus after it had been constructed, as evidenced by the connections between the foundations of the houses and the Stoa and by their locations specifically between the columns of the Stoa. This would suggest a dating during the third century CE, and small finds within grave house 7 confirmed a dating to the latter half of the third century. On the grave walls were found small inset niches for reliefs, some still intact. Within the vicinity, excavators found four reliefs in reasonable states of preservation, three of which depict gladiators. Wolfgang Pietsch and Elisabeth Trinkl, "Der Grabungsbericht der Kampagnen 1992/93," in *Grabungen und Forschungen 1992 und 1993*, vol. 2 of *Via Sacra Ephesiaca*, ed. Dieter Knibbe and Hilke Thür, BerMatÖAI 6 (Vienna: Schindler,

Over several years, not only was the necropolis excavated, but the bones of the men and women buried were carefully examined using a variety of techniques. In this paper, I offer a new interpretation of the stories these bones can tell about the lives of gladiators. The physical analysis of the gladiators' bones has provided evidence of a kind of gladiatorial care of the self, an extensive series of practices by which gladiators would prepare to perform and fight. Recent scholarly discussions of ancient Jewish and Christian martyrdom suggest that similar practices of preparation may have been part of the training of potential martyrs. I argue that better understanding of the lives of gladiators can offer possible insight and revision of our understanding of ancient martyrdom as well.

Before turning to the martyrs, I need to explain how this gladiator graveyard was identified. The key evidence was reliefs discovered at the site. The reliefs found at this site have been numbered 1–4 in the figures on the page opposite, and I will focus on reliefs 1, 3, and 4, as they each depict a gladiator (top row of images and bottom left image).[3] Both reliefs 1 and 3 depict a front-facing figure minimally clothed, armor sitting off to the side, a weapon in hand. This form, quite common on grave reliefs of gladiators from the Greek world, was named by Louis Robert "le gladiateur dans sa glorie."[4]

The reliefs allow us to identify not only that these men were gladiators, but also that they were a particular class of gladiator. Generally, gladiators did not simply fight with whatever weapons might be at hand, but instead they learned a particular style of combat paired with particular weapons and iconography. Often, gladiatorial bouts paired two different types. The

---

1995), 35–39. Pietsch suggests elsewhere that the entire Via Sacra, or at least its two key sections near Ephesus, the Anodos and the Kathodos, may have functioned as the city's primary necropolis. Pietsch, "Ausserstädtische Grabanlagen von Ephesos," in *100 Jahre österreichische Forschungen in Ephesos: Akten des Symposions Wien 1995*, ed. Herwig Friesinger and Fritz Krinzinger (Vienna: ÖAW, 1999), 1:455.

3. Three of these reliefs (1, 2, and 4) were found in situ, in niches cut into their respective grave stones. The other (3) was found among the debris in the area, and comparison to the other three reliefs suggests it once sat in a niche of its own. Each is made of course, white crystalline marble, about 40 cm high, 20–30 cm wide, and 6–9 cm deep. The lettering is about 2 cm high, with forms that date to the late second or early third century. Pietsch and Trinkl, "Der Grabungsbericht der Kampagnen 1992/93," 42–45.

4. Louis Robert, *Les Gladiateurs dans l'Orient grec*, BEHEH 278 (Paris: Champion, 1940), 47–50.

Grave Relief 1 (Palumbus)

Grave Relief 3 (Valerius)

Grave Relief 2 (Serapias)

Grave Relief 4 (Euxeninus)

Dieter Knibbe and Hilke Thür, eds., *Via Sacra Ephesica II: Grabungen und Forschungen 1992 und 1993*, Berichte und Materialen herausgegeben vom Österreichischen Archäologischen Institut 6 (Vienna: Schindler, 1995), figs. 25–27, 29.

crested helmets found in reliefs 1 and 3 are typical of two types, the *murmillo* and the *thraex*. The *thraex* had a square shield, while the *murmillo* carried a taller shield of proportions quite similar to those depicted in the relief. Further, the short sword held by the figure in relief 3 corresponds to the *gladius* wielded by a *murmillo*. These were *murmillos*.[5]

One common opponent of the *murmillo*, based on evidence from inscriptions of fight advertisements and visual depictions of fights, was a peculiar fighter called the *retiarius*. The name *murmillo* derives from a Greek word for "fish," and the *retiarius* or "net man" carried the implements of a fisherman, a large net and a trident, while wearing little armor besides some pads over the neck and arm.[6] The male figure sketched on relief 4 stands facing forward with a cloth wrapped around his waist, thick padding covering his entire left arm, and a long trident grasped in both hands. His left hand somewhat awkwardly holds a dagger, as well. This figure is identifiable then as a *retiarius*, and the depiction, more of an outline than a relief, may be a version of the "gladiator in his glory" pose.[7]

---

5. Markus Junkelmann, "Familia Gladiatoria: The Heroes of the Amphitheatre," in *Gladiators and Caesars: The Power of Spectacle in Ancient Rome*, ed. Ralph Jackson, trans. Anthea Bell (Berkeley: University of California Press, 2000), 49–56.

6. Junkelmann, "Familia Gladiatoria," 59–61.

7. The content of the inscriptions further confirms the identification of the figures as gladiators, based on the names recorded. The inscription names the figure in relief 1 as Paloumbos. This name has been identified as a Greek transliteration of the Latin *palumbes*, meaning "pigeon," a popular stage name for gladiators beginning in the first century, when a gladiator by that name found a fan in the emperor Claudius. The dedicators of relief 4, Peritina and Margarites, were likely gladiatorial colleagues of Euxeinos who identified themselves by their stage names. Margarites, a transliteration from Latin meaning "pearl," is evidenced in other inscriptions as a gladiatorial stage name, and Pietsch and Trinkl theorize that Peritina would be a fitting appellation for a *retiarius*, whose most effective attack would be to hurl a net "around someone," that is, περί τινά. Wolfgang Pietsch, "Der Gladiatorenfriedhof von Ephesos, der archäologische Befund," in *Gladiatoren in Ephesos: Tod und Nachmittag; Eine Ausstellung im Ephesos Museum Seluk, seit 20. April 2002*, ed. Karl Grossschmidt and Fabian Kanz (Vienna: ÖAI, 2002), 16. The full inscriptions run as follows, with my translations: Relief 1: ΥΜΝΙΣ ΠΑΛΟΥΜΒΩ | ΙΔΙΩ ΑΝΔΡΙ ΜΝΕΙΑΣ | ΧΑΡΙΝ—"Hymnis (erected this monument) for Paloumbos, her own husband, in memory"; Relief 3: ΤΥΧΗ ΒΑΛΕΡΙΩ | ΑΝΔΡΙ ΓΛΥΚΤΑΤΩ—"Tyche (erected this monument) for Valerios, her dearest husband"; Relief 4: ΠΕΡΙΤΙΝΑ | ΚΑΙ ΜΑΡΓ | ΑΡΙΤΗΣ | ΕΥΞΕΙΝΩ | ΜΝΕΙΑΣ ΧΑ | ΡΙΝ—"Peritina and Margarites (erected this monument) for Euxeinos, in memory." See also fig. 3. Pietsch and Trinkl, "Der Grabungsbericht der Kampagnen 1992/93," 42–45.

These reliefs, then, confirm variously the hypothesis that the area of the grave stones was a burial place for gladiators.[8]

If the gravestones mark a space where gladiators were buried, that means that this find included a cache of gladiator bones. The analysis of the bones first provided further confirmation of the gladiator graveyard hypothesis and second offered some new and striking evidence about the practices of ancient gladiators. For this analysis, the scholars also undertook similar analyses of five other sets of bones from the necropolis as a control group. The first finding was that the vast majority of the bodies were male, between 75 percent and 95 percent depending on the methods used for counting.[9] As the research of Karl Grossschmidt and Fabian

---

8. The other relief, number 2, is a special case. It was discovered in situ but only partially preserved on block 10, with the remaining half of the relief depicting a woman's chiton-clad lower body. The relief is cut into a block of white, medium-grain marble, and its remaining half measures 23 cm x 24 cm x 5.5 cm. The lettering, also datable to the third century, is 1–1.3 cm high and is marked by the use of semilunar sigmas and epsilons. It reads ΑΧΑΙ ΣΕΡΑΠΙΑΔΙ | ΘΥΓΑΤΡΙ ΜΝΕΙΑΣ | ΧΑΡΙΝ—"Achai (erected this monument) for Serapias, her daughter, in memory." Pietsch and Trinkl suggest that the woman was a slave, based on the lack of a mantle in the depiction and the inscription coming from her mother ("Der Grabungsbericht der Kampagnen 1992/93"). Given the slave status of many gladiators, they theorize she may have been a social relation in some way. I want to note the possibility that Serapias was herself a gladiator. As the other reliefs depict gladiators, and the evidence of bones (see below) further confirms that the men buried here were gladiators, it seems the starting hypothesis should be that Serapias was a gladiator as well, given the clear evidence that women did fight and train as gladiators. While the relief does not depict her in clothes designed for the arena, it is not necessary on the grave reliefs of male gladiators that they appear as such, either ("Der Grabungsbericht der Kampagnen 1992/93," 44). On female gladiators, see Kathleen Coleman, "Missio at Halicarnassus," *HSCP* 100 (2000): 487–500. For other depictions of gladiators, see Robert, *Les Gladiateurs dans l'Orient grec*, plate 23.

9. Due to the constant stream of new construction in the area in the first centuries CE, from the competing grave stones to the grave houses and the Stoa of Damianus itself, the bones had been disturbed several times over. Techniques most commonly applied in the analysis of mass graves were necessary to sort out the disarray, as Suzanne Fabrizii-Reuer estimated the number of bodies buried through Minimum Number of Individuals (MNI) analysis, a process of collecting and counting discrete finds of certain bones most likely to be preserved intact. The identifiable partial skeletons so collected showed peculiar demographic traits. Depending on how broadly or narrowly one draws the boundaries of the gladiatorial cemetery, it contained at least either 124 or 68 bodies. Fabrizii-Reuer used a broad definition and found that, of these

Kanz indicates, this is an anomalous finding, unlikely to have occurred by chance.[10]

Grossschmidt and Kanz have demonstrated via more graphic evidence that these bones once belonged to gladiators—evidence that came from ante- and postmortem trauma to the bones—that is, trauma that occurred either well before death or around the time of death.[11] Ten of the sixty-eight people buried in this graveyard can be identified as having died from head trauma, strongly supporting the hypothesis that the site was a graveyard for gladiators. Most suggestively, one of the skulls suffered two symmetrical, round perimortem wounds 50 centimeters apart, of a size and shape that matches nearly perfectly the tines of a fisherman's trident found near the harbor in Ephesus, dated likewise to the turn of the third century CE. Grossschmidt and Kanz argue that they have found a man killed by a *retiarius*.[12]

The forensic analysis of the bones, which had revealed the high incidence of fatal cranial trauma, also revealed a peculiar arrangement of perimortem wounds. Not a single person who had died of cranial trauma had suffered other perimortem trauma. By contrast, similar analyses of medieval battlefields found extensive perimortem trauma on bodies of those killed in the midst of battle.[13] Gladiators, then, died of traumatic injuries at a rate far higher than the normal population, but they did not die of the accumulation of many injuries in a short period of time in the manner of soldiers. Gladiator bouts must have been quite different from actual war to produce such a result.

---

124 bodies, 75 percent were men, 17 percent were women, and only 8 percent were children ("Gräber im Bereich der Via Sacra Ephesiaca [Kurzfassung]," in Friesinger and Krinzinger, *100 Jahre österreichische Forschungen*, 1:461–62). Later analysis by Grossschmidt and Kanz (Karl Grossschmidt and Fabian Kanz, "Stand der anthropologischen Forschungen zum Gradiatorenfriedhof in Ephesos," *JÖAI* 74 [2005]: 103–23) used a narrower definition of the gladiatorial cemetery, which gave them 68 bodies to analyze, 67 of them male. Numbers like this almost certainly could not occur by chance.

10. Grossschmidt and Kanz, "Stand der anthropologischen Forschungen," 118–21.

11. Ante- and perimortem trauma can be distinguished by the relative smoothness or roughness of the bone in the area of the fracture. A smoother break suggests that the body had time to heal, slowly regrowing bone at the point of injury, while a jagged break suggests that this wound killed. Karl Grossschmidt and Fabian Kanz, "Head Injuries of Roman Gladiators," *FSI* 160 (2006): 210–11.

12. Ibid., 211–14.

13. Ibid., 213–15.

Indeed, recent scholarship has confirmed that death in the arena, among gladiators, was limited. Georges Ville analyzed inscriptional evidence of the careers of gladiators from late republican Rome, and he found that a gladiator stood an approximately one in ten chance of death in a single bout.[14] To fight in the arena was exceptionally dangerous, no doubt, but most matches ended without a kill. One common structure for combat was called *ad digitum*, in which the bout would end when one fighter lifted a finger in surrender. The *editor* of the games held authority in most cases to grant *missio*, declaring the bout a draw and honoring both fighters. There are rare cases of games being given *sine missione*, in which the *editor* cannot end the fight alone. Such games were banned by Augustus, though they are occasionally attested still afterward, but it should be noted that the restriction merely meant that the editor could not end a fight. Surrender *ad digitum* would still be a possible outcome.[15] Thus, the majority of gladiatorial games offered multiple possible conclusions that did not require anyone to die. *Editores*, it should be noted, often had a financial interest in seeing both fighters survive. Gladiators were often either enslaved persons who were the property of the *editor* or leased to the *editor* on the condition that the full price of the gladiator would be paid in the event of death.[16]

This incidence of death is supported by various inscriptional records that make special note, for example, of fights being staged "to the death" (περὶ τῆς ψυχῆς) or with the use of "sharp weapons" (τοῖς ὀξέσι σιδήροις).[17]

---

14. Georges Ville, *Le Gladiature en Occident des Origenes à la Mort de Domitien*, BEFAR 245 (Rome: École française de Rome, 1981), 318–23. Many gladiator gravestones, especially in the Latin West, follow a structure quite different from those found in Ephesus. They list a gladiator's statistical record: fights, victories, draws, and defeats. From this data, Ville was able to extrapolate the expected outcomes of gladiatorial bouts.

15. Michael J. Carter, "Gladiatorial Combat: The Rules of Engagement," *CJ* 102 (2006): 102–3. Coleman, "Missio at Halicarnassus," 488–91.

16. Carter, "Gladiatorial Combat: The Rules of Engagement," 101.

17. Ibid., 100–1; Carter, "Gladiatorial Combat with 'Sharp' Weapons (τοῖς ὀξέσι σιδήροις)," *ZPE* 155 (2006): 161–75; Kathleen M. Coleman, *Bonds of Danger: Communal Life in the Gladiatorial Barracks of Ancient Rome; The Fifteenth Todd Memorial Lecture Delivered in the University of Sydney 15 August 2002* (Sydney: Department of Classics and Ancient History University of Sydney, 2005), 3–4. For inscriptions, see, respectively, J. P. Touratsoglou, "Δύο νέαι ἐπιγραφικαὶ μαρτυρίαι περὶ τοῦ Κοινοῦ τῶν Μακεδόνων κατὰ τὸν τρίτον μεταχριστιανικὸν αἰώνα" ["Two New Epigraphic Testimonies on Common Rules in Macedonia during the Third Century CE"], in *Ancient Macedonia: Papers Read at the First International Symposium Held in Thessaloniki*

The advertisement of violence suggests its relative rarity. One does not advertise that which is common and expected. The "to the death" inscription makes this insight plain by proclaiming also the special imperial indulgence by which they were allowed to stage such an extreme spectacle. We expect to see, then, a high but well-below-universal rate of death by trauma among gladiators. But what should be made of the lack of other perimortem injuries?

In their analysis of the bone data, Grossschmidt and Kanz emphasize two factors. The first is the possibility that gladiators carried extra weight, a fat layer protecting the bones. I will address this possibility later. Second, they note the strikingly "rule-bound" nature of gladiatorial spectacle.[18] Scholarship on gladiatorial combat demonstrates that these fights had strict rules and structures for action. Two referees oversaw a typical bout. Each carried a long switch and was empowered to call fouls and enforce proper technique. Chalk lines would be drawn in the dirt, and gladiators had to respect these boundaries.[19] Relatedly, Thomas Wiedemann has demonstrated that gladiatorial instructors offered training not in effective combat in general but in the techniques proper to a single class of gladiators, such as *secutores* or *retiarii*.[20] The training and practice of gladiatorial combat was aimed less toward killing by whatever means available than toward a controlled and structured performance of technique proper to a particular appearance and training. More confirmation comes from the evidence of organizations of gladiator fans, who named their groups in accordance with their appreciation of particular kinds of gladiators.[21] Thus, evidence suggests that the appreciation of gladiatorial

---

August 26–29 1968, ed. Basil Laourdas and Ch. J. Makaronas, HMCH 122 (Thessaloniki: Salonica Institute for Balkan Studies, 1970), 280–90; Georg Petzl, *Die Inschriften von Smyrna*, 2 vols. (Bonn: Rheinisch-Westfälische Akademie der Wissenschaften, 1982–1990), 2:66 n. 637. These inscriptions come from Beroea in Macedonia and Smyrna, respectively.

18. Grossschmidt and Kanz, "Head Injuries," 216.

19. Carter, "Gladiatorial Combat: The Rules of Engagement," 102–4; Junkelmann, "Familia Gladiatoria," 67–68.

20. Thomas Wiedemann, *Emperors and Gladiators* (London: Routledge, 1992), 117. See also Michael J. Carter, "A Doctor Secutorum and the Retiarius Draukos from Corinth," *ZPE* 126 (1999): 264–65.

21. David M. Potter, Review of *Emperors and Gladiators*, by Thomas Wiedemann, *JRS* 84 (1994): 231.

combat mirrored its training and practice. Proper technique and skillful actions within structured limits were the goal.

This evidence suggests that a focus on the strict "rules" of combat will lead us to mistake the nature of these bouts. Fighters did not, it seems, typically attempt to land fatal blows except in particular and particularly advantageous moments. Otherwise we would expect to see multiple perimortem traumas attested. The bulk of the match, then, would be a performance of skill, control, and technique. The fans of gladiators appreciated the performance of skill in certain defined and structured roles, and gladiatorial training likewise emphasized the proper performance of a *murmuillo*'s fighting style or that of a *retiarius*. When these men died, they often displayed not their record of victories, but the iconography of the role they played.

Carlin Barton has noted how both literary and material sources betray a fascination with the "moment of truth," when one gladiator stands at the mercy of the other, at the mercy of the *editor*, and at the mercy of the crowd.[22] This suggests perhaps that such a moment of truth would be the proper moment for a killing blow ought to be struck, and the gladiators typically fought with the knowledge that one ought to reach a crowd-pleasing moment of truth before launching any final attack.

I suggest that Pierre Bourdieu's notion of practical reason is useful here.[23] Actions within a particular cultural system, for Bourdieu, can be deeply structured and predictable without being determined or necessarily rule bound. Skillful performance within such structures requires creativity and improvisation even though the ultimate outcome will consistently resemble previous outcomes. The "script" of the gladiatorial bout does not determine its outcome, but a knowledgeable observer would recognize the beats being played. Gladiators may be imagined less as purely desperate combatants on the edge of death, though on its edge they were, and more as highly trained fighters possessed of an embodied practical reason that enabled them to perform for the crowd and menace their opponents with the same actions, producing a pleasing spectacle organized along predictable but not determined lines.

---

22. Carlin Barton, *The Sorrows of the Ancient Romans: The Gladiator and the Monster* (Princeton: Princeton University Press, 1993), 35–46.

23. Pierre Bourdieu, *Outline of a Theory of Practice*, trans. Richard Nice (Cambridge: Cambridge University Press, 1977), 72.

The analysis of the injuries of the gladiators suggests the importance of the particular training of gladiators. Such training forms a useful framework for understanding the results of other analyses of these bones. Further forensic analysis considered several antemortem injuries, and found evidence of high-quality medical care. One femur was cut off smoothly, evidencing the skillful and successful amputation of a leg. One broken radius was healed so fully and cleanly that only by computerized tomography could technicians identify clearly where the original break had occurred. Two cranial traumas had been cared for such that the bone healed cleanly around the break.[24] Each of these individual cases suggests that gladiators received medical care of a high quality, which fits well with literary evidence from antiquity. Galen worked for several years as the physician to a team of gladiators, and he claims to have learned many new techniques and treatments from the experience (*Comp.* 203–208). The transfer of insights gained in the care of gladiators to medical care for the broader population likewise appears in Pliny's *Natural History*, where he lists a variety of cures learned from treating gladiators (26.135).[25] Given the significant economic value a trained gladiator had to his master or trainer, such quality care should not be surprising.

I take a slightly different perspective on this evidence, compared to most of the scholarship on gladiators and physicians. As Kathleen Coleman puts it, "These people were expensive instruments, and they had to be kept in working order and repaired."[26] There can be little question that trainers and masters provided care for the gladiators in their charge. However, neither in the contemporary world nor, certainly, in antiquity is medical care best understood only as a series of actions performed by one person upon another. To heal a fractured radius fully and cleanly requires not only the skillful setting of the bone and the proper application of bandages or casts, but it also requires the person whose arm was broken to diligently care for and protect that injured arm throughout

---

24. The theorized protection of the brain and its surrounding fluid is a conclusion from computer modeling of the likely shape of the break and position of the brain. Karl Grossschmidt and Fabian Kanz, "Stand der anthropologischen Forschungen zum Gradiatorenfriedhof in Ephesos," *JÖAI* 74 (2005): 118–21.

25. Wiedemann, *Emperors and Gladiators*, 116–18.

26. Kathleen M. Coleman, "Valuing Others in the Gladiatorial Barracks," in *Valuing Others in Classical Antiquity*, ed. Ineke Sluiter and Ralph Rosen, MnemSup 323 (Leiden: Brill, 2010), 430.

the healing process. Surviving major surgery such as a leg amputation would likewise require careful maintenance of the wound, which could not be the responsibility of a physician alone. In the evidence of the positive health outcomes for wounded gladiators, there is thus evidence of work performed by a gladiator upon himself as well as the care provided to gladiators from their superiors.

Gladiatorial practices can also be glimpsed through the chemical analysis of the bones from the Ephesian cemetery. Grossschmidt and Kanz, together with Sandra Lösch, Negahnaz Moghaddam, and Daniele U. Risser, analyzed a variety of trace elements in the bones of gladiators that may mark differences in diet.[27] They compared the preponderance of trace elements in the bones of gladiators to rates of occurrence in the bones of non-gladiators taken from nearby graveyards. While most of these trace element analyses found no clear evidence of differences in diet between the gladiators and other people from Ephesus, there was one highly significant finding. Gladiators had ratios of strontium to calcium on average double that of the control groups, a highly significant difference.[28] As Lösch and her coauthors explain, the gladiators must have had a dietary source of calcium that was different in kind and quantity from the usual ways that non-gladiators in Ephesus ingested calcium.

While ancient literary evidence for gladiatorial dietary restrictions is weaker than it is for their medical care, various sources do offer some confirmation of this chemical analysis. Both Galen and Pliny the Elder call gladiators *hordearii* or "barley men," a mocking term that Pliny states arose from an earlier practice among gladiators of eating barley porridge exclusively (Galen, *Troph. dyn.* 1.19; Pliny, *Nat.* 18.72). Given the strength of the chemical evidence for a special diet among the Ephesian gladiators, this literary evidence can serve as confirmation even though it is little more than suggestive. In their paper, Lösch and her coauthors push for a

---

27. Sandra Lösch et al., "Stable Isotope and Trace Element Studies on Gladiators and Contemporary Romans from Ephesus (Turkey, Second and Third Ct. AD)—Implications for Differences in Diet," *PLoS ONE* 9.10 (2014): 1–17.

28. Lösch et al., "Stable Isotope and Trace Element Studies," 13. On the interpretation of Sr:Ca ratio, see also James H. Burton and T. Douglas Price, "The Use and Abuse of Trace Elements for Paleodietary Research," in *Biochemical Approaches to Paleodietary Analysis*, ed. Stanley H. Ambrose and M. Anne Katzenberg, AAMS 5 (New York: Kluwer Academic/Plenum, 2000), 159–171; Andrew Sillen and Maureen Kavanaugh, "Strontium and Paleodietary Research: A Review," *YPA* 25 (1982): 67–90.

strong interpretation of this evidence, suggesting that a drink of plant ash referenced by Pliny could be the missing calcium substitute. While this is certainly possible, what is most pertinent for this analysis is the physical evidence of dietary practices, however these might have been specifically articulated. As in the case of medical care, I emphasize that the eating of particular calcium-rich foods requires affirmative engagement by the gladiators themselves to look after their eating practices and choices.

Grossschmidt and Kanz argue that these dietary practices can help explain the lack of nonfatal perimortem trauma among the gladiator remains. The gladiators' diet, they suggest, could have served to allow fighters to pack on pounds and produce a protective layer of fat that prevented bone injuries during bouts.[29] I have already argued that gladiatorial training in practical reason provides a better explanation of the lack of perimortem bone injuries.

So, if the gladiatorial diet was not about weight gain, how does it connect to the other gladiatorial practices discussed so far? It is striking that the two affirmative practices we can see gladiators undertaking relate to their medical care and diet. Philosophical literature under the Roman Empire developed a deep and wide-ranging concern for the health of the body, engaging both diet and medical practice.[30] Ancient writing on medicine confirms the notion that medical care was undertaken as care of the self. For example, Plutarch asserts that philosophers ought not be reproached for undertaking to learn medicine and practice it upon themselves, but rather all should endeavor to understand medicine and philosophy as composing "a single field" of inquiry and cultivation (*Tu. san.* 122d–e). Furthermore, in Plutarch, the admonition to undertake the practice of medicine is immediately linked to practices of diet, the renunciation of certain foodstuffs in certain situations and the eating of others (*Tu. san.* 123b–d). The exhortation to work on oneself as subject and object of philosophical, medical, and dietetic care in order to attain a transformation to health, success, and the right deployment of reason appears strongly in various medical and philosophical literature of which Plutarch is paradigmatic. It makes sense, in considering the Ephesian

---

29. Andrew Curry, "The Gladiator Diet," *Arch* 61.6 (2008): 28–30.

30. Michel Foucault, *The Care of the Self*, vol. 3 of *The History of Sexuality*, trans. Robert Hurley (London: Penguin, 1990), 41–43, 54–58. See also Judith Perkins, *The Suffering Self: Pain and Narrative Representation in the Early Christian Era* (London: Routledge: 1995).

gladiators, to see a similar link between their peculiar dietary practices and their undertaking of medical care. In antiquity, in a manner not alien to contemporary medicine, dietary and medical care ran inevitably into one another as significantly overlapping discourses and practices.

The material analysis of gladiator remains from the cemetery of Ephesus thus provides evidence of a kind of gladiatorial *askēsis*. As Musonius Rufus explained in his treatise *On Training*, "upon the learning of the lessons appropriate to each and every excellence, practical training (ἄσκησιν) must follow invariably, if indeed from the lessons we have learned we hope to derive any benefit" (*Diatr.* 6).³¹ These intellectual and bodily exercises formed the basis of philosophy or of any field that aimed toward the training and transformation of people, of bodies. The gladiator's training in practical reason, designed to develop capacities for skillful performance in the arena, followed structures we also see in the elite philosophical literature of the time. The gladiator's peculiar diet and careful medical care again match the physical and bodily focus of *askēsis* in the ancient Mediterranean world.

I am drawing, then, a series of connections between our evidence of ancient gladiators and our evidence of ancient philosophical practice. This practice enabled skillful semiscripted performance in the arena. These connections that we can see through the gladiatorial data resemble in important ways a series of hypotheses put forward in recent scholarship about martyrdom. Studies of martyrdom texts emphasize the scripted nature of executions in the arena and the ways in which Christian texts aimed to dramatize a counterscript that challenged Roman

---

31. Translation from C. E. Lutz, "Musonius Rufus: 'The Roman Socrates,'" *YCS* 10 (1947): 3–150. For Pierre Hadot, *askēsis* denotes purely "inner activities of the thought and of will," to be distinguished from various practices of bodily renunciation that could accompany them (*Philosophy as a Way of Life: Spiritual Exercises from Socrates to Foucault*, trans. Michael Chase, ed. and intro. Arnold I. Davidson [Oxford: Blackwell, 1995], 128). James A. Francis shows, though, that *askēsis* could refer to a range of practices from athletic training to dietary restriction to moral discipline, all of which typically intersected with each other (*Subversive Virtue: Asceticism and Authority in the Second-Century Pagan World* [University Park, PA: Pennsylvania State University Press, 1995], xvii–xviii). In this paper, I follow Teresa Shaw in using the terms "*askēsis*" and "ascetic practice" both to refer to this array of ancient disciplines for transformation of the self in which bodily and intellectual practices cannot be fully disentangled (*The Burden of the Flesh: Fasting and Sexuality in Early Christianity* [Minneapolis: Fortress, 1998], 5–10).

authority. As Elizabeth A. Castelli puts it, "For the characters in the narratives, controlling the spectacle means acting out of turn, upsetting expectations, even stage-managing the events. For the narrators of these stories, it means providing a counternarrative so that the scene cannot be misread."[32] Christian martyr texts—if not, perhaps, Christian martyrs themselves—sought a counterscript to the arena, a skillful performance that would upset expectations rather than fulfilling them. When Polycarp, threatened in the arena by a fed-up proconsul and a hostile crowd, responds to the proconsul's demand that he say "away with the atheists" by not merely refusing to renounce his Christianity but indeed by condemning the entire crowd, he has flipped the script of the arena with a clever improvisation (Mart. Pol. 9).

Furthermore, Nicole Kelley and Karen King have argued that martyrdom texts sought not only to describe this process of counterscripting but also to enable readers and hearers to perform it themselves. Kelley and King both look to identify the key strategies martyrdom texts use to train potential martyrs. Kelley focuses on comparanda in ancient philosophy, read through the methodology of Pierre Hadot. Following Hadot, Kelley calls these practices of training "spiritual exercises," while King draws on Michel Foucault's language of "practices of the self."[33] Comparison with relevant ancient models of training, Kelley argues, draws out "the mechanisms by which the martyr acts shaped the perspectives of the ancient Christians."[34] Certain methods of training were imagined to produce these new perspectives. She points to practices of scriptural recitation and meditation upon future benefits that could enable potential martyrs to train in preparation for martyrdom. The philosophical exercises of the early Christians, thus, were focused specifically on training to develop capaci-

---

32. Elizabeth A. Castelli, *Martyrdom and Memory: Early Christian Culture Making* (New York: Columbia University Press, 2004).

33. Nicole Kelley, "Philosophy as Training for Death: Reading the Ancient Christian Martyr Acts as Spiritual Exercises," *CH* 75 (2006): 723–47; Karen King, "Martyrdom and Its Discontents in the Tchacos Codex," in *The Codex Judas Papers: Proceedings of the International Conference on the Tchacos Codex Held at Rice University, Houston, Texas, March 13–16, 2008*, ed. April D. DeConick, NHMS 71 (Leiden: Brill, 2009), 23–47.

34. Kelley, "Philosophy as Training for Death," 730. Kelley's study looks exclusively at Acts of the Martyrs for their description and exhortation of spiritual exercises, but she does not at any point exclude the possibility or likelihood that other sorts of martyrdom texts might also be engaged in such a didactic program.

ties that could in theory enable skillful performance in the arena. We can read martyrdom texts, she argues, as practical exhortations to preparation for martyrdom based in the sort of "spiritual exercises" or "practices of the self" that are likewise found in philosophical literature.

Recent scholarship on martyrdom, then, has identified a Christian *askēsis*, structured like the spiritual exercises of the philosophers, aimed at "preparation for martyrdom" that possibly enabled Christians (and others) to enact a "counterscript," by which they skillfully performed in the arena a new narrative for a hostile audience. My reading of the evidence of the gladiatorial cemetery suggests that gladiators were likewise engaging in "preparation for combat," again with structures similar to those of philosophical care of the self, and this preparation helped produce in gladiators the capacity to perform skillfully according to the "scripts of the arena."

It is possible, furthermore, to draw a clearer link between the recognizable gladiatorial practices, which focused more on food and medical care, and practices of preparation for martyrdom that seem to have involved more clearly intellectual practices of calming the passions. In Tertullian's *To the Martyrs*, he mentions in the first paragraph that imprisoned members of the community have received "provision … for your bodily wants in prison," referring to gifts of food (*Mart.* 1 [*ANF*]).[35] Further, he continues, it is best that those preparing for martyrdom maintain a careful regimen with regard to food. He draws an explicit comparison here between the potential martyrs and the athletes of the arena.

---

35. It might be objected here that my analysis has moved from the Greek to Roman worlds and across the Mediterranean. There is no question that a variety of differences apply between different geographical spaces. However, recent scholarship on gladiators in the Greek East has emphasized that Greek gladiators were engaging in their own negotiation of "the spaces between Greek athletic traditions and Roman spectacle practice" (Cavan Concannon, "'Not for an Olive Wreath, but Our Lives': Gladiators, Athletes, and Early Christian Bodies," *JBL* 133 [2014]: 202). The gladiator and the area did not mean the same thing in different spaces, but all were engaged with particularly Roman ideas and norms, which could then be negotiated in various ways in various places. While this space of negotiation can be mined for evidence of particular ways of practicing and understanding gladiatorial life and the arena, it also provides a fertile ground for comparison. See also Michael D. Carter, "Gladiators and Monomachoi: Greek Attitudes to a Roman Cultural Performance," in *Sport in the Cultures of the Ancient World*, ed. Z. Papakonstantinou (London: Routledge, 2009), 150–74; Christian Mann, "Gladiators in the Greek East: A Case Study in Romanization," *IJHS* 26 (2009): 272–97.

> For the athletes, too, are set apart to a more stringent discipline, that they may have their physical powers built up. They are kept from luxury, from daintier meats, from more pleasant drinks.... We, with the crown eternal in our eye, look upon the prison as our training-ground, that at the goal of final judgment we may be brought forth well-disciplined by many a trial, since virtue is built up by hardships as by voluptuous indulgence it is overthrown. (*Mart.* 3 [ANF])

The potential martyrs, he suggests, must likewise engage in bodily and spiritual discipline in preparation for their own, higher combat within the arena. The food of the martyrs, he argues, should be undertaken in the same way as athletes take to theirs. As Andrew McGowan puts it, "This particular strategy of scarcity forms the body by *askēsis*, refiguring the inner as well as the outer realities."[36] The martyrs, like the athletes, must engage in bodily practices in order to transform not only their bodies but also their mentalities and capacities, in preparation for what Tertullian imagined as this greatest competition.

I think this may also be the context for the otherwise odd postscript to the Martyrs of Lyons and Vienne. The author writes to the communities in Asia and Phrygia, a region that would include Ephesus. After telling the story of the martyrs Attalus, Sanctus, and Blandina, the letter turns back to an earlier time before the death of Attalus. It relates that a Christian named Alcibiades was held in prison and maintaining a strict diet.

> He ate only bread and water. He tried to continue this practice in prison. But it was revealed to Attalus after his first conflict in the amphitheater that Alcibiades was not pursuing the right course. In refusing to use the creatures of God he was leaving an example which might be a stumbling-block to others. And Alcibiades was persuaded and partook freely of all kinds of food, and thanked God. (Eusebius, *Hist. eccl.* 5.3.2–3)[37]

The story does not obviously connect to any earlier passage in the text, and the unusual break in the timeline of the narrative requires explanation. The text here uses Attalus's martyrdom, previously narrated, to

---

36. Andrew McGowan, "Discipline and Diet: Feeding the Martyrs in Roman Carthage," *HTR* 96 (2003): 472.

37. Translation from Herbert Musurillo, *The Acts of the Christian Martyrs* (Oxford: Clarendon, 1972).

authorize him to determine Christian dietary practices. This Alcibiades has been maintaining a particular kind of diet, but the letter writer wants to emphasize that the potential martyr in prison should be free to partake of all kinds of food. Here we see, I think, a continuing Christian debate about the *askēsis* of the martyr, with particular highly restricted diets being rejected. Once again, the preparation for martyrdom becomes intertwined with debates over diet and care of the self.

I want to conclude by thinking about the status of gladiators, martyrs, and philosophers—how they were arrayed among the relations of power in the ancient world. While most gladiators were slaves and some were condemned criminals, a significant number were freepersons who submitted to the rigors and restrictions of gladiatorial training.[38] Decrees of the Roman Senate repeatedly forbid its members from competing in the arena, suggesting the great appeal of being a gladiator to even the most privileged in the empire.[39] Concurrently, however, gladiators were outcasts of society, depicted commonly as subhuman. The gladiator as a type became a major site for philosophical reflection. Seneca held up the disciplined gladiator, the man whose training leads him to face death unmoved by his passions, as the embodiment of manliness and Romanness, but condemned those fighters who could not attain to this state. Barton refers to the "inverse exaltation" of the gladiator, to describe how the significant honor to which a gladiator can attain is conditioned on the marginality of his or her status.[40] The fraught status of the gladiator, the abject capable of unexpected honor, bears similarities to the status of the martyr.

Such an analysis of gladiatorial status should caution us against reading too much of a truly free agency into the Christian martyrs and their training. The undertaking of practices of medical care and dietary management by gladiators were enjoined upon them by their masters or their superiors. I have emphasized how gladiators did not just passively receive medical care and a restricted diet but should be imagined as undertaking such projects upon themselves. But this undertaking would likewise not have been possible without the work of trainers, physicians, and cooks. For many gladiators, it may not have been undertaken at all were it not for the

---

38. Wiedemann, *Emperors and Gladiators*, 102–7; Catharine Edwards, *Death in Ancient Rome* (New Haven: Yale University Press, 2007), 47–51.

39. Barton, *Sorrows of the Ancient Romans*, 25–27.

40. Ibid., 12–24. On the gladiator as philosopher, see Seneca, *Tranq.* 11. On the damnable character of the failed gladiator, see Seneca, *Ep.* 7.

exigent circumstances that placed them into slavery or otherwise disposed them to submit to gladiatorial training. The exhortation to the care of the self, in which Foucault and Hadot have found such great possibility for contemporary ethical work, may also have been experienced by some as profoundly disabling—training demanded by a master, directed toward a deadly, violent practice. It is useful to remember, here, that the imprisoned martyrs to whom Tertullian spoke may have been not only under arrest by the state but enslaved or otherwise dependent persons themselves. The most famous martyrdom story out of Carthage tells only obliquely the story of the enslaved Felicitas, who dies alongside Perpetua with her personal story untold. Undertaking preparation for martyrdom, for many Christians and other potential martyrs, might likewise have been enjoined in a situation of quite extreme constraint. When we select new ancient comparanda, gladiators rather than philosophers, it is easier to evoke the complex situations of enabling and constraint under which potential martyrs began their training practices.

Bibliography

Barton, Carlin. *The Sorrows of the Ancient Romans: The Gladiator and the Monster.* Princeton: Princeton University Press, 1993.

Bourdieu, Pierre. *Outline of a Theory of Practice.* Translated by Richard Nice. Cambridge: Cambridge University Press, 1977.

Burton, James H., and T. Douglas Price. "The Use and Abuse of Trace Elements for Paleodietary Research." Pages 159–71 in *Biochemical Approaches to Paleodietary Analysis.* Edited by Stanley H. Ambrose and M. Anne Katzenberg. AAMS 5. New York: Kluwer Academic/Plenum, 2000.

Carter, Michael J. "A Doctor Secutorum and the Retiarius Draukos from Corinth." *ZPE* 126 (1999): 262–68.

———. "Gladiatorial Combat: The Rules of Engagement." *CJ* 102 (2006): 97–113.

———. "Gladiatorial Combat with 'Sharp' Weapons (τοῖς ὀξέσι σιδήροις)." *ZPE* 155 (2006): 161–75.

———. "Gladiators and Monomachoi: Greek Attitudes to a Roman Cultural Performance." Pages 150–74 in *Sport in the Cultures of the Ancient World: New Perspectives.* Edited by Z. Papakonstantinou. London: Routledge, 2009.

Castelli, Elizabeth A. *Martyrdom and Memory: Early Christian Culture Making*. New York: Columbia University Press, 2004.
Coleman, Kathleen M. *Bonds of Danger: Communal Life in the Gladiatorial Barracks of Ancient Rome; The Fifteenth Todd Memorial Lecture Delivered in the University of Sydney 15 August 2002*. Sydney: Department of Classics and Ancient History University of Sydney, 2005.
———. "Missio at Halicarnassus." *HSCP* 100 (2000): 487–500.
———. "Valuing Others in the Gladiatorial Barracks." Pages 419–46 in *Valuing Others in Classical Antiquity*. Edited by Ineke Sluiter and Ralph M. Rosen. MnemSup 323. Leiden: Brill, 2010.
Concannon, Cavan. "'Not for an Olive Wreath, but Our Lives': Gladiators, Athletes, and Early Christian Bodies." *JBL* 133 (2014): 193–214.
Curry, Andrew. "The Gladiator Diet," *Arch* 61.6 (2008): 28–30.
Edwards, Catharine. *Death in Ancient Rome*. New Haven: Yale University Press, 2007.
Fabrizii-Reuer, Suzanne. "Gräber im Bereich der Via Sacra Ephesiaca (Kurzfassung)." Pages 461–64 in *100 Jahre österreichische Forschungen in Ephesos: Akten des Symposions Wien 1995*. Edited by Herwig Friesinger and Fritz Krinzinger. Vienna: ÖAW, 1999.
Foucault, Michel. *The Care of the Self*. Vol. 3 of *The History of Sexuality*. Translated by Robert Hurley. London: Penguin, 1990.
Francis, James A. *Subversive Virtue: Asceticism and Authority in the Second-Century Pagan World*. University Park, PA: Pennsylvania State University Press, 1995.
Grossschmidt, Karl, and Fabian Kanz. "Head Injuries of Roman Gladiators." *FSI* 160 (2006): 207–16.
———. "Stand der anthropologischen Forschungen zum Gradiatorenfriedhof in Ephesos" *JÖAI* 74 (2005): 103–23.
Hadot, Pierre. *Philosophy as a Way of Life: Spiritual Exercises from Socrates to Foucault*. Translated by Michael Chase. Edited and with an Introduction by Arnold I. Davidson. Oxford: Blackwell, 1995.
Junkelmann, Markus. "Familia Gladiatoria: The Heroes of the Amphitheatre." Pages 31–74 in *Gladiators and Caesars: The Power of Spectacle in Ancient Rome*. Edited by Ralph Jackson. Translated by Anthea Bell. Berkeley: University of California Press, 2000.
Kelley, Nicole. "Philosophy as Training for Death: Reading the Ancient Christian Martyr Acts as Spiritual Exercises." *CH* 75 (2006): 723–47.
King, Karen. "Martyrdom and Its Discontents in the Tchacos Codex." Pages 23–47 in *The Codex Judas Papers: Proceedings of the Interna-*

tional Conference on the Tchacos Codex Held at Rice University, Houston, Texas, March 13–16, 2008. Edited by April D. DeConick. NHMS 71. Leiden: Brill, 2009.

Knibbe, Dieter. "Via Sacra Ephesiaca: New Aspects of the Cult of Artemis Ephesia." Pages 141–55 in *Ephesos, Metropolis of Asia: An Interdisciplinary Approach to Its Archaeology, Religion, and Culture.* Edited by Helmut Koester. HTS 41. Valley Forge, PA: Trinity Press International, 1995.

Knibbe, Dieter, and Wolfgang Pietsch. "Via Sacra—Damianos Stoa." *JÖAI* 63 (1994): 17–20.

Lösch, Sandra, Negahnaz Moghaddam, Karl Grossschmidt, Daniele U. Risser, and Fabian Kanz. "Stable Isotope and Trace Element Studies on Gladiators and Contemporary Romans from Ephesus (Turkey, Second and Third Ct. AD)—Implications for Differences in Diet." *PLoS ONE* 9.10 (2014): 1–17.

Lutz, C. E. "Musonius Rufus: 'The Roman Socrates.'" *YCS* 10 (1947): 3–150.

Mann, Christian. "Gladiators in the Greek East: A Case Study in Romanization." *IJHS* 26 (2009): 272–97.

McGowan, Andrew. "Discipline and Diet: Feeding the Martyrs in Roman Carthage." *HTR* 96 (2003): 455–76.

Musurillo, Herbert. *The Acts of the Christian Martyrs.* Oxford: Clarendon, 1972.

Perkins, Judith. *The Suffering Self: Pain and Narrative Representation in the Early Christian Era.* London: Routledge: 1995.

Petzl, Georg. *Die Inschriften von Smyrna.* 2 vols. Bonn: Rheinisch-Westfälische Akademie der Wissenschaften, 1982–1990.

Pietsch, Wolfgang. "Ausserstädtische Grabanlagen von Ephesos." Pages 455–60 in *100 Jahre österreichische Forschungen in Ephesos: Akten des Symposions Wien 1995.* Edited by Herwig Friesinger and Fritz Krinzinger. Vienna: ÖAW, 1999.

———. "Der Gladiatorenfriedhof von Ephesos: Der archäologische Befund." Pages 15–17 in *Gladiatoren in Ephesos: Tod und Nachmittag; Eine Ausstellung im Ephesos Museum Seluk, seit 20. April 2002.* Edited by Karl Grossschmidt and Fabian Kanz. Vienna: ÖAI, 2002.

Pietsch, Wolfgang, and Elisabeth Trinkl. "Der Grabungsbericht der Kampagnen 1992/93." Pages 19–48 in *Grabungen und Forschungen 1992 und 1993.* Vol. 2 of *Via Sacra Ephesiaca.* Edited by Dieter Knibbe and Hilke Thür. BerMatÖAI 6. Vienna: Schindler, 1995.

Potter, David M. Review of *Emperors and Gladiators*, by Thomas Wiedermann. *JRS* 84 (1994): 229–31.
Robert, Louis. *Les Gladiateurs dans l'Orient grec*. BEHEH 278. Paris: Champion, 1940.
Shaw, Teresa. *The Burden of the Flesh: Fasting and Sexuality in Early Christianity*. Minneapolis: Fortress, 1998.
Sillen, Andrew, and Maureen Kavanaugh. "Strontium and Paleodietary Research: A Review." *YPA* 25 (1982): 67–90.
Touratsoglou, J. P. "Δύο νέαι ἐπιγραφικαὶ μαρτυρίαι περὶ τοῦ Κοινοῦ τῶν Μακεδόνων κατὰ τὸν τρίτον μεταχριστιανικὸν αἰῶνα" ["Two New Epigraphic Testimonies on Common Rules in Macedonia during the Third Century CE"]. Pages 280–90 in *Ancient Macedonia: Papers Read at the First International Symposium Held in Thessaloniki August 26–29 1968*. Edited by Basil Laourdas and Ch J. Makaronas. HMCH 122. Thessaloniki: Salonica Institute for Balkan Studies, 1970.
Ville, Georges. *Le Gladiature en Occident des Origenes à la Mort de Domitien*. BEFAR 245. Rome: École française de Rome, 1981.
Wiedemann, Thomas. *Emperors and Gladiators*. London: Routledge, 1992.

Ἐκκλησία in Ephesians as Godlike in the Heavens, in Temple, in γάμος, and in Armor: Ideology and Iconography in Ephesus and Its Environs

Fredrick J. Long

The so-called epistle "to the Ephesians" was most likely a circular letter for Asia Minor commencing with Ephesus.[1] It prominently features God as Benefactor, Jesus the Messiah as his Regent, and the ἐκκλησία as a "(convened) assembly."[2] As a political body, the convened assembly "was

---

1. The textual location ἐν Ἐφέσῳ is very doubtful (omitted in P46, ℵ*, B*, 1739, Marcion, and Origen), which would then either require a location to be supplied (depending on the reading location) or stress the adjective πιστοῖς with the adverbial-additive use of καί, *also*. For a treatment of these matters and the view that Paul was its author writing from Caesarea Maritima in 58–60 CE, see my essay "Ephesians: Paul's Political Theology in Greco-Roman Political Context," in *Christian Origins and Classical Culture: Social and Literary Contexts for the New Testament*, vol. 1 of *Early Christianity in Its Hellenistic Context*, ed. Stanley E. Porter and Andrew W. Pitts, TENTS 9 (Leiden: Brill, 2012), 255–309, esp. 268, n. 52 on the text-critical issue.

2. Gustav Adolf Deissmann argued that " 'the (convened) assembly' ... is the most literal translation of the Greek word ἐκκλησία. This self-bestowed name rested on the certain conviction that God had separated from the world His 'saints' in Christ, and had 'called' or 'convened' them to an assembly, which was 'God's assembly,' 'God's muster,' because God was the convener" (*Light from the Ancient East: The New Testament Illustrated by Recently Discovered Texts of the Graeco-Roman World*, trans. L. R. M. Strachan, 2nd ed. [London: Hodder & Stoughton, 1910], 112–13). See also Hans-Josef Klauck, *The Religious Context of Early Christianity: A Guide to Greco-Roman Religions*, trans. Brian McNeil (Minneapolis: Fortress, 2003), 46. Klauck, in the context of describing the sparse use of the term in voluntary associations, indicates that the term "denotes the official assembly of the association members, in an obvious analogy to the assembly of the citizens of the *polis*." Klauck also suggests the choice of ἐκκλησία may have enabled Christ worshippers to distinguish themselves from other religious associations (54).

founded" (κτισθέντες [2:10]) by God's beneficent, sovereign, and wise design with Jesus the Messiah as its triumphant Lord, Head, Son of God, and Savior. Indeed, the epistle is replete with imperial-political topoi that have not been adequately accounted for altogether.[3] Compared to the Pauline epistles, the sociopolitical word ἐκκλησία has the highest concentration in Ephesians, occurring nine times (equal to 2 Corinthians), with only 1 Corinthians having more occurrences (twenty-one).[4] More

---

3. I have attempted to describe this context comprehensively when interpreting Ephesians in presentations starting in 2006 at annual Society of Biblical Literature meetings and in various published research: Nijay K. Gupta and Fredrick J. Long, "The Politics of Ephesians and the Empire: Accommodation or Resistance?," *JGRChJ* 7 (2010): 112–36; Long, "Ephesians: Paul's Political Theology; Long, "Ephesians, Letter to the (ΠΡΟΣ ΕΦΕΣΙΟΥΣ)," in *The Lexham Bible Dictionary*, ed. John D. Barry (Bellingham, WA: Logos Bible Software, 2012); Long, "Roman Imperial Rule under the Authority of Jupiter-Zeus: Political-Religious Contexts and the Interpretation of 'the Ruler of the Authority of the Air' in Ephesians 2:2," in *The Language of the New Testament: Context, History and Development*, vol. 3 of *Early Christianity in Its Hellenistic Context*, ed. Stanley E. Porter and Andrew W. Pitts, LBS 6 (Leiden: Brill, 2013), 113–54. Other interpreters have seen individual themes or treated individual passages (like 2:11–22): on military triumph, see Eberhard Faust, *Pax Christi et Pax Caesaris: Religionsgeschichtliche, Traditionsgeschichtliche und Sozialgeschichtliche Studien zum Ephesebrief*, NTOA 24 (Freiburg: Freiburg Universitätsverlag, 1993); focusing on Eph 2, see Tet-Lim N. Yee, *Jews, Gentiles, and Ethnic Reconciliation: Paul's Jewish Identity and Ephesians*, SNTSMS 130 (Cambridge: Cambridge University Press, 2005); on 2:11–22, see Gosnell Yorke, "Hearing the Politics of Peace in Ephesians: A Proposal from an African Postcolonial Perspective," *JSNT* 30 (2007): 113–27; on Hellenistic kingship (missing many Roman imperial connections), see Julien Smith, *Christ the Ideal King: Cultural Context, Rhetorical Strategy, and the Power of Divine Monarchy in Ephesians*, WUNT 2/313 (Tübingen: Mohr Siebeck, 2011). Notable exceptions include Jennifer G. Bird, "The Letter to the Ephesians," in *A Postcolonial Commentary on the New Testament Writings*, ed. Fernando F. Segovia and R. S. Sugirtharajah, BP 13 (London: T&T Clark, 2007), 265–80. Bird, however, assumes a later dating and sees the author as reinscribing imperialism rather than exposing and subverting it. See also Harry O. Maier, *Picturing Paul in Empire: Imperial Image, Text and Persuasion in Colossians, Ephesians and the Pastoral Epistles* (London: Bloomsbury T&T Clark, 2013). Maier's analysis, however, is limited (see ch. 3, and *passim*) and assumes a later dating of Ephesians during the reign of Vespasian-Titus, thus limiting his analysis of imperial parallels/ideology to that latter time period.

4. Only 3 John has a higher percentage (20 percent) compared to Ephesians (5.8 percent) and 1 Corinthians (4.8 percent) based on data from BibleWorks 9. The occurrences across the New Testament are Matt 16:18; 18:17; Acts 5:11; 7:38; 8:1, 3; 9:31; 11:22, 26; 12:1, 5; 13:1; 14:23, 27; 15:3–4, 22, 41; 16:5; 18:22; 19:32, 39–40; 20:17, 28;

importantly, the assembly of believers is heavenly located and seated (1:3; 2:6), is the body of Christ who is its head (1:22-23; 2:16; 3:6; 4:4, 12, 15-16; 5:23, 30), is a temple structure bringing glory to God (2:11-22; 3:17-21), is personified as Christ's consort bride (5:22-33), and is standing against the devil's stratagems and donned with divine Roman-like armor (6:10-20). Indeed, this high view of the church in Ephesians is among the reasons for interpreting the epistle as embodying gnostic thought or, at a minimum, a more "mature" ecclesial-theological development, and hence as deutero-Pauline.[5] This view persists despite James D. G. Dunn's emphatic claim that "we cannot say that Paul would have disapproved of the subsequent usage [of the church] in Ephesians."[6]

Rom 16:1, 4-5, 16, 23; 1 Cor 1:2; 4:17; 6:4; 7:17; 10:32; 11:16, 18, 22; 12:28; 14:4-5, 12, 19, 23, 28, 33-35; 15:9; 16:1, 19; 2 Cor 1:1; 8:1, 18-19, 23-24; 11:8, 28; 12:13; Gal 1:2, 13, 22; Eph 1:22; 3:10, 21; 5:23-25, 27, 29, 32; Phil 3:6; 4:15; Col 1:18, 24; 4:15-16; 1 Thess 1:1; 2:14; 2 Thess 1:1, 4; 1 Tim 3:5, 15; 5:16; Phlm 1:2; Heb 2:12; 12:23; Jas 5:14; 3 John 1:6, 9-10; Rev 1:4, 11, 20; 2:1, 7-8, 11-12, 17-18, 23, 29; 3:1, 6-7, 13-14, 22; 22:16.

5. For Ephesians embodying gnostic thought, see Heinrich Schlier, *Der Brief an die Epheser: Ein Kommentar*, 6th ed. (Düsseldorf: Patmos, 1968), 266-76. Those issues identified by Andrew T. Lincoln for why Ephesians is to be rejected as Pauline are: (1) its style, consisting of "long sentences with numerous relative and participial clauses, strings of prepositional phrases, and the piling up of synonyms"; (2) it made use of Colossians; (3) it reflects a later date than Paul, in that the Jew-gentile issue and the law is settled (2:11-22) and Paul's grace and ministry is retrospective in perspective (3:1-13); and (4) its emphasis of thought "is more on Christ's exaltation and cosmic lordship than on his death, on realized eschatology rather than an imminent parousia, on the universal church rather than the local assembly" ("Ephesians," in *The Cambridge Companion to St. Paul*, ed. James D. G. Dunn, CCR [Cambridge: Cambridge University Press, 2003], 135). I have switched the ordering of the second and fourth items. For a full treatment, see T. Lincoln, *Ephesians*, WBC 42 (Dallas: Word, 1990). James D. G. Dunn raises similar issues, although discounting Colossians, and thus adding the problem of *Haustafel* in both letters (*The Theology of Paul the Apostle* [Grand Rapids: Eerdmans, 1998], 732-33).

6. Dunn, *Theology of Paul*, 541. This statement occurs within his discussion "§20 The body of Christ" (pp. 533-64) when treating "the Church" (ch. 7). Dunn notes a move to universal reference (rather than a local reference) in Col 1:18 and 1:24 heading towards the universal usage in Ephesians. Yet Dunn immediately states, "To recognize this as a late (or later) development in Pauline theology should not be overdramatized. Paul had no thought of his churches as a set of independent foundations. His conception of 'the church of God' and regular appeal to 'all the churches' would rule

However, these ecclesial depictions are not simply understandable, but locally relevant and strategic within the ideological environs of Ephesus and Asia Minor in the mid-first century CE. Specifically, I argue that the church assembly's elevation and personification corresponds to the widespread phenomenon of personification of political entities at all levels of society, not least of which was *Roma* in relation to her Caesar in temples.[7] All such personifications were prevalent in Ephesus and Asia Minor and indeed the whole of the Greco-Roman world.[8] The audiences of Ephesians would have readily recognized how and why the church assembly was being comparably described. Yet, in contrast to the defeated and bedraggled personifications of the nations in Roman victory art present in Asia Minor, the church assembly is seated in the heavenly realms with Christ as his bride. Moreover, she is built into a temple and dressed in armor in a resistant and even forward-marching, prayerful pose for proclaiming the gospel of the peace of Christ.

In support of this thesis, I have attended to sociorhetorical interpretive data—philological, literary, argumentative, visual, and archeological—to investigate networks of themes arising from a shared "cognitive environment" of critical spaces within Ephesians.[9] Elsewhere, I have described

---

that out. We cannot say that Paul would have disapproved of the subsequent usage in Ephesians" (p. 541).

7. Such personification is to be differentiated from, e.g., Sin and Death in Paul's argumentation, as studied in Joseph R. Dodson, *The "Powers" of Personification: Rhetorical Purpose in the Book of Wisdom and the Letter to the Romans*, BZNW 161 (Berlin: de Gruyter, 2008), see esp. ch.1 on Dodson's definition of the rhetorical device.

8. For a detailed treatment of but one, see Lajos Juhász, "The Personifications of Gallia in the 1st Century BC and AD," in *Studia Archaeologica Nicolae Szabó LXXV Annos Nato Dedicata*, ed. László Borhy, Károly Tankó, and Kata Dévai (Budapest: L'Harmattan, 2015), 149–60.

9. I am here indebted to the heuristic approach of Vernon K. Robbins and the Rhetoric of Religious Antiquities (RRA) commentary research group, from whom I have learned so much through conversations, presenting my work and receiving their feedback, and their writings; see, esp., Vernon K. Robbins, *Exploring the Texture of Texts: A Guide to Socio-rhetorical Interpretation* (Valley Forge, PA: Trinity Press International, 1996); Robbins, *The Tapestry of Early Christian Discourse: Rhetoric, Society, and Ideology* (London: Routledge, 1996); Robbins, "Rhetography: A New Way of Seeing the Familiar Text," in *Words Well Spoken: George Kennedy's Rhetoric of the New Testament*, ed. C. Clifton Black and Duane Frederick Watson, SSR 8 (Waco, TX: Baylor University Press, 2008), 81–106; Robbins, *The Invention of Christian Discourse: From Wisdom to Apocalyptic*, RRA 1 (Blandford Forum, UK: Deo, 2009). For a dis-

the network of political topoi across Ephesians.[10] Here, I will focus on the major topoi pertaining to ἐκκλησία—seated in heavenly places, as temple, as head-body, as bride of Christ, and divinely armored—showing their intersection with the broader material culture of the Roman Empire, Asia Minor, and especially Ephesus. Specifically, I will treat the following subjects:

1. Imperial monumentation in Ephesus from Augustus to Nero
2. The sociopolitical use of ἐκκλησία in Asia Minor
3. Personifications of people groups in the Greco-Roman world
4. God's people are seated with Christ "in the heavenly realms" (ἐν τοῖς ἐπουρανίοις [1:3, 20–21; 2:4–7])
5. The church assembly as the body of Christ, its head (1:22–23; 2:16; 3:6; 4:4, 12, 15–16; 5:23, 30)
6. The church assembly constructed as a temple for God (2:11–22)
7. Christ, the Savior of the church body (5:23)
8. God's armor on God's people (6:10–18)

My discussions will appeal to the lexical, grammatical, and pragmatic features of these passages that have alerted me to consider sociorhetorically significant topoi in need of more intensive research.[11] I have attempted to move from careful observation of these topoi in their discursive context to

---

cussion of "cognitive environment," see Dan Sperber and Deirdre Wilson, *Relevance: Communication and Cognition*, 2nd ed. (Oxford: Blackwell, 2001); Deirdre Wilson and Dan Sperber, "Outline of Relevance Theory," *Hermes* 5 (1990): 35–56; Wilson and Sperber, "Relevance Theory," in *The Handbook of Pragmatics*, ed. Laurence R. Horn and Gregory L. Ward, BHL 16 (Malden, MA: Blackwell, 2004), 607–32; Wilson and Sperber, *Meaning and Relevance* (Cambridge: Cambridge University Press, 2012). Relevance theory is a field within "pragmatics." On imperial conceptions of critical space in Ephesus, see the very helpful study of Gerhard van den Heever, "Space, Social Space, and the Construction of Early Christian Identity in First Century Asia Minor," *R&T* 17 (2010): 205–43 and the sources cited there.

10. Long, "Ephesians: Paul's Political Theology," 269–71.

11. For discussions of my view of pragmatic features of New Testament Greek for studying discourse, see Long, *2 Corinthians: A Handbook on the Greek Text*, BHGNT (Waco, TX: Baylor University Press, 2015); Long, *Koine Greek Grammar: A Beginning-Intermediate Exegetical and Pragmatic Handbook*, AGROS (Wilmore, KY: GlossaHouse, 2015). David M. Schaps has correctly stated its importance for classical studies: "The use of pragmatics as an approach to the understanding of ancient texts has opened up a window to understanding many aspects of our texts that seemed arbi-

ubiquitous and/or localized data and archeological artifacts, while attempting to avoid imposing such data onto Ephesians.[12] I constantly have this question in mind: what meaning and significance would these ecclesial topoi have had for audiences in Ephesus and Asia Minor in the mid-first century CE?

1. Imperial Monumentation in Ephesus from Augustus to Nero

To help reconstruct the shared cognitive environment of Ephesians, it is necessary to understand the vigorous Romanization in the first half of the first century CE, even more notable given Ephesus's prominence. Fortunately, a happy host of excellent studies describe the imperial climate of Asia Minor, and at times specifically Ephesus.[13] Peter Scherrer in his essay "The City of Ephesos: From the Roman Period to Late Antiquity" begins the collection of essays *Ephesos, Metropolis of Asia*, edited by Helmut Koester,

---

trary or meaningless when looked at from a purely syntactical point of view" (*Handbook for Classical Research* [New York: Routledge, 2011], 97).

12. On methodological grounds such is required, as studied and illustrated by James D. G. Dunn, "On the Relation of Text and Artifact: Some Cautionary Tales," in *Text and Artifact in the Religions of Mediterranean Antiquity: Essays in Honour of Peter Richardson*, ed. Stephen G. Wilson and Michel Desjardins, CSJud 9 (Waterloo, ON: Wilfrid Laurier University Press, 2000), 192–206. Dunn particularly scrutinizes Clinton Arnold's interpretation of "worship of angels" in Col 2:18 as not attending to the text in its literary and argumentative context (198–99). More recently, I have formally responded to and critiqued Maier's *Picturing Paul in Empire* at the Annual Society of Biblical Literature Meeting in Atlanta (2015) during the joint RRA and Disputed Paulines session devoted to reviewing Maier's book. In particular, I argued that Maier's adoption of the dating schema of Colossians/Julio-Claudian, Ephesians/Vespasian-Titus, and Pastorals/Flavian, while allowing him opportunity to pursue possible relevant archeological data in each imperial era, nevertheless presents a quite incomplete picture since relevant local archeological data exists during the Julio-Claudian period for each of these New Testament books and the themes or ideology treated by Maier. As creative and helpful as Maier's work is, then, it perpetuates a dating schema at the expense of relevant earlier data that may help establish an earlier dating of each of these New Testament books.

13. E.g., Cornelius C. Vermeule, *Roman Imperial Art in Greece and Asia Minor* (Cambridge: Harvard University Press, 1968); Simon R. F. Price, *Rituals and Power: The Roman Imperial Cult in Asia Minor* (Cambridge: Cambridge University Press, 1984); see also Benjamin B. Rubin, "(Re)presenting Empire: The Roman Imperial Cult in Asia Minor, 31 BC–AD 68" (PhD diss., University of Michigan, 2008).

with a chronological description of building projects and dedications.¹⁴ L. Michael White follows Scherrer with his essay "Urban Development and Social Change in Imperial Ephesos."¹⁵ Within New Testament treatments, attention is typically paid to such details pertaining to Ephesus at the end of the first century in order to interpret the book of Revelation and John's Gospel.¹⁶ Seemingly an exception to this would be Paul Trebilco, *The Early Christians in Ephesus from Paul to Ignatius*; however, Trebilco hardly treats Ephesians, on the grounds that it is likely pseudepigraphal and dated later (80–90s CE).¹⁷ Trebilco helpfully offers a concise statement of the imperial context, however, concluding, "architecturally and symbolically, then, the emperor was extraordinarily 'present' in Ephesus."¹⁸ He also quotes Simon R. F. Price approvingly regarding Ephesus: "The emperor, whose name or image met the eye at every turn, received a striking position in this process of transformation."¹⁹ Indeed, at Ephesus imperial building and reorganization of space "monumentalized city-scapes" (to use van den Heever's expression).²⁰ Although we ought not to envision all city spaces as imperialized, the general pattern and most visible effects displayed the grandeur of Rome and Rome's right to rule the nations.²¹ In what follows, I selectively

---

14. Peter Scherrer, "The City of Ephesos: From the Roman Period to Late Antiquity," in *Ephesos, Metropolis of Asia: An Interdisciplinary Approach to Its Archaeology, Religion, and Culture*, ed. Helmut Koester, HTS 41 (Valley Forge, PA: Trinity Press International, 1995), 1–25.

15. L. Michael White, "Urban Development and Social Change in Imperial Ephesos," in Koester, *Ephesos*, 27–79.

16. See, respectively, the excellent monograph of Steven J. Friesen, *Imperial Cults and the Apocalypse of John: Reading Revelation in the Ruins* (Oxford: Oxford University Press, 2001) and the fascinating study of van den Heever, "Space, Social Space."

17. Paul Trebilco, *The Early Christians in Ephesus from Paul to Ignatius*, WUNT 166 (Tübingen: Mohr Siebeck, 2004). Of the Pauline epistles, Ephesians has the least scriptural references cited or discussed (with 27), apart from 2 Thessalonians (14) and Philemon (7), located in Macedonia. The closest are Galatians (44), Colossians (37), Philippians (30), and 1 Thessalonians (31). Trebilco treats Ephesians as likely pseudonymous, perhaps even authored in Ephesus by a Pauline school that gathered Paul's letters (*Early Christians in Ephesus*, 89–94; cf. 6–7).

18. Ibid., 36.

19. Price, *Rituals and Power*, 136; Trebilco, *Early Christians in Ephesus*, 36.

20. Van den Heever, "Space, Social Space," 210.

21. See, e.g., Barbara Burrell, "False Fronts: Separating the Aedicular Facade from the Imperial Cult in Roman Asia Minor," *AJA* 110 (2006): 437–69. She shows how, despite "the Emperor Mystique" of earlier interpreters of archeological sites, the gym-

summarize imperial building and reorganization of space beginning with Augustus and extending through Nero's reign.

- 29 BCE—Augustus made Ephesus the provincial capital of Asia.
- 29 BCE—the State Agora was established, and contained a small temple, possibly "the temple that Octavian dedicated to the *conventus civium Romanorum* ("assembly of the Roman citizens") for Divus Julius and Dea Roma in 29 BCE."[22]
- Under Augustus, the prytaneion and bouleuterion were constructed, and between them was located a three-sided peristyle shrine, possibly the location of cults to Artemis and Augustus.
- 25 BCE or later—a statue of Augustus with the *corona civica* and inscription was found, indicating a Sebasteion existed as early as 25 BCE (*JÖAI* 56 [1985] 62; IEph 3.902).
- 4–2 BCE—the victory gate (or triumphal arch) of Mazaeus and Mithridates "demonstrates the dominance of the imperial freedman in Ephesian politics"; "statues of Augustus, his designated heirs Gaius and Lucius Caesar, and their parents looked down upon those who were passing through this gate."[23] The gate was placed at the holy intersection of the Via Sacra and the Processional Way to Ortygia. It was dedicated to Augustus, Agrippa, Livia, and Julia, containing Greek and Latin.[24]
- 5 CE—Cornelius C. Vermeule reports that a sanctuary for Roma and Augustus was placed within the precinct of the Artemision; also a bilingual inscription to Augustus is found in the peribolos wall of the Artemision from the proconsul C. Asinius Gallus (*CIL* 3.6070).[25]
- 11 CE—the Basilica Stoa was built and dedicated to Artemis, Augustus, Tiberius, and the city of Ephesus (IEph 2.404); at one end, monumental statues of Augustus and Livia as well as of Germanicus, have been found (CIL 3.426).[26] It is possible that this

---

nasia and bath houses should not be understood as *Kaiseräle* at Ephesus and elsewhere in Asia Minor.

22. Scherrer, "City of Ephesos," 4.
23. Ibid., 6.
24. Vermeule, *Roman Imperial Art*, 464.
25. Ibid., 463.
26. Ibid., 464.

stoa was dedicated to the worship of the imperial family; Scherrer argues, "Imperial propaganda is the dominating element in this area."²⁷

- Under Augustus the imperial freedman C. Julius Nikephoros secured his position as prytanis for life within the prytaneion by giving money for the perpetual sacrifices to Roma and Artemis, changing also his name from *Caesaris libertus* to *Augusti libertus*.
- 43 CE—an equestrian statue of Claudius was erected as part of a reopened Tetragonus Agora; another statue of Claudius and possibly one of Messalina have been found.²⁸
- 54 CE and later—the Eastern Hall of this reconstructed Tetragonus Agora was dedicated to Artemis, Nero, and Agrippina (IEph 7.1.3003); a municipal building (fish market?) was dedicated to Nero and Agrippina.²⁹
- 54 CE and later—repairs to the Basilica Stoa under Nero were dedicated to him (IEph 2.410).
- 54 CE and later—additionally, the Curetes, who administered the mysteries of Artemis, in the mid-first century began to refer to themselves also as *philosebastoi* (IEph 4.1008).³⁰
- Of the nineteen urban development projects during the Julio-Claudian period listed by White (31–81 CE), ten are sponsored by the emperor(s) or a provincial official. These include (not mentioned above): the Doric Stoa of the Marble Road, the so-called

---

27. Scherrer, "City of Ephesos," 5.
28. Ibid., 8; Vermeule, *Roman Imperial Art*, 464.
29. Ibid.
30. Trebilco, *Early Christians in Ephesus*, 36; he cites Guy MacLean Rogers, *The Sacred Identity of Ephesos: Foundation Myths of a Roman City* (London: Routledge, 1991), 168. Rogers there explains: "It is true that in the Kouretes' inscriptions from the mid-first century A.D. the Roman emperors were not accorded a status equal to that of Artemis. Nor were the Iulio-Claudian emperors called gods in the lists of Kouretes. Yet the Kouretes' proclamation of their devotion to the Iulio-Claudian emperors in the lists from the reign of Nero clearly parallels the ritual assimilation of the Roman emperors into the celebration of other mysteries in the city and anticipates the language used later in inscriptions from Ephesos and other cities of the province, which document the creation of a provincial cult explicitly dedicated to the Roman emperors, both living and dead."

Palace of the Proconsul (?), the Harbor Gate, and both the theater's completion and renovation.[31]

This extensive monumentation indicates that indeed Ephesus had capacity for Romanization.[32] Steven J. Friesen summarizes the broader impact on Asia Minor:

> Imperial worship touched most or all aspects of life in the cities of Asia, but it did not constitute the sum total of religious life. Rather, imperial cults extended religious activities in new ways. No other symbolic system had such a range of effective meaning. Other cults might be useful in municipal religion, in household cult, in group activity, or in combinations thereof. Only imperial cults could operate in all of these spheres while providing a cultic expression for the empire. The worship of the Olympian[god]s nearly approximated this range of applicability; thus, their worship was closely allied with that of the imperial institutions.[33]

For interpreting Ephesians, then, this imperial environment is not merely ancillary, but it is integral at the center of the shared cognitive environment of the epistle's messaging and conceptualization of space and identity. In this regard, while surveying this topic for Ephesus, Gerhard van den Heever helpfully describes two dimensions or "differentials in social positionality" through Romanization and its monumentation. Vertically, one found "at the top of the scale—emperors (divinised) and imperialised gods—and at the bottom, religious adepts and "non-enfranchised" inhabitants of Roman imperial society, translated into servants, with the sliding scale in between filled by systems of mediation of hierarchised authority"; horizontally, one sees a "dominant class-ethnicity in which dominion is attained and held over increasing domains of peoples who retain their ethnic identity but are politically and economically subordinate to the emperor, ... which encapsulates the essence of empire." The location along this horizontal scale "defines the degree to which social identity, social honour, and group status is achieved through assimilation

---

31. White, "Urban Development," 52.
32. White importantly discusses the wealth needed for such projects that were fueled by benefaction and social elevation even to the status of "founder" (κτίστης) of the city (ibid., 27–33). For Paul's succinct statement of God-in-Christ's founding of the church assembly, see the use of κτίζω in Eph 2:10.
33. Friesen, *Imperial Cults*, 126–27.

and adaptation to the ideals and practices of the centre."³⁴ The smallest units of social organization like families and voluntary associations would have to negotiate degrees of assimilation to the common Roman values, expectations, and practices.

2. The Sociopolitical Use of ἐκκλησία in Asia Minor

Karl L. Schmidt's question on how best to translate ἐκκλησία is still apropos: "Why did [the New Testament community] avoid a cultic term and choose instead a secular one?"³⁵ An ἐκκλησία was a localized "summoned legislative body" in the city-state; but under the Roman Empire the term was used by groups and associations for legitimization. For Christians, the term's use maintained "continuity with Israel" and allayed "any suspicion, esp. in political circles" of disorderliness.³⁶ Wayne O. McCready has further contextualized the relationship of ἐκκλησία and voluntary associations, summarizing his research as follows:

> The concept of *ekklēsia* as a vehicle for claiming universal salvation was matched with a social institution capable of transcending a local village, town, or city to unite the church into a collective whole.... Early churches shared significant common features with voluntary associations.... Indeed, the diversity of voluntary associations was an attractive feature, for it allowed experimentation and development by

---

34. Van den Heever, "Space, Social Space," 215–16.

35. Karl L. Schmidt, "ἐκκλησία," *TDNT* 3:503–4. The question occurs as Schmidt muses over the best translation for the term: "Finally, we must ask whether a single rendering cannot be found to cover all Gk. usage, secular as well as sacred. 'Community' or 'assembly' might be suggested. But this again leads us a step further and raises the question of the special term which the NT community had for itself. Why did it avoid a cultic term and choose instead a secular one? 'In both the secular and the biblical use of ἐκκλησία the dictionaries distinguish between the assembling of men and the men thus assembled. Hence a *prima facie* case can be made out for a word like "assembly," which has both an abstract and a concrete sense.'"

36. BDAG, s.v. "ἐκκλησία." The first definition is "a regularly summoned legislative body, *assembly*, as generally understood in the Greco-Roman world." After the final third definition ("people with shared belief, *community*, *congregation*") is found this explanation: "the term ἐ. apparently became popular among Christians in Greek-speaking areas for chiefly two reasons: to affirm continuity with Israel through use of a term found in Gk. translations of the Hebrew Scriptures, and to allay any suspicion, esp. in political circles, that Christians were a disorderly group."

the *ekklēsiai* while at the same time providing a special type of belonging that created a form of community definition that was distinct from the larger society.³⁷

Socially, because it was a fairly rare designation, for Christians to refer to themselves as an ἐκκλησία, argues Wendy Cotter, would indicate that they saw themselves as "an assembly of the citizens of a 'free' city, gathered as God's holy people."³⁸ This would have appealed to gentiles, given the variety of existing associations, since it would have allowed for flexibility in developing organizational structures (see esp. 4:7–16). More recently, Philip A. Harland helpfully summarizes the data:

> Among the self-designations in the literature, the most common term within Pauline circles was "assembly," or "congregation" (ἐκκλησία, often anachronistically translated "church"). This term is drawn from civic life in the Greek East, where a particular gathering or assembly of the civic institution of "the people" (δῆμος), namely, the citizen body, was frequently called an "assembly" (ἐκκλησία). Paul's (or other Jesus-followers') adaptation of this term from its origins in reference to an occasional assembly or meeting to an ongoing title for a group reflects a common process that can be seen with many other associations and their titles.... Although the term does not seem to have become a widespread group self-designation, there is clear evidence that certain associations did use it in reference to a specific "assembly" or "meeting."³⁹

It is reasonable to conclude from such research that, first, the early-Christian deployment of ἐκκλησία was strategic sociopolitically, and, second, the presentation of ἐκκλησία in Ephesians was a localized extension and embodiment of the import of this sociopolitical term intimating legitimization.

---

37. Wayne O. McCready, "Ekklēsia and Voluntary Associations," in *Voluntary Associations in the Graeco-Roman World*, ed. John S. Kloppenborg and Stephen G. Wilson (London: Routledge, 1996), 69.

38. Wendy Cotter, "Women's Authority Roles in Paul's Churches: Countercultural or Conventional?," *NovT* 36 (1994): 370.

39. Philip A. Harland, *Dynamics of Identity in the World of the Early Christians: Associations, Judeans, and Cultural Minorities* (London: T&T Clark, 2009), 44–45.

3. Personifications of People Groups in the Greco-Roman World

The personification of groups was pervasive: the local councils of elders or βουλή (e.g., the Roman Senate), individual cities as a δῆμος, (e.g., Athenians or Ephesians), nationalities or ἔθνη (Armenia, Judaea, etc.), regional leagues (the *Koinon* of Asia, of Aetolia, etc.), whole continents (Asia, Europe, Africa), the Roman populous (*Roma*), and the inhabited Roman world (οἰκουμένη). The ubiquity of this phenomenon is amply found in the extant literature, inscriptions, coins, statuary, reliefs, and other artifacts (gems, cups, engravings, etc.). Percy Gardner has surveyed the development in the Mediterranean World through representations of (1) a guardian deity, (2) an eponymous hero or founder, (3) an allegorical figure (including a simple depiction by ethnic dress and appearance), and/or (4) *Tyche* or *Fortuna*. Gardner gives the greatest treatment to the third category and concludes his study generally, "As we approach Roman times the class of personifications is greatly enlarged."[40]

Ideologically, an important shift occurred in the Roman period, according to R. R. R. Smith. Whereas in the Hellenistic era such personifications represented cities, geographic areas, and concepts more generically, Roman personifications were "victory art" and conveyed the "visual enumeration of victories." "Female versions of such figures were then made to personify whole conquered peoples—*nationes captae* or *gentes devictae*—which appear in a considerable variety of forms and contexts. These conquered personifications were made by combining the 'typical prisoner' figures with forms and style borrowed from the large Hellenistic repertoire of draped women."[41] It is intriguing that the book of Acts records Paul having a vision of "a certain Macedonian man" (ἀνὴρ Μακεδών τις) asking for assistance (16:9); such a vision may have entailed a personification.[42] If so, the male personification would reflect an older practice of occasionally representing a country by a male, possibly indicating the nation or region is not for subjugation, in contrast to Roman victory art that featured

---

40. Percy Gardner, "Countries and Cities in Ancient Art," *JHS* 9 (1888): 80.

41. R. R. R. Smith, "Simulacra gentium: The Ethne from the Sebasteion at Aphrodisias," *JRS* 78 (1988): 71.

42. Also in a dream, Aeschylus, *Pers.* describes two women visiting the queen Atossa, whom she identified by their Doric and Persian dress as representing Hellas and Asia, respectively (180–182).

subjected females. Typically, male personifications could be found for a demos, a river, a mountain, or an abstraction like Nomos.[43]

To illustrate the interpretive complexities of identifying and interpreting personifications, we may consider "The Boscoreale Figure Paintings" (ca. late first century BCE), which originally contained nine painting panels, of which only six survive.[44] The north wall panels featured Venus supporting a shooting Cupid and on either side the three Graces and then Bacchus and Ariadne. The eastern wall features in its center a naked man and dressed women seated on a double throne. The facing central composition on the western wall shows two women, both seated with a Macedonian shield between them. The more elevated woman wears a Macedonian καυσία [a mountaineer's cap] with diadems holding a spear or staff; the other, in the lower right, is a rather large woman, heavily garbed with the distinctive headdress of a Persian tiara crumpled with forehead vailed, showing subjection. After surveying four interpretations, Martin Robertson considers the identification of the more elevated woman:

> We take the figure with the καυσία for a personification of Macedonia. Local personifications are, of course, common in Hellenistic art. A particularly good parallel to our figure is offered by the Aetolia on coins issued towards the middle of the third century by the Aetolian League. The figure on the coins is probably copied from an image of Aetolia as an armed woman which Pausanias mentions as dedicated at Delphi by the League after the repulse of the Gauls in 279 B.C.... She holds a spear, and even wears a καυσία [a mountaineer's cap] but without the diadem. She sits on a pile of Gallic, or in some dies Macedonian, shields-trophies of war, unlike the single, boldly displayed shield in the Boscoreale picture.[45]

Robertson posits that what was represented is the Macedonian victory over Persia. Indeed, the gaze of each woman is telling: The Macedonian stares resolutely at Persia, and Persia in thoughtful pose angrily glares back. Consequently, on the facing western wall, the enthroned couple is most likely the husband representing Macedonia, Alexander, and the woman, Persia, as the wife, Statira, the eldest daughter of Darius. Taken as a whole, the composition signifies "the unity of the world, and the

---

43. Martin Robertson, "The Boscoreale Figure-Paintings," *JRS* 45 (1955): 63.
44. My description and wording is dependent on Robertson, "Boscoreale Figure-Paintings." However, the resolute gazes of Macedonia and Persia is my interpretation.
45. Ibid., 61.

absorption of East and West under one rule, was a theme of deep and immediate concern to Romans of the first century B.C."[46] In the end, this brief example demonstrates the replication of prototypical scenes and attributes, the ubiquity of the imagery, and the structural and thematic representation of power relations in the Roman era.

Increasingly during the period of Augustus, the subjugated nations and islands were featured prominently on Roman victory art as ethnic female personifications in the following monuments:[47]

- Pompey's Theater (fourteen nations; Pliny, *Nat.* 36.41; Suetonius, *Nero* 46)
- Porticus ad Nationes (all the nations) by Augustus (Servius, *Ad Aen.* 8.721; Pliny, *Nat.* 36.39)
- Ara Pacis with small ethnic figures
- Forum Augusti (Spain and other nations named, although perhaps not personified in form; Velleius, *Hist. rom.* 2.39.2)
- The Altar of Augustus at Lugdunum was decorated with sixty nations (Strabo, *Geog.* 4.192)
- Augustus's funeral (all the nations acquired by him were carried in the procession; Cassius Dio, *Hist. rom.* 56.34.2; Tacitus, *Ann.* 1.8.4)

The nations and islands so depicted were "similar to the categories of the [Augustan] *Res Gestae*, chs. 26–33: some 'recovered,' some defeated, some 'pacified' (= Romanized)."[48]

Much nearer to Ephesus, Augustus's national personifications of subjugated nations were programmatically replicated in the remarkable Sebasteion at Aphrodisias.[49] The privately constructed imperial temple complex in the Julio-Claudian period contained reliefs and statuary "to create visual allegory for imperial rule."[50] The temple's construction by wealthy local families began during Tiberius's reign and was finished

---

46. Ibid., 64.
47. Smith, "Simulacra gentium," 71–74; Smith, "The Imperial Reliefs from the Sebasteion at Aphrodisias," *JRS* 77 (1987): 96.
48. Smith, "Simulacra gentium," 59.
49. Joyce M. Reynolds, "New Evidence for the Imperial Cult in Julio-Claudian Aphrodisias," *ZPE* (1981): 226–27; followed by Smith, "Simulacra gentium," 58.
50. Smith, "Imperial Reliefs," 119.

under Nero; it was dedicated "to Aphrodite, the Sebasteion gods, and to the demos." The three-storied temple structure contained relief panels on the upper two tiers. On the north portico, the surviving upper tier panels show Day and Ocean personified, portraying the unbounded scope of Roman rule. On the facing southern upper tier, the motif of Roman Victory is heralded. For example, godlike naked Claudius subdues half-naked and fallen Britannia and Nero is victorious over naked Armenia—these nations represented Roman conquest from the rising (Armenia) to the setting sun (Britannia).[51] Also here, panels show Roma standing over the earth and in another deified Augustus with nimbus as savior-benefactor of personified Land and Sea. Returning to the north portico, the second story showed fifty personified nations under Roman rule. Smith summarizes the purpose of the north-portico allegories "to suggest and illustrate a grandiose identification of the physical world and the Roman Empire. Taken together, the north-portico reliefs seem to speak the language of empire without end, imperial conquest by land and sea, night and day."[52]

Among these top tiered reliefs at Aphrodisias, Roman imperial dominance is shown by fifty named female nations personified in various states of conquest and civility, from naked and fallen dead to properly dressed and standing upright (representing Romanization), and differing states in between. For example, some nations like "the Thracian Bessi, stand in classical pose with arms free, hair properly coiffed, head covered and peplos properly arranged, to signify full incorporation and civilization under Roman rule."[53] Differently, Dacia was presented in the process of civilization: arms crossed as if bound (but not tied), uncovered and uncoiffed hair, peplos falling off of one shoulder with a bare breast, and Jupiter's eagle standing behind, ominously gazing upward checking her state of Romanization.[54] Typically, "the bared breast and the gesture of the crossed arms are parts of the regular iconography of conquered 'barbarian' female figure."[55] If such personification was commonly occurring on dedicatory inscriptions and repeatedly observed visually in monumentation, what

---

51. Descriptions from Smith, "Simulacra gentium," 77.
52. Smith, "Imperial Reliefs," 96.
53. Maier, *Picturing Paul in Empire*, 87.
54. My summary of Dacia (minus Jupiter's eagle and unbound hands [see also Smith, "Simulacra gentium," 64]) is also dependent on Maier. See his discussion of these personifications in view of Colossians (pp. 77–80, 87–89).
55. Smith, "Simulacra gentium," 63.

implications might this have for the representation of the church assembly in Ephesians?

4. God's People are Seated with Christ "in the Heavenly Realms" (ἐν τοῖς ἐπουρανίοις [1:3, 20–21; 2:4–7])

The first spatial indicator in Ephesians is the recurring phrase "in the heavenly realms" (1:3, 20; 2:6; 3:10; 6:12).[56] Among commentators, no consensus exists on the origins or importance of the term ἐπουράνιος, which ranges from understanding it against a Jewish or early Christian liturgical background as well as often simultaneously in a modern existential-spatial sense.[57] For example, Frank Thielman interprets ἐπουράνιος

---

56. We observe in 1:3 that this prepositional phrase (PP) participates in an aurally emphatic list of three PPs all beginning with ἐν. Furthermore, each PP is emphatic: the first PP because of its inclusive scope with πᾶς and additional adjective (ἐν πάσῃ εὐλογίᾳ πνευματικῇ); the last PP because of the final position, repetition (used 4x prior!), and referentiality of the agent Christ (ἐν Χριστῷ); and the second PP because of the prepositional affix ἐπ- on the adjective οὐράνιος, transforming it into the socially recognizable pagan/imperially occupied space (ἐν τοῖς ἐπουρανίοις). See further below.

57. Andrew T. Lincoln is only able to conclude of ἐν τοις ἐπουρανίοις that it has a local meaning in all five occurrences in Ephesians ("A Re-Examination of 'the Heavenlies' in Ephesians," *NTS* 19 [1973]: 468–83). Again, Lincoln concludes, "The origin of the expression is uncertain, though it may well have been a traditional formulation from the worship of the early church on analogy with such expressions as ἐν τοῖς ὑψίστοις (Mark 11:10) or ἐν ὑψηλοῖς (Heb 1:3)" (*Ephesians*, 20). Rudolf Schnackenburg relates its origin to "the Jewish apocalyptic conception of the world," although it is significantly altered in Ephesians (*The Epistle to the Ephesians: A Commentary*, trans. Helen Heron [Edinburgh: T&T Clark, 1991], 77). Schlier's existentialist view is summarized by his comment: "τὰ ἐπουράνια means the 'transcendent' as the dimension of encompassing, manifold power, which enlarges and raises (or deepens), approaches and demands and places in the conflict the earthly existence as if in this heaven. In it, however, at the predominate place and in the predominate rule a person also dwells, if one is 'in Christ'" (*Der Brief an die Epheser*, 45–48, quote at 48). This compares with the conclusion of Walter Wink: "'The heavenlies,' in short, is that dimension of reality of which the believer becomes aware as a result of being 'raised up' by God with Christ. It is a heightened awareness, the consciousness of a noumenal realm in which the final contest for the lordship of all reality is being waged.... But it is not simply a state of rapture. It is an actual, new, epistemic standpoint which surpasses gnosis (Eph. 3:19), and the believer's comprehension pertains not just to the things of God, but also to the reality, deceptions, and delusionary snares of evil" (*Naming the Powers: The Language of Power in the New Testament* [Philadelphia: Fortress, 1984], 89, 92). However, Wesely

within a Jewish context and concludes that it refers to "a dimension of existence that is beyond common, everyday experience."[58] However, such a view completely ignores the Greco-Roman understanding of the space as signifying the highest spatial realm of the gods and deceased apotheosized political rulers. Thus, the occurrences of ἐπουράνιος in Ephesians betray a "contested space."

In Ephesians, the heavenly realms are the location of God's blessings in Christ (1:3). This verse is elaborated grammatically in 1:4–14, moving from past (precreation), to present, to future time. Within this section, 1:10 describes the grandest view of Christ's role: "to sum up/head up [ἀνακεφαλαιώσασθαι] all things, the things in the heavens and the things in the earth [τὰ ἐπὶ τοῖς οὐρανοῖς καὶ τὰ ἐπὶ τῆς γῆς]." What is meant by "all things"? In the LXX, ἐπί ("on," "in," "upon") with οὐρανός in the accusative case always describes God's complete supremacy of position over, above, and riding on the heaven(s) (Deut 33:26; Pss 56:6, 12; 67:34; 107:6; 112:4; Ps. Sol. 2:30 [with the genitive]).[59] However, in Eph 1:10, ἐπί takes the dative case and the prepositional phrase belongs to an appositional nominalization in which τὰ πάντα ("all things") are further described in the space of the heavens and earth. Two points must be made here. First, ἐπί with the dative answers the question "where?"[60] In the plural within the New Testament, the phrase refers to a place of location "within which."[61] Thus, whatever the meaning of the "things," their locations are

---

Carr's understanding of its use in Ephesians is only partially correct: the term arises out of a "Christologically determined world view" aiming to achieve "the glorification of Christ" (*Angels and Principalities: The Background, Meaning, and Development of the Pauline Phrase Hai archai kai hai exousiai*, SNTSMS 42 [Cambridge: Cambridge University Press, 1981], 98, cf. 96–97). For Carr, τὰ ἐπουράνια has a "Christological-local sense" and "figuratively local sense" that avoids a metaphysical dualism while maintaining a moral dualism and only serves to magnify and glorify the Messiah.

58. Frank Thielman, *Ephesians*, BECNT (Grand Rapids: Baker, 2010), 47.

59. So unusual is this expression that a number of Greek manuscripts use the conjunction ἐν "in" rather than ἐπί "upon" (ℵ² A F G K P Ψ 33 81 104 323 365 945 1175 1739 1881 2464 *pm* sy^h Ambrose).

60. BDAG, s.v. "ἐπί," 1.b.α. and 2.b.

61. Thus, Mark 1:45 ("in the unpopulated areas"); Heb 11:38 ("in deserts and mountains and caves and holes in the ground"). It designates a specific location, though, in Rev 21:12 ("at the gates"), as is often the case in the singular: John 4:6 ("at the well"); Acts 3:11 ("at the portico"); Eph 2:20 ("on the foundation"); Rev 4:9; 5:13; 7:10; 19:4; 21:5 "on the throne"; 9:14 ("at the great river").

in the heavens and earth. Second, the exact referent of "all things" is best delimited to "*events* in the heavens and on the earth." Typically, however, interpreters understand τὰ πάντα to refer to the whole cosmos and/or all beings and creatures.[62] However, "events" are more likely in view since the infinitive construction "to sum/head up all things in the Messiah" either explains God's appointment of him "for management of the fulfillment of the times" (εἰς οἰκονομίαν τοῦ πληρώματος τῶν καιρῶν) or is a further development of this notion. In either case, God's plan of salvation history as "times" (καιροί) is in view; such "times" are attested in Jewish-Christian apocalyptic texts.[63] Second, the idea of "all things" is surrounded in Eph 1:9 and 1:11 by the enactment of God's "good pleasure" (εὐδοκία), "will" (θέλημα), "purpose" (πρόθεσις), and "plan" (βουλή), which more naturally describe events in salvation history than to creatures in creation.[64] So, Eph 1:10 envisions the heavenly and earthly spaces within time that are under the management of the Christ.

Outside of 1:4-14, ἐπουράνιος occurs in prominent locations. First, Christ himself is seated in the heavenly realms at God's right hand far above over "every rule and authority and power and lordship and every named being named" (1:20-21); this list is presented with polysyndeton (καί ... καί ... καί ... καί) and thus stresses the individual members of the list and "produces the impression of extensiveness and abundance by means of an exhausting summary" (BDF §460). Christ is above these positions of human and suprahuman political power "in this age and in the age to come."[65] Second, believers are elevated to a position of sitting with Christ (2:6), probably at death. Sitting on a throne commonly depicted

---

62. For example, Schnackenburg, *Epistle to the Ephesians*, 60-61; John Muddiman, *The Epistle to the Ephesians*, BNTC 10 (London: Continuum, 2001), 76. Harold W. Hoehner sees the creation in view, but he sees implications of reconciliation especially for its beings (*Ephesians: An Exegetical Commentary* [Grand Rapids: Baker Academic, 2002], 223). Markus Barth is tempted to understand "all things" as meaning the whole world, but finally understands them as "beings" in 1:10 (*Ephesians 1–3: A New Translation with Introduction and Commentary*, AB 34 [New York: Doubleday, 1974], 89, 175).

63. Luke 21:23-24; see also Acts 1:6-8; Rom 11:25; Gal 4:4; Tob 14:5; 2 Bar. 40:3; 4 Ezra 4:33-37; T. Benj. 11.3; 1QpHab VII, 13-14; 1QM I, 12.

64. In this regard, interpreters often see Eph 1:10 in light of Col 1:16-17; but the context in Col 1:16 is very different from that in Eph 1:10, evoking as it does "the creation of all things" (ἐκτίσθη τὰ πάντα).

65. Long, "Roman Imperial Rule," 124-33.

a god reigning.⁶⁶ Also, conquering rulers sitting on thrones was a commonplace in the Mediterranean world. For example, the *Gemma Augustea* shows divine Augustus sitting Jupiter-like over the conquered nations. Again, a silver cup from Boscoreale depicts Augustus receiving abject homage from those captured from Tiberius's campaign. Commonly, Jupiter is shown sitting on a throne in coinage of Nero (Corinth, Rome) and Vindex (Gaul) in the mid- to late 60s.⁶⁷ Presumably, such believers seated with Christ on thrones are counted among "the heavenly ones." Third, in 3:10 the church assembly on earth displays God's wisdom to "the (earthly) rulers and to the authorities in the heavenly places" (ταῖς ἀρχαῖς καὶ ταῖς ἐξουσίαις ἐν τοῖς ἐπουρανίοις). We must notice that the two Greek articles differentiate these two groups; arguably the "rulers" are human scale and the "authorities" represent heavenly scale. Finally, in 6:12 believers struggle "against the spiritual entities of evil in the heavenly places" (πρὸς τὰ πνευματικὰ τῆς πονηρίας ἐν τοῖς ἐπουρανίοις). What entities inhabit the heavenly realms against which the church assembly struggles and might benefit by the show of God's wisdom within the church assembly?

Looking at the philological data the answer is clear: "pagan deities," including increasingly deceased, apotheosized emperors and their family members. From Homer onward, the adjective ἐπουράνιος, used substantively or attributively, could refer to one spatially localized class of pagan gods, the heavenly ones.⁶⁸ In inscriptions, mostly from Asia Minor, the adjective denoted named and unnamed gods. A full treatment of this term in relation to Phil 2:10—"of the heavenly ones, the earthly ones, and the subterranean ones" (ἐπουρανίων καὶ ἐπιγείων καὶ καταχθονίων)—is forthcoming.⁶⁹ Suffice

---

66. In the Apoc. Sedr. 7:2, the seer while pleading the fate of sinful asks before God in heaven asks "Am I alone supposed to fill the heavenly realms?" (μὴ γὰρ ἐγὼ μόνος γεμίσω τὰ ἐπουράνια;). The assumption is that the heavenly realms can be filled only by those worthy. Cf. the discussions of the heavenly realms in T. Job 36.3; 38.5; and 40.3 with Job's wife Sitis, who sees her children "crowned with the glory of the heavenly One" (ἐστεφανωμένα παρὰ τῇ δόξῃ τοῦ ἐπουρανίου).

67. *BMC* 1:209 (no. 67), 212 (no. 87), 214 (no. 110), and 297 (no. 31); cf. 267 (no. 338; Lugdunum) with Securitas seated on a throne (rev.) and head of Nero (obv.) and 212 (no. 87; Rome) with Salus seated on a throne; these are cited by E. Mary Smallwood, *Documents Illustrating the Principates of Nerva, Trajan and Hadrian* (Cambridge: Cambridge University Press, 1966), 34 (nos. 59–60), 35 (no. 61), 37 (no. 66), and 38 (no. 70d).

68. LSJ, s.v. "ἐπουράνιος," §§1–2.

69. Fredrick J. Long and Ryan Giffin, "'Every Knee Bowed': Christ as Reign-

it to say here that these three terms (plus, less frequently, ἐνάλιοι ["marine"]) describe the major domains of the gods, who are understood spatially as occupying such locations. Thus, Julius Pollux, the second-century CE Egyptian Greek grammarian, describes this regional taxonomy of gods by listing Attic synonyms and phrases by subject matter. Herein, he identified each of these four regional deities (heavenly, earthly, marine, and subterranean).[70] The taxonomy is nearly identical to that of Aelius Aristides (from Asia Minor), who in his encomium "For Zeus" (Εἰς Δία, section 18) delivered circa 149 CE at Smyrna, describes four regions of the gods—heaven, air, sea, and earth—by design of Zeus. The taxonomy, however, is much earlier than is reflected formally in these authors, since Vergil praises Octavian by appeal to the fourfold pattern of identifying him with the earth, sea, and sky gods, but rejecting the gods of the lower realms (*Geor.* 1.25–39). It is as if Vergil was musing, "It is doubtful which society of gods you are to join, gods of earth, of sea, or of sky (certainly not gods of the underworld)."[71]

Additionally, the Roman aristocracy in the first century BCE to the second century CE increasingly conceived of their deceased family members as populating heaven. Through Scipio's Dream, Cicero affirmed that worthy human spirits entered the heavenly places as gods under the "supreme God" (*princeps deus* [*Rep.* 6.26]). Central in the dream is how to attain to this reward (6.13, 15, 16, 18, 20, 25, 26, 29), which is the spirit's proper "seat and home" (*sedem et domum* [6.29]). The elder Scipio explains: "To all who have preserved, assisted, and increased their fatherland a special place is prepared for them in heaven.... Their rulers and protectors have come from here, and to here do they return" (6.13).[72]

---

ing Lord over 'the Heavenly, the Earthly, and the Subterranean gods' (Phil 2:10)," in *Philippi*, vol. 4 of *The First Urban Christians*, ed. James R. Harrison and Laurence L. Welborn (Atlanta: SBL Press, forthcoming).

70. Julius Pollux (*Onom.* apud Suda 1.23.4–24.10) presents the following (given here in the order preserved, with only my comments in parentheses): (heavenly =) θεοὶ ὑπερουράνιοι, ἐνουράνιοι, ἐπουράνιοι, ἐναιθέριοι, ἐναέριοι· (earthly =) ἐπίγειοι, οἱ αὐτοὶ καὶ ἐπιχθόνιοι· (marine =) ἐνάλιοι, θαλάττιοι, οἱ αὐτοὶ καὶ ἐνθαλάττιοι, (subterranean =) ὑπόγειοι, χθόνιοι καὶ ὑποχθόνιοι καὶ καταχθόνιοι (various gods in what follows).

71. So summarizes Gertrude Hirst, "A Discussion of Some Passages in the Prologue to the Georgics (I. 14, 15 and 27)," *TAPA* 59 (1928): 28–29.

72. Cicero's views on this point correspond with the Orphic view, as explained by Max Radin: "We have only to remember the Orphic conception, emphasized in a hundred ways by writers from Euripides to Aristotle, to the effect that the human soul does not merely become divine at the death of the body, but that it always was divine,

Ovid affirmed that Romulus was "placed in heaven" (*inponere caelo*) and given a form "more dignified for the divine seats of honor" (*pulvinaribus altis dignior* [*Metam.* 14.805–828]). So, too, the emperor (exemplified by Augustus) displays wisdom before ascending at death to "the heavenly seats [*aetherias sedes*] and his related stars" (15.832–839). By the mid-second century CE, Lucian's satire, "Parliament of the Gods," describes heavenly conversations to determine which humans have divine descent and may be admitted. The humorous scene depicts the gods holding a hearing before taking a vote on the bill proposed by Momus that a divine commission be established to vet new claims to deity status (humans must bring witnesses to that effect) and that each god must work within their apportioned profession (prophecy, music, medicine, etc.).

Importantly, in Asia Minor we also observe the adjective ἐπουράνιος ascribed to Caesar Augustus, placing him among the heavenly gods. The demos of Erythrai (a coastal Ionian city of Asia Minor) makes this dedication: "The demos to Gaius Julius Augustus Caesar heavenly god" (ὁ δῆμος Γαίωι Ἰουλίωι Σεβαστῶι Καίσαρι θεῶι ἐπουρανίωι [IErythrai 63 (n.d.)]). In Northern Asia Minor (Pontus and Paphlagonia) during Claudius's reign (45–54 CE) another inscription acknowledges the peace (εἰρήνη) of Augustus, honors Caesar Claudius, and affirms Gaius Aquila as "the high priest of the heavenly god Augustus" (ὁ τοῦ ἐπουρανίου θεοῦ Σεβαστοῦ ἀρχιερεύς).[73] In 62 CE, Nero was deemed "heavenly Zeus" (οὐρανίοιο Διός) in an epigram of Leonides of Alexandria, one of Nero's flattering clients.[74] Just how common such accolades were, we cannot

---

and that at bodily death it returns to its divine condition.... To the masses, no doubt, each deification of an emperor merely added a new denizen to Olympus. But to some it was more intelligible to consider the process, a return of an incarnated deity to his former state. Thus Julius Caesar was worshipped as Iuppiter Iulius, Livia was Ceres. Later, Hadrian, too, was Jupiter" ("Apotheosis," *CR* 30 [1916]: 45).

73. Text published in Christian Marek, "Katalog der Inschriften von Amastris," in *Stadt, Ära und Territorium in Pontus-Bithynia und Nord-Galatia*, IF 39 (Tübingen: Wasmuth, 1993), no. 1c; cf. 1a. The opening of the Greek version is as follows: "On behalf of the peace of Augustus and for the honor of Tiberius Claudius Germanicus Caesar Augustus, the high priest of the heavenly god Augustus for life Gaius Aquila, praefect twice." The parallel Latin inscription makes no reference of "heavenly" and simply has *divi Augusti* ("divine Augustus"), likely indicating the attributive importance of ἐπουράνιος in the Greek conceptions of divinity.

74. Denys L. Page, ed., *Further Greek Epigrams: Epigrams before A.D. 50 from the Greek Anthology and Other Sources, Not Included in 'Hellenistic Epigrams' or*

know for certain. However, the praise of the emperor went beyond words and was pervasively visual, including the imperial Sebastoi gods. Many images across the empire depict the Caesar and/or family members ascending or already ascended (*apotheosis*; *consecration*) as heavenly gods.[75] Already, mention has been made of the ideological nature of reliefs at the Sebasteion at Aphrodisias involving Julio-Claudian members as gods. Nero struck a coin near to his inauguration (54 CE) depicting the recently deceased emperor Claudius as a god (*divus*) gloriously radiate (with pointed crown) alongside Augustus who was acclaimed god on thrones riding the four-elephant chariot (indicating godlike status) in heavenly splendor (*RIC* 1 Nero 10). The heavenly placement and residence of the Sebastoi (deceased emperor and select family members) is presupposed in the dozens of imperial temples and shrines found across Asia Minor, especially Ephesus.[76] Fernado Lozano produces a chart that compares the more prevalent celebration of apotheosis in Athens to those in Rome; this chart is apropos for Asia Minor too, since Lozano admits such charts could be produced for each city.[77] Thus, the stress placed on the church assembly in Ephesians as occupying the heavenly realms elevates it to a coruling position of Christ at God's right hand as a counterclaim, if even a trumping claim, to the elitist claim of Roman imperial apotheosis.

5. The Church Assembly as the Body of Christ, Its Head (1:22–23; 2:16; 3:6; 4:4, 12, 15–16; 5:23, 30)

The most prominent metaphor for the church assembly is "body" in relation to Christ as the "head." In 1:22, Christ "as head [κεφαλή] over all

---

'*The Garland of Philip*' (Cambridge: Cambridge University Press, 1981), 533, no. 29, translated in Robert K. Sherk, *The Roman Empire: Augustus to Hadrian*, TDGR (Cambridge: Cambridge University Press, 1988), 110, no. 70a.

75. See, esp., Fernando Lozano, "Divi Augusti and Theoi Sebastoi: Roman Initiatives and Greek Answers," *CQ* 57 (2007): 142. He helpfully distinguishes Theoi Sebastoi (a larger set in the Greek East) and the Divi Augusti (a smaller set for Rome and the West): "*Sebastoi* are then the group of members of the imperial family, male and female, whose divine worship has been approved by the competent institution of a particular political entity, city or league" (146).

76. For a discussion of which, see Lozano, "Divi Augusti." For the proliferation and an accounting of the imperial cult sites and temples, see Price, *Rituals and Power*.

77. Lozano, "Divi Augusti," 143.

things for the convened assembly" employs a well-known *political* topos, already found in some form in the notion of "head/tail" (Deut 28:13, 44) and "head" as "ruler" (ἄρχων) in the LXX (see esp. Ps 18 LXX).[78] The head-body analogy existed in the early to mid-first century within Hellenistic, Stoic political thought (Q. Curtius Rufus, *Hist. Alex.* 10.9.1; Philo, *Praem.* 114, 125) and subsequently (see, e.g., Tacitus, *Ann.* 1.12.12; Plutarch, *Galba* 4.3).[79] Seneca in 54 CE deploys the metaphor strategically in *De clementia* (1.3.5; 1.5.1; 2.2.1) relating the Roman state to the "body" of the emperor.[80] For example, Seneca made a request of Nero: "For if ... you are the soul of the state and the state your body [*corpus*], you see, I think, how requisite is mercy: for you are merciful to yourself when you are seemingly merciful to another. And so even reprobate citizens should have mercy as being the weak members [*membris*] of the body" (*Clem.* 1.3.5).[81] Political headship is explicitly related to power: "For while Caesar needs power, the state also needs a head," argued Seneca (*Clem.* 1.4.3).[82] The predominance of the head-body imagery throughout Ephesians parallels the political metaphor in currency at the middle of the first century CE.

Corresponding to Caesar as the head of the empire was Rome deified as the goddess Roma, a phenomenon of the Greek East.[83] Ronald Mellor explains the history and religious significance of Roma:

---

78. Schlier, "κεφαλή, ἀνακεφαλαιόομαι," *TDNT* 3:674–76. Barth overstates the case when he says: "The proclamation of Christ's resurrection in Eph 1:20–23 is made in political terms, couched in the political language of OT royal psalms; the term 'head' has a distinctly political meaning which is not Greek but Hebrew" (*Ephesians 1–3*, 169).

79. References are from Lincoln, who supports this background (*Ephesians*, 69). See the discussion and conclusions of Charles H. Talbert, *Ephesians and Colossians*, Paideia (Grand Rapids: Baker Academic, 2007), 86–88. See also the very carefully argued dismissal of the gnostic background to the head-body imagery in J. Paul Sampley, *"And the Two Shall Become One Flesh": A Study of Traditions in Ephesians 5:21–33*, SNTSMS 16 (Cambridge: Cambridge University Press, 1971), 61–66.

80. See also the discussion of Michelle V. Lee, *Paul, the Stoics, and the Body of Christ*, SNTSMS 137 (Cambridge: Cambridge University Press, 2006), 37–38.

81. The quotation is from Sampley, *Two Shall Become One Flesh*, 65.

82. Quotation from John W. Basore, trans., *Seneca: Moral Essays*, vol. 1, LCL 214 (Cambridge: Harvard University Press, 1928). Allan P. Ball argues that, "considered as the head of the empire, the imperial figure was a concrete illustration of the principle of a world-wide Providence" ("Theological Utility of the Caesar Cult," *CJ* 5 [1910]: 307).

83. David E. Aune summarizes, "The goddess Roma was not known in Rome

The goddess Roma had always played a political role.... Roma existed solely as a divine embodiment of the Romans themselves and thus would not be honored by them.... She [Roma], like *patria*, symbolized Rome past as well as Rome present. This use of Roma enabled the destinies of the imperial house to be linked with those of the state—the title *pater patriae* is one expression of this and the association of Roma and Augustus is another. The goddess was represented as a traditional divinity. Sometimes a warrior, sometimes a mother-figure, she had always to draw on the attributes of other gods since she herself had no history, no myth.[84]

Historically, Roma's bust was used first on coinage before being eclipsed by the Caesars starting with Julius.[85] The importance of the historical relationship—Caesar added to Roma rather than replacing her—was seen in the Greek East. "In the provinces the regulation was that temples were acceptable only if Dea Roma shared in the cult" with the emperor (Suetonius, *Aug.* 52).[86] Such a temple was built by the Asian League at Pergamum (Tacitus, *Ann.* 4.37.4); an altar was found even in the small village of Choriani near Hierocaesareia, and in Galatia a cult to Caesar and Roma existed during the reign of Tiberius.[87] Herod built a very notable temple at Caesarea Maritima containing statues of Caesar Augustus (in imitation of Jupiter Olympius) and Roma (like Juno at Argos) that could be seen from a far distance out in the sea as one came into the harbor (Josephus, *J.W.* 1.414; *Ant.* 15.339).[88] The apostle Paul was held two years at Caesarea

---

itself before the beginning of the second century A.D. Hadrian (A.D. 117–38) was the first emperor actually to introduce the cult of Roma to the city of Rome" (*Revelation 17–22*, WBC 52C [Dallas: Word, 1998], 922).

84. Ronald Mellor, ΘΕΑ 'ΡΩΜΑ: *The Worship of the Goddess Roma in the Greek World*, Hypomnemata 42 (Göttingen: Vandenhoeck & Ruprecht, 1975), 199–200.

85. Never before had a person been so featured on Roman coins. See Larry Kreitzer, "Apotheosis of the Roman Emperor," *BA* 53 (1990): 212.

86. Duncan Fishwick, "Dio and Maecenas: The Emperor and the Ruler Cult," *Phoenix* 44 (1990): 270.

87. Thomas Robert Shannon Broughton, "Roman Landholding in Asia Minor," *TAPA* 65 (1934): 216; *OGIS* 2.533, translated in Sherk, *Roman Empire*, 73–75.

88. Fishwick, "Dio and Maecenas," 270; Kenneth G. Holum, "Caesarea's Temple Hill: The Archaeology of Sacred Space in an Ancient Mediterranean City," *NEA* 67 (2004): 184–99; "Building Power—The Politics of Architecture," *BAR* 30.5 (2004): 36–45, 57.

Maritima when he appealed to Caesar (Acts 23:23; 25:8–12, 21; 26:32; 27:24; 28:19). Specifically in Ephesus, Mellor summarizes the evidence,

> Ephesus shows the clearest historical development of the cults of Roma: ... [first] a temple of Roma established with the priesthood; a statue of Caesar erected in 48 with a cult after 40; the temple of 29 dedicated to Rome and Divus Julius; a new (or rebuilt) temple dedicated to Roma and Augustus and called the Augusteum ... placed in or adjacent to, the temenos of the Artemision by the Ephesians before 5/6 BCE.[89]

Mellor adds, "The Cult of Roma was important at Ephesus and a temple of the goddess is likely." In this way, imperial worship invaded even the magnificent Temple of Artemis in Ephesus. Importantly, the temple phenomenon of Roma as a consort of the Caesars is a foil for the church assembly in Ephesians.

6. The Church Assembly Constructed as a Temple for God (2:11–22)

A striking metaphor in 2:11–22 blends humans with sacred place of temple. This discourse unit, arranged chiastically, is replete with Jewish and Roman political themes—for example, political leadership, covenants, citizenship, law, peace, unity, reconciliation, and temple construction.[90] Of these, the discourse concludes with the latter climactically in Eph 2:20–22: The new humanity in one body has been built "into a holy temple in the Lord ... a dwelling place of God in the Spirit" (εἰς ναὸν ἅγιον ἐν κυρίῳ ... εἰς κατοικητήριον τοῦ θεοῦ ἐν πνεύματι). Robert L. Foster has also argued persuasively for extending the temple imagery into 3:19.[91] Also, Christ's triumphal parade with gifts to persons (4:7–8) and offer of persons as gifts

---

89. Mellor, ΘΕΑ ῬΩΜΑ, 138. For a religious history of Ephesus in relation to Rome, see pp. 56–59; see also Christine M. Thomas, "At Home in the City of Artemis: Religion in Ephesos in the Literary Imagination of the Roman Period," in Koester, *Ephesos*, 107–15. Aune helpful directs us to David Magie, *Roman Rule in Asia Minor*, 2 vols. (Princeton: Princeton University Press, 1950), 2:1613–14, "for a list of cults of Roma alone and Roma together with Augustus" (*Revelation 17–22*, 922–23).

90. For a discussion of the chiasm in relation to specific political topoi, see Long, "Ephesians: Paul's Political Theology," 285–90, 308–9.

91. Robert L. Foster, "'A Temple in the Lord Filled to the Fullness of God': Context and Intertextuality (Eph 3:19)," *NovT* 49 (2007): 85–96.

(4:11) would quite naturally extend the temple metaphor, since generals erected temples from their military "spoils" (*manubiae*).⁹² On this basis, Pompey and others showered Rome with extravagant temples and public works.⁹³

The building of temples became an imperial prerogative. Before the principate, building temples was central for claiming divine approval. The emperor Augustus strategically and quickly co-opted temple building: "After 33 BCE only Augustus and members of his family built temples in Rome.... Temple building placed the emperor in a unique relationship with the gods."⁹⁴ Augustus's self-published *Res gestae* (with Divi Augusti added later) was likely his justification for apotheosis, that is, to become a *divus*.⁹⁵ The work was published in the Greek East; portions have been found at Ancyra of Galatia and Apollonia and Antioch of Pisidia.⁹⁶ He boasted of rebuilding eighty-two temples in Rome (para. 20; for this Ovid

---

92. Olivier Hekster and John Rich, "Octavian and the Thunderbolt: The Temple of Apollo Palatinus and Roman Traditions of Temple Building," *CQ* 56 (2006): 152–55.

93. Hekster and Rich summarize this building: "The tradition of manubial temples and public works was, however, exploited by the two military dynasts of the late Republic, Pompey and Caesar. Pompey's great theatre complex incorporated a temple of Venus Victrix and various lesser shrines, and he also built temples to Hercules and Minerva. Caesar responded by building a new forum from his spoils, incorporating a temple of Venus Genetrix.... In the triumviral and early Augustan periods manubial building by lesser commanders revived. Numerous commanders undertook such work following their triumphs, from L. Munatius Plancus (triumphed 43) to L. Cornelius Balbus, whose triumph in 19 B.C. was the last celebrated by a non-member of the imperial family. Some, like Balbus with his theatre, built new utilitarian structures, but most opted for the grandiose rebuilding of existing monuments. The temples rebuilt in this way were Saturn (Plancus), Apollo in the Circus Flaminius (C. Sosius, triumphed 34), and Hercules of the Muses and Diana on the Aventine (respectively L. Marcius Philippus and L. Cornificius, following triumphs in 33 or 32)" ("Octavian and the Thunderbolt," 153).

94. Simon R. F. Price, "The Place of Religion: Roman in the Early Empire," in *The Augustan Empire 43 B.C.–A.D. 69*, ed. Alan K. Bowman, Edward Champlin, and Andrew Lintott, 2nd ed., CAH 10 (Cambridge: Cambridge University Press, 1996), 831. Older temples were "Romanized" in form (e.g., the Temple of Cybele).

95. Brian Bosworth, "Augustus, the Res Gestae and Hellenistic Theories of Apotheosis," *JRS* 89 (1999): 1–18.

96. See Frederick W. Danker, *Benefactor: Epigraphic Study of a Graeco-Roman and New Testament Semantic Field* (St. Louis, MO: Clayton, 1982), 256–80. Danker records that fragments were found in Ancyra of Galatia, Apollonia in Pisidia, and Antioch of Pisidia (257).

praised him [*Fasti* 2.55–66]). But Augustus strategically took over temples by having his image replace previous political rulers, as, for example, in Thebes, in which he replaced the cult of Ptolemy Soter with Augustus Soter, thus paving the way for the growth of his cult in Egypt.[97]

Matters were much easier in Asia Minor where cities competed for official imperial temples.[98] At the time of Paul's ministry, more than sixty imperial temples and shrines were in use in Asia Minor.[99] For example, despite Tiberius's general refusal of divine honors,[100] "26 deputations from eleven cities of Asia pleaded with Tiberius for the privilege of building a temple in honor of himself, Livia, and the Senate. Smyrna was favored for its past service to Rome."[101] Placement of temples and shrines—in central locations (e.g., the statue of the divine Augustus in the Corinthian forum), at the acropolis, or in areas that allowed for expansion—was strategic and symbolic.[102] The cult rewarded the local

---

97. For details of Augustus's stratagem, which appears limited according to A. D. Nock ("Σύνναος Θεός," *HSCP* 41 [1930]: 42–43), see Walter Otto, "Augustus Soter," *Hermes* 45 (1910): 448–60.

98. On the provincial, civic, and social motivation for the establishment of the cult and its benefits, see Sara Karz Reid, *The Small Temple: A Roman Imperial Cult Building in Petra, Jordan*, GSCLA 9 (Piscataway, NJ: Gorgias, 2005), 154–56; Dominique Cuss, *Imperial Cult and Honorary Terms in the New Testament*, Paradosis 23 (Fribourg: University Press, 1974), 101–4. Asia Minor was apparently the first place to venerate the Roman emperors at the end of the first century BCE. Augustus declined worship from Roman citizens, but accepted it from Greco-Asians. Pergamum erected the first temple to Augustus and Roma that involved a chorus "of God Augustus and Goddess Roma" (θεοῦ Σεβαστοῦ καὶ θεᾶς Ρώμης). Another similar temple is found at Ancyra in Galatia (*OGIS* 533.2). With regard to Julius while stilling living, an inscription in Ephesus reads "the god descended from Ares and Aphrodite, manifest and common savior of human life" (τὸν ἀπὸ Ἄρεως κιὰ Ἀφροδείτης θεὸν ἐπιφανῆ καὶ κοινὸν τοῦ ἀνθρωπίνου βίου σωτῆρα [*SIG* 347.6]). His apotheosis followed upon his death in 42 BCE (H. A. A. Kennedy, "Apostolic Preaching and Emperor Worship," *Expositor* 7 [1909]: 295–96).

99. These are described in Price, *Rituals and Power*, 249–74, and listed in Long, "Roman Imperial Rule," 135, n. 73.

100. On this topic, see Martin Percival Charlesworth, "The Refusal of Divine Honours: An Augustan Formula," *PBSR* 14.2 (1939): 1–10; Lily Ross Taylor, "Tiberius' Refusals of Divine Honors," *TAPA* 60 (1929): 87–101; cf. E. A. Fredricksmeyer, "Divine Honors for Philip II," *TAPA* 109 (1979): 39–61.

101. Donald L. Jones, "Christianity and the Roman Imperial Cult," *ANRW* 23.2:1025, citing Tacitus, *Ann.* 4.55–56.

102. Reid, *Small Temple*, 153–54.

aristocracies with citizenship, *priestly* prestige in the imperial cult functions, and high political status within the imperial court or as knights or members of the senatorial order.[103] Not surprisingly, the most common architectural designs on imperial coins are temples and altars, especially in Asia Minor.[104] Jonathan Williams argues, "A further aspect to the spread of temple types on early provincial coins ... was that many of the temples represented were associated with the imperial cult. The coins therefore reflect the Romanization of the religious culture of many eastern cities."[105] In Ephesians, then, believers as a unified political body

---

103. Keith Hopkins summarizes: "local leaders were rewarded with Roman citizenship for aiding and abetting their own subordination.... The greatest provincials, or the most ambitious, progressed from the hierarchy of their own cities to the hierarchy of the provincial council. Some became Priests or High Priests of the imperial cult of the province; and for their pains and in return for their generosity to the provincial metropolis or to the festivities surrounding the cult, they were rewarded with the governor's favour and patronage. Others went on embassies to the capital, to the emperor's court. Through their connections and because of their wealth, some provincials became Roman knights or were given membership of the senatorial order" (*Death and Renewal*, SSRH 2 [Cambridge: Cambridge University Press, 1983], 187; cf. 176).

104. Harold Mattingly says, "The Romans, both individually and as a State, always displayed a passion for building, which finds its full expression in the imperial coinage" (*Roman Coins from the Earliest Times to the Fall of the Western Empire*, 2nd ed. [Chicago: Quadrangle, 1960], 177). He continues, "Temples are naturally well represented" and lists examples (p. 178). Not surprisingly, there are many coins in Asia Minor depicting temples dating from Augustus to Nero. Searching the American Numismatic Society Collection Database at http://numismatics.org/search/, we find emperors (obverse) and temples (reverse) or emporers within temples (obverse): with Augustus minted at Pergamum and Sardis 27 BCE–14 CE (Identifier: 1947.97.386 American Numismatic Society), at Teos 27 BCE–14 CE (*RPC* 1.2511), at Pergamum 27 BCE–14 CE (*RPC* 1.2357, 2364), 19–18 BCE (*RIC* 1² Augustus 506, 507), 4–14 CE (*RPC* 1.2364); with Augustus and Tiberius at Smyrna 14 CE (Identifier: 1944.100.47015 American Numismatic Society); with Tiberius 14–29 CE (*RPC* 1.2369); with Claudius at Pergamum 41–45 CE (*RIC* 1² Claudius 120), at Pergamum 41–54 CE (*RPC* 1.2370), at Ephesus 41–42 CE (*RIC* 1² Claudius 118); with Nero at Koinon Asia 54–68 CE (*RPC* 1.2563, 3558).

105. Jonathan Williams, "Religion and Roman Coins," in *A Companion to Roman Religion*, ed. Jörg Rüpke (Malden, MA: Blackwell, 2007), 150. Regarding the importance of identity formation, Williams also argues, "Images of temples on Roman coins bespeak the emperor's exemplary devoutness, especially when he is their author or restorer.... Temples served as potent emblems of communal religious identity, which was also an important element in the civic and ethnic identities of ancient communities" (148).

could worship and have access to God because Christ's blood and sacrifice reconciled them and became the centerpiece for the construction of a temple space. In short, God in Christ brought salvation (2:5, 8).

7. Christ, the Savior of the Church Body (5:23)

In Ephesians, the traditional household code is completely reframed around Jesus as "Lord" (5:22; 6:1, 4, 7–9) and "Messiah" (5:23–25, 29, 32; 6:5–6).[106] The reframing begins with wives–husbands. Within this, however, is a *hieros gamos* ("sacred marriage") theology, explained well by J. Paul Sampley, who, however, only understands this by analogy to YHWH's relationship to Israel.[107] Also problematic is that Sampley believes that 5:23, "He being the Savior of the body" (αὐτὸς σωτὴρ τοῦ σώματος) breaks up the nice chiasm and is merely parenthetical, meant to distinguish the husband-wife relationship from the Christ-church relationship.[108] However, Sampley assumes that the chiastic center is not in fact the paired

---

106. I have treated this elsewhere with Gupta (Gupta and Long, "Politics of Ephesians," 112–36), but here I am extending this research.

107. Sampley, *Two Shall Become One Flesh*, 37–38; he argues, "It is ultimately possible to see the milieu of the Ephesian hieros gamos in that elusive portrait of YHWH's marriage to Israel. There are, to be sure, reflections of such an understanding already to be found in Hosea, Ezekiel, Jeremiah and other writings in the OT; the idea is carried on, developed and, one suspects, at times even suppressed in later Jewish tradition. At this point, however, such a broad background may be assumed while the antecedent task of finding more specific parallels is carried out." Here, he sees Ezek 16:8–14 as a "highly relevant parallel" depicting YHWH's marriage to Jerusalem (38; so also Hoehner, *Ephesians*, 759). Indeed, the church has taken over much of the imagery once associated with Jerusalem in relation to God (42). Other portions of Hebrew Scripture that are relevant include Song 45–49 and Ps 45, one of the royal psalms (Pss 49–51).

108. As Sampley argues, "What is meant by Christ being the savior of his body, the church, is explicated more fully by the author in his expansion of the section of the Haustafel addressed to the husbands (vv. 25 ff.). On the basis of what has been said in the chapters prior to 5:21, the author of Ephesians can rest his case by simply inserting the parenthetical statement (v. 23 c) as a means of qualifying the correlation of Christ and the husband." The only explanation given is that 5:23c "distinguishes between the husband and Christ and makes clear in this context what the author has stated earlier: there is no power or authority co-extensive with that of Christ" (*Two Shall Become One Flesh*, 125).

element (savior/body) since, in his view, this pairing is not very relevant for the audience.[109]

However, one can describe fairly readily two important points of relevancy. First, in Ephesus and Asia Minor, Caesar was "Savior."[110] In 48 BCE, at Ephesus Julius Caesar was hailed as "the god manifest from Ares and Aphrodite and common savior of human life" (τὸν ἀπὸ Ἄρεως καὶ Ἀφροδε[ί]της θεὸν ἐπιφανῆ καὶ κοινὸν τοῦ ἀνθρωπίνου βίου σωτῆρα [*SIG* 2.760, l. 7]). In 9 BCE, "the Letter of Paulus Fabius Maximus and Decrees by Asians concerning the Provincial Calendar"[111] for the annual swearing in of every public official hailed Augustus as Savior: "She [Providence] gave [χαρισαμένη] to us and those who will come after us a Savior [σωτῆρα] who not only stopped war, but who shall arrange peace [κοσμήσοντα δὲ εἰρήνην]." The inscription in Greek and/or Latin has been found throughout Asia Minor: Priene, Apameia, Eumeneia, Dorlyaion, and the rather small town of Maioneia.[112] A second relevancy is observed across 5:22–33, where Christ and the church are referentially abutted in their grammatical placement five times (5:23, 25, 27, 29, 32). The pair is constantly correlated. Thus, the pairing of Christ as Savior and the church assembly as his body in 5:23 seems strategic ideologically. But why? The pragmatic effect of correlating Christ and the church assembly underscores the latter entity as fully personified and embodied as Christ's consort bride.

---

109. See Talbert, who observes a chiasm of only five elements in 5:23a, 23b, 23c, 24a, and 24b (*Ephesians*, 140). Lincoln states that he does not agree with the assertion that this serves as a chiastic focal point; rather, it is "simply to provide an additional description of Christ's relationship to the Church" (*Ephesians*, 370–71).

110. As summarized by Eva Matthews Sanford, "The oriental idea of a golden age ushered in by a ruler who should be at once the conqueror and savior of mankind, the ruler of the world and the prince of peace, had been established at Rome by the writers of the late republican and the Augustan periods and was a significant aspect of the composite character of the *princeps*" ("Nero and the East," *HSCP* 48 [1937]: 77).

111. This title and the treatment of this honorific inscription are from Danker, *Benefactor*, 215–22. For a further bibliographic reference, see Holland L. Hendrix, "On the Form and Ethos of Ephesians," *USQR* 42 (1988): 14 n. 30. See also Umberto Laffi, "Le iscrizione relative all'introduzione nel 9 a.C. del nuovo calendario della provincia d'Asia," *SCO* 16 (1967): 5–98.

112. For bibliographic information, see Danker, *Benefactor*, 215–16.

Chiastic Structure of Ephesians 5:22–24

5:22 αἱ γυναῖκες [submitting] τοῖς ἰδίοις ἀνδράσιν ("wives *submitting* to their own husbands")
↑ ὡς τῷ κυρίῳ ("as to the Lord") [COMPARISON]

23	A ὅτι <u>ἀνήρ</u> ἐστιν κεφαλὴ	a <u>husband</u> is head
	B τῆς <u>γυναικὸς</u>	of the <u>wife</u>
	C ὡς καὶ ὁ <u>Χριστὸς</u> κεφαλὴ	as <u>Christ</u> is head
	D τῆς <u>ἐκκλησίας</u>,	of the <u>ekklēsia</u>
	E αὐτὸς σωτὴρ	He is Savior
	E' τοῦ σώματος	of the body
24	D' ἀλλὰ ὡς ἡ <u>ἐκκλησία</u> ὑποτάσσεται	As the *ekklēsia* submits
	C' τῷ <u>Χριστῷ</u>,	to <u>Christ</u>
	B' οὕτως καὶ αἱ <u>γυναῖκες</u>	thus also the <u>wives</u>
	A' τοῖς <u>ἀνδράσιν</u> ἐν παντί.	to the husbands.

Throughout Ephesians, the church assembly's relationship with her risen, ascended Lord Messiah Jesus above all other positions of power (1:21–23; 2:5–7; 3:10, 21) corresponds to the most prominent pairing of ruler and ruled in early to mid-first-century Asia Minor, and certainly in Ephesus: Caesar with Roma. In Ephesians, we observe Christ the Savior with church assembly as a deliberate ideological counterposition to Caesar the Savior with Roma.

Moreover, given Christ's priestly offering of himself out of love for the church (5:25; cf. 5:1–2), done to present her as "glorious" (ἔνδοξον [5:27]) within a marital context, it is probably not inconsequential that imperial priesthoods reflected the imperial family pattern of the emperor and his wife: "The contrast with the provincial and civic Roman imperial cult is striking: imperial priests were husband and wife teams, and even if the priestess was separately responsible for the female members of the imperial household the joint 'front' presented was that of a married couple."[113] Likewise, in Ephesians, the married couple reflects the priestly couple of Christ and the church assembly.

---

113. Riet van Bremen, "Family Structures," in *A Companion to the Hellenistic World*, ed. Andrew Erskine (Oxford: Blackwell, 2003), 327.

8. God's Armor on God's People (6:10–18)

Finally, most commentators agree that Eph 6:10–20 represents the epistle's conclusion, summarizing the entire discourse with emotional impact. Graphically, the exalted and personified church assembly aptly dons God's armor while espousing core virtues of truth (belt), justice (breastplate), peace (footwear), faithfulness (shield), salvation (helmet), and the Word of God (sword). Recently, David Janssen has provided an excellent visual exegesis of the armor language in 1 Thess 5:8 and Rom 13:12 against the backdrop of statuary, imperial ideology, and the cuirassed representations of the emperors.[114] The armor of God in Ephesians far surpasses these passages in displaying opposition to the imperial ideology of conquest and subjugation while promoting a different vision for living in the world.

The primary statuary type of emperors is cuirassed (as opposed to divine naked or civilian). Price argues that "it was extremely rare for anyone except the emperor to be shown in armour."[115] However, the gods were commonly depicted in armor, as Ernst H. Kantorowicz has so well described historically; this especially occurs under Roman domination, although the practice predates Rome.[116] Among Kantorowicz's six conclusions to account for this, the final two are most germane: "(5) the interrelation of *imitatio deorum* ["imitation of the gods"] on the part of the emperors and *imitatio imperatorum* ["imitation of the empire"] on the part of the gods; (6) the tendency to romanize the *dii peregrini* ["foreign gods"] by means of displaying them in military attire."[117] Although "Christ in military attire ... is rather rare,"[118] rather strikingly, in Ephesians believ-

---

114. David Janssen, "The Roman Cuirass Breastplate Statue and Paul's Use of Armour Language in Romans 13:12 and 1 Thessalonians 5:8," *Colloq* 46 (2014): 55–85. For his visual exegesis, he draws upon the work of Vernon K. Robbins, Harry O. Maier, and Rosemary Canavan. See Canavan, *Clothing the Body of Christ at Colossae: A Visual Construction of Identity*, WUNT 2.334 (Tübingen: Mohr Siebeck, 2012); and, most recently, Canavan, "Visual Exegesis: Interpreting Text in Dialogue with Its Visual Context," *Colloq* 47 (2015): 141–51; Maier, "Come and See: The Promise of Visual Exegesis," *Colloq* 47 (2015): 152–57.
115. Price, *Rituals and Power*, 180–88, quote at 186.
116. Ernst H. Kantorowicz, "Gods in Uniform," *APSP* 105 (1961): 368–93.
117. Ibid., 384.
118. Ibid., 385.

ers wear Roman-like armor. In the end, Christ's consort, the personified church assembly, rivals the goddess Roma.[119]

Such armor, then, represents a counterideology opposed to what was reflected within the environs of Ephesus. Believers stand ready to advance an alternative gospel of peace that does not subject and assimilate the nations as the Romans had done. In contrast to the reliefs of Aphrodisias that depict fallen nations dominated by Roman emperors as ineffectual, the church assembly is urged to "stand against" (ἀντιστῆναι) and to "stand firm" (στῆναι)—a civic if not even cultic virtue.[120] At the same time, the church assembly continues to pray for Paul to proclaim boldly the mystery of the gospel, even as he is an "ambassador in chains" (6:20, πρεσβεύω ἐν ἁλύσει). In this resisting and military-like stance, the church assembly imitates the suffering and dying Christ (1:7; 2:13, 15–16; 5:1–2, 25) and the suffering imprisoned Paul (3:1–13; 6:20).

9. Conclusion

Ephesians speaks to the highest Roman imperial spaces and positions especially with respect to its program of graceful benefaction and bringing salvation and peace while subjugating the nations. The epistle effectively trumps these imperial prerogatives by showing God's elevation of Christ to

---

119. The goddess Roma was modeled after Minerva/Athena. In the republic period, she is shown on coins helmeted. In the Imperial period, she is often shown standing as a warrior. Under Nero (60–64 CE), coinage featuring the emperor (obv.) was printed in Rome with the goddess Roma or Virtue (*Pietas*) in military garb triumphant on the reverse; see *RIC* 1.25, 26, 31, 32, 36, 37, 40, 41 (Aureus and Denarius with helmeted Virtue right foot on a pile of spoils/armor with right hand holding the honorary short sword [*parazonium*] and left hand a spear); 1.27, 28, 33, 34, 38, 39, 42, 43 (Aureus and Denarius with helmeted Roma left foot on helmet with dagger and bow and right hand inscribing shield held with left hand on knee; cf. 1.54, 65, 70 [dating from 64–68 CE]). For Claudius Asses were printed with Constantia helmeted in military dress holding a long spear (*RIC* 1.95) or Minerva helmeted throwing javelin with shield (1.100, 116). On reliefs, Roma was also depicted as a warrior; see, e.g., Diane Favro, "The IconiCITY of Ancient Rome," *UH* 33 (2006): 29, fig. 10. Favro describes the late first-century Cancelleria relief: "Roma as warrior; with bearded *genius Senatus*."

120. Among other deities, within the ideal state, Cicero urged establishing a cult to Stata "standing firm": "But if we must invent names for gods, we ought rather to choose such titles as Vica Pota, derived from Victory and Power, and Stata, from the idea of standing firm [*standi*]" (Cicero, *Leg.* 2.11.28; cf. *Nat. d.* 2.61).

God's right hand as Lord, head of the body, Son of God, and Savior, above all rule and by demonstrating love, offering grace, bringing salvation, and establishing peace between opposing political entities. Such a representation was especially relevant for the Christians of Asia Minor in the middle of the first century. Ideologically, such a situation very plausibly intersects with the apostle Paul's circumstances, having just delivered the collection to Jerusalem, being arrested and then essentially exiled and escorted by Roman soldiers to Caesarea Maritima (ca. 58–60 CE), where Herod had built an imperial temple dedicated to Augustus and Roma. Awaiting further developments, Paul, reflecting on the nature of God's purposes in Christ and the phenomenon of the church assembly comprised of Jews and the Nations, conceivably would have made good use of his imprisonment by writing epistles to Christ followers in Asia Minor, especially given the fact that certain Jews of Asia Minor were responsible for the charges brought against him at the temple in Jerusalem (Acts 21:27–29).

Closely attached and correlated to the resurrected and ascended Christ is the church assembly. Corresponding to the prevailing sociopolitical practices, the personification of the church assembly would have contributed to the "plausibility structure" of early Christianity.[121] Michelle V. Lee, applying this notion, argues concerning the body metaphor in 1 Corinthians that "Paul is setting forth the Christian gatherings as substitutes for the state."[122] The depiction of the church assembly in Ephesians creates a sociopolitical plausibility structure through creative adaptive and subversive spatial blending that occurs in heavenly spaces and regularly experienced places of ideological display: temples, statues, coins, marriage relationships, military struggle, victory, and urbanized monumentation.

---

121. This phrase is described in Peter L. Berger and Thomas Luckmann, *The Social Construction of Reality: A Treatise in the Sociology of Knowledge* (New York: Doubleday, 1966), 158–59, and discussed in Lee, *Paul, the Stoics, and the Body of Christ*, 20, n. 71.

122. See the discussion of this concept theoretically as applied to Paul in Lee, *Paul, the Stoics, and the Body of Christ*, 22. Similarly, Mark T. Finney's conclusion regarding 1 Corinthians applies also to Ephesians: "Writing to a predominantly Gentile audience, Paul may well have employed *ekklesia* not only to represent a 'cultic community' as such, but more pertinently to represent the assembly of those who are 'in Christ,' in pointed juxtaposition and 'competition' with the official city assembly (cf. 1 Cor 11:18; 1 Thess 1:1; Acts 19:39; 1 Cor 16:1, 19; 2 Cor 8:1; Gal 1:2; 1 Thess 2:14)" ("Christ Crucified and the Inversion of Roman Imperial Ideology in 1 Corinthians," *BTB* 35 [2005]: 27).

Christ and the church assembly, even if not physically occupying such spaces, have ideologically and theologically infiltrated them.

Bibliography

Aune, David E. *Revelation 17–22*. WBC 52C. Dallas: Word, 1998.

Ball, Allan P. "The Theological Utility of the Caesar Cult." *CJ* 5 (1910): 304–9.

Barth, Markus. *Ephesians 1–3: A New Translation with Introduction and Commentary*. AB 34. New York: Doubleday, 1974.

Basore, John W., trans. *Seneca: Moral Essays*. Vol. 1. LCL 214. Cambridge: Harvard University Press, 1928.

Berger, Peter L., and Thomas Luckmann. *The Social Construction of Reality: A Treatise in the Sociology of Knowledge*. New York: Doubleday, 1966.

Bird, Jennifer G. "The Letter to the Ephesians." Pages 265–80 in *A Postcolonial Commentary on the New Testament Writings*. Edited by Fernando F. Segovia and R. S. Sugirtharajah. BP 13. London: T&T Clark, 2007.

Bosworth, Brian. "Augustus, the Res gestae and Hellenistic Theories of Apotheosis." *JRS* 89 (1999): 1–18.

Bremen, Riet van. "Family Structures." Pages 313–30 in *A Companion to the Hellenistic World*. Edited by Andrew Erskine. Oxford: Blackwell, 2003.

Broughton, Thomas Robert Shannon. "Roman Landholding in Asia Minor." *TAPA* 65 (1934): 207–39.

Burrell, Barbara. "False Fronts: Separating the Aedicular Facade from the Imperial Cult in Roman Asia Minor." *AJA* 110 (2006): 437–69.

Canavan, Rosemary. *Clothing the Body of Christ at Colossae: A Visual Construction of Identity*. WUNT 2/334. Tübingen: Mohr Siebeck, 2012.

———. "Visual Exegesis: Interpreting Text in Dialogue with Its Visual Context." *Colloq* 47 (2015): 141–51.

Carr, Wesley. *Angels and Principalities: The Background, Meaning, and Development of the Pauline Phrase Hai archai kai hai exousiai*. SNTSMS 42. Cambridge: Cambridge University Press, 1981.

Charlesworth, Martin Percival. "The Refusal of Divine Honours: An Augustan Formula." *PBSR* 14.2 (1939): 1–10.

Cotter, Wendy. "Women's Authority Roles in Paul's Churches: Countercultural or Conventional?" *NovT* 36 (1994): 350–72.

Cuss, Dominique. *Imperial Cult and Honorary Terms in the New Testament*. Paradosis 23. Fribourg: University Press, 1974.
Danker, Frederick W. *Benefactor: Epigraphic Study of a Graeco-Roman and New Testament Semantic Field*. St. Louis, MO: Clayton, 1982.
Deissmann, Gustav Adolf. *Light from the Ancient East: The New Testament Illustrated by Recently Discovered Texts of the Graeco-Roman World*. Translated by L. R. M. Strachan. 2nd ed. London: Hodder & Stoughton, 1910.
Dodson, Joseph R. *The "Powers" of Personification: Rhetorical Purpose in the Book of Wisdom and the Letter to the Romans*. BZNW 161. Berlin: de Gruyter, 2008.
Dunn, James D. G. "On the Relation of Text and Artifact: Some Cautionary Tales." Pages 192–206 in *Text and Artifact in the Religions of Mediterranean Antiquity: Essays in Honour of Peter Richardson*. Edited by Stephen G. Wilson and Michel Desjardins. CSJud 9. Waterloo, ON: Wilfrid Laurier University Press, 2000.
———. *The Theology of Paul the Apostle*. Grand Rapids: Eerdmans, 1998.
Faust, Eberhard. *Pax Christi et Pax Caesaris: Religionsgeschichtliche, Traditionsgeschichtliche und Sozialgeschichtliche Studien zum Ephesebrief*. NTOA 24. Freiburg: Freiburg Universitätsverlag, 1993.
Favro, Diane. "The IconiCITY of Ancient Rome." *UH* 33 (2006): 20–38.
Finney, Mark T. "Christ Crucified and the Inversion of Roman Imperial Ideology in 1 Corinthians." *BTB* 35 (2005): 20–33.
Fishwick, Duncan. "Dio and Maecenas: The Emperor and the Ruler Cult." *Phoenix* 44 (1990): 267–75.
Foster, Robert L. "'A Temple in the Lord Filled to the Fullness of God': Context and Intertextuality (Eph 3:19)." *NovT* 49 (2007): 85–96.
Fredricksmeyer, Ernst A. "Divine Honors for Philip II." *TAPA* 109 (1979): 39–61.
Friesen, Steven J. *Imperial Cults and the Apocalypse of John: Reading Revelation in the Ruins*. Oxford: Oxford University Press, 2001.
Gardner, Percy. "Countries and Cities in Ancient Art." *JHS* 9 (1888): 47–81.
Gupta, Nijay K., and Fredrick J. Long. "The Politics of Ephesians and the Empire: Accommodation or Resistance?" *JGRChJ* 7 (2010): 112–36.
Harland, Philip A. *Dynamics of Identity in the World of the Early Christians: Associations, Judeans, and Cultural Minorities*. London: T&T Clark, 2009.

Heever, Gerhard van den. "Space, Social Space, and the Construction of Early Christian Identity in First Century Asia Minor." *R&T* 17 (2010): 205–43.

Hekster, Olivier, and John Rich. "Octavian and the Thunderbolt: The Temple of Apollo Palatinus and Roman Traditions of Temple Building." *CQ* 56 (2006): 149–68.

Hendrix, Holland L. "On the Form and Ethos of Ephesians." *USQR* 42 (1988): 3–15.

Hirst, Gertrude. "A Discussion of Some Passages in the Prologue to the Georgics (I. 14, 15 and 27)." *TAPA* 59 (1928): 19–32.

Hoehner, Harold W. *Ephesians: An Exegetical Commentary*. Grand Rapids: Baker Academic, 2002.

Holum, Kenneth G. "Building Power—The Politics of Architecture." *BAR* 30.5 (2004): 36–45, 57.

———. "Caesarea's Temple Hill: The Archaeology of Sacred Space in an Ancient Mediterranean City." *NEA* 67 (2004): 184–99.

Hopkins, Keith. *Death and Renewal*. SSRH 2. Cambridge: Cambridge University Press, 1983.

Janssen, David. "The Roman Cuirass Breastplate Statue and Paul's Use of Armour Language in Romans 13:12 and 1 Thessalonians 5:8." *Colloq* 46 (2014): 55–85.

Jones, Donald L. "Christianity and the Roman Imperial Cult." *ANRW* 23.2 (1980): 1023–54.

Juhász, Lajos. "The Personifications of Gallia in the 1st Century BC and AD." Pages 149–60 in *Studia archaeologica Nicolae Szabó LXXV annos nato dedicata*. Edited by László Borhy, Károly Tankó, and Kata Dévai. Budapest: L'Harmattan, 2015.

Kantorowicz, Ernst H. "Gods in Uniform." *APSP* 105 (1961): 368–93.

Kennedy, H. A. A. "Apostolic Preaching and Emperor Worship." *Expositor* 7 (1909): 289–307.

Klauck, Hans-Josef. *The Religious Context of Early Christianity: A Guide to Greco-Roman Religions*. Translated by Brian McNeil. Minneapolis: Fortress, 2003.

Kreitzer, Larry. "Apotheosis of the Roman Emperor." *BA* 53 (1990): 210–17.

Laffi, Umberto. "Le iscrizione relative all'introduzione nel 9 a.C. del nuovo calendario della provincia d'Asia." *SCO* 16 (1967): 5–98.

Lee, Michelle V. *Paul, the Stoics, and the Body of Christ*. SNTSMS 137. Cambridge: Cambridge University Press, 2006.

Lincoln, Andrew T. "Ephesians." Pages 133–40 in *The Cambridge Companion to St. Paul*. Edited by James D. G. Dunn. CCR. Cambridge: Cambridge University Press, 2003.

———. *Ephesians*. WBC 42. Dallas: Word, 1990.

———. "A Re-Examination of 'the Heavenlies' in Ephesians." *NTS* 19 (1973): 468–83.

Long, Fredrick J. *2 Corinthians: A Handbook on the Greek Text*. BHGNT. Waco, TX: Baylor University Press, 2015.

———. "Ephesians, Letter to the (ΠΡΟΣ ΕΦΕΣΙΟΥΣ)." In *The Lexham Bible Dictionary*. Edited by John D. Barry. Bellingham, WA: Logos Bible Software, 2012.

———. "Ephesians: Paul's Political Theology in Greco-Roman Political Context." 255–309 in *Christian Origins and Classical Culture: Social and Literary Contexts for the New Testament*. Vol. 1 of *Early Christianity in Its Hellenistic Context*. Edited by Stanley E. Porter and Andrew W. Pitts. TENTS 9. Leiden: Brill, 2012.

———. *Koine Greek Grammar: A Beginning-Intermediate Exegetical and Pragmatic Handbook*. AGROS. Wilmore, KY: GlossaHouse, 2015.

———. "Roman Imperial Rule under the Authority of Jupiter-Zeus: Political-Religious Contexts and the Interpretation of 'the Ruler of the Authority of the Air' in Ephesians 2:2." Pages 113–54 in *The Language of the New Testament: Context, History and Development*. Vol. 3 of *Early Christianity in Its Hellenistic Context*. Edited by Stanley E. Porter and Andrew W. Pitts. LBS 6. Leiden: Brill, 2013.

Long, Fredrick J., and Ryan Giffin. "'Every Knee Bowed': Christ as Reigning Lord over 'the Heavenly, the Earthly, and the Subterranean gods' (Phil 2:10)." Pages in *Philippi*. Vol. 4 of *The First Urban Christians*. Edited by James R. Harrison and Laurence L. Welborn. Atlanta: SBL Press, forthcoming.

Lozano, Fernando. "Divi Augusti and Theoi Sebastoi: Roman Initiatives and Greek Answers." *CQ* 57 (2007): 139–52.

Magie, David. *Roman Rule in Asia Minor*. 2 vols. Princeton: Princeton University Press, 1950.

Maier, Harry O. "Come and See: The Promise of Visual Exegesis." *Colloq* 47 (2015): 152–57.

———. *Picturing Paul in Empire: Imperial Image, Text and Persuasion in Colossians, Ephesians and the Pastoral Epistles*. London: Bloomsbury T&T Clark, 2013.

Marek, Christian. "Katalog der Inschriften von Amastris." Pages 157–87 in *Stadt, Ära und Territorium in Pontus-Bithynia und Nord-Galatia.* IF 39. Tübingen: Wasmuth, 1993.

Mattingly, Harold. *Roman Coins from the Earliest Times to the Fall of the Western Empire.* 2nd ed. Chicago: Quadrangle, 1960.

McCready, Wayne O. "Ekklēsia and Voluntary Associations." Pages 59–73 in *Voluntary Associations in the Graeco-Roman World.* Edited by John S. Kloppenborg and Stephen G. Wilson. London: Routledge, 1996.

Mellor, Ronald. ΘΕΑ ῬΩΜΑ: *The Worship of the Goddess Roma in the Greek World.* Hypomnemata 42. Göttingen: Vandenhoeck & Ruprecht, 1975.

Muddiman, John. *The Epistle to the Ephesians.* BNTC 10. London: Continuum, 2001.

Nock, Arthur D. "Σύνναος Θεός." *HSCP* 41 (1930): 1–62.

Otto, Walter. "Augustus Soter." *Hermes* 45 (1910): 448–60.

Page, Denys L., ed. *Further Greek Epigrams: Epigrams before A.D. 50 from the Greek Anthology and Other Sources, Not Included in 'Hellenistic: Epigrams before A.D. 50 from the Greek Anthology and Other Sources, Not Included in 'Hellenistic Epigrams' or 'The Garland of Philip'.* Cambridge: Cambridge University Press, 1981.

Price, Simon R. F. "The Place of Religion: Roman in the Early Empire." Pages 812–47 in *The Augustan Empire 43 B.C.–A.D. 69.* Edited by Alan K. Bowman, Edward Champlin, and Andrew Lintott. CAH 10. 2nd ed. Cambridge: Cambridge University Press, 1996.

———. *Rituals and Power: The Roman Imperial Cult in Asia Minor.* Cambridge: Cambridge University Press, 1984.

Reid, Sara Karz. *The Small Temple: A Roman Imperial Cult Building in Petra, Jordan.* GSCLA 9. Piscataway, NJ: Gorgias, 2005.

Reynolds, Joyce M. "New Evidence for the Imperial Cult in Julio-Claudian Aphrodisias." *ZPE* (1981): 317–27.

Robbins, Vernon K. *Exploring the Texture of Texts: A Guide to Socio-rhetorical Interpretation.* Valley Forge, PA: Trinity Press International, 1996.

———. *The Invention of Christian Discourse: From Wisdom to Apocalyptic.* RRA 1. Blandford Forum, UK: Deo, 2009.

———. "Rhetography: A New Way of Seeing the Familiar Text." Page 367 in *Words Well Spoken: George Kennedy's Rhetoric of the New Testament.* Edited by C. Clifton Black and Duane Frederick Watson. SSR 8. Waco, TX: Baylor University Press, 2008.

―――. *The Tapestry of Early Christian Discourse: Rhetoric, Society, and Ideology*. London: Routledge, 1996.
Robertson, Martin. "The Boscoreale Figure-Paintings." *JRS* 45 (1955): 58–67.
Rogers, Guy MacLean. *The Sacred Identity of Ephesos: Foundation Myths of a Roman City*. London: Routledge, 1991.
Rubin, Benjamin B. "(Re)presenting Empire: The Roman Imperial Cult in Asia Minor, 31 BC–AD 68." PhD diss., University of Michigan, 2008.
Rubin, Max. "Apotheosis." *CR* 30 (1916): 44–46.
Sampley, J. Paul. *"And the Two Shall Become One Flesh": A Study of Traditions in Ephesians 5:21–33*. SNTSMS 16. Cambridge: Cambridge University Press, 1971.
Sanford, Eva Matthews. "Nero and the East." *HSCP* 48 (1937): 75–103.
Schaps, David M. *Handbook for Classical Research*. New York: Routledge, 2011.
Scherrer, Peter. "The City of Ephesos: From the Roman Period to Late Antiquity." Pages 1–25 in *Ephesos, Metropolis of Asia: An Interdisciplinary Approach to Its Archaeology, Religion, and Culture*. Edited by Helmut Koester. HTS 41. Valley Forge, PA: Trinity Press International, 1995.
Schlier, Heinrich. *Der Brief an die Epheser: Ein Kommentar*. 6th ed. Düsseldorf: Patmos, 1968.
Schmidt, Karl L. "ἐκκλησία." *TDNT* 3:501–36.
Schnackenburg, Rudolf. *The Epistle to the Ephesians: A Commentary*. Translated by Helen Heron. Edinburgh: T&T Clark, 1991.
Sherk, Robert K. *The Roman Empire: Augustus to Hadrian*. TDGR. Cambridge: Cambridge University Press, 1988.
Smallwood, E. Mary *Documents Illustrating the Principates of Nerva, Trajan and Hadrian*. Cambridge: Cambridge University Press, 1966.
Smith, Julien. *Christ the Ideal King: Cultural Context, Rhetorical Strategy, and the Power of Divine Monarchy in Ephesians*. WUNT 2.313. Tübingen: Mohr Siebeck, 2011.
Smith, R. R. R. "The Imperial Reliefs from the Sebasteion at Aphrodisias." *JRS* 77 (1987): 88–138.
―――. "Simulacra gentium: The Ethne from the Sebasteion at Aphrodisias." *JRS* 78 (1988): 50–77.
Sperber, Dan, and Deirdre Wilson. *Relevance: Communication and Cognition*. 2nd ed. Oxford: Blackwell, 2001.

Talbert, Charles H. *Ephesians and Colossians*. Paideai. Grand Rapids: Baker Academic, 2007.
Taylor, Lily Ross. "Tiberius' Refusals of Divine Honors." *TAPA* 60 (1929): 87–101.
Thielman, Frank. *Ephesians*. BECNT. Grand Rapids: Baker, 2010.
Thomas, Christine M. "At Home in the City of Artemis: Religion in Ephesos in the Literary Imagination of the Roman Period." Pages 107–115 in *Ephesos, Metropolis of Asia: An Interdisciplinary Approach to its Archaeology, Religion, and Culture*. Edited by Helmut Koester. HTS 41. Valley Forge, PA: Trinity Press International, 1995.
Trebilco, Paul. *The Early Christians in Ephesus from Paul to Ignatius*. WUNT 166. Tübingen: Mohr Siebeck, 2004.
Vermeule, Cornelius C. *Roman Imperial Art in Greece and Asia Minor*. Cambridge: Harvard University Press, 1968.
White, L. Michael. "Urban Development and Social Change in Imperial Ephesos." Pages 27–79 in *Ephesos Metropolis of Asia: An Interdisciplinary Approach to Its Archaeology, Religion, and Culture*. Edited by Helmut Koester. HTS 41. Valley Forge, PA: Trinity Press International, 1995.
Williams, Jonathan. "Religion and Roman Coins." Pages 141–63 in *A Companion to Roman Religion*. Edited by Jörg Rüpke. Malden, MA: Blackwell, 2007.
Wilson, Deirdre, and Dan Sperber. *Meaning and Relevance*. Cambridge: Cambridge University Press, 2012.
———. "Outline of Relevance Theory." *Hermes* 5 (1990): 35–56.
———. "Relevance Theory." Pages 607–32 in *The Handbook of Pragmatics*. Edited by Laurence R. Horn and Gregory L. Ward. BHL 16. Malden, MA: Blackwell, 2004.
Wink, Walter. *Naming the Powers: The Language of Power in the New Testament*. Philadelphia: Fortress, 1984.
Yee, Tet-Lim N. *Jews, Gentiles, and Ethnic Reconciliation: Paul's Jewish Identity and Ephesians*. SNTSMS 130. Cambridge: Cambridge University Press, 2005.
Yorke, Gosnell. "Hearing the Politics of Peace in Ephesians: A Proposal from an African Postcolonial Perspective." *JSNT* 30 (2007): 113–27.

From Zeus or by Endoios? Acts 19:35 as a Peculiar Assessment of the Ephesian Artemis

Stephan Witetschek

In Acts 19:35, the Ephesian γραμματεύς manages to calm down the agitated crowd by reasserting, and thus reassuring them of, the "sacred identity" of Ephesus:[1] the city is "temple warden" (νεωκόρος) of Artemis and (that is) of the διοπετές. The latter term most probably means something that has fallen down (πίπτω) from Zeus (τοῦ Διός)[2]—quite understandable for Artemis as a daughter of Zeus. Thus, the cult statue in the famous Temple

---

When revising this Society of Biblical Literature paper, I greatly profited from the preparation of the workshop "Götterbilder" for the joint conference *Inter Disciplinas* (organized by the Graduate School Distant Worlds, LMU Munich, and the Berlin Graduate School for Ancient Studies, October 4–6, 2014 in Munich) together with Prof. Stefan Ritter, Prof. Friedhelm Hoffmann (both LMU Munich), and Prof. Felix Mundt (HU Berlin). Moreover, I am most grateful to my former colleague Dr. Anna Anguissola for reading the paper and advising me on archaeological matters.

1. See Guy MacLean Rogers, *The Sacred Identity of Ephesus: Foundation Myths of a Roman City* (London: Routledge, 1991). The title of this study expresses very well what is at stake, even more so since the inscription discussed in the book (IEph 1a.27) dates from roughly the same time as Luke-Acts.

2. See LSJ, s.v. "διοπετής." Most translations and commentaries, however, render it as "fallen down from heaven/from the sky." A different rendering and interpretation of Acts 19:35 has recently been suggested by Sabine Szidat, "Diopetes oder Endoios? Zum Kultbild der Artemis in Ephesos," *JDAI* 127/128 (2012/2013): 1–50, here esp. 2–17. She strongly stresses the fact that, different from other pertinent texts (see below), τὸ διοπετές in Acts 19:35 is not an attributive adjective but a noun. From this valid observation, she questionably concludes that the adjectival use is of no significance at all to the interpretation of Acts 19:35, and hence, via the attestation of ὁ διοπετής as a noun referring to Christ in the "Religious Discussion at the Court of the Sassanids" (TU 19/3 [fifth/sixth century CE]), she jumps to the somewhat circumstantial, if not fanciful, proposal that τὸ διοπετές (or, then, rather: ὁ διοπετής) in Acts 19:35

of Artemis is here said to be of divine/heavenly origin. This idea about the origins of a given cult statue is not unheard of in traditional Greek religion. The most prominent instance seems to be the Palladium (διοπετὲς Παλλάδιον) of Troy, a statue of Athena that, according to Dionysius of Halicarnassus (*Ant. rom.* 2.66.5), was kept in the Temple of Vesta at Rome in republican times.[3] In the case of Artemis, one may refer to the statue that Iphigenia had set out to get from the Taurians—a διοπετὲς ἄγαλμα (Euripides, *Iph. taur.* 977–979).[4] In Acts 19:35, the city clerk is apparently asserting the same for the cult statue in the Artemision of Ephesus.

1. The Statue in the Artemision

This is where things become interesting. Acts 19:35 is in fact the only known instance of a claim that the cult statue in the Artemision of Ephesus was a διοπετές. The verse could thus offer valuable insight into the local mythology of Ephesus in the late first century. However, there are competing accounts about the origin of the statue. The more current version is that the statue was erected by Amazons in primeval times, even long before any proper temple was built, according to Callimachus's hymn to Artemis (*Hymni* 3.237–39, 248–50).[5] Pausanias, too, reports that the cult statue in the Artemision was set up by Amazons, but he does not mention

---

is the emperor—of whom Ephesus was in fact νεωκόρος by the late first century. But the entire scene (esp. Acts 19:28, 34) is focused on Artemis only.

3. See Francesca Prescendi, "Palladium," *DNP* 9:192–93.

4. ἐντεῦθεν αὐδὴν τρίποδος ἐκ χρύσου λακὼν Φοῖβος μ᾿ ἔπεμψε δεῦρο διοπετὲς λαβεῖν ἄγαλμ᾿ Ἀθηνῶν τ᾿ ἐγκαθιδρῦσαι χθονί. "Then uttering a voice from his golden tripod, Phoibos sent me here to take the statue that fell from Zeus and set it up on the soil of the Athenians." For the terminological nuances in view of ἄγαλμα (here: "statue"), ξόανον (here: "sculpture"), and βρέτας (here: "divine image"), see Tanja S. Scheer, *Die Gottheit und ihr Bild: Untersuchungen zur Funktion griechischer Kultbilder in Religion und Politik*, Zetemata 105 (Munich: Beck, 2000), 8–34.

5. Σοὶ καὶ Ἀμαζονίδες πολέμου ἐπιθυμήτειραι ἔν ποτε παρραλίῃ Ἐφέσῳ βρέτας ἱδρύσαντο φηγῷ ὑπὸ πρέμνῳ, τέλεσεν δέ τοι ἱερὸν Ἱππώ· ... κεῖνο δέ τοι μετέπειτα περὶ βρέτας εὐρὺ θεμείλον δωμήθη, τοῦ δ᾿ οὔτε θεώτερον ὄψεται ἠὼς οὐδ᾿ ἀφνειότερον· ῥέα κεν Πυθῶνα παρέλθοι. "To you (sc. Artemis) the Amazons, lovers of war, too, have set up in Ephesus on the sea a divine image under an oak trunk, yet it was Hippo who completed the sanctuary for you.... That building was later constructed around the divine image. The sunrise will never see anything more godlike and more lavish; easily could it surpass Python (sc. of Delphi)!" For the rendering of βρέτας as a statue of divine efficacy, see Scheer, *Die Gottheit und ihr Bild*, 24–33.

an interval between the establishment of the statue and the construction of the first temple.[6] Later in his work, Pausanias even seems to suggest that the sanctuary (i.e., place of asylum), with or without a temple, predates the involvement of Amazons (*Descr.* 7.2.7). The mythical story of the Amazons is recalled in local coinage from the 90s of the first century CE, where the ὁμόνοια (concord, partnership) of Ephesus and Smyrna is represented by two Amazons (recognizable by their double axes) shaking hands (*RPC* 2.1080).[7]

Neither of these accounts tells us, however, where the statue originally came from, that is, whether the Amazons or someone else produced it—or whether indeed it fell down from Zeus. Yet if the latter had been part of the statue's story, at least Callimachus in his hymnic praise of Artemis would presumably have mentioned it.

In the late first century, however, the mythical story about primeval Amazons establishing the statue was not universally believed. Pliny the Elder mentions the statue in the Artemision

Figure 1. *RPC* 2.1080. © Staatliche Münzsammlung München

---

6. Pausanias, *Descr.* 4.31.8: Ἐφεσίαν δὲ Ἄρτεμιν πόλεις τε νομίζουσιν αἱ πᾶσαι καὶ ἄνδρες ἰδίᾳ θεῶν μάλιστα ἄγουσιν ἐν τιμῇ· τὰ δὲ αἴτια ἐμοὶ δοκεῖν ἐστιν Ἀμαζόνων τε κλέος, αἳ φήμην τὸ ἄγαλμα ἔχουσιν ἱδρύσασθαι, καὶ ὅτι ἐκ παλαιοτάτου τὸ ἱερὸν τοῦτο ἐποιήθη. τρία δὲ ἄλλα ἐπὶ τούτοις συνετέλεσεν ἐς δόξαν, μέγεθός τε τοῦ ναοῦ τὰ παρὰ πᾶσιν ἀνθρώποις κατασκευάσματα ὑπερηρκότος καὶ Ἐφεσίων τῆς πόλεως ἡ ἀκμὴ καὶ ἐν αὐτῇ τὸ ἐπιφανὲς τῆς θεοῦ. "It is the Ephesian Artemis whom all cities and men estimate and, among the gods, hold in most particular honor. The reason, it seems to me, is the fame of the Amazons who are reputed to have set up the statue and that this sanctuary was built in most ancient times. Beyond these, three other things add up for glory: the greatness of the temple that surpasses all human constructions and the excellence of the city of the Ephesians, and in the latter, the manifest presence of the goddess."

7. For the lasting significance of Amazons in connection with the mythology of the Ephesian asylum, see, e.g., Robert Fleischer, "Die Amazonen und das Asyl des Artemisions von Ephesos," *JDAI* 117 (2002): 185–216.

in the context of a discussion about durable wood and seems to be quite skeptical when it comes to the primeval origin, or at least extreme antiquity, of this wooden statue (*Nat.* 16.79.213–215).[8] Mildly mocking his source, the consular Mucianus, Pliny states a contradiction between the alleged antiquity of the statue and the fact that the name of the artist, Endoios,[9] is known. Thus, according to Pliny, this wooden statue is not a relic from a mythical past, but the work of a known and renowned artist from the historically identifiable past. Pausanias, too, views cult statues as a historian of art, when he discusses them in his *Description of Greece* from the third quarter of the second century; he even discerns the individual style or ἐργασία of certain sculptors (Pausanias, *Descr.* 1.26.4–1.27.3, esp. 1.26.6).[10] This becomes quite

---

8. Maxime aeternam putant hebenum et cupressum cedrumque, claro de omnibus materiis iudicio in templo Ephesiae Dianae, utpote cum tota Asia extruente CXX annis peractum sit. Convenit tectum eius esse e cedrinis trabibus. De simulacro ipso deae ambigitur: ceteri ex hebeno esse tradunt, Mucianus III cos. ex iis qui proxime viso eo scripsere, vitigineum et numquam mutatum septies restituto templo, hanc materiam elegisse Endoeon, etiam nomen artificis nuncupans, quod equidem miror, cum antiquiorem Minerva quoque, non modo Libero Patre, vetustatem ei tribuat. Adicit multis foraminibus nardo rigari, ut medicatus umor alat teneatque iuncturas—quas et ipsas esse modico admodum miror—valvas esse e cupresso et iam CCCC prope annis durare materiem omnem novae simile. "It is believed that ebony is the most durable material, and also cypress and cedar wood. A clear verdict about all these materials is given by the temple of the Ephesian Artemis, which, although all of Asia constructed it, took 120 years to be completed. Appropriately, its roof is of beams of cedar, but as to the very statue of the goddess, opinions diverge: all others tell us that it is made from ebony. Among those who have seen it most recently (or: most closely), Mucianus, three times consul, has written that it was made from (the wood of) a vine and never changed, although the temple has been restored seven times, and that Endoios selected the material—he even specifies the name of the artist, which I find astonishing, since he attributes it such antiquity as makes it more ancient than not only Liber Pater, but even Minerva. He adds that it is impregnated with nard through many openings, so that the soothing liquid may nourish (the wood) and keep together the joints—whereas I am quite astonished that there are any in something so small—and that the door leaves are from cypress and that all the material, after almost 400 years, is like new." This information should at least challenge the view often found in commentaries on Acts 19:35 that the διοπετές was a meteorite; see, e.g., Charles Kingsley Barrett, *A Critical and Exegetical Commentary on the Acts of the Apostles*, ICC, 2 vols. (London: T&T Clark International, 1998), 2:936.

9. An Athenian sculptor from the sixth century BCE; see Richard Neudecker, "Endoios," *DNP* 3:1026.

10. On the latter and for a collection of pertinent passages, see Jaś Elsner, "Ancient

evident, for example, when he discusses the temples of Ageira: in the Temple of Artemis he mentions a cult statue of rather modern fabrication (ἄγαλμα τέχνης τῆς ἐφ' ἡμῶν) along with an ancient statue representing Iphigenia (*Descr.* 7.26.5). When discussing the Temple of Apollo, he attributes the archaic wooden sculpture (ξόανον) to the sculptor Laphaes (*Descr.* 7.26.6).[11] His method of comparison comes quite close to that of modern art historians when he compares the object in question to a similar and more clearly attributable statue in order to state stylistic proximity.[12]

Such a connoisseurial attribution of cult statues to individual artists came to be appreciated from a rather unexpected side, as this knowledge of the individual sculptors of famous cult images was grist on the mills of a Christian apologist in the second century CE: Athenagoras.[13] In a fairly polemical passage against traditional Greek polytheism (*Leg.* 17), he puts the cult statues of traditional Greek gods into the context of art history: they only came into existence when plastic or pictorial art was sufficiently developed (17.3). Therefore, all of them were produced within memory—that is, relatively recent history, and even the artists are known

---

Viewing and Modern Art History," *Métis* 13 (1998): 417–37, here esp. 419–28 (= Jaś Elsner, *Roman Eyes: Visuality and Subjectivity in Art and Text* [Princeton: Princeton University Press, 2007], 49–66, here esp. 51–58). In the case of the Athenian Acropolis, however, Pausanias mentions the reputation of one very old statue (ἄγαλμα) of Athena Polias as having fallen down from heaven (φήμη δὲ ἐς αὐτὸ ἔχει πεσεῖν ἐκ τοῦ οὐρανοῦ), yet without giving any judgment about the veracity of that tradition (καὶ τοῦτο μὲν οὐκ ἐπέξειμι εἴτε οὕτως εἴτε ἄλλως ἔχει [1.26.6]); instead he goes on the next attraction, a golden lampstand made by Callimachus. See also Massimo Osanna, "Pausania sull'acropoli. Tra l'Atena di Endoios e l'Agalma caduto dal cielo," *MEFR* 113 (2001): 321–40, esp. 335–36.

11. This, however, seems to be the only instance when Pausanias attributes a sculpture identified as ἀρχαῖον to a known artist; see A. A. Donohue, *Xoana and the Origins of Greek Sculpture*, ACS 15 (Atlanta: Scholars Press 1988), 147.

12. See Elsner, "Ancient Viewing," 420 (= *Roman Eyes*, 51–52): "A description, bald and restrained enough for a museum catalogue, though perhaps insufficiently vivid for a modern museum label!"

13. In fact, other Christian apologists, too, exploited this perceived inconsistency in traditional Greek (and Roman) religion; see, e.g., Justin, *1 Apol.* 9.1–2; Diogn. 2. The argument goes back to Old Testament and Early Jewish polemics against the cultic use of statues; see Ps 115:1–8; Isa 44:9–20; Jer 10:2–5; but most importantly, Wis 13–15. This polemic, however, mainly targets the cultic images used in popular or domestic religion, made from affordable materials like wood.

by name (17.4).[14] What is more, these statues are obviously younger than the artists who produced them (17.5).[15] As one instance, the statue of Artemis in Ephesus is known to be the work of Endoios, so it cannot possibly be of any divine quality. Athenagoras thus radically exploits the point observed by Pliny (see above): the attribution of a statue to a known artist precludes its origin in the mythical past.

Different from the Christian apologist, Pausanias apparently did not perceive this as a serious problem, nor did Pliny. He states the issue quite clearly, but all he does is *mirari*. Another thinker in the late first and early second century, however, did discuss the question of how a work of art that has been produced by a known artist at a given moment in time could be an adequate representation of a god: Dion of Prusa—or Chrysostomos—in his "Olympian Speech" (*Dei cogn.*). Towards the end of this speech, he

---

14. Ὁ μὲν δὴ χρόνος ὀλίγος τοσοῦτος ταῖς εἰκόσι καὶ τῇ περὶ τὰ εἴδωλα πραγματείᾳ, ὡς ἔχειν εἰπεῖν τὸν ἑκάστου τεχνίτην θεοῦ. Τὸ μὲν γὰρ ἐν Ἐφέσῳ τῆς Ἀρτέμιδος καὶ τὸ τῆς Ἀθηνᾶς—μᾶλλον δὲ Ἀθηλᾶς· ἀθήλη γὰρ ὡς οἱ †μυστικώτερον οὕτω γάρ†—τὸ τῆς Ἀλέας τὸ παλαιὸν καὶ τὴν Καθημένην Ἔνδοιος εἰργάσατο μαθητὴς Δαιδάλου, ὁ δὲ Πύθιος ἔργον Θεοδώρου καὶ Τηλεκλέους καὶ ὁ Δήλιος καὶ ἡ Ἄρτεμις Τεκταίου καὶ Ἀγγελίωνος τέχνη, ἡ δὲ ἐν Σάμῳ Ἥρα καὶ <ἡ> ἐν Ἄργει Σμίλιδος χεῖρες καὶ [Φειδίου τὰ λοιπὰ εἴδωλα] ἡ Ἀφροδίτη <ἡ> ἐν Κνίδῳ ἑτέρα Πραξιτέλους τέχνη, ὁ ἐν Ἐπιδαύρῳ Ἀσκληπιὸς ἔργον Φειδίου. "There is in fact such a short time to the images and the fabrication of the idols that one can name the craftsman of each god: the (image) of Artemis in Ephesus and that of Athena—rather of Athela, for she was not suckled, †as the initiates have it†—the old one of (Athena) the Shelter, and the Sitting One crafted Endoios, the student of Daidalos. The Pythian (Apollo) is the work of Theodoros and of Telekles, and the Delian (Apollo) and Artemis are the art of Tektaios and of Angelion. The Hera on Samos, however, and the one in Argos (were made by) the hands of Smilis †and of Pheidias the other idols†. The Aphrodite in Knidos is another work of art by Praxiteles, the Asclepius in Epidaurus is a work Pheidias." According to Donohue, *Xoana*, 204–5, Athenagoras here seems to have connected the traditional iconoclastic argument (see above n. 13) with information about the origins of art, which, according to Donohue, is "badly out of context" (204)—if one expects the author to stick to the desired subject matter. (For readers unfamiliar with the symbol †, which is used in the Greek text and English translation above, it indicates a corrupt text.)

15. Συνελόντα φάναι, οὐδὲν αὐτῶν διαπέφευγεν τὸ μὴ ὑπ' ἀνθρώπου γεγονέναι. Εἰ τοίνυν θεοί, τί οὐκ ἦσαν ἐξ ἀρχῆς; Τί δέ εἰσιν νεώτεροι τῶν πεποιηκότων; Τί δὲ ἔδει αὐτοῖς πρὸς τὸ γενέσθαι ἀνθρώπων καὶ τέχνης; Γῆ ταῦτα καὶ λίθοι καὶ ὕλη καὶ περίεργος τέχνη. "Taking it all together, none of them gets away (with the notion) that they are not made by a human. But if they are gods, why did they not exist from the beginning? Why are they younger than those who made them? Why did they require men and art in order to come into being? Those are earth and stones and matter and useless art."

has the sculptor Pheidias defend his art by asserting that the statue of Zeus in Olympia by its particular features symbolically represents certain traditional (positive) attributes of Zeus (*Dei cogn.* 77).[16] The apology of the artist thus leads to a rather spiritualized and philosophically quite palatable understanding of the relationship between the gods and their images.[17]

---

16. Ὅσον δὲ ἦν ἐπιδεῖξαι ταῦτα μὴ φθεγγόμενον, ἆρα οὐχ ἱκανῶς ἔχει κατὰ τὴν τέχνην; τὴν μὲν γὰρ ἀρχὴν καὶ τὸν βασιλέα βούλεται δηλοῦν τὸ ἰσχυρὸν τοῦ εἴδους καὶ τὸ μεγαλοπρεπές· τὸν δὲ πατέρα καὶ τὴν κηδεμονίαν τὸ πρᾶον καὶ προσφιλές· τὸν δὲ Πολιέα καὶ Νόμιμον ἥ τε σεμνότης καὶ τὸ αὐστηρόν· τὴν δὲ ἀνθρώπων καὶ θεῶν ξυγγένειαν αὐτό που τὸ τῆς μορφῆς ὅμοιον ἐν εἴδει συμβόλου· τὸν δὲ Φίλιον καὶ Ἱκέσιον καὶ Ξένιον καὶ Φύξιον καὶ πάντα τὰ τοιαῦτα ἁπλῶς ἡ φιλανθρωπία καὶ τὸ πρᾶον καὶ τὸ χρηστὸν ἐμφαινόμενα· προσομοιοῖ δὲ τὸν Κτήσιον καὶ τὸν Ἐπικάρπιον ἥ τε ἁπλότης καὶ ἡ μεγαλοφροσύνη, δηλουμένη διὰ τῆς μορφῆς. ἀτεχνῶς γὰρ διδόντι καὶ χαριζομένῳ μάλιστα προέοικε τἀγαθά. "As far as this is to be displayed without speaking, is it not sufficient according to the standard of art? The powerful and majestic appearance is meant to express his rule and kingship, the gentle and friendly trait (expresses that he is) a father and his care, the holy and strict trait (expresses that he is) the 'Protector of the City' [Πολιεύς] and 'Guardian of Law' [Νόμιμος]. The quite similar appearance (expresses) the relatedness of gods and humans in a symbolic way. (That he is) 'Guarantor of Friendship' [Φίλιος], Protector of Those Seeking Sanctuary [Ἱκέσιος], the Guardian of Hospitality [Ξένιος], the God of Refuge [Φύξιος], and all such attributes (is expressed by) the benevolence and the gentle and kind traits as they appear (in the statue). (That he is) the Keeper of Property [Κτήσιος] and the Producer of Fruit ['Επικάρπιος] (is expressed by) both the simplicity and the greatness as they are made plain by the shape. For, to put it simply, he is most similar to one who gives and graciously supplies the good." In the following paragraph, Dio has Pheidias explain that he would not have been able to figure the negative and violent traits of Zeus's character in the same way.

17. See also Hans-Josef Klauck, "Interpretationen," in *Dion von Prusa. Olympische Rede*, ed. Hans-Josef Klauck and Balbina Bäbler, SAPERE 2 (Darmstadt: Wissenschaftliche Buchgesellschaft, 2000), 160–216, esp. 205–13. For a broad survey of reflections on this problem, see Scheer, *Die Gottheit und ihr Bild*, 96–108. A very particular approach to this issue may be seen in the dossier of the Salutaris foundation (IEph 1a.27–37, see below). The statues of Artemis are referred to as "the golden Artemis" (ἡ Ἄρτεμις χρυσέα [IEph 1a.27, ll. 157–58]) or a "silver Artemis" (Ἄρτεμις ἀργυρέα [IEph 1a.27, ll. 164, 168, 173(?), 178(?), 182, 186(?), 190(?), 194(?)]), whereas the other statues belonging to the foundation are not identified with what they represent, but are maintained in their mediality by being referred to as εἰκόνες. Some of the inscriptions on the statue bases, too, show this habit, mentioning that Salutaris donated "a silver Artemis" (*Dianam argenteam*/Ἄρτεμιν ἀργυρέαν [IEph 1a.28, ll. 7, 17; 1a.29, ll. 8, 17; 1a.30, ll. 8, 17; 1a.31, ll. 7, 18; 1a.34, ll. 6, 18; 1a.35, ll. 7, 17]). But in the case of the statues of other deities, persons, or bodies, they speak of "silver images" (*imagines argenteas*/εἰκόνες ἀργυρέας) of Augustus and the phylae Sebaste (IEph 1a.28, ll. 7–8,

Dion's approach may not represent the most widespread understanding of cult statues, but it shows how a thinker around 100 CE—just in Luke's time—could make sense of the idea that gods were somehow thought to be present in their statues.[18]

2. The City Clerk's View in Luke's View

Compared to such philosophical reflections about the significance of cult statues, the assertions the Ephesian γραμματεύς makes in Acts 19:35 appear crudely unenlightened. Whereas Dion rationalizes the physiognomy of Pheidias's statue of Zeus by referring it to positive character traits of the god, and while Pliny the Elder deconstructs the mythical story of Amazons setting up the statue of Artemis by naming the historical artist—unwittingly providing ammunition for a Christian apologist—the Ephesian city clerk, as a literary character in the narrative of Acts, seems

---

17–18), of Lysimachos and the phyle of the Teians (IEph 1a.29, ll. 8–9, 18), of a hero (?) and the phyle of the Karenaioi (IEph 1a.30, ll. 8–9, 17–18), of Mount Pion and the phyle of the Bembinaioi (IEph 1a.31, ll. 8, 18–19), of Athena Pammousos (IEph 1a.33, ll. 10, 20), of the equestrian order and the *ephebeia* (IEph 1a.34, ll. 7–8, 18–19), and of the city of Rome and the gerousia (IEph 1a.35, ll. 7–8, 17–18). For what it is worth, this observation may serve as one indication of the special and particularly intense relationship of the Ephesians to their city goddess Artemis.

18. For a quite comprehensive collection of sources on the issue see Hermann Funke, "Götterbild," *RAC* 11:659–828, esp. 714–16; Donohue, *Xoana*, 85–150. Writing after, and probably in reaction to, Christian apologists like Athenagoras, Porphyry provides some basic reflections on the mediality of images of gods (and gladly declares people like Athenagoras effective illiterates): Φθέγξομαι οἷς θέμις ἐστί, θύρας δ' ἐπίθεσθε βέβηλοι, σοφίας θεολόγου νοήματα δεικνύς, οἷς τὸν θεὸν καὶ τοῦ θεοῦ τὰς δυνάμεις διὰ εἰκόνων συμφύλων αἰσθήσει ἐμήνυσαν ἄνδρες, τὰ ἀφανῆ φανεροῖς ἀποτυπώσαντες πλάσμασιν, τοῖς καθάπερ ἐκ βίβλων τῶν ἀγαλμάτων ἀναλέγειν τὰ περὶ θεῶν μεμαθηκόσι γράμματα. θαυμαστὸν δὲ οὐδὲν ξύλα καὶ λίθους ἡγεῖσθαι τὰ ξόανα τοὺς ἀμαθεστάτους, καθὰ δὴ καὶ τῶν γραμμάτων οἱ ἀνόητοι λίθους μὲν ὁρῶσι τὰς στήλας, ξύλα δὲ τὰς δέλτους ἐξυφασμένην δὲ πάπυρον τὰς βίβλους. "I shall speak to those to whom it is lawful to speak—close the doors, you who are uninitiated—to display the ways of thinking in divinely revealed wisdom, whereby men have pronounced the perception of the deity and of the powers of the deity through cognate images. Thus they have represented the invisible through visible figures for those who have acquired knowledge in reading, just like from the books of statues, the letters concerning the gods. It is nothing astonishing that the most unlearned consider the sculptures to be wood and stone, just as those ignorant of letters regard (inscribed) stelae as stones, writing tablets as wood, and books as woven papyrus" (Porphyry, *Agalm.* 351f = Eusebius, *Praep. ev.* 3.7.1).

to live in a different world. Far from any need of an argument, he states, quite in passing, as a piece of common, even universal knowledge that the city of Ephesus is the temple warden (νεωκόρος) of the Great Artemis, that is, of the διοπετές.[19]

To be sure, this statement is to be seen and understood in the literary context of the riot story of Acts 19:23–40. The riot of the Ephesian silversmiths started in reaction to Paul's Christian mission that denied the divinity of cult statues, implicitly including that of the Ephesian Artemis, a point clearly made in the speech of the silversmith Demetrius (Acts 19:25–27).[20] Accordingly the silversmiths, and then the larger crowd gathered in the theater, shout out their loyalty in the acclamation μεγάλη ἡ Ἄρτεμις Ἐφεσίων (Acts 19:28, 34). In this heated situation, so a common interpretation runs, the city clerk cleverly calms down the crowd by accommodating to the polytheistic views of traditional Greek religion and by referring to the sacred identity of Ephesus as something indisputably obvious: there is no need to risk one's good reputation by a riot.[21] The implicit assumption is that the Christian mission as represented by Paul is no threat to the established cult; in other words, the Ephesians can afford to tolerate this dissenting voice in their city because they are assured in their worship of Artemis. In this interpretation, Luke would make the Ephesian official an involuntary ally of the Christian mission, albeit at the cost of having to give a positive assessment of "pagan" religion.

This understanding of Acts 19:35 tends to minimize Paul's mission over against the established cult of Artemis, which is not easy to reconcile with Luke's general interest in Paul as a successful missionary—and as challenging traditional Greek religion (Acts 17:22–31). Another type of interpretation, that has gained some following in recent years, seems to do more justice

---

19. The διοπετές appears almost as an afterthought: the precise object of common knowledge (τίς γάρ ἐστιν ἀνθρώπων ὃς οὐ γινώσκει) is the fact that Ephesus is νεωκόρος; the special quality of the cult statue is simply presupposed.

20. Two recent articles argue that this incident as narrated in Acts 19:23–40, involving Artemis as the goddess of hunting and "mistress of the beasts," is to be seen as the background to Paul's mentioning of "fighting with wild beasts" in 1 Cor 15:32: Morna Hooker, "Artemis of Ephesus," *JTS* 64 (2013): 37–46, esp. 43–44; Daniel Frayer-Griggs, "The Beasts at Ephesus and the Cult of Artemis," *HTR* 106 (2013): 459–77.

21. See Rudolf Pesch, *Apg 13–28*, vol. 2 of *Die Apostelgeschichte*, EKKNT 5.2 (Zürich: Benziger; Neukirchen-Vluyn: Neukirchener Verlag, 1986), 182; Osvaldo Padilla, *The Speeches of Outsiders in Acts: Poetics, Theology and Historiography*, SNTSMS 144 (Cambridge: University Press, 2008), 183–84.

to both Paul and the city clerk. In this interpretation, the reference to the διοπετές is the strategic center of the city clerk's exordium, the intention being both to acquit Paul and to flatter Ephesian civic pride: when Paul claims that things made by hand are not gods (Acts 19:26), he may be right—but that is not a problem for Ephesus, since the cult statue in the Artemision is not made by human hands, but has fallen down from Zeus. The Ephesian Artemis would thus be no target of Paul's criticism.[22] On the other hand, Paul would thus avoid the confrontation with the Great Artemis of Ephesus. This seems to be a fairly elegant solution at first glance. However, on second thought, it would fit even less, for, in this case, it would make Paul's criticism of pagan cults pointless and support instead the worship of Artemis rather than the Christian faith propagated by Paul.[23]

3. Acts 19:35 in Late First-Century Ephesus

It may be a more promising avenue to read the city clerk's statement in Acts 19:35 as a piece of local color of Ephesus in Luke's time—in my view the end of the first century CE.[24] This implies that this speech of an outsider is not meant to be an "objective" statement or something that Luke would consider correct. Luke has this literary character say what he thinks an Ephesian γραμματεύς would appropriately say to his fellow citizens in such a situation—what rhetoric calls *ethopoeia*.[25] The stock Ephesian thus appears as a convinced adherent to, and eager practitioner of, the cult of the Ephesian Artemis, perfectly happy to believe stories like that of the διοπετές.

---

22. See Hans-Josef Klauck, *Magie und Heidentum in der Apostelgeschichte des Lukas*, SBS 167 (Stuttgart: Katholisches Bibelwerk, 1996), 124; Scott Shauf, *Theology as History, History as Theology: Paul in Ephesus in Acts 19*, BZNW 133 (Berlin: de Gruyter, 2005), 255–57; see also C. L. Brinks, "'Great Is Artemis of the Ephesians': Acts 19:23–41 in Light of Goddess Worship in Ephesus," *CBQ* 71 (2009): 776–94, esp. 791; similarly, Rick Strelan, *Paul, Artemis, and the Jews in Ephesus*, BZNW 80 (Berlin: de Gruyter, 1996), 151.

23. See Ernst Haenchen, *Die Apostelgeschichte*, KEK 3 (Göttingen: Vandenhoeck & Ruprecht, 1956), 516, n. 3; Richard I. Pervo, *Acts: A Commentary*, ed. Harold W. Attridge, Hermeneia (Minneapolis: Fortress, 2009), 498, n. 117.

24. See Stephan Witetschek, *Ephesische Enthüllungen 1: Frühe Christen in einer antiken Großstadt; Zugleich ein Beitrag zur Frage nach den Kontexten der Johannesapokalypse*, BTS 6 (Leuven: Peeters, 2008), 245–55.

25. Quintilian renders ἠθοποιία by *imitatio morum alienorum* (*Inst.* 9.2.58).

It may come as a bit of a surprise that this should be a plausible picture of Ephesus at the end of the first century: since 89/90 CE, the city had another cultic center, the provincial temple of the Σεβαστοί.[26] This temple gave Ephesus a prominent position among the cities of Asia, as the city of Ephesus and its institutions adopted the title νεωκόρος (temple warden). It seems that this new cult made its presence strongly felt in Ephesus, not only through the new temple that had been funded by the assembly of Greek cities in the province of Asia and not only through the regular festivals of the cult. The momentum of this new cult included all parts of the city, as a fragmentary decree of the city council and assembly, IEph 2.449, shows.[27] The main part of the decree is lost, but the introduction makes clear that, in view of the new imperial buildings (Σεβαστεία ἔργα), it was considered appropriate (ἔπρεπεν) to renew older buildings in the city as well. Building inscriptions in the theater (IEph 6.2034, 2035) and on fountains and aqueducts (IEph 2.413–16, 419, 419a) as well as a dedication for a marble pavement on the processional way (IEph 7.1.3008) show that the 90s of the first century CE indeed saw a number of public building projects. Moreover, the new "harbor gymnasium," a combination of baths and sports ground, was explicitly termed "imperial baths" (βαλανεῖα τῶν Σεβαστῶν/Σεβατοῦ [IEph 4.1104, 1125, 1155]).

The city clerk's speech appears completely untouched by all this, which may be somewhat understandable for two reasons: (1) what is at stake in

---

26. For the precise dating of the inauguration, see Steven J. Friesen, *Twice Neokoros: Ephesus, Asia and the Cult of the Flavian Imperial Family*, RGRW 116 (Leiden: Brill, 1993), 41–49; Michael Dräger, *Die Städte der Provinz Asia in der Flavierzeit: Studien zur kleinasiatischen Stadt- und Regionalgeschichte*, EHS.G 576 (Frankfurt am Main: Lang, 1993), 129.

27. [Ἀγα]θῇ τυχῇ. [Ἔ]δοξεν τῇ βο[υλῇ κ]αὶ τῷ νεωκόρ[ῳ δήμῳ] φιλοσεβάστοι[ς·] πε[ρὶ ὧν] ἐνεφάνι[σ]αν Μᾶρκος Τιγέλλ[ιος Μ]άρκου υἱὸς Μαικ[ία] Λ[οῦπος] φιλόκαισαρ ὁ γρ[αμ]ματεὺ[ς τ]οῦ δήμου [καὶ] οἱ στρατηγοὶ τῆς πόλεως φιλ[ο]σέβαστοί· ἐπεὶ τοῖς νέοις τῶν Σεβαστείων ἔ[ρ]γων μεγέθεσιν καὶ ἡ τῶν παλαιῶν κτισμά[τω]ν ἀνανέωσις ἔπρεπεν, [.]ντα[…]ωρούντων τῶν εὐ[τυχ]εστ[ά]των καιρῶν τοῦ [θεῶν ἐμφ]ανεσάτου Αὐτο[κράτορος …] "To good fortune. It was pleasing to the Council and the temple-warding citizenry, the Augustus-loving: concerning what Marcus Tigellius, son of Marcus, of the *tribus* Maecia, Lupus, the Caesar-loving, clerk of the citizenry, and the captains of the city, the Augustus-loving, proposed: since, due to the new magnificence of the Augustus-constructions, a renovation of the old buildings was appropriate, … the most blissful times of the most manifest of the gods, the Emperor…." For the following, see also Stephan Witetschek, "Der provinziale Kaiserkult in Ephesos," in *Ephesos*, ed. Tobias Georges, COMES 2 (Tübingen: Mohr Siebeck, 2017), 101–41.

Acts 19:23–40 is not the imperial cult, but the cult of Artemis, and (2) a reference to the imperial cult would have been rather out of place in a story that is situated in the early 50s of the first century CE, when Ephesus only had an imperial cult at the municipal level. Nevertheless, the strong emphasis on the significance of the Artemis cult for Ephesus is still remarkable in Luke's time, when the provincial imperial cult seems to have exercised such pervasive influence in the city. But did it in fact?

A glance at the local coinage of Ephesus in the 90s of the first century CE gives a slightly different impression: there are no clear references to the imperial cult.[28] The most pertinent issue[29] is a bronze coin that features Domitian and Domitia on the obverse and on the reverse a Nike with the legend ΝΕΙΚΗ ΔΟΜΙΤΙΑΝΟΥ (*RPC* 2.1076).

Most other local issues have the cult statue of the Ephesian Artemis on their reverse sides, mostly identified by the "breasts" (whatever these objects may have been) and the ribbons hanging down from the wrists.[30] On local coinage, thus, Artemis seems to be the unchallenged emblem of Ephesus, regardless of such a thing as a provincial imperial cult.

---

28. The most recent catalog is Stefan Karwiese, *Katalog*, part 1 of *Katalog und Aufbau der römerzeitlichen Stadtprägung mit allen erfassbaren Stempelnachweisen*, vol. 5 of *Die Münzprägung von Ephesos*, VING 14 (Vienna: ÖFN, 2012). One could mention *RPC* 2.F1064 (and F1065), a local bronze coin where Ephesus appears as "twice neōkoros." However, the reverse side of this coin seems to have been "reworked," i.e., falsified; see Dietrich O. A. Klose, "Münz- oder Gruselkabinett, Zu einigen alten Fälschungen kaiserzeitlicher Lokalmünzen Kleinasiens in der Staatlichen Münzsammlung München," in *Internationales Kolloquium zur kaiserzeitlichen Münzprägung Kleinasiens, 27.–30. April 1994 in der Staatlichen Münzsammlung München*, ed. Johannes Nollé, Bernhard Overbeck, and Peter Weiss, Nomismata 1 (Milano: Ennerre, 1997), 255–63, esp. 257. Following Klose are the commentary on *RPC* 2.1064 and Barbara Burrell, *Neokoroi: Greek Cities and Roman Emperors*, CCS 9 (Leiden: Brill, 2004), 65. On the other hand, however, this falsification must have happened before 1840 (since the coin was then documented in the Staatliche Münzsammlung in Munich), that is, at a time when very little was known about the imperial cult in Ephesus. So the question remains whether the falsifier created something entirely new or imitated existing coinage. See also Witetschek, *Ephesische Enthüllungen*, 1, 115, n. 414.

29. The pertinence lies in the victory imagery that enjoyed remarkable prominence on the coinage of the Flavian period; see Jane M. Cody, "Conquerors and Conquered on Flavian Coins," in *Flavian Rome. Culture, Image, Text*, ed. Anthony James Boyle and William J. Dominik (Leiden: Brill, 2003), 103–23.

30. See *RPC* 2.1070–72, 1078, 1079, 1091, 1082, 1083–86, 1089, 1091.

Figure 2. *RPC* 2.1076. © The Trustees of the British Museum

Figure 3. *RPC* 2.1089. © Staatliche Münzsammlung München

The silence about the imperial cult or the newly acquired city title of νεωκόρος may be due to the specific political agenda that these Ephesian local coins carry with them. Most of them celebrate the ὁμόνοια (concord, partnership) between Ephesus and Smyrna.[31] According to the legends of these coins, this partnership was celebrated in particular under the proconsuls P. Calvisius Ruso (92/93) and L. Iunius Caesennius Paetus (early to mid-90s), hence a few years after the provincial Temple of the Sebastoi in Ephesus had been inaugurated.[32] Quite understandably, it was necessary at that time to stress the concord between the cities after one of them had been awarded the privilege to host the provincial imperial temple and even to celebrate itself as νεωκόρος (temple-warden) of said sanctuary. The celebration of ὁμόνοια seems to have been a carefully negotiated settlement to calm down the rivalry between the cities of Asia that was to escalate with remarkable momentum in the second and early third centuries.[33]

The stress on Artemis in Ephesian local coinage is nicely illustrated even by a coin type (*RPC* 2.1073) that seems to be closely related to a current motif in imperial coinage: it is a rare type that features on the reverse side an enthroned Zeus with a small statuette of the Ephesian Artemis

---

31. Since it is not entirely clear whether these coins (*RPC* 2.1079–93) were struck in Ephesus or in Smyrna, they do not figure in Karwiese, *Katalog*.

32. For P. Calvisius Ruso, see *RPC* 2.1079–84; For L. Iunius Caesennius Paetus, see *RPC* 2.1085–93.

33. See, e.g., Dräger, *Die Städte der Provinz Asia*, 189–200; Witetschek, "Der provinziale Kaiserkult," 128–32.

on his palm, replacing the Victoria that would occupy this place on the respective *sestertii* from imperial coinage.³⁴

This impression is supported by the building inscriptions and dedications of the buildings mentioned above. As a consistent pattern, the dedication is firstly to the Ephesian Artemis, secondly to the emperor, and thirdly sometimes to the demos or the city of Ephesus (for the time of Domitian, see IEph 2.413, 414, 418[?]; 6.2034, 2035; 7.1.3008; see also IEph 2.508).³⁵ Again, the Ephesian Artemis maintains her position in the first rank.

Figure 4. *RPC* 2.1073. © The Trustees of the British Museum

The same appears in an inscription from the year 104 CE that reports the institution of a foundation for an annual festival including a procession from the Artemision to the theater and back: the famous Salutaris foundation (IEph 1a.27).³⁶ C. Vibius Salutaris, a Roman of equestrian rank and Ephesian citizen, donated nine statues of Artemis (one from gold, eight from silver) and another twenty silver statues of persons or bodies of significance for Ephesus, including the founder Androklos and the demos of Ephesus, but also the emperor Trajan, his wife Plotina, the Roman Senate, and the Roman people. For display in the theater, the statues were to be arranged in groups of two or three, so that each of them would be accompanied by a statue of Artemis (see IEph 1a.27, ll. 150–213). Again, the Roman emperor, this time Trajan, and his cult are clearly present in Ephesus, but just as clearly, they are integrated into the existing religious fabric of the city. In other words, in the Salutaris foundation, too, Artemis is *the* dominant factor in Ephesus.

---

34. Since only one die type is known so far (Karwiese, *Katalog*, no. 109), this coin type seems to have been produced in small quantity. During Domitian's reign—more precisely, between 85 CE (*RIC* 2.1 Domitian 275) and 95/96 CE (*RIC* 2.1 Domitian 794)—the imperial mint issued several editions of *sestertii* that featured on the reverse side an enthroned Jupiter with a small Victoria on his right palm and the dedicatory legend *Iovi Victori*.

35. In fact, this pattern existed already in the time of Augustus; see IEph 2.404. Thus the epigraphic habit in this respect appears quite unimpressed by the imperial cult.

36. On this, see Rogers, *Sacred Identity*.

In this context, the city clerk's statement about the Ephesian Artemis becomes more understandable as a piece of local color that catches Ephesian civic pride at the end of the first century.[37] The image Luke draws of the Ephesians—including their γραμματεύς—matches the religious stance that also finds expression in the Salutaris foundation. To be sure, this long inscription does not refer to any particular quality or foundation myth of the original statue of Artemis in the Artemision—it is all about gold and silver *copies* of it. But the consistent high appreciation for Artemis,[38] as even sources from the late first and early second century reveal, provides a plausible background for a mythological story about Artemis's statue being a διοπετές: it is perfectly possible that Luke has in fact captured a piece of Ephesian local mythology that was current in the time around 100 CE.

At this point, it may be in order to ask what the city clerk's speech means for Luke. In the result, the speech ends the riot and leads the chaotic crowd to dissolve. Departing from the common ground that the honor of the Great Ephesian Artemis is anyway unassailable, the city clerk points out that the assembly in this form is completely unwarranted and certainly not suitable for legal proceedings for a very simple reason: there is no proper defendant. The city clerk does not mention Paul at all, but it seems evident for him that those men whom the crowd has dragged into the theater (τοὺς ἄνδρας τούτους [19:37]), namely, Gaius and Aristarchos (19:29), are not temple robbers or blasphemers of Artemis—whatever Paul may have said and done. He leaves open the possibility that Demetrius and company may have a case against somebody else (πρός τινα), but that is not a matter for this particular assembly. This observation increases the sense of Paul's absence from this scene and points to Luke's tendency to keep Paul out of all trouble in Ephesus.[39]

---

37. See also Stephan Witetschek, "Artemis and Asiarchs: Some Remarks on Ephesian Local Colour in Acts 19," *Bib* 90 (2009): 334–55, esp. 348–54.

38. The construction of a new *ōdeion* in the precincts of the Artemision may be seen in the wider context of this consistently high appreciation of Artemis in the early imperial period. However, the archaeological evidence does not allow a more precise date for the construction than "second half of the 1st century CE." See Lilli Zabrana, "Vorbericht zur sogenannten Tribüne im Artemision von Ephesos: Ein neues Odeion im Heiligtum der Artemis," *JÖAI* 80 (2011): 341–64. These findings will find their definitive publication in a forthcoming volume of the series Forschungen in Ephesos (FiE). My thanks to Lilli Zabrana for this information.

39. See the vivid comment in Richard I. Pervo, *Profit with Delight: The Literary*

The city clerk, on the other hand, does not appear especially sympathetic towards Christianity, let alone towards Paul. He is just correct and interested in public order and the reputation of the city—and thus he happens to provide a good basis for Christian mission, too. For Luke and his readers, who may have in mind the speech of Acts 17:22–31 with its philosophical inclination (even if they do not share the art-historical knowledge of Pliny or Pausanias—or Athenagoras), the reference to the διοπετές makes the Ephesians and their γραμματεύς appear in a rather dubious light: if they believe such crude stories, Paul's Christian mission can appear as superior to the traditional cults, even if Paul does not say anything of philosophical or theological significance during Luke's account of his stay in Ephesus (Acts 19).[40]

4. Conclusion

Acts 19:35 is and, for the time being, remains the only indication that the cult statue of Artemis in the Artemision of Ephesus was considered to be a διοπετές (ἄγαλμα). It appears even more isolated in the context of a philosophical and art-historical discourse in the first and second centuries CE that reflected on the production of cult statues, whether positively in view of a philosophical conception of God or the gods (Dion) or negatively as criticism of Greek polytheism (Athenagoras). However, in the context of Ephesus at the end of the first century, the γραμματεύς's statement makes sense as an instance of the high appreciation of the Ephesian Artemis as the emblem and guarantee of Ephesian identity in the large cosmos of the Roman Empire. In Luke's narrative, however, it stands in contrast to the philosophically more amenable conception of God that the Lukan Paul has presented in the Areopagus speech (Acts 17:22–31). In this literary context, the mention of a διοπετές contributes to the caricature of the Ephesian popular assembly as an anti-*ekklēsia*.[41]

Genre of the Acts of the Apostles (Philadelphia: Fortress, 1987): "Where was Paul? Sipping sherry with the high priests of the imperial cult" (p. 10).

40. See also Brinks, "Great Is Artemis of the Ephesians," 792–93.
41. For the latter, see also Klauck, *Magie und Heidentum*, 125.

Bibliography

Barrett, Charles Kingsley. *A Critical and Exegetical Commentary on the Acts of the Apostles*. ICC. 2 vols. London: T&T Clark, 1998.

Brinks, C. L. "'Great Is Artemis of the Ephesians': Acts 19:23–41 in Light of Goddess Worship in Ephesus." *CBQ* 71 (2009): 776–94.

Burrell, Barbara. *Neokoroi: Greek Cities and Roman Emperors*. CCS 9. Leiden: Brill, 2004.

Cody, Jane M. "Conquerors and Conquered on Flavian Coins." Pages 103–23 in *Flavian Rome: Culture, Image, Text*. Edited by Anthony James Boyle and William J. Dominik. Leiden: Brill, 2003.

Donohue, Alice A. *Xoana and the Origins of Greek Sculpture*. ACS 15. Atlanta: Scholars Press, 1988.

Dräger, Michael. *Die Städte der Provinz Asia in der Flavierzeit: Studien zur kleinasiatischen Stadt- und Regionalgeschichte*. EHS.G 576. Frankfurt am Main: Lang, 1993.

Elsner, Jaś. "Ancient Viewing and Modern Art History." *Métis* 13 (1998): 417–37.

———. *Roman Eyes: Visuality and Subjectivity in Art and Text*. Princeton: Princeton University Press, 2007.

Fleischer, Robert. "Die Amazonen und das Asyl des Artemisions von Ephesos." *JDAI* 117 (2002): 185–216.

Frayer-Griggs, Daniel. "The Beasts at Ephesus and the Cult of Artemis." *HTR* 106 (2013): 459–77.

Friesen, Steven J. *Twice Neokoros: Ephesus, Asia and the Cult of the Flavian Imperial Family*. RGRW 116. Leiden: Brill, 1993.

Funke, Hermann. "Götterbild." *RAC* 11:659–828.

Haenchen, Ernst. *Die Apostelgeschichte*. KEK 3. Göttingen: Vandenhoeck & Ruprecht, 1956.

Hooker, Morna. "Artemis of Ephesus." *JTS* 64 (2013): 37–46.

Karwiese, Stefan. *Katalog*. Part 1 of *Katalog und Aufbau der römerzeitlichen Stadtprägung mit allen erfassbaren Stempelnachweisen*. Vol. 5 of *Die Münzprägung von Ephesos*. VING 14. Vienna: ÖFN, 2012.

Klauck, Hans-Josef. "Interpretationen." Pages 160–216 in *Dion von Prusa: Olympische Rede*. Edited by Hans-Josef Klauck and Balbina Bäbler. SAPERE 2. Darmstadt: Wissenschaftliche Buchgesellschaft, 2000.

———. *Magie und Heidentum in der Apostelgeschichte des Lukas*. SBS 167. Stuttgart: Katholisches Bibelwerk, 1996.

Klose, Dietrich O. A. "Münz- oder Gruselkabinett: Zu einigen alten Fälschungen kaiserzeitlicher Lokalmünzen Kleinasiens in der Staatlichen Münzsammlung München." Pages 255–63 in *Internationales Kolloquium zur kaiserzeitlichen Münzprägung Kleinasiens, 27.–30. April 1994 in der Staatlichen Münzsammlung München*. Edited by Johannes Nollé, Bernhard Overbeck, and Peter Weiss. Nomismata 1. Milano: Ennerre, 1997.

Neudecker, Richard. "Endoios." *DNP* 3:1026

Osanna, Massimo. "Pausania sull'acropoli: Tra l'Atena di Endoios e l'Agalma caduto dal cielo." *MEFR* 113 (2001): 321–40.

Padilla, Osvaldo. *The Speeches of Outsiders in Acts: Poetics, Theology and Historiography*. SNTSMS 144. Cambridge: University Press, 2008.

Pervo, Richard I. *Acts: A Commentary*. Edited by Harold W. Attridge. Hermeneia. Minneapolis: Fortress, 2009.

———. *Profit with Delight: The Literary Genre of the Acts of the Apostles*. Philadelphia: Fortress, 1987.

Pesch, Rudolf. *Apg 13—28*. Vol. 2 of *Die Apostelgeschichte*. EKKNT 5.2. Zürich: Benziger; Neukirchen-Vluyn: Neukirchener Verlag, 1986.

Prescendi, Francesca. "Palladium." *DNP* 9:192–93.

Rogers, Guy MacLean. *The Sacred Identity of Ephesus: Foundation Myths of a Roman City*. London: Routledge, 1991.

Scheer, Tanja S. *Die Gottheit und ihr Bild: Untersuchungen zur Funktion griechischer Kultbilder in Religion und Politik*. Zetemata 105. Munich: Beck, 2000.

Shauf, Scott. *Theology as History, History as Theology: Paul in Ephesus in Acts 19*. BZNW 133. Berlin: de Gruyter, 2005.

Strelan, Rick. *Paul, Artemis, and the Jews in Ephesus*. BZNW 80. Berlin: de Gruyter, 1996.

Szidat, Sabine. "Diopetes oder Endoios? Zum Kultbild der Artemis in Ephesos." *JDAI* 127/128 (2012/2013): 1–50.

Witetschek, Stephan. "Artemis and Asiarchs: Some Remarks on Ephesian Local Colour in Acts 19." *Bib* 90 (2009): 334–55.

———. "Der provinziale Kaiserkult in Ephesos." Pages 101–41 in *Ephesus*. Edited by Tobias Georges. COMES 2. Tübingen: Mohr Siebeck, 2017.

———. *Ephesische Enthüllungen 1: Frühe Christen in einer antiken Großstadt; Zugleich ein Beitrag zur Frage nach den Kontexten der Johannesapokalypse*. BTS 6. Leuven: Peeters, 2008.

Zabrana, Lilli. "Vorbericht zur sogenannten Tribüne im Artemision von Ephesos: Ein neues Odeion im Heiligtum der Artemis." *JÖAI* 80 (2011): 341–64.

Ephesian Cultic Officials, Their Benefactors, and the Quest for Civic Virtue: Paul's Alternative Quest for Status in the Epistle to the Ephesians

James R. Harrison

In the eastern Mediterranean basin, one of the many pathways for local elites to establish their superiority and precedence over other powerful families in the city was the acquisition of priesthoods in the imperial and indigenous cults. The social capital of prestige accruing from these priesthoods redounded to the praise of the elite family involved as much as to the particular priest or priestess at Ephesus. The Ephesian honorific inscriptions provide us with many examples of such civic recognition. Furthermore, the benefactions of the wealthy Ephesian elites to the local cults ensured the continuance of piety and honor to the gods that was not only vital for the future prosperity of the city but also another source of social capital for the elites through the civic reciprocation of honor for their benefactions.

Not surprisingly, the study of benefaction in the Ephesian inscriptions has grabbed the attention of classical scholars in recent years.[1] Further, the

---

1. Among recent examples, see Guy MacLean Rogers, *The Sacred Identity of Ephesos: Foundation Myths of a Roman City* (London: Routledge, 1991); Angela V. Kalinowski, "Patterns of Patronage: The Politics and Ideology of Public Building in the Eastern Roman Empire (31 BCE–600 CE)" (PhD diss., University of Toronto, 1996), 36–132; Kalinowski, "The Vedii Antonini: Aspects of Patronage and Benefaction in Second Century Ephesos," *Phoenix* 56 (2003): 109–49; C. P. Jones, "Atticus in Ephesus," *ZPE* 124 (1999): 89–94; Sheila Dillon, "The Portraits of a Civic Benefactor of 2nd Century Ephesos," *JRA* 9 (1996): 261–74; Beate Dignas, *Economy of the Sacred in Hellenistic and Roman Asia Minor*, OCM (Oxford: Oxford University Press, 2002); Dieter Knibbe, "Private Euergetism in the Service of the City-Goddess: The Most Wealthy Ephesian Family of the Second Century CE Supports Artemis in Her Struggle against

pivotal study of Gabrielle Frija has contributed enormously to our understanding the role of imperial priests in the cities of Asia, allowing scholars the additional benefit of having online access to the corpus of priestly inscriptions, with the original texts and French translations provided for further scholarly study.[2] Steven J. Friesen has enriched our understanding of the imperial priestly context of ancient Ephesus, including Flavian benefaction culture.[3] Guy MacLean Rogers also has written a significant exposition of the mysteries of Artemis at Ephesus, including the city's various cultic personnel involved in the worship of the mysteries.[4] Some of this emphasis on the Ephesian inscriptions has trickled into New Testament exegetical studies, but surprisingly little effort has been made to relate the documentary evidence to the exegesis of Ephesians, though the excellent works of Clinton E. Arnold and Paul Trebilco are significant exceptions.[5]

---

the Decline of Her Cult after the Meteorological Catastrophe of 186 CE," *MedAnt* 5 (2002): 49–62; Craig S. Keener, "Paul's 'Friends' the Asiarchs (Acts 19:31)," *JGRChJ* 3 (2006): 134–41. More generally, see Frederick W. Danker, *Benefactor: Epigraphic Study of a Graeco-Roman and New Testament Semantic Field* (St. Louis, MO: Clayton, 1982); Arjan Zuiderhoek, *The Politics of Munificence in the Roman Empire: Citizens, Elites and Benefactors in Asia Minor*, GCRW (Cambridge: Cambridge University Press, 2009).

2. Gabrielle Frija, *Les prêtres des empereurs: Le culte impérial civique dans la province romaine d'Asie*, Collection Histoire (Rennes: Presses Universitaires de Rennes, 2012). For the website, see https://tinyurl.com/SBL4209i. See also Rosalinde A. Kearsley, "Asiarchs, 'Archiereis,' and the 'Archiereiai' of Asia," *GRBS* 27 (1986): 183–92.

3. Steven J. Friesen, *Twice Neokoros: Ephesus, Asia and the Cult of the Flavian Imperial Family*, RGRW 116 (Leiden: Brill, 1993), esp. 158–60. See also Jan N. Bremmer, "Priestly Personnel of the Ephesian Artemesion: Anatolian, Persian Greek, and Roman Aspects," in *Practitioners of the Divine: Greek Priests and Religious Officials from Homer to Heliodorus*, ed. Beate Dignas and Kai Trampedach, HS 30 (Washington, DC: Center for Hellenic Studies, 2008), 37–53; Marietta Horster and Anja Klöckner, eds., *Cities and Priests: Cult Personnel in Asia Minor and the Aegean Islands from the Hellenistic to the Imperial Period*, RVV 64 (Berlin: de Gruyter, 2013); James R. Harrison, *Paul's Language of Grace in Its Graeco-Roman Context*, WUNT 2/172 (Tübingen: Mohr Siebeck, 2003; repr., Eugene, OR: Wipf & Stock, 2017); Harrison, "The 'Grace' of Augustus Paves a Street at Ephesus," *NewDocs* 10:59–63.

4. Guy MacLean Rogers, *The Mysteries of Artemis of Ephesos: Cult, Polis, and Change in the Graeco-Roman World*, Syncrisis (New Haven: Yale University Press, 2012).

5. See Clinton E. Arnold, *Ephesians, Power and Magic: The Concept of Power in Ephesians in Light of Its Historical Setting*, SNTSMS 63 (Cambridge: Cambridge University Press, 1989, repr., Grand Rapids: Baker, 1992). On Ephesus in regards to Acts 19:23–40 and 20:17–35, the Pastorals, the Johannine letters, and Rev 2:1–7, see Paul

This lacuna in Ephesian studies is not occurring owing to the disputed status of Ephesians as an authentic letter of Paul because the equally disputed Pastorals have, by contrast, been brought into substantial dialogue with the Ephesian inscriptional evidence.[6] Some exegetes, while being aware of the vast Ephesian inscriptional corpus, dismiss it outright for the study of Ephesians.[7] Other scholars expend great labor in investigating the sociological understanding of honor with a view to its intersection with the honor and shame rhetoric in Ephesians, while ignoring the "honor" and "glory" terminology present in the Ephesian inscriptions.[8] Surely the Ephesian inscriptional models of honor and glory are more relevant to understanding Paul's eulogistic terminology and rituals than modern sociological models helpful as they may be? In sum, the neglect of the documentary evidence in the exegetical study of Ephesians remains puzzling.

This chapter will explore the benefaction culture of the Ephesian elites in its cultic expression and contrast this with Paul's benefaction hymn in Eph 1:3-14.[9] After examining the cult of the Julio-Claudian

---

Trebilco, *The Early Christians in Ephesus from Paul to Ignatius*, WUNT 166 (Tübingen: Mohr Siebeck, 2004, repr., Grand Rapids: Eerdmans, 2007), passim. For examples of Ephesian inscriptions influencing other New Testament Studies, see on 1 Cor 15:32, Daniel Frayer-Griggs, "The Beasts at Ephesus and the Cult of Artemis," *HTR* 106 (2013): 459-77. Regarding the Gospel of John, see Sjef van Tilborg, *Reading John in Ephesus*, NovTSup 83 (Leiden: Brill, 1996); Warren Carter, "Festivals, Cultural Intertextuality, and the Gospel of John's Rhetoric of Distance," *HvTSt* 67 (2011): https://tinyurl.com/SBL4209a. On Revelation, for example, see Steven J. Friesen, "The Beast from the Land: Revelation 13:11-18 and Social Setting," in *Reading the Book of Revelation: A Resource for Students*, ed. David L. Barr (Atlanta: Society of Biblical Literature, 2003), 49-64. More generally, see Rick Strelan, *Paul, Artemis, and the Jews in Ephesus*, BZNW 80 (Berlin: de Gruyter, 1996).

6. Korinna Zamfir, *Men and Women in the Household of God: A Contextual Approach to Roles and Ministries in the Pastoral Epistles*, NTOA 103 (Göttingen: Vandenhoeck & Ruprecht, 2013), 325-28.

7. Peter Thomas O'Brien writes: "A specific knowledge of the ancient city of Ephesus, in spite of the increasing amount of information available to us, especially through the inscriptions, does not assist us a great deal in interpreting the letter" (*The Letter to the Ephesians* [Grand Rapids: Eerdmans, 2009], 49).

8. Peter W. Gosnell, "Honor and Shame Rhetoric as a Unifying Motif in Ephesians," *BBR* 16 (2006): 105-28.

9. The debate as to whether Ephesians is an authentic epistle of Paul or the product of a later Pauline school will not be discussed here. For differing conclusions, see, Ernest Best, *A Critical and Exegetical Commentary on Ephesians*, ICC (Edinburgh: T&T Clark, 1998), 6-40; Harold W. Hoehner, *Ephesians: An Exegetical Commentary*

"world benefactors" and the corruption in the civic leadership of Ephesus during the Claudian period, the civic virtue of Ephesian priestesses and benefactors will be examined. Against this backdrop we will be able to determine to what degree Paul establishes a new quest for alternative status in Christ in Eph 1:3–14. A blend of the inscriptional, numismatic, and material evidence will be employed.

1. The Cult of the Julio-Claudian Benefactors and Corruption in Civic Leadership at Ephesus

1.1. Artemis, Ephesus, and the Julio-Claudian Benefactor of the World

1.1.1. Inscriptional Evidence

In discussing benefactors and their involvement in cults at Ephesus, we must commence with the "benefactor of the world": namely, the Julio-Claudian ruler and his house.[10] The Ephesian inscriptional evidence is replete with examples of how central the imperial cult was to the operation of Ephesian society in the Julio-Claudian period. The picture that emerges, while initially clear, is subtler and more complex than first assumed. A series of Julio-Claudian Ephesian inscriptions, consisting of honors to the Roman ruler or honors from the Roman ruler to Artemis, provide suf-

---

(Grand Rapids: Baker Academic, 2002), 2–61. Either way, I will be arguing that the writer, whether pseudonymous or the apostle Paul, is certainly conversant with the Ephesian context of the letter and alert to the intersections of the Jewish and epigraphic language in Eph 1:3–14. If the epistle is a pseudonymous product, I would place its composition very close after the martyrdom of Paul during Nero's reign (cf. Eph 3:13), whenever that took place. A Pauline dating for the composition of Ephesians, in my opinion, would be during the apostle's Roman imprisonment—thereby rejecting the proposed Caesarean and Ephesian "incarceration" theories—in ca. 60–62 CE. Nevertheless, throughout the text, I will retain the traditional attribution of authorship in the epistle, because, even if it is concluded that the text is deutero-Pauline, the Pauline attribution was the intention of the original pseudonymous writer.

10. See E. A. Judge, "Thanksgiving to the Benefactor of the World, Tiberius Caesar," *NewDocs* 9:22. The term εὐεργέτην τοῦ κόσμου is attributed, e.g., to Tiberius (SEG 36.1092 [Sardis, 41–54 CE]), Vespasian (*TAM* 2.275 [Lycia, 69 CE]), Trajan (T. B. Mitford, "Inscriptiones Ponticae—Sebastopolis," *ZPE* 87 [1991]: 191 [Sebastopolis, 105–106 CE] = SEG 41.1110), Hadrian (*IG* 11.3.1396 [Thera, 117–138 CE]), Antoninus Pius (*MAMA* 4.235 [Phrygia, Tymandos, 140 CE]).

ficient insight for our purposes into how the indigenous deities of the Ephesians related to the "godlike" world benefactor at Rome.

In the period prior to the assassination of Caesar, an honorary inscription from the Asian cities, dedicated to Julius Caesar, eulogizes the ruler as "the god manifest (descended) from Ares and Aphrodite [τὸν ἀπὸ Ἄρεως καὶ Ἀφροδε[ί]της θεὸν ἐπιφανῆ] and the common savior of the life of mankind" (IEph 2.251 [48 BCE]).[11] In the triumviral period after the assassination of Julius Caesar, an Ephesian law establishes ceremonies in honor of the deified Julius Caesar (IEph 7.2.4325), probably datable to 41 BCE. Another decree honors the deified Augustus and his house with sacrifices and libations (IEph 4.1393). Income from unspecified properties, given to the Temple of Artemis by the "[grac]e of Caesar August[us]," was used to pave a street at Ephesus (IEph 2.458 [22/21 BCE]), discussed more fully later (§4.1.2.1 below).[12] A series of highly fragmentary inscriptions are dedicated to the health of Tiberius and the permanence of Roman hegemony (IEph 2.510), the latter motif also being recapitulated in IEph 2.599.[13] In a Latin and Greek dedication, Claudia Metrodora and her husband render honor to Artemis Ephesia, the divinized Claudius, and Nero (IEph 7.1.3003),[14] whereas Gaius Stertinius Orpex and his family dedicate a wall and other parts of the stadium to Artemis Ephesia and Nero (IEph 2.411). The guild of the fishermen and fishmongers of Ephesus, comprising about one hundred members, built a customs house at the harbor of

---

11. On how the Julio-Claudian house legitimated its rule at Aphrodisias by virtue of its association with Aphrodite, see the evidence of the propylon of the Sebasteion with the inscription on its inner and outer faces: "To Aphrodite, the Divine Augusti, and the People" (Kenan T. Erim, *Aphrodisias: City of Venus Aphrodite* [London: Muller, Bond & White, 1986], 112). Not only are the Julio-Claudian rulers depicted in heroic, military, and mythic poses, but also amidst the plethora of divine figures interspersed among the imperial iconography is the figure of Aphrodite herself. See R. R. R. Smith, *The Marble Reliefs from the Julio-Claudian Sebasteion*, vol. 6 of *Aphrodisias* (Darnstadt: von Zabern, 2013), 202–6.

12. Harrison, "'Grace' of Augustus."

13. The translation of IEph 2.599 is "Rome, queen over all, your power will never end."

14. See also the Latin and Greek dedication of a base and statues for Divus Claudius and Nero from the Procurator of Asia (?) and the tribe Arniensis at Ephesus (SEG 39.1178). In a bilingual Ephesian monument for the divinized Claudius and Nero, the procurator of Asia (?) erects at his own expense and consecrates the pedestal of the monument and its statues (SEG 39.1178).

Ephesus for the fishery toll from their own subventions (IEph 1a.20; cf. 5.1503), but, nevertheless, strategically dedicated the monument to Nero, his mother Agrippina, and his wife Octavia. Finally, an inscription honors Nero for having restored an aqueduct (?) for Artemis (SEG 55.1245).

These inscriptional vignettes of Ephesian cultic life reveal that the Julio-Claudian rulers, as benefactors of humankind and of Ephesian Artemis herself, had secured the loyalty of the Asian city-states and their wealthy elites by accommodating to the reciprocity rituals of the Hellenistic ruler cult. This remained the case even though Tiberius had refused divine honors from the Greek East because, in his view, such honors were only appropriate for the divinized Augustus (DocsAug 102b [Gytheion, 15 CE]; cf. Tacitus, Ann. 4.38; Cassius Dio, Hist. rom. 56.35–42; Suetonius, Tib. 26). The initiative for this process of imperial incorporation into indigenous cult, as Simon Price has shown,[15] came from the Asian cities, their councils, aristocratic elites, and local associations, who wished to enter into client-patron relationships with the Julio-Claudian benefactor of the world. But such relationships were not entered into naively by the Greek city-states. In the case of Ephesus, the apotropaic power of Artemis against the malevolent arts of a sorcerer was known well beyond the boundaries of her territory and the Ephesian inscriptions highlight the international fame of the goddess.[16] Consequently, although the Julio-Claudian rulers are incorporated into the Ephesian pantheon, wherever Artemis is mentioned in dedications alongside the Roman rulers, she is invariably listed first (e.g., IEph 2.411; 7.1.3003).

Nor are the imperial rulers themselves passive regarding the ideology promulgated by the Greek city-states. The inscriptional link of Caligula's descent with Aphrodite at Ephesus, for example, is primarily prompted by the Julio-Claudian propaganda relating to the descent of their house from Aeneas, the son of Aphrodite.[17] To cite another example, the prefect of Asia, as we will see, promptly intervenes when the treasury of the Temple of Artemis was being put at risk by corrupt practices (IEph 1a.18b). Simi-

---

15. Simon R. F. Price, *Rituals and Power: The Roman Imperial Cult in Asia Minor* (Cambridge: Cambridge University Press, 1984), 101–32.

16. James R. Harrison, "Artemis Triumphs over a Sorcerer's Evil Art," *New Docs* 10:37–47.

17. Karl Galinsky, *Augustan Culture: An Interpretive Introduction* (Princeton: Princeton University Press, 1996), 5. Elsewhere Drusilla, Caligula's sister, is identified with Aphrodite: "the games of the goddess new Aphrodite, Drusilla" (*SIG* 2.798).

larly, the bequest of the Ephesian benefactor C. Vibius Salutaris (IEph 1a.27 [104 CE]), while pretentiously highlighting the civic importance of Salutaris by its enormous size, is nonetheless a carefully constructed document. As Rogers, observes, the Ephesian boule, the demos, and Roman authorities were involved in every aspect of the supervision of the bequest from beginning to end,[18] with the Roman *legatus pro pratore*, Afranius Flavianus, inserting his own commendation of Salutaris and stipulations regarding potential changes to the bequest (IEph 1a.27, ll. 370–413). Nevertheless, the Julio-Claudian rulers are still very keen to ingratiate themselves with the city by funding civic works in honor of Artemis from their own funds or from imperial funds given directly to the goddess (IEph 2.458; *SEG* 55.1245).

Notwithstanding these caveats from each side of the client-patron relationship, the Ephesians strategically link the worship of the Roman rulers seamlessly to their city's worship of its founding goddess. Moreover, the Ephesian benefactors reciprocate with their own munificence in the city, dedicating it to the praise of Artemis and the Roman ruler. Even the members of the Ephesian guild of fishermen and fishmongers—hardly an impoverished group of men and reflecting a diverse social constituency—"mark the event with a very large, pretentious stele."[19] Each member is ranked according to the size of his donation, ranging from fifty to twelve denarii, but, significantly, they all bask in the reflected glory of their honorific attachment to the imperial house. Thus the beneficence of the Julio-Claudian world-benefactors elicits enthusiastic and loyal responses from the Ephesian elites and guild members alike, inspiring them to their own acts of generosity within the city.

1.1.2. Numismatic Evidence

The Ionian provincial coins of Ephesus reveal a similar but more complex and nuanced picture from the time of the second triumvirate through to the reign of Nero, though there are no surviving Ephesian issues from the reign Caligula.[20] The triumviral coin issues show the bare heads of

---

18. Rogers, *Sacred Identity of Ephesos*, 29.
19. Greg H. R. Horsley, "A Fishing Cartel in First-Century Ephesos," *NewDocs* 5:99.
20. See the discussion of Michael P. Theophilos, "Ephesus and the Numismatic Background to νεωκόρος," in this volume. For another helpful discussion of the Ephe-

the triumvirs (Antony, Octavian, Lepidus) on the obverse, with ΕΦΕ ("Ephe[sus]") on the reverse facing the cult statue of Artemis. The coins are signed on the reverse ΑΡΧΙΕΡΕΥΣ ΓΡΑΜ(ΜΑΤΕΥΣ) ΓΛΑΥΚΩΝ ("*archiereus gram*[*mateus*] Glaucon" [*RPC* 1.1.2569–74]), Glaucon being a local Ephesian magistrate who holds the posts of priest and secretary.[21] The Augustan issues—minted by eight moneyers who hold either the single post of *grammateus* or *archiereus*—display either (1) the jugate heads of Augustus (laureate) and Livia on the obverse, accompanied on the reverse by Artemis's stag, reclining or standing, with either a torch or a quiver, or (2) the bare head of Augustus on the obverse, with the cult statue of Artemis on the reverse (*RPC* 1.1.2575–612). The latter issue is replicated in the laureate-headed coins of Tiberius (*RPC* 1.1.2613–19). In the Augustan coin issues above, the rule of Augustus and his household, symbolized by the presence of Livia, is not only linked to the foundation myths of the city, but it is also incorporated as imperial benefactor with the divine blessing of Artemis upon the city.

More wide-ranging motifs occur on the reverses of the Augustan silver coinage from the mint of Ephesus. These situate the city within some of the more defining moments of Augustan rule in the wider empire and at Rome herself, as opposed to, in the coin issues above, strategically accommodating Augustus to the chief goddess of the city. On the obverse of a tetradrachm, the laureate head of Augustus is represented and the

---

sian coinage, see Lyn Kidson, "Minting in Ephesus: Economics and Self-Promotion in the Early Imperial Period," *JNAA* 23 (2012/2013): 27–36.

21. The material evidence from Ephesus from the Kunsthistorisches Museum (Vienna) touching on priests from the Caesar cult postdates the Julio-Claudian period, but it is nonetheless instructive. There is a bust of a middle-aged imperial priest (260–268 CE) clothed in a tunic and cloak (*FES* 170, fig. 98). His head wears a laurel wreath enclosed by rolled ribbons, the crown type perhaps identifying him as the *archiereus*, the chief priest of the imperial temple. A head fragment of an imperial priest/priestess (200 CE) shows another wreath with eight dressed busts on it (*FES* 180). It is possible that the middle, bearded bust is to be identified with Caesar Septimius Severus (193–211 CE). This style of wreath crown corresponds to what we learn from an honorific inscription at Rhodiopolis dedicated to a lifelong priestess of Meter Theon (Angelos Chaniotis, "Epigraphic Bulletin for Greek Religion 2006," *Kernos* 22 (2009): 229–30, §63, citing a Turkish article editing several new inscriptions from Lycia and Pamphylia). It is said in the Rhodiopolis inscription regarding the priestess that "she had constructed at her own expense a golden crown with inlaid stones and with representations of the emperors [χρυσοῦν στέφανον ἔνλιθον σὺν τοῖς ἀπευκονίσμασιν τῶν Σεβαστῶν]."

coin securely dated to 28 BCE (COS VI): the reverse, however, displays the personified and draped Pax ("Peace") standing on the left and holding a caduceus (winged staff with two snakes wrapped around it) in her right hand, while a snake emerges from a *cista mystica* (a wickerwork box) on the right (*BMC* 1:112.691-93). Here the Augustan peace is ready to strike down any emerging threat to it, symbolized by the snake.[22] The continuing legacy of Augustus's victory at Actium (31 BCE) is thereby underscored. Another silver tetradrachm, depicting a bare-headed Augustus on the obverse, reveals a garlanded and wreathed altar with the name AVGVSTVS above it and the two hinds of Artemis standing left and right of the altar, facing each other (*BMC* 1:112-13.694-95). In this case, it is important that the name of Augustus is strategically positioned above the altar, implicitly reminding the Ephesians who really is the pontifex maximus (high priest), imperator (general), and world benefactor. We must remember in this regard that the power and influence of Artemis stretched well beyond the city boundaries of Ephesus, so the absolute ascendancy of Augustus would be worth reiterating in the coin's iconography for Ephesus. On another reverse we see Capricorn, the astrological sign prophetically associated with Augustus's birth (Suetonius, *Aug.* 94.12; Cassius Dio, *Hist. rom.* 56.25.5; Manilius, *Astr.* 507-509), with head turned to his back, on which is placed a cornucopiae, a symbol of plenty (*BMC* 1:113.696). Prophetic and benefaction motifs are intertwined here, whereas another reverse, displaying six corn ears knotted in a bundle (*BMC* 1:113.697), probably alludes to the fertility goddess Ceres, highlighting the blessings of peace and prosperity for provincial Ionia dispensed through Augustus's reign.

Another series of silver tetradrachms, datable to the year 19-18 BCE (TR POT V), show the bare-headed Augustus on the obverse, accompanied by a series of important motifs on the reverse. A triumphal arch, surmounted by a quadriga (a four-horse chariot), with an *aquila* (the Roman eagle legionary standard) before each side wall, has the message: S·P·R SIGNIS RECEPTIS ("The senate [and] the Roman people: the standards recovered" [*BMC* 1:114.703]). This alludes to the much anticipated (but not actual) triumph of Augustus over Parthia (20 BCE), which was entirely diplomatic in nature. Phraates, the barbarian Parthian king, was simply pressured into returning the captured Roman military

---

22. For discussion of the coin issue in relation to Rom 16:20, see James R. Harrison, *Paul and the Imperial Authorities at Thessalonica and Rome: A Study in the Conflict of Ideology*, WUNT 273 (Tübingen: Mohr Siebeck, 2011), 161-63.

standards. Another reverse shows a circular domed temple with four columns, mounted upon a podium of five steps and with a military standard within the middle (*BMC* 1:114.704). The legend MART VLTO ("Mars the avenger") would have reminded Ephesians of Augustus's desire to avenge his adoptive father's assassination at the battle of Philippi in 42 BCE. The (then) Octavius vowed that he would construct a temple to Mars Ultor, ideally represented on the coin, should he be militarily victorious (Suetonius, *Aug.* 29.2; Ovid, *Fasti* 5.569–578). This vow was fulfilled many years later in the construction of the Augustan forum at Rome in 2 BCE. A final reverse shows the Temple of Roma and Augustus (ROM·ET·AVGVST), highlighting for the Ephesians who is the protector of the capital, the empire, and Augustus: the goddess Roma. As important as the goddess Artemis was for Ephesians and for the neighboring cities that experienced her blessing, ultimately, the province of Asia was guarded and blessed by the goddess Roma and the Julian ruler of the empire (*BMC* 1:114.705–6).

The majority of the Claudian issues, dated to circa 49–51(?)/54 CE, show the laureate head of Claudius facing the draped bust of Agrippina II on the obverse (though one variation shows the bare and draped bust of Nero), whereas the reverse employs the motif of ΕΦΕΣΙΑ facing the cult statue of Artemis (*RPC* 1.1.2620–25).[23] The sole Claudian exception to the rule in terms of iconography on the reverse is a rendering of the Temple of Roma and Augustus (ROM·ET·AVGVST), with Claudius placed between its columns holding a spear in his right hand and a shield in his left, with a female figure extending a crown over his head (*BMC* 1:44.228). It is impossible to determine whether this figure is intended to be Victoria, Roma herself, or a generic goddess.[24] Interestingly, a later relief from Aphrodisias shows Nero being crowned by a divinity with the features of Agrippina.[25] Certainty is unachievable. What is unequivocally clear is that imperial succession occurs, in the iconographic rendering of this

---

23. Note the Ephesian coins]Π(?) ΜΕΜΜΙΟΥ [ΠΗΓ]ΟΥΛΟΥ ΑΝΘΥΠΑΤΟΥ, ΚΟΥΣΙΝΙΟΣ ΕΠΙΣΚΟΠΟΣ (*RPC* 1.2623, rev.) and ΚΟΥΣΙΝΙΟΣ ΤΟ Δ, ΕΦΕ (1.2624, rev.). The proconsul of Asia, P. Memmius Regulus, is known and held the magistracy 47–51(?)/54 CE (*LP* 1.43). Kousinios (presuambly the moneyer) and his magistracy (ἐπίσκοπος) are unknown (*RPC* 1.1:433). For the variation, see Claudius and Agrippina: *RPC* 1.1.2620–24. Laureate head of Claudius: *RPC* 1.1.2625

24. On Victoria, see James R. Harrison, "'The Fading Crown': Divine Honour and the Early Christians," *JTS* 54 (2003): 493–529, esp. 509–13.

25. Paul Zanker, *The Power of Images in the Age of Augustus*, trans. A. Shapiro, JL 16 (Ann Arbor: University of Michigan Press, 1988), 303, fig. 235.

coin, through the providential appointment of Roma and, consequently, all prosperity in the empire is mediated through Rome.

Finally, the obverses of Nero are more varied: the laureate head of Nero (*RPC* 1.1.2626), the bare head of Nero (with the head of Statilia Messalina on the obverse [*RPC* 1.1.2631]), the draped bust of Agrippina facing laureate head of Nero (with a turreted bust of Roma on the reverse [*RPC* 1.1.2629]), and the draped bust of Messalina (with Roma standing holding both the scepter and the cult statue of Artemis on the reverse [*RPC* 1.1.2632]). Fascinating are the prominence given to Messalina on the obverse and reverse issues and the fact that Roma not only holds the scepter but also Artemis herself. Once again the dominance of the Roman gods and the imperial household is asserted, even though Artemis is brought into special relationship with Roma and the Julio-Claudian household.

But most important of all are the two issues of Nero, presented bare headed and laureate. On the reverse in each case is ΝΕΟΚΩΡΟΝ, ΕΦΕ (*RPC* 1.1.2626, 2628) accompanied by either a three-quarter view of a temple or a temple with six columns. The name of the proconsul, ΑΟΥΙΟΛΑ ΑΝΘΥΠΑΤΩ ΑΙΧΜΟΚΛΗΣ ("Aviola Aichmokles, proconsul") secures the date to 65/66 CE.[26] As Andrew Burnett, Michel Amandry, and Pere Pau Ripollès have convincingly argued, this is probably a genuine temple of the imperial cult rather than, as has formerly been proposed, a temple of Artemis. The "neocorate for a second time" coins of Domitian have been shown to be cut at a later date and thus do not demonstrate that by the time of Domitian, a temple of Artemis and of Sebastos existed at Ephesus for the first time.[27] As Burnett, Amandry, and Ripollès conclude, speaking of the Neronian coin issues displaying a *neōkoros* temple:

> Furthermore, why is no cult statue shown in this temple, when it was standard practice to show Artemis both earlier … and later? Thus the view that the Neronian coins refer to and depict a neocorate temple in his honor seem to merit reconsideration.[28]

---

26. The name is M. Acilius Aviola: *PIR* 1.A.49; *LP* 1.59.

27. *RPC* 1.1:433. For the evidence for the later numismatic cut, see James R. Harrison, "The First Urban Churches: Introduction," in *Methodological Foundations*, vol. 1 of *The First Urban Churches*, ed. James R. Harrison and L. L. Welborn, WGRWSup 7 (Atlanta: SBL Press. 2015), 5–6, n. 15.

28. *RPC* 1.1:433.

What do we learn about the relationship between Artemis, Ephesus, its priests, and the Julio-Claudian benefactors of the world from their provincial coinage issued in the city? The Ephesian coins articulate how the Romans conceived of the relationship between Rome, their ruler, and the indigenous gods of the provincial cities during the Julio-Claudian period. Divine blessing flowed from Roman ruler to his provincial clients in conjunction with the blessing extended to their cities by their founding deities. What is obvious, however, is that there is a progression beyond the "mutuality" evinced in the Augustan coins. A more assertive iconographic statement about the dominance of the goddess Roma gradually emerges. Notwithstanding the reciprocity of blessing and recognition represented in the Augustan issues, the Ephesians are reminded in other Augustan coin issues of key diplomatic and military highpoints in Augustus's rule stretching from his triumviral years (42 BCE) to his principate (20 BCE). The prosperity of Augustus as world benefactor is also highlighted, along with the astrological and prophetic conjunctions associated with his birth. Undoubtedly, the Ephesian moneyers issuing these coins are asserting the *fides* ("faithfulness") of Ephesus to the Roman ruler and his household. Furthermore, the dominant place of the goddess Roma, personifying the city of Rome and the Roman people more widely, is underscored in the numismatic iconography. Thus the deities Roma and Victoria (?) endorse the succession of Claudius to power: it is Roma who holds the scepter, symbol of her divine authority and rule, along with the bust of Artemis herself. That the Julio-Claudian household governs the empire, with its descendants destined to imperial rule, is also emphasized by the presence of the imperial women on the coins (Livia, Agrippina II, Messalina). Furthermore, their role as benefactors is also being highlighted. Last, it is possible that Nero established the first *neōkoros* temple in Ephesus for the worship of the Roman ruler, asserting thereby the appropriateness of Ephesus showing its gratitude to the world benefactor in cultic sacrifice and prayer rituals.

In sum, as world benefactor and imperator of a far-flung military empire, the Julio-Claudian ruler acknowledged the beneficence of the provincial deities and their importance in the foundation stories of their cities, but they did so within the very strict boundaries of Roman superiority. Lest we overstate our case, it should be noted that these coins were minted by elite Ephesian moneyers, whose accession to civic posts had profited from the imperial *cursus honorum* (*archiereus, grammateus, episkopos* [?]) in the provinces. The turnover of eight moneyers/magistrates during the long reign of Augustus emphasizes the point. In other words, the numismatic messages at Ephesus are carefully constructed with the involvement and endorsement of the pro-Roman Ephesian elites and confirmed in the Claudian and Neronian issues by the presence of the name of the proconsul of Asia in the legend.

1.2. The Corruption of the Priests of Artemis

From the Roman provincial point of view, sound moral practices had to inform the operations of the sanctuary of Artemis so that not only would the divine majesty of both the city's goddess and the Roman gods, including the ruler and his family, be upheld through the imperial priests regulating the cult, but also the city itself would not be bankrupted by financial incompetence or corruption. As far as the proconsul of Asia, Paullus Fabius Persicus was concerned, the exemplum of their beneficent ruler, Claudius, should motivate the Roman provincial civic officials to act ethically (IEph 1a.18a, ll. 4–6 [ca. 44 CE]).[29] This should not surprise us because the Roman Senate had similarly averred in a decree that its ethical exemplum in government was Augustus and Tiberius.[30] In the case of Persicus's edict, the proconsul makes explicit the connection between ethical leadership and the beneficence of Claudius:

> While it is my own view, above all else, that magistrates in charge of provinces must perform the office entrusted to them with all steadfastness and good faith, in such a way that they give thought to the long-term good of the individual, of the whole province and of each city, and not only to that of his own office, for all that I freely acknowledge that I have been drawn to this view by the example of the greatest and the most truly just princeps, who has taken the whole race of men into his personal care

---

29. On the issue of exemplum, see James R. Harrison, "The Imitation of the Great Man in Antiquity: Paul's Inversion of a Cultural Icon," in *Christian Origins and Classical Culture: Social and Literary Contexts for the New Testament*, vol. 1 of *Early Christianity in Its Hellenistic Context*, ed. Stanley E. Porter and Andrew W. Pitts, TENTS 9 (Leiden: Brill, 2013), 213–54.

30. Alison E. Cooley (*Res Gestae Divi Augusti: Text, Translation, and Commentary* [Cambridge: Cambridge University Press, 2009], 40) cites a senatorial decree that asserts that the senate modeled its behavior on Augustus and Tiberius (Eck, Werner, Antonio Caballos, and Fernando Fernández, eds., *Das Senatus Consultum de Cn. Pisone Patre*, Vestigia 48 [Munich: Beck, 1996], 44).

and, amongst his benefactions, one and all most welcome, has conferred this favour—he has restored to each person what is his own.[31]

While we must take into account the proconsul's shameless flattery of the Roman ruler in this instance, nevertheless, the proconsul deliberately spotlights the beneficent example of Claudius as a foil to the self-absorption and corruption of the Ephesian priests. The generous donations of Augustus for the care and decoration of the dedications to Artemis and her temple were being siphoned off by the Ephesian leaders of the *koinon* of Asia for their own purposes (IEph 1a.18b, ll. 11–20). As Persicus explains,

> The temple of Artemis itself, the jewel of the whole province on account of the grandeur of the building and the antiquity of the cult of the goddess and because of the abundance of funds which have been restored to the goddess by Augustus, is being deprived of its own money which would have sufficed for the care and decoration of the dedications. For whenever rather good news comes from Rome they exploit it to their own profit: using the condition of the divine house as a veil, they sell priesthoods in the manner of a public auction and they call together men of every kind to buy them; then they do not choose those most suitable to have the appropriate crown placed on their heads. They allot to the priests as much of the revenues as they are willing to take, so that they may pocket as much as possible … (11 lines are missing; trans. G. H. R. Horsley)

The city officials had auctioned off the priesthoods of Artemis to the highest bidder, while the city continued to allow them to borrow from temple revenues, depleting and (without the prompt intervention from the Romans) bankrupting the treasury of the temple.[32] Although the extract from the decree cited above is missing the next eleven lines, Persicus later stipulates that the city must bear the expenses of the priesthood so that the man most deserving of the honor might be chosen, thereby returning to the financial arrangements previously made by Vedius Pollio under Augustus (IEph 1a.18c, ll. 1–11). Although not explicitly stated, it seems that the corrupt priests were dismissed from their office, with the priests receiving back only 1 percent of the price paid.

---

31. For translation, see David C. Braund, *Augustus to Nero: Sourcebook on Roman History 31 BC–AD 68* (Totowa, NJ: Barnes & Noble, 1985), §586.

32. Rogers, *Sacred Identity of Ephesos*, 11–12.

In terms of civic ethics, we are witnessing here prior to Paul's arrival in Ephesus the unraveling, to some degree, of the moral integrity required for the officials presiding over the worship of Artemis. Indeed, the perilous situation had precipitated the direct intervention of the proconsul of Asia. This Ephesian ethos of financial cupidity, revealed in the mid-40s CE, is further underscored by the perceived financial threat to the trade of the association of the Ephesian silversmiths (IEph 2.425 [81–117 CE]; 2.586 [second to third century CE]) occasioned by the preaching of Paul (Acts 19:23–27).[33] While the silversmiths were genuinely concerned about the desecration of the goddess's honor, ultimately cupidity was at the heart of their complaint, as its polemical foregrounding by Luke highlights (Acts 18:25; cf. 18:19).[34] Both the Ephesian elites and the local associations, therefore, were wedded to the status and financial advantages that the imperial cult had at its disposal, though that was expressed differently in each case.[35] Having seen how the reputation of the cult of Artemis and its interconnection with the imperial cult had been sullied just prior to the time of the apostle's visit to the city, we might ask what "roll calls" of civic and cultic virtue still remained within Ephesus into the late first century CE and beyond.

2. The Civic Virtue of Ephesian Priestesses and Their Families

We will concentrate on the priestesses of Augustus in this section, although it should be realized that priestesses at Ephesus officiated at other cults (e.g., of Hestia).[36] With the exception of four Ephesian inscriptions,

---

33. For a translation of IEph 2.425 (+IEph 3.636), where the high priest of Asia (T. Claudius Aristion) is honored by the guild of silversmiths for his beneficence, see Richard S. Ascough, Philip A. Harland, and John S. Kloppenborg, eds., *Associations in the Greco-Roman World: A Sourcebook* (Waco, TX: Baylor University Press, 2012), §164.

34. See C. Kavin Rowe, *World Upside Down: Reading Acts in the Graeco-Roman Age* (Oxford: Oxford University Press, 2009), 44–45.

35. The Ephesian silversmiths are clear about the priority of the glory of Artemis (Acts 19:27b–28, 34), notwithstanding the important place of the imperial rulers in the cult of Artemis and their readiness to bring the issue of sacrilege to the attention of the town clerk (19:37), probably with a view to handing the apostle Paul over to the Roman proconsul (19:38).

36. See Mustafa Büyükkolanci and Helmut Engelmann, "Inschriften aus Ephesus," *ZPE* 120 (1998): 65, no. 1. See also IEph 4.1062.

the priestesses of Ephesian Artemis held the office for a year, undoubtedly marrying a male of high social status after she had completed her prestigious service of the goddess. Significantly, nineteen of the twenty priestesses of Artemis in the Ephesian inscriptions have Roman names and often vaunt the fact that their families are φιλοσεβάστος ("Augustus loving"). This is evident in IEph 7.1.3059 (second to third century CE).[37] The moral epithets accorded to the priestess in the eulogy are conventional (εὐσεβῶς ["piously"], κοσμίως ["modestly," "with decorum"]), erecting in her case the moral scaffolding required for worthy service of the Ephesian mysteries. As the inscription outlines,

> [- - - Aurelia - - -] priestess of Arte]mis, completed her term of priestess piously [εὐσεβῶς] and with decorum (κοσμίως), restored all the mysteries [τὰ μυστήρια] of the goddess and funded (them) in accord with ancient custom, daughter of M. Aur(elius) Hierokleos Apolinarius the Augustus-honoring [φιλοσεβάστου] general, market Director, council chairman, father of the priestess. (trans. Baugh, "Cultic Prostitution")

Intriguing, too, is the fleeting mention that her family funded the celebration of these mysteries.[38] We know from another Ephesian inscription that funds of five thousand denarii had to be provided to the Ephesian city council for the young woman to acquire the priestesshood.[39] Only the Ephesian elites, mostly of Roman background, could afford this stratospheric cost. IEph 3.987 (first century CE) confirms this, adding that the council of elders was included in the administration of this hefty

---

37. Steven M. Baugh, "Cultic Prostitution in New Testament Ephesus: A Reappraisal," *JETS* 42 (1999): 443–60.

38. The parental funding of the priestesshoods is stated explicitly in IEph 3.989: "Ulpia Euodia Mudiane the Priestess of Artemis, daughter of Mudianus and of Euodia the descendant of (Upius) Strato and (daughter) of Dionisius, whose family often held the office of priestess and *kosmēteira*, sister of Ulpia Strato the *kosmēteira*, performed the rites and made all the expenses through her parents."

39. See Dieter Knibbe, Helmut Engelmann, and Bülent İplikçioğlu, "Neue Inschriften aus Ephesos XI," *JÖAI* 59 (1989): 163–237, §8 (ca. 165 CE): "[...] served as priestess of Artemis piously and generously, and (she) zealously supplied all that which was to be given to the city to the sum of five thousand denarii in accordance with the Council's measure, and she furthermore gave the customary distributions. T(itus) Aulius Priscus, the secretary and imperial freedman, her foster father, set up this honor" (p. 76).

donation, and specifying that repairs to the basilica were effected by the money contributed:

> The Council and People honored Vipsania Olympias, daughter of Lucius Vipsanius Apelleus, son of Neo of the Cornelian tribe, and of Claudia Polemonis, the daughter of Pythos, having completed her term as priestess of Artemis as befits a sacred office, fulfilling both the mysteries [τὰ μυστήρια] and sacrifices worthily [ἀξίως]; she wreathed the shrine and all its precincts in the days of the goddess's manifestations [ἐπιφαν εστάταις], making the public sacrifices and the distributions (of money) to the state council and to the council of elders, and bestowing in addition for repairs of the basilica the sum of five thousand denarii. She served her priestly term during the prytany of Gaius Licinnius Dionysodorus. (trans. Baugh, "Cultic Prostitution")

In sum, as Rogers concludes,[40] these inscriptions demonstrate how intensely the powerful Ephesian elites competed among each other for these prestigious positions. In the end, money buys civic virtue for the powerful.

Finally, an inscription from Ephesus (IEph 7.1.3072) unfolds the remarkable roll call of ancestral glory belonging to the aristocratic Ephesian family of the Vedii. Vedia, a priestess of Artemis, had made the customary distributions to the guilds and completed the mysteries worthily of her family (ll. 28–32).[41] But the inscription also lists all the civic magistracies that her relatives had achieved: asiarch, high priest, priestess, and *kosmēteira* prytanis, secretary, and agonothete (l. 27). Indications of Roman rank (*eques*) and female social importance—*matrona stolata* ("woman wearing a stole")—are emphasized, as well as imperial connections—φιλοσεβάστος ("Augustus-loving" [ll. 8–9, 12, 18]). While Vedia's contribution to this rich repository of civic virtue has been modest, her inherited glory was incalculable.

3. The Civic Virtue of Ephesian Benefactors

Three examples of Ephesian civic virtue, spanning the first and second centuries CE, illustrate well the dynamics of the Greco-Roman reciprocity system and how conspicuous virtue has to be recorded and recompensed

---

40. Rogers, *Mysteries of Artemis of Ephesos*, 157.
41. Cf. IEph 3.730: "The benefactors descended from ancestors and a family (of benefactors)."

publicly. First, a first-century CE Ephesian inscription (IEph 3.683a) speaks about its priestly honorand in this manner:

> [(This honors) Heraclides, priest of Arte]mis
> and benefactor [εὐεργέτην] of the people, for
> his own comprehensive virtue [τὴν ἰδίαν αὐτοῦ περὶ πάντα ἀρετὴν]
> and for his piety [εὐσέβειαν] towards Artemis
> 5 and for his scholarly power [ἐν τῷ μαθήματι δύναμιν]
> and trustworthiness [πίστιν] and for his public
> goodwill [εὔνοιαν].
> [(This honors) Ammion (daughter) of Perigenes,
> th]e wife of Heraclides Didymus, (son) of Menis,
> 10 for her own moderation [σωφροσύνην]
> and for her husband
> Heraclides's good will [εὔνοιαν]. (trans. E. A. Judge)

Many of the qualities for which the priest Heraclides is praised belong to the conventional eulogistic canon of benefaction terminology.[42] There is one exception. The word ἀρετή ("virtue") is routinely assigned to benefactors in inscriptions but, very unusually in this instance,[43] it is given extra moral force by the addition of περὶ πάντα to the noun. Thus the moral range of Heraclides's "goodness" or "excellence" is not merely confined to his civic benefactions or to his priestly duties. We are left wondering how his innate goodness so spectacularly exceeds the normal boundaries of beneficence.

This notwithstanding, the remaining words applied to Heraclides in the inscription are entirely conventional. In priestly contexts, for example, the word εὐσέβεια ("piety") is applied to cultic faithfulness to the gods through the official scrupulously carrying out the sacrifices and rituals in their honor. The term πίστις ("trustworthiness") refers to the benefactor's thorough reliability in carrying out what he had promised. The public relations disaster that Dio Chrysostom faced because he did not carry out his promise of beneficence to his native city promptly enough is a case in

---

42. See Danker, *Benefactor*.
43. In a web search of all the regional catalogues of the Packard Humanities Institute Greek Epigraphy Project, only three uses of the phrase περὶ πάντα ἀρετήν occurred: *MAMA* 9 list 179, p. 47; *SEG* 29.1380; IEph 3.683a. Given the ubiquity of ἀρετή in the honorific inscriptions, the addition of περὶ πάντα is a striking compliment to the honorand.

point (*Conc. Apam.* 3–6).⁴⁴ The term εὔνοια ("goodwill") is often a circumlocution for the benefactor's money, though we should not eliminate the nuance of the benefactor being kindly disposed to requests for beneficence as opposed to demonstrating reservation or recalcitrance.

Seemingly, by way of elimination, the one area in which Heraclides excels in *aretē* over the other priests or benefactors is in his "scholarly power." The force of this observation is underscored by the fact that the phrase ἐν τῷ μαθήματι δύναμιν only occurs once in the entire regional epigraphic corpora—in our Ephesian inscription.⁴⁵ The area of scholarly specialization in which Heraclides dominated over his peers remains undefined, though the Greek word μάθημα could refer to the mathematical sciences (arithmetic, geometry, astronomy) and astrology.⁴⁶ It would be worthwhile to speculate what his "scholarly power" might consist of in an Ephesian context. It may refer to his intimate familiarity, at the highest scholarly level, with all the traditions concerning Ephesian Artemis: the mythology of the cult and its history in the city from its foundation and its spread elsewhere; the roll call of Ephesian families associated with the service of the goddess; the cult's benefaction history, both in terms of benefactions received and the benefactions dispensed by the goddess herself; the protocols of worship required at every level to ensure divine blessing upon the city, and so on. The complexity of the procession and donations of the foundation of C. Vibius Salutaris would, as we will see, require an advisor like Heraclides. In sum, here is a man who demonstrates his virtue not only by contributing to the religious and civic needs of Ephesus but also by shaping its intellectual culture, however understood, in ways now not clear to us.

Second, the foundation of C. Vibius Salutaris (IEph 1a.27 [104 CE]), consisting of 568 lines in the inscription, outlines in minute detail how the money was to be used by the boule and demos of Ephesus. A procession took place through the streets of Ephesus for important festivals and occasions, probably as regularly as every two weeks, if Rogers is correct, occurring on the days that the assembly met.⁴⁷ In terms of Salutaris's

---

44. See Harrison, *Paul's Language of Grace*, 312–13.
45. In a web search of all the regional catalogues of the Packhard Humanities Institute Greek Epigraphy Project, the phrase ἐν τῷ μαθήματι δύναμιν only occurs in IEph 3.683a.
46. LSJ, s.v. "μάθημα," §§3, 4.
47. Rogers, *Sacred Identity of Ephesos*, 83.

bequest, the inscription mentions a yearly scheme of lotteries and distributions, from which were given

1. monetary donations to the crowds in the Temple of Artemis on the reenactment of her birthday and to the provincial officials of the imperial cult for the sacrifices during the celebration of the mysteries;[48]
2. the donation of thirty-one gold and silver type-statues for the "procession of the statues," which moved in a circular route throughout the city, beginning and ending at the Temple of Artemis, as well as money for the care of the statuary;[49] and
3. donations for unspecified tasks, in strict hierarchical order, to the citizens of the tribes, members of the boule, members of the gerousia, and the ephebes.[50]

The birth of Artemis, an Olympian deity, legitimized the social hierarchy of Ephesus, pointed to her existence before the Greek city, affirmed the Roman contribution to the city through the processional map, and gave the city its sacred identity and civic unity.[51]

Our interest, however, is more focused on how Salutaris is honored in highly adulatory moral terms that define what true civic virtue was for elite Ephesians:

> [Gaius] Vibius Salutaris, a man
> 15 of the equestrian order, conspicuous by birth and personal worth,
> and with military commands
> and procuratorships by our lord *imperator* adorned,
> our citizen and (a member) of the bouleutic council, and in the sight of (his) father
> managing (his life) with a good disposition, since, from fortune to the better
> (intending) to crown (his) prosperity by the gravity of (his) morals, piously making

---

48. Ibid., 1, 48–50.
49. Ibid., 45–48, 83–86. Nine of the statues depicted Artemis, with dedications from different groups within the city (see the table on pp. 84–85).
50. Ibid., 50–65.
51. Ibid., 69, 112–151.

20 donations he has been zealous regarding the foundress with diverse plans concerning
the cult, and with generous donations he has honored the city in every way,
and further now coming forward in the assembly he has promised
to dedicate nine type-statues, one of gold, on which is
gold-gilded silver, and eight other type-statues, and twenty silver images.
(IEph 1a.27, ll. 14–24; cf. 1a.27d, ll. 370–89)

This densely worded accolade resonates with the high morality expected of Ephesian benefactors. Salutaris's life is lived out before the watchful eyes of his father, causing Salutaris to demonstrate the type of internal disposition that invariably leads to a controlled lifestyle. The gravity (σεμνότητι ["dignity"]) of his morals (ἠθῶν ["character"]) is the secret of his success, with the result that he shows *eusebeia* ("piety") towards Artemis, the foundress of the city, generously (φιλοτεί[μως]) carrying out his promises about honoring her cult. As the preamble has already articulated, precisely because of the qualities of benefactors like Salutaris, the honors of the present had to be commensurate with those accorded to benefactors of the past so that it would act as an incentive to a new generation of benefactors seeking the same honors in the future. Consequently, Afrianus Flavianus, the *legatus pro praetore*, emphasizes the importance for the Ephesians to reciprocate Salutaris commensurately by a fitting acknowledgement of his favors and personal merit:

> Wherefore I think it is owed to him by you, with a view toward being more equally enthusiastic, if this man should appear to be worthy of recompense according to merit. And it would be especially gratifying and the sweetest of things to me if the man, whom especially of friends I honor and love, among you should be seen as worthy of recognition and honor. (IEph 1a.27, ll. 389–395)[52]

---

52. Note Dieter Knibbe's assessment of C. Vibius Salutaris. He argues that the processions had "no relationship to the cult of Artemis," but were honoring instead Salutaris, who had become very rich in serving tax-collectors in Sicily and in his equestrian career. As Knibbe concludes, "Returning to Ephesos as a private citizen, he did something that would make him immortal" ("*Via Sacra Ephesiaca*: New Aspects of the Cult of Artemis Ephesia," in *Ephesos, Metropolis of Asia: An Interdisciplinary Approach to Its Archaeology, Religion, and Culture*, ed. Helmut Koester, HTS 41 [Valley Forge, PA: Trinity International, 1995], 154). In my view, two motives drove Salutaris:

Third, an inscription (IEph 1.24a–c [162–164 CE]) deals with a decree from the Ephesian assembly relating to the administration of the festivals and sacrifices to Artemis during the Artemisia and the maintenance of the sanctity of the month Artemision. The inscription comprises three parts: the edict of the Roman proconsul ratifying the Ephesian decree (1.24a, ll. 1–21); the original Ephesian decree itself (1.24b, ll. 1–34); and an honorific decree eulogizing the role of the agonothete T. Aelius Marcianus Priscus (1.24c, ll. 1–18). In the edict of the proconsul, it is mentioned that the edict was promulgated

> 18 while Titus Aelius Marcianus Priscus,
>   son of Aelius Priscus, a man very well thought of [ἀνδρὸς δοκιμωτάτου]
> 20 and worthy of all honor and acceptance [πάσης τειμῆς καὶ ἀποδοχῆς ἀξίου],
>   was leader of the festival and president of the games.

The moral esteem in which Priscus was publicly held necessarily results, according to the operations of the Greco-Roman reciprocity system, a worthy return of honor and praise to the agonothete. Here we see how the quest for honor in the Greek East and Latin West, by means of the acquisition of civic magistracies by the local aristocracies, resulted in virtue and moral esteem being credited to its members.[53] But what did

---

honor of Artemis and, equally, honor of himself. The more that Salutaris honored Artemis, the more Salutaris, as the benefactor of the goddess, was honored by Ephesus and immortalized in the city's memory.

53. The centrality of honor is emphasized in many other Ephesian inscriptions. See my discussion of the preamble to the decree of the benefactor C. Vibius Salutaris (IEph 1.27, ll. 8–14) in Harrison, "Fading Crown," 495. More generally, see James R. Harrison, "Paul and Ancient Civic Ethics: Redefining the Canon of Honour in the Graeco-Roman World," in *Paul's Graeco-Roman Context*, ed. Cilliers Breytenbach, BETL 277 (Leuven: Peeters, 2015), 75–118. Also, an inscription honoring Titus Flavianus highlights how in his secretaryship of the city he paid for grain and how, at the same time as panegyriarch, he hosted the Great Ephesia and promised to pay for a room in the Varius Bath (IEph 3.672). Consequently, the inscription concludes: "Erected by those in the agora for the honor of a man in all things incomparable [ἀσυνκρίτου]" (ll. 20–24). IEph 3.728, too, depicts the continuous pursuit of honor by its benefactor honorand: "... and who with many great projects adorned the city and at every opportunity actively [προθύμως] and voluntarily pursued honor [ἐκουσίως πεφιλοτειμημένον]" (ll. 27–32).

Priscus the agonothete do to merit these accolades? The honorific decree eulogizes Priscus thus:

> His own city honors
> Titus Aelius Marcianus Priscu[s], son of Titus,
> of the Cl(audian tribe),
> the president of the games [ἀγωνοθετήν] and the leader of the festival [πα[νηγυριάρχην]]
> 5 of the great Artemisia, (because)
> he was first [πρῶτον] to conduct the
> festival in its entiret[y] [κατὰ τέλειο[ν]]
> and obtained festal holidays for the entire
> month [εἰς ὅλον μῆνα] named after the goddess and
> 10 established the Artemisiac
> contest and increased
> the prizes for the contestants
> and erected statues
> for the ones who won.
> 15 L. Faenius Faustus,
> his relative,
> erected this in his honor. (trans. S. R. Llewelyn)

While Priscus's "devotional and moral character" is "couched in terms entirely typical for such texts," as Richard E. Oster correctly notes,[54] there are interesting features in this honorific inscription which elevate it from the merely formulaic. This rhetorical use of the word πρῶτος ("first"), although frequently used in other inscriptions, locates Priscus's boasting in the eulogistic tradition of the Roman elites in the Latin West.[55] The routine mention of his father ensures that his achievements enhance his family honor, whereas the deflected honor also accorded the Claudian tribe ensures its prominence in the hierarchy of Ephesian tribal organization.[56] The emphasis on the entire completion of the Artemisia and the provision of festal holidays for the whole of Artemision underscores the faithfulness of Priscus to his responsibilities as an official. As Oster

---

54. Richard E. Oster, "Holy Days in Honour of Artemis," *NewDocs* 4:77.

55. Harrison, *Paul and the Imperial Authorities*, 223–34.

56. Note the alternative suggestion of Strelan regarding Priscus and the Claudian tribe: "Interestingly, he is identified as being of the Claudian tribe (IEph 1a.24). Was that tribe, in that year, responsible for the festival?" (*Paul, Artemis, and the Jews*, 67 n. 106).

observes, "Apparently, the fidelity and scrupulousness with which the sacred time and accompanying festivals of Artemis had been kept were waning."[57] Last, Priscus's faithfulness to his word and office is matched by his readiness to increase beneficence to the Artemisiac contest. In other words, in an era of declining commitment to the Artemisia among some in the city,[58] Priscus evinces costly piety towards the goddess of Ephesus.

4. An Alternative Quest for Status in Ephesians 1:3–14

A series of intriguing questions emerge at this juncture. How did Paul differentiate the beneficence of Christ from that of Artemis and the Julio-Claudian rulers? What would have been Paul's response to the corrupt civic leadership issues discussed above, or was his attention totally focused elsewhere? What moral standards for the leaders of the body of Christ did the apostle establish within his communities of grace? What alternative honorific culture did he develop and was it polemically aimed at the Ephesian cultic context?

4.1. Redefining Benefaction, Honor, and Status

4.1.1. What Type of Eulogy Is Ephesians 1:3–14?

Holland L. Hendrix has proposed that the opening blessing of Eph 1:3–14 fits the genre of the honorific decree in "its expansive recital of divine benefactions."[59] This is not to deny that Paul's eulogy reflects elements of Old Testament eulogies, rabbinic prayer blessings (e.g., the Shemoneh Esrei),[60] and Psalm-like hymns and the Qumran *Hodayot*. However, there are also crucial differences between these writings and Paul's eulogy, such as (1) the much greater length of the Shemoneh Esrei with its eighteen benedictions; (2) the transitions in Old Testament hymns to genres

---

57. Oster, "Holy Days," 77.

58. See the discussion of Rogers on the decline of the Artemis cult from the late second CE onwards due to her failure to protect the polis and herself (*Mysteries of Artemis of Ephesos*, 275–85).

59. Holland L. Hendrix, "On the Form and Ethos of Ephesians," *USQR* 42.2 (1988): 8.

60. See David Instone-Brewer, "The Eighteen Benedictions and the Minim before 70 CE," *JTS* 54 (2003): 25–44.

of confession, exhortation, and prayer, unlike Paul's eulogy; and (3) the stubborn refusal of Eph 1:3–14 to fit the conventional literary characteristics of hymns (e.g., the absence of Greek meter).[61] At best, the category of "eulogy" captures its essence, but the type of eulogy, notwithstanding its Jewish elements and vocabulary, still eludes scholars. Thus the suggestion of Hendrix has merit. It allows scholars to infer correctly that Paul is drawing upon the tradition of Jewish eulogy. But the apostle is casting his eulogy in the form of the honorific decree of the eastern Mediterranean basin, while still further adapting that genre for his own purposes. We see this in the way the eulogy leads to the cosmic climax of all things in Christ (Eph 1:14), but it returns to the praise of God where the entire eulogy began (Eph 1:3, 14), thereby creating a liturgical climax to round off the eulogy. We should, however, note the role that the three members of the Trinity in the unfolding of the eulogy: God (Eph 1:3–6), Christ (1:7–12), and Spirit (1:13–14).

Paul's eulogy is a single sentence in the Greek, with the main verb "to be" (εἶναι) omitted in verse 3 because it is understood ("blessed *be* the God and Father of our Lord Jesus Christ"). The sentence's structure is supported by three participial clauses that spell out the blessings that God has conferred, which are further amplified in each case with subsidiary clauses:

- "having blessed us [εὐλογήσας] with every spiritual blessing in the heavenlies in Christ" (Eph 1:3b)
- "having predestined us [προορίσας] to sonship through Jesus Christ" (Eph 1:5)
- "having made known to us [γνωρίσας] the mystery of his will" (Eph 1:9)[62]

The participial clauses, with their long elaborations of blessings, are reminiscent of the lengthy participial clauses often found in honorific benefaction decrees. There, the benefits of the benefactor are listed relentlessly one after the other before the official proclamation of the decree and before the awards in honor of the benefactor are publicly proclaimed and

---

61. See the excellent discussion of Chrys C. Caragounis, *The Ephesian Mysterion: Meaning and Content*, ConBNT 6 (Lund: Gleerup, 1977), 39–45.

62. Rudolf Schnackenburg, *The Epistle to the Ephesians: A Commentary*, trans. Helen Heron (Edinburgh: T&T Clark, 1991), 46.

recorded for posterity in the erection of the monument at a prominent site. Rather than Eph 1:3–14 being the "most monstrous sentence conglomeration" encountered in Greek literature, as the classicist Eduard Norden opined, it is instead, as Frederick W. Danker has justifiably written, "a marvellous spiral ... without rival in Greek literature."[63] The spiral-like effect is achieved by the amplifications of each participial phrase and by the repetitions throughout:

- "blessing" terminology (3x)—εὐλογητός, ὁ εὐλογήσας, ἐν πάσῃ εὐλογίᾳ πνευματικῇ (Eph 1:3)
- "in Christ" terminology (11x)—ἐν αὐτῷ ("in him"), ἐν Χριστῷ ("in Christ"), ἐν τῷ Χριστῷ ("in Christ"), ἐν ᾧ ("in whom"), ἐν τῷ ἠγαπημένῳ ("in the beloved one" [Eph 1:3b, 4a, 6b, 7a, 9b, 10b, 10c, 11a, 12b, 13a, 13b])
- language of "grace" (3x)—δόξης τῆς χάριτος αὐτοῦ ἧς ἐχαρίτωσεν ἡμας, τὸ πλοῦτος τῆς χάριτος αὐτοῦ (Eph 1:6, 7b)
- language of Christ's or God's "will" (3x)—τὴν εὐδοκίαν τοῦ θελήμματος αὐτοῦ, τὸ μυστήριον τοῦ θελήμματος αὐτοῦ, τὴν βουλὴν τοῦ θελήμματος αὐτοῦ (Eph 1:5b, 9a, 11b)
- "glory" terminology (3x)—δόξης τῆς χάριτος αὐτοῦ, δόξης αὐτοῦ, τῆς δόξης αὐτοῦ (Eph 1:6, 12, 14)
- "praise" terminology (3x)—εἰς ἔπαινον δόξης τῆς χάριτος αὐτοῦ, εἰς ἔπαινον δόξης αὐτοῦ, εἰς ἔπαινον τῆς δόξης αὐτοῦ (Eph 1:6, 12, 14)
- "good pleasure" terminology (2x)—τὴν εὐδοκίαν τοῦ θελήμματος αὐτοῦ, τὴν εὐδοκίαν αὐτοῦ (Eph 1:5b, 9)
- "heavenlies" terminology (2x)—ἐν τοῖς ἐπουρανίοις (Eph 1:3b, 10b)
- "inheritance" terminology (2x)—ἐκληρώθημεν, τῆς κληρονομίας (Eph 1:11a, 14a)
- "redemption" terminology (2x)—τὴν ἀπολύτρωσιν, εἰς ἀπολύτρωσιν (Eph 1:7a, 14b)

---

63. Eduard Norden, *Agnostos Theos: Untersuchungen zur Formengeschichte religiöser Rede* (Leipzig: Teubner, 1913), 253, n. 1. Frederick W. Danker writes: "As a syntactical salmagundi, the marvellous spiral of Eph 1:13–14 is probably without rival in Greek literature" ("Ephesians, Epistle to the," in *E–J*, vol. 2 of *International Standard Bible Encyclopaedia*, ed. Geoffrey William Bromiley [Grand Rapids: Eerdmans, 1982], 110). Note Caragounis's comment: "Among the eulogies of the LXX, the NT and Judaism the Eph Eulogy is incomparable for its thought" (*Ephesian Mysterion*, 40).

In sum, there is a fullness in the language, expressing a liturgical majesty, with the result that a perceptible rhythm in the flow of the sentence is created from beginning to end.[64] To some extent, it approximates the quasi-lyrical way in which Artemis is occasionally praised in the Ephesian inscriptions.[65] Ephesians 1:3-14 is a processional hymn of praise that culminates in the glory of God (1:14), eulogizing him for all his benefits in a magnificent way, reminiscent, to some extent, of the Salutaris procession of the statues from and to the Artemision. Moreover, when we connect Paul's processional hymn, moving across the ages from pretemporal predestination to eschatological redemption (Eph 1:4, 14), with the founder traditions of Androclus interspersed along the Via Sacra Artemis route, we come to understand the most prominent feature of Paul's rhetoric: the relentless mention, some eleven times, of our incorporation into our soteriological founder, Christ. It has polemical reference not only in terms of the Artemis traditions but also is in light of the founder mythology of Ephesus.[66]

4.1.2. Transitions between Praise and Polemic: The Two Conversations Underlying Paul's Eulogy in Ephesians 1:3-14

If one expected a wholesale polemical employment of the language of the Ephesian inscriptions by Paul in Eph 1:3-14, one is disappointed: only the language of "grace," "glory," "mystery," and "salvation" have significant overlaps between Paul, the LXX, and the Ephesian epigraphic tradition in our sentence. Indeed, the methodological question might be raised whether Paul is drawing upon the LXX semantic fields more than the language of the Ephesian inscriptions. Undoubtedly, Paul wanted to underscore the new status of the gentiles believers at Ephesus, who have been blessed by God's benefactions, by means of his strong emphasis upon LXX terminology and theological motifs. This is hardly surprising. The story of Israel had absolute primacy for Paul and his gentile converts as the apostle sought to locate their identity in the messianic king, crucified

---

64. Charles Masson notes: "One is struck by the fullness of the language, its liturgical majesty, its perceptible rhythm from beginning to end" (*L'Épître de Paul aux Éphésiens*, CNT 9 [Neuchâtel: Delachaux & Niestlé, 1953], 149).

65. See especially SEG 41.981, translated in Harrison, "Artemis Triumphs."

66. For full argumentation, see James R. Harrison, "An Epigraphic Portrait of Ephesus and Its Villages," in this volume.

and risen, who is the culmination of the Jewish prophetic and covenantal tradition. This notwithstanding, particular phrases and motifs from Paul's eulogy may well have had more polemical force than is first realized when they are considered against the backdrop of the terminology, social conventions, and the civic Ephesian eulogistic inscriptions.

In conclusion, two conversations are occurring in Paul's eulogy. One conversation, transitioning from the divine election of believers in Christ to the eschatological summing up of history in the risen and ascended Lord, results in an ever-increasing spiral of praise to God. The other conversation, achieved through Paul's evocative use of Ephesian inscriptional language, polemicizes against the powers and principalities enslaving the Ephesians, but likewise it transitions into a spiral of praise of God for Christ's soteriological rescue of his dependents from the spiritual powers in the city and their own deadness of sin.

4.1.2.1. Paul's Eulogy and the Ephesian Understanding of Grace

The phrase "the wealth of his grace" (τὸ πλοῦτος τῆς χάριτος αὐτοῦ [Eph 1:7b]) may have triggered for Paul's auditors a contrast between the prosperity of the Artemis and imperial cults at Ephesus and the incalculable soteriological wealth offered to the elect in Christ for eternity. Paul's language of grace helps to evoke this contrast. Ephesian auditors were certainly aware of the overflowing grace of Augustus throughout the entire Mediterranean basin, including the province of Asia. An Ephesian inscription honors Augustus for paving a street in Ephesus (22/21 BCE), employing the language of grace to describe the munificence of the Roman ruler to Artemis:

> By means of [t]he [favo]r [[χάριτ]ι] of Caesar August[us]
> from the sacred reven[ues]
> [t]hat he himself [gave] freely [ἐχαρ[ίσατο]] to the goddess
> a road was laid under (the) proconsul
> Sextos Appoleios. (IEph 2.459)[67]

We should also remember that Paul's eulogy in honor of God's beneficence in Christ (Eph 1:3–14) is followed by further cognates of χάρις in

---

67. Note also the latest restoration of [χάριτ]ι for the IEph editor's proposal of [κρίσει]; see Harrison, "'Grace' of Augustus."

Paul's thanksgiving prayer (1:15-23; e.g., 1:16a: οὐ παύομαι εὐχαριστῶν ὑπὲρ ὑμῶν). Indeed, Paul's language of thanksgiving flows from the overflowing grace adumbrated in the eulogy (1:15a: διὰ τοῦτο κἀγώ ["for this reason I also"]).[68] Paul's thankfulness to God for his fellow believers in his prayers stands in contrast to the very formal reciprocation of gratitude rendered by individual Ephesians to Artemis (IEph 3.961)[69] and Hestia in the honorific inscriptions. In these inscriptions, there is no prayer for or gratitude to the gods for fellow cult initiates, though one's family can sometimes be included among those rendering thanks (IEph 4.1066).[70] The transaction is entirely focused on the individual, cult ritual, and the deity. In Eph 1:16a we see, by contrast, the importance that communal thanksgiving brings to the ministry of the body of Christ, as opposed to the private rituals of thanksgiving in the cults of Artemis and Hestia. Rudolf Schnackenburg correctly notes that Paul's remembrance of the saints (ὑμων μνείαν ποιούμενος [Eph 1:16b]) is grammatically dependent on the apostle's reference to his not stopping giving thanks for the believers at Ephesus (οὐ παύομαι εὐχαριστῶν [1:16a]).[71] In other words, Paul's thankfulness for God's anterior grace in his life, evinced in his gratitude for his fellow believers and intercession for them (Eph 1:18-23), drives and replenishes his ministry to others. Paul's understanding of divine grace, therefore, is vastly different to the manipulation of the favors of the gods by correct cultic practice in the Greco-Roman reciprocity system and in the Ephesian mysteries in particular (*do ut des*: "I give that you may give").

Last, the large amounts of money invested by prominent Ephesian families such as the Vedii in the Artemis cult, along with C. Vibius Salutaris's sponsorship of the procession of the statues in the city, bought them commensurately substantial civic virtue and social prominence among the other provincial elites. Paul's understanding of God's overflowing grace, which cannot be reciprocated and which redounds to his glory alone, not only pinpricked the boasting of the Ephesian elites in their beneficence

---

68. Schnackenburg writes: "διὰ τοῦτο refers to the whole Eulogy" (*Epistle to the Ephesians*, 72).

69. εὐχαριστῶ σοι κυρία Ἄρτεμι ("I give thanks to you mistress Artemis"); cf. 3.960, 963, 967.

70. εὐχαριστῶ τῇ δεσποίνῃ Ἑστίᾳ καὶ πᾶσιν τοῖς θεοῖς ("I give thanks to mistress Hestia and to all the gods"); cf. IEph 4.1060, 1065. On family being included in thanksgiving to Artemis, see IEph 3.961, 966; 5.1501.

71. Schnackenburg, *Epistle to the Ephesians*, 73.

and social prominence but also installed a God-glorifying denial of self in the service of others as the basis for a new personal, ecclesial, and civic ethic on the part of believers.

4.1.2.2. Paul's Eulogy and the Ephesian Understanding of Mystery

The phrase "the mystery of his will" (τὸ μυστήριον τοῦ θελήματος αὐτοῦ [Eph 1:9a]) may also have had polemical reference for Ephesian auditors. The full unveiling of what Paul meant by this phrase is unfolded in the progression of the epistle. What has been hidden with God in the past (Eph 3:9), inaccessible to human prying, has now been revealed to his apostles and prophets in the present (3:4–5).[72] While contextually "the mystery of his will" might initially seem to refer to the culmination of all things in Christ (Eph 1:10), Paul narrows the focus of the mystery in Eph 2:11–3:13 to the creation of a unified body of believers, consisting of Jews and gentiles, the wall of hostility having been broken down by Christ who establishes peace (2:14). This extraordinary theological and social construct spotlights the wide gulf between the Ephesian understanding of the mysteries and the μυστήριον of the early believers living in the city. As we have seen in our discussion of the Artemis priestesses above (§2), their administration of τὸ μυστήριον is entirely cultic in its understanding. This is confirmed by what we can glean from the Ephesian inscriptions elsewhere, especially IEph 3.987, lines 1–27.[73] Also important for our understanding of mystery in Ephesians is the total absence of the singular τὸ μυστήριον in the Ephesian inscriptions: the plural τὰ μυστήρια is always used, in contradiction to its consistently singular usage in Ephesians (1:9; 3:3, 4, 9; 5:32; 6:19).[74] Chrys C. Caragounis correctly notes that the singular τὸ μυστήριον in the New Testament, and in Ephesians in particular, is used "most conspicuously of

---

72. Hoehner, *Ephesians*, 214.

73. For discussion, see James R. Harrison, "Family Honour of a Priestess of Artemis," *NewDocs* 10:34–35.

74. IEph 2.213; 3.667a, 702, 987–89; 4.1058, 1060, 1069, 1077, 1080a; 5.1597; 6.2913; 7.1.3059, 3072; 7.2.4330; SEG 34.1104. For discussion of the occurrences of τὸ μυστήριον and τὰ μυστήρια in the New Testament, see Caragounis, *Ephesian Mysterion*, 119–20. Caragounis observes that of the twenty-eight occurrences of "mystery" terminology in the New Testament, there are only five instances of τὰ μυστήρια, whereas the remaining twenty-three are τὸ μυστήριον.

God's plan or purpose," whereas the plural τὰ μυστήρια, in the case of the mystery religions, "is a designation of the whole rite of initiation."[75]

In Eph 3:9, Paul expands on the mystery motif by referring to "the stewardship of the mystery [ἡ οἰκονομία τοῦ μυστηρίου] hidden for ages in God." Contextually, this refers to Paul's apostolic role, allocated to him by divine grace (τὴν δωρεὰν τῆς χάριτος τοῦ θεοῦ [Eph 3:7a], ἡ χάρις αὕτη [3:8a]) and mediated to the apostle through the apocalyptic revelation of the mystery (ἀποκάλυψιν ἐγνωρίσθε μοι τὸ μυστήριον [3:3]). Paul is enlisted as an apostle to unfold the mystery of the unsearchable riches of Christ to the gentiles (ἐν τῷ μυστηρίῳ τοῦ Χριστοῦ [3:4], τὸ ἀνεξιχνίαστου πλοῦτος τοῦ Χριστοῦ [3:8b]).[76] While the language of mystery is certainly used in the LXX and Second Temple Judaism for God's revelatory purposes (e.g., Dan 2:18, 19, 27, 28, 29, 30; Wis 12:5; 14:15, 23; cf. 1QpHab VII, 1–4, 13–14; VIII, 1–3),[77] it is again possible that Paul's polemic, in an Ephesian context, is directed against the threat posed to the Asian house churches by the Lydian-Phrygian mysteries. Paul has already highlighted God's unprecedented admission of the idolatrous gentiles—"without hope and without God in the world (Eph 2:12)—into his people through Christ. The apostolic mystery, however, is not one hidden away with its priestly personnel, only to be shared with initiates of the cult, as was the case with Lydian-Phrygian mysteries in Ephesus. The openness of Paul's apostolic

---

75. Caragounis, *Ephesian Mysterion*, 119.

76. As Schnackenburg observes, in contrast to Jewish apocalyptic, the eschatological mystery unveiled is Christ, "the Secret per se." As the apostolic *oikonomos* of the mystery of salvation, Paul "becomes the enlightened interpreter of the divine enterprise already extolled in the Great Eulogy—the enterprise which God planed 'before the foundation of the world' (1.4) and had decided to carry out in 'the fullness of the times' (1.9)" (*Epistle to the Ephesians*, 138).

77. On the mysteries at Ephesus, see Rosalinde A. Kearsley, "The Mysteries of Artemis at Ephesus," *NewDocs* 6:196–202. On mystery in the Greco-Roman world and in Second Temple Judaism more generally, see Caragounis, *Ephesian Mysterion*, 1–26; Hoehner, *Ephesians*, 428–34. The most extensive discussion of the Jewish background is Markus Bockmuehl, *Revelation and Mystery in Ancient Judaism and Pauline Christianity*, WUNT 2.36 (Tübingen: Mohr Siebeck, 1990, repr., Grand Rapids: Eerdmans, 1997), 8–126. On the mysteries and the apostle Paul, see Günter Wagner, *Pauline Baptism and the Pagan Mysteries: The Problem of the Pauline Doctrine of Baptism in Romans VI.1–11, in the Light of Its Religio-historical "Parallels"* (Edinburgh: Oliver & Boyd, 1967); Alexander J. M. Wedderburn, *Baptism and Resurrection: Studies in Pauline Theology against Its Graeco-Roman Background*, WUNT 44 (Tübingen: Mohr Siebeck, 1987), 90–163, 296–359.

proclamation of God's mystery in Christ to the gentiles stands in contrast to the secrecy of the mystery cults (Eph 6:19).⁷⁸

Moreover, as noted, a new entity informs the full unfolding of God's mystery. It is given a sharply defined shape in the body of Christ, a "joint body" (σύσσωμα [Eph 3:6]) consisting of Jew and gentile "joint heirs" (συγκληρονόμα [cf. 2:14, 19, 20, 21]).⁷⁹ The "multifaceted wisdom of God" (ἡ πολυποίκιλος σοφία τοῦ θεοῦ [Eph 3:10b]) is now made known (ἵνα γνωρισθῇ νῦν [3:10a]; cf. 1:9a: γνωρίσας ἡμῖν τὸ μυστήριον τοῦ θελήματος αὐτοῦ) through the church to the principalities and powers in the heavenly places (3:10). The eschatological shift of the νῦν ("now") in Eph 3:5 and 3:10 is potent.⁸⁰ The revelation of the mystery, hidden to former generations, has now been fully unveiled through the Spirit via the apostles and prophets of Christ's church. Moreover, the Ephesian believers, along with the rest of the body of Christ, are presently seated with the risen, ascended, and reigning Christ at God's right hand in the heavenly places (Eph 1:20; 2:6). The proclamation of the mystery of Christ through the church liberates believers from the evil and hostile powers in the heavens (Eph 1:21; 6:12) and from the destructive activities of the Evil One in his sphere of darkness on the earth (2:2; 5:11–12; 6:11, 13, 16). In reality, the Lydian-Phrygian mysteries, along with the meticulous rituals of the elite priestesses at Ephesus, are spent forces. God's revelation of his mystery, no longer hidden but now accessible to all, displays his eternal wisdom (3:10). We see this in how heaven and earth finds its cosmic *anakephalaiōsis* in Christ (ἀνακεφαλαιώσασθαι τὰ πάντα ἐν τῷ Χριστῷ [Eph 1:10]),⁸¹ brought

---

78. Andrew T. Lincoln, *Ephesians*, WBC 42 (Dallas: Word, 1990), 31.

79. Max Zerwick perceptively writes regarding Paul's invention of the word σύσσομα in Eph 3:6: "The absolute novelty of what he wished to say needed a new word. Hence we should translate the word as it stands, by 'co-body,' awkward though it sounds. The Greek '*syssoma*' of Paul must have sounded just as harsh to the ears of his first readers" (*The Epistle to the Ephesians*, NTSR 16 [London: Burns & Oates, 1969], 78). On συγκληρονόμα (Eph 3:6), see Hoehner, *Ephesians*, 445–46.

80. See Lincoln, *Ephesians*, 186.

81. Caragounis, *Ephesian Mysterion*, 143–46, and note p. 112: "In the Eulogy the *mysterion* is God's inscrutable plan conceived by Him before the creation of the world.... The *mysterion* has an aim, namely, the *anakephalaiōsis* of the whole *cosmos* in Christ. Things are now moving towards that end." Bockmuehl writes: "the notion of a universal, *cosmic* encompassment in Christ, while not entirely alien to Pauline theology (1 Cor 15:28; Col 1:15–20), has not hitherto been a part of the Pauline μυστήριον" (*Revelation and Mystery*, 200, emphasis original).

about for benefit of his redeemed people (3:8-18) and, above all, for the magnification of God's glory in the coming ages (1:6, 12, 14, 17, 18; 3:13, 16; 21; cf. 2:7).

4.1.2.3. Paul's Eulogy and the Ephesian Understanding of Stewardship

Another intriguing terminological overlap is found in the *oikonomos/oikonomia* terminology of the Ephesian inscriptions. Paul's stewardship of the gospel mysteries is different from the *oikonomiai*, the written "conditions" undergirding Salutaris's bequest of the statue procession to Ephesian Artemis ("concerning the things he dedicated on the conditions written below [ταῖς ὑπίσγεγραμμέναις οἰκονομίαις], to the greatest Ephesian Artemis" [IEph 1a.27, ll. 141-43]). My guess is that οἰκονομίαι is a technical term for the proper legal arrangement of such bequests to Artemis,[82] though, undoubtedly, this bequest is in a league different from anything offered before. However, the stewardship of other bequests to Artemis and the city would have been known to the Ephesians well before the Salutaris bequest of 104 CE. Paul may have been aware of this in his choice of *oikonomia* for his stewardship of the gospel. Furthermore, John K. Goodrich, citing IEph 4.1415,[83] points to a decree directing the *oikonomos* (τὸν δὲ οἰ[κονό]μον) to distribute (ἀποδοῦναι) money so that the victorious athlete in a contest could buy the crown himself (ἀργύριον εἰς τὸν στέφανον). How, then, does Paul's understanding of stewardship intersect with this Ephesian inscriptional background?

In Eph 1:9b-10a, Paul speaks of God's purpose in Christ "for a stewardship of the fullness of the times" (εἰς οἰκονομίαν τοῦ πληρώματος τῶν καιρῶν [1:10a]). As noted, *oikonomiai* refers to the careful legal arrangements put in place for bequests to the city.[84] The term *oikonomos* also designates the organizer of the monetary gifts for the city's games and its honorific awards. Thus the stewardship terminology emphasizes the

---

82. In a decree that defers and annuls legal actions and replaces them with incentives during the Mithridatic war, we hear of "the former arrangements [τὰς προυπαρχούσας οἰκονομίας] in accord with the laws" (IEph 1a.8, ll. 34-35 [86/85 BCE]). In a highly fragmentary honorific decree of Ephesus for Tiberius (IEph 4:1398: 14/15? CE), the phrase μετ' οἰκονομία[ς] appears.

83. John K. Goodrich, *Paul as an Administrator of God in 1 Corinthians*, SNTSMS 152 (Cambridge: Cambridge University Press, 2012), 52.

84. See Lincoln, *Ephesians*, 186.

distribution of beneficence to the city of Ephesus, its goddess, games and people. While *oikonomos* involves the notion of careful planning in Eph 1:10, well brought out by commentators,[85] the nuance of overflowing beneficence, gleaned from the Ephesian inscriptional context, must be kept to the forefront in discussion of what has actually been planned. This is particularly appropriate, given the spectacular cosmic *anakephalaiōsis* highlighted subsequently by Paul. The accompanying language of grace (δόξης τῆς χάριτος αὐτοῦ ἧς ἐχαρίτωσεν ἡμας [Eph 1:6b], τὸ πλοῦτος τῆς χάριτος [1:7b]) and "overflow" (ἐπερίσσευσεν [1:8a]) further underscores the benefaction context.[86] The appropriate response to an infinitely generous benefactor whose benefits bring about cosmic resolution must be the language of "praise" (ἔπαινος [Eph 1:6, 12, 14]), terminology also employed throughout the eulogy. The Ephesian inscriptions, therefore, allow us to see better the nuance of *planned beneficence* underlying the *oikonomos* metaphor in Eph 1:10.

Ephesians 3:2 speaks of his calling as apostle for the gentiles (εἰς ὑμᾶς ["for you"]) with the phrase τὴν οἰκονομίαν τῆς χάριτος τοῦ θεοῦ τῆς δοθείσης μοι ("the stewardship of the grace of God which has been given to me"). Later, in Eph 3:9, Paul speaks of his "stewardship of the mystery" (ἡ οἰκονομία τοῦ μυστηρίου), which, up till then, had been divinely hidden for ages. Little more needs to be said other than that the benefaction context again still dominates. This is the case whether Paul is talking about the origins of his apostolic ministry to the gentile nations (Eph 3:2), with a view to his fuller apocalyptic unveiling of God's mystery in the "co-body" of Jews and gentiles (3:3, 6), or his revelatory role in expounding the mystery of God's plan and wisdom, now made known universally through the church (3:9–10).

---

85. Caragounis, *Ephesian Mysterion*, 94; Schnackenburg, *Epistle to the Ephesians*, 58–59; Best, *Critical and Exegetical Commentary on Ephesians*, 138–39; Margaret Y. MacDonald, *Colossians and Ephesians*, SP 17 (Collegeville, MN: Liturgical Press, 2000), 202; John Muddiman, *The Epistle to the Ephesians*, BNTC 10 (London: Continuum, 2001), 75; Hoehner, *Ephesians*, 216–17. Markus Barth gives οἰκονομία a christological interpretation, arguing that the word refers to Christ's "stewardship over all possessions and the administration of all plans" (*Ephesians 1–3: A New Translation with Introduction and Commentary*, AB 34 [New York: Doubleday, 1974], 128). However, this reads too much theologically into Paul's text.

86. On the language of "overflow" in benefaction terminology, see Harrison, *Paul's Language of Grace*, 231, n. 74.

4.1.2.4. Paul's Eulogy and the Ephesian Understanding of Glory

The prominent use of the language of "praise of his glory" (εἰς ἔπαινον (τῆς) δόξης, ἔπαινον δόξης [Eph 1:6b, 12a, 14b])—in each case referring to God's glory—undermines the quest for personal status and ancestral glory on the part of the Ephesian elites. Cognates of δόξα (e.g., ἔνδοξος) are widely used in the Ephesian inscriptions. The city of Ephesus, we are told in IEph 1.24b, is made "more illustrious ([ἐ]νδοξοτέρα) and more blessed for all time" (ll. 33–34) through the correct honoring of Artemis.[87] Paul's theocentric redirection of the focus of glory away from the elites, who, as priests and priestesses, basked in the deflected glory of Artemis and the Roman ruler, is potent. Significantly, ἔνδοξος is never used for Artemis herself, but only for the city of Ephesus and the achievements of its inhabitants. Consequently, there are honorific decrees eulogizing "Augustus-loving" civic magistrates who are praised for their "glorious public service" (λιτουργὸν ἔνδοξον [IEph 3.624, 792; cf. 5.1575; 7.1.3058]).[88] An asiarch of Asia carries out his magistracy gloriously (ἐνδόξω[ς] [IEph 3.686; cf. 6.2063]). Finally, an athlete triumphs gloriously (ἐνδόξως) at the great Pythian games in Ephesus (IEph 4.1107). In terms of δόξα, we could also refer to Cn. Pompeius Quartinus who is honored on account of his good will towards the people and "glory in paideia" (τῆς ἐν παιδείᾳ δόξης [IEph 3.710]).

Here we see how glory at Ephesus concentrates upon human achievement in the imperial *cursus honorum* and in the athletic contests or upon the city of Ephesus itself. The entire spiral of Paul's praise in Eph 1:3–14, however, culminates in the glory of God alone, thereby consigning the luminaries of Ephesus to historical insignificance in the face of the surpassing wealth of God's grace and kindness in the coming ages (2:7). Elsewhere in the epistle, δόξα is reserved for the Father of glory (Eph 1:17), God's glorious inheritance for the saints (1:18), God's glory experienced in Christ's indwelling and strengthening of the believer (3:16), and God's glory in the church and Christ (3:21).

---

87. See also IEph 1a.24B: "Since the goddess Artemis, leader of our city, is honored not only in her own homeland, which she has made the most illustrious [ἐνδοξοτέραν] of all cities through her own divine nature, but also among Greeks and barbarians ..." (ll. 8–11).

88. In an inscription honoring a *grammateus* and gymnasiarch, he is spoken of as "glorious advisor of a plan" (βούλαρχον ἔνδοχον [IEph 7.1.3071, l. 4]).

Only once in Ephesians does Paul speak of the glory of human beings. There Paul inverts the operations of the Ephesian honor system by asserting that his sufferings on behalf of his converts in the city are paradoxically their glory (δόξα ὑμῶν [Eph 3:13]).[89] Margaret Y. MacDonald rightly locates Paul's thought here in the honor and shame discourse of antiquity, but she draws the wrong conclusion. Paul, she proposes, is appealing to afflictions "as external manifestations of honor."[90] While this works in a military context,[91] it does not square with the carefully constructed politics of public esteem cultivated by the elites in the Ephesian inscriptions. The shame of Paul's sufferings in ministry is reconfigured as the "glory" of his converts precisely because of the radical redefinition of suffering found in the cross of Christ and its soteriological benefits allocated to others through the vindication of the dishonored, but now resurrected and reigning, Messiah.

4.1.2.5. Paul's Eulogy and the Ephesian Gospel of Salvation

The "gospel of salvation" (τὸ εὐαγγέλιον τῆς σωτηρίας ὑμῶν [Eph 1:13]) stands in contrast to the arrival of "the happy announcement" (ἄν ἀπὸ Ῥώμης ἱλαρωτέρα ἔλθῃ ἀγγελία [IEph Ia.18b, l. 10]) from Claudian Rome. IEph 5.1448 stipulates that all Ephesian residents "wear garlands in view of the happy events which have been announced, [and that they make a thank offering] for the good tidings to Artemis [[εὐ]αγγέλια τῆι Ἀρτέμιδι]" because of the benefactions of King Demetrius to the city (306/301 BCE). The use of ἀγγελία ("announcement") and εὐαγγέλιον ("good tidings") in relation to the imperial and early Hellenistic Artemis cult at Ephesus in these two Ephesian inscriptions is surely significant as an ideological backdrop to Paul's use of εὐαγγέλιον in Eph 1:13. In light of the summation of cosmic history in Christ (Eph 1:10), including his supreme exaltation over all powers and the subordination of all things under his feet (1:20-22), it is hard not to conclude that an implicit critique of the imperial cult is

---

89. See Muddiman on why Eph 3:12 points to the "implausibility of a purely pseudepigraphical account of the origin of Ephesians" (*Epistle to the Ephesians*, 163-64).

90. MacDonald, *Colossians and Ephesians*, 267.

91. Peter Marshall cites literary sources where Roman generals glory in their weakness, shame, and suffering (*Enmity in Corinth: Social Conventions in Paul's Relations with the Corinthians*, WUNT 2/23 [Tübingen: Mohr Siebeck, 1987], 362-63).

occurring, as much as a decisive demonstration of the overthrow of the demonic powers.[92]

The language of salvation is also significant here. It is used in the Ephesian inscriptions of Julius Caesar: "The god manifest and common savior [σωτῆρα] of all human life, descended from Ares and Aphrodite" (IEph 1a.251). Similarly, it is used for Hadrian: "benefactor and savior [σωτῆρα]" (IEph 5.1501). Once again, the imperial cult background to such terminology lifts Paul's language to a more polemical dimension, even if such soteriological language is much more prominent in the LXX. To be sure, this language was also used of rulers in the Hellenistic ruler cult, but its immediate terminological transfer to Julius Caesar by the Ephesians ensured continuity between the Hellenistic ruler cult and the imperial ruler cult at Ephesus. Again, Paul's location of salvation in Christ alone implicitly critiques all the alternative savior figures of antiquity, divine and human.

4.1.2.6. Paul's Eulogy and Ephesian Identity

Lastly, we point to other features of the passage that may have had Ephesian resonances as well. We have noted the "roll call" of honor and civic virtue attached to the wealthy Ephesian families. The sense of marginalization for the majority who did not belong to these elite groups must have been intensely felt in a culture where the chatter of the honorific inscriptions reinforced the social hierarchy of merit and privilege in every public space of the city. However, Paul teaches the Ephesians that they have been predestined to "sonship" through Christ according to God's good pleasure (εἰς υἱοθεσίαν διὰ Ἰησοῦ Χριστοῦ [Eph 1:5]). Their status, by virtue of its attachment to the infinite God, excels the powerful elites of Ephesus. Notably, this election has occurred before "the foundation of the world" (Eph 1:5). Not only does this emphasize the unilateral initiative of divine grace and the ultimate security of the believer's destiny, but it also deflates the Ephesian foundation myths about the birth of Artemis and her residence in the Artemision at the city. These myths cannot compare with the anteriority of the believer's election into the family of God before all creation. This plan, devised before time, is spectacularly fulfilled "in the fullness of the times" (Eph 1:10) and will redound to God's glory in the coming ages (2:7). The

---

92. Arnold, *Ephesians, Power and Magic*, 70–85.

eternity of Roman rule and the international fame of Artemis belong to the passing age of darkness whereas believers, as children of light, now live in the age of Christ's resurrection light (5:8–14).

Furthermore, all this is accomplished in Christ, as the relentless *en Christō* language spotlights. Believers are incorporated into Christ, the beloved one, and into his love. All of God's favor, therefore, is given to those who are in the realm of Christ.[93] Thus the intimate association of Augustus and Roma with the goddess Artemis, articulated in numismatic reconfiguration of Ephesian civic identity in the Julio-Claudian period, does not bring security to the inhabitants of Ephesus, and the Roman Empire more generally, or provide them with a meaningful identity as citizens. That idolatrous ideology belongs to the deceitful thinking that will face the coming wrath (Eph 5:6) and that believers at Ephesus must expose as the works of darkness (5:10; cf. Acts 1:1–41). The believer's identity resides in Christ alone and not in the city and its rulers, human or divine. The gentile Ephesian believers, who are secure in Christ, are now citizens with the saints and belong to the household of God (ἐστὲ συμπολῖται τῶν ἁγίων καὶ οἰκεῖοι τοῦ θεοῦ [Eph 2:13, 19]).

This new citizenship and membership of God's household would have been especially meaningful for the new Ephesian believers, given that non-Ephesian benefactors were given citizenship in reciprocation of their benefits and that the citizenship grant was then inscribed in the Temple of Artemis (IEph 5.1449–55, 1458, 1460–61, 1465).[94] Paul seizes upon this in emphasizing that in Christ the Ephesians, as Jews and Gentiles, are joined together and grows into a holy temple in the Lord. There, as citizens, they become a dwelling place for God as opposed to Artemis (Eph 2:22). Paul's exposition of the new status of the believers at Ephesus in Eph 2:19–22 could not be more culturally pointed. As total outsiders to the covenant with Israel, with nothing to offer or to commend them to God, the Ephesian believers had achieved citizenship and familial status. In conclusion, Eph 1:3–14 reduces the Artemis cult, the Roman rulers, and their clients to

---

93. Constantine R. Campbell, *Paul and Union with Christ: An Exegetical and Theological Study* (Grand Rapids: Zondervan, 2012), 91.

94. For example: "To inscribe the grant of citizenship [πολιτείαν] to him in the temple of Artemis where the rest of such grants have been inscribed, and to allot a place for him both in a tribe and in a thousand, in order that the people of Ephesus honors with appropriate gifts the benefactors of the temple and the city" (IEph 5.1499, ll. 7–9).

insignificance in comparison to the overflowing and spiraling beneficence of God in Christ.

4.1.2.7. Divine Beneficence and the Ethical Transformation of Ephesian Believers: Paul's Challenge to Ephesian Civic Ethics

A final question remains. Does Paul, by implication, have anything to say specifically about the ethical corruption of the officials of the *koinon* of Asia and the pretentious and acquisitive quest for priesthoods by the elites? I doubt it. His concerns are fundamentally elsewhere. But Paul sets new standards for the leaders in Christ's alternative community. In our passage Paul highlights that believers have been chosen to be holy and blameless before God in love (Eph 1:4). Elsewhere, they are called ethically to resist the demonic powers of Ephesian life (Eph 6:10–20), discarding the old self and putting on the new self (4:24). Thus Paul warns believers about the idolatry of greed in Eph 5:4, a pointed reminder of the cupidity underlying Ephesian culture.

But most intriguing of all is Paul's adaptation of Ps 67:18 LXX (68:18 MT) in Eph 4:8.[95] The LXX original depicts the victory procession of the warrior God after his conquest of his enemies on earth. God, as victor over his captured enemies, ascends to Mount Zion in triumph, whereupon he receives tribute ("gifts") from the defeated rebels to signal their submission (ἔλαβες δόματα ἐν ἀνθρώπῳ [Ps 67:18 LXX]). But, in Paul's messianic reconfiguration of the Psalm, the ascended Christ gives gifts to men (ἔδωκεν δόματα τοῖς ἀνθρώποις [Eph 4:8]) instead of receiving them. Thus Paul moves the Psalm's imagery from honor and triumph, where the victor is acknowledged with tribute from the captured rebels, to one of overflowing beneficence, where the victor dispenses gifts to his dependents and allies. What the risen Christ gives, however, are *gifted leaders* to his church (Eph 4:11). The role of the gifted leaders is to prepare God's people for the work of service so that believers might attain the fullness of Christ, demonstrated in a stable faith that is characterized by a commitment to truth and love (Eph 4:12–16). The contrast between the self-effacement of the leaders in the body of Christ and the self-aggrandizement of the wealthy civic and cultic elites at Ephesus could not be clearer.

---

95. For full discussion, see W. Hall Harris III, *The Descent of Christ: Ephesians 4:7–11 and Traditional Hebrew Imagery*, BSL (Grand Rapids: Baker, 1998).

5. Conclusion

We have argued that in Eph 1:3–14, Paul interweaves Jewish motifs with the civic benefaction language of the Ephesian inscriptions. This long sentence spiral of God's benefactions finds its rhetorical counterpart in the cumulative participial phrases of the honorific inscriptions in which the munificence of the benefactor is recounted in intricate detail. We have noted six important motifs that would have resonated with an Ephesian audience familiar with the eulogies of the civic inscriptions (§§4.1.2.1–6). God's public unveiling of his eternal mystery in Christ, of which Paul was the apostolic *oikonomos*, totally outshone the civic statue processions funded by the bequest of C. Vibius Salutaris. The annual stewardship of the mysteries of Artemis, overseen by the priestess daughters of the wealthy Ephesian aristocratic elites, remained closed to everyone else outside that privileged circle. But the *mystērion* of Christ was now opened, by an unprecedented act of predestinating grace, to the entire world, including the godless gentiles who did not belong to Israel and who had never sought her God. The cruciform Lord of grace provided a selfless soteriological benefaction that stood in contrast to the self-seeking elites of Ephesus vying for imperial priesthoods, as well as the ephemeral "facelifts" that the Roman world benefactor, his governor, and the local Ephesian benefactors gave to the roads and buildings of Ephesus. The varied iconographic motifs of the local Ephesian provincial coinage, which praised Roma, the Roman ruler, and Artemis, the protecting deity of Ephesus, would also have been sidelined by Paul's spiraling paean of praise to the God of Israel and to his risen messianic Son, who had triumphed over the demonic ruler of the spirit world through the cross. Rather than a monstrous conglomeration of inelegant phrases, as the classicist Norden had ventured, Eph 1:3–14 is one of the most carefully written sentences in the New Testament. Paul's sentence implicitly critiques the city's propaganda about the Roman ruler, its gods, its benefactors, and its priests, employing both the terminological heritage of the LXX and the considerable opportunities provided by the Ephesian honorific inscriptions.

Bibliography

Arnold, Clinton E. *Ephesians, Power and Magic: The Concept of Power in Ephesians in Light of Its Historical Setting.* SNTSMS 63. Cambridge: Cambridge University Press, 1989. Repr., Grand Rapids: Baker, 1992.

Ascough, Richard S., Philip A. Harland, and John S. Kloppenborg, eds. *Associations in the Greco-Roman World: A Sourcebook.* Waco, TX: Baylor University Press, 2012.

Barth, Markus. *Ephesians 1–3: A New Translation with Introduction and Commentary.* AB 34. New York: Doubleday, 1974.

Baugh, Steven M. "Cultic Prostitution in New Testament Ephesus: A Reappraisal." *JETS* 42 (1999): 443–60.

Best, Ernest. *A Critical and Exegetical Commentary on Ephesians.* ICC. Edinburgh: T&T Clark, 1998.

Bockmuehl, Markus. *Revelation and Mystery in Ancient Judaism and Pauline Christianity.* WUNT 2.36. Tübingen: Mohr Siebeck, 1990. Repr., Grand Rapids: Eerdmans, 1997.

Braund, David C. *Augustus to Nero: Sourcebook on Roman History 31 BC–AD 68.* Totowa, NJ: Barnes & Noble, 1985.

Bremmer, Jan N. "Priestly Personnel of the Ephesian Artemesion: Anatolian, Persian Greek, and Roman Aspects." Pages 37–53 in *Practitioners of the Divine: Greek Priests and Religious Officials from Homer to Heliodorus.* Edited by Beate Dignas and Kai Trampedach. HS 30. Washington, DC: Center for Hellenic Studies, 2008.

Burnett, Andrew M., Michel Amandry, and Pere Pau Ripollès. *Introduction and Catalogue.* Part 1 of *From the Death of Caesar to the Death of Vitellius (44 BC–AD 69).* Vol. 1 of *Roman Provincial Coinage.* Paris: Bibliothèque nationale de France; London: British Museum Press, 1992.

Büyükkolanci, Mustafa, and Helmut Engelmann. "Inschriften aus Ephesos." *ZPE* 120 (1998): 65–82.

Campbell, Constantine R. *Paul and Union with Christ: An Exegetical and Theological Study.* Grand Rapids: Zondervan, 2012.

Caragounis, Chrys C. *The Ephesian Mysterion: Meaning and Content.* ConBNT 6. Lund: Gleerup, 1977.

Carter, Warren "Festivals, Cultural Intertextuality, and the Gospel of John's Rhetoric of Distance." *HvTSt* 67 (2011): https://tinyurl.com/SBL4209a.

Chaniotis, Angelos. "Epigraphic Bulletin for Greek Religion 2006." *Kernos* 22 (2009): 209–43.

Cooley, Alison E. *Res Gestae Divi Augusti: Text, Translation, and Commentary.* Cambridge: Cambridge University Press, 2009.

Danker, Frederick W. *Benefactor: Epigraphic Study of a Graeco-Roman and New Testament Semantic Field.* St. Louis, MO: Clayton, 1982.

———. "Ephesians, Epistle to the." Pages 109–13 in *E–J*. Vol. 2 of *International Standard Bible Encyclopaedia*. Edited by Geoffrey William Bromiley. Grand Rapids: Eerdmans, 1982.

Dignas, Beate. *Economy of the Sacred in Hellenistic and Roman Asia Minor*. OCM. Oxford: Oxford University Press, 2002.

Dillon, Sheila. "The Portraits of a Civic Benefactor of 2nd Century Ephesos." *JRA* 9 (1996): 261–74.

Eck, Werner, Antonio Caballos, and Fernando Fernández, eds. *Das Senatus Consultum de Cn. Pisone Patre*. Vestigia 48. Munich: Beck, 1996.

Erim, Kenan T. *Aphrodisias: City of Venus Aphrodite*. London: Muller, Bond & White, 1986.

Frayer-Griggs, Daniel. "The Beasts at Ephesus and the Cult of Artemis." *HTR* 106 (2013): 459–77.

Friesen, Steven J. "The Beast from the Land: Revelation 13:11–18 and Social Setting." Pages 49–64 in *Reading the Book of Revelation: A Resource for Students*. Edited by David L. Barr. RBS 44. Atlanta: Society of Biblical Literature, 2003.

———. *Twice Neokoros: Ephesus, Asia and the Cult of the Flavian Imperial Family*. RGRW 116. Leiden: Brill, 1993.

Frija, Gabrielle. *Les prêtres des empereurs: Le culte impérial civique dans la province romaine d'Asie*. Collection Histoire. Rennes: Presses Universitaires de Rennes, 2012.

Galinsky, Karl. *Augustan Culture: An Interpretive Introduction*. Princeton: Princeton University Press, 1996.

Goodrich, John K. *Paul as an Administrator of God in 1 Corinthians*. SNTSMS 152. Cambridge: Cambridge University Press, 2012.

Gosnell, Peter W. "Honor and Shame Rhetoric as a Unifying Motif in Ephesians." *BBR* 16 (2006): 105–28.

Harris, W. Hall, III. *The Descent of Christ: Ephesians 4:7–11 and Traditional Hebrew Imagery*. BSL. Grand Rapids: Baker, 1998.

Harrison, James R. "Artemis Triumphs over a Sorcerer's Evil Art." *NewDocs* 10:37–47.

———. "'The Fading Crown': Divine Honour and the Early Christians." *JTS* 54 (2003): 493–529.

———. "Family Honour of a Priestess of Artemis." *NewDocs* 10:30–36.

———. "The First Urban Churches: Introduction." Pages 1–40 in *Methodological Foundations*. Vol. 1 of *The First Urban Churches*. Edited by James R. Harrison and L. L. Welborn. WGRWSup 7. Atlanta: SBL Press, 2015.

———. "The 'Grace' of Augustus Paves a Street at Ephesus." *NewDocs* 10:59–63.

———. "The Imitation of the Great Man in Antiquity: Paul's Inversion of a Cultural Icon." Pages 213–54 in *Christian Origins and Classical Culture: Social and Literary Contexts for the New Testament*. Vol. 1 of *Early Christianity in Its Hellenistic Context*. Edited by Stanley E. Porter and Andrew W. Pitts. TENTS 9. Leiden: Brill, 2013.

———. "Paul and Ancient Civic Ethics: Redefining the Canon of Honour in the Graeco- Roman World." Pages 75–118 in *Paul's Graeco-Roman Context*. Edited by Cilliers Breytenbach. BETL 277. Leuven: Peeters, 2015.

———. *Paul and the Imperial Authorities at Thessalonica and Rome: A Study in the Conflict of Ideology*. WUNT 273. Tübingen: Mohr Siebeck, 2011.

———. *Paul's Language of Grace in Its Graeco-Roman Context*. WUNT 2/172. Tübingen: Mohr Siebeck, 2003. Repr., Eugene, OR: Wipf & Stock, 2017.

Hendrix, Holland L. "On the Form and Ethos of Ephesians." *USQR* 42 (1988): 3–15.

Hoehner, Harold W. *Ephesians: An Exegetical Commentary*. Grand Rapids: Baker Academic, 2002.

Horsley, Greg H. R. "A Fishing Cartel in First-Century Ephesos." *NewDocs* 5:95–114.

Horster, Marietta, and Anja Klöckner, eds. *Cities and Priests: Cult Personnel in Asia Minor and the Aegean Islands from the Hellenistic to the Imperial Period*. RVV 64 Berlin: de Gruyter, 2013.

Instone-Brewer, David. "The Eighteen Benedictions and the Minim before 70 CE." *JTS* 54 (2003): 25–44.

Jones, C. P. "Atticus in Ephesus." *ZPE* 124 (1999): 89–94.

Judge, E. A. "Thanksgiving to the Benefactor of the World, Tiberius Caesar." *NewDocs* 9:22.

Kalinowski, Angela V. "Patterns of Patronage: The Politics and Ideology of Public Building in the Eastern Roman Empire (31 BCE–600 CE)." PhD diss., University of Toronto, 1996.

———. "The Vedii Antonini: Aspects of Patronage and Benefaction in Second Century Ephesos." *Phoenix* 56 (2003): 109–49.

Kearsley, Rosalinde A. "Asiarchs, 'Archiereis,' and the 'Archiereiai' of Asia." *GRBS* 27 (1986): 183–92.

———. "The Mysteries of Artemis at Ephesus." *NewDocs* 6:196–202.

Keener, Craig S. "Paul's 'Friends' the Asiarchs (Acts 19:31)." *JGRChJ* 3 (2006): 134–41.

Kidson, Lyn. "Minting in Ephesus: Economics and Self-Promotion in the Early Imperial Period." *JNAA* 23 (2012/2013): 27–36.

Knibbe, Dieter. "Private Euergetism in the Service of the City-Goddess: The Most Wealthy Ephesian Family of the Second Century CE Supports Artemis in Her Struggle against the Decline of Her Cult after the Meteorological Catastrophe of 186 CE." *MedAnt* 5 (2002): 49–62.

———. "Via Sacra Ephesiaca: New Aspects of the Cult of Artemis Ephesia." Pages 141–55 in *Ephesos, Metropolis of Asia: An Interdisciplinary Approach to Its Archaeology, Religion, and Culture*. Edited by Helmut Koester. HTS 41. Valley Forge, PA: Trinity Press International, 1995.

Knibbe, Dieter, Helmut Engelmann, and Bülent İplikçioğlu. "Neue Inschriften aus Ephesos XI." *JÖAI* 59 (1989): 163–237.

Lincoln, Andrew T. *Ephesians*. WBC 42. Dallas: Word, 1990.

MacDonald, Margaret Y. *Colossians and Ephesians*. SP 17. Collegeville, MN: Liturgical Press, 2000.

Marshall, Peter. *Enmity in Corinth: Social Conventions in Paul's Relations with the Corinthians*. WUNT 2/23. Tübingen: Mohr Siebeck, 1987.

Masson, Charles. *L'épître de Paul aux Éphésiens*. CNT 9. Neuchâtel: Delachaux & Niestlé, 1953.

Mattingly, Harold. *Augustus to Vitellius*. Vol. 1 of *Coins of the Roman Empire in the British Museum*. London: Trustees of the British Museum, 1965.

Mitford, T. B. "Inscriptiones Ponticae—Sebastopolis." *ZPE* 87 (1991): 181–243.

Muddiman, John. *The Epistle to the Ephesians*. BNTC 10. London: Continuum, 2001.

Norden, Eduard. *Agnostos Theos: Untersuchungen zur Formengeschichte religiöser Rede*. Leipzig: Teubner, 1913.

O'Brien, Peter Thomas. *The Letter to the Ephesians*. Grand Rapids: Eerdmans, 2009.

Oster, Richard E. "Holy Days in Honour of Artemis." *NewDocs* 4:74–82.

Price, Simon R. F. *Rituals and Power: The Roman Imperial Cult in Asia Minor*. Cambridge: Cambridge University Press, 1984.

Rogers, Guy MacLean. *The Mysteries of Artemis of Ephesos: Cult, Polis, and Change in the Graeco-Roman World*. Syncrisis. New Haven: Yale University Press, 2012.

———. *The Sacred Identity of Ephesos: Foundation Myths of a Roman City*. London: Routledge, 1991.

Rowe, C. Kavin. *World Upside Down: Reading Acts in the Graeco-Roman Age*. Oxford: Oxford University Press, 2009.
Schnackenburg, Rudolf. *The Epistle to the Ephesians: A Commentary*. Translated by Helen Heron. Edinburgh: T&T Clark, 1991.
Smith, R. R. R. *The Marble Reliefs from the Julio-Claudian Sebasteion*. Vol. 6 of *Aphrodisias*. Darnstadt: von Zabern, 2013.
Strelan, Rick. *Paul, Artemis, and the Jews in Ephesus*. BZNW 80. Berlin: de Gruyter, 1996.
Tilborg, Sjef van. *Reading John in Ephesus*. NovTSup 83. Leiden: Brill, 1996.
Trebilco, Paul. *The Early Christians in Ephesus from Paul to Ignatius*. WUNT 166. Tübingen: Mohr Siebeck, 2004. Repr., Grand Rapids: Eerdmans, 2007.
Wagner, Günter. *Pauline Baptism and the Pagan Mysteries: The Problem of the Pauline Doctrine of Baptism in Romans VI.1–11, in the Light of Its Religio-historical "Parallels."* Edinburgh: Oliver & Boyd, 1967.
Wedderburn, Alexander J. M. *Baptism and Resurrection: Studies in Pauline Theology against Its Graeco-Roman Background*. WUNT 44. Tübingen: Mohr Siebeck, 1987.
Zamfir, Korinna. *Men and Women in the Household of God: A Contextual Approach to Roles and Ministries in the Pastoral Epistles*. NTOA 103. Göttingen: Vandenhoeck & Ruprecht, 2013.
Zanker, Paul. *The Power of Images in the Age of Augustus*. Translated by A. Shapiro. JL 16. Ann Arbor: University of Michigan Press, 1988.
Zerwick, Max. *The Epistle to the Ephesians*. NTSR 16. London: Burns & Oates, 1969.
Zuiderhoek, Arjan. *The Politics of Munificence in the Roman Empire: Citizens, Elites, and Benefactors in Asia Minor*. GCRW. Cambridge: Cambridge University Press, 2009.

Ephesus and the Numismatic Background to νεωκόρος

Michael P. Theophilos

The term νεωκόρος is a New Testament *hapax legomenon*, which occurs in the speech of the unnamed Ephesian town clerk (γραμματεύς) in Acts 19:35. The context of his speech is that of the ensuing riot instigated by Demetrius the silversmith (Acts 19:21–41), who was concerned for the economic viability of his trade guild in light of Paul's message, "[gods] made with hands are not gods" (οὐκ εἰσὶν θεοὶ οἱ διὰ χειρῶν γινόμενοι [19:26]).[1] Demetrius subsequently protests that "the temple of the great goddess Artemis will be regarded as worthless and she whom all of Asia and the world worship will even be dethroned from her magnificence" (τὸ τῆς μεγάλης θεᾶς Ἀρτέμιδος ἱερὸν εἰς οὐθὲν λογισθῆναι, μέλλειν τε καὶ καθαιρεῖσθαι τῆς μεγαλειότητος αὐτῆς ἣν ὅλη ἡ Ἀσία καὶ ἡ οἰκουμένη σέβεται [19:27]). This, in turn, generates a series of ideological objections by the inhabitants of the city who had assembled in the theatre to engage in a verbal demonstration of support for Artemis, "great is Artemis of the Ephesians" (μεγάλη ἡ Ἄρτεμις Ἐφεσίων [19:28]). In response, the town clerk (γραμματεύς), seeking to placate the crowds, reassured the inhabitants that the great reputation of Ephesus as the "guardian of the temple of the great Artemis and of the image which fell down from heaven" (νεωκόρον οὖσαν τῆς μεγάλης Ἀρτέμιδος καὶ τοῦ διοπετοῦς [19:35]) was not at risk. Citing the decrees of Ephesus, A. N. Sherwin-White notes that the "[γραμματεύς] appears in conjunction with the *strategoi* as a senior partner, acting as the director of affairs in council or assembly,"[2] providing evidence that his role was akin to a magistrate, rather than an administrative assistant. Paul Trebilco notes that the position was of such significance that "inscriptions

---

1. All translations are my own unless otherwise noted.
2. A. N. Sherwin-White, *Roman Society and Roman Law in the New Testament: Sarum Lectures, 1960–1961* (Oxford: Clarendon, 1963), 86.

were often dated by the clerk's year in office."[3] The γραμματεύς is thus well placed to "take control of the assembly."[4]

One of the pertinent questions that arises within this pericope is the precise meaning of the Ephesian town clerk's reference to the city as the νεωκόρον. The term is variously translated in English versions as "guardian of the temple" (NASB, NIV), "temple guardian" (HCSB), "official guardian of the temple" (NLT), "keeper of the temple" (NET, GW), "temple keeper" (ASV, ESV), "worshipper" (KJV, DRB), and "devotee" (YLT). This paper brings to bear the relevant numismatic material and the manner in which it can be employed to illuminate this designation.

1. Method

One of the early modern scholarly endeavors to grapple with, and incorporate, critical numismatic material into the emerging discipline of Greek lexicography was Franz Passow's *Handwörterbuch der griechischen Sprache* (1831).[5] A century later, the pioneering linguistic work by Friedrich Preisigke and Emil Kiessling, *Wörterbuch der griechischen Papyrusurkunden mit Einschluss der griechischen Inschriften, Ausschriften, Ostraka, Mumienschilder usw. aus Ägypten*, also drew on numismatic material, as did the work's revisions and supplements.[6] Although later studies have occasionally drawn

---

3. Paul Trebilco, "Asia," in *Graeco-Roman Setting*, vol. 2 of *The Book of Acts in Its First Century Setting*, ed. David W. J. Gill and Conrad Gempf (Grand Rapids: Eerdmans, 1994), 351.

4. I. Howard Marshall, *Acts: An Introduction and Commentary*, TNTC (Grand Rapids: Eerdmans, 1980), 360.

5. The work, Franz Passow, *Handwörterbuch der griechischen Sprache*, 2 vols. (Leipzig: Vogel, 1831), appropriately acknowledged as precursor to LSJ, is itself essentially the fourth edition of a work begun by Johann Gottlob Theaenus Schneider (see John A. L. Lee, *A History of New Testament Lexicography*, SBG 8 [New York: Lang, 2003], 347–48). Upon Passow's death in 1833, work was continued on the project by V. Rost and F. Palm with a four-volume revision published in 1841–1857. See also Wilhelm Crönert, *Passow's Wörterbuch der griechischen Sprache*, 3 vols. (Göttingen: Vandenhoeck & Ruprecht, 1913).

6. The full details of the original work are Friedrich Preisigke and Emil Kiesssling, *Wörterbuch der griechischen Papyrusurkunden mit Einschluss der griechischen Inschriften, Ausschriften, Ostraka, Mumienschilder usw. aus Ägypten*, 3 vols. (Berlin: Erbe, 1925–1931); Kiessling and others gradually produced a still incomplete fourth volume in five parts, covering the alphabetic sequence ἀ–ζωφυτέω, and also three supplements, the last appearing in 2000.

on the material evidence of the numismatic record (with some notable exceptions), characteristically, this material is neglected in technical discussions of Greek lexicography.

The eminent numismatist Harold Mattingly has noted the relationship of coins to forms of propaganda in the Roman world, stating, "Coin types are constantly changing, and constantly emphasising definite events and policies, and, as they change move in close agreement with the political changes of the time."[7] Mattingly continues by stating, "The possible influence of such coinage on public opinion could not possibly be overlooked or minimized by the Emperor. He must ... have censored, if not inspired

---

7. Harold Mattingly, *Nerva to Hadrian*, vol. 3 of *Coins of the Roman Empire in the British Museum* (London: British Museum, 1936), xlv. On the use of coins in Roman propaganda, see Christopher J. Howgego, *Ancient History from Coins* (London: Routledge, 1995), 62–87; A. H. M. Jones, "Numismatics and History," in *The Roman Economy: Studies in Ancient Economic and Administrative History*, ed. Peter Brunt (Oxford: Blackwell, 1974), 61–81; Michael H. Crawford, "Roman Imperial Coin Types and the Formation of Public Opinion," in *Studies in Numismatic Method presented to Philip Grierson*, ed. C. N. L. Brooke et al. (Cambridge: Cambridge University Press, 1983), 47–64; Barbara Levick, "Propaganda and the Imperial Coinage," *Antichthon* 16 (1982): 104–16; C. T. H. R. Ehrhardt, "Roman Coin Types and the Roman Public," *JNG* 34 (1984): 41–54; Andrew Meadows and Jonathan Williams, "Moneta and the Monuments: Coinage and Politics in Republican Rome," *JRS* 91 (2001): 27–49. For earlier Republic coins see Andrew M. Burnett, "The Iconography of Roman Coin Types in the Third Century B.C.," *NC* 146 (1986): 67–75; Andreas Alföldi, "The Main Aspects of Political Propaganda on the Coinage of the Roman Republic," in *Essays in Roman Coinage presented to Harold Mattingly*, ed. Robert Andrew Glindinning Carson and Carol Humphrey Vivian Sutherland (Oxford: Oxford University Press, 1956), 63–95; Harriet I. Flower, *Ancestor Marks and Aristocratic Power in Roman Culture* (Oxford: Clarendon, 1996); Philip V. Hill, "Coin Symbolism and Propaganda during the Wars of Vengeance (44–36 B.C.)," *QT* 4 (1975): 157–207. For discussion of propaganda and coins of the Imperial period, see Tonio Hölscher, *Staatsdenkmal und Publikum: Vom Untergang der Republik bis zur Festigung des Kaisertums in Rom* (Konstanz: Universitätsverlag Konstanz, 1984); Pierre Bastien, *Le buste monétaire des empereurs romains*, 3 vols., NR 19 (Wetteren: Éditions numismatiques romaines, 1992–1994); Niels Hannestad, *Roman Art and Imperial Policy*, JASP 19 (Aarhus: Aarhus University Press, 1986); Sutherland, *Coinage in Roman Imperial Policy 31 B.C—A.D. 68* (London: Methuen, 1951); Andrew Wallace-Hadrill, "The Emperor and His Virtues," *Historia* 30 (1981): 298–323; Carlos F. Noreña, "The Communication of the Emperor's Virtues" *JRS* 91 (2001): 146–68; Paul Zanker, *The Power of Images in the Age of Augustus*, trans. A. Shapiro, JL 16 (Ann Arbor: University of Michigan Press, 1988); Wallace-Hadrill, "Image and Authority in the Coinage of Augustus," *JRS* 76 (1986): 66–87.

it."[8] In similar regard, Warren Carter states, "coins demonstrated Roman sovereignty ... [and] symbolized Roman accomplishments and the blessings of the gods which the emperor mediated to the people. There was no escaping Roman presence even in daily transactions."[9] In first-century Mediterranean village life, Keith D. Dyer suggests, the circulation of coinage operated as one of the most efficient and concrete forms of communication.[10] This would suggest, *prima facie*, that the numismatic record has preserved a wealth of cultural, social, and—most importantly for our purposes—linguistic material from a period contemporaneous with the composition of the New Testament. A strong and relatively sophisticated methodological case has been put forward by Richard E. Oster, who advocates for the inclusion of numismatic material by New Testament academicians. Surprisingly, however, his excellent treatment has largely fallen on deaf ears.[11] In Oster's analysis, coins are to be seen as a valid "source for ancient economics, art, political science, history of religions, and general history" (and we might add one further—lexicographic), yet

---

8. Mattingly, *Nerva to Hadrian*, xlv.

9. Warren Carter, *Matthew and the Margins: A Sociopolitical and Religious Reading* (Sheffield: Sheffield Academic Press, 2000), 38.

10. Keith D. Dyer, *The Prophecy on the Mount: Mark 13 and the Gathering of the New Community*, ITS 2 (Bern: Lang, 1998), 112; Dyer, "'But Concerning That Day ...' (Mark 13:32): 'Prophetic' and 'Apocalyptic' Eschatology in Mark 13," in *1999 Seminar Papers*, SBLSP 38 (Atlanta: Scholars Press, 1999), 104–22; Richard E. Oster has also argued at length that coinage was one of the main methods of disseminating ideas and information in antiquity ("Numismatic Windows into the Social World of Early Christianity: A Methodological Inquiry," *JBL* 101 [1982]: 195–223). On Roman provincial coinage, see Andrew M. Burnett, Michel Amandry, and Pere Pau Ripollès, *Roman Provincial Coinage* (London: British Museum Press; Paris: Bibliothèque nationale, 1992–); K. Butcher, *Roman Provincial Coins: An Introduction to the Greek Imperials* (London: Seaby, 1988); Christopher J. Howgego, "The Supply and Use of Money in the Roman World 200 B.C.–A.D. 300," *JRS* 82 (1992): 1–31; Michael H. Crawford, "Money and Exchange in the Roman world," *JRS* 60 (1970): 40–46; Jean Andreau, *Banking and Business in the Roman World*, KTAH (Cambridge: Cambridge University Press, 1999). Attention to the numismatic record also helps define the circulation and models of the monetary economy; see Howgego, "Coin Circulation and the Integration of the Roman Economy," *JRA* 7 (1994): 5–21; Keith Hopkins, "Taxes and Trade in the Roman Empire (200 B.C.–A.D. 400)," *JRS* 70 (1980): 101–25; Richard P. Duncan-Jones, *Structure and Scale in the Roman Economy* (Cambridge: Cambridge University Press, 1990); Duncan-Jones, "Mobility and Immobility of Coin in the Roman Empire," *AIIN* 36 (1989): 121–37.

11. Oster, "Numismatic Windows," 195–223.

he notes that "historians of earliest Christianity have repeatedly failed to give appropriate and significant attention to the analysis and application of data preserved on ancient coins."[12]

The serious, scientific, and academic incorporation of numismatic material into historical analysis was significantly impeded by the disparaging comments by A. H. M. Jones:

> If a modern analogy is to be sought for the varying types and legends of Roman imperial coins it is perhaps to be found in the similar variations in the postage stamps of modern countries other than our own (England). These often show a certain propagandistic tendency, its artistic monuments, or its principal industries. They are also sometimes topical, or commemorative of great events in national history. They throw a sidelight on the history of the period, but they mainly reflect the mentality of the post-office officials. No serious historian would use them as a clue which revealed changes of government policy, even if other evidence were totally lacking. It would be better if numismatists took the coin types and legends less seriously, and if historians of the empire, instead of building fantastic history upon them, frankly admitted that the political history of periods when coins are the sole evidence is irrecoverable, apart from the bare bones of chronology of the reigns, the areas which the various emperors effectively controlled, and any salient events which the coins directly celebrate.[13]

A swift and satisfying rebuttal of Jones was forthcoming in the work of Carol Humphrey Vivian Sutherland:

> Analogy is of course always tempting, but very often dangerous, especially when the precise degree of parallelism—upon which the efficacy of analogy depends most powerfully—is open to serious question. At best it can serve as a stimulating suggestion—that is, where no direct causal connection exists: at worst it may be fallacious. Thus when the function and behaviour of Roman imperial coin types is likened to that of modern postage-stamps the analogy is to be regarded with the utmost skepticism. It is true that both authenticate a government product, and that both, without question, reflect the activity of government officials, and that both, again, incorporate the principle of variety, but there the like-

---

12. Ibid., 195.
13. A. H. M. Jones, "Numismatics and History," in *Essays in Roman Coinage Presented to Harold Mattingly* (Oxford: Oxford University Press, 1956), 15–16.

ness ends. The modern postage stamp has always existed in an age when official propaganda of news has depended on organs of information far more ample than mere stamp-design, which is therefore devoted, apart from its essential symbolism of authority, to often quite formal aspects of general national interest. In imperial coinage, however, not only is there seen to be an overwhelming desire to vary types, but those types play so constantly and (even to modern eyes) so skillfully with different concepts of imperial government that, in an age when news could not be propagated by newspaper and radio, their intention cannot be doubted. They were, in essence, organs of information.[14]

The trajectory of this paper is part of a larger project that explores the implications of the numismatic material for contributions to lexicography, particularly as it pertains to linguistic features of postclassical Greek.[15] The working aim and methodology adopted in both that larger work and this paper can be summarized as follows: to employ dated and geographically legitimate comparative numismatic data to refine, illuminate, and clarify the relevant semantic domains of New Testament vocabulary, with a particular interest in New Testament *cruces interpretationis*. This study will necessarily focus on the Roman provincial coinage that enjoyed greater flexibility than its imperial counterpart and indeed featured a rich diversity of representations of local rulers and their concerns, including themes related to religion, myth, emperor worship, personification, general history, local interest, military types, and buildings. The evidence in all of these categories is voluminous and provides a rich resource of material into the linguistic fabric of the New Testament period.[16]

---

14. Carol Humphrey Vivian Sutherland, "The Intelligibility of Roman Imperial Coin Types," *JRS* 49 (1959): 54, cited in Oster, "Numismatic Windows," 197.

15. Michael P. Theophilos, *Numismatics and Greek Lexicography* (Edinburgh: T&T Clark, forthcoming).

16. A specific area of concern is the social origin of the coins and the way in which this influences our historical reconstruction. Historians have frequently noted that coins are issued by the narrow, upper stratum of society, and as such, forming a historical picture based only on numismatic evidence is not only methodologically suspicious but may in many circumstances be seriously misleading. Rather than dismissing the numismatic material as evidence for reconstructing history, a more plausible solution is to acknowledge that the distillation of historical reconstruction on coinage does not represent the full spectrum of the contemporary social world. However, this does not discount the valid contribution of the evidence, albeit of a section of elite social life.

2. Context and Background

Ephesus was the leading city in the Roman province of Asia. It could boast a rich and complex history of occupation dating back, at the very least, to the Mycenaean period (ca. 1400 BCE).[17] Its coastal location offered the ideal conditions for developing into a large seaport, which in turn generated considerable wealth for the city and created a prosperous commercial entity. So much so that Strabo states, "Such, then, is the harbour; and the city, because of its advantageous situation in other respects, grows daily, and is the largest emporium in Asia this side [of] the Taurus" (ὁ μὲν οὖν λιμὴν τοιοῦτος· ἡ δὲ πόλις τῇ πρὸς τὰ ἄλλα εὐκαιρίᾳ τῶν τόπων αὔξεται καθ' ἑκάστην ἡμέραν, ἐμπόριον οὖσα μέγιστον τῶν κατὰ τὴν Ἀσίαν τὴν ἐντὸς τοῦ Ταύρου [*Geogr.* 14.1.24]).[18]

In the first century CE, it is estimated that the population of Ephesus exceeded two hundred thousand.[19] Amid the cosmopolitan population of Ionians, Lydians, Phrygians, and Mysians, there was a substantial Jewish population. Josephus notes that Dolabella, the governor of Asia, exempted Ephesian Jewish Roman citizens from military service "because they are not allowed to bear arms, or to travel on the Sabbath days, nor there to procure themselves those sorts of food which they have been used to eat from the times of their forefathers" (διὰ τὸ μήτε ὅπλα βαστάζειν δύνασθαι μήτε ὁδοιπορεῖν ἐν ταῖς ἡμέραις τῶν σαββάτων, μήτε τροφῶν τῶν πατρίων καὶ συνήθων κατὰ τούτους εὐπορεῖν [*Ant.* 14.226; cf. 14.223–227, 262–264]).

---

17. See further Ekrem Akurgal, *Ancient Civilizations and Ruins of Turkey: From Prehistoric Times until the End of the Roman Empire*, 6th ed. (Ankara: Haşet Kitabevi, 1985); Machteld J. Mellink, "Archaeology in Asia Minor," *AJA* 63 (1959): 73–85; Veronika Mitsopoulos-Leon, "Ephesus," in *The Princeton Encyclopedia of Classical Sites*, ed. Richard Stillwell, William L. MacDonald, and Marian Holland McAllister (Princeton: Princeton University Press, 1976), 306–10.

18. Translation from Horace Leonard Jones, trans., *Strabo: Geography; Books 13–14*, LCL 223 (Cambridge: Harvard University Press, 1929), 231.

19. Otto Friedrich August Meinardus estimates 200,000 (*St. Paul in Ephesus and the Cities of Galatia and Cyprus*, IFS [New Rochelle, NY: Caratzas, 1979], 54). Thomas Robert Shannon Broughton estimates less than 225,000 ("Roman Asia," in *Roman Africa, Syria, Greece, and Asia*, vol. 4 of *An Economic Survey of Ancient Rome*, ed. Tenney Frank [Baltimore: Johns Hopkins Press, 1938], 813). Richard E. Oster estimates 250,000 ("Ephesus, Ephesians," in *Encyclopedia of Early Christianity* [Chicago: St. James, 1990], 301). It is notable that only Rome and Alexandria were more populous during this period.

It would thus appear that the Ephesian Jewish community had a "cordial relationship with the civic officials and the local populace."[20]

One of the ways the local inhabitants chose to bestow acclamation upon the emperor was to build a temple in his honor and thus to provide a central location for the cities of the province to sacrifice to the emperor. It was in the first century CE that a transition of terminology occurred. As will be discussed below, before the first century CE, the term νεωκόρος referred to a temple official (or the like) whose duties ranged from priestly to economic and administrative support for a temple; later, however, this term underwent a significant evolution.

Etymologically, the derivation of the compound νεωκόρος comes from two Greek words. The first part, ναός, denotes a "place or structure specifically associated with or set apart for a deity," in which the "deity is worshipped."[21] Barbara Burrell, however, cites Pierre Chantraine who distinguishes ναός, as a built structure, from a sacred unroofed enclosure.[22] Moisés Silva further distinguishes the term from τέμενος, which he defines as "a space fenced in, or at least clearly marked as an area a theophany has once occurred and is expected again on the ground of tradition," as distinct from ναός, which is "a dwelling for the gods; used for sacrifice, worship and the reception of oracles," and a place that "required a local priesthood."[23] Nonetheless, a definition of the term ναός, which at its core has linkage with a sacred place and associated deity, is readily evident.

The second part of the compound -κόρος is more ambiguous. Burrell notes that Hesychius of Alexandria identifies the derivation of the term as "keep in order" and, specifically, "sweep."[24] This indeed is the definition that Wilhelm Büchner attributes to the term on the basis of Euripides's *Ion*, in which one of his tasks was to sweep the Temple of Apollo (ll. 54–55).[25]

---

20. Clinton E. Arnold, "Ephesians," in *Romans to Philemon*, vol. 3 of *Zondervan Illustrated Bible Backgrounds Commentary*, ed. Arnold (Grand Rapids: Zondervan, 2002), 301–2.

21. BAGD, s.v. "ναός"; Johannes Petrus Louw and Eugene Albert Nida, *Greek-English Lexicon of the New Testament Based on Semantic Domains* (New York: United Bible Societies, 1989), 83, §7.15.

22. Barbara Burrell, *Neokoroi: Greek Cities and Roman Emperors*, CCS 9 (Leiden: Brill, 2004), 4; Pierre Chantraine, *Dictionnaire étymologique de la langue grecque*, 4 vols. (Paris: Klincksieck, 1968–1980), s.v. "ναός."

23. Moisés Silva, "ναός, νεωκόρος," *NIDNTTE* 3:370.

24. Burrell, *Neokoroi*, 4.

25. Wilhelm Büchner, *De neocoria* (Gissae: Ricker, 1888), 2–21.

Burrell accurately counters, however, that Ion is never specifically referred to as a νεωκόρος by Euripides but only as χρυσοφύλαξ ("guard for gold") and ταμίας ("steward"). Furthermore, the Suda (s.v. κόρη, κόρος, νεωκόρος, ζάκορος, νεωκορήσει) primarily identifies the derivation as "maintain," with the meaning "sweeper" as only a secondary derivation.[26]

The role and function of the human νεωκόρος as documented in later literary sources includes an impressive variety of duties. A papyrus from the early third century BCE, P.Magd. 35, preserves νακόρος (the Doric form of νεωκόρος) in reference to Nicomachus, apparently an official of a Jewish synagogue in a local Egyptian village.[27] The νεωκόρος as a temple functionary could include a variety of tasks, such as (1) priestly duties, (2) being involved in sacrificial procedures, (3) performing and receiving sacrifices on behalf of the god, (4) acting as key holder for the temple, (5) being responsible for other valuables in the temple, (6) collecting pilgrim fees, (7) issuing tickets, (8) listing names and cities on wooden tablets. These composite duties incline Burrell to conclude that "it is possible that 'neo-koros' was the title that the chief priest used in his practical or financial functions."[28] In this light, the term encompasses a diverse and wide-ranging set of referents.

The term occurs twice in Josephus. In *J.W.* 1.153, Josephus refers to certain individuals who were responsible for the cleansing of the Jerusalem temple,

> yet did not he touch the money, nor anything else that was there reposited; but he commanded the ministers about the temple, the very next day after he had taken it, to cleanse it, and to perform their accustomed sacrifices.

---

26. Burrell, *Neokoroi*, 4. See further Chantraine, *Dictionnaire*, 2, s.v. "κορε- κορέω." Linear B tablets from the Mycenaean period include references to a "da-ko-ro" and "da-mo-ko-ro" without reference to any kind of "sweeper" but rather indicating "a high official." See Cornelis J. Ruijgh, "Observations sur κορέσαι, κορέω, myc. da-ko-ro δακόρος, etc.," in *O-o-pe-ro-si: Festschrift für Ernst Risch zum 75 Geburtstag*, ed. Annemarie Etter (Berlin: de Gruyter, 1986), 376–92; M. Petrusevki, "Aukewa damokoro," *Živa Antika* 15 (1965): 12, cited by Burrell, *Neokoroi*, 4.

27. See further James Hope Moulton and George Milligan, *The Vocabulary of the Greek Testament: Illustrated from the Papyri and Other Non-Literary Sources* (London: Hodder & Stoughton, 1929), 425. An even earlier occurrence of νεωκόρος is attested in IPriene 231; see further below.

28. Burrell, *Neokoroi*, 4–5.

οὔτε δὲ τούτων οὔτε ἄλλου τινὸς τῶν ἱερῶν κειμηλίων ἥψατο, ἀλλὰ καὶ μετὰ μίαν τῆς ἁλώσεως ἡμέραν καθᾶραι τὸ ἱερὸν τοῖς νεωκόροις προσέταξεν καὶ τὰς ἐξ ἔθους ἐπιτελεῖν θυσίας. (trans. Whiston)

The second reference to the term occurs in Josephus's own account of his speech to those who had yet to surrender during the siege of Jerusalem:

> Who is there that does not know that Egypt was overrun with all sorts of wild beasts, and consumed by all sorts of distempers? How their land did not bring forth its fruits? Now the Nile failed of water; how the ten plagues of Egypt followed one upon another? And how, by those means, our fathers were sent away, under a guard, because God conducted them as his peculiar servants? (trans. Whiston)
> τίς οὐκ οἶδεν τὴν παντὸς θηρίου καταπλησθεῖσαν Αἴγυπτον καὶ πάσῃ φθαρεῖσαν νόσῳ, τὴν ἄκαρπον [γῆν], τὸν ἐπιλείποντα Νεῖλον, τὰς ἐπαλλήλους δέκα πληγάς, τοὺς διὰ ταῦτα μετὰ φρουρᾶς προπεμπομένους πατέρας ἡμῶν ἀναιμάκτους ἀκινδύνους, οὓς ὁ θεὸς αὑτῷ νεωκόρους ἦγεν;

Herein, the title is used with reference to an entire people, that is, all Jews as νεωκόροι. The element of particular interest here is that Josephus is referring to a historical time period during which the people were in exile and no temple per se stood in Jerusalem. Burrell thus concludes that this indicates "that the Jews' ward over their temple … was a spiritual one."[29]

The term νεωκόρος occurs even more frequently in Philo, most often in reference to the tribe of Levi. A typical example is *Fug.* 1.90, when it states:

> Either, therefore, it is for this reason alone, or perhaps for this other also, that the Levitical tribe of the persons set apart for the service of the temple ran up, and at one onset slew those who had made a god of the golden calf, the pride of Egypt, killing all who had arrived at the age of puberty, being inflamed with righteous danger, combined with enthusiasm, and a certain heaven-sent inspiration. (trans. Yonge)
> ἆρ' οὖν διὰ τοῦτο μόνον ἢ καὶ δι' ἐκεῖνο, ὅτι ἡ τῶν νεωκόρων Λευιτικὴ φυλὴ τοὺς θεοπλαστήσαντας τὸν χρυσοῦν μόσχον, τὸν Αἰγυπτιακὸν τῦφον, ἡβηδὸν ἐξ ἐπιδρομῆς κατέκτειναν, ὀργῇ δικαίᾳ σὺν ἐνθουσιασμῷ καί τινι κατοκωχῇ θεοφορήτῳ χρησάμενοι.

Although several other passages could be cited and discussed, it is sufficient for our purposes to note that Philo consistently uses the term

---

29. Burrell, *Neokoroi*, 5.

νεωκόρος in reference to the tribe of Levi, "especially in their function as priests…, guardians, gatekeepers, purifiers, and general caretakers of the temple at Jerusalem."[30] Philo does, however, distinguish between an ἱερεύς and a νεωκόρος, as per *Mos.* 2.276 where he states,

> There were two classes of ministrations concerning the temple; the higher one belonging to the priests, and the lower one to the keepers of the temple;[31] and there were at this time three priests, but many thousand keepers of the temple. (trans. Yonge)
> τῶν περὶ τὸν νεὼν λειτουργῶν δύο τάξεις εἰσίν, ἡ μὲν κρείσσων ἱερέων, ἡ δ᾽ ἐλάττων νεωκόρων· ἦσαν δὲ κατ᾽ ἐκεῖνον τὸν χρόνον τρεῖς μὲν ἱερεῖς, νεωκόρων δὲ πολλαὶ χιλιάδες.

Commentators have thus detected a diachronic development of νεωκόρος, shifting from a reference to human individuals, initially, to a term that officially designated a particular type of temple "a provincial temple for the cult of the emperor."[32] Frederick Fyvie Bruce acknowledges this shift in stating that the term "was applied as a title of honor, first to individuals and later to cities."[33] Greg H. R. Horsley similarly concludes that "the claim of a city to be the *neōkoros* of a temple and its deity was an important feature of its political self-promotion in the context of inter-city rivalry, especially (from the end of the first century) in relation to temples of the Imperial cult."[34]

On the basis of the voluminous material culture of the period, it can thus be stated with some confidence that during the first century, the term νεωκόρος became a special title bestowed upon cities that dedicated a temple to the current emperor. In addition to imperial favor, Burrell identifies two further criteria essential for a city's securing of the title, namely the "koinon's backing … and the Senate's approval."[35] Ephesus wanted to have

---

30. Ibid. For other passages, see *Fug.* 1.93–94; *Mos.* 1.316, 318; 2.72, 159, 174, 276; *Spec.* 2.120; *Praem.* 1.74; *QG* 2:17.

31. For νεωκόρος as "ἐν τῇ δευτέρᾳ τάξει," see *Spec.* 1.156.

32. Burrell, *Neokoroi*, 5.

33. Frederick Fyvie Bruce, *Acts of the Apostles: Greek Text with Introduction and Commentary*, 3rd rev. and enl. ed. (Grand Rapids: Eerdmans, 1990), 420.

34. Greg H. R. Horsley, "The Inscriptions of Ephesos and the New Testament," *NovT* 34 (1992): 136–37.

35. Barbara Burrell, "Neokoros," in *The Encyclopedia of Ancient History*, ed. Roger S. Bagnall et al. (Malden, MA: Blackwell, 2013), 8:4743.

such an honor with regard to Augustus, but this distinction was first given to Pergamon in Mysia, primarily on the basis that Ephesus was perceived to be wholly devoted to Artemis (Tacitus, *Ann.* 4.55). The significance of Ephesian devotion to Artemis within the context of both the numismatic evidence (see below) and the use of νεωχόρος in Acts 19 (see above) justifies the full citation of the passage in Tacitus:

> To divert criticism, the Caesar attended the senate with frequency, and for several days listened to the deputies from Asia debating which of their communities was to erect his temple. Eleven cities competed, with equal ambition but disparate resources. With no great variety each pleaded national antiquity, and zeal for the Roman cause in the wars with Perseus, Aristonicus, and other kings. But Hypaepa and Tralles, together with Laodicea and Magnesia, were passed over as inadequate to the task: even Ilium, though it appealed to Troy as the parent of Rome, had no significance apart from the glory of its past. Some little hesitation was caused by the statement of the Halicarnassians that for twelve hundred years no tremors of earthquake had disturbed their town, and the temple foundations would rest on the living rock. The Pergamenes were refuted by their main argument: they had already a sanctuary of Augustus, and the distinction was thought ample. The state-worship in Ephesus and Miletus was considered to be already centred on the cults of Diana and Apollo respectively: the deliberations turned, therefore, on Sardis and Smyrna. The Sardians read a decree of their "kindred country" of Etruria. "Owing to its numbers," they explained, "Tyrrhenus and Lydus, sons of King Atys, had divided the nation. Lydus had remained in the territory of his fathers, Tyrrhenus had been allotted the task of creating a new settlement; and the Asiatic and Italian branches of the people had received distinctive titles from the names of the two leaders; while a further advance in the Lydian power had come with the despatch of colonists to the peninsula which afterwards took its name from Pelops." At the same time, they recalled the letters from Roman commanders, the treaties concluded with us in the Macedonian war, their ample rivers, tempered climate, and the richness of the surrounding country.
> Sed Caesar quo famam averteret, adesse frequens senatui legatosque Asiae, ambigentis quanam in civitate templum statueretur pluris per dies audivit. Undecim urbes certabant, pari ambitione, viribus diversae. Neque multum distantia inter se memorabant de vetustate generis, studio in populum Romanum per bella Persi et Aristonici aliorumque regum. Verum Hypaepeni Trallianique Laodicenis ac Magnetibus simul tramissi ut parum validi; ne Ilienses quidem, cum parentem urbis Romae Troiam referrent, nisi antiquitatis gloria pollebant. Paulum addubita-

tum, quod Halicarnasii mille et ducentos per annos nullo motu terrae nutavisse sedes suas vivoque in saxo fundamenta templi adseveraverant. Pergamenos (eo ipso nitebantur) aede Augusto ibi sita satis adeptos creditum. Ephesii Milesiique, hi Apollinis, illi Dianae caerimonia occupavisse civitates visi. Ita Sardianos inter Zmyrnaeosque deliberatum. Sardiani decretum Etruriae recitavere ut consanguinei: nam Tyrrhenum Lydumque Atye rege genitos ob multitudinem divisisse gentem; Lydum patriis in terris resedisse, Tyrrheno datum novas ut conderet sedes; et ducum e nominibus indita vocabula illis per Asiam, his in Italia; auctamque adhuc Lydorum opulentiam missis in insulam1 populis, cui mox a Pelope nomen. Simul litteras imperatorum et icta nobiscum foedera bello Macedonum ubertatemque fluminum suorum, temperiem caeli ac ditis circum terras memorabant.[36]

After Pergamon was bestowed this honor under Augustus, Smyrna in Ionia was next to receive it under Tiberius, then Miletus in Ionia under Gaius, and finally Ephesus in Ionia under Nero.[37] Pergamon also had the prestigious honor of being the first city to become twice *neōkoros* (under Trajan). In sum, "thirty-seven cities in fifteen koina called themselves neokoroi on inscriptions and coins up to the Christianization of the empire."[38] Of significance for our own discussion is that Ephesus was only one of three cities (together with Aizanoi and Magnesia) that was permitted to extend the title to their patron god's temple, a subject to which we will return below.[39]

---

36. Text and translation from John Jackson, trans., *Tacitus: Annals; Books 4–6, 11–12*, LCL 312 (Cambridge: Harvard University Press, 1937), 96–101.

37. Moving forward chronologically in the *koinon* of Asia: Kyzikos in Mysia under Hadrian; Sardis in Lydia under Antoninus Pius; Aizanoi and Laodicea in Phrygia under Commodus; Philadelphia and Tralles in Lydia, and Antandros in the Troad under Caracalla; Hierapolis in Phrygia under Elagabalus; Magnesia in Ionia under Severus Alexander; and Synnada in Phrygia under the Tetrarchy.

38. Burrell, "Neokoros," 4743.

39. Ibid. It is worth noting that the apparent decline of the Artemis cult in Ephesus is based on E. L. Hicks's reconstruction of *IBM* 3.1.482b, ll. 8–9: [Ἐπειδὴ ἡ π]ροεστῶσα τῆς πόλεως ἡμων θεὸς Ἄρτε[μις οὐ μόνον] ἐν τῇ ἑαυτῆς πατρίδι ἀτιμᾶται ("[Since the] guardian of our city, the goddess Artemis, is dishonored [not only] in her own native city"). This is a misreading that has produced erroneous conclusions. For example, Lily Ross Taylor states, "About a century later [mid-second century CE] the cult of the goddess was again on the wane, and we find the Ephesian senate taking active measures to restore the goddess to her former prominence. Again, it was probably the growing power of Christianity which caused the decline of Ephesian Artemis" ("Arte-

3. Numismatic Evidence

The earliest scholarly attempt to explore the manner in which the term νεωκόρος was adopted as a title for cities was Büchner's *De neocoria* in 1888.[40] Other monographs and technical studies since then have significantly supplemented this earlier work with more recent literary, numismatic, epigraphic, and archaeological evidence.[41] The present study will focus on the contribution of numismatic material, insofar as it might elucidate the term's usage in reference to Ephesus and Acts 19:35.

Our introductory comments have already noted the paucity of attention generally afforded to numismatic material. We will here attempt to present an exhaustive account of the relevant numismatic material, noting not merely the economic function of the coinage but also its political and symbolic value. Appropriate caution must be employed when interpreting depictions of temples and their associated symbols so that one does not fail to distinguish between ancient reality and the medium of the symbolic representation.[42] Our analysis in the present paper will focus solely on

---

mis of Ephesus," in *The Beginnings of Christianity: The Acts of the Apostles*, ed. F. J. Foakes-Jackson and Kirsopp Lake, 5 vols. [London: Macmillan, 1933], 5:255). Richard E. Oster restores the corrected reading as follows: [Ἐπειδὴ ἡ π]ροεστῶσα τῆς πόλεως ἡμων θεὸς Ἄρτε[μις οὐ μόνον] ἐν τῇ ἑαυτῆς πατρίδι τειμᾶται ("[Since the] guardian of our city, the goddess Artemis, is honored [not only] in her own native city"). See further Oster, "Acts 19:23–41 and an Ephesian Inscription," *HTR* 77 (1984): 233–37. This reconstruction is in accordance with Pausanius, writing in the late second century CE: "But all cities worship Artemis of Ephesus and individuals hold her in honour above the gods.... Three other points have contributed to her renown, the size of the temple, surpassing all buildings among men, the eminence of the city of the Ephesians, and the renown of the goddess who dwells there" (*Descr.* 4.31.8). Translation from W. H. S. Jones, trans., *Pausanias: Description of Greece; Books 3–5*, LCL 188 (Cambridge: Harvard University Press, 1926).

40. Büchner, *De neocoria*, 2–21.

41. Simon R. F. Price, *Rituals and Power: The Roman Imperial Cult in Asia Minor* (Cambridge: Cambridge University Press, 1984), 64–65; Steven J. Friesen, *Twice Neokoros: Ephesus, Asia and the Cult of the Flavian Imperial Family*, RGRW 116 (Leiden: Brill, 1993); Burrell, *Neokoroi*.

42. The spectrum is, as expected, broad ranging. On the points of connection with history, Martin Jessop Price, Bluma L. Trell, and Cornelius C. Vermeule are optimistic; see Price and Trell, *Coins and Their Cities: Architecture on the Ancient Coins of Greece, Rome, and Palestine* (London: Vecchi, 1977); Vermeule, *The Cult Images of Imperial Rome* (Rome: Bretschneider, 1987). Thomas Drew-Bear and Johannes Nollé

those coins with a clear and unambiguous, unobscured legend—νεωκόρος and/or its abbreviations and derivatives.

Before proceeding it would be remiss not to mention two methodological hurdles in such an analysis. First, it is a rather crude and obvious fact that we possess only a fraction of a fraction of a fraction of the numismatic material that originally circulated in antiquity. Edwin Yamauchi astutely notes the severely limited view that archaeological excavation affords in this regard: "Only a fraction of what is made or what is written survives, only a fraction of that material is preserved in archaeological sites that have been surveyed, only a fraction of the surveyed sites have been excavated, only a fraction of any excavated site is actually examined, and only a fraction of materials are actually published."[43] Numismatic material that is published generally consists of the large and prestigious museum collections, which naturally marginalizes poor quality or illegible coins that do not find their way into those collections. There is also the problem of unprovenanced coins that appear in private collections and auction catalogues. As will be demonstrated in our present discussion, problems abound with inaccurate attribution or failure to recognize inauthentic examples, especially so in the older collections.[44] These can mislead and have misled scholars in the recent past on the very topic of consideration. We therefore will limit our discussion to those numismatic examples that have appeared in bona fide peer-reviewed publication outlets and carefully weigh, where necessary, questions of authenticity.

---

are highly skeptical: Drew-Bear, "Representations of Temples on the Greek Imperial Coinage," *ANSMN* 19 (1974): 27–63; Nollé, "Zur neueren Forschungsgeschichte der kaiser-zeitliche Stadtprägungen Kleinasiens," in *Internationales Kolloquium zur kaiser-zeitlichen Münzprägung Kleinasiens, 27.–30. April 1994 in der Staatlichen Münzsammlung München*, ed. Johannes Nollé, Bernhard Overbeck, and Peter Weiss, Nomismata 1 (Milan: Ennerre, 1997), 11–26. For a nuanced discussion see Andrew M. Burnett, "Buildings and Monuments on Roman Coins," in *Roman Coins and Public Life under the Empire*, ed. George M. Paul, ETSP 2 (Ann Arbor: University of Michigan Press, 1999), 137–64.

43. Edwin M. Yamauchi, *The Stones and the Scriptures*, EP (Philadelphia: Lippincott, 1972), 146–54.

44. See, for example, Joseph Hilarius von Eckhel, *Doctrina numorum veterum*, 8 vols. (Vienna: Degen, 1792–1839), 4:288–306, which catalogues a list of misreadings in Théodore Edme Mionnet, *Description des médailles antiques, grecques et romaines*, 6 vols. (Paris: Toulouse, 1806–1808), 105. Cited in Burrell, *Neokoroi*, 12.

The first step of our analysis is to list out in tabular form the relevant numismatic evidence for discussion. Table 1 draws on the work of Barbara Burrell, the inventory of Wolfgang Leschhorn, and the location list catalogue of the Heberden Coin Room, Ashmolean Museum, Oxford.[45]

	Ruler	Legend/Title	Publication	Collection(s)
1	Nero	*neōkoros*	SNGvA 7863	Berlin (3x), London (2x), Oxford, Paris, Vienna
2	Trajan	*neōkoros*	CGCI 223; SNGvA 1884	Berlin (2x), New York, Oxford
3	Hadrian	2x *neōkoros*	CGCI 227, 228; SNGMün 127	Berlin, New York, Paris (3x), Vienna (2x)
4	Hadrian and Aelius Verus	2x *neōkoros*		Paris
5	Antoninus Pius	2x *neōkoros*	CGCI 233–36; SNGCop 397; SNGvA 1888; SNGMün 132, 133	Berlin (7x), London (2x), New York (2x), Oxford (5x), Paris (7x), Vienna (5x), Warsaw
6	Marcus Aurelius Caesar	2x *neōkoros*	CGCI 242	Berlin (2x), Oxford, Paris (2x)
7	Marcus Aurelius Augustus	2x *neōkoros*	CGCI 243; SNGCop 400; SNGvA 1890, 1891; SNGMün 141–45; SNGLewis 1448	Berlin (10x), London, New York (2x), Oxford (4x), Paris (4x), Vienna (9x), Warsaw

---

45. Burrell, *Neokoroi*, 59–85; Wolfgang Leschhorn, *Lexikon der Aufschriften auf griechischen Münzen*, VNK 37 (Vienna: ÖAW, 2002), 210–14. Burrell lists a number of coins that are in collections but not yet published in corpora, which are taken up and adapted for our listing here. The collections are adapted from Burrell, *Neokoroi*, 84–85. Abbreviations for locations of extant examples are as follows: Berlin (Münzkabinett, Staatliche Museen), Boston (Classical Department, Museum of Fine Arts), London (British Museum, Department of Coins and Medals), New York (American Numismatic Society), Oxford (Heberden Coin Room, Ashmolean Museum), Paris (Cabinet des Médailles, Bibliothèque nationale), Vienna (Münzkabinett, Kunsthistorisches Museum), Warsaw (Narodowe Museum).

8	Faustina the Younger	2x *neōkoros*	*CGCI* 235; *SNGCop* 402	Berlin (4x), Oxford, Paris, Vienna (2x)
9	Lucius Verus	2x *neōkoros*	*CGCI* 247	Berlin (3x), Oxford, Paris
10	Commodus Caesar	2x *neōkoros*	*CGCI* 254	Berlin, Boston, New York, Paris
11	Commodus Augustus	2x *neōkoros*	*CGCI* 255; *SNGCop* 409	Berlin (2x), London, New York, Paris (5x), Vienna (2x)
12	Septimius Severus	2x *neōkoros*	*CGCI* 259, 260; *SNGCop* 411; *SNGvA* 1893, 7869; *SNGMün* 152–55; *SNGRighetti* 853	Berlin (7x), London (3x), New York (3x), Oxford (10x), Paris (12x), Vienna (7x)
13	Julia Domna	2x *neōkoros*	*CGCI* 263, 265; *SNGCop* 415, 416; *SNGvA* 1895; *SNGMün* 158; *SNGLewis* 1449	Berlin (2x), Oxford (2x), Paris (3x), Vienna (4x)
14	Caracalla	2x *neōkoros*	*CGCI* 271–75; *SNGCop* 419–23; *SNGvA* 1896–98; *SNGMün* 160, 161, 163, 164	Berlin (9x), London, New York (2x), Oxford (7x), Paris (6x), Vienna (10x)
15	Geta Caesar	2x *neōkoros*	*SNGCop* 425; *SNGvA* 7874; *SNGMün* 168	Oxford, Paris (2x), Vienna (2x)
16	Geta Augustus	2x *neōkoros*	*CGCI* 281, 282; *SNGCop* 431; *SNGvA* 1902, 1903, 7877; *SNGMün* 173	Berlin (4x), Boston, London, New York, Oxford (3x), Paris (5x), Vienna (4x)
17	Geta Augustus	3x *neōkoros*		Gotha (genuine?)
18	Julia Domna	3x *neōkoros* and of Artemis		Berlin, London, Paris
19	Caracalla	3x *neōkoros* and of Artemis	*SNGvA* 7871	Berlin

20	Caracalla and Geta	3x *neōkoros* and of Artemis	*CGCI* 292; *SNGCop* 436; *SNGvA* 1904	Berlin (2x), Paris
21	Geta Augustus	3x *neōkoros* and of Artemis		Berlin, London
22	Caracalla	2x *neōkoros* and of Artemis	*CGCI* 269	
23	Julia Domna	3x *neōkoros*	*CGCI* 266, 267; *SNGCop* 417	Berlin (4x), New York, Oxford (2x), Paris (3x), Vienna (5x)
24	Caracalla	3x *neōkoros*	*CGCI* 276–79, Adramyttium 24, 25; *SNGvA* 1899, 1900, 7872, 7873; *SNGMün* 162, 165, 166; *SNGLewis* 1450; *SNG-Paris* Adramyttium 59	Berlin (17x), London (2x), New York (6x), Oxford (6x), Paris (11x), Vienna (13x), Warsaw
25	Elagabalus	3x *neōkoros*	*CGCI* 300, 302–5, 307; *SNGCop* 442–448165; *SNGvA* 1905, 1906; *SNGMün* 184; *SNGRighetti* 854	Berlin (21x), London (7x), New York (4x), Oxford (8x), Paris (19x), Vienna (13x)[45]
26	Julia Paula	4x *neōkoros*	*CGCI* 308; *SNGCop* 453, 454; *SNGvA* 1907; *SNGRighetti* 856	Berlin (4x), London, Oxford (2x), Paris (3x), Vienna (2x)
27	Annia Faustina	4x *neōkoros*	*CGCI* 309; *SNGvA* 1908; *SNGMün* 187[46]	Berlin (2x), London, Paris (4x), Vienna
28	Julia Soaemias	4x *neōkoros*		New York, Paris (2x)

---

45. Hans-Dietrich Schultz notes that *SNGCop* 444 and several of the Berlin examples appear to be cast copies ("Fälschungen ephesischer Münzen," *MONG* 35 [1995]: 7–14). Cited in Burrell, *Neokoroi*, 84.

46. Dietrich O. A. Klose argues that this coin is inauthentic ("Münz- oder Gruselkabinett? Zu einigen alten Fälschungen kaiserzeitlicher Lokalmünzen Kleinasiens in der Staatlichen Münzsammlung München," in Nollé, Overbeck, and Weiss, *Internationales Kolloquium*, 253–64).

29	Julia Maesa	4x *neōkoros*	*CGCI* 310	Paris (3x)
30	Severus Alexander Caesar	4x *neōkoros*	*CGCI* 312; *SNGMün* 189	Berlin (2x), Oxford, Paris (4x), Vienna
31	Severus Alexander Augustus	4x *neōkoros*	*CGCI* 311, 314, 318; *SNGCop* 460-62; *SNGvA* 7880; *SNGMün* 190, 193, 196; *SNGLewis* 1453; *SNGRighetti* 857	Berlin (4x), London, New York, Oxford (3x), Paris (8x), Vienna (5x)
32	Julia Mamaea	4x *neōkoros*	*CGCI* 328	Berlin
33	Maximinus	3x *neōkoros*	*CGCI* 329, 330; *SNGCop* 472, 473; *SNGvA* 1912; *SNGMün* 208, 209	Berlin (5x), Boston, London (3x), New York, Oxford (4x), Paris (8x), Vienna (6x)
34	Maximus Caesar	3x *neōkoros*	*SNGMün* 212	London, Paris
35	Gordian III	3x *neōkoros*	*CGCI* 331; *SNGvA* 1913; *SNGMün* 213-15; *SNGLewis* 1454; *SNGRighetti* 860	Berlin (2x), New York, Oxford (2x), Paris (5x), Vienna (4x)
36	Otacilia	3x *neōkoros*	*CGCI* 342, 343; *SNGCop* 486	Berlin, New York (2x), Oxford, Paris, Vienna
37	Philip Caesar	3x *neōkoros*	*SNGCop* 488, 489; *SNGvA* 1914; *SNGMün* 224	New York, Oxford, Paris, Vienna (2x)
38	Trajan Decius	3x *neōkoros*	*SNGvA* 1916	Berlin, London, Oxford, Paris (2x), Vienna
39	Valerian	3x *neōkoros*	*CGCI* 350-58; *SNGCop* 496-00; *SNGvA* 1921-23; *SNGMün* 234-38, 240, 241, 243; *SNGLewis* 1457; *SNGRighetti* 861-63	Berlin (23x), Boston (2x), London (8x), New York (12x), Oxford (12x), Paris (19x), Vienna (12x), Warsaw

40	Gallienus	3x *neōkoros*	CGCI 370–76; SNGCop 510–12; SNGvA 1928–30, 7887; SNGMün 249–54, 263; SNGLewis 1459	Berlin (20x), Boston, London (5x), New York (3x), Oxford (10x), Paris (12x), Vienna (7x)
41	Salonina	3x *neōkoros*	CGCI 390–91, 393–94; SNGCop 532–34; SNGvA 1933, 1934; SNGMün 266–68, 270; SNGLewis 1461	Berlin (6x), London (3x), New York (4x), Oxford (7x), Paris (8x), Vienna (6x), Warsaw (2x)
42	Valerianus	3x *neōkoros*	SNGMün 276; SNGLewis 1463	Berlin, New York, Oxford, Paris (2x)
43	Saloninus	3x *neōkoros*	SNGCop 541	Berlin, London, Paris
44	Valerian	3x *neōkoros*	CGCI 359–63; SNGCop 501–3; SNGvA 1924, 1925;	Berlin (4x), London, New York (2x), Oxford (5x), Paris (3x), Vienna (3x)
45	Gallienus	4x *neōkoros*	CGCI 377–79, 381–84; SNGCop 513–20; SNGvA 1931, 7888, 7889; SNGMün 257–60; SNGRighetti 864, 868	Berlin (12x), London (6x), New York (6x), Oxford (9x), Paris (13x), Vienna (10x)
46	Salonina	4x *neōkoros*	CGCI 395; SNGCop 535, 536; SNGMün 275; SNGRighetti 869	Berlin (4x), New York (3x), Oxford (2x), Paris (4x), Vienna (2x)
47	Valerianus	4x *neōkoros*	SNGCop 538	Berlin, Vienna. Saloninus: Paris

Modern scholarship on the coinage of Ephesus has suffered considerably from issues related to the (in)authenticity of some material. Typically, problems range from naive misattribution, such as the Ephesian coin in the Landesarchiv Saarbrücken attributed to Julia and Agrippa, to the complete fabrication or tooling of inscriptions, such as more than a dozen examples cited by Andrew M. Burnett, Michel Amandry, and Pere Pau Ripollès in *Roman Provincial Coinage*.[48] Misattribution and forgery are not, of course,

---

48. *Griechische Münzen*, part 3 of *Sonder Münzenauktion: Sammlung Apostololo*

problems unique to the numismatic material of Ephesus,[49] yet the problem is felt in a unique manner when considering the history and function of the νεωκόρος.

The identification of coins as modern forgeries involves a range of observational and analytic approaches, including: comparison of coin die typology, observation of the characteristics of the metal and the coin surface, diagnosing additional coercions, and identifying artificial patination. There are multiple cases where the νεωκόρος coins are demonstrably Renaissance casts of genuine ancient coins. Particularly notable examples are *CGCI* 380, 384, 392; *SNGCop* 444, 521; *SNGRighetti* 867.[50] As Michael H. Crawford notes however, these cast copies of genuine ancient coins "do not ... falsify the picture totally, [but] they can ... give a wrong impression of how common a particular coin is."[51] More problematic, of course, are those coins that are complete fabrications or that have been recut or tooled to alter the inscription or iconography. Such is the case with two important coins listed in *RPC* 2 that "seem to attest to a second neocorate temple for Domitian at Ephesus."[52] *RPC* 2.1064 is a bronze coin (30 mm, 19.83 g) that, on the obverse, depicts the laureate head of Domitian facing right with aegis. The inscription reads ΔΟΜΙΤΙΑΝΟΣ ΚΑΙΣΑΡ ΣΕΒΑΣ-ΓΕΡΜ ΑΥΤΟΚΡΑΤ ("Domitian Caesar Augustus Germanicus Emperor"). The reverse has a temple with four columns enclosing a

---

Zeno (Vienna: Dorotheum, 1957), no. 3969 (M S6.126.322 Sestini), a specimen that Burnett, Amandry, and Ripollès attribute to a worn example of *RPC* 1.2620 (*RPC* 1:433–34).

49. Dimitar Dimitrov, Ilya Prokopov, and B. Kolev, *Modern Forgeries of Greek and Roman Coins*, EHS.G 576 (Sofia: n.p., 1997); David Hendin, *Not Kosher: Forgeries of Ancient Jewish and Biblical Coins* (New York: Amphora, 2005); S. Hurter, "The Black Sea Hoard: The Cache of an Ancient Counterfeit Mint," *Bulletin on Counterfeits* 15 (1990): 2–4; Constantin A. Marinescu, "Modern Imitations of Ancient Coins from Bulgaria," *Minerva* 9.5 (1998): 46–48; Wayne G. Sayles, *Classical Deception: Counterfeits, Forgeries and Reproductions of Ancient Coins* (Iola: Krause, 2001), 61–65, 87–89; Ilya Prokopov, Kostadin Kissyov and Eugeni Paunov, *Modern Counterfeits of Ancient Greek and Roman Coins from Bulgaria*, CCCHBulg (Sofia: n.p., 2003); Prokopov, *Contemporary Coin Engravers and Coin Masters from Bulgaria*, CCCHBulg (Sofia: n.p., 2004); Prokopov and Paunov, *Cast Forgeries of Classical Coins from Bulgaria*, CCCHBulg (Sofia: n.p., 2004).

50. See further Schultz, "Falschungen ephesischer Münzen," 7–14.

51. Michael H. Crawford, "Numismatics," in *Sources for Ancient History*, ed. Crawford (Cambridge: Cambridge University Press, 1983), 188.

52. *RPC* 2:165.

cult statue of Atemis with the inscription ΕΦΕΣΙΟ-Ν Β ΝΕΟΚΟΡΩΝ ("Ephesus twice *neōkoros*"). *RPC* 2.1065 is a bronze coin (30 mm, 22.10 g) that, on the obverse, portrays the draped bust of Domitia facing right with the inscription ΔΟΜΙΤΙΑ ΣΕΒΑΣΤΗ ("Domitia August"). The reverse has a temple with eight columns enclosing a statue of Artemis, with the inscription [ΝΕΩ]ΚΟΡΟΝ ΕΦΕΣΙΟΩΝ ("Ephesus Neocorate").[53] Both *RPC* 2.1064 and 1065 were accepted as genuine by Steven J. Friesen and utilized to reconstruct the developments in cultic traditions within the city. Friesen states that on the basis of "at least two coins of the Domitianic period, the Ephesians called themselves 'twice neokoros,' i.e., of Artemis and of the Sebastoi," and "these two coins present a vivid visual image of the city's new religious situation." Friesen concludes that the city thus had "two dominant cults of equivalent significance: that of Ephesian Artemis, and that of the Emperors."[54] Michael Dräger similarly accepts these coins as genuine and comes to comparable conclusions.[55]

Unfortunately, however, both Friesen and Dräger have uncritically followed the error of Josef Keil in accepting the coins as genuine.[56] As Burnett notes, both coins display obvious signs of having been altered (*RPC* 2.1064) or completely reworked by tooling (*RPC* 2.1065). That the coins were recut or altered from existing types, for example, *RPC* 2.1064 from *RPC* 2.1070, has been subsequently confirmed in more recent analysis.[57] Burnett's conclusion that the possibility of a second neocorate at Ephesus under Domitian, or for that matter a temple of Domitian, "seems extremely doubtful"[58] is entirely justifiable.

The earliest attestation of the titular νεωχόρος occurs on an Ephesian coin under Nero. *SNGvA* 7863 (cf. *RPC* 2.2626) is a bronze issue (26 mm, 11.72 g) that, on the obverse, has the laureate head of Nero facing right

---

53. See Behrendt Pick, "Die Neokorien von Ephesos," in *Corolla Numismatica: Numismatic Essays in Honour of Barclay V. Head*, ed. George Francis Hill (Oxford: Oxford University Press, 1906), 234–44.

54. Friesen, *Twice Neokoros*, 56–57.

55. Michael Dräger, *Die Städte der Provinz Asia in der Flavierzeit: Studien zur kleinasiatischen Stadt- und Regionalgeschichte*, EHS.G 576 (Frankfurt am Main: Lang, 1993), 118; 123, n. 2; 292–93.

56. Josef Keil, "Die erste Kaiserneokorie von Ephesos," *NZ* 12 (1919): 118–20. Trebilco also accepts uncritically the assumptions of Friesen and others, which are adopted without further consideration ("Asia," 329–30).

57. Klose, "Münz- oder Gruselkabinett," 253–64; Burrell, *Neokoroi*, 65.

58. *RPC* 2:165.

with the accompanying inscription ΝΕΡΩΝ ΚΑΙΣΑΡ ("Nero Caesar"). The reverse has a three-quarter view of a temple on a three-step podium and an inscription reading ΑΟΥΙΟΛΑ ΑΝΘΥΠΑΤΩ ΑΙΧΜΟΚΛΗΣ, ΝΕΟΚΟΡΩΝ, ΕΦΕ ("Aviola Aichmokles proconsul, *neōkoros* Ephesus").[59] By virtue of the preservation of the name of the proconsul, M. Acilius Aviola, the coin can be dated to 65/66 CE (*PIR* 1.A.49).[60] A second type during the same period, *RPC* 2.2626, has the head of Nero facing right on the obverse with the inscription ΝΕΡΩΝ ΚΑΙΣΑΡ ("Nero Caesar"). The reverse depicts a six-column temple on a three-step podium, a disc in the pediment, and a bee on either side with the accompanying inscription ΕΦΕΣΙΟΝ ΝΕΟΚΟΡΟΝ ("Ephesus *neōkoros*").

4. Implications for the νεωκόρος of Acts 19:35

We now turn to the question of how our discussion above might illuminate a reading of Acts 19:35. Within the speech of the town clerk (γραμματεύς) in Acts 19:35–40, Ephesus is directly identified as the "guardian of the temple of the great Artemis" (νεωκόρον οὖσαν τῆς μεγάλης Ἀρτέμιδος [19:35]). Critically weighing evidence from the Pauline letters, and Acts of the Apostles (particularly with reference to the edict of Claudius, the Delphi inscription, and the proconsulship of Gallio) scholars typically are inclined to date Paul's reported stay in Ephesus to August 52 CE–October 54 CE.[61] If this is so, then an acute historical problem arises for the text of Acts, for the term νεωκόρος is applied to Ephesus under Claudius (nephew of Tiberius) rather than a decade later under Nero (great-great-nephew of Tiberius). As per numismatic evidence surveyed above, Ephesus seems to be claiming the title, according to the book of Acts, before our earliest evidence for the use of the term in a titular sense.

In light of this apparent tension Stephan Witetschek asks, "Does the narrative of Acts 19 report what really happened in the mid-50s of the 1st

---

59. *RPC* 2.2627 is of the same type but with laureate head facing left on the obverse.

60. John Anthony Crook, *Consilium Principis: Imperial Councils and Counsellors from Augustus to Dicoletian* (Cambridge: Cambridge University Press, 1955), 148; George Woodard Houston, "Roman Imperial Administrative Personnel during the Principates of Vespasian and Titus (A.D. 69–81)" (PhD diss., University of North Carolina, Chapel Hill, 1971).

61. Jerome Murphy-O'Connor, *Paul: A Critical Life* (Oxford: Oxford University Press, 1996), 1–31.

C.E., when Paul was in Ephesos?"[62] He concludes in the negative, stating that the passage "addresses the concerns of Luke's readers in the late 1st century, when Christianity in Asia Minor would already have become a factor that made some impact on the economy," and that "Acts is a source not so much for the narrated time of Paul, but rather for Luke's own time, and as such of interest for both exegetes and historians."[63] L. Michael White similarly concludes that "at best it [i.e., νεωκόρος] would seem to have been a new accolade for the city in Paul's day; at worst, if one posits a date later in Nero's reign, the phrase would not yet have been operative," and that "the setting in Acts seems anachronistic, even if it does suggest direct knowledge of Ephesus at a later date."[64]

There is, however, an alternative, more nuanced historical approach that seems to account for the reference in Acts, the numismatic evidence, as well as the inscriptional data. First, it is important to note that Acts 19 does not explicitly use the title with reference to the imperial cult, but rather applies the title to the Ἐφεσίων πόλιν (19:35). The references surveyed above from Josephus and Philo indicate that the term νεωκόρος underwent a significant shift in the first century CE, at which point it was commonly used with reference to a representative people or city rather than a particular individual(s) necessarily.[65] Second, of interest is IEph. 3.647, which consists of a statue base of white marble with an inscription that documents that by 211–212 CE, Ephesus was "metropolis of Asia and temple warden of Artemis and three times temple warden of the emperors" (μητροπόλεως τῆς Ἀσίας καὶ νεωκόρου τῆς Ἀρτέμιδος καὶ τρὶς νεωκόρου τῶν Σεβαστῶν). In Rosalinde A. Kearsley's discussion of this inscription, she notes the manner in which the inscription sheds further light on the "importance of Artemis to Ephesus and therefore also assists

---

62. Stephan Witetschek, "Artemis and Asiarchs: Some Remarks on Ephesian Local Colour in Acts 19," *Bib* 90 (2009): 334.

63. Ibid., 352, 355.

64. L. Michael White, "Urban Development and Social Change in Imperial Ephesos," in *Ephesos, Metropolis of Asia: An Interdisciplinary Approach to Its Archaeology, Religion, and Culture*, ed. Helmut Koester, HTS 41 (Valley Forge, PA: Trinity Press International, 1995), 37. Similarly, Richard I. Pervo states that "[νεωκόρος] may be a bit of an anachronism here," see Pervo, *Acts: A Commentary*, Hermeneia (Minneapolis: Fortress, 2009), 498, n. 117.

65. Marshall notes simply that "when applied to Ephesus as temple keeper of Artemis in the third century, the usage is an extension of the imperial use" (*Acts*, 360).

understanding of the incident recorded in Acts 19."[66] It is noteworthy that the titulature is used in later inscriptions with reference to both the name of the city (IEph 7.3005) and the citizens themselves (IEph 3.857). A. N. Sherwin-White cautions, however, that "the late inscriptions do not illustrate the usage in Acts."[67] Although this may be technically accurate, both the inscriptional and numismatic evidence demonstrate a trajectory that is consistent with the later material. Sherwin-White does, however, note an honorary base inscription from Priene (IPriene 231) dated to 333 BCE that records the following, "Megabyzos, son of Megabyzos, temple warden in Ephesus" (Μεγάβυζος Μεγαβύζου νεωκόρος τῆς Ἀρτέμιδος τῆς ἐν Ἐφέσωι).[68] As such, Luke could hardly be charged with anachronism if he was using the term metaphorically, contra Stephan Witetschek, L. Michael White, and Richard I. Pervo.[69] When the term νεωκόρος was uttered by the town clerk in Acts 19:35 (52–54 CE), it was presumably a metaphor drawing on the long and illustrious association of Artemis with Ephesus, and indicative of the city's civic pride. It was thus no coincidence that approximately a decade later, the word would appear so prominently on the coinage of the city under Nero. Burrell notes that "it is possible that at this point it meant what it came to mean later, that Ephesos possessed a koinon temple for the cult of the Emperor, in this case for Nero."[70]

Several commentators have noted the religious, social, and political knowledge displayed in Acts 19:21–40, so much so that Helmut Koester has suggested that the entire volume was, in fact, composed in Ephesus.[71] One need not, however, accept Koester's conclusions regarding the provenance of Acts to validly identify the obvious local features, such as the

---

66. Rosalinde A. Kearsley, "Ephesus: Neokoros of Artemis," *NewDocs* 6:203.

67. Sherwin-White, *Roman Society*, 89.

68. Ibid., 89. In addition to this, Craig S. Keener's comment is intuitively satisfying: "A term's first appearance in our surviving, fragmentary sources is rarely its first actual occurrence" (*15:1–23:35*, vol. 3 of *Acts: An Exegetical Commentary* [Grand Rapids, Michigan: Baker Academic, 2014], 2930).

69. Witetschek, "Artemis and Asiarchs," 355; White, "Urban Development," 37; Pervo, *Acts*, 498, n. 117.

70. Burrell, *Neokoroi*, 4. Strangely, however, no mention of this historical conundrum is made in the otherwise excellent treatment of the historical issues in Paul Trebilco, *The Early Christians in Ephesus from Paul to Ignatius*, WUNT 166 (Tübingen: Mohr Siebeck, 2004), 155–96.

71. Helmut Koester, "Ephesos in Early Christian Literature," in Koester, *Ephesos*, 130–31.

reference to νεωκόρος, the sale of silver shrines, asiarchs as political figures, and the mention of "the scribe of the demos."[72]

5. Conclusion

Throughout this study we have sought to identify a distinctive contribution of the numismatic material for our understanding of the history of Ephesus, particularly as it pertains to Acts 19:35 and the use of the term νεωκόρος. The arguments put forward in our discussion allowed a fruitful comparison of both the continuity and discontinuity of motifs across several historical periods. There are principally five outcomes of our investigation. First, scholarly endeavors to incorporate numismatic material into New Testament studies generally, and Greek lexicography in particular, are in their infancy. Much work remains to be done in this area, in regard both to methodology and to disseminating numismatic collections in published, well-illustrated catalogues. Second, there continues to be a lack of discernment of relevant authentic numismatic material. In the present study, this expresses itself as (1) the uncritical acceptance of the inauthentic νεωκόρος coinage and (2) attempting to apply the numismatic material too generally, which necessarily leads to inaccuracies. Both these issues persist in the literature, but they are especially pronounced in New Testament commentaries.[73] Third, there is a clear diachronic development of νεωκόρος from a reference to human individuals to a term that officially designated a particular type of temple in service of the cult of the emperor. Fourth, the allegiance of the Ephesians to Artemis is readily appreciated through the extended quotation and discussion of Tacitus's account of intercity rivalry and Ephesus's apparent complete devotion to Artemis (*Ann.* 4.55). Finally, rather than posing a genuine historical conundrum, the reference to the νεωκόρος in Acts 19:35 should be situated within the larger trajectory of the city's devotion to Artemis, which is documented from as early as the fourth century BCE.

---

72. Koester, "Ephesos," 130, n. 42; Ben Witherington III, *The Acts of the Apostles: A Socio-rhetorical Commentary* (Grand Rapids: Eerdmans, 1998), 585; Colin J. Hemer, *The Book of Acts in the Setting of Hellenistic History*, ed. Conrad H. Gempf, WUNT 49 (Tübingen: Mohr Siebeck, 1989), 121–22.

73. For example, Luke Timothy Johnson notes that "for Ephesus, the title ["νεωκόρος"] appears on coins of the period" (*The Acts of the Apostles*, SP 5 [Collegeville, MN: Liturgical Press, 1992], 350).

Bibliography

Akurgal, Ekrem. *Ancient Civilizations and Ruins of Turkey: From Prehistoric Times until the End of the Roman Empire*. 6th ed. Ankara: Haşet Kitabevi, 1985.

Alföldi, Andreas. "The Main Aspects of Political Propaganda on the Coinage of the Roman Republic." Pages 63–95 in *Essays in Roman Coinage Presented to Harold Mattingly*. Edited by Robert Andrew Glindinning Carson and Carol Humphrey Vivian Sutherland. Oxford: Oxford University Press, 1956.

Andreau, Jean. *Banking and Business in the Roman World*. KTAH. Cambridge: Cambridge University Press, 1999.

Arnold, Clinton E. "Ephesians." Pages 300–41 in *Romans to Philemon*. Vol. 3 of *Zondervan Illustrated Bible Backgrounds Commentary*. Edited by Clinton E. Arnold. Grand Rapids: Zondervan, 2002.

Bastien, Pierre. *Le buste monétaire des empereurs romains*. 3 vols. NR 19. Wetteren: Éditions numismatiques romaines, 1992–1994.

Broughton, Thomas Robert Shannon. "Roman Asia Minor." Pages 499–918 in *Roman Africa, Syria, Greece, and Asia*. Vol. 4 of *An Economic Survey of Ancient Rome*. Edited by Tenney Frank. Baltimore: Johns Hopkins Press, 1938.

Bruce, Frederick Fyvie. *Acts of the Apostles: Greek Text with Introduction and Commentary*. 3rd rev. and enl. ed. Grand Rapids: Eerdmans, 1990.

Büchner, Wilhelm. *De neocoria*. Gissae: Ricker, 1888.

Burnett, Andrew M. "Buildings and Monuments on Roman Coins." Pages 137–64 in *Roman Coins and Public Life under the Empire*. Edited by George M. Paul. ETSP 2. Ann Arbor: University of Michigan Press, 1999.

———. "The Iconography of Roman Coin Types in the Third Century B.C." NC 146 (1986): 67–75.

Burrell, Barbara. *Neokoroi: Greek Cities and Roman Emperors*. CCS 9. Leiden: Brill, 2004.

———. "Neokoros." Pages 4742–43 in vol. 8 of *The Encyclopedia of Ancient History*. Edited by Roger S. Bagnall et al. Malden, MA: Wiley-Blackwell, 2013.

Burnett, Andrew M., Michel Amandry, and Pere Pau Ripollès. *Roman Provincial Coinage*. 2 vols. in 4 parts. London: British Museum Press, 1992–1999.

Butcher, K. Roman *Provincial Coins: An Introduction to the Greek Imperials*. London: Seaby, 1988.
Carter, Warren. *Matthew and the Margins: A Sociopolitical and Religious Reading*. Sheffield: Sheffield Academic Press, 2000.
Chantraine, Pierre. *Dictionnaire étymologique de la langue grecque*. 4 vols. Paris: Klincksieck, 1968–1980.
Crawford, Michael H. "Money and Exchange in the Roman World." *JRS* 60 (1970): 40–46.
———. "Numismatics." Pages 185–233 in *Sources for Ancient History*. Edited by Michael H. Crawford. Cambridge: Cambridge University Press, 1983.
———. "Roman Imperial Coin Types and the Formation of Public Opinion." Pages 47–64 in *Studies in Numismatic Method Presented to Philip Grierson*. Edited by C. N. L. Brooke, B. H. I. H. Steward, J. G. Pollard, and T. R. Volk. Cambridge: Cambridge University Press, 1983.
Crönert, Wilhelm. *Passow's Wörterbuch der griechischen Sprache*. 3 vols. Göttingen: Vandenhoeck & Ruprecht, 1913.
Crook, John Anthony. *Consilium Principis: Imperial Councils and Counsellors from Augustus to Dicoletian*. Cambridge: Cambridge University Press, 1955.
Dimitrov, Dimitar, Ilya Prokopov, and B. Kolev. *Modern Forgeries of Greek and Roman Coins*. EHS.G 576. Sofia: n.p., 1997.
Dräger, Michael. *Die Städte der Provinz Asia in der Flavierzeit: Studien zur kleinasiatischen Stadt- und Regionalgeschichte*. EHS.G 576. Frankfurt am Main: Lang, 1993.
Drew-Bear, Thomas. "Representations of Temples on the Greek Imperial Coinage." *ANSMN* 19 (1974): 27–63.
Duncan-Jones, Richard P. "Mobility and Immobility of Coin in the Roman Empire." *AIIN* 36 (1989): 121–37.
———. *Structure and Scale in the Roman Economy*. Cambridge: Cambridge University Press, 1990.
Dyer, Keith D. "'But Concerning that Day…' (Mark 13:32): 'Prophetic' and 'Apocalyptic' Eschatology in Mark 13." Pages 104–22 in *1999 Seminar Papers*. SBLSP 38. Atlanta: Scholars Press, 1999.
———. *The Prophecy on the Mount: Mark 13 and the Gathering of the New Community*. ITS 2. Bern: Lang, 1998.
Eckhel, Joseph Hilarius von. *Doctrina numorum veterum*. 8 vols. Vienna: Degen, 1792–1839.

Ehrhardt, C. T. H. R. "Roman Coin Types and the Roman Public." *JNG* 34 (1984): 41–54.
Flower, Harriet I. *Ancestor Marks and Aristocratic Power in Roman Culture.* Oxford: Clarendon, 1996.
Friesen, Steven J. *Twice Neokoros: Ephesus, Asia and the Cult of the Flavian Imperial Family.* RGRW 116. Leiden: Brill, 1993.
Griechische Münzen. Part 3 of *Sonder Münzenauktion: Sammlung Apostololo Zeno.* Vienna: Dorotheum, 1957.
Hannestad, Niels. *Roman Art and Imperial Policy.* JASP 19. Aarhus: Aarhus University Press, 1986.
Hemer, Colin J. *The Book of Acts in the Setting of Hellenistic History.* Edited by Conrad H. Gempf. WUNT 49. Tübingen: Mohr Siebeck, 1989.
Hendin, David. *Not Kosher: Forgeries of Ancient Jewish and Biblical Coins.* New York: Amphora, 2005.
Hicks, E. L. *Ephesos.* Vol. 3.2 of *The Collection of Ancient Greek Inscriptions in the British Museum.* Oxford: Clarendon, 1890.
Hill, Philip V. "Coin Symbolism and Propaganda during the Wars of Vengeance (44–36 B.C.)." *QT* 4 (1975): 157–207.
Hölscher, Tonio. *Staatsdenkmal und Publikum: Vom Untergang der Republik bis zur Festigung des Kaisertums in Rom.* Konstanz: Universitätsverlag Konstanz, 1984.
Hopkins, Keith. "Taxes and Trade in the Roman Empire (200 B.C.–A.D. 400)." *JRS* 70 (1980): 101–25.
Horsley, Greg H. R. "The Inscriptions of Ephesos and the New Testament." *NovT* 34 (1992): 105–68.
Houston, George Woodard. "Roman Imperial Administrative Personnel during the Principates of Vespasian and Titus (A.D. 69–81)." PhD diss., University of North Carolina, Chapel Hill, 1971.
Howgego, Christopher J. *Ancient History from Coins.* London: Routledge, 1995.
———. "Coin Circulation and the Integration of the Roman Economy." *JRA* 7 (1994): 5–21.
———. "The Supply and Use of Money in the Roman World 200 B.C.–A.D. 300." *JRS* 82 (1992): 1–31.
Hurter, S. "The Black Sea Hoard: The Cache of an Ancient Counterfeit Mint." *Bulletin on Counterfeits* 15 (1990): 2–4.
Jackson, John, trans. *Tacitus: Annals; Books 4–6, 11–12.* LCL 312. Cambridge: Harvard University Press, 1937.

Johnson, Luke Timothy. *The Acts of the Apostles.* SP 5. Collegeville, MN: Liturgical Press, 1992.
Jones, A. H. M. "Numismatics and History." Pages 61–81 in *The Roman Economy: Studies in Ancient Economic and Administrative History.* Edited by Peter Brunt. Oxford: Blackwell, 1974.
Jones, Horace Leonard, trans. *Strabo: Geography; Books 13–14.* LCL 223. Cambridge: Harvard University Press, 1929.
Jones, W. H. S., trans. *Pausanias: Description of Greece; Books 3–5.* LCL 188. Cambridge: Harvard University Press, 1926.
Kearsley, Rosalinde A. "Ephesus: Neokoros of Artemis." *NewDocs* 6:203–5.
Keener, Craig S. *15:1–23:35.* Vol. 3 of *Acts: An Exegetical Commentary.* Grand Rapids: Baker Academic, 2014.
Keil, Josef. "Die erste Kaiserneokorie von Ephesos." *NZ* 12 (1919): 115–20.
Klose, Dietrich O. A. "Münz- oder Gruselkabinett? Zu einigen alten Fälschungen kaiserzeitlicher Lokalmünzen Kleinasiens in der Staatlichen Münzsammlung München." Pages 255–63 in *Internationales Kolloquium zur kaiserzeitlichen Münzprägung Kleinasiens, 27.–30. April 1994 in der Staatlichen Münzsammlung München.* Edited by Johannes Nollé, Bernhard Overbeck, and Peter Weiss. Nomismata 1. Milano: Ennerre, 1997.
Koester, Helmut. "Ephesos in Early Christian Literature." Pages 119–40 in *Ephesos, Metropolis of Asia: An Interdisciplinary Approach to Its Archaeology, Religion, and Culture.* Edited by Helmut Koester. HTS 41. Valley Forge, PA: Trinity Press International, 1995.
Lee, John A. L. *A History of New Testament Lexicography.* SBG 8. New York: Lang, 2003.
Leschhorn, Wolfgang. *Lexikon der Aufschriften auf griechischen Münze.* VNK 37. Vienna: ÖAW, 2002.
Levick, Barbara. "Propaganda and the Imperial Coinage." *Antichthon* 16 (1982): 104–16.
Louw, Johannes Petrus, and Eugene Albert Nida. *Greek-English Lexicon of the New Testament Based on Semantic Domains.* New York: United Bible Societies, 1989.
Marinescu, Constantin A. "Modern Imitations of Ancient Coins from Bulgaria." *Minerva* 9.5 (1998): 46–48.
Marshall, I. Howard. *Acts: An Introduction and Commentary.* TNTC. Grand Rapids: Eerdmans, 1980.
Mattingly, Harold. *Nerva to Hadrian.* Vol. 3 of *Coins of the Roman Empire in the British Museum.* London: British Museum, 1936.

Meadows, Andrew, and Jonathan Williams. "Moneta and the Monuments: Coinage and Politics in Republican Rome." *JRS* 91 (2001): 27–49.
Meinardus, Otto Friedrich August. *St. Paul in Ephesus and the Cities of Galatia and Cyprus.* IFS. New Rochelle NY: Caratzas, 1979.
Mellink, Machteld J. "Archaeology in Asia Minor." *AJA* 63 (1959): 73–85.
Mionnet, Théodore Edme. *Description des médailles antiques, grecques et romaines.* 6 vols. Paris: Toulouse, 1806–1808.
Mitsopoulos-Leon, Veronika. "Ephesus." Pages 306–10 in *The Princeton Encyclopedia of Classical Sites.* Edited by Richard Stillwell, William L. MacDonald, and Marian Holland McAllister. Princeton: Princeton University Press, 1976.
Moulton, James Hope, and George Milligan. *The Vocabulary of the Greek Testament: Illustrated from the Papyri and Other Non-literary Sources.* London: Hodder & Stoughton, 1929.
Murphy-O'Connor, Jerome. *Paul: A Critical Life.* Oxford: Oxford University Press, 1996.
Nollé, Johannes. "Zur neueren Forschungsgeschichte der kaiser- zeitliche Stadtprägungen Kleinasiens." Pages 11–26 in *Internationales Kolloquium zur kaiserzeitlichen Münzprägung Kleinasiens, 27.–30. April 1994 in der Staatlichen Münzsammlung München.* Edited by Johannes Nollé, Bernhard Overbeck, and Peter Weiss. Nomismata 1. Milano: Ennerre, 1997.
Noreña, Carlos F. "The Communication of the Emperor's Virtues." *JRS* 91 (2001): 146–68.
Oster, Richard E. "Acts 19:23–41 and an Ephesian Inscription." *HTR* 77 (1984): 233–37.
———. "Ephesus, Ephesians." Pages 300–4 in *Encyclopedia of Early Christianity.* Edited by Everett Ferguson. Chicago: St. James, 1990.
———. "Numismatic Windows into the Social World of Early Christianity: A Methodological Inquiry." *JBL* 101 (1982): 195–223.
Passow, Franz. *Handwörterbuch der griechischen Sprache.* 2 vols. Leipzig: Vogel, 1831.
Pervo, Richard I. *Acts: A Commentary.* Hermeneia. Minneapolis: Fortress, 2009.
Petrusevki, M. "Aukewa damokoro." *Živa Antika* 15 (1965): 12.
Pick, Behrendt. "Die Neokorien von Ephesos." Pages 234–44 in *Corolla Numismatica: Numismatic Essays in Honour of Barclay V. Head.* Edited by George Francis Hill. Oxford: Oxford University Press, 1906.

Preisigke, Friedrich, and Emil Kiessling. *Wörterbuch der griechischen Papyrusurkunden mit Einschluss der griechischen Inschriften, Ausschriften, Ostraka, Mumienschilder usw. aus Ägypten.* 3 vols. Berlin: Erbe, 1925–1931.

Price, Martin Jessop, and Bluma L. Trell, *Coins and Their Cities: Architecture on the Ancient Coins of Greece, Rome, and Palestine.* London: Vecchi, 1977.

Price, Simon R. F. *Rituals and Power: The Roman Imperial Cult in Asia Minor.* Cambridge: Cambridge University Press, 1984.

Prokopov, Ilya. *Contemporary Coin Engravers and Coin Masters from Bulgaria.* CCCHBulg. Sofia: n.p., 2004.

Prokopov, Ilya, Kostadin Kissyov, and Eugeni Paunov. *Modern Counterfeits of Ancient Greek and Roman Coins from Bulgaria.* CCCHBulg. Sofia: n.p., 2003.

Prokopov, Ilya, and Eugeni Paunov, *Cast Forgeries of Classical Coins from Bulgaria.* CCCHBulg. Sofia: n.p., 2004.

Ruijgh, Cornelis J. "Observations sur κορέσαι, κορέω, myc. da-ko-ro δακόρος, etc." Pages 376–92 in *O-o-pe-ro-si: Festschrift für Ernst Risch zum 75 Geburtstag.* Edited by Annemarie Ette. Berlin: de Gruyter, 1986.

Sayles, Wayne G. *Classical Deception: Counterfeits, Forgeries and Reproductions of Ancient Coins.* Iola: Krause, 2001.

Schultz, Hans-Dietrich. "Falschungen ephesischer Münzen." *MONG* 35 (1995): 7–14.

Sherwin-White, A. N. *Roman Society and Roman Law in the New Testament: Sarum Lectures, 1960–1961.* Oxford: Clarendon, 1963.

Silva, Moisés. "ναός, νεωκόρος." *NIDNTTE* 3:370–74.

Sutherland, Carol Humphrey Vivian. *Coinage in Roman Imperial Policy 31 B.C.–A.D. 68.* London: Methuen, 1951.

———. "The Intelligibility of Roman Imperial Coin Types." *JRS* 49 (1959): 46–55.

Taylor, Lily Ross. "Artemis of Ephesus." Pages 251–56 in *The Beginnings of Christianity: The Acts of the Apostles.* Edited by F. J. Foakes-Jackson and Kirsopp Lake. 5 vols. London: Macmillan, 1933.

Theophilos, Michael P. *Numismatics and Greek Lexicography.* Winona Lake, IN: Eisenbrauns, forthcoming.

Trebilco, Paul. "Asia." Pages 291–362 in *Graeco-Roman Setting.* Vol. 2 of *The Book of Acts in Its First Century Setting.* Edited by David W. J. Gill and Conrad Gempf. Grand Rapids: Eerdmans, 1994.

———. *The Early Christians in Ephesus from Paul to Ignatius.* WUNT 166. Tübingen: Mohr Siebeck, 2004.
Vermeule, Cornelius C. *The Cult Images of Imperial Rome.* Rome: Bretschneider, 1987.
Wallace-Hadrill, Andrew. "The Emperor and His Virtues." *Historia* 30 (1981): 298–323.
———. "Image and Authority in the Coinage of Augustus." *JRS* 76 (1986): 66–87.
White, L. Michael. "Urban Development and Social Change in Imperial Ephesos." Pages 27–79 in *Ephesos, Metropolis of Asia: An Interdisciplinary Approach to Its Archaeology, Religion, and Culture.* Edited by Helmut Koester. HTS 41. Valley Forge, PA: Trinity Press International, 1995.
Witetschek, Stephan. "Artemis and Asiarchs: Some Remarks on Ephesian Local Colour in Acts 19." *Bib* 90 (2009): 334–55.
Witherington, Ben, III. *The Acts of the Apostles: A Socio-rhetorical Commentary.* Grand Rapids: Eerdmans, 1998.
Yamauchi, Edwin M. *The Stones and the Scriptures.* EP. Philadelphia: Lippincott, 1972.
Yonge, C. D. *The Works of Philo: Complete and Unabridged.* Peabody, MA: Hendrickson, 1993.
Zanker, Paul. *The Power of Images in the Age of Augustus.* Translated by A. Shapiro. JL 16. Ann Arbor: University of Michigan Press, 1988.

Contributors

Bradley J. Bitner (PhD, Macquarie University, 2013) is Tutor in New Testament, Greek, and Biblical Theology at Oak Hill College, London, and an Honorary Associate in the Ancient History Department of Macquarie University. He is the author of *Paul's Political Strategy in 1 Corinthians 1–4: Constitution and Covenant* (Cambridge University Press, 2015).

James R. Harrison studied Ancient History at Macquarie University and graduated from the doctoral program in 1997. Professor Harrison is the Research Director at the Sydney College of Divinity and an Honorary Associate of Macquarie University Ancient History Department. His recent publications include *Paul's Language of Grace in Its Graeco-Roman Context* (Mohr Siebeck, 2003; repr., Wipf & Stock, 2017) and *Paul and the Imperial Authorities at Thessalonica and Rome* (Mohr Siebeck, 2011); he coedited with S. R. Llewelyn volume 10 of *New Documents Illustrating Early Christianity* (Eerdmans, 2012). His new book, *Paul and the Ancient Celebrity Circuit*, will appear with Mohr Siebeck in 2018.

Mikael Haxby received his PhD from Harvard University and taught at Harvard, Pace University, and Rutgers University. He is now a stay-at-home parent, a community activist, and a freelance writer. His soccer writing has appeared in FiveThirtyEight, *The Economist* and the *Washington Post* under the pseudonym Michael Caley.

Fredrick J. Long (PhD, Marquette University; MA Classics, University of Kentucky; MDiv, Asbury Theological Seminary) is Professor of New Testament and Director of Greek Instruction at Asbury Theological Seminary as well as the International Coordinator of Gamma Rho Kappa Greek Honor Society. He is the author of several books, including *Ancient Rhetoric and Paul's Apology: The Compositional Unity of 2 Corinthians* (Cambridge University Press, 2004), *2 Corinthians: A Handbook on the Greek Text* (Baylor

University Press, 2015), *Koine Greek Grammar: A Beginning-Intermediate Exegetical and Pragmatic Handbook* (GlossaHouse, 2015), and *In Step with God's Word: Interpreting the New Testament with God's People* (GlossaHouse, 2017).

Guy MacLean Rogers was Chairman of the History Department of Wellesley College from 1997 to 2001 and in 2012. From 2008 to 2013 he held the Mildred Lane Kemper endowed Chair at Wellesley College. Since 2013 he has served on the Advisory Board of the Madeleine Korbel Albright Institute for Global Affairs and the Freedom Project at Wellesley College. In 2014 he was elected to the William R. Kenan Jr. endowed Professorship of Classics and History at Wellesley College. His first book, *The Sacred Identity of Ephesos: Foundation Myths of a Roman City*, won the 1989 Routledge Ancient History Prize. In 2014 *The Sacred Identity of Ephesos* was reprinted in the Routledge Revival Program of distinguished works from the past one hundred years. In 2013 Yale University Press published his most recent book, *The Mysteries of Artemis of Ephesos: Cult, Polis, and Change in the Graeco-Roman World*. In 1997 he held a senior visiting fellowship at All Souls College Oxford, and in 2003 he was the recipient of the "Perennial Wisdom Medal" from the Monuments Conservancy in New York City.

Michael P. Theophilos studied New Testament at Oxford University and graduated from the doctoral program in 2008. Dr. Theophilos is Senior Lecturer of Biblical Studies and Ancient Languages in the Faculty of Theology and Philosophy at the Australian Catholic University, Melbourne. He is the author of *Jesus as New Moses in Mathew 8–9: Jewish Biographical Typology in First Century Greek Literature* (Gorgias, 2011), *The Abomination of Desolation in Matthew 24:15* (T&T Clark, 2012), and for the last decade has worked on *editiones principes* of the Oxyrhynchus papyri in conjunction with the Faculty of Classics, Oxford University. He is currently writing a commentary on the *Matthean and Lukan Infancy Narratives* for the Papyrologische Kommentare zum Neuen Testament series (Vandenhoeck & Ruprecht) and a monograph on the methodology and application of the contribution of numismatics to Greek lexicography entitled *Numismatics and Greek Lexicography* (T&T Clark).

Paul Trebilco (PhD, 1987) studied theology at the University of Otago, New Zealand, and completed his PhD at the University of Durham in the United Kingdom. He is currently Professor of New Testament Studies in the Department of Theology and Religion, University of Otago. His recent publications include *The Early Christians in Ephesus from Paul to Ignatius* (Mohr Siebeck, 2004), *Self-Designations and Group Identity in the New Testament* (Cambridge University Press, 2012,) and *Outsider Designations and Boundary Construction in the New Testament: Early Christian Communities and the Formation of Group Identity* (Cambridge University Press, 2017).

L. L. Welborn (PhD, 1992) studied New Testament and early Christianity at Vanderbilt University and the University of Chicago and is currently Professor of New Testament and Early Christianity at Fordham University and Honorary Professor of Ancient History at Macquarie University. Recent publications include *Paul, the Fool of Christ: A Study of 1 Corinthians 1–4 in the Comic-Philosophic Tradition* (T&T Clark, 2005), *An End to Enmity: Paul and the "Wrongdoer" of Second Corinthians* (de Gruyter, 2011), and *Paul's Summons to Messianic Life: Political Theology and the Coming Awakening* (Columbia University Press, 2015).

Stephan Witetschek studied Catholic theology in Eichstätt, Augsburg, Rome, and Munich and obtained his doctorate (Drtheol, 2007) and *Habilitation* in New Testament Exegesis (2013) at the Ludwig-Maximilians-Universität Munich, where he is Privatdozent in the Faculty of Catholic Theology. His major publications are *Ephesische Enthüllungen 1: Frühe Christen in einer antiken Großstadt; Zugleich ein Beitrag zur Frage nach den Kontexten der Johannesapokalypse* (Peeters, 2008) and *Thomas und Johannes–Johannes und Thomas: Das Verhältnis der Logien des Thomasevangeliums zum Johannesevangelium* (Herder, 2015). Research interests include the study of canonical and apocryphal gospels, the Apocalypse of John, the memory of apostolic figures in early Christian literature, and the political and cultural history of the first and second centuries CE.

Primary Sources Index

Old Testament

Exodus
- 3:14 — 24

Deuteronomy
- 5:6 — 27
- 25:1–3 — 104
- 28:13 — 216
- 28:44 — 216

Joshua
- 3:10 — 27

Ezra
- 3:12–13 — 135

Psalms
- 18 — 216
- 45 — 222
- 67:18 — 291
- 115:1–8 — 239
- 115:3–7 — 27
- 131:15–16 — 1

Song of Solomon
- 45–49 — 222

Isaiah
- 41:21–24 — 27
- 43:10–13 — 27
- 44:6–23 — 27
- 44:9–20 — 239
- 45:20 — 27

Jeremiah
- 10:1–16 — 27
- 10:2–5 — 239
- 10:10 — 27
- 29:7 — 27

Ezekiel
- 16:8–14 — 222

Daniel
- 2:18 — 283
- 2:19 — 283
- 2:27 — 283
- 2:28 — 283
- 2:29 — 283
- 2:30 — 283

Deuterocanonical Books

Tobit
- 14:5 — 211

Wisdom of Solomon
- 12:5 — 283
- 13–15 — 239
- 14:15 — 283
- 14:23 — 283

Bel and the Dragon
- 18 — 135
- 41 — 135

1 Maccabees
- 15:16–25 — 94

Pseudepigrapha

Apocalypse of Sedrach
  7:12   212

2 Baruch
  40:3   211

4 Ezra
  4:33–37   211

Testament of Benjamin
  11.3   211

Testament of Job
  36.3   212
  38.5   212
  40.3   212

Sibylline Oracles
  5.293–299   163

Dead Sea Scrolls

1 QM
  I, 12   211

1QpHab
  VII, 1–4   283
  VII, 13–14   211, 283
  VIII, 1–3   283

Ancient Jewish Writers

Josephus, *Antiquitates judaicae*
8.2	136
12.119–121	94
12.125–126	93, 94
12.125–128	94, 99
14.223–227	94, 305
14.226	305
14.227	23, 94
14.228	100
14.228–230	23, 94
14.230	98
14.231–232	23
14.234	23, 94, 100
14.238–240	23
14.240	23, 94, 100
14.262–264	23, 94, 95, 98, 100, 305
16.2	136
16.27	101
16.27–28	98
16.27–30	94, 95, 100
16.28	99
16.45	99
16.57–60	98
16.59–60	94
16.160–165	23, 96
16.162–165	94, 100
16.163	100
16.164–165	100
16.167–168	23, 95, 96, 98, 100
16.168	96
16.172–173	23, 95, 96, 98, 100

Josephus, *Bellum judaicum*
  1.153   307, 308

Josephus, *Contra Apionem*
  2.39   93

Josephus, *Vita*
  48   136

Philo, *De fuga et inventione*
  1.90   308
  1.93–94   309

Philo, *De praemiis et poenis*
  114   216
  125   216
  174   309

Philo, *De specialibus legibus*
  2.120   309

Philo, *De vita Mosis*
  1.316   309
  1.318   309

Primary Sources Index

2.72	309	Acts	
2.159	309	1:1–11	154
2.174	309	1:1–41	290
2.276	309	1:1–6:7	154
		1:6–8	211
Philo, *Legatio ad Gaium*		1:12–14	154
31	23	1:12–8:4	154
245	101	5:11	194
315	94, 98	6:7	154, 157
315–316	23	6:8–9:31	154
		7:38	194
Philo, *Questions and Answers on Genesis*		8:1	194
2.17	309	8:1b–4	154
		8:3	194
NEW TESTAMENT		8:16–14:28	154
		9:31	194
Matthew		9:32–12:24	154
16:18	194	11:22	194
18:17	194	11:26	194
26:47–56	115	12:1	194
27:21–26	135	12:5	194
		12:20–23	135
Mark		12:22	136, 157
14:43–47	115	12:24	157
15:13–14	135	12:25–16:5	154
		13:1	194
Luke		13:1–28:31	155
9:51–52	155	13:13–14	104
21:23–24	211	13:42	104
22:47–53	115	13:44–52	104
23:18–25	135	13:45	104
		13:50	104
John		14:5	104
8:44	115	14:23	194
9:22	110	14:27	194
10:28	110	14:27–28	154
12:42	110	14:27–16:5	154
15:18	110	15:3–4	194
16:2	110	15:22	194
18:2–12	115	15:35–16:5	154
19:6	135	15:35–19:22	154
19:12	135	15:41	194
19:15–16	135	16:5	154, 194
		16:6–19:20	154
		16:9	205

Primary Sources Index

Acts (cont.)

Reference	Pages
17:1–5	104
17:2	104
17:5–9	104
17:13–14	104
17:22–31	243, 250
18:2–20:1	155
18:5–7	104
18:12	104
18:19	23, 94, 267
18:19–21	103
18:22	194
18:25	267
18:26	23, 94, 103
18:27	103
19	250, 310, 321, 322
19:1	103, 155
19:1–7	155, 157, 158
19:1–17	158
19:1–20	155
19:1–40	155
19:4	158
19:5	158
19:8	164
19:8–9	23, 94
19:8–10	95, 103, 119
19:8–12	156
19:9	104, 105
19:10	105, 130
19:11	163
19:13	149, 158
19:13–16	23
19:13–17	156, 157
19:14	23
19:15	158
19:17	156–59, 162, 163
19:18–19	156
19:18–20	154, 156
19:20	156–57, 159, 162, 163
19:20–21	154
19:20–22	154
19:21	154
19:21–22	155, 156
19:21–40	323
19:21–41	299
19:21–28:31	154
19:23	128
19:23–24	159
19:23–27	267
19:23–40	127, 129, 154–56, 158–59, 243, 246, 254
19:23–41	15, 22, 105
19:24	158
19:25a	159
19:25–27	159, 160, 243
19:26	160, 244, 299
19:27	103, 158, 160, 299
19:27b–28	267
19:28	127–30, 133, 154, 158–60, 162, 243, 299
19:29	128, 249
19:29–34a	159
19:31	17, 154
19:32	128, 194
19:33	160
19:33–34	105
19:33–40	130
19:34	127–31, 133, 158–63, 243, 267
19:35	158, 162, 235–36, 243–44, 250, 324
19:35–36	162
19:35–39	159, 161
19:35–40	321
19:37	162, 249, 267
19:38	162, 267
19:38–40	164
19:39	162, 227
19:39–40	194
19:40	128, 159, 162
19:41–20:1	159
20:1	128, 155
20:17	194
20:21	164
20:25	164
20:28	194
20:31	84
21–28	155
21:27–29	227
23:23	218
25:8–12	218

25:21	218	7:21	42		
26:32	218	7:22	41		
27:24	218	9:19–23	104		
28:14b–16	154	9:20	104		
28:14b–31	154	11:18	227		
28:19	218	11:22	195		
		12:28	195		
Romans		13:2	85		
1:5	104	14:4–5	195		
1:13–14	104	14:12	195		
1:14	15	14:19	195		
1:16	104	14:23	195		
2:9–10	104	14:28	195		
3:9	104	14:33–35	195		
9:1–5	104	15:9	195		
9:30–33	104	15:28	284		
10:1	104	15:32	103, 243, 255		
10:12	104	15:51	84		
10:16–19	104	16:1	195, 227		
10:21	104	16:8–9	103		
11:1	104	16:19	195, 227		
11:7	104				
11:11–15	104	2 Corinthians			
11:20	104	1:1	195		
11:25	104, 211	3:14	104		
11:28	104	8:1	195, 227		
13:12	225	8:18–19	195		
15:15–21	104	8:23–24	195		
15:16	104	11:8	195		
16:1	195	11:24	104, 119		
16:4–5	195	11:26	104		
16:6–15	82	11:28	195		
16:16	195	12:13	195		
16:23	195				
		Galatians			
1 Corinthians		1:2	195, 227		
1:24	104	1:13	195		
2:1	85	1:16	104		
2:6–7	84	2:7–9	104		
3:5–4:5	133	3:28	42, 104		
4:1	84	4:4	211		
4:9	44	4:29	104		
5:1–13	42				
6:12–20	42	Ephesians			
7:18	104	1:1	86, 106		

Primary Sources Index

Ephesians (cont.)

1:3	7, 195, 197, 209, 277, 278	2:19	16, 284, 290
1:3–6	277	2:19–22	290
1:3–14	7, 255–56, 276–80, 290, 292	2:20	284
1:4	7, 278–79, 291	2:20–22	218
1:5	277, 278, 281, 289	2:21	284
1:6	7, 278, 281, 285–87	2:21–22	16
1:7	7, 226, 278, 280, 286	2:22	290
1:7–12	277	3:1–13	195, 226
1:8a	286	3:2	286
1:9	7, 277, 278, 282	3:3	86, 282, 283
1:9b–10:a	285	3:4	282, 283
1:10	7, 211, 278, 282, 284–86, 288–89	3:4–5	282
1:11	7, 278	3:6	195, 197, 215, 284
1:12	7, 278, 285–87	3:7	283
1:13	7, 278, 288	3:8–18	285
1:13–14	277, 287	3:9	282, 283
1:14	277–79, 285–87	3:9–10	286
1:15–23	281	3:10	195, 209, 224, 284
1:17	285, 287	3:13	256, 285, 287
1:18	285, 287	3:16	285, 287
1:18–23	281	3:17–21	195
1:20	209, 284	3:19	218
1:20–21	197, 209	3:21	195, 224, 285, 287
1:20–22	288	4:4	195, 197, 215
1:21	284	4:7–8	218
1:21–23	224	4:8	291
1:22	195, 215	4:11	219, 291
1:22–23	195, 215	4:12	195, 197, 215
2:2	284	4:12–16	291
2:4–7	197, 209	4:15–16	195, 197, 215
2:5	222	4:22	42
2:5–7	224	4:24	291
2:6	195, 209, 284	5:1–2	224, 226
2:7	285, 287, 289	5:3–5	42
2:8	222	5:4	291
2:10	194	5:6	290
2:11–22	106, 195, 197, 218	5:8–14	290
2:11–3:13	282	5:10	290
2:12	16, 283	5:11–12	284
2:13	226, 290	5:20–6:9	42
2:14	15, 282, 284	5:22	222, 224
2:15–16	226	5:22–23	195, 223
2:16	195, 215	5:22–24	224
		5:23	195, 197, 215, 222, 223
		5:23–25	195, 222

Primary Sources Index

5:25	223, 224, 226	2 Thessalonians	
5:27	195, 223, 224	1:1	195
5:29	195, 222, 223	1:4	195
5:30	195, 197, 215	2:8	15
5:32	195, 222, 223, 282		
6:1	222	1 Timothy	
6:4	222	1:3–4	108
6:5–6	222	1:4	108
6:5–9	42	1:5–6	107
6:7–9	222	1:7–11	108
6:10–18	197, 225	1:8–11	108
6:10–20	195, 291	1:9–10	108
6:11	284	2:8–15	108
6:12	209, 212, 284	3:5	195
6:13	284	3:15	195
6:16	284	4:1–3	108
6:19	282, 284	4:11	107
6:20	226	5	108
		5:16	195
Philippians			
1:18–27	85	2 Timothy	
2:10	212	1:10	15
2:12	86	2:18	107, 108
2:24	86	2:26	106
3:6	195	3:8	107
4:15	195	3:13	106
		4:1	15
Colossians		4:8	15
1:15–20	284		
1:16	211	Titus	
1:16–17	211	1:10	107
1:18	195	1:14	107
1:24	195	2:13	15
3:11	42	3:9	107
3:21–4:1	42		
4:15–16	195	Philemon	
		2	41, 195
1 Thessalonians		11	41
1:1	195, 227	11–13	41
2:14	195, 227	15–16	41
2:15–16	104	16b	41
4:3–8	42	17	41
4:4–6a	42	17b	41
5:8	225		

Hebrews		2:11	113
2:12	195	2:11–12	195
12:23	195	2:17	113
		2:17–18	195
James		2:23	195
5:14	195	2:29	113, 195
		3:1	195
1 John		3:6	113
1:4	111	3:6–7	195
2:2	111	3:9	112
2:15–17	111	3:13	113
2:18	111	3:13–14	195
2:18–26	110	3:22	113, 195
2:19	110	4:9	210
2:22	110, 111	5:13	210
2:22–24	111	7:10	210
3:1	111	9:14	210
3:12	111	12:10	112
3:13	111	13:1	112
4:1	111	13:5	112
4:1–6	110	13:6	112
4:3	111	13:9	113
4:5	111	13:11–18	255
4:9	111	17:3	112
4:14	111	19:4	210
5:4–5	111	21:5	210
5:19	111	21:12	210
		22:16	195

2 John	
7	111
7–9	110

Early Christian Literature

Acts of John	
42–43	163
94	115

3 John	
6	195
9–10	195

Athenagoras, *Legatio pro Christianis*	
17	239
17.3	239
17.4	240
17.5	240

Revelation	
1:4	195
1:11	195
1:20	195
2:1	195
2:1–7	111–12, 254
2:7	113
2:7–8	195
2:9	112

Diognetus	
2	239

Primary Sources Index

Eusebius, *Historia ecclesiastica*
4.18.6	115
5.3.2–3	186
5.24.2–7	116

Eusebius, *Praeparatio evangelica*
3.7.1	242

Ignatius, *To the Ephesians*
9	87
12.2	87

Ignatius, *To the Magnesians*
8–10	113
10.3	113

Ignatius, *To the Philadelphians*
6.1	113

John Chrysostom, *Homiliae in Acta apostolorum*
42.3	162
45.3	155
45.4	160, 162

Justin, *Apologia 1*
9.1–2	239

Martyrdom of Polycarp | 184

Tertullian, *Ad martyras*
1	185
3	186

Tertullian, *De spectaculis*
16	134

Greco-Roman Literature

Achilles Tatius, *Leucippe et Clitophon*
6.4–5	75

Anthologia Graeca
5.38	54
6.285	54
11.10	54

Apuleius, *Metamorphoses*
11.17	140

Aristophanes, *Vespae*
393–94	55

Arrian, *Epicteti dissertations*
1.19.32	38

Athenaeus, *Deipnosophistae*
8.361d–e	3
13.573a	77

Callimachus, *Hymni*
3.237–239	236
3.248–250	236

Cassius Dio, *Historia Romana*
56.25.5	261
56.34.2	207
56.35–42	258

Catullus, *Carmina*
37	55

Cicero, *De natura deorum*
2.61	226
3.3	30

Cicero, *De legibus*
2.11.28	226

Cicero, *De republica*
6.13	213
6.15	213
6.16	213
6.18	213
6.20	213
6.25	213
6.26	213
6.29	213

Dio Chrysostom, *De Concordia cum Apamensibus*
3–6   271

Dio Chrysostom, *De dei cognition*
77   240, 241

Dio Chrysostom, *Rhodiaca*
109   136

Euripides, *Iphigeni Taurica*
977–979   236

Galen, *De comparanda medicina*
203–208   180

Galen, *Peri trophon dynameos*
1.19   181

Historia Augusta, *Caracalla*
5.7   55

Horace, *Ars poetica*
470–472   55

Horace, *Satirae*
1.8.37–39   55

Julius Pollux, *Onomasticon*
1.23.4–24.10   213

Livy, *Historia Romae*   30

Lucian, *Apologia*
1   38

Lucian, *De morte peregrine*
33   137

Manilius, *Astronomica*
507–509   261

Martial, *Epigrammata*
6.42   54

Musonius Rufus, *Diatribai*
6   183

Ovid, *Fasti*
2.55–66   220
5.569–578   262

Ovid, *Metamorphoses*
14.805–828   214

Pausanias, *Graeciae descriptio*
1.26.4–1.27.3   238
1.26.6   238, 239
4.31.8   237
7.2.6–9   6
7.2.7   236, 237
7.2.8–9   3
7.26.5   239
7.26.6   239

Persius, *Satirae*
1.112–114   55

Petronius, *Satyricon*
71.8   55

Pliny the Elder, *Naturalis historia*
16.79   238
18.72   181
26.135   180
36.39   207
36.41   207

Pliny the Younger, *Epistulae*
6.31   21

Plutarch, *Galba*
4.3   216

Plutarch, *De Stoicorum repugnantiis*
22.2   55

Plutarch, *De tuenda sanitate praecepta*
122d–e   182
123b–d   182

Polyaenus, *Stratagemata*
5.18   77

Porphyry, *Peri agalmatōn*
351f   242

Q. Curtius Rufus, *Historiae Alexandri Magni Macedonensis*   216

Quintilian, *Institutio oratoria*
9.2.58
244

Res gestae divi Augusti
20   219
26–33   207

Seneca, *De beneficiis*
3.28.1   41

Seneca, *De clementia*
1.3.5   216
1.4.3   216
1.5.1   216
2.2.1   216

Seneca, *De tranquillitate animi*   187

Seneca, *De vita beata*
24.3   41

Seneca, *Epistulae*
7   187
31.11   41
44.1   41
47.10   41
47.16–20   41

Servius, *Ad Aeneid*
8.721   207

Statius, *Thebaid*
1.5   54

Strabo, *Geographica*
4.192   207
13.3.2   10
14.1.24   305
14.1.24b   35
14.1.20   81
14.1.29   74
14.12.21   3

Suetonius, *Divus Augustus*
29.2   262
94.12   261

Suetonius, *Nero*
20   139
46   207
56   55

Suetonius, *Tiberius*
26   258

Tacitus, *Annales*
1.8.4   207
1.12.12   216
4.38   258
4.55   310, 311, 324
16.23   35

Varro, *De lingua latina*
25.8.21   35

Velleius, *Historia Romana*
2.39.2   207

Vergil, *Georgica*
1.25–39   213

COINS

BMC
1:44.228   262
1:112.691–93   261
1:112–13.694–95   261
1:114.703   261
1:114.704   262

Primary Sources Index

BMC (cont.)
1:114.705–6	262
1:209	212
1:212	212
1:214	212
1:267	212
1:297	212

CGCI
223	
227	
233–36	
235	314
242	314
243	314
247	315
254	314
255	314
259	315
263	315
265	315
266	315
267	315
269	315
271–75	316
276–79	316
281	316
282	315
292	316
300	315
302–5	316
307	316
308	316
309	316
310	316
311	317
312	317
314	317
318	317
328	317
329	317
380	317
384	319
392	319
	319

RIC
1.10	215
1.25	226
1.26	226
1.27	226
1.28	226
1.31	226
1.32	226
1.33	226
1.34	226
1.36	226
1.37	226
1.38	226
1.39	226
1.40	226
1.41	226
1.42	226
1.43	226
1.54	226
1.65	226
1.70	226
1.95	226
1.100	226
1.116	226
1.118	221
1.120	221
2.1	248

RPC
1.2357	221
1.2364	221
1.2369	221
1.2370	221
1.2511	221
1.2563	221
1.1.2620–24	262
1.2623	262
1.3558	221
1.1.2569–74	260
1.1.2575–612	260
1.1.2613–19	260
1.1.2620–25	262
1.1.2625	262
1.1.2626	263
1.1.2628	263

Primary Sources Index

1.1.2631	263	*SNGMün*	
1.1.2632	262	127	314
2.1064	319, 320	132	314
2.F1064	246	133	314
2.1065	319, 320	141–45	314
2.F1065	246	152–55	315
2.1070	320	158	315
2.1070–72	246	162	316
2.1073	247, 248	165	316
2.1076	246, 247	166	316
2.1078	246	184	316
2.1079	246	187	316
2.1079–84	247		
2.1079–93	247	*SNGParis*	
2.1080	237	59	316
2.1082	246		
2.1083–86	246	*SNGRighetti*	
2.1085–93	247	853	315
2.1089	246, 247	854	316
2.1091	246	856	316
2.2626	320, 321	867	319
2.2627	321		
		SNGvA	
SNGCop		1884	314
397		1888	314
402	314	1890	314
409	315	1893	315
411	315	1895	315
415	315	1896–98	315
416	315	1899	316
417	316	1900	316
419–23	315	1902	315
425	315	1903	315
431	315	1904	316
436	316	1905	316
442–44	316	1906	316
444	316, 319	1907	316
453	316	1908	316
454	316	7863	314, 320
521	319	7872	316
		7873	316
SNGLewis		7874	315
1448	314	7871	315
1449	315	7877	315
1450	316		

Primary Sources Index

INSCRIPTIONS

CIL

1.1297	30
1.1298	30
2.1809	30
3.426	200
3.1966	55
3.6070	200
4.7716	55
5.600	37
6.1816	30
6.7861	37
6.13740	55
9.5125	37
10.202	37
11.4382	37
14.4506	37

FES

170	260
180	260

IAG

84	46

IBM

3.1.482b	311

IEph

1a.2	14
1a.7	7
1a.8	8, 285
1a.9b	73
1a.10	11, 17
1a.13	22
1a.17–19	38
1a.18b	38, 39, 258, 266, 288
1a.18c	266
1a.18d	17, 22
1a.20	17, 22, 258
1a.20a	36
1a.20a–b	36
1a.20b	36
1a.21	17, 45
1a.22	22, 74
1a.24	14, 15, 35, 36
1a.24b	287
1a.24c	46
1a.26	80, 85
1a.27	6, 11, 43, 87, 235, 241, 248, 259, 271–73, 285
1a.27–37	241
1a.28	241, 242
1a.29	241, 242
1a.30	241, 242
1a.31	241, 242
1a.33	242
1a.34	241, 242
1a.35	241, 242
1a.41	21
1a.47	76
1a.251	289
1.24a–c	274
1.24b	151, 152, 274, 287
1.24c	274
1.27	148, 149
1.33	148
1.36	148
1.585	151
2.101	76
2.102	76
2.103	76
2.104	76
2.213	72, 282
2.215	22
2.219	27
2.234	5
2.235	5
2.237	5
2.239	5
2.241	5
2.251	257
2.267–71a	17
2.274	16, 35
2.275	74, 76, 77
2.276	77, 151
2.293	75, 76
2.404	200, 248
2.410	201

2.411	30, 257, 258	3.456	52
2.413	248	3.606	148
2.413–16	245	3.616	53
2.414	248	3.622	27
2.418	248	3.624	287
2.419	245	3.636	22, 151, 267
2.419a	245	3.638	5
2.424	5	3.644	4
2.424a	5	3.646	37, 38
2.425	5, 22, 151, 267	3.647	322
2.425a	5	3.661	74
2.427	5	3.667a	282
2.431	19	3.672	274
2.433	56	3.675	74
2.434	74	3.683a	270, 271
2.449	245	3.686	287
2.454a	20	3.690	3
2.454a–f	19	3.695	147
2.455	51	3.702	282
2.458	257, 259	3.710	287
2.459	280	3.719	28
2.461	5	3.720	30
2.476	76	3.727	20
2.501	4	3.728	20, 274
2.502	74, 77	3.730	269
2.502a	74, 77	3.742	87
2.504	148	3.789	53
2.505	148	3.792	87. 287
2.508	5, 248	3.802	8
2.510	257	3.810	45
2.541	84	3.851	34
2.547	22, 150	3.853	38
2.560	52	3.857	38, 323
2.561	53, 54	3.858	38
2.561c	55	3.859	38
2.562	38	3.859a	38
2.566	56	3.875	87
2.567	54	3.892	87
2.568a	54	3.902	73, 77, 200
2.569	54	3.946	27
2.577	56	3.956a	27
2.580	50, 51	3.960	281
2.585	22	3.961	281
2.586	22, 151, 267	3.963	281
2.599	55, 257	3.966	281

IEph (cont.)	
3.967	281
3.980	87
3.983	87
3.984	87
3.987	268, 282
3.987–89	282
3.989	87, 268
3.993	87
3.994	87
4.1001	84
4.1005–8	84
4.1008	201
4.1020	76
4.1058	282
4.1060	17, 85, 281, 282
4.1061	75
4.1062	267
4.1064	4
4.1065	281
4.1066	281
4.1069	282
4.1075	76
4.1077	83, 86, 282
4.1080a	282
4.1086a	46
4.1099	74, 77
4.1104	245
4.1107	287
4.1125	245
4.1129	76, 77
4.1133	47
4.1155	245
4.1161–67	27
4.1162	28
4.1182	44
4.1202	77
4.1210	72
4.1211	74
4.1228	72
4.1233	72
4.1240	17
4.1250	75
4.1251	25, 94
4.1265	148
4.1267	74
4.1268	75
4.1270	72, 73, 76
4.1305	73
4.1351	16, 163
4.1393	257
4.1398	285
4.1408	14
4.1415	285
5.1448–55	15
5.1449–55	290
5.1458	290
5.1460–61	290
5.1465	290
5.1486	72
5.1491	18
5.1492	22
5.1499	290
5.1501	281, 289
5.1503	36, 258
5.1506	72
5.1523–24	16
5.1538	72
5.1544	38
5.1548	4, 53
5.1564	38
5.1575	287
5.1595	71, 73, 77
5.1597	282
5.1600	73, 75, 76, 77
5.1601	75
5.1601a	75, 76
5.1601c	75
5.1602	75
5.1605	46
5.1606	14
5.1613	47
5.1618	46
5.1655	87
5.1676	25, 26, 97
5.1677	25, 26, 96, 97
5.1786	8
5.1872a	87
5.1932a	74
5.1958	53

Primary Sources Index

5.1982	75	7.1.3217a–b	5
6.2034	245, 248	7.1.3217b	72
6.2035	245, 248	7.1.3239	27
6.2038	72	7.1.3250	10, 12
6.2044	4	7.1.3251	9, 11, 12
6.2061	35, 45	7.1.3252	11, 73, 145
6.2063	287	7.1.3253–54	10
6.2065	20, 28	7.1.3256	12
6.2066	53	7.1.3262	12
6.2070–71	46	7.1.3263	10, 12
6.2078	19	7.1.3271	9
6.2083–87	43	7.1.3271–75	9
6.2103	98	7.1.3272	9
6.2104	73	7.1.3273	9
6.2113	31, 32	7.1.3274	10
6.2200a	98	7.1.3276	8
6.2212	22, 26, 98, 150	7.1.3287	12
6.2213	22, 98	7.1.3292	9
6.2226	98	7.1.3329	73, 74
6.2304	28, 98	7.1.3453	9
6.2306k	25	7.2.3513a	84
6.2402	98	7.2.3513b	84
6.2441	22	7.2.3701	9, 12
6.2446	98	7.2.3801	17
6.2709	22	7.2.3850	12
6.2902	87	7.2.3901	53
6.2913	282	7.2.4101	27
7.3005	323	7.2.4105	5
7.1.2350	9	7.2.4117	98
7.1.2352	9	7.2.4123	30, 32, 38
7.1.3003	201, 257–58	7.2.4130	23
7.1.3006	33, 35	7.2.4301	1
7.1.3007	34	7.2.4325	257
7.1.3008	245, 248	7.2.4330	282
7.1.3025	37	7.2.4337	17, 27, 71, 87
7.1.3058	287	7.2.4340	53
7.1.3059	85, 268, 282	7.2.5110	21
7.1.3064	74	7.2.5113	5
7.1.3070	45		
7.1.3071	287	IErythrai	
7.1.3072	87, 269, 282	63	214
7.1.3075	20		
7.1.3079	4	*IG*	
7.1.3090	151, 157	7.2711	137
7.1.3216	98	7.2712	137

IG (cont.)

11.3.1396	256
12.8.549	44

IJO

2.26	116
2.31	24
2.32	25, 26, 97
2.33	25, 26, 97
2.34	25
2.35	25
44.3	116
181.2	116
206.5	116

IKyme

46	46

IMagnMai

127	46

IPergamon

1.10–12	46

IPriene

231	307, 323

IStratonikeia

10	144

MAMA

4.235	256
5.1.260	37
6.260	37
9	270

OGIS

2.524	37
2.533	220

SEG

29.1380	270
31.952	53
33.960	53
34.1094	151
34.1104	282
34.1168a–d	43
36.1092	256
39.1178	257
41.981	279
41.1110	256
43.812	97, 98
48.1363	98
49.2427	98
53.1344	143, 144
55.1245	259
55.1275	258
56.1219	53

SIG

2.760.1	223
2.760.7	223
2.798	258

TAM

2.275	256
5.1	134, 160

Modern Authors Index

Adams, Edward	119, 122	Beard, Mary	9, 57
Agamben, Giorgio	135, 152–53, 164	Beck-Brandt, Barbara	50, 62
Akurgal, Ekrem	305, 325	Becker, Adam H.	119, 120–23, 125
Aldrete, Gregory S.	133–34, 164	Belayche, Nicole	132, 164
Alföldi, Andreas	301, 325	Berger, Peter L.	227, 228
Amandry, Michel	293, 302, 318–19	Best, Ernest	255, 286, 293
Ameling, Walter	101, 122	Betori, Giuseppe	154, 164
Ando, Clifford	133, 164	Binder, Donald D.	94, 96, 100–01, 122
Andreau, Jean	302, 325	Bird, Jennifer G.	194, 228
Anguissola, Anna	235	Bitner, Bradley J.	v, 15, 127, 133–34, 164, 333

Arnold, Clinton E.   13, 57, 254, 289, 292, 306, 325
Arnold, Irene Ringwood   42, 57, 254
Ascough, Richard S.   17, 19, 20, 44, 57, 98, 122, 267, 293
Attridge, Harold W.   114–15, 122, 244, 252
Aune, David E.   216, 218, 228
Aurenhammer, Maria   75, 77, 89
Bagnall, Roger S.   49, 57, 309, 325
Bailey, Colin   18, 29, 31, 32, 57
Baird, Jennifer A.   49, 57, 58, 134, 165
Baldwin, B.   133, 164
Ball, Allan P.   216, 228
Barclay, John M. G.   xii, 23, 57, 88–89, 93–94, 98–100, 104, 122, 320, 329
Barrett, C. K.   129, 164, 238, 251
Barth, Markus   86, 89, 211, 216, 228, 286, 293
Barton, Carlin   179, 187, 188
Basore, John W.   216, 228
Bastien, Pierre   301, 325
Bauckham, Richard   110, 116, 122
Baugh, Steven M.   25–26, 29, 39, 57, 268–69, 293

Bockmuehl, Markus   283, 293
Bonnet, Jacques   13, 57
Bosworth, Brian   219, 228
Botermann, Helga   101, 122
Bourdieu, Pierre   179, 188
Bradley, Keith R.   29, 57
Braund, David C.   266, 293
Bremen, Riet van   224, 228
Bremmer, Jan N.   254, 293
Brent, Allen   87. 89
Brinks, C. L.   128–29, 164, 244, 250–51
Broughton, Thomas Robert Shannon   217, 228, 305, 325
Brown, Raymond   84, 89
Bruce, Frederick Fyvie   309, 325
Brunet, Stephen Andrew   42, 46–48, 57
Büchner, Wilhelm   306, 312, 325
Burkert, Walter   69–70, 75, 81, 85–86, 89, 156, 164
Burnett, Andrew M.   293, 301, 313, 318, 319, 325
Burrell, Barbara   199, 228, 246, 251, 306, 307, 308, 309, 311–14, 316, 320, 323, 325

Burton, James H. 181, 188
Butcher, K. 302, 326
Büyükkolanci, Mustafa 44, 57, 267, 293
Büyükkolanci, P. 43, 58
Callahan, Allen Dwight 29, 58
Cameron, Archibald 39, 58
Campbell, Constantine R. 290, 293
Canavan, Rosemary 225, 228
Caragounis, Chrys C. 277–78, 282–84, 286, 293
Carr, Wesely 210, 228
Carson, Donald A. 111, 122
Carter, Michael J. D. 42, 44–45, 58, 177–78, 185, 188
Carter, Warren 255, 293, 302, 326
Casel, Odo 69, 89
Castelli, Elizabeth A. 184, 189
Chaniotis, Angelos 49, 58, 131–34, 137, 141, 142, 144–45, 150, 160, 162, 164–65, 260, 293
Chantraine, Pierre 306, 326
Charlesworth, Martin Peruval 220, 228
Clarke, John R. 55, 58
Cody, Jane M. 246, 251
Cohoon, J. W. 136, 165
Coleman, Kathleen 134, 165, 175, 177, 180, 189
Colin, Jean 133, 134, 165
Concannon, Cavan 185, 189
Cooley, Alison E. 265, 293
Cotter, Wendy 204, 228
Cottier, Michel 35, 58
Cotton, Hannah 33, 39, 144, 165
Crawford, Michael H. 301–2, 319, 326
Crönert, Wilhelm 300, 326
Crook, John Anthony 321, 326
Crosby, H. Lamar 136, 165
Crowther, Nigel B. 47, 58
Curry, Andrew 182, 189
Cuss, Dominique 220, 229
Danker, Frederick W. 219, 223, 229, 254, 270, 278, 293, 294
Debord, Guy 152, 153, 165
Deissmann, Gustav Adolf 193, 229
De Ruggiero, Ettore xii, 133, 165

Dignas, Beate 253–54, 293, 294
Dillon, Sheila 253, 294
Dimitrov, Dimitar 319, 326
Dodson, Joseph R. 196, 229
Donohue, A. A. 239, 240, 242, 251
Dräger, Michael 245, 247, 251, 320, 326
Drew-Bear, Thomas 312, 326
Duffy, Maureen E. 159, 160, 165
Duncan-Jones, Richard P. 302, 326
Dunbabin, Katherine M. 54, 58
Dunn, James D. G. 195, 198, 229, 231
Dyer, Keith D. 302, 326
Ebner, Martin 152, 165
Eck, Werner 33, 58, 265, 294
Eckhel, Joseph Hilarius von 313, 320, 326
Edwards, Catherine 187, 189
Ehrhardt, C. T. H. R. 301, 327
Eliav, Yaron Z. 28, 55, 58
Elsner, Jas 238, 239, 251
Engelmann, Helmut xiv, 98, 114, 122, 123, 267–68, 293, 296
Eplett, Chris P. 45, 59
Erdemgil, Selahattin 34, 59
Erim, Kenan T. 161, 167, 257, 294
Fabrizii-Reuer, Suzanne 175, 189
Faust, Eberhard 194, 229
Favro, Diane 226, 229
Feuser, Stefan 43, 48, 59
Finley, Moses I. 29, 59
Finney, Mark T. 227, 229
Fischer-Hansen, Tobias 149, 165
Fishwick, Duncan 217, 229
Fitzmyer, Joseph A. 84, 85, 89
Fleischer, Robert 237, 251
Flower, Harriet I. 301, 327
Foss, Clive 95, 122
Foster, Robert L. 218, 229
Foucault, Michel 182–84, 188–89
Francis, James A. 183, 189
Frankfurter, David 112, 123
Frayer-Griggs, Daniel 243, 251, 255, 294
Fredricksmeyer, E. A. 220, 229
Friesen, Steven J. 13, 59, 199, 202, 229, 245, 251, 254–55, 294, 312, 320, 327

Frija, Gabrielle 254, 294
Funke, Hermann 242, 251
Furnish, Victor Paul 89
Galinsky, Karl 258, 294
Gardner, Percy 205, 229
Gathercole, Simon J. 89
Giffin, Ryan 212, 231
Gilleland, Michael 55, 59
Glancy, Jennifer A. 29, 41, 42, 59
Goodrich, John K. 285, 294
Gosnell, Peter W. 255, 294
Gregory, Andrew P. 7–10, 12, 59
Grossschmidt, Karl 43–44, 58, 59, 62, 67, 174–76, 178, 180–82, 189–90
Gruen, Erich S. 94, 100, 123
Guarducci, Margherita 51, 59
Gupta, Nijay K. 194, 222, 229
Hadot, Pierre 183–84, 188, 189
Haenchen, Ernst 105, 123, 129–30, 165, 244, 251
Hannestad, Niels 301, 327
Hanson, J. Arthur 140, 166
Harland, Philip A. 17, 19–20, 28, 44, 57, 59, 71, 73, 75, 89, 98, 122, 151, 166, 204, 229, 267, 293
Harrill, J. Albert 29, 59
Harris, W. Hall 291, 294
Harrison, James R. 7, 13–14, 18, 21, 27, 47, 52–53, 59, 60, 128, 166, 254, 257–58, 261–63, 265, 271, 274–75, 279–80, 282, 286, 294–95
Haxby, Michael 43
Heil, John Paul 86, 89
Hekster, Olivier 219, 230
Hemer, Colin 324, 327
Hendin, David 319, 327
Hendrix, Holland L. 223, 230, 276–77, 295
Hezser, Catherine 134, 166
Hicks, E. L. 311, 327
Hill, Philip V. 301, 327
Hirschberg, Peter 113, 123
Hirst, Gertrude 213, 230
Hoehner, Harold W. 211, 222, 230, 255, 282–84, 286, 295
Hölscher, Tonio 301, 327
Hoffmann, Friedhelm 235
Holum, Kenneth G. 217, 230
Hooker, Morna 243, 251
Hopkins, Keith 221, 230, 302, 327
Horner, Timothy J. 115–16, 123
Horsley, Greg H. R. xvi, 1, 23–25, 36–38, 60, 94–95, 123, 145, 149–51, 166, 259, 266, 295, 309, 327
Horsley, Richard A. 29, 58
Horst, Peter Willem van der 26–27, 60, 101, 117, 123
Horster, Marietta 254, 295
Houston, George Woodard 321, 327
Howgego, Christopher J. 301–2, 327
Hurter, S. 319, 327
Huttner, Ulrich 117, 123
Içten, C. 44, 67, 98, 123
Instone-Brewer, David 276, 295
İplikçioğlu, Bülent 1, 2, 62, 78, 90, 98, 123, 268, 296
Jackson, John 311, 327
Jacobs, Andrew S. 119, 123
Jansen, David 225, 230
Jobst, Werner 50, 51, 60
Johnson, Luke Timothy 324, 328
Jones, A. H. M. 301, 303, 328
Jones, C. P. 253, 295
Jones, Donald L. 220, 230
Jones, Horace Leonard 10, 60, 81, 91, 305, 328
Jones, Tamara 43, 60
Jones, W. H. S. 312, 328
Joshel, Sandra R. 29, 61
Judge, E. A. 256, 270, 295
Juhász, Lajos 196, 230
Junkelmann, Markus 174, 178, 189
Junod, Eric 115, 123
Kaestli, Jean-David 115, 123
Kalinowski, Angela V. 3, 18, 19–20, 22, 33–34, 61, 253, 295
Kantorowicz, Ernst H. 225, 230
Kanz, Fabian 43, 58, 59, 62, 67, 174, 176, 178, 180–82, 189–90
Karwiese, Stefan 246–48, 251

Kavanaugh, Maureen 181, 191
Kearsley, Rosalinde A. 12–13, 18, 34, 61, 254, 283, 295, 322–23, 328
Keegan, Peter 49–50, 61, 64, 134, 166
Keener, Craig S. 128, 130–31, 155, 157, 166, 254, 296, 323, 328
Keil, Josef 24, 39, 58, 61, 74, 77, 89, 95, 320, 328
Kelley, Nicole 184, 189
Kennedy, H. A. A. 220, 230
Kidson, Lyn 260, 296
Kiessling, Emil 300
King, Karen 184, 189
Kirbihler, François 8, 13, 18, 20, 61
Kissyov, Kostadin 319
Klauck, Hans-Josef 193, 230, 241, 244, 250–51
Klauser, Theodore 133–34, 166
Kleijwegt, Marc 73, 90
Klöckner, Anja 254, 295
Kloppenborg, John S. 17, 19, 20, 44, 57, 98, 122, 204, 232, 267, 293
Klose, Dietrich O. A. viii, 246, 251, 316, 320, 328
Knibbe, Dieter 1, 2, 13, 24, 61, 62, 69, 78, 81, 90, 90, 98, 123, 171, 173, 190, 253, 268, 273, 296
Kodell, Jerome 157, 166
Koester, Helmut 2, 5, 35, 62, 66–67, 75, 82, 86, 88–90, 128, 168, 171, 190, 218, 233–34, 273, 296, 323–24, 328, 331
Kolev, B. 319
Kraabel, A. Thomas 24, 62
Kreitzer, Larry 217, 230
Kruse, Thomas 133, 137, 138, 139, 166
Ladstätter, Sabine 40, 44, 50, 52–53, 62, 67
Ladstättoweverer, S. 43, 62
Laffi, Umberto 223, 230
Lalleman, Pieter J. 114–15, 123
Lambrecht, Jan 112, 123–24
Lampe, Peter 7, 62, 130, 166
Lane, Eugene N. 73, 90
Latte, Kurt 77–78, 90
La Torre, Martino 19, 65

Lee, John A. L. 228, 300
Lee, Michelle V. 216, 227, 230
Léger, Ruth M. 13, 62
Leschhorn, Wolfgang 314, 328
Levick, Barbara 301, 328
Levinskaya, Irina 95, 124
Lieu, Judith M. 111, 115, 124
Lifshitz, Baruch xi, 27, 62
Lincoln, Andrew T. 195, 209, 216, 223, 231, 284–85, 296
Llewelyn, S. R. xvi, 15, 16, 39, 275
Loisy, Alfred 129, 166
Long, Fredrick, J. v, 16, 193, 194, 197, 211–12, 218, 220, 222, 229, 231
Lösch, Sandra 181, 190
Louw, Johannes Petrus 306, 328
Lozano, Fernando 215, 231
Luckman, Thomas 227–28
Lüdemann, Gerd 130, 166
Lutz, C. E. 183, 190
MacDonald, Margaret Y. 286, 288, 296
Maier, Harry O. 194, 198, 208, 225, 231
Malay, Hasan 144, 166
Mann, Christian 185, 190
Magie, David 218, 231
Magness, Jodi 101, 124
Marek, Christian 214, 232
Marinescu, Constantin A. 319, 328
Markschies, Christoph 129, 131, 167
Marshall, I. Howard 107–8, 124, 300, 322, 328
Marshall, Peter 288, 296
Martin, Dale B. 29, 62
Masson, Charles 279, 296
Mattingly, Harold xi, xviii, 221, 232, 296, 301–3, 325, 328
McCready, Wayne O. 203, 204, 232
McGing, Brian 100–101, 124
McGinn, Thomas 51, 62
McGowan, Andrew 186, 190
Meadows, Andrew M. 301, 329
Meeks, Wayne A. 101, 124
Meinardus, Otto Friedrich August 51, 62, 305, 329
Mellink, Machteld J. 305, 329

Mellor, Ronald	216–18, 232	Park, Joseph S.	26, 33
Meriç, Recep	7, 63	Passow, Franz	300, 329
Merkelbach, Reinhold	xiv, 56, 63, 73, 90	Paton, W. R.	54, 63
Miller, John F.	35, 63	Paunov, Eugeni	319, 330
Milligan, George	307, 329	Perkins, Judith	182, 190
Milnor, Kristina	49, 63	Pervo, Richard I.	114–15, 124, 128–30, 155–57, 167, 244, 249, 252, 322–23, 329
Mionnet, Théodore Edme	313, 329		
Mitford, T. B.	256, 296		
Mitsopoulos-Leon, Veronika	305, 329	Pesch, Rudolf	243, 252
Molthagen, Joachim	158, 166	Peterson, Erik	129, 131, 133–34, 161, 167
Moore, Casey C.	55, 63		
Moretti, Jean-Charles	49, 63	Petrusevki, M.	329
Moulton, James Hope	307, 329	Petzl, Georg	xiv, 178, 190
Mounce, William D.	107–8, 124	Pick, Behrendt	320, 329
Mouritsen, Henrik	38, 63	Pietsch, Wolfgang	171–72, 174–75, 190
Muddiman, John	211, 232, 286, 288, 296	Pillinger, Renate	96, 124
		Pleket, Harry W.	11, 64, 73, 90
Mundt, Felix	235	Portefaix, Lilian	42, 49, 64
Murphy-O'Connor, Jerome	2, 63, 321, 329	Potter, David M.	178, 191
		Poulsen, Birte	150, 165
Murray, Michele	112–14, 124	Preisigke, Friedrich	300, 330
Muss, Ulrike	13, 63	Preisshofen, Felix	54
Musurillo, Herbert	186, 190	Prescendi, Francesca	236, 252
Nani, Teresa Giulia	39, 63	Price, Martin Jessop	312, 330
Neudecker, Richard	238, 252	Price, Simon R. F.	198–99, 215, 219–20, 225, 232, 258, 296, 312, 330
Ng, Diana Y.	5, 6, 63		
Nida, Eugene Albert	306, 328	Price, T. Douglas	181, 188
Nock, A. D.	220, 232	Prokopov, Ilya	330
Nollé, Johannes	312–13, 316, 329	Pucci Ben Zeev, Miriam	94, 125
Norden, Eduard	278, 292, 296	Radin, Max	213
Noreña, Carlos F.	301, 329	Rajak, Tessa	94, 125
Noy, David	xiv, 97, 124	Rathmayr, Elisabeth	3, 5, 50, 64
O'Brien, Peter Thomas	255, 296	Rautman, Marcus	101, 125
Ogereau, Julien	35, 52, 63	Read-Heimerdinger, Jenny	127, 130, 158, 167
Oliver, J. H.	21, 65		
Olson, Emily Victoria	33–35, 63	Reed, Annette Yoshiko	119–23, 125
Osanna, Massimo	239, 252	Reid, Sara Karz	220, 232
Oster, Richard E.	13, 16, 63, 74, 78, 90, 120, 124, 128, 166, 275–76, 296, 302, 304–5, 312, 329	Reitzenstein, Richard	69, 90
		Reumann, John Henry Paul	86, 90
		Reynolds, Joyce M.	133, 167, 207, 232
Otto, Walter	220, 232	Rich, John	7, 64, 219
Overbeck, Bernhard	313, 316	Ricl, Marijana	39, 64
Padilla, Osvaldo	243, 252	Riesner, Rainer	84, 86, 90
Page, Denys L.	214, 232	Ripollès, Pere Pau	293, 318–19
Palm, F.	300	Ritter, Bradley	98, 125

Ritter, Stefan 235
Rius-Camps, Josep 130, 158, 167
Robbins, Vernon K. 196, 225, 232
Robert, Jeanne 71, 90
Robert, Louis 42, 44, 45, 64, 71, 90, 133, 167, 172, 175, 191
Robertson, Martin 206, 233
Robinson, Thomas A. 7, 64, 101, 119, 125
Rogers, Guy MacLean 12–15, 18, 42, 64, 80, 83–86, 90, 97, 125, 128, 145–50, 154, 156, 162–63, 167, 201, 233, 235, 248, 252–54, 259, 266, 269, 271, 276, 296
Rose, Charles Brian 33, 34, 64
Rost, V. 300
Roueché, Charlotte 50, 64, 133–34, 161, 167
Rowe, C. Kavin 130, 160, 167, 267, 297
Rowe, Gregory 133–34, 167
Rubin, Benjamin B. 198, 233
Ruijgh, Cornelis J. 307, 330
Rüpke, Jörg 139, 167
Sampley, J. Paul 216, 222, 233
Sanford, Eva Matthews 223, 233
Sayles, Wayne G. 319, 330
Schaferdiek, Knut 163, 167
Schaps, David M. 197, 233
Scheer, Tanja S. 236, 252
Scherrer, Peter 2, 24, 50, 65, 198–201, 233
Schindler, Friedrich 1
Schlier, Heinrich 195, 209, 216, 233
Schmidt, J. 133, 168
Schmidt, Karl L. 203, 233
Schmithals, Walter 107, 125
Schnackenburg, Rudolf 209, 211, 233, 277, 281, 283, 297
Schneider, Johann Gottlob Theaenus 300
Schultz, Hans-Dietrich 316, 330
Schürer, Emil 116, 125
Schüssler Fiorenza, Elisabeth 112, 125
Schwindt, Rainer 128, 168
Selinger, Reinhard 131, 168
Servadei, Cristina 49, 65

Shanor, Katherine Ann 29, 36–40, 65
Shauf, Scott 132, 155–58, 160, 162–63, 168, 244, 252
Shaw, Teresa 183, 191
Sherk, Robert K. 215, 233
Sherwin-White, A. W. 299, 323, 330
Sillen, Andrew 181, 191
Silva, Moisés 306, 330
Slater, William J. 46, 65
Small, Alastair 9, 65
Smallwood, E. Mary 212, 233
Smith, Abraham 29, 58
Smith, Julien 194, 233
Smith, R. R. R. 205, 207–8, 233, 257, 297
Sperber, Dan 197, 233
Spier, Jeffrey 134, 168
Steskal, Martin 19, 50, 65
Stevenson, Gregory 14, 65
Stoops, Robert F. 106, 125, 128–29, 168
Stowers, Stanley K. 104, 125
Streett, Daniel R. 110, 125
Strelan, Rick 13, 65, 101–2, 107, 125, 128, 148, 168, 244, 252, 255, 297
Strocka, Volker Michael 24, 53, 54, 65
Strong, Anise K. 51
Strubbe, Johan 55, 65
Sutherland, Carol Humphrey Vivia 301, 303–4, 330
Swift, L. J. 21, 65
Szidat, Sabine 235, 252
Taeuber, Hans 49, 65
Talbert, Charles H. 128–29, 155, 168, 216, 223, 234
Taylor, Claire 49
Taylor, Justin 106, 125
Taylor, Lily Ross 220, 234, 311, 330
Tellbe, Mikael 119, 120, 126, 161, 168
Theissen, Gerd 135, 168
Theissen, Werner 13, 65, 109, 126
Theophilos, Michael P. 259, 304, 330
Thielman, Frank 210, 234
Thomas, Christine M. 128, 168, 218, 234
Thompson, Leonard L. 112, 116, 126
Thür, Hilke 5, 66, 171, 173
Tilborg, Sjef van 29–31, 66, 255, 297

Tomson, Peter J.	28, 66	Yorke, Gosnell	194, 234
Topai, Cengiz	28, 56, 66	Zabehlicky, Heinrich	35, 66
Touratsoglou, J. P.	177, 191	Zabrana, Lilli	13, 249, 252
Towner, Philip H.	107, 124, 126	Zamfir, Korinna	255, 297
Trebilco, Paul	13, 23–27, 66, 79, 86–87, 91, 93, 94, 98, 100–103, 105–11, 113, 126, 128, 130, 168, 199, 201, 234, 254, 297, 300, 323, 330–31	Zanker, Paul	262, 297, 301, 331
		Zerwick, Max	284, 297
		Ziesler, John A.	157, 169
		Zimmermann, Norbert	40, 44, 50, 53, 67
Treggiari, Susan	38, 66		
Trell, Bluma L.	312, 330	Zuiderhoek, Arjan	254, 297
Trinkl, Elisabeth	171, 174, 190	Zülkadiroglu, A.	44, 67
Tripp, Jeffrey M.	128, 160, 168		
Vermeule, Cornelius C.	198, 200–201, 234, 312, 331		
Ville, Georges	177, 191		
Wagner, Günther	283, 297		
Wagner, J. Ross	84, 88, 91		
Wallace, Rex E.	49, 66		
Wallace-Hadrill, Andrew	7, 301, 331		
Wasserstein, Abraham	100, 126		
Wedderburn, Alexander J. M.	283, 297		
Weiss, Peter	313, 316		
Westermann, William Linn	29, 66		
White, L. Michael	2, 66, 199, 202, 234, 322–23, 331		
Wiedemann, Thomas	29, 66, 178, 180, 187, 191		
Wiemer, Hans-Ulrich	133, 168		
Williams, Jonathan	221, 234, 301		
Williams, Margaret H.	121, 126		
Wilson, Deirdre	197, 234		
Wilson, Stephen G.	111–12, 114, 116, 126		
Wink, Walter	209, 234		
Wiplinger, Gilbert	2, 20, 32, 35, 66		
Witetschek, Stephen	13, 95, 126, 130, 168, 244, 245, 246, 247, 249, 252, 321, 322, 323, 331		
Witherington, Ben	154, 155, 169, 324, 331		
Wlach, Gudrun	2, 20, 32, 35		
Yamauchi, Edwin M.	50–51, 66, 313, 331		
Yee, Tet-Lim N.	194, 234		
Yonge, C. D.	331		

www.ingramcontent.com/pod-product-compliance
Lightning Source LLC
Chambersburg PA
CBHW051205300426
44116CB00006B/447